About the Author

LIEUTENANT COLONEL CARLO W. D'ESTE retired from the U.S. Army in 1978 to write full-time. Of his first book, *Decision in Normandy: The Unwritten Story of Montgomery and the Allied Campaign*, Max Hastings wrote, "the superb book establishes him at a stroke as a major military historian." He is emerging as one of the most exciting and stimulating military historians now writing. He lives with his family in Massachusetts.

FATAL
DECISION

ANZIO AND THE
BATTLE FOR ROME

CARLO D'ESTE

HARPER PERENNIAL

NEW YORK • LONDON • TORONTO • SYDNEY • NEW DELHI • AUCKLAND

Grateful acknowledgment is made to the following for permission to quote from copyrighted material:

From *Tug of War: The Battle for Italy 1943–45*, by Dominick Graham and Shelford Bidwell, © 1986 by St. Martin's Press and Hodder & Stoughton, Ltd.

The Trustees of the Liddell Hart Centre for Military Archives, King's College London: the Papers of the Field Marshal Lord Alanbrooke and Major General W. R. C. Penney.

Maps by Paul Pugliese except as noted:

Map 1 from *Bitter Victory*, by Carlo D'Este. © 1988 by Carlo D'Este. Map 3 from *The Royal Inniskilling Fusiliers in the Second World War*, by Sir Frank Fox. Maps 14 and 15 from *World War II in the Mediterranean, 1942–1945*, by Carlo D'Este. © 1990 by Carlo D'Este. Maps 4 and 16 from *The Times Atlas of the Second World War*. © 1989 by Times Books Limited.

A hardcover edition of this book was published in 1991 by HarperCollins Publishers.

FIRST HARPER PERENNIAL EDITION PUBLISHED 1992, REISSUED 2008.

Designed by Alma Orenstein

The Library of Congress has catalogued the hardcover edition as follows:
D'Este, Carlo.
    Fatal Decision: Anzio and the battle for Rome / Carlo D'Este.
       p.   cm.
    Includes bibliographical references and index.
    ISBN 978-0-06-015890-3
    1. Anzio Beachhead, 1944. 2. World War, 1939–1945—Campaigns—Italy—Rome (City). 3. Rome (City)—History—1870–1945. I. Title.
D763.I82A554 1991
940.54'21—dc20   90-55833

ISBN 978-0-06-057649-3 (reissue)

08 09 10 11 12 RRD 10 9 8 7 6 5 4 3 2 1

Yet always with victory there is an accompanying sense of disappointment. Rome had been so long delayed . . . it had been a long journey, and everyone was very weary. And too many had died.

—CHRISTOPHER BUCKLEY, *ROAD TO ROME*

Anzio was a prime example of the horror of war. It was a place where thousands died and death had no regard for nationality or status. Some who died disappeared forever in the mud and swamps. And, of many of those who survived, it can be said that Anzio took their souls.

The dead of both sides are now honored in the war cemeteries.

This book is dedicated to the survivors.

May Anzio never happen again.

Contents

Prologue   1

Part I: The Road to Rome

1 Alamein to Messina: The Origins of the "Soft
   Underbelly"   11
2 The Path to Stalemate   30
3 The American Eagle and the Gentleman-General   48
4 The Decision to Launch Shingle   67
5 "Smiling Albert"   86
6 Mr. Churchill Takes Charge   93
7 Final Preparations   104

Part II: The Anzio Beachhead

8 The Invasion   119
9 Missed Opportunities   137
10 Calamity at Cisterna and Campoleone   159
11 The Battle for the Thumb   182

Part III: "Lancing the Abscess"

12 The German Onslaught   205
13 "Deafening, Mad, Screaming Senseless Hatred"   222
14 A House Divided   252
15 The Changing of the Guard   264

Part IV: Stalemate

16 The Ordeal of the Caves   283
17 Impasse   291

18 "Will I Be All Right, Sir?"   299
19 Plans and Controversies   326

Part V: Breakout

20 The Great Allied Offensive   347
21 The Battle for Valmontone Gap   366
22 All Roads Lead to Rome   383

    Epilogue   400

    Postscript   413
    Appendixes   431
    Notes   465
    Sources and Selected Bibliography   541
    Acknowledgments   549
    Index   553

Illustrations follow pages 118 and 374.

Maps

1. Mediterranean Theater of Operations   viii–ix
2. Allied Military Operations in 1943   23
3. Liri Valley   73
4. Anzio   125
5. The Anzio Beachhead   128
6. Expansion of the Anzio Beachhead   139
7. Allied Attacks on Campoleone Station   180
8. First German Attacks   191
9. German Capture of Carroceto and the Factory   214
10. German Counteroffensive, First Day   231
11. German Counteroffensive, Second Day   238
12. Battle for the Flyover   247
13. The Caves   289
14. Diadem   351
15. Breakout at Anzio   357

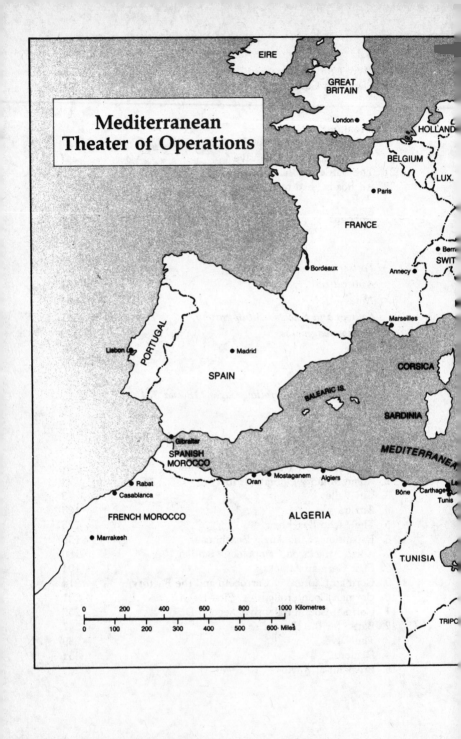

Prologue

Shortly before dark on the afternoon of February 7, 1944, the pilot of a Luftwaffe fighter attempting to evade an Allied plane jettisoned his five antipersonnel bombs near Anzio, a small coastal resort city some thirty-five miles south of Rome. Without warning all five fell on the U.S. 95th Evacuation Hospital, virtually wrecking the facility, killing twenty-two, and wounding sixty others. Among the dead were three nurses, a Red Cross worker, and Private Robert P. Mulreaney, who was visiting his wounded brother Eugene in one of the recovery tents. As the official report later stated, "when the bombs fell, Private Robert Mulreaney covered the body of his wounded brother and was killed by fragmentation." Eugene was not injured.[1]

One morning near the front line of the Anzio beachhead two GI riflemen of the 45th Infantry Division were observed digging a new foxhole. Curious because no one had ordered them to move, their platoon leader, 2d Lieutenant Howard D. Anderson, asked them why they were digging. "They said they didn't know but just thought they'd like a new place. They finished the hole and moved into it that afternoon." The next morning someone yelled, "Hey, Lieutenant!" "During the night a 150-mm [shell] had come and hit directly on their old hole."[2]

In another nearby 45th Division regiment two GIs named Stanley and Massack had just dug a new foxhole and were returning to their old position to move their weapons and equipment when they were struck by an incoming artillery shell and killed instantly.[3]

North of the town of Anzio a British soldier was washing his mess kit in the sea when suddenly a shell landed between his legs and splashed water into his face but miraculously failed to explode. Thinking a nearby Commando was having fun at his expense, the soldier yelled, "That was a bloody silly trick!" When shown what really happened, the man collapsed and had to be revived with a shot of whiskey.[4]

Elsewhere, after a typically heavy German shelling, Staff Sergeant Sidney Gilliam, the amiable mess sergeant of a 1st Armored Division tank company, got down on his knees and in a mock prayer intoned to the sky above, "God, help us. You come yourself. Don't send Jesus; this is no place for Children."[5]

At Anzio it was common for men who were recuperating from minor wounds or illness to request to be sent back to the front lines where it was deemed "safer." At the front, others concealed minor wounds in order not to be evacuated to the rear. Although generally located near the front, throughout the campaigns of World War II the evacuation hospitals were normally safe havens. Such was not the case at Anzio, where they quickly became such dangerous places that they were dubbed "Hell's Half Acre" and routinely avoided by front-line soldiers.

By those who fought there, the Anzio beachhead is remembered as "that" kind of campaign, a series of battles unique in the history of World War II. During the winter and spring of 1944, nearly 250,000 German and Allied forces were locked in a life-and-death struggle for control of the cold, damp lowland plains of the Pontine Marshes, which extend over a wide area east and northeast of Anzio and its nearby twin resort city of Nettuno.* Anzio's "only claim to fame was that it was the birthplace of the Roman Emperor Nero, and Nero is the only man who is known to have loved Anzio."[6] During the 125-day siege of Anzio both sides suffered grievously. Allied losses were 4,400 dead, 18,000 wounded, and nearly 7,000 captured by the Germans—whose losses were even higher. "It was a very difficult place to stay alive," remembers 1st Sergeant Jerome Lowrey. During just the first two weeks in the Anzio beachhead the rifle battalions of the British 1st Division lost an average of 50 percent of their strength. Some units were so badly decimated that they could muster only a fraction of their preinvasion strength.

Not only were battle losses exceptionally heavy, but Anzio also claimed some 37,000 so-called "nonbattle casualties": men who suffered from exhaustion, frostbite, trench foot, shell shock, and madness. At the height of the stalemate, the AWOL and desertion rates rose to alarming

*On November 27, 1939, the names *Anzio* and *Nettuno* were suppressed when King Victor Emmanuel III signed a sanction fusing the two towns into a single entity called Nettunia. Under this decree Anzio in 1944 was known as Nettunia Porto. In May 1945 the new Italian government scrapped the wartime decree and returned the two cities to their original prewar names of *Anzio* and *Nettuno*. (Information furnished by Silvano Casaldi, an Italian journalist and a native of Nettuno, letter, October 9, 1990.)

proportions, and the most worrisome problem facing the commanders was not their enemy but morale.

What made Anzio so different from other campaigns for the Allied soldiers who fought there was that it was a place where everyone was exposed to death—where the usual distinctions between front-line and rear-area-support troops simply did not exist. In the so-called rear area the soldier who baked bread in a quartermaster bakery, the ordnance mechanic who repaired vehicles, or the dentist who fixed teeth was as likely to be wearing a Purple Heart as someone at the front. As one American division commander noted, "All of us were in the same boat. We were to stay or die . . . I have never seen anything like it in the two World Wars of my experience. There was at Anzio a confidence in unity, an unselfish willingness among troops to help one another, that I never saw again."[7]

At Anzio, artillery was king, and to counter the invasion the Germans massed the largest guns in their arsenal and pounded the beachhead day and night. Movement during daylight hours was suicidal. The two largest were huge railway guns nicknamed Anzio Annie and Anzio Express. Cleverly hidden in caves in the Alban Hills overlooking the plains of Anzio, these massive guns could hurl a 280-mm shell over thirty miles. There was no place in the beachhead these monsters could not reach, and throughout the campaign they also regularly shelled Allied shipping offshore and killed a number of Allied sailors and merchantmen.

Many survivors of Anzio are still haunted by their horrific experiences. Nurse Grace Newton served in the 93d U.S. Evacuation Hospital, and she vividly recalls:

> the chattering of artillery, the explosions and resulting fires signifying that bombs had found their targets; the breathtaking display of vermillion ack-ack tracers in the night sky; the sight of ambulances weaving their way through grain fields to bring their sad cargo to the nearest hospital; the tight-lipped faces of men in pain trying to hide the fact, as if we couldn't see the beads of sweat on their brow and the clenched fists, as if they thought they must act out a charade of bravery—even when dying. I can't ever forget one young soldier whose bravery collapsed in a last desperate cry as the medical officer walked away, unable to do anything more to save him. "Nurse, don't let me die." Kneeling beside his cot, I could only hold him as he died. What little we had to offer! Sometimes only a prayer that God would grant a quick death.[8]

Famed correspondent Ernie Pyle covered every major campaign in the Mediterranean and European theaters of war, but he never reported from a more godforsaken place than Anzio. Pyle barely escaped death early one morning when the Luftwaffe raided the Anzio waterfront.

Several five-hundred-pound bombs exploded thirty feet from the villa housing the war correspondents covering Anzio. Pyle had been asleep and had rushed to the window when nearby antiaircraft guns began firing at the raiders. His room was demolished and his bed buried under hundreds of pounds of debris.

In his unique style, Pyle described Anzio as a place where, after a few hours, "you wish you were back on the boat . . . a new kind of warfare for us. . . . The whole beachhead is the front line . . . so small you stand on high ground in the middle of it and see clear around the thing. That's the truth and it ain't no picnic feeling either."[9]

At Anzio men lived a miserable, molelike existence in order to survive. To expose oneself to daylight was tantamount to a death sentence from snipers or artillery. Comparisons with the trench warfare of World War I were common. Wynford Vaughan-Thomas reported Anzio for the BBC and later wrote of trenches, no-man's land, and the constant need, as one senior British commander ordered his men, to "dig, dig, dig your way to safety."[10]

Lieutenant Anderson recalls the devastating effect of a German mortar barrage that "started out with a number of salvos of Screaming Meemies followed by mortar shells that came down like rain [in] the neighborhood of 500 in the first five minutes."[11] To a GI in the 3d Division, Anzio was "just plain hell all through the day, and the nights were worse . . . the hole got about six inches of water and you couldn't do anything but try and bale it out with your helmet. We wrapped shelter halves and blankets around us but . . . they got soaked with rain and then you . . . sat and shivered and cussed. . . . Jerry threw in a lot of artillery and mortars. The best thing to do was to pull in your head and pray. . . . If you got it at night you were lucky, because they could get you out right away. God help you if you got hit in the daytime."[12]

What turned into a 125-day siege and one of the bloodiest campaigns of World War II opened on January 22, 1944, when an Anglo-American amphibious task force consisting of the 36,000 men of the U.S. VI Corps landed at Anzio and Nettuno, barely an hour's drive from Rome. Under the command of American Major General John Porter Lucas, a veteran artillery officer, the operation was code-named Shingle. Despite considerable misgivings on the part of many senior Allied officers, including Lucas himself, the Shingle landings were a stunning success.

Only a handful of German troops contested the landings, and Allied losses were only 13 killed, 97 wounded, and 44 missing in action. The Allies had gained strategic surprise and by the end of the first day had not only landed 36,000 men and 3,000 vehicles but the first of an enormous quantity of supplies and ammunition.

Although the Germans had no major defenses established at Anzio, they had been expecting the Allies to launch an amphibious end run somewhere into their rear. Any such Allied operation was regarded as a potentially lethal threat to their aspirations for defending Italy. Thus, even though German forces in Italy were spread too thin to protect all potential landing sites, the German high command had prepared contingency plans to deal with Allied landings at various places on the Italian coast, including Anzio.

After the successful landings almost nothing at Anzio went according to plan for either side. The Germans moved swiftly to contain the Allies, prevent the fall of Rome, and protect their lines of communication to the Gustav Line, eighty miles to the south at Cassino, where General der Panzertruppen Heinrich von Vietinghoff's Tenth Army occupied formidable defensive positions in the mountains overlooking the Liri Valley.

Within a week the fleeting advantage gained by the surprise of Shingle was lost, VI Corps became mired in a dangerously narrow beachhead, and Anzio turned into a nightmare of unprecedented proportions. Ringed against the Allied force was the entire German Fourteenth Army, commanded by General Eberhard von Mackensen. His mission was plainly stated by his superior, Generalfeldmarschall Albert Kesselring, the German commander in chief[13] in Italy, and his Führer, Adolf Hitler: Hold Anzio at all costs and then lance "the abscess south of Rome." In a stunning turnaround, it was now the Germans who threatened to annihilate VI Corps, thus forcing the Allies to rush reinforcements that swelled the Anzio beachhead to more than 110,000 troops.

During the autumn of 1943 the wily Kesselring had brought the advancing Allied 15th Army Group of General Sir Harold R. L. G. Alexander to a halt at Cassino, thwarted the capture of Rome, and precipitated a crisis within the Allied high commands in Washington and London. At Anzio Kesselring would once again stalemate his foe.

The Anzio landings set off a chain reaction that within two weeks turned into siege warfare reminiscent of World War I. The two sides became locked in a deadly struggle as the beleaguered Allies fought to retain a small, semicircular strip of ground known as the Anzio beachhead against the German forces determined to drive them into the sea. Later, in the late spring of 1944, when the roles were reversed and the Allies were finally able to launch a great breakout offensive, the campaign would culminate in another series of equally savage and bloody battles.

Brutality in all its disparate and repellent forms has always been an inevitable hallmark of warfare, but the catastrophic world war of 1939–45 refined its odiousness to heretofore unequaled heights. Anzio, however, is remembered as a campaign in a class by itself: a place where, during one of the coldest Italian winters in memory, men suffered and died in unprecedented numbers from napalm, bullets, shell fragments, mines, bombs, rockets, booby traps, and grenades. Even by the standards of World War II, Anzio was regarded as among the most brutal of its many campaigns. The ferocity of the battles fought for the Anzio beachhead shocked even the most battle-hardened combat commanders.

To tell the story of Anzio is to recount the incredible stubbornness and courage of two determined protagonists, neither of whom was prepared to give up the fight. The Germans were under a mandate from Hitler to battle to the death, but those who fought at Anzio were mostly veteran soldiers who did not require the fanatical ravings of their Führer to inspire them to fight with a fury that was equaled only at Monte Cassino.

Above all, Anzio was a saga of courage, missed opportunities, bungled planning, and the misguided perceptions of its architects. In the forty-five years since it was fought, the campaign has been the subject of endless debate and controversy. Its lessons have become a case study both of the perils of faulty planning and of the inevitable fiasco that results whenever political aims take precedence over sound military practice.

At the center of the debate are Lucas, the task force commander, and the military architects of Shingle, Alexander and Lieutenant General Mark Clark, the U.S. Fifth Army commander. At the highest political level was British Prime Minister Winston Churchill, whose pressure on the Allied commanders in Italy ensured that the operation was carried out despite its obvious flaws.

In war the blame for failure traditionally falls on the lower end of the military chain of command, and Anzio was no exception. Lucas was perceived to have botched an opportunity to break the stalemate at Cassino, capture Rome, and in the process shorten the war in Italy. The allegation is that he failed to seize the Alban Hills (the Colli Albani, also known as the Colli Laziali) a volcanic mass that rises above the Anzio plain twenty miles inland from the sea. The Alban Hills bisect two railroad lines and Highways 6 and 7, which in 1944 were the vital German lifelines linking Cassino with Rome and their supply routes from northern Italy. By failing to capture the Alban Hills and Rome early in the campaign, when both were allegedly unprotected, Lucas's critics charge, he needlessly brought about the bloody campaign that followed.

Others argue with equal conviction and logic that Lucas was a victim of the ineptness of his superiors, Clark and Alexander. Many of those critical of Lucas's leadership at Anzio nevertheless fully supported his decision not to advance on Rome or to the Alban Hills immediately after the Shingle landings. They include his strongest critic, the commander of the 1st British Division, Major General W. R. C. Penney, who scoffed at the notion. "We could have had one night in Rome and 18 months in P.W. camps," he wrote after the war.[14]

What has never been in dispute is that Anzio was a campaign that went dreadfully wrong. The mistakes of Anzio were both political and military and extended from the battlefields of Italy to the boardrooms of Whitehall and Washington.

My aim in this book remains unchanged from those of my two previous accounts of World War II campaigns: to examine Anzio from the perspective of both the Allied and German commanders and the ordinary soldiers, NCOs, and junior officers at the sharp end, whose often impossible task it was to carry out the orders of their superiors.

The story of Anzio is an essential—indeed inseparable—part of the larger campaign fought in Italy. The events occurring at Anzio and on the southern front along the German Gustav Line, anchored on Monte Cassino, were vital ingredients that made up the larger canvas that was the Italian campaign. As one historian has noted, "Somewhere along the way Anzio means and Cassino ends became juxtaposed."[15] Thus the reader should be aware that the occasional digression to record the events occurring along the southern front fulfills the need to relate Anzio and Cassino to one another.

The archives of Britain, Canada, and the United States contain extensive primary source material about Anzio, and virtually all the major players on both sides have left either published or unpublished accounts of their version of events. The German side of the campaign was extensively documented after the war by several teams of Allied historians who painstakingly reconstructed the events of what British historian Sir Basil Liddell Hart so aptly titled "the other side of the hill."

To the Germans, British, Canadians, and Americans who fought there, Anzio was a living hell that fully tested and, indeed, often exceeded the limits of human endurance. Some men became heroes, others broke under the strain; some went mad, others deserted to the enemy or deliberately maimed themselves to escape the front.

This, then, is the story of a desperate campaign fought by determined men on one of the most godforsaken battlefields on earth.

PART I

The Road
to Rome

We took a chance on Churchill's persuasive
eloquence, his conviction that we could "slit this
soft underbelly of the Mediterranean." It turned
out to be not so soft.

—GENERAL MARK CLARK

1

Alamein to Messina: The Origins of the "Soft Underbelly"

Once North Africa is secure we must go forward to
the attack on Italy, with the object of preparing the
way for a very large-scale offensive on the underbelly
of the Axis in 1943.

—WINSTON S. CHURCHILL[1]

An eminent World War II historian has described Anzio as a "gamble" conceived in impatience and carried out in haste, the result of a large measure "of resentment and conflict between allies. The seed of Anzio was a difference of opinion, and the seed was nourished on long-term argument."[2] Anzio was an extension of the conflict of purpose that plagued the Allied effort in the Mediterranean virtually from the moment the United States formally entered World War II in December 1941. To understand what occurred at Anzio in 1944, we must first examine how the Allies came to fight the campaign in Italy.

The broad outlines of the Italian campaign were drawn by the Combined Chiefs of Staff at the Quebec Conference (also called the Quadrant Conference) in August 1943, when the Allied commander in chief in the Mediterranean, General Dwight D. Eisenhower, was given the green light to invade Italy at the conclusion of the Sicily campaign, which had begun on July 10.

By pursuing military action in Sicily the Allies hoped to knock Italy

11

out of the war; establish air bases from which the air forces, with their growing might, could continue their strategic bombing effort[3] throughout the "soft underbelly" of Europe; and capture Corsica and Sardinia. Most important, by electing to carry the Mediterranean war into Italy, the Allies intended to stage a major diversion by forcing Hitler to maintain large numbers of troops there and away from northern France, where they were scheduled to launch the long-delayed cross-Channel invasion in the late spring of 1944 along the coast of Normandy (Operation Overlord), along with a secondary invasion in southern France (Operation Anvil).

After decisive victories over the Germans at Stalingrad and Kursk, the Red Army had at last gained the upper hand on the Eastern Front, at a terrible cost to both sides. Nevertheless, the Wehrmacht still posed a considerable threat, and Stalin was anxious to ease the burden of the Red Army. For some time the Soviet leader had been demanding that the Allies open a second front in the west. The inability of the two western Allies to agree on a timetable for the cross-Channel invasion made the British, whose motivation to continue operations in the Mediterranean had both a political and a military basis, regard Italy as an attractive alternative.

Although Pearl Harbor brought about the formal entry of the United States into the war against the Axis in December 1941, the British were nevertheless destined to fight alone for most of 1942, a year of transition during which the United States mobilized for the forthcoming battles in Europe and the Pacific. It was also a period of stormy conflict between the aggressive British, led by Prime Minister Winston Churchill, who championed Allied military operations in the Mediterranean, and their reluctant new ally, whose strategy consistently called for the defeat of Nazi Germany by the most direct means, irrespective of political considerations.

At the Arcadia Conference in Washington in December 1941 the two Allies had agreed to place priority on the defeat of Germany. The architect and senior military spokesman of American policy was U.S. Army Chief of Staff General George C. Marshall, and from the outset he feared the consequences of getting bogged down in military operations against the Axis in the Mediterranean. Marshall believed that the decisive battles of the war would be fought in northwestern Europe, and he attempted to dissuade President Franklin D. Roosevelt from succumbing to Churchill, who began to articulate the view that the "soft underbelly" of the Mediterranean was Germany's Achilles' heel. Churchill argued that a cross-Channel operation in 1942 was impossible, but that in the Mediterranean there existed an opportunity to defeat Axis forces and eliminate Italy from the war.

The military options were only one aspect of British motivation.

The far-flung British colonial empire in the Far East had been swept away by the Japanese Army, whose seizure of Burma, Hong Kong, and Malaya culminated in the greatest humiliation in the history of the British Army, when Singapore fell in early 1942 and 85,000 British troops were lost.

From the spring of 1940, when Dunkirk climaxed the defeat of France and of the British Expeditionary Force (BEF), there had been one military defeat after another as the German Army occupied Denmark, Norway, Holland, and Belgium. Hitler regarded the Mediterranean as a secondary theater of war belonging to Mussolini. However, in late 1940, when the ineptly led Italian Army earned its own disgrace in Cyrenaica at the hands of a small British force under Lieutenant General Sir Richard O'Connor, Hitler elected to send a small German expeditionary force to North Africa under the command of the dashing, unconventional General Erwin Rommel.

After Rommel's arrival the British Eighth Army suffered sharp reverses in North Africa. Gazala and Tobruk became the latest entries in the lexicon of British military disasters and by the summer of 1942, Rommel had driven the British back to Alam Halfa, only thirty miles from Alexandria, and was threatening to annihilate the thoroughly dispirited Anglocolonial army of General Sir Claude Auchinleck. If Rommel's Panzerarmee Afrika were able to break the British defenses at Alam Halfa, there was nothing to stop a drive into the rich Nile Delta toward Cairo, beyond which lay the precious oil fields of the Middle East.

In August 1942 Churchill's patience ran out, and he acted to restore the situation before it was too late. He summoned General Sir Harold Alexander from Burma to replace Auchinleck as British commander in chief, Middle East, and an obscure, eccentric lieutenant general named Bernard Montgomery from England to take command of the Eighth Army.

Within several weeks Montgomery revitalized the Eighth Army and won a great defensive victory over Rommel at Alam Halfa. Two months later, after painstaking preparation, Montgomery launched the battle that was to catapult him to fame and win the first major British victory of World War II at El Alamein. The thirteen-day battle that began in late October 1942 was the turning point of the war in the west. Montgomery put the British back on the offensive, enabling them to regain the initiative they were never again to lose for the duration of the war. A rejuvenated Churchill, who only months before was forced to stave off a vote of confidence in Parliament, could later proclaim that "Before Alamein we never had a victory. After Alamein we never had a defeat."[4]

* * *

At the high-level meetings held after Pearl Harbor to hammer out a joint strategy for defeating Germany, Marshall fought tooth and nail for British acceptance of a cross-Channel invasion as the cornerstone of Allied strategy. One of his junior staff officers, an obscure brigadier general named Dwight Eisenhower, was the author of the U.S. position paper. Known as the Marshall Memorandum, it called for an enormous buildup of American forces in the United Kingdom—as part of an operation code-named Roundup—as the first vital step toward a future cross-Channel operation.

Churchill had first conceived of such a venture in the black days of 1940, after Dunkirk, but insisted that when an Allied expeditionary force invaded France it must succeed. Failure was unthinkable, thus the operation must be deferred until the odds favored Allied success. It became British policy to accept the concept of an eventual cross-Channel invasion but to oppose adamantly any attempt to carry it out in 1942.

Roosevelt was far more concerned that a suitable role be found for American combat forces as quickly as possible and was unwilling to tolerate a delay into 1943. The only practical possibility for joint operations in 1942 lay in the Mediterranean, but after more than six months of debate the two allies had failed to formulate a mutually agreeable strategy for the defeat of Germany. With the Red Army facing a serious prospect of defeat after Hitler launched his invasion of Russia the previous summer,[5] the pressure for action became too much even for Marshall. Intense Anglo-American negotiations took place throughout the summer of 1942, and at Roosevelt's insistence the two sides reached a compromise that would bring U.S. forces into active operations in the Mediterranean.

The United States agreed to participate in Operation Torch, an Anglo-American invasion of French North Africa, in the autumn of 1942. In return for this American commitment to the Mediterranean, the British agreed to Roundup. To demonstrate their good faith, they also agreed to the appointment of an American to command the Allied force. That officer was the newly promoted Lieutenant General Dwight D. Eisenhower.

Torch, the first of many compromises between the two partners, was a solid victory for Churchill and the British, who gave up virtually nothing in return. Churchill would have been the first to concede that Roundup was inevitable, but now it would be carried out according to a British rather than an American timetable. What Churchill understood with great clarity and Marshall was to learn with even greater dismay was that once committed, the United States would never untangle itself from the Mediterranean. Churchill's military assistant, Brigadier Ian Jacob, summed up American suspicions when he observed in his diary, "The U.S. regarded the Mediterranean as a kind of dark hole into which one entered at one's own peril."[6]

Torch took place on November 8, 1942, when an Allied fleet carrying three separate invasion forces from the United States and Britain landed simultaneously along a nearly-thousand-mile front, at Casablanca, Oran, and Algiers. The French were torn between loyalty to the odious Vichy regime and a desire to join the Allied cause and avenge the defeat of France. After sharp exchanges at Oran and Casablanca, French forces were neutralized and the Allies thrust quickly into Tunisia to capture the key ports of Bizerte and Tunis before Axis forces in North Africa could be reinforced. Then, while Montgomery pursued Rommel into Tunisia, the Torch forces would drive east to Tripolitania and trap Panzerarmee Afrika.

Fearing the loss of Bizerte and Tunis, which the Allies would certainly utilize to mount an invasion of southern Europe, Hitler quickly lost his lethargy for operations in the Mediterranean and ordered the immediate reinforcement of Tunisia. While the Luftwaffe made Allied movement on land a costly proposition, at sea, German U-boats sank Allied shipping with distressing regularity.

The troops of Montgomery's Eighth Army, exhausted after the battles of Alam Halfa and El Alamein, were now stretched across nearly a thousand miles of Libyan desert. His critics have charged that Montgomery forfeited an opportunity to defeat Rommel once and for all by cutting off his retreat. Montgomery, however, was quite unwilling to risk a setback from Rommel, whom he considered an ever-dangerous foe.[7] By mid-November, as the Torch forces were struggling to establish a fully operational front in western Tunisia, the Eighth Army reached Tobruk, the scene of its dreadful defeat six months earlier.

After Alamein, Rommel had urged Hitler to remove German forces from North Africa while there was still time, arguing that prolonged operations there would serve no useful purpose and only result in their senseless annihilation. Hitler angrily spurned Rommel's advice and instead created the Fifth Panzer Army under General Jürgen von Arnim. More than one hundred thousand German and Italian reinforcements began pouring into Tunisia about the time the Allies were attempting to capture Tunis in early November. In contrast to the inexperience of the Anglo-American Torch force, von Arnim's army consisted mostly of veteran troops, whose mandate from Hitler was nothing less than the destruction of the Allied force, thus setting the stage for the first major confrontation of the war in the West.

The five-hundred-mile supply line between Algeria and Tunisia, heavy winter rains, and uninspired leadership combined to turn the overoptimistic timetable established for Torch into a shambles. Moreover, the Allies had not counted upon Hitler's countermove and received two bloody noses attempting to capture Tunis in December 1942. The result was stalemate.

In February 1943, a major German offensive inflicted heavy losses on the inexperienced American troops of Major General Lloyd R. Fredendall's U.S. II Corps at Sidi Bou Zid and Kasserine Pass. Although internecine squabbling between Rommel and von Arnim kept the Germans from striking a killing blow that might well have changed the outcome of the campaign, the result for the Americans was still more than six thousand battle casualties and the humiliation of a major setback in their first major engagement of the war. The British regarded American inexperience and leadership at Kasserine as evidence of the unpreparedness of the U.S. Army to fight a first-class foe and attempted to relegate II Corps to minor roles for the remainder of the campaign.

Kasserine served as a cruel object lesson to those who misunderstood the difficulty of defeating the German Army on the battlefield. It also left American commanders with the problem of restoring the confidence of their ally and the shattered morale of their troops. Eisenhower belatedly sacked Fredendall and appointed Major General George S. Patton, Jr., as the new corps commander. Major General Omar N. Bradley became the deputy commander. The reversal of American fortunes was swift and dramatic. In one of the outstanding leadership feats of the war, Patton and Bradley led II Corps to victories at El Guettar[8] and during the climactic battles of the campaign in the spring of 1943. In less than three months American forces demonstrated the accuracy of war correspondent Drew Middleton's observation that "Armies never learn from other armies. They have to learn by themselves, and a lot of the tactics that we used were those the British had used disastrously two years earlier and discarded."[9]

The British remained skeptical and several unpleasant high-level incidents demonstrated all too clearly that U.S. forces were not yet regarded as trustworthy partners. Sensing a growing lack of confidence in Eisenhower, General Sir Alan Brooke, the Chief of the Imperial General Staff, orchestrated the assignment of Alexander as the Allied ground commander in Tunisia. When he arrived in February 1943, Alexander was quickly dismayed by the American performance. Later, despite the superb leadership of Patton, Bradley, and the commander of the U.S. 1st Armored Division, Major General Ernest N. Harmon, the example of Kasserine and the ineptness of Fredendall still lingered in the minds of Alexander and the other senior British commanders.

Alexander privately criticized the American GI and his leaders. Calling them "soft, green and quite untrained," he noted, "is it surprising then that they lack the will to fight?" Alexander believed the situation was so serious that it threatened the future of Allied operations in both the Mediterranean and Europe. "I have only the American 2d

Corps. There are millions of them elsewhere who must be living in a fool's paradise. If this handful of Divisions here are their best, the value of the rest may be imagined," he wrote to Brooke.[10]

Throughout Tunisia the growing pains of the new alliance abounded and were by no means confined to national rivalries. The veterans of the Eighth Army were as contemptuous of their comrades in the British First Army as they were of the U.S. II Corps. The unhappy result was a poisoning of the atmosphere that extended across service lines and was typified by a rancorous incident over close air support between Patton and the Allied tactical air commander, British Air Vice Marshal Sir Arthur Coningham. Allied Air Commander in Chief Sir Arthur Tedder moved swiftly to avert what might have been "a major crisis in Anglo-American relations" by sending Coningham to apologize personally to Patton for an intemperate signal suggesting that II Corps was not battleworthy. This incident was regarded with such gravity at Allied Force Headquarters (AFHQ) that Eisenhower nearly resigned.

Alexander's continued mistrust of American fighting ability remained evident in his plan for the decisive battle of the campaign, in which II Corps was relegated to the minor mission of protecting the Allied left flank, while the British made the main effort to trap Army Group Afrika on the Cape Bon Peninsula.[11]

Marshall believed that Eisenhower had yielded too much to his British ally, and that American troops were being given menial tasks on the battlefield. Cabling his feelings to Eisenhower, he questioned the diminished American role, which he rightly viewed as a matter of national pride and prestige. Marshall's message was a polite but unmistakable directive to act at once. The final Allied offensive that began on April 19, 1943, crushed Army Group Afrika. Under Bradley's aggressive leadership, II Corps performed brilliantly by capturing Bizerte and cutting off von Arnim's only escape route, forcing the surrender of the Axis army on May 12, 1943.

Allied inexperience and miscalculations in North Africa were more than offset by the inconsistency of their adversary. The cost of Axis intervention in North Africa resulted in the loss of an entire army group of about 240,000 men, when Hitler ruthlessly left von Arnim and his troops to wither and die in the Allied trap after urgent appeals for food, fuel, and ammunition were ignored by Berlin.[12] Germany could ill afford to lose nearly 250,000 troops to a hopeless venture when Wehrmacht units were being annihilated with shocking rapidity on the Eastern Front.

For the Allies the Tunisian venture was a testing ground. As Bradley later noted, "In Africa we learned to crawl, to walk—then run."[13] That Tunisia was a battlefield laboratory was all too evident by the experience of Kasserine, which, for all its bitter aspects, became a valuable lesson American commanders were doggedly determined never to repeat. The campaign also marked the emergence of a new generation of American battlefield generals, whose performance during the remainder of the war was first class. Unfortunately, as events that summer in Sicily would show, this redemption was not recognized by Alexander and other senior British officers.

With the Allies in complete control of North Africa, a turning point in the war had come whereby they, not Hitler, would henceforth dictate the time and place of future engagements. Although the Führer refused to acknowledge that the Axis effort in North Africa was anything more than a sideshow, the defeat of Army Group Afrika was the second disastrous setback of 1943 for Germany.

The Tunisian campaign[14] had run dangerously long and severely threatened the timetable for the next Allied venture in the Mediterranean, the invasion of the island of Sicily. Once "in for a penny," Churchill knew, the United States was "in for a pound." Torch was an excellent example of the opportunistic nature of Britain's Mediterranean policy, which was again demonstrated in January 1943, when the Allied leadership met at Casablanca to debate future strategy after the end of the North African campaign and, as Churchill reminded Roosevelt, "because we have no [suitable] plan for 1943."

Churchill and the British chiefs of staff were fully committed to the removal of Mussolini and the Italians from the war once and for all. In the autumn of 1942, Churchill favored a cross-Channel invasion in the late summer of 1943, but when it became evident that the Tunisian campaign was badly behind schedule, he began to insist on playing out the Mediterranean option. Thus, while continuing to affirm the eventual necessity of a cross-Channel invasion, the prime minister sought to buy time for its planning and preparation by nibbling away at what he termed "the soft underbelly" of Germany. Any action to restore the balance in the Far East was clearly out of the question for the foreseeable future, but in the Mediterranean the Allies had the Axis on the run and must not, argued Churchill, surrender the initiative.[15]

The bargaining chip Churchill had gained six months earlier with Torch was played at the Casablanca Conference. Stalin refused to attend but nevertheless cast a long shadow over the deliberations of his two allies. Although they were soon to win the most important victory of the war on the Eastern Front at Stalingrad, Stalin continued to badger both Churchill and Roosevelt during the second half of 1942 to open a second front without delay and further relieve the pressure upon the beleaguered Red Army by forcing Hitler to maintain a full commitment of forces in the west.

An Anglo-American clash at Casablanca was inevitable when the

Combined Chiefs of Staff[16] began the stormiest negotiations ever to occur between the two Allies. Brooke, the chief British strategist and military spokesman, came to Casablanca fully committed to an invasion of Sicily following the Tunisian campaign. Sicily seemed an obvious choice for the Allies to reinforce their success in the Mediterranean and, at the same time, gain a foothold in southern Europe.

During ten arduous days of wrangling, the major sticking point became the allocation of resources between Europe and the Pacific, with the U.S. chiefs insisting on a 70–30 percent split, while the British demanded virtually 100 percent for Europe. Finally a compromise on Pacific operations was reached that satisfied the U.S. chief of naval operations, Admiral Ernest J. King, and it then became a matter of finding common ground for a joint strategy for the defeat of Germany.

The deadlock over European strategy continued to center on the fundamental differences about the timing and form of the cross-Channel invasion.[17] As Brooke's biographer writes, Marshall continued to insist that "the Mediterranean was a blind alley to which American forces had only been committed because of the President's insistence that they should fight the Germans somewhere; and reinforced in that view by the protracted nature which the North African campaign was assuming."[18] Marshall demanded the transfer of Allied forces in North Africa to the United Kingdom for Roundup, while the British chiefs of staff continued to insist on Churchill's avowed goal of the "cleansing of North Africa to be followed by the capture of Sicily."[19] The final four days of strenuous debate resulted in a second major compromise, which Churchill loftily proclaimed was "the most complete strategic plan for a world-wide war that had ever been conceived."[20] One of its main provisions was the invasion of Sicily, code-named Operation Husky.

Another of the British triumphs at Casablanca was their manipulation of the command structure for Husky. Disturbed both by Eisenhower's lack of high-level command experience and the state of the campaign in Tunisia, Brooke engineered the appointment of Alexander not only as the ground commander in chief in Tunisia but also for Husky. Tedder and Admiral Sir Andrew Cunningham were appointed to command the air and naval forces, while Montgomery and Patton were selected to command the respective Anglo-American invasion forces.

From its inception as a strategic compromise at Casablanca, the planning of Operation Husky was plagued by interminable problems of organization and command. The planning began in early February 1943 at the very moment when the invasion commanders found themselves preoccupied with the faltering campaign in Tunisia. As the commander in chief of the ground forces, it was Alexander's responsibility to develop the invasion plan. However, both he and Eisenhower became so engrossed with the problems in Tunisia that neither was able to give more than token attention to Husky, even though only a full-time commander could have resolved a growing list of problems. The joint Anglo-American planning staff attempted without success to fill the void but were unable to maintain the June timetable decreed by Churchill and Roosevelt at Casablanca. Although five months seemed a sufficiently wide margin, the British official history later noted that "brute facts were to show that it was narrow."[21]

The initial invasion plan called for a series of small amphibious landings from D day* to D plus 5, along the six-hundred-mile coast of Sicily. When he first learned of the proposed plan, Montgomery was horrified by what, in reality, was a return to the "penny packet"[22] tactics that had been so disastrously employed under his predecessor, Auchinleck, and in the early days of Tunisia by the Torch forces. Calling it "a dog's breakfast," Montgomery denounced the entire Husky planning effort as "a hopeless mess" and repeatedly warned his superiors that unless a sensible plan were developed soon, the results would be calamitous.

Eisenhower's worst fears soon became a reality when the committee system, imposed on him by the British at Casablanca, exacerbated the ever-widening divisions between the force commanders.[23] Tedder was insistent on the prompt acquisition of airfields in southern Sicily for his tactical aircraft, while Cunningham demanded maximum security for his ships by backing the multiple-invasion plan, which dispersed the Allied fleet. Acting in the absence of Alexander, Montgomery contended that the only acceptable plan which would guarantee the success of the invasion was to concentrate all ground forces in the south-eastern corner of Sicily.

For three months the debates raged within the Allied high command, as various options were proposed, none of which satisfied the full committee. Even worse, there was mounting evidence of Allied conservatism. In April Churchill became irate when presented with a pessimistic signal from Eisenhower, stating that the Husky planners feared failure if the invaders encountered more than two German divisions. The prime minister scathingly replied that "these pusillanimous and defeatist doctrines . . . would make us the laughing stock of the world."[24]

As concern mounted in both Washington and London, the solution came from within, when a calculated act of insubordination by Montgomery at last broke the impasse. In late April, frustrated by the inac-

*Although commonly (and mistakenly) thought of as referring only to the Normandy landings on June 6, 1944, *D day* is a military term used to denote the start of a military operation. It was employed in numerous amphibious landing operations during World War II, including North Africa, Sicily, Salerno, and Anzio.

tion and deeply worried that the planning stalemate might never be broken in time for the invasion, Montgomery, at considerable risk to his reputation, deliberately precipitated a crisis by signaling Alexander that he intended to proceed with planning for the employment of the entire Eighth Army in southeastern Sicily.

A turbulent meeting on April 29, 1943, not only failed to resolve Allied differences but further exacerbated the bad feelings toward the Eighth Army commander. Finally, on May 2, the Allied leadership approved Montgomery's plan. Tedder was assured of the highest priority for the capture of Axis airfields in the Gela sector, but Cunningham was never comfortable with the plan, which he believed exposed the Allied fleet to greater risk of enemy retaliation. In a short speech to the assembled Allied leadership, Montgomery said, "I have seen so many mistakes made in this war, and so many disasters happen, that I am desperately anxious to try and see that we have no more . . . a disaster in Sicily . . . would be dreadful."[25]

Although conservative, Montgomery's was the soundest of the five plans the Allies had considered and rejected. The approved invasion plan called for the Eighth Army to land four divisions and one independent infantry brigade along a fifty-mile front in southeastern Sicily, from Syracuse to the Pachino Peninsula. At the same time, Patton's U.S. Seventh Army would make its primary landings along the south coast, at Gela, with the reinforced U.S. 1st Infantry Division. Secondary landings at Licata and Scoglitti by two other U.S. divisions were to protect the flanks of the Seventh Army.

The landings were to be preceded the night before by U.S. airborne and British glider landings to capture and control several key choke points near Gela and Syracuse. A parachute regiment of the U.S. 82d Airborne Division and a British glider brigade were the spearhead forces of a bold night operation, the first of its kind ever attempted. Once ashore, the Eighth Army's mission was the capture of the ports of Syracuse and Augusta, and then the strategically important plain of Catania, along the southern edge of Mount Etna. Eventually, the British were to drive north to capture the port city of Messina, which served as the primary Axis logistic lifeline to the Italian mainland across the narrow Strait of Messina.

Montgomery's plan relegated Patton's army to the unimportant role of protecting the British left flank. Although disappointed at playing second fiddle to Montgomery, Patton believed that future circumstances would inevitably alter the mission of the Seventh Army. Several senior Allied commanders urged him to protest, but Patton emphatically refused, with the comment, "No, goddammit, I've been in this Army thirty years and when my superior gives me an order I say, 'Yes, Sir!' and then do my goddamndest to carry it out."[26]

* * *

The calamitous defeat of Axis forces in North Africa left the German and Italian high commands in no doubt that the Allies would soon employ their massive sea, air, and ground forces elsewhere in the Mediterranean. The only question was whether they would invade southern Europe via Italy or the Balkans. Among the possible sites were the lightly defended Aegean, mainland Italy, and—most obvious of all—the islands of Sardinia and Sicily.

Sicily had long been a remote outpost of Mussolini's modern-day Roman empire, and the Sicilians had welcomed neither the Italian Army nor its German ally. Theoretically, the island was a military fortress, garrisoned by an Italian army of more than three hundred thousand men, backed by a small German contingent that, up to June 1943, never consisted of more than the equivalent of a division. Moreover, until 1943 the island was paid only token attention as a possible Allied target. This quickly changed with the loss of North Africa and when the new Axis commander, Italian General Alfredo Guzzoni, arrived in May, he found Sicily's naval defenses virtually nonexistent, its air defenses inadequate, and the ground forces woefully trained and their equipment archaic.

Among the senior Axis commanders, only Guzzoni was convinced the Allies intended to invade southeastern Sicily. His dilemma was that the Italian Sixth Army was not only badly positioned to repel an enemy invasion, but its state of preparedness was so woeful that in some units the officers did not even know how to operate their own guns. Italian morale was dreadful and there was too little time for Guzzoni to alter the deeply rooted inferiority complex that had pervaded the Italian Army since the beginning of the war. His dire warnings of the sorry state of Sicily's defenses went unheeded in Rome, where Mussolini had fallen victim to his own fantasies about the invincibility of the Italian Army. Il Duce's response was to boast that any invader would be smashed "at the water's edge."

After the debacle in Tunisia, Hitler seemed less inclined to so casually sacrifice German troops to lost causes and, in response to Italian requests for assistance, agreed only to send the newly re-created Hermann Göring Division to augment the also recently formed 15th Panzer Grenadier Division.[27] He also ordered a corps headquarters, commanded by a veteran panzer general, Hans Valentin Hube, positioned in southern Calabria to take over tactical command of all German forces in the event of an Allied invasion.

Although the two German divisions were in position to assist in repelling an invasion by early July, Kesselring and Guzzoni disagreed over the defense of the island. Recognizing that he could not protect the entire Sicilian coastline, Guzzoni proposed the formation of a pow-

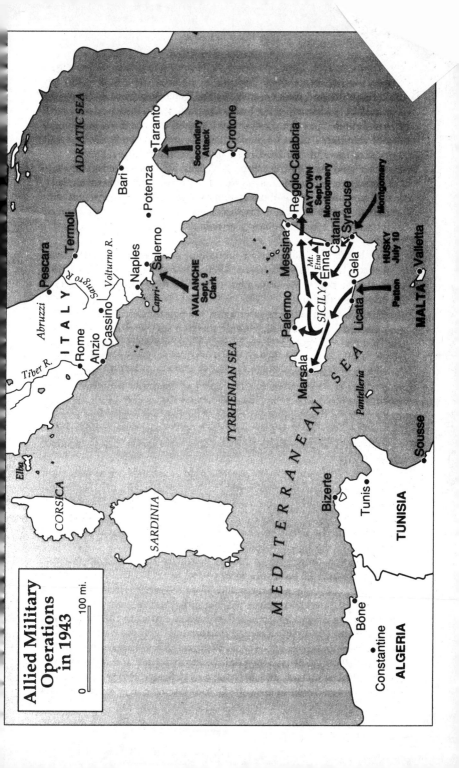

Allied Military Operations in 1943

0   100 mi.

ADRIATIC SEA

Taranto
Crotone
Secondary Attack
Bari
Potenza
Termoli
Pescara
Santoro R.
Volturno R.
Naples
Salerno
Capri
AVALANCHE Sept. 9 Clark
Abruzzi
Rome
Anzio
Cassino
Tiber R.
ITALY
Elba
CORSICA
SARDINIA
TYRRHENIAN SEA
Reggio-Calabria
BAYTOWN Sept. 3 Montgomery
Messina
Syracuse
Montgomery
Palermo
Mt. Etna
Enna
Catania
SICILY
Gela
HUSKY July 10
Licata
Patton
Marsala
Pantelleria
MALTA
Valletta
MEDITERRANEAN SEA
Bizerte
Tunis
TUNISIA
Sousse
Bône
Constantine
ALGERIA

erful counterattack force, utilizing as its core the armor of the two German panzer grenadier divisions then in Sicily. These mobile forces would be positioned in the eastern half of Sicily, safely out of range of naval gunfire, poised to deliver a crushing blow while the invaders were still vulnerable. Kesselring overruled Guzzoni by personally ordering most of the 15th Panzer Grenadier Division to western Sicily.[28]

A vital part of the Husky plan was for the Allied air forces to conduct round-the-clock bombing of targets in Sicily, Sardinia, Italy, and elsewhere in the Mediterranean, with the object of neutralizing Axis air capability. The effort was an exceptional success; both Axis air forces were left a shambles. The Italians were destroyed as a fighting force and the Luftwaffe severely crippled.

A vast battle armada of nearly 2,600 Allied naval vessels participated in Husky. Under the command of Vice Admiral H. Kent Hewitt and Admiral Sir Bertram Ramsay, eight naval task forces were formed for the invasion on July 10.

The invasion of Sicily began tragically when the British glider force encountered dangerously high winds, smoke from the island, and heavy flak from enemy guns and from friendly naval vessels that, contrary to orders, mistakenly fired on the aerial armada of aircraft and gliders. Coordination and cooperation between the air forces and the naval and ground forces was extremely poor and had for some time been the object of serious contention. Losses were very heavy, and only a fraction of the glider forces landed on target. The U.S. airborne force met a similar fate when most of its more than 5,000 troops were dropped far from Gela and became scattered over a thousand square miles of south-eastern Sicily.

The British landings met generally light resistance, but at Gela the U.S. 1st Infantry Division was heavily counterattacked by the Hermann Göring Division and Italian forces on the first two days.[29] The attacks on D day were beaten off by American paratroopers and infantrymen, but on July 11 the Germans launched a heavy tank attack that nearly penetrated to the beaches before being repulsed.

Thereafter, there was no further threat to the American beach-head, and by July 12 the Allies were poised to exploit the absence of a coordinated Axis defense of the island. The problem was that both army commanders found themselves without either a firm plan of action or guidance from Alexander. Before the invasion Patton and Montgomery never once met to discuss strategy; thus among the three senior ground commanders there was not even a consensus of how the campaign was expected to unfold. Alexander preferred to await actual developments before asserting himself, and after the war indicated that he never had any intention of doing so until the Seventh Army had seized the Gela airfields and the Eighth Army had control of the ports of Syracuse and Augusta and the plain of Catania.

Alexander failed to develop either a strategic or tactical plan for the capture of Sicily. His notion of strategy was for Patton to act as the shield in his left hand, while the Eighth Army served as the sword in his right. But, as one of Montgomery's senior staff officers has written, "The two armies were left largely to develop their operations in the manner which seemed most propitious in the prevailing circumstances."[30] Although both Montgomery and Patton identified Messina as the only worthwhile objective in Sicily, Alexander nevertheless elected to allow the land battle to develop before deciding the strategy his two armies would employ.[31]

Alexander's inaction stemmed in part from his unwillingness to entrust to the Seventh Army anything more than a minor role in the campaign. The improved American performance in Tunisia in the spring of 1943 had failed to alter his conviction that American fighting ability was still inferior to that of the British Army, even though the U.S. Army now fighting in Sicily bore scant resemblance to the one that had been humiliated at Kasserine five months earlier. Alexander firmly believed that the troops of the Eighth Army were more experienced and reliable than any American troops, despite the fact that most of Montgomery's veteran formations were worn out from too many months of combat in North Africa.

By failing to develop a plan or anticipate the speed with which the two armies would secure such sizable bridgeheads, Alexander was unprepared to fight the campaign in Sicily. The inevitable result was that his two strong-willed subordinates began to act independently of Alexander—and of each other. Thus, when Montgomery proposed on July 12 what Alexander had envisioned all along, that the Eighth Army make the main effort to cut Sicily in two, he found ready acceptance from the Allied ground commander in chief. The proposed route of advance cut across the interarmy boundary and directly across the axis of advance of the U.S. 45th Division. Montgomery signaled Alexander that he wanted the troublesome boundary line moved farther to the west. Neither took cognizance of the fact that the 45th Division was not only better prepared but advantageously positioned to carry out this task.

Alexander ordered Patton to hand over the disputed highway to the Eighth Army, which, in turn, required Bradley to move the entire 45th Division back to the Gela beaches, and then north to new positions on the left flank of the 1st Division. It was the most contentious and militarily unsound decision of the campaign and, at a stroke, forfeited an opportunity to encircle the German XIV Panzer Corps.

Although the order disgusted Patton, he complied without protest.

Bradley was thunderstruck. "My God," he told Patton, "you can't let him do that." However, the root of this problem was neither Montgomery nor Patton, but Alexander's unwillingness to take control of the campaign at its most crucial moment, which played directly into German hands by granting Hube precious time to prepare a defensive line centered along Mount Etna and thus dictate the timetable for the campaign.[32]

On July 17 Patton decided the time had come to take matters into his own hands, and he arrived unexpectedly at Alexander's headquarters in North Africa to make a personal plea for a greater American role. Patton recognized that Montgomery's offensive to capture Messina was in serious trouble on the plain of Catania, where repeated attempts to break the German left flank had failed. Patton knew that Montgomery, having committed the 13th Corps along the coast and the 30th Corps inland, had forfeited most of his options. Alexander found himself unable to refuse Patton after giving Montgomery free rein. He agreed to Patton's plan to use Bradley's II Corps for a drive to the north coast to cut the island in two, while the remainder of the Seventh Army was detached for a secondary offensive to clear western Sicily. Patton did not bother telling Alexander that this included the capture of Sicily's capital city, Palermo.

In reality this was merely a clever ploy by Patton to maneuver the Seventh Army into a position to capture Messina. At that moment his army was ideally placed to break through the Etna Line and encircle XIV Panzer Corps, who were now giving the 30th Corps the same kind of bloody nose they had administered on the plain of Catania to Lieutenant General Sir Miles Dempsey's 13th Corps. In the rough, mountainous terrain of central Sicily, where the road net was poor and vehicular mobility severely limited, the Germans mounted an effective defense, giving ground when necessary, then forcing their attackers to start all over again. Every advance had to be paid for in blood.

For the second time during the campaign, Alexander failed to seize an opportunity to strike a killing blow with the Seventh Army. The Etna Line defenses were incomplete and were the weakest precisely where II Corps might have been used to break them and tighten a noose from which the only escape was retreat or surrender.

The American offensive into western Sicily rapidly crushed all Italian resistance in its path. Palermo fell on July 21, and American troops entering the capital city were greeted by thousands of flag-waving, cheering Sicilians. When the 45th Division reached the north coast on July 23, Patton immediately ordered II Corps to begin a fresh offensive toward Messina.

Although Alexander had given the Eighth Army the exclusive use of the only four roads leading to Messina, thus effectively excluding the

Seventh Army from any role in its capture, Montgomery nevertheless proposed on July 25 that the Seventh Army capture the city. Although Patton privately questioned Montgomery's motive, the Eighth Army commander firmly believed that the Seventh Army was better positioned to capture Messina and end what had become a frustrating and increasingly bloody campaign.

For three weeks the Germans had skillfully carried out a succession of delaying actions by using the mountainous terrain to maximum advantage. Time and again, they managed to plug the gaps in the Etna Line by concentrating their defenses along key terrain and the obvious routes of approach, despite having to contend with unending harassment from the air, where the Allied air forces now exercised total dominance. They were also feeling the effects of a rapidly growing shortage of supplies, ammunition, and fuel, not from any interruption of their efficient ferry service across the Strait of Messina but rather from Allied interdiction of the road and rail net in central and southern Italy. With time rapidly running out, Hube's staff began to prepare plans for a series of delaying actions to Messina and a mass evacuation across the strait to mainland Italy.

The Germans elected to stand and fight for the mountain city of Troina, and for nearly a week one attack after another by the U.S. 1st Division was beaten off in what Bradley described as "the most bitterly fought battle of the campaign."[33] Although the Germans suffered sixteen hundred killed, their sacrifice bought sufficient time for Hube to finalize his plans for the evacuation.

When the Germans began their evacuation of Sicily, they fully expected catastrophic losses. A preliminary evacuation began in early August, and by the time the final evacuation commenced on the night of August 11, they had already withdrawn more than thirteen thousand troops and considerable equipment. Ferry traffic in the Strait of Messina was efficiently organized and performed flawlessly under the cover of heavy German and Italian antiaircraft gunfire.

The Allied air forces made a halfhearted and largely futile effort to interdict the evacuation. However, they not only failed to attack the correct targets, but deliberately avoided employing their B-17 strategic bomber force, the only weapon which could have made a difference. The result was that instead of enormous losses, the Germans pulled off a stunningly successful strategic withdrawal. By the time it ended on the morning of August 17 they had evacuated nearly 55,000 troops, 9,789 vehicles, 51 tanks, and 163 guns, mostly by daylight.

When the U.S. 3d Division entered the smoking ruins of Messina that same morning, the last German had long since departed. The German naval commander who had masterminded the evacuation had every right to exult: "We have not given up a single German soldier, weapon or vehicle into enemy hands."[34]

The last days of the battle for Sicily were a dismal conclusion to a campaign that had been beset from the outset by controversy and indecision. For thirty-eight days the Allies fought some of the most difficult battles of the war, in terrain every bit as harsh as they would find ahead of them in Italy. Yet their enemy had not only defied them to the end but had accomplished one of the most impressive strategic withdrawals in military history.

At Dunkirk British ingenuity and grit had saved the British Expeditionary Force but not its precious equipment. In Sicily the Germans had not only saved themselves, but virtually everything capable of being ferried to the mainland. Defiant to the end, the Germans emerged from the campaign with justifiable pride in having acquitted themselves well against overwhelmingly superior air, sea, and ground forces.

From the time of Alexander's decision to force the Seventh Army into a secondary role, and Montgomery's decision to switch his main effort from the plain of Catania to the highlands, the Germans had been in control of the timetable for the Sicilian campaign. One historian has aptly described Sicily as "an Allied physical victory, a German moral victory."[35] Others have been less charitable.

The Allies needlessly prolonged the reduction of Sicily by ponderous and largely ineffective tactics. The reasons were varied: Eisenhower's lack of direct involvement; Alexander's failure to take command of the ground campaign; Montgomery's unfortunate changes of strategy; the failure of the air forces to make more than a token effort[36] to impede the German evacuation, and the navy's failure to block the Strait of Messina. The German commanders were scornful of Allied tactics. Kesselring believed that Calabria ought at least to have been a secondary target, while another senior German general called the failure to seize the Strait of Messina "incomprehensible."[37]

From the outset, the Allies had taken the safe, conservative path. The invasion plan was Montgomery's version, which opted for safety in numbers, and was in no small part the result of the misjudgment of the Allied planners, who overestimated the resistance the Italians would offer. Even so, as the campaign unfolded there were numerous opportunities to win a decisive victory, which were wasted, and the Allied ground forces were left to fight a needless, frontal battle of attrition. Thus, a German army corps that was devoid of air and naval support, and never exceeded 60,000 men, managed to thwart two Allied armies, whose combined strength exceeded 450,000 troops, for thirty-eight days at a considerable cost.[38]

Secondary landings elsewhere along the Sicilian coast were never seriously pursued, even though the Allies controlled both the air and the sea. In some instances Allied strategy was downright foolish. Air attacks on Sicilian towns and cities—which, as British war correspondent Christopher Buckley caustically observed, were "blotted out by bombing from the air on a scale unprecedented in the history of war"— failed miserably when the Germans made a point of not defending urban areas.[39]

The key to Sicily was not in the air but on the sea. Husky was an enormous improvement over Torch and provided valuable lessons in the development of airborne and amphibious warfare that would be put to good use the following summer in Normandy. To defeat the Axis evacuation of Sicily required an integrated, joint air-naval effort, which was never forthcoming. Sea power was the greatest weapon the Allies possessed, and it was never pressed anywhere near its full capability. Too often, in fact, it was treated as a commodity too precious to be employed in any operation involving risk.

Sicily ought to have served as a example to the Allied leadership that faintheartedness and the absence of clearly defined strategic goals ensured that the same blunders would shortly be repeated time and again during the bloodiest campaign of the entire war.

2

The Path to Stalemate

Italy is like a boot. You must, like Hannibal, enter it from the top.

—NAPOLEON

The invasion of Sicily hastened the downfall of the Italian dictator, Benito Mussolini, and plunged the Italian government into a crisis from which it never recovered. By mid-July 1943, Il Duce's Fascist regime was already on the brink of collapse from within, brought about by the woeful performance of the Italian Armed Forces and by intense Allied pressure in the form of the invasion of Sicily and saturation bombing of targets on the island and the mainland.

The blows had come with numbing regularity, commencing with the Husky landings, followed by the near-total collapse of the Italian Army in Sicily as an effective fighting force. On July 19, the first Allied bombing attack against Rome struck directly at the heart of the Fascist state. The decision to bomb the Eternal City was made by the Combined Chiefs of Staff for sound military reasons: Rome's two huge marshaling yards were the hub of all rail movement between northern and southern Italy, and their destruction would seriously impair the movement of Axis supplies. In addition to successfully disrupting Axis rail movements for several days, the attack also—as expected—had a powerful effect on Italian morale. Although sparing Rome's precious landmarks, it created panic among the populace and deepened the sense of gloom that had surrounded the Italian dictator for months. Thinly veiled hints from King Victor Emmanuel III that Mussolini ought to consider resignation were pointedly ignored.

The deteriorating position of Italy as a middleman in the larger conflict between the Allies and Nazi Germany led to the hatching of two unrelated plots to remove Mussolini, one of which was led by the dictator's own son-in-law, Count Galeazzo Ciano, the former foreign minister. The other was led by General Vittorio Ambrosio, the outspoken anti-German head of the Commando Supremo; Marshal Pietro Badoglio, the former head of the Armed Forces and a longtime opponent of Mussolini; and King Victor Emmanuel III, the man who had brought Mussolini to power in 1922.

After refusing to accept a no-confidence vote at a meeting of the largely ceremonial Grand Council on July 24, 1943, Mussolini turned to the king for support. It was not forthcoming, and Mussolini was arrested and exiled to the tiny island of Ponza, where enemies of the Fascist state had been previously banished. Victor Emmanuel immediately appointed Badoglio to head the Italian government. Although he proclaimed that the war would go on as before, the new Italian leader began secretly negotiating an armistice with the Allies that led, in September 1943, to Italy's secession from the Rome-Berlin Axis.

The fall of Mussolini came as a shock to the German leadership, and despite Badoglio's assurances of Italian loyalty, there was a storm of derision from Hitler, who jeered, "They say they'll fight but that's treachery! We must be quite clear: it's pure treachery! . . . the biggest impudence in history. Does that man imagine that I will believe him?"[1] The enraged Führer was dissuaded from attempting a coup. Instead, the Germans moved quickly to revive earlier contingency plans for a series of military actions to be taken in the event of an Italian collapse.

Rommel, who had been in disfavor since his recall from North Africa, was hastily recalled from a special mission to Greece, given command of the newly formed Army Group B, and ordered to organize the defense of northern Italy across the Apennines from Pisa to Rimini and the Alpine passes.[2] For the moment there remained an uneasy truce between the two Axis partners, with neither side trusting the pledges of the other. As Rommel made preparations to intervene, the Germans began moving fresh troops into northern Italy under the pretense of reinforcing Kesselring if the Allies invaded southern Italy. Despite his distrust of the Italians, Hitler retained a soft spot for Mussolini and was determined to remove him from the hands of his captors. (Less than two months later Mussolini would be dramatically rescued from captivity in the Apennines in a superbly executed raid, masterminded and led by thirty-five-year-old Lieutenant Colonel Otto Skorzeny, who commanded an elite German commando unit that carried out the most daring and successful special operations of the war.)

While the Germans pondered their survival and the Italians their future, after months of indecision, the Allies had at last acted on Eisenhower's recommendation that an invasion of Italy follow the fall of Sicily. At Casablanca the Allied leadership failed to clarify whether the invasion of Sicily was a stepping-stone to a larger objective in Italy or merely an end in itself, and by August 1943 the question had still not been resolved. Overlord was not scheduled until May 1944, and the large Allied ground force in the Mediterranean could hardly be left in Sicily and North Africa without a new mission.

Eisenhower was authorized to begin planning two operations directed against Italy. The U.S. Fifth Army had been organized in the spring of 1943 to plan and execute operations in Italy, and for months Mark Clark's troops had been preparing for an amphibious invasion at a point south of Naples, which was identified in August as Salerno. Toward the end of operations in Sicily, Montgomery withdrew Dempsey's 13th Corps to begin planning an invasion of Calabria, code-named Operation Baytown.

At the Quadrant conference in Quebec in August 1943, the U.S. and British military chiefs clashed over the scope of future operations in the Mediterranean, including Avalanche, the Salerno landings. They finally agreed that Overlord would take precedence and that Eisenhower would have to carry out operations in Italy with considerably reduced forces and logistic support. Seven divisions were to be transferred to the United Kingdom to prepare for the cross-Channel attack. Eisenhower would have to make do with what remained.

What was lacking at Quebec or indeed at any time during the Italian campaign was a statement of Allied grand strategy. If the political goals were vague, even less clear were those of the forthcoming military operations. Churchill's Mediterranean strategy envisioned continued Allied operations in Italy, including an offensive that would carry them into its northern provinces, where the Allied air forces could be employed in a direct support role in Overlord operations.* The British continued to believe that a strong Allied presence in the Mediterranean was a vital ingredient in the defeat of Germany. As one U.S. official historian has written, "Although the basic decision of 'Europe First' held throughout the war, the question of how it was to be interpreted and applied arose early in the conflict and remained almost to the end."[3]

---

*A controversial plan to invade southern France in support of the cross-Channel invasion was also under consideration. An invasion along the Riviera was deemed essential by those who saw a pressing need to divert German attention and troops from Normandy during the critical days immediately after the D-day landings. The result was code-named Anvil (later redesignated Dragoon), and it eventually became the most hotly debated Allied operation of the war. Headed by Churchill, the cross-Channel's detractors argued that it was unnecessary, would necessitate using forces urgently needed in Italy, and so weaken the Allies that the stalemate in the autumn and winter of 1943, after Salerno, might never be broken.

The British had long feared that the United States would insist on ceasing further active military operations in the Mediterranean once Sicily was successfully conquered and Allied control of the region in the air and on the sea was supreme. This fear drew Churchill to North Africa in May 1943 to dissuade the American leadership from such a decision. According to Eisenhower, "He frankly said that he wanted to do his utmost to see that no such 'disaster'—as he called it—would occur."[4] The decision to continue operations in Italy after Sicily again hinged on British backing for cross-Channel operations. According to Eisenhower, the decision to invade Italy brought jubilation to Churchill.[5]

The Mediterranean campaigns sharply focused on the fundamental differences between a European colonial maritime power and the insularity of a great industrial nation. The British considered it both prudent and pragmatic to disperse the Allied effort and take advantage of opportunities. "The British placed a correspondingly high value on strategic flexibility, in preference to rigid adherence to a long-prepared plan," wrote an official British historian. But, for the United States:

> Strategy implied concentration of effort, in the Napoleonic sense. Unused to long wars against numerically superior Continental powers, and rightly confident in their application of ingenuity to unparalleled strength, they had no need or experience of the devious approach. Their strategic resource and tactical boldness [were] exercised in the service of a single strategic target and of a single well-prepared design. . . . The Americans thus disliked the "side-shows" which to the British were an inherent element of warfare; and the Mediterranean had always seemed to them to bear all the marks of the "side-show." Every division sent to the Mediterranean "was a division lost for the main battle."[6]

The inevitable result was that the Allies launched their campaign in Italy with only a short-term vision of what was to become a long-term problem.

During August the Allies pursued secret negotiations with the new Badoglio government for the surrender of Italy. When the Allies refused to budge from their insistence on unconditional surrender, the Italians soon learned they had virtually no bargaining position. Deeply concerned about what was certain to be a violent German reaction, they pleaded that the announcement of the Italian surrender should be withheld until the Allies landed and could protect Rome. However, unless Italian forces could be severed from their German ally, the combined Axis forces in Italy would number approximately thirty-five divisions and pose a considerable threat to the Allies, whose numbers were far smaller. A compromise was finally agreed on, whereby a proclamation of Italian capitulation would coincide with the Salerno landings.

The principal factor in the decision to invade Salerno was the range of Allied tactical aircraft. Naples represented the maximum range of Tedder's Sicily-based squadrons, but even at that distance, air cover would only amount to approximately twenty minutes over the battle front. Hence the Allied planners recommended that the Fifth Army invade Italy along the Gulf of Salerno, approximately twenty miles south of Naples.

They were also worried about control of the Italian boot and the vital shipping lanes of the Strait of Messina. Eisenhower decided that a force in southern Italy was necessary to draw valuable German reserves away from Salerno, to cope with the Baytown invasion. No consideration seems to have been given to the possibility that the Germans might refuse to do battle in southern Calabria.

The shortage of landing craft was to prove the single greatest impediment to Allied operations in the Mediterranean and Northwest Europe. There were never enough, and with priorities split between Europe and the Pacific, it became a constant struggle to obtain adequate craft with which to mount amphibious operations. Even worse for the Italian theater was the knowledge that, by early 1944, most Mediterranean-based shipping would be shifted to the United Kingdom for Overlord. Because there were too few landing craft for simultaneous landings, Baytown necessarily had to precede Avalanche. Once Montgomery gained a foothold on the toe of southern Calabria, the landing craft were to be committed to the Salerno landings, scheduled for September 9, a week after Baytown.

Among those who considered Baytown a wasteful and unnecessary operation was Montgomery, who complained to Brooke that the same lack of coordination and strategic goals that had characterized operations in Sicily now threatened the forthcoming campaign in Italy. The focus of his concern was Alexander, whom he esteemed as a friend but about whom he had few illusions when it came to masterminding a major operation of war. The end of the Sicily campaign only reinforced his doubts about what lay ahead in Italy. "The trouble is there is no higher-up grip on this campaign. CUNNINGHAM is in MALTA; TEDDER is at TUNISIA; ALEXANDER is at SYRACUSE. It beats me how you can run a campaign in that way, with each of the three Commanders of the three Services about 600 miles from each other."[7]

However unpleasant to his critics, Montgomery's criticism had considerable merit.[8] Years later he called Baytown "a unique incident in the history of war," in which "I had been ordered to invade the mainland of Europe with the Eighth Army—but had been given no object."[9] Montgomery's premise was, Why bother with a costly and laborious drive north through southern Italy in the first place? His chief of staff, Major General Francis de Guingand, asked the question no one seemed willing to address: "If Avalanche is a success, then we should reinforce that front for there is little point in laboriously fighting our way up Southern Italy. It is better to leave the enemy to decay there or let him have the trouble of moving himself up from the foot to where we are concentrated."[10]

No one spelled out for Montgomery or anyone else who was going to do what. His diary for September 5 records his frustration: "Before we embark on major operations on the mainland of Europe we must have a master plan and know how we propose to develop these operations. I have not been told of any master plan and I must therefore assume that there was none."[11]

Montgomery attempted without success to persuade Eisenhower to cancel Baytown and use the threat of landings in Calabria as a means of tying down forces which might otherwise imperil the Fifth Army at Salerno. The truth was that there was little Montgomery could do to alter Allied thinking. His uncompromising stand over Husky had all but worn out his welcome as an arbitrator of Allied policy. Consequently, his complaints about the futility of Baytown were ignored and merely provided additional ammunition to his critics, who were anxious to discredit him.

The decisions made by the Allied high command during this period of the war in the Mediterranean reflected both a lack of strategic goals for the Italian campaign, and an occasional, uncharacteristic rashness. An example of the latter was Giant II, an operation to seize Rome using the U.S. 82d Airborne Division. Its most powerful advocate was the AFHQ chief of staff, Walter Bedell Smith, who sold both Alexander and Eisenhower on its merits. The plan was to drop the division outside Rome, where they would link up with approximately four divisions of Italian troops and, together, seize Rome by *coup de main*, assisted by the Roman citizenry who, according to Smith, would "drop kettles, bricks, [and] hot water on the Germans in the streets of Rome."[12] The result, argued Smith, would have been a mandatory retreat to the north by German forces then in central and southern Italy.

Among the opponents of Giant II was Clark, who lost his only strategic reserve for Avalanche, which he intended to employ in blocking positions along the Volturno River to prevent panzer reserves from rushing from the north to the aid of General Heinrich von Vietinghoff's Tenth Army at Salerno. An irate Clark told Eisenhower, "No! That's my division! . . . Taking away the Eighty-Second just as the fighting starts is like cutting off my left arm." Eisenhower refused to budge, and Clark was left with a vague assurance that he would get the division back as soon as Giant II was completed.[13]

Major General Matthew B. Ridgway refused to commit his division on the assurance of AFHQ staff officers whom he distrusted, and with

Eisenhower's consent his division artillery commander, Brigadier General Maxwell Taylor, undertook a secret mission to Rome. Taylor soon learned that Smith's claims were absurd. Not only was the Italian will to fight dubious, but the notion that two nearby German Panzer Grenadier Divisions would be deterred by a small U.S. airborne force without heavy supporting weapons or air support was sheer fantasy.[14]

Only hours before the operation was to commence, Taylor urgently radioed Eisenhower to abort Giant II. Not only did the situation bear scant relation to its backers' claims, but as Taylor pointed out, there was only sufficient airlift capability to move the equivalent of a reinforced regiment to Rome.[15] Had this ill-advised scheme been carried out, there is little doubt of the probable fate of the 82d Airborne.

Operation Avalanche was designed by its architects to take advantage of the imminent collapse of Italy, and to gain an Allied foothold on the Italian mainland. A major consideration was Salerno's proximity to Naples, which the Allies urgently required for its excellent port facilities. The basic concept of the plan was that, once ashore, Clark's Fifth Army would link up with Montgomery's Eighth Army driving north from Calabria. Together they would continue offensive operations toward Rome under the aegis of Alexander's 15th Army Group.

The shortage of landing craft reduced the scope of the Salerno landings to three divisions and a small U.S. Ranger and British Commando force. The Anglo-American assault elements of Avalanche consisted of the British 10th Corps, commanded by an outspoken former cavalry officer who had been Alexander's chief of staff in the Middle East, Lieutenant General Richard McCreery, and the U.S. VI Corps, commanded by Major General Ernest J. Dawley.[16]

In reality the initial stages of Avalanche were to be little more than a corps-size operation. 10th Corps consisted of two infantry divisions that had fought in North Africa, while VI Corps consisted of a single assault division, Major General Fred L. Walker's 36th (Texas National Guard) Division.[17] The Rangers and Commandos were to land west of Salerno, seize the mountain passes leading from Salerno to Naples, and establish blocking positions against German reinforcements attempting to reach the Salerno bridgehead. The British mission was to land between the Sele River and the city of Salerno and capture the vital Montecorvino airfield.

Backed by tanks, Walker's Texans were to land south of the Sele River at Paestum to anchor the right flank. On the second day, the reserve force of Major General Troy Middleton's two 45th Division regimental combat teams was to land and assist the 36th Division. In all, the Avalanche force would by nightfall on D day consist of twenty-seven infantry battalions, 150 supporting Sherman tanks, and a large number of antitank guns, backed by nearly 400 guns and assorted self-propelled artillery. The invasion force would also be supported by the naval guns of Vice Admiral Hewitt's Western Naval Task Force and Rear Admiral Sir Philip Vian's Support Carrier Force, consisting of Royal Navy carriers, battleships, cruisers, and destroyers. Although the numbers of men and weapons on the ground looked impressive on paper, in practice they were to prove woefully inadequate when deployed over an invasion front of nearly thirty-five miles.

During the war Montgomery frequently complained that far too many combat operations were being planned by inexperienced staffs, and Avalanche turned out to be a classic example of what he meant. Its most serious flaw was that the missions assigned the invasion force far exceeded the sum of its parts. Both 10th Corps and VI Corps were dangerously overextended and assigned frontages far in excess of their capability to either defend or attack. Even worse, the plan split the two corps so that neither force was in a position to initially provide mutual support to the other. The U.S. 36th Division was virtually a separate invasion force, and the British 56th Division, on the VI Corps' left flank, was ten miles away and itself obliged to cover a frontage of some fifteen miles. The Sele River and several tributaries constituted a formidable obstacle to mutual support.

The Rangers and Commandos were dependent on relief by the British 46th Division, yet no consideration seems to have been given to the consequences if the division were unable to complete the linkup. The invasion force was to land directly in the line of fire of German gun emplacements in the hills overlooking the Gulf of Salerno. Finally, the forces allocated to a breakout from the bridgehead were inadequate. As the authors of a superb study of the Italian campaign note, "The whole plan was an example of the Fifth Army staff's propensity to make plans on the map without any study of the ground or of possible enemy reaction. The result was that of the nine brigades [of infantry] . . . available only two were allotted to the task of breaking out of the bridgehead; both infantry, marching on foot."[18]

Although Eisenhower had confidence in his protégé, Mark Clark, he had learned from previous amphibious operations to mistrust the optimism of his planners. Clark himself had not been satisfied with Salerno as the invasion site, preferring that the landings be made north of Naples, in the Gulf of Gaeta, which was devoid of the mountainous terrain advantageous to a defender. He was overruled, and the deciding factor had become the limitations of air support. As Clark later explained, "I was forced to go in there because the Airman [Tedder] says I won't support you north—I can't. The Navy [Cunningham] says I won't support you north because your transports are too unprotected. . . . There was no one man to say, 'You'll do it!' "[19]

Nevertheless, Clark was generally optimistic about the chances of Allied success. Others were less enthusiastic, among them Alexander, who, on August 30, called the operation "a dangerous gamble" because inadequate forces had been allocated. Nevertheless, his misgivings about Salerno did not sway his conviction that the Allies would capture Rome by mid-October at the latest.

The Germans expected an Allied invasion somewhere near Naples; the only major question was when. The Allied commanders had no illusions that they could gain either strategic or tactical surprise, but Clark told Admiral Hewitt that he believed the Italian Army would forestall a German takeover of the vital coast defenses.[20]

The most controversial decision became Clark's election to forgo a preliminary naval bombardment in an effort to achieve tactical surprise. Hewitt vehemently protested that "any officer with a pair of dividers could figure out that the Gulf of Salerno was the northernmost practicable landing place for the Allies; reconnaissance planes would snoop the convoys; in short, that it was fantastic to assume we could obtain tactical surprise."[21] Clark's refusal to accept Hewitt's advice was based on the assumption that naval gunfire would unnecessarily attract German reinforcements to Salerno.

Badoglio lost his battle with the Allies to withhold the announcement of Italy's capitulation until after the invasion of Salerno, and on September 8 the BBC announced: "The Italian armed forces have accepted unconditional surrender." Over Radio Algiers came a similar proclamation from Eisenhower. Communications to Kesselring's headquarters had been knocked out during an Allied bombing raid, and he suffered the embarrassment of learning of the surrender from Oberkommando der Wehrmacht (OKW).[22] By most members of the war-weary Italian Army the news was greeted with a sense of relief. There were few true Fascists left with a desire to continue fighting as an ally of Nazi Germany.

Clark thought the public announcement might make a difference in the resistance his army would face the following day on the beaches of Salerno. He told his key staff officers that, "at best, we could steam into Naples harbor unopposed. At worst, we could have a hell of a fight." Despite warnings by the invasion commanders not to take the capitulation of Italy as a sign that Salerno would be a walkover, many did.[23]

In Berlin this announcement was not unexpected, and OKW immediately ordered Kesselring to implement the contingency plan that would ensure German control of northern Italy, the evacuation of Sardinia, and the seizure of the Italian government. Kesselring's message to the troops of the Tenth Army complained that the Italians had "committed the basest treachery by concluding an armistice with the enemy behind our backs. We Germans must continue to fight . . . for the salvation of Europe and Italy. No mercy must be shown to traitors. *Heil Hitler!*"[24]

The Italian campaign officially commenced during the early morning hours of September 3, 1943, when Allied guns fired massive barrages against suspected enemy positions on the Italian side of the Strait of Messina. More than four hundred tons of high explosive were hurled into Calabria in advance of three brigades of Canadian and British infantry, who led the Allied invasion of Italy only to find that their enemy had prudently withdrawn several days earlier into the rough, mountainous terrain of central Calabria, at the neck of the Italian boot.

The British 13th Corps advanced rapidly north, and its only danger came from mines and the thorough demolition job performed by the German engineers, whose deadly handiwork had to be undone by British sappers before the drive could resume along the sparse road net of southern Calabria. During the first five days of the new campaign, the Eighth Army advanced some one hundred miles to the point where the foot of the Italian boot joins the leg. This was the only period of the Italian campaign that could be labeled easy. From there on the Italian campaign would become a grim epic of endurance, in which the weather and terrain were as formidable as the enemy.

The Avalanche landings ran into immediate trouble as the veteran German panzer division defending the Salerno sector reacted with fury. Unlike the invasion of Sicily, which had encountered only scattered opposition when it began, the Allied invasion of Salerno was bitterly resisted by 16th Panzer Division with every weapon in its arsenal. The landing craft ferrying the assault troops were assailed by seemingly endless tracer fire from machine guns emplaced along the beachfront; from mortars, antiaircraft guns, antitank guns, and tanks farther inland; and especially from the dreaded 88-mm guns of the German artillery.

Many never made it to the beaches. Some landing craft were hit by shellfire and blew up; others exploded after hitting mines emplaced in the bay or were hit by marauding Luftwaffe fighters, which bombed and strafed the invaders in the heaviest aerial resistance ever encountered during the war in the Mediterranean. As the correct beaches were missed and the timetable disintegrated, the landings quickly turned chaotic, and troops, vehicles, and supplies were landed in a haphazard, sporadic manner. Units designated to assault specific objectives never appeared. Even so, the naval performance at Salerno was a dramatic improvement over Sicily, with the majority of the assault forces landed on time, under exceptionally difficult circumstances.[25]

The German Tenth Army commander, General von Vietinghoff, at once recognized that this was a *Grosslandung* and not a diversionary feint. The 26th Panzer Division, then fighting a delaying action against the Eighth Army in southern Calabria, was ordered to disengage at once and hurry north to reinforce the Salerno front. Other units in the Rome and Naples areas were alerted for movement to Salerno.

The situation at Salerno deteriorated so badly in the week following the landings that it was uncertain if the Allies could even retain their foothold. Eisenhower was heard to say that he would probably be out if the battle ended in disaster. A pessimistic cable to the Combined Chiefs of Staff noted that Avalanche would "be a matter of touch and go for the next few days . . . we are in for some very tough fighting."[26]

The relentless defense of the Salerno beachhead by the German Army was typical of what the Allies encountered in their battles in the Mediterranean. When they could, the Germans fought tenaciously to defend their positions; when it was impossible or militarily impractical, they fought delaying actions until they could establish new defenses elsewhere. In Sicily they had been outnumbered, outgunned, outmaneuvered, and unable to meet the Allied invaders on the beaches. Despite its large area of responsibility at Salerno, the 16th Panzer Division was able to mount an effective defense from the outset.

Although vastly outnumbered, the Germans controlled the high ground and the exits from the invasion beaches and, from the first appearance of the invasion fleet, demonstrated that they had every intention of driving the Allies back into the sea. As the official naval historian points out, "Unfortunately for us, the Germans were almost as well prepared to contest landings at Salerno as the Japanese would be at Tarawa two months later."[27]

The gravest threat to the Allies lay in an enormous seven-mile gap between the British 10th Corps and U.S. VI Corps, which Clark optimistically called "not too serious" but which in reality would have to be corrected to prevent the Germans from exploiting it and rolling up the Allied flanks.

The crisis at Salerno was traceable to the flawed invasion plan. The numbers of troops in the initial assault force were limited to the landing craft available, but their method of employment left a great deal to be desired. It was correctly assumed that the Germans would concentrate their defenses to prevent the Fifth Army from capturing the city of Salerno and the passes leading to Naples. Nevertheless, of the three assault divisions, two were assigned defensive missions: the U.S. 36th to guard the southern flank, and the British 56th, whose objective of seizing and holding Montecorvino airfield was also defensive. This left the British 46th Division with the principal offensive role, yet they were landed too far from Salerno to assure that they could accomplish their mission. The result was that the desperate battle for the Salerno beachhead was never a single, coordinated operation, but rather individual battles fought by three separate forces.

The fate of the Allies hung in the balance for nearly a week. At one point Clark directed planning for the reembarkation of one of the two corps and its relocation to the sector of the other. To help alleviate the German threat, the Fifth Army commander ordered the 82d Airborne Division to the rescue. Two regimental combat teams parachuted into the beachhead on successive nights, in what came to be regarded as the most successful Allied airborne operation of the entire war. Their presence became a major factor in the outcome of the battle for Salerno.[28]

What appeared to be a disaster in the making greatly disturbed Eisenhower, who questioned if his longtime friend had lost his nerve. His naval aide recorded that the commander in chief thought that "Clark should show the spirit of a naval captain. If necessary, he should go down with his ship." Nevertheless, Eisenhower was determined to "move heaven and earth" to save the Fifth Army. Cunningham and Tedder lent their support by sending additional naval reinforcements to Salerno and by increasing air support, which included B-17 strategic bombers to attack German positions.

With commendable understatement, Cunningham later wrote of the proposed evacuation that it "would have resulted in a reverse of the first magnitude—an Allied defeat which would have completely offset the Italian surrender, and have been hailed by the Germans as a smashing victory."[29]

Clark restlessly prowled the front offering encouragement and inspiration, and American troops in the VI Corps sector responded by holding their ground. In the 10th Corps sector the Germans had enjoyed little success against the British 46th Division, and despite von Vietinghoff's unwarranted optimism, his two corps commanders at the front realized there was little to be gained from another all-out attack, except the senseless destruction of the German Tenth Army. Although there was to be more heavy fighting, the tide had clearly turned in favor of the Allies.

The arrival of Allied reinforcements and the gradual stabilization of their foothold at Salerno precipitated a critical decision by the German high command. Despite the arrival of reinforcements from all over Italy, numerous German counterattacks had failed to dislodge the Allies. All hope of a German strategic victory at Salerno was lost by September 13, when it became clear that the Allies could not be pushed back into the sea.

The sheer tenacity of the front-line troops and superb gunnery on the part of the Allied navy and the artillerymen ashore had enabled the Fifth Army to hold on long enough for reinforcements to arrive, and for the Germans to shoot their bolt in a series of unsuccessful counterattacks. When Kesselring realized that there could be no strategic victory at Salerno, he ordered von Vietinghoff to implement a phased withdrawal that would disengage the Tenth Army without further serious losses. By September 17, LXXVI Corps was withdrawing to the north, while XIV Panzer Corps fought a stiff rearguard action, halting their retreat to the north only long enough to thwart any pursuit by the skillful use of demolitions and the terrain.

The Fifth Army was a spent force,[30] unable to mount a serious pursuit operation. Although Naples fell to the Allies on October 1, Clark found little joy in becoming its liberator when he made what was intended to have been a grand entrance into the city. In his memoirs he noted: "There was little that was triumphant about our journey" through the wreckage of Naples, whose deserted streets left the eerie impression it was "a city of ghosts."[31]

The British were dismayed by American leadership at Salerno, which they believed had continued to display its inexperience. Although the airborne force, the Ranger and Commando force, and the field artillery had performed flawlessly, the senior commanders remained suspect. Someone had to pay for the muddle that had been Salerno, and it was Dawley. Neither Clark nor Alexander had confidence in Dawley's leadership, and at Alexander's instigation—and Eisenhower's prodding—he was relieved of command by Clark.[32] Although Dawley was no ball of fire as a corps commander, his relief was partly a face-saving gesture by the Allied high command, and he became the first of several senior field commanders who would pay a high price for a faulty plan during the Italian campaign.

As they had in North Africa, the British senior commanders continued to be critical of the American performance, believing that, Sicily notwithstanding, little had changed since Kasserine. McCreery held Clark in utter contempt, and in return the Fifth Army commander scornfully referred to the British 10th Corps commander as a "feather duster."[33] Alexander revealed his true feelings after the war in a little-known interview with the official U.S. Army historians.[34] With few exceptions, the American generals under his command did not rank highly.

The British had no cause for smugness. Salerno was the scene of one of the most humiliating episodes in the tradition-filled history of the British Army: a mutiny. Although little publicized, on September 16, some seven hundred replacement troops sat down on the beach and refused a series of orders to report to their units. Finally McCreery personally intervened and managed to persuade the majority to obey. The 192 Tommies who refused were mostly veterans of the 50th Northumbrian and 51st Highland divisions and were court-martialed.[35]

* * *

Salerno failed to dampen the Allied belief that Rome would fall within the next six weeks. This optimism was directly attributable to Ultra, which intercepted German message traffic in mid-August that indicated an intention to establish their main defenses in the northern Apennines. A month later this was reaffirmed in a signal that noted, "Germany had no intention of fighting a decisive battle in the center or south of Italy," and that even Salerno "had been carried out with the purpose of inflicting as great a loss as possible on the enemy," to be followed by a retirement to the north, regardless of the outcome of the battle.[36]

Sir David Hunt, one of Alexander's staff officers, drafted the official campaign dispatch, and he points out: "It is because of this mass of firm and reliable information that Allied commanders such as Alexander forecast a rapid advance to the Pisa-Rimini Line by the autumn of 1943. No one would have supposed such a thing likely if the enemy offered resistance . . . [and] raised in acute form the question whether the object prescribed for the Mediterranean forces could be achieved. Containment is impossible if the enemy refuses to allow himself to be contained."[37]

This was the crux of the great dilemma facing the Allies in Italy. *Initiative* is an elusive term, which—as Alexander later described it— meant, "We had the initiative in operations but the Germans had the initiative in deciding whether we should achieve our object since they were free . . . to refuse to allow themselves to be contained in Italy. Had they decided to withdraw altogether, for instance, they could have defended the line of the Alps, or one of the strong river lines in northeastern Italy, with the minimum of forces and, instead of us containing them, they would be containing us."[38]

When Hitler changed his mind and supported Kesselring's view that southern Italy should be defended, it was in the belief that the Allied aims in Italy were Rome and the establishment of air bases from which to launch further operations into either southern France or the Balkans.[39] By early October Ultra had provided conclusive evidence that the Germans would defend south of Rome during the winter of 1943–44. This news relieved Alexander's anxiety that the Germans would fail to cooperate in the Allied strategy of tying down the maximum number of German divisions in Italy. Everything has its price, and this strategic decision meant that Kesselring's twenty-five divisions were fully capable of limited offensive action against the Allies.

Disciples of the Italian campaign point to Hitler's decision to fight for Italy as evidence of the soundness of Allied strategy. Others, such as Marshall, the staunchest opponent of the Mediterranean option, believed that Hitler had blundered. "It was a great mistake on his part, and like the Battle of the Bulge, it was successful at first but fatal in the end. Hitler should have withdrawn from Italy and placed troops in France to meet our impending attack there."[40]

Despite their inability to defeat the Allied invasion, Kesselring and the German Army had considerable cause for optimism. Outgunned, lacking the air superiority possessed by the Allies, and at the end of a long logistical lifeline, the Germans nevertheless had managed to stifle the invasion landings and in the process had come close to inflicting a major defeat on their enemy. Most important, however, Salerno was the proof Kesselring required to convince Hitler that his forces could indeed successfully defend central Italy. Had the Allies employed their resources better at Salerno, Kesselring might have drawn a different conclusion and thus altered the entire course of the war in Italy.

Even though the Tenth Army had voluntarily withdrawn from the Salerno bridgehead and offered little resistance on the road to Naples, it still managed to make the Fifth Army's advance very difficult. Kesselring's strategy included creating every possible obstacle to Allied movement, which was vividly illustrated on September 27, when German engineers demolished virtually every culvert and bridge between Salerno and Naples. The result was that "the pace of the victorious advance on Naples was to be determined by the speed at which the engineers could sweep for land-mines and bridge the gaps. That was to be the pattern of war in Italy until the bitter end."[41]

Sicily and Salerno were unmistakable evidence of what lay in store for the Allies in Italy. Even as the Tenth Army was withdrawing from Salerno, Kesselring was hastening completion of his defenses, which were to be anchored across the mountains overlooking Cassino at the southern end of the Liri Valley. To gain the necessary time, the retreating Tenth Army was to delay the Allied advance along a series of natural defensive barriers between Naples and the new Gustav Line.

Unless the Allies were to initiate another amphibious landing north of Salerno, the geography of Italy dictated that they must advance on Rome along the Mediterranean side of the great chain of mountains that bisects the center of Italy from the Alps to the boot in Calabria. Hans Valentin Hube's XIV Panzer Corps had the responsibility for defending the primary Allied route to Rome, while to the east a mountain corps covered the sector running from Minturno (on the northern end of the Gulf of Gaeta) to the Adriatic coast. It was at Cassino that Kesselring planned to establish the main German defenses he intended to hold for as long as possible.

At Quebec the Combined Chiefs of Staff had at long last determined that Overlord would occur in Normandy in May 1944. Allied strategy centered on keeping the Wehrmacht in Italy fully committed, so that its veteran divisions could not be shifted to France to help repel the cross-Channel invasion. Although the primary Allied task in Italy was allegedly diversionary, there was considerable pressure on Alexander to act offensively and capture Rome.

The Eternal City was far more important to the Allies than merely as the capital city of their former enemy. Militarily, Rome was of considerable strategic importance for its road and rail net and nearby airfields. The immense political and cultural significance of the Italian capital also made its capture of psychological value to the Allies. Moreover, the elimination of Rome from the Axis sphere of control would send a signal to Adolf Hitler and to the rest of the world that Berlin, which was being pounded into rubble by the round-the-clock combined bombing offensive of the RAF and USAAF, was next.

Churchill was emphatic that Rome must fall by the end of the year, and well before Avalanche he warned Alexander that if its liberation were prolonged, "no one can measure the consequences."[42] Alexander's task was thus the precise opposite of Kesselring's, and to accomplish it speed was of the essence before the Germans were able to strengthen their defenses between Naples and Rome.

The mountainous terrain of central Italy became Kesselring's greatest ally. Not only are the mountains themselves formidable obstacles, but the many rivers, the freezing winters, the wind, mud and rain, and the limited road net made any advance a potential nightmare against a well-prepared defender. The mountains could only be negotiated via mule train by sweating, weary soldiers who had to take over the portage of guns, ammunition, and supplies when the trails became too steep even for mules. However, even to test the Gustav Line, the Allies found they first had to get past a series of hastily fortified defensive belts manned by crack German troops. In short, it was the worst imaginable terrain in which to fight a large-scale military campaign.

Dawley's replacement as VI Corps commander was fifty-two-year-old Major General John Porter Lucas, an artilleryman who had served in Sicily with Patton as Eisenhower's "eyes and ears." Soon after Lucas's appointment Clark wrote in his diary: "Since General Lucas has taken command of the VI Corps, there appears to be a general improvement in the morale of the entire corps headquarters."[43]

In his diary Lucas recorded the incredible hardships faced by the soldiers who fought in Italy:

> Rain, rain, rain. Military operations are always conducted in the rain. The roads are so deep in mud that moving troops and supplies forward is a terrific job. Enemy resistance is not nearly as great as that of Mother Nature, who certainly seems to be fighting on the side of the German. . . . This is a

> heart-breaking business. An advance of a few miles a day, fighting a terrible terrain and a determined enemy, building bridges, removing mines, climbing mountains. The men get punch drunk.[44]

What had been anticipated as an offensive of short duration to capture Rome turned out to be a methodical and deadly advance. The first German obstacle was based along the Volturno River, thirty-five miles north of Naples. Here, the terrain limited the routes of advance and von Vietinghoff's 60,000 men were dispersed between the Mediterranean and the Adriatic. The German anchor was opposite the Fifth Army, where XIV Panzer Corps had 35,000 defenders, most of them veterans of Sicily and Salerno. Their mission was to delay along the Volturno River until at least mid-October, so that German engineers could complete their fortification of the Gustav Line.

Mountains were not the only formidable obstacle to the advance on Rome. No less difficult were river-crossing operations, where the logistics were enormous, the execution demanding, and rapid exploitation essential. In Italy the Allies were forced to breach such obstacles during the most difficult time of year, when the wretched weather grounded the Allied air forces that Eisenhower regarded as being worth another ten divisions.[45] Italian rivers run mostly west or east, thus the old adage about "one more river to cross" took on a grim reality throughout the campaign.

The Tenth Army's defenses along the Volturno would have been even more troublesome had von Vietinghoff not had to deal with a surprise amphibious landing by the Eighth Army on October 3 behind German lines at Termoli, on the Adriatic end of the Volturno line. Von Vietinghoff balked at Kesselring's order to shift the 16th Panzer Division to the east to meet this new threat, believing it should remain committed against the Fifth Army. Nevertheless, despite the tardy commitment of the 16th Panzer Division, the great potential of the British operation was lost because of the advent of vile weather.

The arrival of the rainy season had swollen the Volturno and flooded lowland areas. Roads turned into quagmires that made vehicular travel virtually impossible. The mud became the Germans' greatest ally, delaying the Fifth Army offensive until nearly mid-October when 10th Corps and VI Corps launched attacks that gained footholds north of the river at heavy cost. The British bore the brunt of the casualties, losing more than six hundred men.

What was so discouraging and difficult in Italy for the Allies was that the successful crossing of a river or a mountain merely led them to yet another set of identical obstacles. After the time-consuming and costly operations to gain a bridgehead north of the Volturno, the Allies then faced the hasty defenses along the outer boundary of what the Germans called the Bernhard Line and the Allies, the Winter Line.

Anchored on the Garigliano River on the left, and with a formidable mountain barrier in the center and on the right, the Winter Line was the most serious obstacle the Allies had yet encountered in their march on Rome. Many of their formations were exhausted after months of combat and in poor shape to sustain an offensive under the conditions they faced in Italy. Worst effected was the Eighth Army, many of whose veteran units were simply worn out from endless combat that, for most, dated to Alamein the previous year.

Most senior American commanders, including Clark, believed that the British were overcautious on the battlefield. Few understood the magnitude of the British growing manpower shortages or that, by the end of 1943, they faced a major crisis wherever they fought. Four years of global war had stretched Britain's manpower reserves to the breaking point. Most seriously affected was the infantry arm, whose casualty losses were always the highest. In a secondary theater of war like Italy, infantry replacements were not being furnished on a scale anywhere approaching losses. The grim news from the War Office was personally given to the British commanders by the adjutant general, Sir Ronald Adam, when he visited Italy in October 1943.[46]

After Salerno the Fifth Army was in equally rough shape as it struggled to gain a foothold across the Volturno. Attempts in November to continue the advance toward the Gustav Line lacked sufficient strength to breach the German defenses along the Winter Line, and it was not until early December that the Fifth Army was able to regroup and launch a fresh offensive. A series of bloody battles lasting into mid-December did gain considerable ground but failed to attain the final objective—the Liri Valley and the capture of the town of Cassino.

As 1943 drew to a close, the Allies had not yet tested the Gustav Line, and there was now little optimism that 15th Army Group could capture Rome without the assistance of an amphibious end run near the Italian capital. Eisenhower and Alexander had already come to this conclusion and had targeted the place where they hoped to outflank Kesselring. It was called Anzio.

3

The American Eagle and the Gentleman-General

Alexander . . . is not a strong commander . . . the higher art of war is beyond him.

—BERNARD MONTGOMERY

The American Eagle

—CHURCHILL'S NICKNAME FOR
LIEUTENANT GENERAL MARK CLARK

The portrayal of the battle for Salerno as a near disaster has obscured the underlying reasons why it was so. Its course was in the hands of Sir Harold Alexander and Mark Clark, and each commander bore a measure of responsibility for the dilemma that faced the Fifth Army in the beachhead. The villain has been seen as Bernard Montgomery, whose Eighth Army dallied in southern Italy while Clark's troops were fighting for their lives against Kesselring's best.

The truth was that the mess at Salerno was of Alexander and Clark's own making. Alexander knew full well that the Fifth Army plan was flawed but permitted Avalanche to go ahead without making the slightest attempt to redress its ills. Even when the situation deteriorated to the point where the entire beachhead was in jeopardy, Alexander still failed to act, although it was clear that Clark was in serious trouble. The solution was not for Montgomery to race to the Fifth Army's rescue, but for the two commanders to make use of the resources immediately available.

The gravest problem facing the Avalanche force was the great ten-mile Sele River gap between the two corps, and its solution was the immediate employment of the 82d Airborne Division, which, in the event, came too late and in the wrong form. Thus, "Clark had in his grasp the quickest, best and most positive way to influence the battle at Salerno, by inserting it complete (plus some heavier artillery and tank-destroyers, not too difficult to supply) into the void between the two corps." But Clark lacked McCreery's and Alexander's battle experience, and he failed to act until the fifth day. "Alexander, true to form, urged Clark to make use of [the 82d Airborne] . . . but never gave the order. For what else do general officers commanding-in-chief exist? Instead, he wasted time in exhorting Montgomery to do what, if not completely impossible, was at least very difficult, and something that officer had no intention of doing."[1]

Salerno was Mark Clark's baptism of fire as a commander, and it taught him the wrong lessons, one of which was that it would pay dividends to "follow Montgomery's advice not to take any notice of what Alexander told him to do because Alexander was a man of straw."[2] Clark deluded himself in the belief that Montgomery shared the blame for his predicament at Salerno. In a postwar interview with Clark, the official historian noted that "there was no excuse, Clark says, for Monty's slowness. . . . If Monty had moved faster he could have helped Fifth Army out of a tough situation. As it was, we at Salerno won the battle by dint of our own efforts."[3]

More important was the fact that Salerno imbued Clark with the clear understanding that his reputation—if not his neck—might not survive another near-run battle. Thus he mistakenly permitted himself to believe that his problems were the fault of others.

In the aftermath of Salerno, Clark was outraged to learn that Alexander's press minions were directing that the Eighth Army get the lion's share of the press coverage at his expense. As the standard bearer of American forces in Italy, he was left, after Salerno, more determined than ever that the Fifth Army would never again be slighted. To gain the public attention he believed his army merited, Clark would have to beat the British at their own game. The obvious solution was for the Fifth Army to capture Rome—without the British.

The emerging campaign in Italy could not have been dominated by two more disparate commanders than Alexander and Clark. One was vain and inexperienced; the other self-effacing and capable but utterly unwilling to assert his authority. Between them, they were a genuine military odd couple. They rarely saw eye to eye with one another, yet Alexander seemed genuinely fond of the man he called

Wayne. The events chronicled in this book are irretrievably linked to the personalities of Alexander and Clark, and it is appropriate, therefore, to pause for a deeper examination of these two remarkable men.

In Italy Alexander reigned as the senior Allied ground commander of the most diverse multinational force ever assembled. The major elements of Allied forces in Italy were:[4]

- Fifth U.S. Army: Lieutenant General Mark Clark
- Eighth British Army: General Sir Bernard Montgomery
- 2d Polish Corps: Lieutenant General Wladyslaw Anders
- Corps Expéditionnaire Français: General Alphonse Juin
- 1st Canadian Corps: Lieutenant General H. D. G. Crerar
- New Zealand Corps: Lieutenant General Sir Bernard Freyberg

At one time or another formations of sixteen nations served under the Allied banner in Italy. In addition to the major participants, there were formations from South Africa, Brazil, Morocco, Algeria, Tunisia, Greece, and, later in the war, units of their former enemy, the Italian Army. Within the Mediterranean Allied Air Forces (MAAF) were flying units of the Royal Canadian Air Force (RCAF), Royal Air Force, U.S. Army Air Force (USAAF), South African Air Force, Rhodesian Air Force, Royal Australian Air Force, the Free French Air Force, and several Greek and free Polish air squadrons.[5]

Presiding over this vast international army group was Alexander, the courtly Guardsman who, along with Eisenhower, was easily the most popular of the Allied generals. Most often referred to by the affectionate nickname Alex, he was one of the most modest and unassuming generals ever to hold high command in the war. In fact, Alexander's style of leadership was so laid back that no one who ever served with him could really claim to know the full measure of the man beneath the exterior facade of the charming aristocrat.

Ulster was the breeding ground for many of the most illustrious names of World War II: Montgomery, Brooke, Auchinleck, Dill, Gort, and Alexander. As his biographer notes, "Alexander was born in London, but he belonged to Ulster, where generations of Alexanders had built a reputation for public service in and out of uniform, and for an unfeignedly patrician style of living."[6] It was he among his fellow Ulstermen who earned the distinction of becoming Churchill's favorite general. Among the Americans, Alexander commanded almost universal admiration and respect. Even when they were angered by his blatant favoritism in Sicily, neither Patton nor Bradley lost their regard for Alex.

Harold Macmillan cites an example of Alexander's tact in handling American officers under his command, when, in Tunisia, Bradley "showed us on a map how the battle was progressing, and there were certain dispositions and movements of troops of which I could see General Alexander did not altogether approve. By a brilliant piece of diplomacy, he suggested to his subordinate commander some moves which he might well make. He did not issue an order. He sold the American general the idea, and made him think he had thought of it all himself. . . . If Montgomery was the Wellington, Alexander was certainly the Marlborough of this war."[7]

Montgomery and Alexander had known each other for many years, and Montgomery's rough edges were in sharp contrast to Alexander's polish; where Montgomery was always controversial, Alexander was diplomatic and avoided the limelight. Possessed of a soldierly bearing that automatically commanded attention and respect, Alexander exuded, as Montgomery once observed, "all those fine qualities that I lack myself."[8]

A professional soldier from the age of nineteen, Alexander had gained a well-deserved reputation for fearlessness in battle. In less than a year during World War I, he rose from platoon leader to battalion commander and in the process became one of the youngest lieutenant colonels in the Army and—indisputably—the most highly regarded officer of his regiment, the Irish Guards.

In retrospect his rise to fame and high command seemed inevitable and took him from the sands of Dunkirk, where he commanded the 1st Division of the BEF in 1940 and was the last Englishman to leave France; to Burma, the Middle East, North Africa, and now, Italy. The story is told of Alexander building sand castles on the beach at Dunkirk during the height of the German dive-bombing and of an excited staff officer rushing up to report to Alexander, "Our position is catastrophic," and receiving the reply, "I'm sorry, I don't understand long words."[9]

Alexander was considered a lucky general whose mere appearance was an omen of good fortune. That luck dated to his days as a student at Harrow and his participation in the historic Fowler's cricket match against Eton at Lords in 1910.* Although Alexander was on the losing side of the most famous match in cricket history, he nevertheless won a reputation throughout his military career as an officer whose very name equated with success. To his men, Alex was a hero. His frequent and highly visible presence at the front sent a message to his troops that

---

*Fowler's match, between Harrow and Eton, took place in July 1910 at Lords cricket ground. Harrow was heavily favored and needed an easily attainable fifty-five runs during its final innings. The Eton captain, Bob Fowler, had other ideas and took eight of Harrow's eleven wickets, the last of which was Alexander's. Harrow lost by nine runs. This stunning upset was forever christened Fowler's match.

he too was prepared to share a common danger. "He not only commanded his men but represented them. He was one of them. . . . He came to inform and enquire and discuss, to encourage and to sympathize. One felt he was capable at any moment of changing places with a subaltern."[10] Instead of a helmet, Alexander deliberately wore his garrison cap with its prominent red band, which usually managed to draw enemy fire whenever he visited the front. Veteran *New York Times* correspondent C. L. Sulzberger asked Alexander why and he replied that "he wanted the men to see that their commander went right up to the front line. He liked to advertise this fact with the red band—unlike our American theory under which officers wear helmets, both for safety and so that, at any distance, they are indistinguishable from GIs."[11]

With this exception, Alexander shunned the trappings of high command and seemed embarrassed whenever a fuss was made. On one occasion he politely ordered the dismissal of a covey of motorcycle outriders who were supposed to clear the road ahead for him. "I have a marked objection to clearing my own troops off the road for me," he said.[12]

A veteran Grenadier Guardsman has captured the essence of Alexander's impact on the ordinary British soldier:

> He was the one general that most of the troops knew by sight . . . he was the only general I ever saw (apart from ceremonial parades) and I was always "running across him." . . . On the edge of the beach at Anzio, on the edge of my slit trench later at Anzio, on a hillside in central Italy, at a villa near Siena, on the quayside when we were going home.
>
> This was I think his appeal to the average soldier—they felt that he had their interests at heart, that he knew what it was all about, and that he identified with them. He had style, he had panache, he was quite unmistakable . . . but he never went around surrounded by a crowd of hangers on and bodyguards. I seldom ever saw him with more than one man and that was usually his driver.[13]

Even generals are not immune from the need to have their morale boosted. Major General Gerald Templer, the commander of the 56th Division at Anzio and a future field marshal, recalls a visit from Alexander in February 1944, during the most crucial period of the fight to save the Anzio beachhead:

> Alex flew in to see, in a single-seater fighter—clamped behind the pilot. He landed on a football ground . . . about 9 a.m. . . . [in Templer's HQ trailer] we sat and talked about this and that—mostly Ireland or Yorkshire. Several times I tried to steer the conversation round to my troubles and problems. Always he adroitly turned the conversation in some other direction. In

desperation, when he was showing signs of wanting to go . . . I asked him to have a drink. To my surprise . . . he asked for some gin—surprise, because I knew he drank sparely and never at such an unearthly hour of the morning. . . . He drank it . . . and then jumped up and said "Gerald, I must be off. I have done all I could to help you, haven't I?" I replied "Yes, indeed, you have, Sir," and I meant it. We hadn't discussed one thing about the battle or any of my problems, but he had instilled hope and courage and determination into me at a moment when I wanted it badly.[14]

Alexander never curried favor with Churchill. In fact, Churchill's long-time personal physician and confidant, Lord Moran, believed the prime minister's near hero worship of Alex was a natural extension of his romantic nature. To Churchill war was:

a romantic calling, the highest man could embrace, but it was a game for gentlemen, which had to be played according to the rules. What he loved in Alex was that he had justified his own feelings about war, tried them out in the field and made sense of them. Alex had redeemed what was brutal in war, touching the grim business lightly with his glove. In his hands it was still a game for people of quality. He had shown that war could still be made respectable.[15]

After the war, Moran once asked Churchill if Alex was a good general and received the reply, "the best we had; better than Monty."[16] There is little doubt that Churchill was aware of Alexander's limitations, yet he often turned to him for advice on the most mundane matters. He once cabled Alexander to seek his advice on the use of malaria pills, leading Moran to wonder "if General Alexander's views on medical matters have the same value as mine on military matters."[17] A significant part of Alexander's appeal to Churchill lay in the fact that he was one of the few senior British officers who never challenged the prime minister, whose relations with others, such as Brooke, Tedder, Portal, and Montgomery, were often adversarial. While these strong-willed men never hesitated to disagree with Churchill, who resented being contradicted or criticized, Alexander never posed a threat to his authority. To the contrary, Alexander would sometimes listen silently to Churchill's ramblings late into the night as a sort of father confessor whose soothing reassurances affected the prime minister like a tonic.[18] Even so, Alexander was always candid in his dealings with Churchill, and in the many signals between the two during the Italian campaign, there is a hint of intimacy not found in the prime minister's correspondence with his other generals.

Nearly everyone aspires to be someone else, and in Churchill's case it was to have been a great battlefield general. He once told Alexander, "I envy you the command of armies in the field. That is what I should have liked." Asked by Moran if Churchill would have made a good general, Alexander remained silent for some time and then replied only: "Winston is a gambler."[19]

The very traits that made Alexander a success were those that also led to his greatest failing. His style of leadership by persuasion was designed to take advantage of his intuition for the art of the possible; for tactfully handling his subordinate generals in different ways, each designed to take advantage of that man's strengths and minimize his weaknesses. Yet this method had mixed results with strong-minded generals like Patton and Mark Clark, who were determined to prevail and often did so by taking advantage of Alexander's reluctance to impose his will.

Thus, despite his outstanding record, there were justifiably grave doubts about Alexander's ability to function as a high-level commander. His style of command was detached, lacking in the essentials of formulating command guidance, and often so vague in execution that his subordinate commanders were unclear as to his intentions. In short, Alexander never fully grasped the reins of high command and this deeply troubled his superiors. Although Churchill "placed Alexander at the center of his Pantheon of heroes,"[20] Brooke questioned his fitness for high command on numerous occasions during the Italian campaign. His doubts are reflected in numerous unflattering entries in his diary, the substance of which appeared after the war in Sir Arthur Bryant's two international best-sellers.[21]

From the time of their first contact at the Staff College, Camberley (the British equivalent of the U.S. Army Command & General Staff College, Fort Leavenworth, Kansas), Brooke had regarded Alexander as a lightweight and dismissed him with an unflattering diary entry that read: "No brains." However, Brooke's biographer has written that, having revised his estimate of Alexander, Brooke "at times seemed to have doubts and to return to it . . . [but] he never stinted his admiration for Alexander's ability to get men working together, particularly in Italy."[22] Although Brooke never lost sight of his positive qualities, he was never comfortable with Alexander in charge of the Allied ground campaign in Italy. En route to the Cairo Conference in November 1943, Alexander joined a meeting of the chiefs of staff, leading Brooke to write that "charming as he is [Alexander] fills me with gloom. He is a very, very small man and cannot see big. . . . He will never have either the personality or the vision to command three services [as a supreme commander]."[23]

The following month when Brooke visited Italy he found no reason to revise his judgment, noting with concern that "Alex fails to grip the show." After the war, however, he softened his view of Alexander:

There is no doubt he held some of the highest qualities of a commander, unbounded courage, never ruffled or upset, great charm and a composure that inspired confidence in those around him. But when it came to working on a higher plane and deciding matters of higher tactics and of strategy he was at once out of his depth, had no ideas of his own and always sought someone to lean on. Up to now he had fitted admirably into the various jobs I had asked him to do but looking ahead I foresaw some stormy seas with rocks, crags and sandbanks and the gravest doubts about Alex's ability to navigate such waters.[24]

Montgomery was characteristically blunt in assessing his longtime friend and colleague:

Alexander is a very great friend of mine, and I am very fond of him. But I am under no delusion whatsoever as to his ability to conduct large-scale operations in the field; he knows nothing about it; he is not a strong commander and he is incapable of giving firm and clear decisions as to what he wants. In fact, no one ever knows what he *does* want, least of all his staff; in fact, he does not know himself. . . . The whole truth of the matter is that ALEXANDER has got a definitely limited brain and does not understand the business.[25]

The problem, noted Monty, was that Alexander "does not understand the offensive and mobile battle":

He cannot snap out clear and concise orders. He does not think and plan ahead. . . . He has never commanded an Army or a Corps in the field. He loves battle schools and minor tactics. The higher art of war is beyond him. . . . *And so ALEXANDER has acquired a false reputation as a great commander in the field, and as a great strategist* [italics added].[26]

More in sorrow than in animosity, Montgomery later said of him: "When he has a conference of commanders, which is very seldom, it is a lamentable spectacle; he relies on ideas being produced which will give him a plan; he does not come to the conference with *his own* plan, and then give out clear orders. No one gets any orders, and we all do what we like."[27] The line between leadership by persuasion and the abrogation of responsibility is thin, and even Eisenhower, who was in virtual awe of Alexander, occasionally discerned signs of his deficiencies as a commander. In June 1943 he observed in a confidential memo: "At times he seems to alter his own plans and ideas merely to meet an objection or suggestion of a subordinate, so as to avoid direct command methods."[28]

In Sicily Alexander had stood mutely on the sidelines and allowed the campaign to degenerate into virtually two private wars fought by Montgomery and Patton to their own ends, while he resided in splendor in North Africa. Churchill's political envoy in the Mediterranean was Harold Macmillan, and his diary is filled with descriptions of days bathing with Alexander on a beach and evenings in the drawing room of his seaside villa, where the topics of conversation were not Sicily, but pheasant driving, philosophy, politics, or architecture "in the usual tone of educated (and there are some *very* well-educated) Englishmen."[29] The battle for Sicily was a mere six days old when Eisenhower began to demonstrate increasing signs of annoyance with Alexander. His naval aide recorded in his diary that Ike was "not too happy with Alexander and staff taking a three-or-four-hour siesta, good for bathing purposes, leaving only duty officers on watch during the heat of battle."[30]

Patton's foray with the majority of his army into western Sicily, where there were only thousands of dispirited Italians eager to surrender, was born of frustration and had limited military value. Had Alexander promised him a meaningful role in the reduction of Sicily, the outcome of this sorry tale might have been far different.

His former chief of staff, Lieutenant General Sir John Harding, relates that Alexander's office in Italy had a peephole in the door, and sometimes "I'd look through the peephole, and I'd see him sort of half asleep with a book in his hand. Then I banged the door pretty hard before walking in, and coughed and so on, whereby of course the book disappeared and he was bright and alert."[31]

During the first four months of the Italian campaign Alexander provided no indication that he had any intention of altering his laissez-faire style of command. His penchant for leaving the mundane details of command and military routine to others was formed early in his career. As his biographer notes, Alexander was bored by such details and took for granted the means by which his men were clothed, fed, and supplied. It was typical of him that he once said, "Just tell me at what time I'm supposed to be on parade."[32]

Alexander's generalship at Salerno varied little from his performance throughout the war in the Mediterranean. He failed to influence the outcome of the battle in any but a negative way. Alexander's task was to ensure that the invasion commander received the optimum support, but he failed to invest the beachhead with additional support at an earlier moment by committing the 82d Airborne when and where their presence would have made an appreciable difference. Although Montgomery took far too long to move north from Calabria and relieve the Fifth Army at Salerno, it was Alexander who failed to instill a sense of urgency in the Eighth Army commander. Moreover, Alexander failed to address the obvious problem of Clark's flawed invasion plan or even so much as state publicly his opinion that he considered it faulty.

Alexander was an intensely reserved and private man who was never known to have shared his thoughts with anyone. Yet, from time to time, he briefly lifted the veil surrounding the private man to reveal a far more complex character behind the aristocratic facade. Sir John Colville remembers Alexander as a man with "surprisingly advanced political views. He was an enemy of class distinction and said he was alarmed by it in his own Brigade of Guards. He was one of the earliest protagonists of a generous policy to defeated Germany, believing she should be invited to join NATO and be treated as an equal in the concourse of nations."[33]

In a rare public display of emotion, Alexander lost his temper during the height of the German counterattacks at Anzio in February 1944. Stories that began appearing in the press about how dire the situation had grown there soon gained Churchill's full attention, resulting in considerable pressure on Alexander to put a stop to such negative reporting. Although it turned out that they were not responsible for the stories, the Anzio correspondents were angrily berated by Alexander, who accused them of sabotaging the war effort.

Alexander did not suffer fools gladly, as John Harding relates in the story of the Russian generals during the Italian campaign, who "were due to come and have lunch with Alexander . . . we waited for them, and they didn't arrive, and so Alex said, 'We'd better start lunch.' We were about half way through lunch when the Russian delegation arrived. . . . And they said they were very sorry for arriving so late but they'd lost their way. So all Alex said was, 'Well, didn't you have a map?' "[34]

Alexander's biographer has candidly assessed his subject this way:

> I don't think he was a very clever man, Alex. I don't think he had much imagination. He had great courage but not much daring. You can never see in any of Alex's battles or campaigns something that makes you gasp with admiration. You see how much he . . . depended on advice from very, very brilliant subordinate generals who often disobeyed his orders, but brought it off! . . . He was an English country gentleman, almost uneducated, who never read a book or had any interest in the arts at all, except for his painting—not other people's painting. . . . He had no philosophy, you see. He had no politics. He wasn't interested in the causes of war, or the cause of that particular war in which he was fighting.[35]

Alexander was an unfathomable enigma whose admirers ran the gamut from front-line soldiers, who loved him for his courage, to generals who served under him, and politicians, like Harold Macmillan, who considered him "first class." Others, like Brooke and Cunningham, saw an entirely different person, as did one of his best division commanders, who wrote of him: "He is quite the least intelligent commander I have ever met in a high position . . . [but] I found that I could not talk to him for more than five minutes: whereas I can talk for hours to intelligent men. Perhaps it is too harsh to say that he's bone from the neck up, but perhaps it isn't."[36]

Alexander's relations with his principal subordinate, Mark Clark, were difficult, even though in public neither officer ever had anything but praise for the other. No Allied officer was more ruthlessly and openly ambitious than Mark Wayne Clark, the Fifth Army commander whom Churchill had nicknamed the American Eagle. After his first-ever meeting with Eisenhower and Clark, the British prime minister later recalled, "I was immediately impressed by these remarkable but hitherto unknown men."[37]

A commander who never left anyone in doubt as to who was in charge, Clark has been accurately described as "big, rawboned, energetic and outspoken, learning and growing as he went, he personified in Italy the power of the United States commitment to the Allied venture."[38]

An ambitious and hard-driving West Pointer, class of 1917,[39] whose ability was exceeded only by his vanity, Clark evinced early in his career a willingness to pay any price to achieve fame. As an infantry battalion commander during World War I, Clark was wounded on his first day of combat in June 1918 and thereafter vowed that he would one day gain the opportunity for history to record his exploits as a great battlefield commander. With Mark Clark there was rarely a middle ground. What some perceived as self-confidence and professionalism others viewed as conceit and extreme arrogance, an image that was not enhanced at Salerno, where Clark would only permit his photograph to be taken from his "good side" (his left) by an Army photographer who always accompanied him.

Clark's Army public relations staff was composed of nearly fifty men, whose task was to gain favorable recognition for the Fifth Army and its commander. This staff operated on what was unofficially called "the three and one rule": every news release was to contain Clark's name three times on the first page and at least one time on all other pages. "It was always 'Lieutenant General Mark W. Clark's Fifth Army.'"[40] The management of news by the Fifth Army could have served as a model for the present day, but to give Clark his due, it was at least in part a reaction to his growing disillusion with the British, who received the lion's share of publicity. "Determined to get justice for his Fifth Army, he surrounded himself . . . [with an] entourage of cameramen and newspaper correspondents who made sure that the accomplishments of his army were recorded and publicized. The crowning achievement and one that he desired ever more ardently to give his army—and incidentally himself—was the glory of liberating Rome."[41]

Sometimes his staff concocted schemes that only made their commander look foolish. Eric Sevareid, then a correspondent, recounts an incident in a movie theater in Caserta when "little mimeographed slips were distributed through the rows of bewildered officer spectators. They contained the words of a song beginning, 'Stand up, stand up for General Clark, let's sing the praises of General Clark.' They stumbled to their feet and uncertainly followed the words with the aid of their flashlights while the General stood stiffly at attention. Somebody said the tune was that of 'Stand Up, Stand Up for Jesus.' "[42]

Some of the correspondents covering the Italian campaign were infuriated by the schemes concocted by Clark's giant publicity machine and troubled by his excessive vanity, which all too often left the impression that his troops were merely the means to a personal end. C. L. Sulzberger, who thought Clark's rangy, hawklike features made him resemble the sheriff in a western movie, occasionally played bridge in Clark's trailer. "He always talked about 'When I take Rome.' Once, when I had been complaining to him about the particular stupidity of his Fifth Army censors, he put his long arm around my shoulder and said: 'Cy, when we make our breakthrough I want you to ride in a jeep with me. I'll see to it when we get there that you can tell the world just how Mark Clark took Rome.' "[43]

The opinions of his subordinate commanders were equally varied. Lucas was among those who were uneasy about Clark and he once described him as an officer of "great physical courage but no moral courage."[44] Yet his drive and unshakable belief in himself were vital traits in Italy, where there was precious little for his troops to be optimistic about. Clark's admirers found in their commander "a soldier, a leader and a driver."[45]

During the battle for San Pietro, Clark made one of his frequent appearances at the front, and in a mountain foxhole he found a small infantry private named Gebhart, whose heavy growth of beard made him resemble one of Bill Mauldin's "Willie and Joe" GI characters. Clark noticed the soldier was wearing overshoes and asked why. Gebhart replied: "Haven't any shoes, sir." The general asked: "Don't you want to wear shoes?" The private answered: "Yes, sir, but mine are worn out, and my feet are so small that I couldn't get any others." Clark learned that Gebhart wore a size 7A, for which the Army produced only sixty-seven pairs out of every one hundred thousand. Undeterred, Clark said, "I'll get you a pair of shoes if there is a pair that size anywhere in the Mediterranean theater." Within hours Clark's G-4 located a pair of 7As, and the next morning Clark's aide returned to San Pietro with the boots: "General Clark sent these shoes." Gebhart accepted with thanks but no visible expression. "Aren't you surprised?" asked the aide. "No," replied the soldier, "he told me he'd send them."[46]

George Biddle, who sketched Clark for *Life* magazine, described him "as a superb study for an artist . . . his bony face looks like an American Indian's, his eyes snap like those of a bird of prey. His mouth, however, is kind. He . . . gives the impression that behind his silence he hides a well of determination. He is hard, sharp, always vigilant."[47]

Clark's standing with the British had never been high. As a long-time friend and protégé of Eisenhower, he served as his deputy in North Africa before assuming command of the newly created Fifth Army in early 1943. The British staff of AFHQ saw Clark as a hugely disruptive influence who intrigued against them, caused immense irritation by his habit of issuing direct and sometimes contradictory orders to the staff, terrified the American officers, and was considered the "evil genius of the force."[48]

Several months earlier Eisenhower had expressed surprisingly strong misgivings about several facets of Clark's character and experience:

> He is the best organizer, planner and trainer of troops I have yet met in the American Army. He thinks in an orderly and logical fashion and is energetic in carrying an adopted plan into execution. While at one stage of the operations it seemed that he was becoming consumed with a desire to push himself. . . . His only drawback now is a lack of combat experience in a high command position. This I tried to give him in the early days of [Tunisia]. . . . He rather resented taking any title except that of Army Commander. . . . This was a bad mistake on Clark's part, but I still think that he could successfully command an army in operations.[49]

Salerno seems to have given Eisenhower little cause to revise his estimate of his friend. Writing to Marshall after the battle, Eisenhower noted that Clark was "not so good as Bradley in winning, almost without effort, the complete confidence of everyone around him, including his British associates. He is not the equal of Patton in his refusal to see anything but victory . . . but he is carrying his full weight and, so far, has fully justified his selection for his present important post."[50]

Only weeks before Eisenhower's letter, Marshall's "eyes and ears" in the Mediterranean for Husky, Brigadier General Albert C. Wedemeyer, delivered this scathing assessment of Clark: "He possesses many fine ideas about training. He is self-seeking and ambitious; not a broad gauged man who would subordinate himself for the 'big picture.' "[51]

Alexander and Clark could not have been more dissimilar. "Where Alexander would discuss endlessly and never give orders, Clark gave orders and refused to discuss them."[52] Alexander's anti-Americanism[53] was cleverly concealed behind his gentlemanly facade, whereas Clark was openly contemptuous of the British and frequently complained that they were attempting to steal the limelight from him and his Fifth

Army. To his detriment, Clark all too often permitted his unfounded suspicions and jealousy to cloud his judgment as a commander.

His rise to high command had been meteoric, not only due to his longtime friendship with Eisenhower but as a consequence of his high standing with Marshall, with whom any American officer destined for high command had to pass muster. There was never any doubt about Clark's remarkable physical courage. In October 1942 he undertook an exceptionally dangerous mission by submarine to North Africa to secretly meet with senior French officers in the hope of avoiding a clash with French forces when the Allies launched Operation Torch the following month. In Italy he became well known for his frequent visits to the front, where he displayed a casual, almost contemptuous disregard for his own safety. Clark's recklessness led his wife to implore him to avoid taking risks. After one such entreaty in early 1944, he shot back a letter saying: "You turn your lamb chops on the stove, and I'll run the Army."[54] It was not unusual for a squad leader in a remote corner of a battlefield to suddenly find the Army commander at his side, offering encouragement, only to disappear as silently as he had arrived. Clark was to be found wherever there were American troops, and most loved him for it. After the war and virtually to the time of his death Clark received enormous quantities of mail. On his birthday it arrived by the truckload.[55]

Clark's impatience and lack of high command experience became a liability in Italy. His career was notable for many staff assignments but few postings with troop units, the most recent of which had been in 1928 as a regimental executive officer. In fact, such inexperience was a problem common to many senior commanders of World War II, including Eisenhower and Bradley, who had not fought in World War I. However, what Clark lacked was that ill-defined but vital ingredient for successful command—the ability to sense instinctively the right course of action on the field of battle. Both Bradley and Patton possessed this quality to a marked degree. Clausewitz called war "the domain of uncertainty" in which "three fourths of the things upon which action in war is based, are hidden in the mist of greater or lesser uncertainty."[56] An early-twentieth-century study of leadership notes that Napoleon's successes "were not due to the gifts of a magician, but to those of a general who incessantly worked out the possibilities on a map."[57] Clark's biographer notes that a senior British officer paraphrased "Clausewitz's well known statement that war is an extension of policy by other means" to describe him as one "who believed war to be an extension of publicity by other means."[58]

Mark Clark's generalship exhibited an unfortunate absence of what Clausewitz called "the genius for war."[59] As British historians Dominick Graham and Shelford Bidwell note, "he lacked something granted to many lesser soldiers, that almost instinctive faculty for discerning what was operationally sound and what was not. His 'schemes of maneuver' were designed mechanically from a set of rules imbibed at the Staff College, drawn on a map and invariably faulty."[60]

Alexander well understood Clark's ambition and hunger for recognition of the Fifth Army, which, in many respects, paralleled those of his other difficult subordinate, Montgomery. According to the notes of an official U.S. historian, Alexander used the kid-gloves approach with Clark and believed that he was:

> extremely ambitious—vain—learned a lot as the campaign went on—frequently spoke sharply and nastily to Alexander—temperamental—very sensitive, especially about any advice or instructions Alexander might give to Clark's subordinates . . . resented any effort by Alexander to tell him how to run the battle based upon Alexander's experience in war—as time went on Clark was not so sensitive . . . would always listen even if he didn't like what Alexander said—learned a lot as time went on—was a driver, a pusher of his troops—pushed hard to get them to take his objectives—Clark was a good army commander.[61]

Alexander's deputy chief of staff was an exceptionally able American officer who would rise to the postwar command of NATO, General Lyman L. Lemnitzer. His assessment was that despite the fundamental difference in their personalities, Alexander respected Clark's ability even though the volatile Clark fully tested Alexander's patience on many occasions. "Clark was aggressive, sure he was right, loved publicity and got plenty of it. . . . Clark was regarded by Alexander as an able commander. He told the Prime Minister that on many occasions and this was reflected in the PM's comments to FDR [about] Clark." Nevertheless, at times "there were sharp exchanges [between the two] . . . but generally Alexander was very patient and handled the sensitive Clark tactfully. In fact there were some occasions when Clark spoke too sharply to Alexander." Several times Lemnitzer expected Alexander to relieve Clark.[62] Clark frequently sneered at Alexander behind his back. After a meeting with Alexander shortly before the Anzio landings, Clark's aide and principal diarist, Lieutenant Colonel Arthur Sutherland, included in his entry for the day: "General Clark said, as he repeatedly had in the past, that General Alexander was a peanut and a feather duster."[63]

Another example of the fundamental disparity between Clark and Alexander was that they rarely agreed on the qualifications of their subordinates. An example was their divergent opinions of Major General W. R. C. Penney, the commander of the 1st British Division, which came under Lucas's command in the Anzio beachhead. Penney had been Alexander's chief signal officer and was regarded by him as an able commander. Clark, on the other hand, referred scornfully to Penney "as a division commander [who] was a good telephone operator."[64]

Salerno typified Clark's strengths and weaknesses as an Army commander. His bravery in restlessly prowling the beachhead and giving orders and encouragement to his men won him both their respect and the Distinguished Service Cross (America's second highest decoration for exceptional bravery in combat). However, it was his inexperience and stubborn disregard of the advice of colleagues that had placed the Fifth Army in such a perilous position. Admiral Hewitt was not known as a naval commander who gave gratuitous advice, but Clark's failure to heed his pleas to be permitted to conduct a preliminary naval bombardment on German positions was a grievous mistake.

If Salerno established Clark as a man of exceptional personal courage, it also marked him as a commander who had a great deal to learn about high command. Clark mistakenly believed he had saved the Allied invasion by his leadership, when in fact it was precisely his inexperience that precipitated most of the problems the invasion force faced. His relations with Alexander, always cordial on the surface, never went beyond the formality of a senior-subordinate relationship and frequently led him to ignore Alexander in the same manner as Montgomery had throughout his tenure as Eighth Army commander. The difference was that Monty had considerable rapport with Alexander, while the Alexander-Clark relationship was essentially adversarial.

Clark saw himself as the American foil to British ambition in the Mediterranean, as the one who had paid the price at Salerno for what he believed was the inefficient performance of the Allied air forces, led by Coningham and Tedder.[65] He viewed Montgomery and Alexander as threats to a fitting role for himself and his Fifth Army. Unfortunately, the tactical lessons of Salerno that Clark ought to have learned were lost in the confusion of recriminations and resentment directed toward the British. In short, pride became a major factor in the conduct of future operations. With near paranoia, Clark suspected virtually every British act as motivated to deny himself and the U.S. Army recognition due them.

Nor were Clark's relations with his own American subordinate commanders cause for elation. He related to most badly and rarely listened to their advice. As the Italian campaign developed, his relations with Fred Walker, the veteran 36th Division commander, worsened. Clark also took most of the blame for the relief of General Dawley at Salerno, but both Alexander and Eisenhower felt Dawley was not up to the job and, when briefed on the problem, Eisenhower said, "Well, God Damn, why in the hell doesn't he [Clark] relieve Dawley?"[66]

* * *

These were by no means the only tempestuous relationships in the Mediterranean Theater of Operations. When Eisenhower departed at the end of 1943 to assume command of Allied invasion forces in England for Operation Overlord, his replacement was Field Marshal Sir Henry Maitland Wilson (a six-foot-seven-inch giant of a man whose large ears, not his height, had earned him the nickname "Jumbo"). Wilson was a man of considerable experience of both the battlefield and the politics of war, whose standing with his colleagues was nonetheless never high. Even though Alexander rarely interfered with the conduct of the campaign in Italy, he held Wilson in utter contempt, noting dismissively that "he could be pushed around." Although Alexander got along with him, he politely ignored any suggestions Wilson made unless they happened to coincide with his own ideas.[67]

Equally ineffectual was Wilson's new American deputy, Lieutenant General Jacob L. Devers, Marshall's personal choice to protect American interests within AFHQ in Algiers. Devers had previously commanded U.S. ground forces in the United Kingdom until Eisenhower's arrival left him superfluous. The new Overlord commander did not know him personally and appears to have had little faith in his ability.[68]

Over Devers, Alexander and Clark for once found themselves in agreement. Alexander asserted that Devers never had the slightest influence on tactical operations and, although a "pleasant fellow," always reminded him of a boy who never grew up.[69] Clark was less charitable. The two despised one another and clashed repeatedly. Clark regarded Devers as a "dope" who likewise had no influence over command decisions. "I made it clear to Jakie when he came to Italy the first time that I had too many bosses already."[70]

According to Lemnitzer, "Clark and Devers got along like cats and dogs. They would not be together three minutes without getting into a fight." So powerful was their enmity that Lemnitzer feared that each visit by Devers to the Fifth Army might end in Clark's relief. The two had clashed earlier in the war, and "Clark had no respect for Devers' tactical military ability. . . . Devers would try to interfere in the tactical operations of the Fifth Army, and it would make Clark boil. Devers looked on Clark as a very ambitious man who was interested only in feathering his own nest. Devers was jealous of Clark and lost few opportunities to belittle Clark's ability and his conduct of the Italian campaign."[71]

Nevertheless, the self-effacing Devers was destined to play an important behind-the-scenes role in the Italian campaign. As Wilson's deputy and the commander of the North African Theater of Operations, U.S. Army, Devers had little to do with the planning of Shingle. "Devers' role was to make sure that the operational forces were receiving the available resources in the amounts needed and using them to advantage" in a thankless and multifaceted job that included the rearming of the French Army in North Africa.[72]

Wilson's selection came as a disappointment to Clark, who nurtured the hope that Alexander might be kicked upstairs to supreme commander, thus leaving Clark himself as the logical choice to become the senior Allied commander in Italy. Clark's only rival to succeed Alexander was Montgomery, whose appointment to command all Allied land forces for Overlord left the Eighth Army under the command of an officer with no experience as an army or army group commander.

Lieutenant General Sir Oliver Leese was, like Alexander, a Guardsman and a protégé of Montgomery who had previously commanded 30th Corps in North Africa and Sicily. Leese was clearly not a candidate to advance higher without experience as an Army commander. Moreover, as the campaign progressed, it was soon evident that Leese was unable to sustain the uncommon spirit that Montgomery had so infused in the Eighth Army. Like Wilson, Leese was a giant of a man whose attempts to emulate Monty's style of command failed miserably.[73] A Canadian officer later described Leese as "a smooth-faced baronet with about as much personal appeal to Canadian troops as a suet pudding in a Sam Browne belt."[74] Leese had been an excellent corps commander, but his tenure as Eighth Army commander displayed flaws that included laziness and lack of initiative.[75]

Moreover, Leese lacked Montgomery's stable temperament and his occasional intemperate outbursts would have dismayed his mentor.[76] More than one of Leese's subordinate commanders deeply resented his imperiousness and his habit of summoning commanders back to his tactical headquarters instead of going forward to see them as military custom dictated.

Although Leese would continue to command the Eighth Army until the autumn of 1944, like Devers and "Jumbo" Wilson, he was never destined to play an influential role during the long campaign in Italy. That mantle fell upon Alexander and Clark, the two commanders who were so vastly different in experience and outlook. As the latest heir of a blue-blooded Scottish–Northern Irish aristocratic family that had served the Crown in various capacities for nearly 150 years, Alexander was a gentleman-general who exemplified the traditions of his forefathers and the British Army. Disdainful of the messy details of routine military matters, his approach to command varied little from that of his warrior ancestors. By contrast, like most Americans, Clark was a man without a pedigree, a product of the great cultural melting pot of the United States.

To Churchill, Mark Clark may have been the American Eagle, but his enemies would argue that his performance to date had shown him to be more like that other bird of prey, the hawk. After toiling in obscurity during the interwar years, Clark's drive and exemplary courage had at last propelled him to the exalted position of Fifth Army commander and the three stars of a lieutenant general.

Both men were considered heroes by the vast majority of their countrymen, and each came to symbolize the strengths and weaknesses of their respective armies. Within the confines of an ill-defined strategy, the leadership exercised by these two men would determine the future course of events of the Allied campaign in Italy.

4

The Decision to Launch Shingle

My plan for the capture of Rome is divided into three
phases. . . . Phase Three [is] an amphibious operation
south of Rome directed on Colli Laziali.

—ALEXANDER TO BROOKE,
November 9, 1943

This should decide the Battle of Rome.

CHURCHILL,
December 26, 1943

In 1943 there were only two roads
leading to Rome from the south. The town of Cassino straddled Highway 6, the only interior road, and Highway 7 (the famed Appian Way),
the other highway to the Italian capital, ran generally along the Mediterranean to Terracina, where it crossed the Pontine Marshes and the
Alban Hills south of Rome. Both highways were strongly defended
where they met the Gustav Line.

However, if the hub of the German defenses at Cassino could be
broken, the terrain to the north along Highway 6 would be far less
defensible. The Allied offensive in December had intended to gain a
foothold in the Liri Valley, but when the Fifth Army was unable to gain
a foothold north of the twin obstacles of the Garigliano and Rapido,
Clark's staff began developing a plan for an assault crossing of both
rivers.

Though Alexander was responsible for the conduct of the ground
operations in Italy, it was Mark Clark who was most affected by the

pressure from above to break the growing stalemate. Churchill had already made his displeasure over the lack of Allied progress well known, but despite his personal liking for the British leader, Clark was no Anglophile. To the contrary, his growing disdain for his British colleagues in Italy began to affect his judgment. He believed that from Alexander on down, the British intended to take Rome and claim the credit at the expense of the Fifth Army. The award of the Distinguished Service Cross for gallantry at Salerno, personally pinned on his breast by Roosevelt, only seemed to increase a growing obsession that it was his personal responsibility to capture Rome. The Eternal City, however, remained a distant illusion unless the Fifth Army could crack the Gustav Line.

The Eighth Army had encountered the same ferocious resistance that the Fifth Army was facing in the west. The end run at Termoli on the Adriatic was met with violent counterattacks by the 16th Panzer Division and sent a clear message that the Germans intended to resist whenever and wherever the Allies attempted to outflank them. After the Termoli landings, Montgomery's operations on the eastern end of the Allied line had succeeded in capturing the important Foggia airfield complex, thus enabling Allied tactical aircraft to provide close-air support within minutes. Although the Allies were able to penetrate the eastern end of the Gustav Line, any hope of rolling up the Adriatic flank was lost when the weather deteriorated so badly that the Eighth Army offensive stalled along the flood-swollen Sangro River. Most of the assault bridges constructed by the engineers were washed away, and progress was measured in yards as the Germans fought furiously to prevent the British from establishing a bridgehead north of the river.

Montgomery recognized that any hope of severing the Adriatic end of the Gustav Line was impossible and would only consume his army in an essentially futile effort. "I am fighting a hell of a battle here . . . [in] a sea of mud . . . and in the most foul conditions you can ever imagine," he lamented. He was dismayed that the Allies "have made a sad mess of it" in Italy and believed it was futile to persist until the weather improved. "Given some clear and firm directive, followed by a firm hand on the tiller which guides the military effort," he wrote to Mountbatten, "we would have been in Rome by now. . . . I understand Caesar used to go into winter quarters about this time, when he commanded an Army in these parts!! And very wise too!!"[1]

The British drive to the Sangro was Montgomery's last battle in the Mediterranean. For months Churchill, Roosevelt, and the Combined Chiefs of Staff had been wrestling with the problem of reorganizing the Allied high command in England and the Mediterranean, which was destined to supply the majority of the senior Overlord commanders. Both Marshall and Brooke passionately desired command of the cross-Channel invasion forces, but neither Roosevelt nor Churchill could afford to part with the men who were the heart and soul of their nation's war effort.

With Marshall and Brooke out of the running, the consensus choice was Eisenhower, whose appointment was announced on December 6. Omar Bradley's brilliant performances in North Africa and Sicily had earned him command of the U.S. invasion force over Patton, whose lonely exile in Sicily as a result of the uproar over his slapping of two soldiers in August was to continue until January 1944.

There was considerable wrangling between Churchill and Brooke over the appointment of the British invasion commander, who would command not only the 21st Army Group but initially all Allied ground forces in Normandy until such time as Eisenhower himself could assume command. Both Eisenhower and the prime minister avidly favored Alexander, while Brooke maneuvered to secure the appointment for Montgomery, whom he considered the best qualified.

Alexander's less-than-inspiring performance in the Mediterranean left Brooke unconvinced that he was fit for the Overlord appointment. He never questioned the gallant Alexander's leadership qualities, but, as we have seen, Brooke believed he lacked the ability to perform in a position that required tactical and strategic decisions. Eventually Brooke won his point, and Churchill agreed to leave Alexander in Italy and appoint Montgomery to command the Allied ground forces for Overlord.

These wholesale shifts of key personnel into and from the Mediterranean theater took place at a critical moment in the Italian campaign. Admiral Cunningham had returned to London to become the First Sea Lord on the untimely death of Admiral Sir Dudley Pound, and Tedder had already left to become Eisenhower's deputy, while Air Vice Marshal "Mary" Coningham would leave shortly to take command of the tactical air force supporting the 21st Army Group. To replace Eisenhower the Combined Chiefs of Staff agreed to the appointment of a British officer, who turned out to be "Jumbo" Wilson. With Eisenhower's departure, the British now had the reins of power in the Mediterranean completely under their control, leaving the key decisions in the hands of British officers, all of whom were subject to the intrigues and enormous influence of Churchill.[2]

Eisenhower was the first to recognize that the optimistic predictions about the capture of Rome were pie in the sky. The U.S. official history records that about October 7, 1943, Eisenhower's optimism suddenly "underwent a startling change." If the Germans elected to defend southern Italy, "there will be very hard and bitter fighting before we can hope to reach Rome," he informed the Combined Chiefs of Staff.[3] Eisenhower tended to rely too heavily on the pronouncements of his intelligence officer, Brigadier Kenneth Strong, whose main claim to fame is that as the AFHQ G-2 he was rarely right about anything. In Sicily, Strong had rejected massive evidence that the Germans were conducting a major withdrawal across the Strait of Messina.[4] As he had in the past, Strong failed to grasp that the Germans were only withdrawing when forced to do so. "Both men paid too little regard to field conditions and too much to the current indulgence in what one staff officer called 'the annual "collapse of Germany" predictions' which were greeted with derision and cynicism in the field."[5]

The supreme commander also believed that the major contribution that could be made in Italy was for Allied forces to drive as far north as the Po Valley, and to that end he asked the Combined Chiefs of Staff for a greater share of the precious landing-craft assets. However, there was no help forthcoming from Washington, where it was believed that the Germans would not resist in southern Italy. Eisenhower was told that the allocations previously agreed upon in Quebec would not be altered. Overlord and the Pacific theater were to receive the lion's share. What remained for the Mediterranean was scarcely enough to move a single division. Like it or not, Eisenhower would have to make do in Italy with what little sealift he possessed.[6] What made the problem even more acute was the fact that the majority of his LSTs were allocated for Overlord and would in December be shifted to the United Kingdom.

Eisenhower and Alexander first discussed the feasibility of amphibious end runs at an October 24 command conference at Carthage. Several weeks earlier Clark had created a special section in the Fifth Army to examine and plan possible amphibious operations.[7] Two days before discussing the subject with Alexander at Carthage, Clark and Eisenhower agreed that an operation should be launched within ten days somewhere behind German lines on the west coast of Italy north of Naples, in the vicinity of Gaeta.

The operation had to be scrapped when "the practical obstacles seemed insuperable . . . mine fields offshore, the strength of coastal defenses, and most important, the distance of the land forces from the projected landing areas, which would make their quick link-up with a beachhead impossible."[8] Under Clark's direction there was to be continued planning but no attempt to launch an operation until the Fifth Army could advance farther north.

As the planners began to examine possible landing sites their focus became Anzio, where there were beaches and a small port. The problem was that Anzio was simply too far out of range for a linkup. Moreover, with sufficient sealift for only a single division and reinforcements more than seventy-five miles away, an amphibious force stood little chance of survival. The planners recognized that there was scant likelihood of capturing the port of Anzio intact; thus, even a two-division force was insufficient unless the Fifth Army could complete a rapid linkup from the Cassino sector.

The desire to find some way to bypass the German lines and initiate an operation that would speed the capture of Rome was in direct conflict with other high-priority movements from North Africa via the woefully inadequate sealift available to Eisenhower. An essential element of the Pointblank bomber offensive was the capture of the vital airfield complex at Foggia, from which Allied heavy bombers could attack strategic targets in the Balkans and inside Germany. The problem was that the movement and maintenance of the heavy bomber force would tie up the entire sealift capacity in the Mediterranean for months. Even by delaying the activation of some units, there was simply no way these requirements could be filled and an amphibious operation undertaken without considerable additional sealift.

A second command conference at Carthage on November 3 resulted in several important decisions that set the stage for Anzio. Allied strategy called for the Fifth Army to continue its attacks up the west coast of Italy in a drive that would carry it into the Liri Valley and as far north as Frosinone on Highway 6, some thirty miles north of Cassino and approximately halfway between Cassino and Rome. The key to the success of the plan was that the offensive had to thrust successfully through the western anchor of the Gustav Line so that the Fifth Army could link up with the Anzio force within ten days at the latest. Concurrently the Eighth Army was to attack along the eastern coast and thrust north of the Sangro to Avezzano, a town about fifty miles east of Rome. This feint was intended to deepen Kesselring's predicament by forcing him to respond to attacks in three separate locations.

Eisenhower believed he could meet both a commitment to Anzio and the air forces if the Combined Chiefs of Staff would approve the retention in the Mediterranean until December 15 of sixty-eight LSTs destined to be sent to England for Overlord. The alternative was to continue with the present series of costly frontal attacks in increasingly bad winter weather.[9] Permission to retain the LSTs was the only part of the Carthage strategy to attain reality. By mid-December Montgomery was bogged down in the mud of the Sangro, and the Fifth Army's painful advance had left them unable to crack the German defenses at the mouth of the Liri Valley. As it would throughout the entire Italian campaign, Allied strategy was not going according to plan.

On November 9, Alexander cabled Brooke that it would most certainly be necessary to plan for an amphibious operation south of Rome into the German rear and threaten, if not actually capture, the Eternal City. Several sites were under consideration, but the primary one was at the twin resort cities of Anzio-Nettuno, thirty-five miles southwest of the capital:

> My plan for the capture of Rome is divided into three phases. Phase One, operations by Eighth Army to get astride the road communications in the area [of] Pescara . . . and from there to threaten the enemy Line of Communications behind Fifth Army via Avezzano. Phase Two, an attack by Fifth Army to drive up the Liri and Sacco Valleys to Frosinone. Phase Three, *an amphibious operation south of Rome directed on Colli Laziali together with a possible airborne landing by one R[egimental] C[ombat] T[eam]* (italics added).[10]

Brooke's papers contain two maps, marked in colored ink, which are based on Alexander's November 9 signal. Both clearly illustrate Alexander's intention that the U.S. VI Corps seize the Alban Hills.[11] A composite of the two maps is shown below. In light of the later controversy over Alexander's intentions for the operation, these maps are important evidence that he fully intended this to be far more than a diversionary operation. In the postwar aftermath of the Anzio landings Winston Churchill has been portrayed as the instigator of the ill-fated Allied end run. Although the British prime minister avidly embraced the scheme when first briefed in late December and became its midwife, the original architects were in reality Alexander and Eisenhower.

Alexander believed that if an Allied force seized and held the Alban Hills, it could block all German reinforcement of Cassino by road and rail, and likely make Kesselring's position so untenable that he would be forced to retreat to the Apennines, where the Germans were thought to have been preparing their main defensive line in Italy.

Alexander designated the Fifth Army to plan and execute the operation, code-named Shingle. Although an outline plan was developed by Clark's staff, there was no conviction that Shingle would ever take place, particularly when it became evident that there were insufficient landing craft available to carry out even a small amphibious operation. Virtually all the available landing craft, particularly the all-important LSTs,* remained earmarked for transfer to England.

---

*The LST, or Landing Ship Tank, was one of the great workhorse vessels of World War II. The first of the standardized LSTs were constructed in Newport News, Virginia, in late 1942. Measuring 328 feet in length and powered by two diesel engines, the LST was capable of carrying 2,100 tons through rough seas and beaching itself in shallow water so that its cargo could be unloaded or driven off using the large front ramp. The LST had the unique capability of transporting on its deck a fully loaded Landing Craft Tank (LCT), the next in size of the U.S. Navy family of seagoing landing craft (see Samuel Eliot Morison, *Operations in North African Waters* [Boston, 1984], p. 268).

Liri Valley

Mountain Village of Villa S. Julia

TO FROSINONE AND ROME

GERMAN POSITIONS ON NORTH SIDE OF LIRI VALLEY

TO CASSINO

CASTROCIELO

PIEDIMONTE

AQUINO

PONTECORVO

PIUMAROLA

L I R I V A L L E Y

GERMAN LINE HOLDING WEST BANK OF RAPIDO

PIGNATARO

S. GIORGIO

S. ANGELO

L I R I R.

PACHIDO

R A P I D O   R I V E R

ALLIED POSITIONS ON EAST BANK

GERMAN POSITIONS ON SOUTH SIDE OF VALLEY

S. AQUILARE

GARIGLIANO R.

Not only was the Fifth Army staff lukewarm, but there was little enthusiasm for Shingle within the Allied naval and air forces and the operation seemed doomed to oblivion. Although the scope of Shingle was increased to corps size and scheduled to be carried out by mid-December by Lucas's VI Corps, problems continued to mount over the acquisition of the necessary landing craft. When Allied operations became hopelessly stalled in front of the Gustav Line, Clark finally decided there was no other option except to cancel Shingle. The Combined Chiefs of Staff had granted a one-month extension for the departure of the landing craft, but even this left Clark doubtful that the Fifth Army could drive north to Frosinone by that date.

The first outline plan was approved by Clark on November 25 and defined Shingle as a diversionary operation by a single reinforced infantry division to assist the Fifth Army in an all-out drive on the Alban Hills. Its basic premise was that the Fifth Army had already successfully driven to Frosinone and that the two forces were to join hands within seven days.[12] Clark's plan was based on Alexander's November 8 directive and, as the Fifth Army history records, was based on the assumption that "a force landed on the enemy flank below Rome, *once Fifth Army had already broken through the main German defenses in the south*, might so threaten Kesselring's communications as to force him into rapid retreat. This appreciation was to result in the Anzio landing [italics added]."[13]

On December 10, Clark suddenly changed the rules of the game by suggesting that if the Frosinone phase line was unattainable, it "might be cut down and Shingle launched without waiting until the overland attack was within supporting distance. Once in, the landing force would consolidate and make a stand until main Fifth Army came up. This conception would demand both a larger force and a resupply."[14]

It also suggested that Clark was willing to compromise on Anzio despite the criteria laid down by Alexander. Nevertheless, after briefing Eisenhower on the morning of December 18, Clark killed Shingle for a more basic reason—the lack of landing craft. He cabled Alexander:

> I feel I must recommend the cancellation of Operation "Shingle" in January. The limiting date of January 15 makes it impracticable. I will continue planning "Shingle" in the hope that craft will be made available at a later date, when it will be possible to execute the operation with proper preparation, supported by the main part of Fifth Army. It is my urgent request that all efforts be made to get necessary craft for a later time.[15]

Clark's decision not to press for Shingle was the only sensible course of action. The Fifth Army was exhausted after nearly four months of bitter combat and in no shape to properly support an end run at Anzio.[16] Shingle thus appeared to be a dead issue. It was only the intervention of Churchill in late December that resurrected Anzio.

Although the stated purpose of the Italian campaign was to divert German battle formations from other fronts and tie them down, the Allied commanders in Italy nevertheless found themselves under mounting pressure from Churchill to break the deadlock along the Cassino front and capture Rome. After the Cairo Conference in early December 1943, the prime minister became seriously ill with pneumonia and was bedridden in Eisenhower's villa in Carthage until December 27, when he was flown to Marrakech to recuperate.

The forthcoming loss of 104 landing craft from the Mediterranean and the painfully slow progress of Alexander's two armies north of Naples had been the objects of increasing concern in London throughout the autumn of 1943. Both Brooke and Churchill sought some means of increasing the emphasis of operations in Italy without creating what the CIGS was certain would be "an almighty row with the Americans who have put us in this position with their insistence to abandon the Mediterranean operations for [Overlord]."[17] Alexander's private cables and letters to Brooke and Churchill had added considerable fuel to the flames of discontent in London. Powerful evidence of this can be found in the minutes of Alexander's commander's conference of October 25, in which he warned that the Foggia airfield complex and Naples would not be considered secure until the 15th Army Group had established "a firm defensive base north of Rome. We cannot afford to adopt a purely defensive role, for this would entail the surrender of the initiative to the Germans."[18]

The first specific reference to Shingle appears to have been made to Churchill sometime between December 19 and 22, 1943. Brooke visited Churchill on December 18 en route to London from a weeklong visit to Italy and deliberately avoided conveying his own pessimistic outlook on the campaign because, "I knew from experience that he would only want to rush into some solution which would probably make matters worse. I had to keep these misgivings to myself and look for a cure."[19]

They did, however, discuss the continuing problem of landing craft, and the following day the prime minister cabled the British chiefs of staff in London to complain: "The stagnation of the whole campaign on the Italian front is scandalous . . . [and] confirmed my worst forebodings. The total neglect to provide the amphibious action on the Adriatic side and the failure to strike any similar blow on the west have been disastrous."[20] Three days later came a return cable agreeing that the "stagnation cannot be allowed to continue" and that the answer to the problem "clearly lies in making use of our amphibious power to strike round on the enemy's flank and open up the way for a rapid advance on Rome."[21]

The British chiefs noted that the withdrawal of landing craft for Overlord would leave Eisenhower with only enough lift for a single division and that "he has a plan to make a landing behind the enemy just south of Rome. The weakness of this plan is that the assault in this strength on the coast cannot be launched until the 5th Army is within supporting distance of the force to be landed." After offering several sources of additional landing craft, they added: "We should decide now to concentrate in the Central Mediterranean sufficient landing craft to enable General Eisenhower to deal the Germans a crushing blow in Italy and secure Rome. This could be fitted in before 'Anvil.' "[22]

This response was precisely what Churchill wanted to hear, and it arrived the same day he met with Alexander, who "altogether demurs to the suggestion that he is not very keen on the 'Shingle' operation. . . . He wants a two-division lift and the problem is how this could be supplied."[23]

Throughout the remainder of December, Anzio dominated Churchill's agenda. On Christmas Eve, he met with Wilson, Alexander, and Tedder to discuss how to obtain the necessary landing craft to make Shingle a reality. During the last week of December there was a virtual torrent of cables between Marrakech and London. On December 24, the British chiefs of staff addressed the assumption that proved to be Shingle's Achilles' heel. Commenting on the feasibility of a one-division assault, they noted:

> The progress of operations in Italy shows clearly that any ideas of a rapid advance of the 5th Army must be abandoned. The nature of the country and the winter weather make it impracticable. *If, however, the amphibious assault could be strengthened, and could be launched with two Divisions in the assault and possibly with one Division as a follow-up, it might well have a decisive effect upon the campaign. The assaulting forces would be strong enough to stand by itself and there would be good prospects of cutting off a portion of the enemy's Army* [italics added].[24]

Churchill never questioned the assumptions presented him with regard to what Anzio was likely to accomplish. The discussions tended to revolve around what the Shingle landings would do to the Germans. Apparently no one took serious note either of the enemy's options or how Kesselring was likely to respond. Although no one had altered the assumption that a linkup was highly improbable, all concerned seem to have been infused with the belief that the increase in size from one to two divisions would be enough to turn failure into success. This was evident when Churchill sealed the British commitment to Shingle in a telegram to Roosevelt the day after Christmas:

> General Alexander is prepared to execute operation SHINGLE about 20th January if he can get a lift of two divisions. This should decide the Battle of Rome and possibly achieve destruction of a substantial part of [the] enemy's army. To strike with less than two divisions would be to court disaster having regard to positions likely to be achieved by that date by Fifth and Eighth Armies. . . . We cannot afford to go forward leaving [a] vast half-finished job behind us. . . . If this opportunity is not grasped we must expect the ruin of [the] Mediterranean campaign in 1944. I earnestly hope therefore that you may agree to three weeks delay in the return of 56 landing craft.[25]

Churchill had anticipated considerable opposition from Marshall and was delighted that the final obstacle to the launching of Shingle was overcome the next day, when Roosevelt replied affirming American approval of the extension of the LSTs in the Mediterranean until mid-February. Although Marshall drafted the U.S. reply, he was not reassured by Churchill's request; thus the approval of Shingle included the blunt admonition that it was only "on the basis that OVERLORD remain the paramount operation and will be carried out on the date agreed at Cairo and Teheran."[26] His biographer notes that these views "reflected Marshall's determination not to let the Italian situation get out of hand. Later, the Chief of Staff said of this period: 'I doubt if I did anything better in the war than to keep Churchill on the main point (he always wanted to take the side shots). I was furious when he wanted to push us further in the Mediterranean.'"[27]

Once Churchill and Alexander gained the necessary landing craft for a two-division assault at Anzio, neither displayed an inclination to question the potential outcome. The two had met extensively over a three-day period at Christmas, and it is reasonable to conclude that the prime minister's telegram to his chiefs of staff on December 26 accurately reflected their belief in Shingle. Virtually every fallacy about Anzio was expressed in Churchill's comments:

> The success of SHINGLE depends upon the strength of the initial landing. If this is two full divisions plus paratroops, it should be decisive, as it cuts the communications of the whole of the enemy's forces facing the Fifth Army. The enemy must therefore annihilate the SHINGLE force by withdrawals from the Fifth Army front or immediately retreat. Nothing less than two divisions will serve for SHINGLE. Weather uncertainties make it essential to put them ashore with at least four days supplies. It is not intended to maintain these divisions for long over the beaches but rather to bring the battle to a climax in a week or ten days and thereafter supply them from Fifth Army. A proportion of L.S.T.s will in fact leave after the

first lift is over in order to start home on 5th February . . . the success or
ruin of our Italian campaign [depends upon] the delay of three weeks in
the return of the 56 L.S.T.s.[28]

Churchill's vision of a cheap, quick victory at Anzio was wishful thinking and counter to everything he had been told regarding the practical-
ity of a linkup between the Shingle force and the Fifth Army. Eisenhower had no contact with Churchill during the three-day period when
the operation was revived, and it must be concluded that the prime
minister was either misled by Alexander that his assumption meant
total control by the Shingle force of the Alban Hills or failed to grasp
that there was no basis whatever for such optimism. His conclusions
were that Anzio would be quite different from Salerno. "At Salerno
there was never any question of building up and supplying the landed
force from the south. . . . In SHINGLE . . . the landed force will only
be perhaps 60 miles from Clark's advancing army and will be supplied
from them as soon as a junction is effected. There is no build-up in this
case."[29]

Throughout the war Brooke played the role of devil's advocate and
successfully curbed the more impetuous schemes that emanated from
Churchill's fertile mind. However, in the case of Anzio, Brooke fully
agreed with Churchill that something must be done quickly to break the
growing stalemate. His visit to Italy merely reinforced his belief that "we
are stuck in our offensive here and shall make no real progress till the
ground dries, unless we make greater use of our amphibious power . . .
the offensive is stagnating badly."[30] In his war memoirs, Churchill
named Brooke a full accessory: "We had a full discussion and I found that
General Brooke had by a separate route of thought arrived at the same
conclusion I had. We agreed on the policy, and also that while I should
deal with the commanders on the spot, he would do his best to overcome
all difficulties at home."[31] Thus, the one man with the influence to have
killed Shingle instead gave the operation his blessing.

There were myriad details yet to be worked out between the various parties, including a further crisis over Alexander's insistence that he
required a total of eighty-eight LSTs rather than the eighty he was to
receive under the terms of the compromise, but the major hurdle to
Shingle had been surmounted by December 29, 1943. Churchill set the
seal on the inevitability of the operation when he cabled Roosevelt, "I
thank God for this fine decision which engages us once again in whole
hearted unity upon a great enterprise . . . here the word is 'Full steam
ahead.' "[32]

We turn now to the other half of the Anzio equation, the Fifth Army
offensive to drive north to Frosinone. The problem facing Clark was

where to attack the Germans. In December 1943, his two remaining corps (the U.S. II and the British 10th) were stalled south of the Garigliano and Rapido rivers. With the date for Shingle now set for January 22, it was essential that the Fifth Army attack to crack the Gustav Line be timed to take place in time to divert Kesselring's attention from Anzio and oblige him to commit German formations to the Gustav Line that might otherwise have been used to counterattack VI Corps. Both Shingle and the river crossings presented an opportunity for Clark not only to erase British and not a few American doubts about his leadership but also to capture the prize of Rome. It was to this end that the Fifth Army planners turned their attention.

Mark Clark's paranoid distrust of the British in general and Lieutenant General Richard McCreery[33] in particular were major factors in the ill-fated offensive he planned for January 20, 1944, to seize a bridgehead north of the Rapido River. He was determined that the main effort be all-American despite the fact that the opportunities offered by shifting the main effort to the Garigliano sector were far more promising.

The intent was to create a diversion by a series of three separate 10th Corps assault crossings along the Garigliano, from its lower reaches near Minturno (by the British 5th Division) on the extreme left flank of the Allied front, to Castelforte some five miles upriver (by the British 56th Division). Finally, at Sant'Ambrogio the British 46th Division was to protect the American left flank by launching a third diversionary assault crossing. The object was to force XIV Panzer Corps to commit its reserves, thus freeing II Corps to assault the Rapido and exploit their breakthrough up Highway 6 to the vital road junction at Cassino. By shattering the right flank of the Gustav Line and gaining a foothold in the Liri Valley, it was thought that not only might the Fifth Army be able to link up with VI Corps at Anzio and seize Rome, but, if they were successful, Kesselring could be expected to abandon the Gustav Line and retreat to the Apennines.

Only one unit was chosen to carry out Clark's plan, Walker's 36th Infantry Division—now assigned to Major General Geoffrey Keyes's II Corps—perhaps the worst of all possible choices. Not only was the 36th Division exhausted from the failed December offensive, but it had suffered heavy casualties, many of which had not yet been replaced. Those who had arrived via the U.S. replacement system were green troops who had yet to experience their first combat. The division commander, Fred Walker, believed the operation had little chance of success and was unable to keep from infecting his subordinates with his pessimism.

Clark's original idea for the Rapido operation had been to use Major General Lucian K. Truscott's veteran U.S. 3d Infantry Division. Truscott and his staff studied the proposed operation and concluded it was "a terrible idea that would cost most of the division if it succeeded."[34]

By itself, this was ample prescription for failure, but to make matters worse, Walker's fears were fully justified. The site chosen by Clark's planners was along the open floodplain of the valley opposite the heavily defended village of Sant'Angelo, which itself was situated on higher ground. There was little cover, and the advance to the river would be under the direct observation and fire of German artillery. The Germans had made any advance here even more difficult by diverting the flow of the river to flood the approach route the 36th Division was obliged to employ. In plain terms, it meant that virtually all vehicular movement was curtailed and the assault troops would have to approach the river on foot, across heavily mined scrub woodland and swamp that was actively patrolled by the Germans.

The necessity for thwarting an Allied breakthrough at this key point was not lost on the German commanders. General Fridolin von Senger had assumed command of XIV Panzer Corps from Hube and, along with Kesselring and von Vietinghoff, was determined at all costs to prevent the Allies from gaining a bridgehead across the Rapido. Defending this sector of the Gustav Line was the 15th Panzer Grenadier Division, the veteran unit that had fought brilliantly in Sicily against the U.S. 1st Infantry Division. By selecting the 15th Panzer Grenadiers to defend the mouth of the Liri Valley, von Senger was shrewdly protecting the one area of the Gustav Line where the Allies could not be permitted to gain a foothold.

The site selected for the assault crossing was only fifty feet wide, but its drawback was that the advantage of narrowness was more than offset by the Rapido's steep banks and its twelve-foot depth, where the icy water flowed at torrential speeds that often exceeded ten miles per hour.

Clark's plan called for the 36th Division to assault and hold a bridgehead across the Rapido for Ernest Harmon's U.S. 1st Armored Division, which was to move up and pass through the Texans and debouch into the Liri Valley. The problem was that the Fifth Army commander's optimism for the operation overlooked the simple fact that the swampy terrain along both sides of the Rapido was the worst possible site for the employment of armor.

Moreover, the exceptionally strong German defense along the outer belts of the Gustav Line ought to have alarmed Clark and the Fifth Army staff. There was absolutely nothing in the past German performance to suggest that they had any intention of permitting the Allies to drive them from the Liri Valley. From the German perspective, defending against such an Allied assault crossing of the Rapido was an obvious necessity. Yet an unfortunate and wholly unjustified aura of optimism pervaded Clark's headquarters, which led to false assumptions about German intentions.

That false optimism was primarily attributable to the fact that major operations were being planned by inexperienced staff officers and not, as Montgomery had lamented, by the commanders who had to carry them out. Clark was unable to recognize that the Fifth Army plan for the Rapido and Garigliano operations was fatally flawed by both the inexperience of his staff and his own anti-British bias. Having decided that the 36th Division would make the main effort, he attempted to mold his plan to fit this premise. There are few more difficult operations in the military repertoire than an assault crossing under enemy fire. In this instance the Fifth Army had two rivers to cross at *night* under the worst possible weather conditions.

The British operation began with an unexpected delay. To protect the vulnerable American left flank, the 46th Division assault at Sant'Ambrogio was scheduled to commence forty-eight hours before the 36th Division assaulted the Rapido. At the last minute, McCreery postponed the operation for twenty-four hours, to the outrage of Clark and Keyes, who were convinced this was a prima facie example of British treachery. McCreery refused to alter his decision, as did Clark, who refused Keyes's request to defer the 36th Division assault for a similar period. The timetable for Anzio left Clark little choice but to order the operation to proceed without delay.

The 10th Corps crossings were a shocking surprise to the Germans. To avoid detection from the German-held heights north of the Garigliano, the British brought their artillery forward under the cover of darkness. The assault troops of the 5th Division managed to cross the river in total silence the night of January 17. Upriver the 56th Division launched its attack to the accompaniment of a heavy bombardment, and within forty-eight hours 10th Corps had successfully established a bridgehead several miles deep across a ten-mile front along the lower Garigliano. At a stroke, McCreery had gained a bridgehead north of the Garigliano, which was tailor-made for exploitation. Von Senger fully expected an imminent attempt to use McCreery's bridgehead to pry open and collapse the right flank of the Gustav Line.

Kesselring immediately perceived the serious threat posed by 10th Corps and was obliged to make his most crucial decision of the Italian campaign: whether or not to commit his only strategic reserve to block McCreery, two panzer grenadier divisions then resting and refitting near Rome. For some time, the Germans had been anticipating an Allied end run into their rear and had been preparing contingency plans to react accordingly. The problem was that there were simply too few formations to meet Kesselring's requirements. If he committed his only strategic reserve to meet the Allied threat on the Garigliano, there would be no forces readily available to counter an amphibious landing near Rome. Nevertheless, without the slightest hesitation—and counter to the advice of some of his senior staff officers—Kesselring elected to commit his reserves then and there. In his judgment the threat posed by McCreery's success on the lower Garigliano was so grave that he must react at once or risk the collapse of the Gustav Line.

Not only had Clark's plan split 10th Corps, but McCreery was never permitted to exploit his success with the 46th Division. The concept of reinforcing success by shifting his main attack to the Garigliano was anathema to Clark, who doggedly stuck to his flawed plan for the 36th Division to assault the Rapido at Sant'Angelo. It was unthinkable that the British should gain the credit for breaking the Gustav Line or do so with merely the support of American troops.

Once again the gods of war smiled favorably on the German Army in Italy as Clark declined to press his advantage, with the predictable result that further British progress along the Garigliano was checked by Kesselring's hastily assembled reinforcements.

Clark never saw the flaws in his plans and strategy and instead blamed the British for fouling up his operation. He was particularly critical of Hawkesworth, the 46th Division commander, whose assault battalions failed to reach their objectives. Describing it as "quite a blow," Clark wrote in his diary, "I was fearful that General Hawkesworth had a mental reservation as to the possibilities of [the] success of his operation. . . . It is a question of 'sending a boy to do a man's job.' " McCreery believed the Rapido attack had little chance of success because of the heavy German defenses west of the Rapido, but was firmly overruled. "I maintain," wrote Clark, "that it is essential that I make the attack fully expecting heavy losses in order to hold all the troops on my front and draw more to it, thereby clearing the way for SHINGLE. The attack is on."[35]

Having committed himself in advance to a fixed plan for assaulting the Garigliano and Rapido rivers, Clark failed to grasp that what he had created was a scheme that embodied the worst features of *both* a hasty and a deliberate river crossing.[36] Instead he destroyed the potential effectiveness of the Fifth Army by a series of separate deliberate assault crossings against an entrenched enemy who was given time to commit his reserves and plug the gaps in his defenses along the Garigliano. Moreover, as Graham and Bidwell point out, there was a fatal flaw in Clark's thinking, which was colored by "his irrational dislike of McCreery and his lack of faith in the fighting power of the 'poor dumb British.' . . . The role of the 10th Corps was to draw in the German Army group reserves, and no more. The role of the 46th Division was simply to secure the left flank of General Walker's crossing place. After that the Gustav Line battle was to be an all-American show."[37]

But what would ultimately doom Clark's plan to ignominious failure was his refusal to permit Americans and British to fight together. Throughout his tenure as Fifth Army commander—with the lone exception of Anzio, where his superiors insisted on an Allied team—Mark Clark repeatedly refused to mix Anglo-American forces even when it would have been militarily sound. The inevitable result was a series of piecemeal attacks that were never individually powerful enough to achieve his objectives. Clark's Anglophobia was too strong to enable him to modify his plan for the Rapido and Garigliano operations. He was not prepared to permit his rival McCreery to steal the limelight by breaking through the Gustav Line. That "honor" belonged to the U.S. Army. The British effort was intended to be a diversion and that was that.

The result was that the 36th Division assault the night of January 20 was one of the bloodiest failures of the war. The 15th Panzer Grenadier Division manned positions astride the west bank of the Rapido that enabled them to pour a devastating volume of fire on the hapless assault troops of the 36th Division, which had no cover, no artillery support, and insufficient infantry to force a successful crossing of the river. The operation was a virtual encyclopedia of mistakes that ran the gamut from no coordinated fire-support plan to the fact that the infantry and engineers had never even seen one another prior to the assault. River-crossing operations require exceptional rapport between engineers and infantry, and at the Rapido both came under devastating fire from the Germans as they attempted to portage their assault craft across the scrub and marshes. Not only did they have to contend with the dark but also with uncharted German mine fields, which took their toll.

The first attempt was repulsed with heavy losses, but Clark remained determined to force a crossing and ordered Walker to renew his assault the afternoon of January 21. The smoke, fire, and noise were terrifying. Confusion and death were the only constants as the 36th Division was soundly repulsed at the Rapido a second time. Many simply fled the battlefield, while others floundered helplessly and became stragglers when unit integrity evaporated. Casualties for the 36th Division numbered 1,681, including 143 killed and 663 wounded.[38] The few who managed to cross the Rapido were trapped there and rounded up by the Germans. Some 875 men were reported missing, and it was later confirmed that 500 had been captured by the 15th Panzer Grenadier Division.

The Rapido-Garigliano river crossings were a shambles that left the Fifth Army stalled at the mouth of the Liri Valley. Walker was appalled by the severe losses to two of his three infantry regiments and fully expected to be sacked by Clark and Keyes "to cover their own stupidity." He was surprised when the Fifth Army commander told him the Rapido failure was partly his responsibility.[39]

In a postmortem on the operation, Clark never wavered in his belief that he had done the right thing. "In deciding upon the attack some time ago, I knew it would be costly but was impelled to go ahead with [it] . . . in order that I could draw to this front all possible German reserves . . . to clear the way for SHINGLE. This was accomplished in a magnificent manner. Some blood had to be spilled on either the land or the SHINGLE front, and I greatly preferred that it be on the Rapido, where we were secure, rather than at Anzio with the sea at our back."[40]

The attempt to breach the Rapido was a major debacle that haunted the survivors and tainted Clark's reputation.[41] It also resulted in a congressional inquiry into the operation in 1946, after the 36th Division veteran's association called for an investigation of the "fiasco" and of a military system "that will permit an inefficient and inexperienced officer [Clark] . . . to [order such an operation and to] prevent future soldiers from being sacrificed wastefully and uselessly."[42]

Although Walker apparently attempted to dissuade the 36th Division Association from pursuing the investigation, he remained extremely critical of the operation. Among his comments was that Clark had assured him that "no crossing [of the Rapido] will be attempted until we hold the high ground on your left." The statement was witnessed by Walker's assistant division commander, who wrote it down and certified to its accuracy within five minutes of Clark's utterance. When the British 46th Division failed to capture this terrain the operation nevertheless went ahead as planned.[43]

Walker's men had been ill prepared, under strength, exhausted from endless weeks of combat during the bloody battle for San Pietro, and asked to accomplish the impossible. Walker himself was unenthusiastic about the operation, and his attitude permeated the entire division.

The disaster at the Rapido shattered once and for all the basic premise that VI Corps could expect relief from the main body of the Fifth Army. The reality was that the Allies hadn't a hope of breaking the Gustav Line in the foreseeable future.

The ultimate irony of the Rapido debacle was that McCreery might not have had to contend with the two German divisions sent to reinforce the Garigliano sector had not Kesselring been fed very inaccurate intelligence. Two days before McCreery opened his diversionary offensive, Kesselring was given an erroneous intelligence assessment of Allied intentions by the head of the German Abwehr, Admiral Wilhelm Canaris, who was on a tour of Italy. Unaccountably, Canaris emphatically stated in mid-January: "There is not the slightest sign that a new landing will be undertaken in the near future."[44] At the same moment that Canaris was issuing his confident pronouncement, the Allies were assembling a fleet in the Bay of Naples for an amphibious landing—scheduled for the following week—that the German high command in Italy now believed would not come for at least another four to six weeks.

5

"Smiling Albert"

"Smiling Albert" he may have been, but no one disobeyed him twice.

—SHELFORD BIDWELL[1]

The senior German commander in the Mediterranean and the officer responsible for the defense of Italy was one of the outstanding German commanders of the war. Field Marshal Albert Kesselring bore the stamp of genius for the defensive operations that seemed to characterize products of the German General Staff. Born in 1885, Kesselring had acquired the nickname Smiling Albert for his perpetually optimistic nature. He served in World War I as an artillery officer and was retained in the small postwar army of one hundred thousand permitted under the terms of the Treaty of Versailles. During the interwar years he rose rapidly from captain to major general and, quick to sense the potential of the new German air arm, transferred to the Luftwaffe in 1935, where he became one of the architects of its emergence as an effective and terrifying force. He was also one of the originators of the *blitzkrieg* and was instrumental in the Polish campaign and in France and Norway in 1940, earning him a promotion to field marshal. In 1942, Kesselring was given command of all Axis air operations in the Mediterranean and in the autumn of 1943 became commander in chief of all German forces as Oberbefehlshaber Süd (OB South).

What made Kesselring unique in an army whose standard of generalship was universally high were his achievements in what amounted to three separate and diverse military careers. A measure of Kesselring's ability is that he was forty-eight years old before he learned to fly an airplane. During World War II he constantly flew over the front lines and survived being shot down five times.[2] In Italy he was most often found at the controls of a Ju-88 fighter-bomber, and on at least one occasion, to von Vietinghoff's consternation, Kesselring insisted on flying over the battlefield to "feel the pulse of the situation."[3]

An outwardly amiable bear of a man, Kesselring's sunny disposition masked an iron will. During the twenty months he commanded German forces in the Mediterranean, where they were generally moving backwards, Kesselring became accustomed to criticism from all levels of the chain of command. Although he tolerated the usual give and take between professionals, his subordinates learned, some of them the hard way, that when Kesselring gave an order, it had better be carried out. Kesselring and von Vietinghoff got on well and respected one another, but even the German Tenth Army commander was not immune to the sting of an angry "Smiling Albert." When he learned that von Vietinghof was shilly-shallying over an order to move 16th Panzer Division to counter the British landings at Termoli in early October 1943, Kesselring ordered that "my instructions be carried out in double-quick time."[4]

Besides Hitler, Kesselring's primary nemesis was Rommel, with whom he had clashed repeatedly in North Africa. By the time of the Italian campaign their relations had reached such animosity that neither could stand the sight of the other. Kesselring appreciated Rommel's fighting spirit and how he had successfully waged a "poor man's war" in North Africa. However, the differing temperaments of the two men were virtual assurance that they would clash. Where Rommel was dashing and impetuous, Kesselring was calm and studious. (Yet shortly before he died Rommel paid tribute to Kesselring's "splendid leadership" in preventing the collapse of the Italian front.[5])

Despite his troubles with Rommel and with Guzzoni in Sicily, Kesselring established himself as a master of the defensive who was able time and again to thwart Allied aims in the Mediterranean with significantly smaller forces. In North Africa, Kesselring exercised command through two independent-minded subordinates, von Arnim and Rommel. His imprint on the battle for Tunisia had been minimal, but this changed dramatically when the fighting shifted to Italy. The prolonged German defense of Italy was a product of Kesselring's genius for defensive operations. Throughout that campaign it was Kesselring who dictated German strategy by the firm exercise of command and by his ability to shrewdly maneuver his forces against the Allies. Graham and Bidwell believe that in Kesselring the Allies faced "as good a general as emerged from the German Army in the Second World War and certainly the best on either side in the Italian theater."[6] Unlike his opposite numbers, Alexander and Clark, Kesselring was a decisive commander whose imprint on the Italian campaign was his and his alone.

The defection of Italy to the Allies in September proved to be a turning point in Kesselring's relations with Hitler. Although he had escaped censure for ordering the evacuation of Sicily prior to receiving Hitler's permission,[7] Kesselring, no exception to the Führer's penchant for blaming his generals for setbacks over which they had little control, was—like General Alfred Jodl, head of the OKW operations staff, and Rommel—no friend at court. On one occasion Hitler scornfully referred to him as "a dupe among those born [Italian] traitors." Nor did Kesselring help his own cause by his support of the Italians and his mistaken belief that the Badoglio government would remain allied with Germany.

Like many other German officers, Kesselring was torn between allegiance to his country and distaste for the Nazi regime. His British biographer notes that, "like others among the cream of the German High Command, he performed a perilous balancing trick, attempting faithfully to serve his country, in the knowledge that it was embarked upon a suicide course, while subtly retaining the ear of men who deeply mistrusted him and to whom he referred, at the time, as 'bandits.' "[8]

Despite intense pressures from the Allies and from his own high command, Kesselring managed successfully to walk a narrow tightrope between the unrealistic, often wild delusions of Hitler and the realities of his position as a commander forced to live from hand to mouth in a secondary theater of war that had a very low priority for reinforcements and resupply.

Nevertheless, Kesselring was rarely free from orders and guidance emanating from OKW or Hitler, and there were occasions when he found his most serious problems were with Berlin rather than the Allies. He had to fight constant battles with OKW and the twin nemeses of all German commanders in the field—Jodl and Field Marshal Wilhelm Keitel.[9]

Kesselring's quarrels with OKW revolved around how the Germans ought to conduct the defense of Italy. One faction in Berlin favored a strong defense in the northern Apennines, while Kesselring was convinced that it was foolish to cede three-quarters of Italy to the Allies without a fight. Although Kesselring realized he could not hold southern Italy indefinitely, he far preferred defending there than in the Apennines and the Po Valley in the north. Despite his own low standing in Berlin, Kesselring eventually persuaded a reluctant Hitler to follow his ideas for a strategic approach to the defense of Italy. He believed it was possible to defend south of Rome along Italy's narrowest point, which ran from the vicinity of Pescara on the Adriatic, through the Liri Valley to the Gulf of Gaeta, north of Naples—the area that later came to be known as the Gustav Line. Such a defense offered the advantage of denying the Allies important air bases in central and northern Italy and discouraged any attempt to invade the Balkans and threaten the crucial sources of raw materials used to feed the German war machine. That Kesselring was able to overcome Rommel's intrigues, Hitler's displeasure, and the second-guessers at OKW and within his own HQ to conduct the Italian campaign largely according to his own conception and strategy was a considerable achievement.[10]

From Ultra it was learned that Kesselring's appointment was "still in the balance" until the last minute. At one point Hitler actually dictated a cable appointing Rommel, only to reverse himself. Rommel had openly lobbied Hitler to become Kesselring's replacement, but what seems to have won the day for Kesselring was his unwavering belief that Italy could and should be defended, and his success in doing so. After the decision, Rommel was immediately sent to France to take charge of the coastal defenses from Belgium to Normandy.[11]

By November 1943 Kesselring's arguments prevailed, and he was given command of the newly created Army Group C, which consisted of von Vietinghoff's Tenth Army and a new formation, the Fourteenth Army, commanded by another Prussian aristocrat, Colonel General Eberhard von Mackensen. His father had been a field marshal, and von Mackensen himself was another of the German tank officers who had fought well in Russia in command of a corps and later of the First Panzer Army.

Kesselring had shrewdly anticipated the Allied invasion of Salerno and had begun preparations to defend the Gustav Line, while at the same time elements of the Tenth Army dealt for as long as possible with the invasion. The repeated setbacks the Germans caused the Fifth Army were unmistakable evidence that Kesselring could deliver on his promises.

Von Vietinghoff was one of the new breed of tough, aggressive armored commanders who had been blooded in Russia leading a panzer division under General Heinz Guderian. His supporting cast of field commanders were also as able a group as the Wehrmacht employed in any theater of operations during the war. In command of XIV Panzer Corps was yet another armored officer whom the Allies already knew only too well from Sicily, the one-armed General der Panzertruppen Hans Valentin Hube, who had previously commanded the First Panzer Army on the Eastern Front under General Erich von Manstein.[12] When Hube was reassigned back to Russia in November, his replacement was General Fridolin von Senger und Etterlin.

Von Senger was one of a growing number of anti-Nazi generals who fought not for a regime they despised but for the honor of Germany. He was a Bavarian, a devout Catholic, a lay Benedictine, and a former Rhodes scholar who had many English friends from his days at

Oxford before World War I. Had it not been for his outstanding record as a commander, von Senger's hatred of Hitler would have resulted in his removal and court-martial on more than one occasion. He was serving in Russia in command of a panzer division when he was suddenly sent by Hitler to Sicily, shortly before the Allied invasion, as a liaison officer to Guzzoni. Because of Hube's presence as the German tactical commander, a role originally given him by Hitler, von Senger played a relatively minor role in Sicily.

Throughout his career von Senger's pragmatism and humanity were often at odds with the Establishment. In Sardinia, in September 1943, he had openly defied a direct order from Hitler to execute a large number of Italian officers and soldiers in retaliation for Italy's defection to the Allies. In favor of peace with the Allies but never one of the active anti-Nazi conspirators, von Senger elected the same middle ground so many others followed: He would do his duty and fight for honor and for Germany. Whether von Senger believed he could accomplish this while still remaining a vital part of an odious regime was the essence of the moral crisis faced by the entire German officer corps. Von Senger seems to have resolved this quandary by turning to St. Thomas Aquinas, whose creed was, he wrote in his diary, that "no man can be blamed for the crimes of others insofar as he has no influence over them. However, the power is not in the hands of the generals but of Hitler and the German people who have voted him into power and who to this day are following him blindly and devotedly on the course he selected."[13]

Many years later his son would argue: "He had indeed served Hitler's state loyally. Within the sphere of his own commands he had permitted not one deviation from the accepted code of Christian morality. It was the state, not its Führer, that he had served; he was never one of Hitler's generals."[14]

None of this was relevant to the Allied battlefield commanders in Italy, who were up against an opponent who would emerge from the war with a reputation as the best tactician of either side.[15] As the commander of XIV Panzer Corps, von Senger was responsible for carrying out Kesselring's orders to hold the Gustav Line for as long as possible. This he did with a skill that in the postwar years earned him the plaudits of his former enemies.

Although caught entirely off guard by the size and success of McCreery's attacks along the lower Garigliano, von Senger was critical but thankful for Clark's response: "The original plan was followed too rigidly. This gave me the chance to draw reserves from the sectors where the attacks had failed, to constantly change the operational boundaries of the divisions, and to parry the blows one by one. Nor did I understand why the enemy attempted to break through at so many points of the front."[16]

At division level were some equally tough customers. Commanding the 1st Parachute Division was the able Lieutenant General Richard Heidrich, a portly, cigar-smoking veteran of France, Crete, and Russia, who was as proud of his resemblance to Churchill as he was of the accomplishments of his paratroopers. In Sicily his tiny, outgunned paratroop force had single-handedly blocked Montgomery's attempt to break through to Messina during the first week of the campaign.[17]

Others included Major General Ernst-Günther Baade, a brilliant and eccentric veteran infantry officer and a strong Anglophile from his days as an expert rider on the horse circuit in Europe, who was fond of wearing kilts and notifying the Allies of the names of their POWs on their own radio frequencies. Baade had fought in North Africa, and in Sicily, as the commandant of the Strait of Messina, he played a key role in the evacuation of the island.[18] As successful division commanders, von Vietinghoff rated Heidrich and Baade "in a class by themselves."[19]

Lieutenant General Paul Conrath, who had commanded the Hermann Göring Division in Sicily and at Salerno, had earned a reputation as an aggressive officer. Also present was his eventual successor in early 1944, Colonel (later Lieutenant General) Wilhelm Schmalz, the commander of a *Kampfgruppe* that had fought brilliantly against the British in Sicily. Near Augusta, during the first days after the invasion, Schmalz's *Kampfgruppe* was literally all that stood between the Eighth Army and an undefended road to Messina. Others, like Eberhardt Rodt of the 15th Panzer Grenadier Division and Walter Fries of the 29th Panzer Grenadier Divison, helped form the backbone of the new Army Group C.[20]

This, then, was the high-caliber opposition the Allies faced in Italy: veteran infantry, panzer, and panzer grenadier and airborne units commanded by combat-experienced officers, all of whom had long since learned to make do with less than a full deck.

With the coming of 1944, the German high command knew they faced a year of decision that would fully test their ability to defend the Fatherland. Except in the minds of the unrealistic fanatics of the Third Reich, it was now clear that Germany had passed from the offensive to the defensive. Nineteen forty-three had been a year of transition and of wholly unnecessary disasters, beginning with the fall of Stalingrad and the loss of Friedrich von Paulus's Sixth Army, followed by the decisive setback at Kursk. In the Mediterranean the Germans were expelled from North Africa with the irreplaceable loss of an entire army group.

It was inevitable that 1944 would see the Allies launch their long-delayed second front somewhere in northern France, against either the Pas de Calais or Normandy. In Italy there was, the German predicament notwithstanding, some justification for cautious optimism. By November 1943, the situation in southern Italy had stabilized sufficiently for OKW to be able to transfer four veteran panzer divisions, a parachute division (less a cadre used to form the core of the new 4th Parachute Division), and one infantry division to the Russian front and replace them with reorganized or low-grade infantry or panzer grenadier divisions. Although the Allies dominated the air and the sea and their ground forces outnumbered the Germans by a very wide margin, to date their campaigns had been singularly lacking in boldness and innovation. Sicily had demonstrated Allied unwillingness to take even mild risks, and the invasion of Calabria continued this conservatism. The decision to require the Eighth Army to march more than three hundred miles to link up with the Fifth Army lost Salerno's potential for exploitation, when an alternative was to use them as a reserve force.

Having elected to defend southern Italy, Kesselring was able to take advantage of the Allied penchant for linear thinking. Now, four months later, the Germans expected the Allies to attempt an amphibious landing somewhere near Rome. The forthcoming battle for Rome would be an attempt by the leopard to change its spots, and its outcome would decide the future course of the war in Italy.

6

Mr. Churchill
Takes Charge

Without risk there is no honour, no glory, no
adventure.

—CHURCHILL

The sudden resurrection of Operation Shingle from the wastebasket of discarded plans was a testament to the powerful influence of Winston Churchill, who bullied the Combined Chiefs of Staff into postponing the shift of amphibious landing craft long enough to participate in the invasion of Anzio. Anxious for a military solution to the flagging Italian campaign, the prime minister elevated Shingle to the center of the turbulent politics that engulfed the Allies at this stage of the war. Virtually overnight, Shingle became the centerpiece in Italy and, in the process, became more of a political football than a military operation.

The Anzio landings had originally been conceived from necessity and then cancelled for compelling military reasons when its success became doubtful. Churchill, however, was blinded by the allure of attaining the glittering prize of Rome and tended to dismiss its military drawbacks as examples of the usual negative thinking of generals, admirals, and planners, whom he liked to refer to as "masters of negation."

For one of the few times during the war, a unique opportunity unexpectedly emerged for Churchill, the politician, to fulfill a lifelong fantasy by taking charge of a military operation and—at least temporarily—playing the role of a commanding general. It never occurred to the prime minister that he possessed no qualifications for the role. His ess had resulted in his presence in North Africa at a propitious ment, when he could exert his considerable influence on a major military operation. Inaction was a trait utterly alien to his nature and, as his wartime assistant private secretary, Sir John Colville, has written, "Patience is a virtue with which he was totally unfamiliar."[1] Thus, it was completely in character that Churchill, whose memos were frequently stamped in red, "Action This Day," would embrace Shingle.

As Britain's warlord and the dominant leader of the Anglo-American alliance, Churchill encountered no one who curbed his tendency to seize on military ventures that appealed to him. By default, that role had fallen to Brooke, but at this moment of the war the chief of the Imperial General Staff was in London, attending to the urgent business of high command. Moreover, as we have already learned, Brooke himself favored Shingle and, in this instance, could have been expected to have supported Churchill.

An example occurred that autumn, when the prime minister's frustration with his inability to sway the U.S. chiefs of staff to the British point of view, and his increasing irritation with the flagging Italian campaign, led him to champion a British invasion of the German-held Greek island of Rhodes, the largest of the Dodecanese Islands, in the eastern Mediterranean. Churchill argued passionately that the boldness of such an operation would pay off by dragging Turkey into the war and setting the Balkans ablaze, thus enabling the Allies to threaten Germany via the "soft underbelly." The problem, however, was more than a shortage of landing craft and the fact that such an operation violated the agreements reached at Quebec, which limited future Allied military operations in the Mediterranean. From the American viewpoint, Churchill's enthusiasm for this scheme smacked of yet another excuse for evading or delaying Overlord. As the prime minister later admitted, the incident produced "the most acute difference I ever had with General Eisenhower," who successfully argued that Allied resources in the Mediterranean were not large enough to carry out operations in both Italy and the Aegean. "We must therefore choose between Rhodes and Rome . . . we must concentrate on the Italian campaign."[2] It also left Marshall more determined than ever that nothing detract from Overlord.[3]

The Rhodes venture was pure Churchill: bold, imaginative, and opportunistic, "an immense but fleeting opportunity." He believed that "it was intolerable that the enemy, pressed on all fronts, could be allowed to continue to pick up cheap prizes in the Aegean."[4] It was also a prime example of Churchill's penchant for imposing his vast authority and intellect to overwhelm opposition and influence the outcome of events. As official British naval historian Stephen Roskill writes, Churchill's "hope of bringing Turkey into the war, which was the principal plank on which he rested his case, was an illusion; for the Turks could not have defended themselves as long as the Germans held Greece and most of the Aegean Islands."[5]

Although he agreed with the basic premise of the invasion of Rhodes, Brooke despaired that Churchill's dogged pursuit of it would upset the delicate balance of U.S.–British relations. "The Americans are already desperately suspicious of him," wrote Brooke, "and this will make matters worse. . . . He has worked himself into a frenzy of excitement about the Rhodes attack, has magnified its importance so that he can no longer see anything else and has set his heart on capturing this one island even at the expense of endangering his relations with the President and the Americans and the future of the Italian campaign. He refused to listen to any arguments or to see any dangers."[6]

During the previous eighteen months, Churchill had successfully persuaded Franklin Roosevelt that the Allies must attack attainable targets in the Mediterranean instead of impossible ones in France. This strategy had successfully driven Italy out of the war, and now was an opportune moment to seize a very important military and political objective that was certain to alter the course of the war in the Mediterranean. That prize was Rome, and by his forceful intervention the prime minister had seen to it that his trusted lieutenant, Harold Alexander, would make it his number-one priority.

The task of carrying out the Anzio-Nettuno landings was assigned to Lucas's VI Corps, whose Shingle force consisted of Major General W. R. C. Penney's 1st British Division, which was to land on the beaches north of Anzio and hold the left flank of the Allied beachhead. South of Nettuno, Major General Lucian K. Truscott's veteran U.S. 3d Division was to seize and hold the right flank.

A Ranger force commanded by Colonel William O. Darby and the independent 509th Parachute Infantry Battalion was given the mission of assaulting and securing the vital port of Anzio. While the Rangers took Anzio, the veteran paratroopers of Salerno, Colonel Reuben Tucker's 504th Parachute Infantry Regiment, were to be dropped along the Anzio-Albano highway, at the base of the Alban Hills, to establish blocking positions pending the arrival of the main Shingle force.[7]

The decision to employ a mixed Anglo-American force was another of the political aspects that engulfed Shingle. From a purely military point of view, it made better sense to leave the force entirely American. Different equipment, guns, and ammunition made the task of the logisticians far more complicated. The day after Christmas, Churchill made it plain to Alexander that he did "not like the idea that the first and most risky operation undertaken in the Mediterranean under British command should fall exclusively upon American forces."[8] To Wilson he confided that without British participation in the capture of Rome, there would be "a feeling of bitterness in Great Britain when the claim is stridently put forward, as it surely will be, that 'the Americans have taken Rome.' "[9]

Shingle was an operation driven by outside factors and by a chain reaction of mistakes and faulty assumptions. The limitations on the size of the invasion force ensured that it became neither fish nor fowl. Yet the success of its mission was conditional on its combat strength, and this was never adequate. To make matters worse, the Allies were again violating the principle for which Montgomery had unsuccessfully fought tooth and nail: that commanders, not staff officers, and certainly not politicians, should plan battles. Nevertheless, during the critical period when the operation developed from concept into reality, Shingle was planned with its commanding general largely filling the role of spectator while his fate was sealed by others.

Logistically, there were barely sufficient landing craft for a two-divisional lift, plus supporting troops, and it was the Navy's judgment that Lucas would have to make do with seven days' supplies on the beachhead, after which the LSTs would be withdrawn and sent to England. Although the period was later raised to ten days, no one addressed the most crucial question of all: How long could Lucas hold out with an undersize force against an unknown German reaction, when the Fifth Army was bogged down behind the Rapido with virtually no chance of linking up with Lucas within ten days?[10]

Clark's papers establish that while "he was genuinely eager to engage in SHINGLE, to the point of committing in it units which he would subsequently have to utilize in ANVIL . . . in effect a pistol was being held at his head because he was told, totally to his surprise, that if he was to engage in SHINGLE it must be done with inadequate craft, that the craft would be available for only two days after the landing and that no resupply or reinforcement thereafter would be available. In effect, therefore, he was asked to land two divisions at a point where a junction with the balance of Fifth Army was impossible for a long period, thereby leaving the two divisions in question out on a very long limb."[11]

Two days later Clark took his case to Alexander and his 15th Army Group staff at Caserta. Before Alexander's arrival in the conference room, Clark made his position clear to the assembled Shingle commanders and Fifth Army staff officers: "We are supposed to go up there, dump two divisions ashore with what corps troops we can get in, with an indeterminate number of craft without resupply or reinforcement, and wait for the rest of the Army to join up. I am trying to find ways to do it, not ways in which we can not do it. I am convinced we are going to do it, and that it is going to be a success."[12]

There followed a tense meeting with Alexander in which Clark laid out the problems in unmistakable terms. He was determined to do Shingle but he was equally determined not to squander two divisions needlessly in the process. Clark also told Alexander that it was his function to determine if the German opposition at Anzio was too great to permit a successful operation and that he did not propose to discuss the question any further. Clark also told Alexander that as an alternative to Shingle he would keep open the option of landing one division north of Gaeta. The two commanders agreed to dispatch a cable immediately to Churchill spelling out that if Shingle was to be carried out, the necessary landing craft must be retained beyond D day.

Privately Clark had little faith in either Churchill or Alexander, and believed that at the Christmas Day meeting:

> The Prime Minister had been inspired with a desire to capture Rome and had determined that SHINGLE would take place, and General Eisenhower and General Alexander, without detailed knowledge of the problems involved, had agreed to it. Unfortunately . . . none of those who thus lightheartedly decided on the SHINGLE operation understood the details of shipping and of loading necessary to put ashore the requisite force and maintain it once ashore.[13]

Clark strongly protested the inadequacy of supplies in the beachhead—the Navy would guarantee less than one-third of VI Corps' requirement of fifteen hundred tons per day. A flurry of urgent cables between Clark and Alexander and Alexander and Churchill eventually led to the retention of the additional landing craft required by Clark. But left unresolved was exactly what Lucas was to accomplish when he landed at Anzio.

By early January Churchill's takeover of Operation Shingle was complete. On January 7, Lucas's G-3 (operations officer), Colonel William H. Hill, and his G-4 (the corps logistician), Colonel E. J. O'Neill, were summoned to Algiers to brief Alexander and Harding on the VI Corps plan. They also rehearsed with Clark exactly what they were to present to Churchill. Above all else, Clark warned, they were to stick to their position that more LSTs were essential and not succumb to Churchill's cajoling. The following day they flew to Marrakech, where a high-level conference had been convened to brief Churchill. Those present comprised a star-studded cast that included Lord Beaverbrook, Wilson, Alexander, Harding, Devers, Bedell Smith, Admiral John Cunningham—the new Allied naval commander in chief, Mediterranean[14]—and a great many staff officers. Incredibly, the two men most vitally concerned with Shingle, Clark and Lucas, were absent. Neither comnander had even been invited. Instead, Lucas was told he could send only two staff officers. "Why I was not allowed to attend in person I have never known as no reason was ever given me."[15]

The prime minister dominated the conference, whose main discussions revolved around the maintenance of the Shingle force.[16] By this time, both AFHQ and Alexander had awakened to the folly of leaving VI Corps at Anzio with a mere seven days' supplies. Clark had been told that of the eighty-six LSTs employed in the assault landings, a mere six would be left at the end of seven days to resupply the beachhead. Although Alexander concurred that Shingle could not be launched unless there was a provision for continued maintenance, he never challenged the briefing of the AFHQ G-2, Brigadier Strong, who told Churchill that the plan envisioned the remainder of the Fifth Army driving north to Anzio within seven days.[17]

Strong then attempted to speak out against the operation but was prevented from doing so by Churchill until after both the prime minister and Alexander had "supported the Anzio operation strongly." He then turned to Strong and said, "Well, we might as well hear the seamy side of the question." In his memoirs Strong writes that he warned:

> Although the landing force might make a deep initial advance, it could not achieve a decisive success in the face of the opposition which could be expected. I also believed that the strength of the Gustav Line was being seriously underestimated. The Germans had been able to construct an enormously strong position. . . . I estimated that they could hold it without taking units or formations away from the Anzio area. I was strongly supported by members of General Clark's staff, but we could make little impression on the others there.[18]

The crux of Strong's message was that the success of Anzio was dependent upon a breakthrough at Cassino, that the Germans were too powerfully entrenched, and that the Allies lacked sufficient strength there for an attack to succeed.[19] An irrevocable decision had been made to carry out Shingle. The matter was beyond dissent, and those who dared to speak out were put firmly in their place. Alexander's newly arrived chief of staff, John Harding, quickly discovered that "the more he heard the less he liked it . . . he did not like the haphazard way in which the operation was being planned and thought little of its prospects."[20]

Harding, however, could do little more than observe. Many years later, he still retained vivid recollections of the December meeting at Carthage, when:

> At one stage Admiral Cunningham said to the Prime Minister, "You know, Prime Minister, this operation is fraught with great risks"—whereupon the Prime Minister turned on him and said, "Admiral, of course there is risk,

but without risk there is no honour, no glory, no adventure," whereupon John Cunningham crumpled up because no admiral of the fleet could admit that he wasn't interested in honour, glory or adventure. . . . I came away, again, rather anxious and uncertain about the whole thing.[21]

British naval historian Richard Hough points out that Churchill held "an inordinate regard for admirals of action," among them John Cunningham's predecessor, his cousin Andrew, and Sir Philip Vian, who had commanded an assault force in the invasion of Sicily and the carrier support force at Salerno. The vast majority were never aggressive enough to suit the former First Lord of the Admiralty, whose love-hate relationships with his admirals more often than not left him complaining that they were not sufficiently aggressive. "Churchill was not only fundamentally insecure—and remained so even when acknowledged as the greatest public hero since Wellington and Nelson, and recognized even by his closest friends as a victim of megalomania—he distrusted admirals from his experiences with them from 1911 to May 1915."[22]

Even though their names were the same, Admiral Sir John Cunningham and his cousin and illustrious predecessor, "ABC," bore no resemblance. Royal Navy Captain Manley Power, who served under both admirals, later observed that, "it would be difficult to find two men less alike than 'ABC' and John D. Cunningham. The former fiery, aggressive, active and intolerant; the latter quiet, thoughtful, rather lethargic, very kind but possessed of an acid tongue. 'ABC' scintillating, successful and inclined to be schoolboyishly boastful. John D. . . . very cautious, cynical and suspicious of adventure. . . . I found myself translated suddenly from reining in a champing charger to goading a reluctant draft horse." Small wonder, then, that John Cunningham did not press his objections to Anzio on Churchill, who, as Stephen Roskill has written, "did not place Sir John among the brightest luminaries of the naval firmament of the period."[23]

The dissenters—and there were many besides Lucas—had no chance so long as Churchill exercised such a dominant influence over the predominantly British Allied leadership in the Mediterranean. They could point out the problems, but with the prime minister so personally involved, little more could be done. Shingle would take place, and it was everyone's task to make it work regardless of their personal views.

In a manner reminiscent of Clark at the Rapido, Churchill became so convinced of the righteousness of his cause that he attempted to orchestrate only solutions that enhanced his premise that Shingle would be a cure-all for the ills besetting the Italian campaign. Later, when the operation failed, Churchill became the first to disavow Shingle.

Without Brooke's restraining presence, the British prime minister took such total charge of all aspects of Shingle that he literally became its commanding general. To suggest that he reveled in this role would be to understate the truth. He passed judgment on all issues that arose in Marrakech. When, for example, Lucas's two representatives argued for a postponement until January 25, so that a rehearsal could be conducted, Churchill naively retorted that all troops were trained and needed no rehearsal. When informed by Colonel Hill that the turnover of personnel in the 3d Division had been so great that only a few were left who had amphibious experience, Churchill insisted that one experienced officer or noncommissioned officer in a platoon was sufficient. When an argument arose between Colonel O'Neill and the Navy over the VI Corps' plan for resupplying the beachhead, Churchill again intervened to side with the Navy. The plan called for what today would be known as a "roll-on, roll-off" operation. Trucks were to be preloaded at Naples and driven off the LSTs directly to a supply dump, while empty trucks from a previous run were to return aboard the LSTs to Naples to be reloaded, and the cycle repeated. As the official naval historian records, the scheme was carried out despite the official disapproval and reduced unloading time at the Anzio beachhead from a full day "to a single hour; without it, Operation SHINGLE would have been doomed to disaster."[24]

Throughout these discussions the Navy expressed concern that they would have difficulty in maintaining two divisions in the beachhead; three would be "precarious," and four divisions "impossible." It was finally agreed that the maintenance of the Shingle force be planned for a period of twenty-eight days.[25]

There is no better example of Churchill's deviousness and ability to get his way by hook or crook than the case of Captain Manley Power, Cunningham's deputy chief of staff (Plans), who was summoned at short notice to Churchill's bedside in Carthage, where he was quizzed about landing craft and required to produce a paper for the prime minister. Power's memorandum argued that the necessary landing craft for Shingle could be readied and used in the operation without an adverse effect on Overlord. An immensely pleased Churchill remarked, "A most remarkable paper. Just what I require," and ordered it cabled to the British chiefs of staff in London.[26]

Power, an outstanding young naval officer who later became a full admiral, had deeply impressed Churchill. Shortly thereafter, he ordered that Power return at once from London, where he was conferring with the Admiralty about Anvil, to attend the Marrakech conference on January 8. Again summoned to the prime minister's bedside, he found Churchill in an irritable mood because of the opposition he had encountered, presumably from Strong and Power's boss, Admiral

John Cunningham. "I want your views," he demanded. Power refused on the grounds that he could not speak for his superior. Never one to take no for an answer, Churchill summoned Major General Leslie Hollis[27] and ordered: "You are to cancel Captain Power's appointment to the staff of the Commander-in-Chief, Mediterranean, and attach him to the staff of the Minister of Defence."[28]

Power protested this high-handed act, but now officially a member of Churchill's personal staff, he complied and produced another report that demonstrated how the present difficulties with shipping could be overcome. The prime minister's delight that Shingle was still feasible for the Navy earned Power a place of honor next to Churchill at lunch. Although Power's appointment was ripped up, Churchill insisted, to his considerable embarrassment, that he read his paper to the conference that night.[29]

Roskill has reproduced, complete with Churchill's famous lisp, the sense of a cat playing with mice. "Thish is jusht what I want," crowed the prime minister. "Now gentlemen can any of you take exsheption to theshe cogent argumentsh for retaining theshe vital veshells for thish great adventure?"[30] None did.

The Marrakech conference erased the final obstacles to the launching of Shingle, and as it ended Churchill said, "Now that's decided we must tell the Chiefs of Staff." When Hollis pointed out that Shingle was properly a matter for the Combined Chiefs of Staff, the prime minister retorted, "No! The British Chiefs of Staff are, by agreement, responsible for the Mediterranean area." Hollis replied: "In that case, it is a matter for the War Cabinet." The quorum for a War Cabinet meeting was two, and with Lord Beaverbrook concurring, Shingle was formally approved and ordered executed. As the meeting ended, Churchill said to Alexander, "I do hope General, that when you have landed this great quantity of lorries and cannon you will find room for a few foot soldiers—if only to guard the lorries."[31]

In his war memoirs, Churchill referred to Anzio as his "cat claw" and somewhat disingenuously observed that he "did not dare to demand the necessary weight and volume for the 'cat claw' . . . in my opinion, if the extravagant claims of the military machine had been reduced, we could . . . have flung ashore south of the Tiber a still larger force with full mobility. . . . If I had asked for a three-division lift, I should not have got anything. How often in life one must be content with what one can get! Still, it would be better to do it right."[32]

To the contrary, the evidence suggests Churchill was well satisfied with the plan and convinced that it was sufficient. His elation over his role in l'affaire Shingle is beyond question. On January 8, 1944, he confidently cabled Roosevelt: "A unanimous agreement for action as proposed was reached by the responsible officers of both countries and of all services as a result of our two conferences. Everyone is in good heart and resources seem sufficient. Every aspect was thrashed out in full detail."[33] The same day he signaled London: "The battle is one of the highest consequence and by no means free from hazard mainly through weather. I am convinced it should be launched as planned and that it is in the most confident and resolute hands."[34] He also sent a note to Clark in which he urged him to launch Shingle on time: "I am deeply conscious of the importance of this battle, without which the campaign in Italy will be regarded as having petered out ingloriously. . . . I know you will do everything in human power."[35]

According to the official historian, Clark's recollection of the letter was that it "quite clearly stated Churchill's belief that the Anzio operation would make the Germans pull back from the southern (Garigliano) front and make the Italian campaign an overwhelming success. The letter was over-optimistic regarding what effect the landing would have on the resistance in Italy. Churchill implied to Clark that he expected Clark to put on the Anzio operation successfully."[36]

Churchill's unique role in the evolution of Shingle was rooted in his earlier experience as a politician, naval warlord, and soldier, where his restlessness and penchant for the dramatic gesture and the bold maneuver can be discerned. During the early years of World War I, Churchill was one of the most powerful men in the War Cabinet of Prime Minister Herbert Asquith, and certainly its most bellicose member, leading Sir Maurice Hankey to comment: "He had a real zest for war." Nevertheless, Churchill thirsted to make the leap from political office to a position of command at the front in France. In 1916, after he had been stripped of his portfolio at the Admiralty for his role in Britain's disastrous venture in the Dardanelles the previous year, Churchill got his wish and spent six months in the squalor of the front lines as a lieutenant colonel commanding a rifle battalion. Even this horrific experience never seemed to tarnish his romantic vision of war.

No matter what the endeavor, Churchill's tempestuousness inevitably led him to be at the center of events. One colleague said of him, "it is no disparagement of Winston's extraordinary qualities to say that his judgment is not quite equal to his abilities." His biographer, William Manchester, notes his fascination with war and destruction, both of which "enthralled the mischievous boy in him . . . he would never entirely outgrow that fascination."[37]

Churchill's unfulfilled ambition to become a warrior-hero was lifelong. As early as 1911, one of his critics noted with insightful accuracy that:

He is always unconsciously playing a part—an heroic part. And he is himself his most astonished spectator. He sees himself moving through the smoke of battle—triumphant, terrible, his brow clothed with thunder, his legions looking to him for victory, and not looking in vain. He thinks of Napoleon; he thinks of his great ancestor [the Duke of Marlborough]. . . . It is not make-believe, it is not insincerity; it is that in this fervid and picturesque imagination there are always great deeds afoot, with himself cast by destiny in the Agamemnon role.[38]

Little had changed in the man who was now the most influential personality of the western alliance. Another biographer, Robert Rhodes James, has said of Churchill that he "saw himself in the role of a Commander cast in the Napoleon mold."[39] Anzio was tailor-made to fit Churchill's love of adventure.

According to Lord Moran, Churchill's deep involvement in Shingle acted as a tonic:

As the P.M. grows in strength, his old appetite for the war comes back. The C.I.G.S. is in England, but the P.M. has a bright idea. He is organizing an operation all on his own. . . . If the Chiefs of Staff are not available, there are plenty of lesser fry to work out the details. . . . Alex too is sympathetic. He sees that the Italian campaign may receive a great fillip. Why, it may even shorten the whole war. The P.M. has become absorbed . . . [and] seems not only to direct the policy of war, he even plans the details.[40]

Once the question of landing craft and a two-division force were resolved, the extensive documentation of this period reflects no questioning of the operation's potentially negative side. There were no hard, "what-if" questions asked or debated. No one dared challenge the assumptions on which Shingle was based. Those who had dared to raise their voices in protest were for the most part junior staff officers whose misgivings had been either dismissed or ignored.

Only much later would Churchill admit that "Anzio was my worst moment of the war. I had most to do with it."[41]

7

Final Preparations

I felt like a lamb being led to the slaughter.

LUCAS

The commander on whom the responsibility for Shingle fell was a fifty-four-year-old veteran artilleryman with a reputation for integrity, fairness, common sense, and a fondness for the poetry of Rudyard Kipling. Lucas was attracted to Kipling because of the poet's love for soldiers and soldiering, traits that he brought to a long career that began in 1911, when he graduated from West Point. Lucas received a severe head wound in France in 1918 and, during the interwar years, gained wide experience in a variety of command and staff jobs. Lucas had passed muster with Marshall as a division commander in 1941, and from March 1942 to April 1943 as the III Corps commander in the United States. With the invasion of Sicily imminent, Marshall rated Lucas an officer of "military stature, prestige and experience" and sent him to Eisenhower, where he won the confidence of both the Supreme Commander and his longtime friend Patton as a liaison officer attached to the Seventh Army.[1] Among those impressed with Lucas was famed airborne commander James M. Gavin, who has described him as "a widely read man of unusual intelligence and sensitivity."[2]

Although the major factor in Lucas's selection by Eisenhower to command VI Corps was his availability, Clark expressed disappointment even though he personally liked the affable Lucas, whose trademark was an ever-present corncob pipe. Apparently Clark's unhappiness never extended to a protest to Eisenhower to find someone else to command VI Corps. A month before Lucas's appointment to replace

Dawley, Eisenhower had written "a special word about Lucas" to Marshall, noting that "I think he would command a combat corps most successfully."[3] In mid-December, when Eisenhower prepared to depart for England to command Overlord, he briefly considered Clark for the position of American theater commander, which eventually went to Devers. His recommendation for the new Fifth Army commander would have been Lucas.[4]

When he first learned of Shingle, Lucas expressed doubts about its viability. Lucas knew he would soon oppose some of the best formations in the Wehrmacht, and that Anzio presented a formidable problem. He had seen for himself in Sicily, as Eisenhower's "eyes and ears," how effectively the German Army could fight. Three months of combat and the brutal conditions in Italy left Lucas skeptical of Clark's plan for breaching the Rapido and of Alexander's optimism that Anzio would not pose a problem. This false optimism disturbed Lucas, who saw no reason to believe that the Gustav Line would suddenly collapse, when the Germans had repeatedly displayed a mastery of the terrain from Salerno to Cassino.

During the brief three weeks before the landings, Lucas became little more than a spectator as his superiors wrangled with each other and higher headquarters over the details of obtaining the necessary landing craft for Shingle. His opinions were not solicited and his misgivings were ignored. On the day of the first high-level meeting, January 4, 1944, Lucas recorded in his diary:

> Everyone agreed we must have the shipping. . . . If we try to pull it off otherwise, a crack on the chin is certain. Anyone can figure that out with a paper and pencil. I will do what I am ordered but these "Battles of the Little Big Horn" aren't much fun and a failure now would ruin Clark, kill many of my men, and certainly prolong the war. These are disagreeable contingencies. I have always watched over my troops as carefully as I could.[5]

Swept along by decisions over which he had no control, Lucas found that his protests to Clark went unheard:

> I was quite disturbed over the diminutive size of the proposed expedition, as well as the distance to which it was projected. The word "amphibious" has become such a legendary military term that its presence often confuses the tactical issue under discussion. . . . To me the proposed maneuver was just another envelopment and the military principles that applied to any envelopment should apply here. It was evident though, that in the eyes of the high command, they did not, but I could say nothing as General Clark, evidently under pressure, said emphatically that the operation would take place, and after that I could only obey orders.[6]

Lucas could never understand the casual manner with which his superiors treated Shingle. On January 10, Alexander not only described the expected effects on Kesselring but remarked "in great glee that Overlord would be unnecessary." The VI Corps commander's concerns were of a practical nature. What about the four to five German divisions that Kesselring was believed to have available to reinforce a landing at Anzio?[7] What reserve could Clark promise for VI Corps? What about the decision to land with supplies sufficient for only seven days?

The answers were not reassuring. "Clark told me he would hold a Regimental Combat Team of another division ready to send in if he could. . . . The force would be landed at Anzio with seven days' supplies and then abandoned to its fate. No build-up and no maintenance. It was stated that the remainder of Fifth Army would catch up before food and ammunition ran completely out, an example of blind optimism that showed such a lack of appreciation of the fighting qualities of the German soldier that I could not believe it to have been seriously considered."[8]

Even Patton was discouraged by what he learned when he visited Naples shortly before the invasion. He found Clark jumpy and worried that Lucas lacked the drive to carry out Shingle successfully. According to Lucas, Patton blurted out, "John, there is no one in the Army I hate to see killed as much as you, but you can't get out of this alive."[9] General Penney was among those who dined with Patton in Naples. "Before lunch we were all given a large tot of Scotch and George Patton gave two toasts. Looking at me he first said, 'Here's to the British,' and then he added a second toast, 'And here's hell and damnation to any God damn commanding General who is ever found at his own C[ommand] P[ost].' "[10]

Two days after Marrakech, Alexander chaired the final commanders' conference before Shingle. Lucas records that "Sir Harold started the conference by stating that the operation would take place on January 22 with the troops as scheduled, and that there would be no more discussion on these two points. He quoted Mr. Churchill as saying, 'It will astonish the world,' and added, 'it will certainly frighten Kesselring.' " Lucas felt "like a lamb being led to the slaughter but thought I was entitled to one bleat, so I registered a protest against the target date as it gave me too little time for rehearsal. This is vital to the success of anything as terribly complicated as this. I was ruled down as I knew I would be, many reasons being advanced. . . . The real reasons cannot be military."[11] As the meeting broke up, Alexander told Lucas, "We have every confidence in you. That is why you were picked."[12] Like Walker at the Rapido, Lucas could find nothing that even faintly encouraged him. In his diary he wrote: "This whole affair had a strong odor of Gallipoli and apparently the same amateur [Churchill] was still on the coaches bench."[13]

Contrary to his claim, Alexander had very little confidence in Lucas but was unwilling to act on his misgivings. Harding found his first encounter with Lucas disquieting. "It seemed to me that General Lucas had not got his heart in the job. He was very anxious . . . about the chances of success, and he was quite determined that it wasn't going to be a failure under his command. . . . I didn't think he had what Monty used to describe as 'the light of battle' in his eyes."[14] Lucas made his "Gallipoli" remark to Admiral Cunningham, who retorted: "If that's how you feel you had better resign."[15]

Harding immediately conveyed to Alexander his belief that Lucas ought to be replaced while there was still time.

> But he came to the conclusion that all this business of fighting on an Allied basis, it would be wrong for him to press Mark Clark to make a change at that stage in the operation. And so that was that. I think it was a mistake. . . . I should have pressed Alexander to have a thorough discussion with Mark Clark about it, and to hammer it out [and] make clear . . . that he, Alexander, hadn't got complete confidence in Lucas, and therefore some change should be made, if necessary delaying the operation accordingly. . . . I was wrong not to do so. So nothing was done and Lucas was left in command.[16]

In Italy the planning went forward at a frantic pace, and with a mere three weeks to work out the complex details of a major amphibious landing, time was clearly working against the Shingle planners. There was a frenzy of activity. VI Corps organized a crash program to train the invasion units in amphibious landings, where the emphasis began at the unit level and moved to battalion- and regimental-level exercises. "Assault battalions studied craft landings and special beach assault tactics, such as the reduction of pill boxes and beach obstacles. . . . Engineers gave instruction in mines and obstacles. The artillery practiced landing and unloading DUKWs [amphibious trucks]. . . . tanks and tank destroyers participated in infantry-tank problems and made practice landings from LCTs."[17]

In early January the various invasion commanders assembled to address the many complex details that still had to be resolved. The British arrived expecting a crisp, well-organized military headquarters, and a staff and commander who had done their homework and were ready to issue plans and orders. Instead, "they found themselves invited to join a debating society."[18] As Penney has recorded:

> We had about 15 days to get ready, rehearse and land and I think it was a remarkable achievement.... The planning technique we were subjected to was fantastic. Lucas for various good reasons was not there at the start. We assembled and the G-3 put up on a board a map giving an outline plan. If it was not acceptable he pulled it down and put up another. I don't remember any conclusion and certainly no ORDERS. Truscott, Derbyshire [*sic*] [Darby], myself and the paratroop commander all had our say and it was a free for all.[19]

Foul weather and insufficient time to adequately prepare VI Corps were among the problems faced by Lucas, who was encouraged neither by the miserable performance of the assault troops during rehearsals carried out five days before the invasion in poor weather conditions nor by what he regarded as a lack of cooperation by the Navy. Both Lucas and Truscott had been adamant that a rehearsal was essential, and both found they had to overcome considerable opposition before one was agreed to. The British 1st Division rehearsal near Salerno was moderately successful, but the American night landings of Truscott's 3d Division were an unmitigated disaster. Truscott, who was by now an authority on amphibious landings from his experience in London on Mountbatten's Combined Operations staff in 1942 and from the Husky landings in Sicily the previous July, noted that "the token rehearsal for the 3d Division [on January 19] was terrible. All because the Navy didn't close on the beach—which they admit." Not one infantry battalion landed on time, in the right location, or in the correct formation. Communications were nonexistent, and landing craft were released so far offshore that most took from three to four hours to reach land. Forty DUKWs were swamped and sank with a loss of considerable equipment, which included nineteen 105-mm howitzers. By daylight no artillery or tanks were ashore.

A senior 3d Division officer called the planning for Shingle "a tremendous undertaking . . . but the rehearsal was a complete fiasco. The Navy merely dumped these people too far out to sea and we lost one whole artillery battalion. . . . The coordination in the landing was just terrible. . . . Oh, God, the whole thing was just a debacle. We were just trying to do too many things in three short weeks."[20]

Deeply troubled by the number of accidents, the Allied Naval commander of Task Force 81 (the Allied naval force for Shingle), Rear Admiral Frank J. Lowry (USN), believed that it "appeared impractical on the face of it to make an assault [landing at Anzio] without further training." However, as Lucas well understood, there was simply no time left for further practice. The Army and Navy would have to learn from their mistakes and do it right on the day or face potential disaster.

Truscott was so disturbed by the fiasco that he sent Clark's chief of staff, Major General Alfred Gruenther, a note asking that if Shingle was "to be 'a forlorn hope' or a 'suicide sashay' then all I want to know is that fact—If so, I'm positive that there is no outfit in the world that can do it better than me—even though I reserve the right (personally) to believe we might deserve a better fate."[21] Clark was disturbed by Truscott's report and complained bitterly to Admiral Lowry about naval mismanagement. A visibly shaken Lowry conveyed his displeasure with the performance of his landing flotilla to his subordinate commanders, admonishing them that failure would bring a swift "kick in a soft spot by a cruiser."[22]

Truscott pressed for another rehearsal, but Clark replied, "Well, Lucian, I've got your report here and it's bad. But you won't get another rehearsal. The date has been set at the very highest level. There is no possibility of delaying it even for a day. You have got to do it."[23]

Admiral John Cunningham dismissed the problem with an assurance to Lucas that he need not worry because "the chances are seventy to thirty that by the time you reach Anzio the Germans will be north of Rome." This cryptic remark left Lucas suspicious that important intelligence was deliberately being withheld from him. "Apparently everyone is in on the secret of the German intentions except me."[24] His suspicions were well founded, for while Cunningham was privy to the Ultra signals flowing from the supersecret facility at Bletchley Park northwest of London, Lucas was not. The 29th and 90th Panzer Grenadier Divisions, both of which were known to be based near Rome, were of special concern to the Shingle planners, as potential reinforcements against the invasion. Although Ultra also revealed that McCreery's diversionary operations along the Garigliano had succeeded in drawing off these two formations, the decrypts were not received in Italy until the day of the landings, January 22, 1944.[25]

Throughout the war the Ultra secret was zealously guarded, and those privy to it were restricted to key personnel at Army level and above. Even though this meant depriving corps commanders like Lucas of information they ought to have had, it was decided that the need to protect Ultra from German detection took precedence. A similar problem had occurred in Sicily, where the 82d Airborne Division was not told the Hermann Göring Division was based in the area of their airborne landings at Gela. Ultra had nearly been compromised in early 1943, which created "an almighty flap" and near paranoia among its guardians that no unnecessary risks be run that might result in its compromise. As one historian has pointed out, this was the Achilles' heel of Ultra, its "inescapable limitation. . . . It was impossible to risk disclosing its intelligence to those in actual contact with the enemy, or liable to capture for other reasons, even though the knowledge might improve their chance of success or survival."[26]

A strong case can be made for Lucas's exclusion, but the suspicion that he was only a bit player in the forthcoming drama that was to be the Anzio beachhead did not enhance his already shaky confidence. As historian Ralph Bennett points out in a new study of Ultra in the Mediterranean, "The upper echelons of the Allied command knew at all relevant times that they would take the enemy far more completely by surprise than [at] Salerno, and that nothing stood in the way of an immediate advance of twenty miles to the Alban Hills, or forty to Rome."[27]

The skepticism over Shingle extended to the 3d Division. In his war memoirs Truscott reveals how he and his staff had first studied the operation in December and come to the inescapable conclusion that "not one of us believe[d] that there was even a remote possibility that the main forces could cross the Rapido and drive up the Liri Valley to join us within a month." Truscott personally briefed Clark on the results of his study and reminded the Fifth Army commander how difficult it had been in Sicily against much lighter opposition. He concluded by telling Clark: "We are perfectly willing to undertake the operation if we are ordered to do so and we will maintain ourselves to the last round of ammunition. But if we do undertake it, you are going to destroy the best damned division in the United States Army for there will be no survivors."[28]

Lucas drew little comfort from the estimates of the expected German opposition prepared by the various Allied intelligence staffs. On December 30, 1943, Clark's own G-2 issued this estimate of the expected German reaction to Shingle:

> An attack on the coast line in the vicinity of ANZIO by a force the size of a corps will become an emergency to be met by all the resources and strength available to the German High Command in ITALY. It will threaten the safety of the Tenth Army. It will also threaten to seize ROME and the airfields in the vicinity thereof.... As soon as the Germans are able to appreciate the magnitude of our landing and that there is no other attack at other points along the coast, it will then become necessary for him to concentrate enough force to defeat the landing attack if possible ... [if not] it then becomes all important to him to endeavor to isolate the landing force and prevent a further build-up and its further advance.[29]

The prediction was that the initial German resistance to the landings would consist of scattered elements of various panzer grenadier formations comprising approximately 12,000 men, three parachute battalions totaling 1,500 men, and some twenty to thirty tanks. In all, the Fifth

Army G-2 reported, VI Corps could expect to face 14,300 German troops. In subsequent days the projected buildup looked like this:

	Estimated Reinforcements	Cumulative Total
D plus 1	5,000	19,300
D plus 2	3,000	22,300
D plus 3	9,000	31,300
D plus 16	30,000	61,300[30]

The estimate given Churchill by Brigadier Strong at Marrakech predicted that the Germans would be able to insert two divisions into the beachhead by D plus 3. Taking note of the D plus 16 projection, which would give the Germans considerably more strength in the beachhead than VI Corps, the British official history notes that, "It therefore seems that an already rather risky enterprise became more risky while it was being planned."[31]

The major postwar controversy about Anzio has focused on the mission assigned to Lucas once VI Corps established a beachhead. On December 27, 1943, the Fifth Army ordered VI Corps to plan for the following:

1. Seize and secure a beachhead in the vicinity of Anzio.
2. Advance and secure Colli Laziali.
3. Be prepared to advance on Rome.[32]

There were major differences of opinion between Alexander and Clark over the mission of VI Corps. Alexander's papers establish beyond doubt that his intention was to strangle Kesselring and open the road to Rome by seizing and holding the Alban Hills. After the January 9 conference Alexander privately told Clark that, "I am frightfully keen for a diversion and for a Commando to crack into the outskirts of Rome." Clark replied that the naval gunfire diversion would take place north of Rome at Civitavecchia, but that further troop landings would dissipate the landing craft available for the main landings. "General Alexander asked whether it could be done the following night, as he felt it would frighten Kesselring and keep Rome garrisoned by the Germans."[33]

In subsequent days contingency plans were developed for an eight-hundred-man British Commando force under Lieutenant Colonel J. M. T. F. ("Mad Jack") Churchill to land in conjunction with Shingle. Churchill (no relation to the prime minister) had led a Commando force in Sicily and had performed brilliantly at Salerno. The idea was to provide the Commandos with jeeps and to turn them loose for raids against Rome the evening after the landings. In addition Clark directed his G-3, Brigadier General Brann, to prepare to land a regimental combat team north of the Tiber River in the event the Germans elected to defend along the river instead of along the plains of Anzio. Neither plan was ever carried out.[34]

Over drinks that evening Alexander asked if Clark would consider taking him along in his PT boat to Anzio on January 22, provided it wouldn't be an intrusion. Clark replied that he would be delighted but "afterwards, when General Alexander had gone, General Clark said, as he repeatedly had in the past, that General Alexander was a peanut and a feather duster."[35]

Clark, on the other hand, had been burned at Salerno, and began to view the problem in terms of avoiding another debacle on the scale of Avalanche. The original planning guidance in December 1943, prepared by Brann, directed Lucas to seize and hold the Alban Hills. However, as the day grew closer, both Clark and Brann began to have second thoughts about Lucas's ability to hold the hills with the force at his disposal and still maintain a twenty-mile logistic lifeline to the beaches.

Clark's mounting conviction that Lucas must be given some latitude was translated into a modification of his instructions on January 12, when the Fifth Army issued its operational order for Shingle. The plan had been significantly modified from the original conception of the operation by two crucial and much-debated changes. The mission of VI Corps was now simply to:

1. Seize and secure a beachhead in the vicinity of Anzio
2. *Advance on COLLI LAZIALI* [italics added][36]

Clark's order was hand carried to VI Corps by Brigadier General Brann, who explained what the Fifth Army commander had in mind. The new order merely directed Lucas, after establishing a beachhead at Anzio, "to advance on Colli Laziali." Neither a timetable for this advance nor mention of seizing Rome was contained in Clark's revised order.

This change affected Lucas like a stone lifted from his shoulders, and he now viewed his mission at Anzio in a completely new light. No longer obliged to seize the Alban Hills, Lucas was given the discretion to conduct the battle on his own terms. "Brann made it clear that my primary mission was to seize and secure a beachhead. He stated that much thought had been put on the wording of this order so as not to force me to push on at the risk of sacrificing my Corps. Should conditions warrant, however, I was free to move to and seize [the] Colli

Laziali."[37] At one point, Clark even told Lucas, "You can forget this God damned Rome business."[38]

In effect Clark was telling Lucas to fight the battle as he saw fit, even though doing so directly contradicted Alexander's intention to capture and hold the Alban Hills. Further evidence of Clark's conservatism came when he cancelled the airborne landings in the Alban Hills. Instead, the 504th Parachute Infantry Regiment would land by LST as ordinary infantry. The official U.S. historian has recorded that the cancellation of the airborne phase removed "a powerful incentive to push the VI Corps out from the landing beaches in order to make contact with the paratroopers . . . [and] coincided with doubts expressed by Brann and Clark that Lucas could do anything more than seize and secure a beachhead. Since Lucas himself had reservations on what was possible, he was sure that a successful landing and capture of a beachhead would be considered in itself a successful operation."[39]

Naples became a gigantic staging area. Warships and cargo ships of all sizes converged on its port, as did the men of the assault force and their 5,200 vehicles, which were waterproofed before being loaded aboard landing craft. In all, the Shingle convoy consisted of more than 250 ships and landing craft. The weather forecast was encouraging, with only moderate swells and a heavy morning haze predicted for the morning of January 22.

With Lucas aboard the flagship USS *Biscayne* of Admiral Lowry's Task Force 81, the convoy slipped out of Naples and several nearby satellite ports before dawn on January 21 and headed into the Gulf of Naples. Task Force 81 was a joint U.S.–Royal Navy command consisting of two assault forces, one to land the 3d Division (X-Ray Force under Lowry) and a second Royal Navy force (Rear Admiral Thomas H. Troubridge's Peter Force) to land Penney's 1st British Division. As the assault fleet approached Anzio-Nettuno it was spearheaded by minesweepers, which probed the waters for the ever-dangerous mines that the Germans were known to have sown offshore. Shortly after 2200 hours on the night of January 21, the *Biscayne*'s radar had located the Anzio lighthouse, and by midnight had dropped anchor four miles away to the southeast to await H hour. The temperature was an unseasonable fifty-five degrees and the seas remained calm with a six-thousand-foot ceiling, which meant that the Allied air forces would have no difficulty supporting the landings.[40]

A night invasion was chosen for the same reasons that pertained for Operation Husky: to increase the chances of tactical surprise and, because the assault beaches were believed to be lightly defended, to gain a beachhead as rapidly as possible before the Germans could react. Waiting to guide the assault forces were two Royal Navy beacon submarines, whose task it was to take fixes on the beaches and help identify the minefields, so that clear channels could be swept for the landing craft.

In order to deceive the Germans, Task Force 81 took a roundabout route south of Capri before entering the Tyrrhenian Sea and heading north for the seventy-five-mile trip to Anzio. The Germans never detected the presence of the Allied fleet until well after the landings were underway. For the two nights preceding the landings, Kesselring had ordered an intensified state of readiness along the Anzio sector; however, in response to complaints from his staff that too many such nights would be counterproductive, the German commander ordered no alert for the night of January 21–22.

The assault troops wedged into the confines of troopships and landing craft had been briefed to expect the worst. A typical example was given one of the first units to go ashore, the 540th Engineer Regiment, whose beach groups were responsible for organizing and controlling the flow of the landings:

> The assault will be opposed initially by units of three German divisions in the vicinity of Rome . . . manned by experienced German troops. It is expected that Germans will move all possible reserves to meet the attack [and] delay contact with our troops from the south. Field defenses consist of concrete pill boxes, strong points surrounded by wire, machine-gun emplacements, tank traps and numerous prepared battery positions. The beaches may be wired with booby traps, tanks and anti-personnel mines.[41]

Six months earlier Lucas had been with Patton aboard a similar command vessel in the waters off southern Sicily in the final hours before the launch of Operation Husky. Now, in the last moments before 0200 hours on January 22, Lucas was in command of a force whose future was uncertain. The latest intelligence reports indicated that all was quiet along the invasion sector and that there was no indication the Germans had yet discovered Task Force 81.

The trappings of a general are great, but so is his accountability. Nothing equals the awesome responsibility of high command in war. The fate of any military force in combat hinges on the actions and decisions of its commanding general. Although Lucas was pessimistic from the outset about the validity of Shingle, he never questioned his ability to lead VI Corps effectively. On the eve of the landings he committed his feelings to his diary:

> I have many misgivings but am also optimistic. I struggle to be calm and collected. . . . I think we have a good chance to make a killing [but] I wish the higher levels were not so over-optimistic. The Fifth Army is attacking violently towards the Cassino line and has sucked away many German

troops to the south and the high command seems to think they will stay there. *I don't see why. They can still slow us up there and move against me at the same time*[42] [italics added].

Within seven days Lucas's prophecy would become a grim reality.

That afternoon, a B-24 of the 721st Squadron, 450th Heavy Bombardment Group (Fifteenth Air Force), was returning to its base in southern Italy after bombing the rail yards at Pisa when the voice of the nose gunner suddenly came over the intercom. "Ships ahead! All over the ocean! There must be a thousand!" The crew speculated that the large armada must be heading for an invasion of southern France. However, the next morning, as their B-24 headed north on another mission, the crew noticed that the ships were now anchored offshore, near a small seaside town southwest of Rome. The ball gunner overheard the following conversation between the pilot and navigator:

> *Pilot:* "What's the name of the town?"
> *Navigator:* "Anzio. It's a resort town dating back to Roman times. I can't imagine it has any military value."[43]

PART II

The Anzio
Beachhead

Anzio will astonish the world.

—CHURCHILL

The whole affair had a strong odor of Gallipoli.

—MAJOR GENERAL JOHN P. LUCAS,
COMMANDING GENERAL, U.S. VI CORPS

Prime Minister Winston Churchill. (*Imperial War Museum*)

General Sir Harold Alexander, the Allied ground commander in chief. (*Hulton Picture Company*)

Lieutenant General Mark Clark, the U.S. Fifth Army commander. (*Official U.S. Army photograph, National Archives*)

General Sir Henry Maitland ("Jumbo") Wilson, Allied commander in chief, Mediterranean, the intermediary between Churchill and Alexander. (*Imperial War Museum*)

The architects of Shingle.

The Allied beachhead commanders.

Major General John P. Lucas, the Shingle force commander. (*Official U.S. Army photograph, National Archives*)

Major General Lucian K. Truscott. (*Official U.S. Army photograph, National Archives*)

Major General Ernest N. Harmon. (*Photo courtesy of Norwich University*)

Major General W. R. C. Penney. (*Imperial War Museum*)

Major General G. W. R. Templer. (*Imperial War Museum*)

Aerial view of Monte Cassino and the Liri Valley, showing Highway 6 to Rome and Naples. (*Official U.S. Army photograph, National Archives*)

Part of the Allied invasion armada offshore, Anzio, January 1944. (*Imperial War Museum*)

Anzio and the Alban Hills (looking southeast toward the Liri Valley); Nettuno is at bottom right. (*Official U.S. Army photograph, National Archives*)

Two aerial views of Anzio and the beachhead.

Anzio and the Alban Hills (looking north toward Albano); the Padiglione Woods are at the left center. (*Official U.S. Army photograph, National Archives*)

The Shingle landings at Anzio-Nettuno, January 22, 1944. (*Official U.S. Army photograph, National Archives*)

DUKWs landing supplies at Anzio under enemy fire. (*Official U.S. Coast Guard photograph, National Archives*)

Allied anti-aircraft guns guarding the port of Anzio. (*Official U.S. Army photograph, National Archives*)

U.S. tanks and infantry move forward, Cisterna sector, January 1944. (*National Archives*)

The Flyover, scene of the desperate battle to save the beachhead in February 1944 (looking north toward Carroceto along the Via Anziate). (*Imperial War Museum*)

Two views of the left flank of the Anzio beachhead.

The Via Anziate and the Fischfang battlefield (looking north from the Flyover toward the Factory, top right). (*Imperial War Museum*)

U.S. troops dug in along the Mussolini Canal, February 1944. (*Official U.S. Army photograph, National Archives*)

German heavy flak guns firing into Allied positions in the Anzio beachhead. (*Von Richthofen Collection, Imperial War Museum*)

Aerial view of Cisterna and the Pantano Ditch, where Darby's Rangers were ambushed on January 30, 1944. (*Official U.S. Army photograph, National Archives*)

British troops marching north along the Via Anziate on January 23, 1944. (*Imperial War Museum*)

Aerial view of the ruins of Aprilia, the "Factory." Campoleone Station is at upper left; Dung Farm is in center of photo; Carroceto is just beyond the bottom left. (*Official U.S. Army photograph, National Archives*)

Campoleone Station, the farthest point of advance by the Allies until the breakout in May 1944. The Factory is in the background, top right. (*Official U.S. Army photograph, National Archives*)

German reinforcements near Carroceto, February 1944. (*Imperial War Museum*)

German tanks and artillery in
the ruins of Carroceto. The
Factory is in the background.
(*Imperial War Museum*)

**Carroceto and the
Factory.**

German troops defending
the Factory. (*Imperial War
Museum*)

Tanks of the British 46th Royal Tank Regiment preparing to counterattack during the struggle to hold the left flank of the beachhead. (*Imperial War Museum*)

Allied wounded awaiting evacuation by LST to Naples. (*Official U.S. Army photograph, National Archives*)

Allied POWs being marched through Rome; the Coliseum is in the background. (*Imperial War Museum*)

The bitter taste of defeat.

German paratroopers captured outside Rome, June 4, 1944. (*Von Richthofen Collection, Imperial War Museum*)

U.S. 155-mm "Long Tom" firing near Nettuno, February 1944. (*Official U.S. Army photograph, National Archives*)

At Anzio artillery was king. LSTs fulfilled the insatiable demand for artillery shells. (*Official U.S. Army photograph, National Archives*)

American walking wounded, Anzio beachhead. (*Official U.S. Army photograph, National Archives*)

"Hell's Half Acre": the Allied field hospitals near Anzio and Nettuno. (*Official U.S. Army photograph, National Archives*)

8

The Invasion

Don't stick your neck out, Johnny. I did at Salerno
and got into trouble.

CLARK TO LUCAS
January 22, 1944

Shingle commenced ten minutes
before zero hour in the early morning hours of January 22, 1944, when
the skies over Anzio were lit by rocket barrages that Lucas described
as "perfectly terrific." The rocket launchers were mounted on LCTs,
which became seaborne gun platforms that delivered nearly eight hundred
dred rockets virtually simultaneously in an awe-inspiring demonstration
of naval firepower that was intended to neutralize not only any
opposition but also the expected enemy minefields and wire defenses.
At the same time the Navy staged an elaborate diversion by bombarding the small port of Civitavecchia, sixty miles to the north, and carrying
out fake landings so successful that Kesselring ordered the regional
commandant to demolish the harbor immediately.[1]

As Lucas later wryly noted in his diary, "We achieved what is
certainly one of the most complete surprises in history. The Germans
were caught off base and there was practically no opposition to the
landing." Lucas had expected "a fight to get ashore but was not disappointed when I did not get it."[2]

No one aboard the vessels anchored off Anzio-Nettuno that night
thought the landings would go so smoothly. A British soldier of the 1st
Division has written of the tension that gripped the troops in those final
moments before zero hour:

Aboard all ships was an intense stillness. . . . All men watched and waited.
The immensity of what was about to happen struck them speechless.

119

The jokes and the conversations of a few minutes ago . . . were now forgotten. . . . Suddenly the shoreline rose in convulsion. Men, trees, houses, earth, stones were flung skywards. An intense rocket barrage had begun. . . . The sky was rent by an insane, howling, shrieking madness. A giant thunder filled all men with fear. The land erupted into great orange flames. . . . As the preliminary bombardment ended there was an ominous silence from the land.[3]

Guided by beacon submarines,[4] the debarkation was "almost unbelievably smooth and accurate," as Truscott later described it. When Darby's Ranger force assaulted Anzio they found the port lightly guarded, and what scant opposition there was soon evaporated as the Rangers gained control of the town by 0800 hours. Lieutenant Colonel William P. Yarborough's 509th Parachute Infantry Battalion then thrust east along the coast road and seized Nettuno. After Gela, where the Rangers had encountered stiff resistance from the Italians, and Salerno, where the Germans had fought furiously, the Anzio landings were a welcome change. A German engineer battalion of the 29th Panzer Grenadier Division sent to Anzio to blow up the breakwater in the harbor was captured before it could carry out its task. This turned out to be the only German combat force of any consequence located within a twenty-five-mile radius of Anzio. This particular unit had been so severely mauled during the recent fighting on the southern front "that it had been sent there the day before to rest and refit and to acquire some training in demolition by blowing up, at its leisure, the small harbor of Anzio."[5] Many of the more-than two hundred German prisoners were captured while still in their beds.

The Shingle landings might best be characterized as a nonevent or, as one of Penney's Irish Guards officers wrote, "very gentlemanly, calm and dignified." A company commander "with a large black umbrella hung on his arm, stepped ashore with the air of a missionary visiting a South Sea island and surprised to see no cannibals. It was quite clear that the landing had achieved complete surprise. 'I only hope we are taking advantage of it' was everyone's unspoken and spoken thought."[6] As the Guardsmen awaited their vehicles and equipment, most of which did not arrive until the following morning, they observed some Italian farm laborers on their way to work who "showed singularly little interest" in the sudden arrival of foreign soldiers in the dark of night. Later that morning Alexander made it a point to visit his former regiment about the time the Germans began shelling the beachhead. A Guardsman remembered that he "came walking up the road as if he was taking a morning stroll."[7] Although he pronounced himself "very satisfied," his reluctant companion, Admiral Troubridge, was heard to complain, "This is most unfair, as really I am a non-combatant on land."[8]

A POW later told his captors that sometime before midnight the German commandant of Anzio became suspicious of inexplicable noises emanating from the sea. He left Anzio by car for another headquarters south of Nettuno but was killed near Yellow Beach by a burst of automatic weapon fire from a Ranger patrol before he could raise the alarm. The next day, when Lucas and his staff occupied the same house, they discovered the commandant had left in such a hurry that there was a half-drunk glass of brandy on his desk.[9]

The POW was taken to the beach where he witnessed the invasion. What he found the most impressive about the landings was:

> He never heard a word of command and yet it seemed that everything went clock-work-like . . . it was like a big market and a medley without muddle. The ease of movement of our big amphibious vehicles impressed him as so much better than he had seen in Russia. He had his first contact with a Jeep and was astounded at its maneuverability. Like beetles they helped each other out by pushing or pulling when stuck in the sand or water. He could appreciate the careful planning . . . when he saw bulldozers being operated only a few hours after the initial landing, grading the ground to make a road on to which wire netting was placed without any loss of time. It was an impressive spectacle where every man knew his place.[10]

In the days that followed the Luftwaffe and German artillery emplaced in the Alban Hills would make life for the Allied naval and merchantmen considerably more difficult. In comparison to the 140 Luftwaffe sorties, the Allied air forces flew more than 1,200 on January 22, attacking road and rail targets in an attempt to seal off the beachhead from enemy reinforcement. As would be true throughout the war, there was a considerable difference of opinion over the effectiveness of the Allied air forces at Anzio.

The Allied air command employed the same approach for Anzio as they had in Sicily. Operations were in three phases:

1. Preliminary bombing from January 1 to 14 to disrupt rail communications in central Italy and to destroy or cripple the Luftwaffe.
2. Intensive efforts from January 15 to 21 to isolate the Anzio battle area by stepped-up attacks on roads and railways north of Rome and all roads leading to Anzio from the south.
3. From the day of the landings, the isolation of the Anzio beachhead through interdiction of German reinforcements and close air support of VI Corps.[11]

Most of the Allied air support came from the former Axis airfields captured during the autumn of 1943. Unlike the suspicion and ill will that existed between the ground forces and the Allied air forces during

Husky, the air support for Shingle was both massive and timely. Under the aegis of the new commander of the Mediterranean Allied Air Forces (MAAF), Lieutenant General Ira C. Eaker, a favorite of both the officers and airmen of the RAF and the USAAF and one of the truly outstanding air commanders of the war, the once-strained relations between airmen and their counterparts in the Army had improved dramatically. Whatever his personal feelings, Eaker, a dedicated advocate of strategic bombing, fresh from England where he had commanded the Eighth Air Force, never questioned the premise that a legitimate (and indeed, vital) role of the air forces was to support the ground campaign in Italy.[12]

Although Eaker arrived barely a week before Shingle he immediately endorsed the air plan. And, unlike his predecessors, Eaker was fully prepared to employ his strategic bomber force in support of a major ground operation. Prior to his arrival the tactical air commanders had become increasingly concerned that without heavy bomber support their efforts to isolate the Anzio battlefield would prove unsuccessful. After some misunderstanding and delay a directive was issued to Major General Nathan F. Twining's Fifteenth Air Force that their number one priority was now to attack rail lines and marshalling yards in northern Italy in support of Shingle.[13]

The air effort was as massive as it was costly: In phase one 5,777 tons of bombs were expended during 12,974 sorties, and in phase two 6,471 tons in 9,876 sorties. German losses included 142 aircraft, but MAAF lost 58 bombers and 86 fighters during the run-up to Shingle, a very high cost indeed.[14]

Despite Lucas's relief at the absence of opposition to the landings, he was never lulled into a false sense of security. He knew that German units would soon be heard from, but for the moment the major task facing VI Corps was the speed with which his troops and equipment could be landed. The first of many difficulties encountered in landing the 1st Division on Peter Beach north of Anzio was the menace of offshore floating mines, which produced some very close calls before a path could be cleared. Although the assault craft landed on time at 0200 hours, the first DUKWs did not land until two hours later, and the first LCTs and LSTs were held up until after dawn.[15] Sandbars and a steep gradient along the shore were particularly troublesome, and many vehicles became mired in the soft sand of the exits. One LST ferrying two batteries of Royal Artillery was stranded on a sandbar two hundred yards offshore. It eventually became necessary to unload the guns by derrick onto LCIs, and the batteries did not get ashore until January 23. Pontoons were laid from the shore to the LSTs but even this improvisation did not always work satisfactorily.[16] To make the landings even more unpleasant, German artillery shelled Peter Force throughout D day but did little damage.

With such minor exceptions the landings of the two infantry divisions could have served as models for the conduct of amphibious warfare. Fortunately, the port of Anzio was cleared and ready for LSTs and LCIs by early afternoon, thus enabling the remainder of the 1st Division to land in the town instead of across their beaches, which were permanently closed down.

The Luftwaffe was more successful and although damage to the Allied fleet was minimal, sporadic harassment took place throughout the day from Messerschmitts and Focke-Wulf fighter-bombers that attacked the landing craft and Red Beach where the 3d Division was disembarking. Some damage was done to vehicles ashore, and one LCI was destroyed when it took a direct hit from a five-hundred-pound bomb. The Allied air forces lost three planes while claiming seven German aircraft.[17] The most serious loss occurred when the minesweeper *Portent* struck a large underwater mine and sank instantly with the loss of eighteen hands. Otherwise, German interference with the Shingle landings was minimal.

At 0800 hours the morale of those still waiting to come ashore was raised by a BBC announcement that troops of the U.S. Fifth Army had landed south of Rome and that all was well. The men of the 1st Division could have been forgiven for believing that Anzio might turn out to be another Pantelleria.[18]

Truscott was ashore at 0600 hours and four hours later was joined at his CP by Clark, who was invited to share breakfast. Truscott's efficient Chinese cook had obtained bacon and some rare fresh eggs. Then Lucas and his chief of staff arrived and more food was dispensed, while the cook grew increasingly annoyed that others were eating his general's precious eggs. Later Truscott overheard his exasperated cook exclaim, "Goddam, General's fresh eggs all gone to hell."[19]

By the evening of January 22 the Allies had landed 36,034 troops, 3,069 vehicles, and large numbers of supplies, totaling 90 percent of the VI Corps assault load. Losses were less than those of the Navy. Total Allied casualties were thirteen killed, ninety-seven wounded, and forty-four missing or captured. Unfortunately for the Allies, one of those captured was found to be carrying a copy of the Shingle plan.

Lucas had every reason to be pleased with the day's events. Not only had his force gotten ashore unscathed, but VI Corps had attained all the preliminary objectives for the initial beachhead laid down in his orders. Infantry and reconnaissance elements of the 3d Division had seized intact all the bridges spanning the Mussolini Canal, which were considered vital to the defense of the right flank of the beachhead. Penney's troops likewise had accomplished a great deal during the day and now controlled some seven miles of the Anzio-Albano road, as far as the Moletta River.

The complete absence of German defenders enabled a jeep patrol to drive undetected to the outskirts of Rome the morning of January 22. 1st Lieutenant John T. Cummings of the 36th Engineer Regiment came ashore attached to a 3d Division reconnaissance unit. Shortly after 0900 hours Cummings and his driver began heading toward Rome. Just south of the city they stopped in the foothills to observe German vehicles crossing a bridge over the Tiber River: "There was no sense of panic; apparently the people had not heard of the invasion. We stayed about an hour, met no enemy or civilian and returned to our unit [at Anzio], made out our report and went about our regular engineer duties."[20]

It was along the Mussolini Canal that the 3d Division encountered the first serious German resistance, when the Hermann Göring Division recaptured most of the canal bridges that night with a tank-infantry force that dislodged the 30th Infantry. On January 23 the Americans struck back with a regimental-size counterattack and by the next day all these bridges were back in Allied hands.

Elsewhere during the first forty-eight hours of Shingle, VI Corps expanded its initial gains to carve out a bridgehead seven miles deep that ran from the Moletta River to the Mussolini Canal. The 3d Division, supported by Tucker's 504th Parachute Infantry and Darby's Rangers, had solidified the Allied right flank by occupying positions along the Mussolini Canal and its western tributary. In the British sector a single brigade held the left flank along the Moletta. Lucas retained the remainder of the 1st Division in corps reserve to repel an expected German counterattack.

Although the Germans had long been expecting the Allies to launch an amphibious landing somewhere near Rome, the Shingle landings nevertheless caught Kesselring flat-footed. Inexplicably, the extensive preparations in and around Naples had somehow escaped the notice of the Abwehr, which assured Kesselring that no Allied amphibious operation was imminent. The Luftwaffe was equally lax in failing to discover until too late that a large fleet was being assembled at Naples. In the absence of intelligence to the contrary, Kesselring expected the Allies to continue their efforts to break the Gustav Line.

Why had the Germans not detected the massive preparations in and around Naples or the presence of Task Force 81? German agents were thought to be operating in Naples, where enterprising Italian street merchants were openly selling postcards of Anzio to anyone who would buy them. At least part of the answer lay in carelessness on the part of German intelligence, which was aware that the landing craft previously in the harbor of Bizerte had disappeared, and that there was

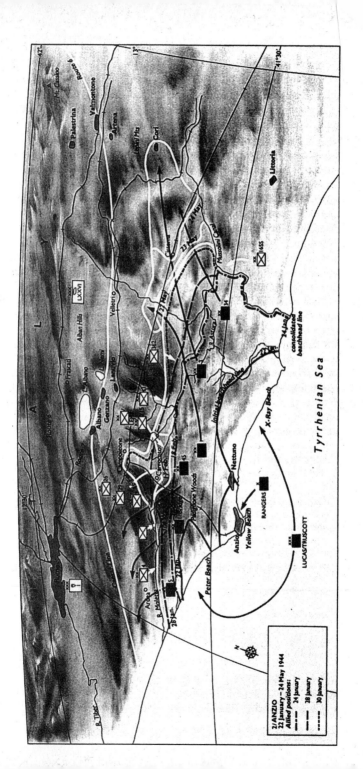

2/ANZIO
22 January–24 May 1944
Allied positions:
24 January
28 January
30 January

a heavy buildup of Allied ships in the Gulf of Gaeta. The German commanders were badly misled by Admiral Canaris, the head of the Abwehr,[21] who visited Kesselring several days before Shingle. An intercepted Allied radio message suggested an impending invasion but when Kesselring's chief of staff, General Siegfried Westphal, asked Canaris for his assessment, the admiral assured him: "There is not the slightest sign that a new landing will be undertaken in the near future." On January 15, Westphal passed on to von Vietinghoff and von Mackensen the news that any large-scale amphibious operation was "out of the question for the next four to six weeks."[22]

The Fifth Army offensive along the Rapido and Garigliano rivers had precipitated a major crisis within the German high command, obliging Kesselring to make one of the most important decisions of the entire Italian campaign: what to do with the 29th and 90th Panzer Grenadier Divisions, his two reserve forces then refitting near Rome. One of the most crucial decisions any combat commander must make is when to commit his reserves. Clark's threat to the Liri Valley was taken very seriously by Kesselring, whose priority was that the Gustav Line remain intact. What particularly worried the German commander in chief was the potential collapse of his right flank if McCreery's 10th Corps was permitted to expand its toehold north of the Garigliano. Correctly interpreting this as a major threat, he telephoned von Vietinghoff the morning of January 18 to state: "I am convinced that we are now facing the greatest crisis yet encountered [in Italy]." There began "a bitter tussle" over what course of action to follow.[23]

After the war Kesselring revealed why he decided to reinforce his right flank along the Garigliano:

> If [an] amphibious operation were mounted, it had to strike, in my opinion, in the Rome area—either north or south of Rome. . . . It was furthermore clear to me that an amphibious landing would be coupled in some manner with a new offensive on the southern front. Strong motorized reserves would be required for both sectors. . . . When I released [the] 29th and 90th Panzer Grenadier Divisions for what was supposed to be a brief counter-attack, I did not expect that an invasion was immediately forthcoming. I felt justified in hoping that the commitment of [these] good divisions could restore the situation on the southern front very rapidly, and that these forces would then be immediately available for employment elsewhere. If I shirked my responsibility toward 10th Army then I had to expect that the right wing of the Army would be pushed back, and no one could say where it might have held.[24]

Kesselring later admitted he had no idea that Clark's offensive was designed to cover Shingle and expected an amphibious landing would take place only after success in the south made such an operation

feasible. In fact, Kesselring's assumption was the same premise o
which Shingle had originally been founded, before its true intention
was lost in the quagmire created by Churchill. Kesselring briefly toyed
with the idea of sending only the 90th Panzer Grenadier Division and
keeping the 29th near Anzio. Even if he had done so, he remained
convinced that "it would still have been by no means certain that the
landing could have been prevented. In that case, we should have suffered from two malignant growths which would have rendered it almost impossible to withdraw forces from the southern front and send
them to Anzio-Nettuno. It was much better to restore order in the one
place first and then to turn our full attention to the second task."[25]

During the first critical days after the Anzio landings, Kesselring
never seriously considered withdrawing from the Cassino front because
of the threat posed by VI Corps. Panic was not in his makeup and,
although disturbed by the threat posed by the landings, Kesselring
calmly reviewed his options. He had no desire to defend in the north,
where the Italian peninsula widened, necessitating more troops to defend fewer natural defensive positions. "The decisive battle had to be
joined somewhere . . . and the 'C'[assino] position seemed to me the
most favorable place and the most hopeful of success."[26]

Although there were few Germans to resist the Allied landings
Kesselring had nevertheless laid elaborate contingency plans for such
an event somewhere in Italy. Five potential invasion sites were selected
in December 1943 and plans laid to react to each. The Germans had
long regarded Rome as the most endangered portion of their flank and
accordingly gave an Allied landing in the vicinity of Rome, code-named
Case Richard, the most attention. It was over von Vietinghoff's objections that Kesselring had insisted in the autumn of 1943 that two divisions must always be stationed nearby to act as an army group reserve.

German plans included units preloaded and ready to react within
eight to twelve hours of an alert, depending on the location of the
invasion. The target sites were fortified with obstacles and defended by
small units. The object in each case was to delay the Allied invaders long
enough to bring in reinforcements to contain them. Fuel and resupply
dumps were established along routes of march and teams deployed to
keep bridges repaired.

Allied deception measures, calculated to suggest the landings
would come north of Rome, were implemented to draw German attention away from Anzio. These included assembling troops and landing
craft in Sardinia and Corsica and heavy air attacks against targets in and
around Civitavecchia and northern Italy. Air force cover operations in
January were designed not only to shift German attention to northern
Italy but at the same time to interdict German lines of communication
to southern Italy.[27] Another deception measure employed by Brigadier

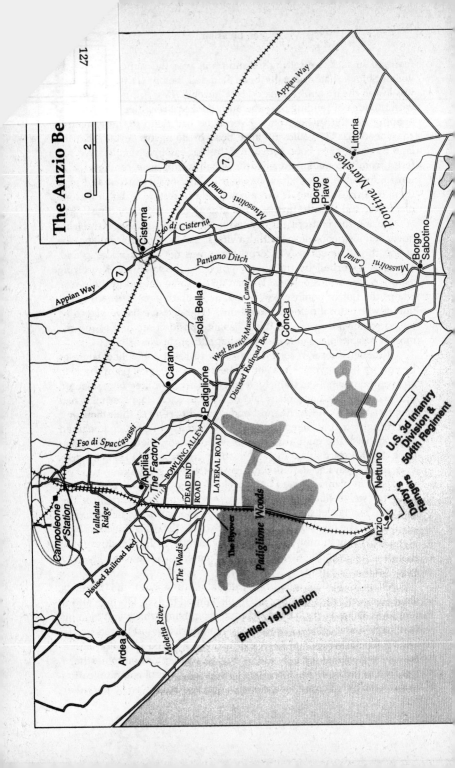

The Anzio Be...

127

Dudley Clarke's A Force (an immensely successful British-run unit whose specialty was deception operations in the Mediterranean) was to send fake wireless messages to Italian resistance forces (in ciphers the Germans were known to be capable of breaking) in which they were told that an invasion was imminent at Civitavecchia.[28]

The British official history credits a German railway engineer corporal stationed at Anzio with being the first to report the Allied landings. Apparently unaware of the presence of the 29th Panzer Grenadier unit in Anzio, or perhaps unable to locate them, he sped off on a motorcycle in search of someone to report to. At Albano he met a German panzer grenadier lieutenant who passed the information on to the German major in charge of Albano. By now it was nearly two hours since the landings had begun, and at about 0400 hours the news was finally passed along to a German headquarters in Rome.[29] It has not been established how Kesselring's headquarters first learned of the invasion, but it may have been as early as 0300 hours on the morning of January 22 that the first report was received by OB South.

In any event, it did not take Kesselring long to assess the seriousness of the landings and order the code-word Case Richard to be flashed throughout the far-flung German chain of command to signal that the Rome area was the site of the invasion. The problem was that without adequate intelligence the initial reports flowing into OB South were at best confusing and at worst wholly misleading. The Navy correctly reported two landings north and south of Anzio but vastly overestimated Allied strength at three to four divisions.[30] "Not until twenty minutes past eight on the morning of 22nd January, six hours after the landings had been carried out, did a Messerschmitt 109 succeed in penetrating the air screen and bringing authentic news to Kesselring that the Allies were behind his right flank."[31]

As the Allies would soon learn, the German reaction to the Anzio landings was a total commitment to containing the beachhead. Throughout the German chain of command there flowed a steady stream of orders by telephone and wireless as Kesselring sought to counter this new complication before it got out of hand. Units from as far away as Germany, Yugoslavia, and France were on the move at once. Three divisions based in northern Italy in reserve under the Fourteenth Army were likewise alerted and headed south within twenty-four hours. For the moment Kesselring was satisfied merely to place in motion stopgap measures to block an Allied advance to the Alban Hills. There would be ample time later for Army Group C to demonstrate its determination to crush the invaders.

One of Kesselring's first acts was to order the counterattack along the Garigliano discontinued, thus freeing additional units that could be sent to Anzio. Later that day he would view for himself the full extent of this new threat, but for the time being there was little he could do except order every available formation based in the Rome area to Anzio to take up blocking positions between the town and the Alban Hills to forestall the expected Allied thrust inland. Beginning at dawn there was a frenzy of activity as units were alerted and began to react with varying degrees of speed.

Because the number of German troops in Italy was barely sufficient to man the Gustav Line, Kesselring wisely rotated formations into and out of the Cassino front. Until Anzio, the Fourteenth Army acted as a training command where units were rested and brought back to strength and then exchanged with a battle-weary division from the Tenth Army. Under an OKW directive issued in December, Kesselring was assured of reinforcements from France, Holland, or the Balkans in the event of an Allied invasion. Until then Kesselring would have to defend as best he could with the forces at his disposal.

On January 22 German forces in and around Anzio-Nettuno proper numbered fewer than one thousand troops. However, three battalions of the 90th Panzer Grenadier Division's Battle Group von Behr along the Tiber were guarding the northern approaches to Rome; farther inland was Battle Group Gericke of the 4th Parachute Division. Near Velletri were two parachute engineer companies of the 4th Parachute, a battle group of the 29th Panzer Grenadier Division, and a reconnaissance battalion near Terracina. In the Alban Hills were several reinforcement holding units of the Hermann Göring Division.[32] Far to the south there were two divisions en route to the Tenth Army front, the 71st Infantry and the 3d Panzer Grenadier, both of which were immediately ordered to halt and turn north to reinforce Anzio. The first elements of these two divisions arrived early on January 23. North of Rome, in the vicinity of Spoleto, were the main elements of the 4th Parachute Division, a new unit that was not yet fully operational.[33] Operational or not, the 4th Parachute nevertheless reacted with great speed, and during the early evening hours of January 22 elements of the division were among the first to reach the Anzio sector, where they were assigned the key mission of blocking all roads leading to Rome from Anzio and to the Alban Hills from the south.

One of Kesselring's most pressing problems was the need for a tactical headquarters to take charge of the German defense of Anzio. Von Mackensen's headquarters was then in northern Italy and could not become operational at Anzio for several days. In the interim Kesselring ordered von Vietinghoff to release a corps headquarters and every unit that could be spared from the Tenth Army. Fortunately for the Germans, the rear echelons of I Parachute Corps had been deployed to Rome several days earlier, and it was this HQ that was summoned to Anzio from the southern front, where the corps commander and his operational staff were directing the defense of the Garigliano. The corps commander, General Alfred Schlemm, arrived about 1700 hours the afternoon of January 22, but until that time Kesselring needed someone to take control of the beachhead defenses. The only available officer was the former commandant of Rome, a bumbling staff officer and brigadier general coincidentally named Schlemmer. His performance on January 22 was inept, and, contrary to Kesselring's instructions, he assembled a force of three or four infantry battalions as local reserves in the Alban Hills instead of along the key choke points on the roads to Rome. When Kesselring learned of Schlemmer's stupidity he immediately replaced him with the commander of XI Air Corps, a Luftwaffe officer who understood what he was supposed to accomplish.

Kesselring was also well served by the local Luftwaffe flak commander, who rushed his batteries with unprecedented speed to new positions along the roads to Rome and the Alban Hills that became the first line of defense against the expected Allied thrust.[34] Until he could somehow stabilize the situation Kesselring was determined to hold every possible foot of ground necessary for defense in order to avoid paying for that same ground later "at a bloody cost."[35] Later would come the expected order from Hitler, which was duly read to all troops: "The Gustav Line must be held at all costs for the sake of the political consequences which would follow a completely successful defense. The Führer expects the bitterest struggle for every yard."[36]

The early hours of the invasion were the most anxious for virtually everyone—including Kesselring, who remained practically unflappable despite the chaotic conditions within his headquarters, which Westphal has described as being in "a state of acute tension."[37] Although a few of the German units sent to Anzio on January 22 seemed to know that they were being sent to defend against an Allied landing, most had been alerted and moved so quickly that they simply had no idea what was afoot or even what they were doing there.

When there was no sign of the expected Allied offensive toward Rome by the end of the morning, Kesselring began to believe "the worst danger had been staved off." As predicted, the weather had turned out clear, and as Kesselring made his presence felt when he inspected the hastily assembled defenses that afternoon, what he would have observed from the Alban Hills was the Allied naval armada well offshore with barrage balloons drifting lazily above many of the vessels. Near the beaches LSTs were busily discharging seemingly endless streams of vehicles and equipment. Overhead, marauding Allied aircraft crisscrossed the skies, attacking road junctions, bridges, and anything that moved on the ground in an effort to seal off the beachhead from the expected German counterattack. Not for the first time in this war Kesselring faced a crisis requiring decisions of such magnitude that they would determine the course of the campaign in Italy. For the moment, if the Allied invasion commander decided to move on Rome and the Alban Hills, he was helpless. However, despite the hodgepodge of units flung into the breech, Kesselring never lost "the confident feeling that the Allies had missed a uniquely favorable chance of capturing Rome and of opening the door on the Garigliano front." Instead, he was now "certain that time was our ally."[38] As one historian has observed: "At this moment, Kesselring might well have offered a sacrifice to the old Roman Goddess of Fortune at Anzio . . . it was clear she had already left the Allied side and come over to the Germans."[39]

Once the Germans became the beneficiaries of extraordinarily good fortune when a copy of the Shingle plan fell into their hands, Kesselring had solid proof that his instincts had been correct. Thus, almost from the outset Kesselring gained a priceless advantage from his knowledge that Lucas would not attempt to cut his lines of communication to Cassino. And, once certain of the limited objectives of the invasion, he could compensate with impunity for the lack of immediately available forces in the Rome-Anzio sector.

By the end of January 22 the broad outlines of a defensive strategy had taken shape. The Germans were expecting a second Allied invasion north of the Tiber, and until it later became clear that Anzio was the only threat, Kesselring disposed the 71st Division to cover his northern flank. The 4th Parachute Division was ordered to cover the critical sector along the approaches to Rome until the arrival of the 3d Panzer Grenadier Division, which was to defend what the German commanders regarded as the most dangerous area of the beachhead, the Campoleone sector on the road to Rome. The badly battered Hermann Göring Division was ordered to guard the less-threatening southern flank, with their defense centered on the important communications center of Cisterna. By 1700 hours I Parachute Corps had moved into the Anzio sector and taken control of the German defenses.

Kesselring symbolized the German defense of Italy, and he became the bedrock upon which it was built. Where others would have drawn the wrong conclusions or overreacted, Kesselring remained composed and was quite literally the glue that held the German Army in Italy together. His actions on January 22 and the equally nervous days that followed gave "the Allied commanders and, indeed, students of the art of war a lesson in clear thinking, sound appreciation and rapid reaction."[40] Kesselring excelled at the art of improvisation, and Anzio may well have been his finest hour.

Nevertheless, the German commander in chief was severely criticized by some second-guessers on his staff who disagreed with his decision to strip the Rome sector of reserves to stem McCreery's attacks along the Garigliano. The bitter debate over whether or not to commit the army group reserve was undoubtedly one of the most important and controversial incidents of the Italian campaign. As Westphal has recounted, Kesselring's fateful decision was based on a solid rationale:

> If the Tenth Army's fears of an enemy break-through into the Liri Valley were realized, the damage would be irreparable. . . . It needed assistance from at least two divisions in order to stabilize the situation [they] would be needed for only a few days; they would be at the disposal of the Army Group again after a few days . . . the Army Group felt they could not refuse Tenth Army's request.[41]

The deciding factor in the decision to send the two panzer grenadier divisions to von Vietinghoff seems to have been Canaris's assurances that the Allies would not launch their end run any time soon. Kesselring was used to being second-guessed and shrugged off the criticism with the observation that "there is no absolute certainty in war. I had to act accordingly."[42]

By the early afternoon Colonel Thomas H. Stanley's 36th Engineer Combat Regiment[43] had cleared what few obstacles had been encountered in the port of Anzio, which was now able to receive and discharge four LSTs and three LCTs simultaneously. As the battle for the Anzio beachhead later developed, the German failure to destroy the port proved to be of immense importance in enabling VI Corps to keep open the vital lifeline between Naples and Anzio.

The initial objective of VI Corps was to carve out a semicircular beachhead seven miles deep and fifteen miles wide around Anzio and Nettuno. Its total perimeter of twenty-six miles "was considered the maximum which could be held by General Lucas' limited forces and yet include the best natural features for defense."[44]

Kesselring was, of course, correct in his conclusion that Lucas would not make a dash for the Alban Hills, and we know that Lucas had long since made up his mind that any such attempt would be suicidal folly. Whatever confidence Lucas may have had in his ability to accomplish his mission at Anzio was certainly not enhanced by Clark's visit to the beachhead on January 22. As he prepared to reembark for Naples, Clark—who was certainly aware of Lucas's doubts—warned him, "Don't stick your neck out, Johnny. I did at Salerno and got into trouble."[45] There is ample evidence that Clark had infected Lucas with what Jumbo Wilson later called the "Salerno complex"—the natural caution exhibited by anyone who has had his nose bloodied by an adversary. Kesselring had done just that to Clark, who had nearly lost the Salerno beachhead and had no intention of placing himself in a similar plight twice. Clark's message to Lucas was therefore unmistakable: He had little confidence in the operation and Lucas was under no circumstances to jeopardize the Shingle force. Clark's Salerno warning, rather than reassure Lucas, simply became the VI Corps commander's *raison d'être* for playing it safe.

Moreover, if Clark and Alexander had been really serious about a drive on the Alban Hills, neither would have approved Lucas's order of battle for the landings. As finally constituted, armor was in short supply and included primarily to support the infantry while the beachhead was secured and later defended. A tank battalion of the Royal Tank Regiment (the 46th RTR) was attached to the 1st Division, and a similar battalion of Shermans (the 751st Tank Battalion) was provided Truscott. Neither had been groomed for mobile operations in an environment where armor was vulnerable and most effectively employed only in a supporting role.

Small wonder, then, that Lucas never quite knew what to make of his masters, both of whom visited Anzio on January 22. Alexander had pronounced himself well satisfied with the landings, telling Lucas, "You have certainly given the folks at home something to talk about." (Before he departed Clark had issued his ominous warning to Lucas about not sticking his neck out.) Lemnitzer accompanied Alexander and Clark on January 22 and later confirmed that on that day Alexander was in full agreement with Lucas's decision not to attempt to push to the Alban Hills: "General Alexander realized that we did not have strength enough to hold the Hills even if we did take them. He thoroughly approved of the caution with which the Corps commander was acting. Neither General Alexander nor Clark gave any sign that they thought Lucas had acted unwisely."[46]

Although perhaps temporarily reassured that he and his superiors were of like mind, in the days that followed, with the great German buildup opposite VI Corps proceeding unabated, Lucas well understood that he faced a steadily mounting problem. He also understood that he was expected to produce results beyond the capability of VI Corps. Unfortunately, Lucas's pessimism served him badly, for—despite the increasing gloominess of the situation—he had made little attempt to be offensive minded while the opportunity existed. Lucas's frame of mind was communicated to his diary: "The strain of a thing like this is a terrible burden. Who the hell wants to be a general."[47]

Lucas's decision played directly into German hands, leaving a surprised but delighted Kesselring with the whip hand. The situation along the Cassino front was stalemate. Both sides had spent themselves in the months since Salerno, and there was not even the remotest possibility of the Allies breaking the German grip on the Gustav Line, as the recent bloody battles along the Rapido and Garigliano had conclusively proved. With this in mind, Kesselring was confident he could detach formations from the Cassino front to relieve this new threat at Anzio.

Lucas was well aware that he must advance at least as far as Cisterna, an important crossroads town on Highway 7, fourteen miles northeast of Anzio, and to the vicinity of Albano along the Anzio-Rome highway. Both sides regarded Campoleone and Cisterna as their most vital objectives: Allied control would block all German road and rail traffic to the south; German control would thwart a successful advance to the Alban Hills.

To occupy the Alban Hills VI Corps would have had to advance inland and seize blocking positions at Albano and Cisterna within the first twenty-four to forty-eight hours of Shingle. Although VI Corps was simply too small to establish and maintain a defensible beachhead and seize the Colli Laziali at the same time, both Cisterna and Albano were attainable objectives. Lucas's failure to press for their capture was a serious mistake.

Despite their tactical importance, taking Cisterna and Albano would not have solved the dilemma facing Lucas. As the official U.S. naval historian points out, seizing the lines of communication on the western side of the hills would still have left the Germans in control of the second rail line and Highway 6 to the east, which were the most important links to the southern front. The Allied beachhead would thus have been "a mere nuisance to the enemy who might be expected to react violently against it. That was the fundamental weakness of Operation SHINGLE. Either it was a job for a full army, or it was no job at all; to attempt it with only two divisions was to send a boy on a man's errand."[48]

The calm lasted less than twenty-four hours as the Luftwaffe began stepping up its attacks on shipping and ground targets in an attempt to forestall any attempted move by Lucas toward Rome and the Alban Hills. By midnight on January 22 the Germans had assembled approximately twenty thousand troops in the vicinity of Anzio, the majority of whom were parachute troops and panzer grenadiers.[49]

As the Allies continued to consolidate their beachhead, the German buildup continued at a relentless pace. By the end of January 24 the number had doubled to forty thousand and when von Mackensen's Fourteenth Army headquarters became operational on January 25 there were elements of eight separate divisions in defensive positions. Allied attempts to counter the buildup by heavy air attacks across the entire front had little effect upon the German ability to flood the plains surrounding Anzio with troops. Although the initial German consideration was defensive, the speed of their reaction to Shingle far exceeded the Allied worst-case scenario. It did not take Lucas long to learn that he was indeed "out there on his own."

Although Eaker's Mediterranean Allied Air Forces had done their best to isolate the battlefield, they were unable to prevent massive German reinforcements from getting through. While Allied air forces did disrupt rail and road movements, their interference was little more than a temporary nuisance to the Germans. One of the lessons of World War II was that air power alone was not enough to turn the tide of a battle such as that fought at Anzio. The Germans had long since learned to live with the threats posed by Allied air and had found ingenious ways to circumvent them. Nevertheless, the Allied airmen would soon play a crucial role in the desperate battles for the Anzio beachhead.

One particularly absurd notion was soon discarded by the Allied command: the original concept whereby VI Corps would be left at Anzio with ten days' supplies while the bulk of the landing craft were withdrawn in accordance with the previously established priorities for Overlord. As both sides prepared for a major battle there was no further mention of withdrawing the vital LST lifeline between Anzio and Naples.

The Germans were satisfied merely to gain vital time to establish defensive blocking positions, despite a gap of nearly five miles between their main line of resistance and the Allied front lines. However, as their reinforcements rose to nearly seventy thousand on January 29, it was only a matter of time before von Mackensen initiated a powerful counterattack to drive the Allies back into the sea. In fact, by the time of von Mackensen's arrival, Kesselring was confident enough to believe that a major counteroffensive could crush the invaders of Anzio.

9

Missed
Opportunities

Lucas must be aggressive. He must take some
chances.

—CLARK
Diary, January 23, 1944

he Anzio beachhead was situated
in East Latium, a region that includes the Alban Hills and the flat, damp
lowlands along the coast southwest of Rome. The hills are in reality
extinct volcanos with two enormous craters that created Lake Albano
(nearby is Castel Gandolfo, the pope's summer home) and the smaller
Lake Nemi. Rising to heights of three thousand feet, the rugged Alban
Hills are covered with dense forests and, near Velletri, numerous vineyards, which give the region its well-deserved reputation as a wine
center. In ancient times the town of Anzio was known as Antium and
was best known as the birthplace of the Emperor Nero, whose reign
(A.D. 54 to 68) saw the persecution of Christians and the excesses associated with the nadir of the Roman Empire.

In 1944 the flat plains of Anzio were flanked on the right by the
Mussolini Canal, beyond which lay the Pontine Marshes. For nearly
thirteen miles these plains were dotted with small villages and isolated,
sturdy, stone farmhouses, or *poderi,* laid out in neat patterns. Around
them were a series of secondary roads and small irrigation canals that
resembled a checkerboard. In 1928 Mussolini initiated a massive effort
to drain the marshes and reclaim the bogs that had for centuries made
the area a mosquito-infested hellhole where malaria was endemic. The

reclamation of the Pontine Marshes had employed thousands of work-
ers and taken nearly fifteen years and enormous cost to accomplish. In
the 1930s Mussolini would boast that this success was a model of the
great "new civilization" created by his enlightened version of fascism.

Only a small section directly north of the two resort towns was left
in its original state of bog, scrub timber, and grazing land. Il Duce's
pride and joy was the canal bearing his name and the brand-new farm-
ing commune of Aprilia, built in 1937. One of five such towns in the
region, designed by town planners as a model village, Aprilia was a
self-contained modern community of brick buildings that fulfilled its
citizens' needs by providing a cinema, school, and medical facilities for
physical needs; a church for spiritual needs; and wine stores to help
sustain both. Rising above the local Fascist headquarters in the town
center was a large bell tower that from afar resembled a factory smoke-
stack, leading the Allies to dub Aprilia "the Factory." Several hundred
yards to the west of the Factory lay the tiny village of Carroceto on the
Anzio-Rome highway. Paralleling the highway was a branch line of the
main Rome-Naples railway that ran from Anzio and Nettuno to Campoleone station. During the savage battles for control of the Factory,
the bell tower would be utilized with great effect as an artillery observation post by its occupants of the moment. The buildings were solidly
constructed of reinforced concrete, and later their ruins would become
fortified strongpoints where the fighting often resembled a miniature
Stalingrad, with each room a separate and deadly battleground.

Aprilia was of considerable military importance not only because
it was built on the only small section of high ground in the immediate
area but, more important, because its location was a natural choke point
astride the road net leading to Campoleone and Albano to the north
and Anzio to the south. Both the German and Allied commanders
quickly recognized the importance of the Factory.

The Mussolini Canal formed the right flank of the beachhead. The
main canal, which was used to drain the northern section of the Pontine
Marshes, was "built like an antitank ditch, with steeply sloping sides and
a shallow, 16-foot wide stream in the middle. The combination of canal
and marshes made the right flank of the beachhead a poor avenue of
attack and enabled us to hold it with a minimum force."[1] In places the
canal and its embankments were 120 feet across. Six miles inland from
its terminus in the Tyrrhenian Sea south of Nettuno, it split into two
forks, one of which continued northeast below Cisterna toward the
Alban Hills. The western fork cut across a considerable portion of the
beachhead to Padiglione, where it dissolved into a small stream fed by
a number of creeks, one of which ran directly through the Factory. This
section of the canal formed a natural tank ditch and an obstacle to both
sides.

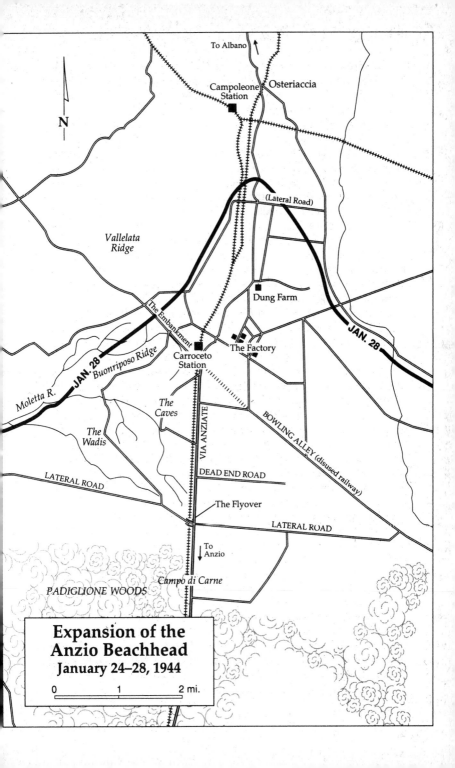

N

To Albano

Campoleone
Station   Osteriaccia

(Lateral Road)

Vallelata
Ridge

Dung Farm

The Embankment

JAN. 28

The Factory

JAN. 28

Moletta R.   Buonriposo Ridge   Carroceto
Station

The
Caves

The
Wadis

BOWLING ALLEY (disused railway)

VIA ANZIATE

LATERAL ROAD   DEAD END ROAD

The Flyover

LATERAL ROAD

To
Anzio

Campo di Carne

PADIGLIONE WOODS

Expansion of the
Anzio Beachhead
January 24–28, 1944

0   1   2 mi.

Another natural defensive barrier was called the "Bowling Alley": a disused railway bed that began at Borgo Piave and ran in a straight line northwest slightly to the south of Padiglione, across the Factory road net, and through Carroceto.

On the left flank, west of the Anzio-Albano-Rome highway, the British 1st Division boundary was the Moletta River. Here the country became more harsh, with a series of steep, rocky gullies that reminded veteran troops of the wadi country of North Africa. In summer, temperatures at Anzio were stifling, often exceeding one hundred degrees, and in winter the rains turned the land and the once-dry watercourses into such a soggy mess that foxholes quickly filled with water. To the north of Anzio along both sides of the Anzio-Albano highway was the thick, mostly cork-oak forest called the Padiglione Woods. Its trees, growing in dense clumps in the boggy soil, were surrounded by tangled undergrowth that made movement impossible except along the few sandy tracks that turned into quagmires in the winter. The winter of 1943–44 was no exception, and those who fought at Anzio were subjected to what sometimes seemed to be endless downpours and numbing cold that froze feet and made existence there under combat conditions a living hell. As the historian of the Irish Guards has written: "The whole area had for centuries been shunned by sensible men."[2]

The road net in and around Anzio was extremely poor. Only the two-lane Anzio-Albano-Rome highway, which joined the Appian Way (Highway 7) four miles northwest of Albano, actually led to Rome. The few other roads were either sandy or gravel tracks and the occasional paved roads that tended to branch off in various directions. In dry weather, vehicles traversing these roads threw up clouds of dust that made them lucrative targets for Allied or German gunners. Along the reclaimed marshes in the 3d Division sector, there was no cover or concealment from German observation either nearby or in the Alban Hills and, as both sides would soon discern, it became suicidal to use the roads in daylight. Except in the British sector the terrain in the beachhead rarely exceeded an elevation of 150 feet, and the 3d Division sector had no high ground at all except at La Ferriere, a wool mill midway between Nettuno and Cisterna, at an elevation of 220 feet. Along the Mussolini Canal the flat land was punctuated by a series of drainage ditches, running from the fields of the reclaimed marshlands, which ranged in size from "small scratches in the ground to a twenty or thirty-foot width, and fifteen or twenty-foot depth."[3]

The entire beachhead frontage was tailor-made for defensive operations, and along the Cisterna–Mussolini Canal sector the Germans took full advantage by establishing strong points in virtually every farmhouse, barn, or outbuilding, where they emplaced antitank guns, automatic weapons, and an occasional tank- or self-propelled gun. Only the direct fire of a tank, tank destroyer, or heavy-caliber artillery had any effect on these simple but nearly impregnable defenses. It was not uncommon for the Germans to occupy the buildings on one side of a crossroads and Allied troops, those across the street. In other parts of the line, foxholes were as close as fifty feet and, when they were not shooting at one another, the occupants often conducted a dialogue between the two sides.

During the first week of the battle several attempts were made by the 1st and 3d Divisions to reach Campoleone and Cisterna, but Lucas did not order an all-out offensive. The 3d Division managed to advance several miles beyond the western fork of the Mussolini Canal toward Cisterna before German resistance forced Truscott to regroup and prepare a stronger attack. On January 24 a reconnaissance force attempting to advance on Cisterna along two parallel roads ran into panzer grenadiers of the Hermann Göring Division, who raked the Americans with machine- and antitank-gunfire from virtually every farmhouse, each of which had been turned into a mutually supporting strongpoint.

On January 26 Tucker's paratroopers of the 2d Battalion, 504th Parachute Infantry, emerged from the shelter of the Mussolini Canal in a diversionary operation on the right flank designed to distract the Hermann Göring Division while the 3d Division renewed its attempt to capture Cisterna. Supported by two destroyers and the cruiser USS *Brooklyn,* Colonel Tucker's airborne captured several villages on the road to Littoria until strong intervention by an armored task force of the Görings surprised Company D of the 504th Parachute Infantry in open ground southeast of Borgo Piave. Having suffered heavy losses and cut off until that night, the paratroopers were forced to withdraw to safe ground. With these exceptions, the right flank of the beachhead continued to be the Mussolini Canal.

His first probe toward Cisterna a failure, Truscott decided to increase his assault forces to two battalions of infantry each and to support them heavily with tanks and the massed fires of the 3d Division artillery. On January 26 and 27 successive attacks were launched toward Cisterna, where they again were fiercely resisted. The Germans were demonstrating iron determination to prevent the fall of Cisterna and the severing of Highway 7. (Truscott himself had a narrow escape from death on January 24 when a shell exploded near him. He received a painful wound from shell fragments in one of his feet, and a nagging case of laryngitis reduced his voice to a rasping whisper.) Despite the stiff German resistance, Truscott was not yet prepared to give up the fight for Cisterna. The 24th Guards Brigade of the 1st Division was being held in corps reserve by Lucas until the 179th Regiment of the 45th Division arrived on January 24 to relieve the Guards and become the reserve force. Truscott proposed that Lucas attach the 179th to the 3d Division for an all-out attack on Cisterna that he was convinced would penetrate the defenses of the Hermann Göring Division, which were spread very thinly, defending the entire German left flank.

For its part, the Hermann Göring Division knew its opponents well. Both had played key roles in the battle for Sicily the previous summer, and although both had fought other opponents, they had met again in southern Italy and, in one of the paradoxes of war, the veterans of the two divisions had developed a grudging respect for one another. In Sicily the Hermann Göring Division had performed so badly on July 10, 1943, and during the counterattacks against the U.S. 1st Division on July 11 that its commander had threatened firing squads for cowardice. Thereafter, the division rapidly developed into a formidable foe and for most of the campaign battled the British and Canadians in the highlands of northeastern Sicily. The division was still commanded by Lieutenant General Paul Conrath, a tough, no-nonsense former state policeman who had joined the Luftwaffe in 1935 and quickly caught Hermann Göring's eye. A veteran of the French and Balkan campaigns, the Eastern Front, and, most recently, Sicily and Salerno, Conrath and his troops typified the Allied concept of Nazi fanaticism.[4]

Lucas was torn between the obvious need to capture Cisterna and Campoleone and his sense of caution. "I must keep in motion if my first success is to be of any value," he wrote on January 24. Unable to resolve the impossible conflict between caution and military necessity, Lucas would take no risks, yet he felt keenly the mounting pressure to seize the initiative, even if on a limited basis. On January 25 Lucas found Clark "greatly disturbed" by the failure of the Rapido crossings:

> That situation will not be relieved, I am afraid, until I can get my feet under me and make some further progress. I am doing my best but it seems terribly slow. After all, though this is the 25th and we landed on the 22d so I am not procrastinating. . . . This is the most important thing I have ever tried to do and I will not be stampeded.[5]

Lucas, however, was not prepared to assume the offensive until the arrival of Combat Command A (CCA) of Harmon's 1st Armored Division in several days, and Truscott's scheme was scrapped.[6] Lucas would have done well to have listened to Truscott, for despite the rapid German buildup there were still huge gaps in their defenses that could have been exploited. Campoleone was still lightly defended, and Penney had already turned loose the 24th Guards Brigade to capture Carroceto and the Factory. However, to avoid an awkward bulge in the front lines as well as capture an important objective, it was essential that the 3d

Division maintain the pressure to complement the British advance.

Here was an opportunity for Lucas to have taken the two most important objectives inside the Anzio beachhead at relatively little cost, without sacrificing the safety of his force. He would have none of it. "I must keep my feet on the ground and my forces in hand and do nothing foolish," he confided to his diary on January 25. With the arrival of the 1st Armored Division imminent and the Germans obviously unprepared to take countermeasures, it was to prove Lucas's best and, as it turned out, final opportunity to gain ground that the Allied force would later pay for at a terrible cost in blood. A calculated, controlled risk would have given Lucas the important anchor it was obvious he would soon need to defend against Kesselring's counteroffensive. For his part, Kesselring had already taken his opponent's measure and found him wanting. Though Albano was the key to a drive on Rome, "judging Lucas too cautious to aim for the moon, Kesselring concentrated his troop strength at Cisterna."[7]

According to his diary entries, within twenty-four hours of his cautionary warning to Lucas on January 22, Clark had changed his mind and begun to think offensively. Instead of a single reserve regiment from the 45th Division, he decided to send not only the remainder of the division to Anzio but the entire 1st Armored Division and Brigadier General Robert T. Frederick's First Special Service Force. Perhaps lulled into overconfidence as a result of the successful landings the day before, Clark began to act aggressively and, with his usual impatience, he began to prod Lucas, demanding answers to a myriad questions about the status of operations on the VI Corps front. To Lucas's dismay and annoyance, within days Clark would establish a forward Fifth Army command post in the Anzio beachhead. Lucas believed with considerable justification that its primary purpose was to keep tabs on his conduct of the battle.

Clark's diary reflected both his anxiety and the recognition that if the Anzio operation was to help break the deadlock at Cassino, Lucas must at least threaten to capture the Alban Hills: "Lucas must be aggressive. He must take some chances. He must use the 3d Division to push out."[8] Apparently convinced that his decision to reinforce the beachhead well beyond the scope of the original Shingle plan would solve the problem of security, and reassured by the smoothly running resupply operation between Naples and Anzio, Clark thought Lucas should start acting offensively about January 25. The steady flow of intelligence detailing the German reinforcement opposite the beachhead did nothing to change Clark's attitude. "I will then strike out and cut the German lines of communication, forcing his withdrawal out of the Cassino area. Then, I will turn my attention to Rome."[9]

Lucas continued to get mixed signals from his superiors. Clark had warned him about "sticking his neck out" but was now beginning to exhibit discontent, while Alexander, who again visited Anzio on January 25, conveyed continued optimism about the future prospects of VI Corps. "What a splendid piece of work," he told Lucas, who "reminded him that it wasn't over yet."[10] Alexander offered a far different version of the January 25 visit. In their postwar interview with him, the U.S. official historians' notes record that Alexander was "very much disappointed that Lucas had not pushed out to the Alban Hills and told him then that Cisterna should be taken. After this visit on 25 January, Alexander felt that Lucas was not measuring up and told Clark after this visit that this was his opinion."[11] He did not, however, tell Lucas.

Alexander's concern is verified by Clark, whose diary for January 26 noted the 15th Army Group commander's concern about "the slowness of the attack. . . . I am too, and have been for at least 48 hours. I know that he has received a personal telegram from the Prime Minister who, from his desk at #10 Downing Street, is going to direct the battles here in Italy. The Prime wants an attack, Rome and a victory, notwithstanding tactical or logistical reasons to the contrary."[12] However, Clark's assurance that he would ride close herd on Lucas temporarily assuaged Alexander's worries. That same day Clark fired off a cable to his VI Corps commander asking when he planned to take Cisterna.[13]

Two days later Alexander conveyed the first formal sign of his growing disenchantment with Lucas when he cabled Churchill that he was "not satisfied with the speed of our advance." For the first week of the campaign the prime minister believed that something dramatic was about to occur at Anzio. "The battle hasn't happened yet. But we are ahead of schedule in landing stuff and we ought to win when the battle comes. We have more men, more guns, more armour and complete air mastery. . . . Everyone [is] mad keen on this new operation." With the exception of air mastery, Churchill was dead wrong on all counts, and his high opinion of the German performance in Italy could have served as an ominous warning of what lay ahead at Anzio. "The Germans are fighting magnificently. Never imagine they are crashing. Their staff work is brilliantly flexible. They improvise units out of unrested remnants and those units fight just as well as the fresh ones. I don't know how the Russians have beaten the main German armies if they are all like the German army in Italy."[14]

Clark's references to Rome were wishful thinking, but Allied intelligence soon confirmed that there was a firm basis for his belief that boldness right then, even if limited to the capture of Campoleone and Cisterna, would pay dividends while the Germans were still content to remain on the defensive. An Ultra intercept of a January 24 message from Kesselring revealed future German intentions. Its essence was that the Fourteenth Army was to take charge of the battle and "throw the Allies back into the sea" while a new force, Army Group von Zangen, was to take over the defense of northern Italy, where a second invasion was still considered likely.[15] Although this intercept was not sent to Italy until early February, it did later confirm that Clark's thinking was correct.

Clark's prodding had little effect on Lucas, who continued to act ultraconservatively. Nothing in Lucas's diary or the records of VI Corps suggests he ever seriously considered that the extreme tactical urgency of enlarging the beachhead as far as Cisterna and Campoleone was worth the risk. Instead he continued to think in terms of the Alban Hills and seemed content to mark time. Clark's visit to Lucas on January 28 had no immediate impact despite the Fifth Army commander's admonition to act boldly and aggressively at once, before the German buildup could remove his initiative. Lucas seems to have confused Clark's intentions regarding Cisterna and Campoleone with the Alban Hills and continued with plans for an offensive to begin on the following day.

A major contributing factor to Lucas's conservatism was that he was not privy to Ultra. As reports of various German formations arriving at Anzio began to be received at VI Corps, Lucas and his staff derived a false impression of German strength defending the beachhead.

A postwar study of Ultra's impact reveals that VI Corps often over-estimated German troop strength.

> General Lucas' diary shows the entire 65th Division arriving on 28 January. In actuality, the 65th arrived in an assembly area less one regiment which never was sent from northern Italy. Ultra portrayed an accurate picture of the units, down to regimental and quite often battalion level. . . . But this information was not available to General Lucas. . . . As each new German division or unit was identified by prisoner of war reports, Y-service or other routine intelligence sources, VI Corps appears to have assumed that the entire German division was present or near by en route. General Clark and General Alexander, on the other hand, had a more realistic estimate of the opposition available through Ultra messages. They could not and did not communicate their knowledge to the corps commander. General Lucas consequently decided to "dig-in."[16]

Various claims have been made for Ultra's contributions, but what is often overlooked is that it was not a real-time source of intelligence. Most of the Ultra intelligence received by the 15th Army Group and the Fifth Army was well after the fact. Thus, Ultra's value was that it tended to confirm (or refute) conclusions already drawn by the G-2s and commanders who received it. An example was Kesselring's January 24 message, which was not forwarded to Italy until February 2.[17]

Time had, in fact, already all but run out on Lucas. The critical date seems to have been January 26, when Truscott proposed attacking Cisterna with the full weight of the 3d Division and the newly arrived 179th Regiment. With each passing day the German buildup continued at a relentless pace. Von Mackensen had arrived on the evening of January 25 to assume command of the Anzio front, and by January 29 German forces outnumbered the Allies by a ratio approaching two to one—71,500 to 41,000. The folly of inaction and its desperate price were soon to become part of the butcher's bill for Anzio.

We turn now to the first operations of the British on the left flank of the beachhead. Until January 24 their five-mile front was thinly held by the 2d Brigade, but with the release of the remainder of the division from corps reserve, Penney was able to begin an offensive aimed at the capture of Campoleone. Many of the British commanders were by now seething with frustration at their inaction. On their own initiative several battalion commanders had concocted their own plan for a tank-infantry attack.[18] Within the Irish Guards frustration grew into:

> a sickening feeling of anti-climax. Every man had been keyed up for a bold, impressive stroke, an enterprise that would probably be bloody, but would certainly be spectacular. The unexpected ease of the landing had raised hopes even higher. There were no Germans, what was stopping the Division? The men could not understand it, and the officers found it difficult to explain . . . the orthodox answers—the necessity of securing a firm base before advancing, the need for landing and accumulating supplies, the inadvisability of doing anything rash—all sounded very unconvincing. The 23rd was a completely wasted day.[19]

On January 24 the 24th Guards Brigade took over the division right flank and that night were given orders to spearhead a limited offensive to capture the Factory and advance toward Campoleone. At dawn on January 25 two troops of Shermans of the 46th Royal Tank Regiment and several self-propelled guns began moving up the Anzio-Albano highway, the Via Anziate, while along both sides of the road marched lines of 5th Battalion Grenadiers that stretched for nearly two miles. They were observed from nearby woods by the Irish and Scots Guards who were awaiting the signal to begin moving forward behind them. The historian of the Irish Guards describes the atmosphere that sunny but chilly morning as "unreal" and more like a training exercise than the start of a combat operation. Along the road small groups of Italian farmers and their families spiritedly waved handkerchiefs and clapped as the Guards marched toward Campoleone. As they passed under an overpass nicknamed the Flyover, three miles south of Carroceto, which was little more than a railroad station on the Rome-Anzio line, they were silently observed from above by "every red hat in the Division—the Divisional Commander, the C.R.A. and the three Brigadiers."[20] The Flyover offered the best vantage point in the entire British sector of the beachhead, but before the morning was over it became a prime target for the German artillery and from then on a deadly place to linger near.

The British expected little opposition at either Carroceto or the Factory, which intelligence reported was guarded by a small tank-infantry force of the 3d Panzer Grenadier Division. It was not until about mid-morning that the calm was broken when the first shots were fired from the direction of the Factory. Mines had been cleared from the area known as the Embankment, and as the Grenadiers resumed their march toward Carroceto, mortars, machine guns, and snipers opened up and within moments the situation was reported as "sticky." The first attempt by the Grenadiers to seize the Factory failed, and among the wounded was the battalion commander, who now carried out his duties from a stretcher.

After capturing Carroceto the Grenadiers launched a second attack in midafternoon that wiped out a company of the 3d Panzer Grenadiers that was defending the Factory. It also cost the Grenadiers the equivalent of a company, as the Germans had to be ferreted out of the maze of cellars and rubble. For the first of many occasions the Factory had changed ownership and claimed its first victims. The Irish Guards took over Carroceto, and the Scots Guards moved into positions farther to the rear as the brigade reserve. More than a hundred prisoners had been bagged. One was a young officer who pointed enviously to a nearby Sherman and announced, "if I had that, I would be in Rome by now."[21] That night, under the cover of the first of the heavy rains and hailstorms that were to pelt the beachhead and plague friend and foe alike, the Germans began infiltrating troops into positions close to the Factory.

Before the Guards could jump off the next morning toward Campoleone to complete the second phase of their mission, the enemy struck back. The Germans had assessed the crucial tactical importance of the Factory and were determined to get it back. At dawn they attacked from the north and the east from the protection of one of the many dry creek beds *(fossos)* that dotted the landscape. Supported by self-propelled guns and a company of Tiger tanks, the German infantry threatened several times to overrun the Factory, only to be thrown back by the Grenadiers, who fought doggedly while suffering heavy losses, including nearly an entire platoon of No. 3 Company. Their situation was made even more critical because the Grenadiers had no support on their right flank. The boundary line between 1st and 3d Divisions was near Padiglione, about four miles east of the Via Anziate.

To plug the gap VI Corps sent the three battalions of Darby's Rangers (1st, 3d, and 4th Ranger Battalions) and Yarborough's 509th Parachute Infantry Battalion to plug the gap and advance north in conjunction with the attack of the 24th Guards Brigade. However, on January 25 the 4th Rangers advanced only as far as an offshoot of the western fork of the Mussolini Canal, near the Embankment and more than one mile southeast of the Factory.

At this early stage of the campaign the Germans were not prepared to take advantage of this gap, but it did give them the opportunity to maneuver freely to the east and southeast during their attempts to retake the Factory on January 26. The Rangers ran into heavy fire and spent most of January 26 consolidating their positions. The following morning the Rangers and paratroopers had a new mission—to capture the road junction approximately a mile east of the Factory. There was bitter fighting as the Rangers had to overcome a German strongpoint in a nearby farm astride the road junction. Fighting was hand to hand in places, and as the Grenadiers had already discovered at the Factory, it was often necessary to fight room to room to clear out the German defenders. The Ranger and paratroop force now occupied positions from the road junction to the banks of Spaccasassi Creek. The British and American sectors were at last tied together.[22]

While the Grenadiers were fighting for their lives to hold the Factory, precisely at 0800 hours all hell broke loose across the entire British front line as the Germans opened up with the massed firepower of their growing arsenal of large-caliber guns situated in the Alban Hills. Their targets were the Factory and the Embankment, where the Bowling Alley passed over the Via Anziate on the southern edge of Carroceto. Soon there were cries of what were to become the most used and dreaded words heard at Anzio: "Stretcher-bearer!" and "Medic!" On the reverse slope of the Embankment the Irish Guards began digging in "like a colony of dispossessed moles . . . with an amazing collection of Italian farm implements."[23]

In their haste to contain Lucas the Germans had amassed a collection of heavy guns, old and modern, from every imaginable source including French, Italian, Yugoslav, Russian, and Czech as well as German. The result was that "the heavens opened [and] the air was full of iron dug from every mine in Europe; the fragments were marked in every known language west of the Urals."[24]

A series of German tank-infantry counterattacks, during which both sides paid a fearful price, was beaten off on January 26. Ambulances and corpsmen lost the battle to keep pace with the steady stream of wounded, who soon overtaxed the front-line medical aid stations. These attacks continued throughout the day as the German artillery pounded British positions and the Luftwaffe bombed the Factory. The

Irish Guards suffered more than ninety casualties, and large numbers of vehicles and equipment were destroyed by German artillery and antitank fire. At Anzio survival depended upon how well and how quickly soldiers adapted to the peculiar battlefield conditions. The first of the rules for survival was that tanks attracted artillery and antitank fire like angry bees attacking an intruder. On January 26 alone, nine Shermans were knocked out in the Carroceto sector. Along the Moletta River the 1st Battalion, the Loyal Regiment,* also came under heavy shellfire but was aided by the naval gunfire support of the destroyer HMS *Loyal* in the first of what would be many direct support roles in the days ahead.[25]

From between two farms, one of which had been given the nickname Dung Farm by the British (and Smelly Farm by the Germans) in recognition of the unpleasant odors of dead livestock and rotting manure emanating from it, a small valley led south to Carroceto.[26] From the Factory a series of secondary roads and tracks merged into a single road that joined the Via Anziate approximately one thousand yards to the north. Here, the road bent to the left toward Campoleone, while to the right a track led to Dung Farm. To the west across the railway line was Vallelata Farm and behind it a slope of high ground called Vallelata Ridge. The Germans had massed their defenses in this sector to protect Campoleone, and it was here that the counterattack force massed for a thrust toward Carroceto and the Factory. From the vicinity of Vallelata Farm, German tanks began firing on the Irish Guards. The main object of their attention was a small farm near the Embankment that anchored the left flank of the Irish Guards' defense. Called Preston's Farm, for the platoon leader of No. 3 Company, it became the scene of savage combat on January 26. German tanks and British antitank guns destroyed one another at close range as the farm became a shambles of burning and broken tanks, guns, smoke, and fire from which could be heard the cries of the wounded. The German commander then launched a battalion-size infantry attack down the Anzio railway line toward Carroceto, which was smashed by a heavy barrage of three-inch mortar fire.

By midday the Germans had managed to move tanks up to Preston's Farm, where they posed a serious menace to the Irish Guards until the British gunners demonstrated that their ability to hit targets was as good as the Germans'. Supporting the Irish Guards was a battery of the 80th Medium Regiment, RA (the Scottish Horse), whose commander, Major Campbell-Preston, fondly referred to as "Little Robin Redbreast," had been battling the chain of command for more than an hour

---

*Originally called the Loyal North Lancashire Regiment, this unit was redesignated the Loyal Regiment (North Lancashire) in 1921.

to obtain permission to fire his guns. After considerable dithering in the rear permission to fire came, but with the admonition to be "very economical." It is impossible to escape the tentacles of bureaucracy even in the heat of battle, and Anzio was no exception. Fortunately, practical men find ways to evade the red tape of officialdom, and Major Campbell-Preston told the CO of the Irish Guards that "if you want it, I'll shoot every shell in the beach-head." On this day it proved unnecessary, as several well-aimed salvos scored a direct hit on a German tank and drove off the remainder that had been making life hell for the Irish Guards.[27]

Most of the fighting that day centered on the Factory and Preston's Farm. Seventeen of Preston's troops were captured by a German force, led by a Tiger, which, in turn, was supported by twelve more tanks in a hull-down position a short distance away. Throughout the day the Guards fought off numerous German forays against Carroceto and the Factory. When it ended and both sides began to count the cost, any illusions either had entertained about what Anzio would be like had been well and truly dispelled. The Irish Guards lost twenty killed and ninety-nine more wounded; losses to the Grenadiers were also heavy in their defense of the Factory. So savage had been the shelling that every Irish Guardsman was dug in below ground level. The battalion chaplain, Father Brookes, called it the worst day he had ever spent in the two world wars. The barrages and bombardments of tank and artillery fire were the equal of those at Flanders and the most severe endured by British troops so far in the war.[28]

Among the most hard-pressed soldiers that day were the medics and ambulance drivers. The front-line aid stations could not even begin to handle the ever-increasing numbers of wounded and dying men and field ambulances shuttled the overflow to a casualty clearing station near Anzio that itself quickly became overtaxed. This description by the Irish Guards historian conveys a chilling description of the sudden hell of Anzio:

> The silent courage of maimed, battered, bleeding Irish Guardsmen lying in the open or, if they were lucky, in some muddy ditch, was a living monument to the strength of the human will in the depths of human misery. A man drained of blood gets very cold; there is not much a man with a shattered thigh can do for himself; a man whose chest has been torn to ribbons by shell-splinters would like to be moved out of the barrage. But they did not say anything, they didn't ask for anything; they smiled painfully when the orderlies put a blanket over them or gave them a drink of water and a cigarette.[29]

The preponderance of casualties at Anzio were from artillery and mortar fire and it was only much later when VI Corps captured the Alban

Hills that they could appreciate just how easily and effectively the German gunners had been able to spot targets and lay fires at virtually any spot in the narrow beachhead. "Officers who climbed Monte Caro afterwards realized that there was, in fact, no single place in which a man could move without being seen. The Germans knew where the Battalion was to a square foot."[30] On a clear day German artillery observers could with virtual impunity and "a cup of coffee in one hand and a telephone in the other . . . direct their guns as if they were playing on a sand-model." One NCO of the 1st Armored Division may have said it best when he told Harmon, "General, with them Krauts lookin' down from the mountains, I feel just like bacteria in a bottle."[31]

Unlike Salerno and, later, Normandy, where the Allied fleet made any attempt to reinforce the front a deadly ordeal, the combination of naval gunfire and air strikes was incapable of stopping the Germans. Initially the need for such support was negligible, but by the time it was urgently needed the targets were beyond the range of all vessels but a heavy cruiser and none was available to assist Lucas. Moreover, a new threat soon emerged in the form of deadly radio-controlled glide bombs, which forced Admiral Lowry to retire his support ships at 1600 hours each afternoon.

After the savage battles of January 26 neither side was prepared to resume the attack. However, by the early hours of January 27 the Scots Guards had moved forward and now controlled Dung Farm as the first step in a limited offensive to capture Campoleone. The plan was for the Scots Guards and the Grenadiers to advance some two thousand yards beyond Dung Farm the following afternoon (January 28) and secure a lateral road halfway between the Factory and Campoleone as the jumping-off point for the uncommitted 3d Brigade, which was to move forward and complete the drive on Campoleone the following day. However, a serious setback occurred in the early afternoon of January 28 when the Grenadier company commanders who were moving forward to Dung Farm where the two battalions were to hold a joint briefing somehow missed the turnoff and continued north on the Via Anziate toward Campoleone. After three-quarters of a mile they ran into a German outpost and were ambushed by antitank guns and a hail of automatic weapons fire that killed three officers and wounded a fourth, who was captured. The regimental history called this "the greatest single disaster to befall the Grenadiers during the Anzio campaign."[32]

In little more than twenty-four hours the Grenadiers had lost nine of their thirteen company officers and with the four surviving officers still in the Factory it was now far too late in the day to organize and initiate the attack during daylight. Penney was compelled to reschedule the attack for the night of January 29–30 and replace the battered

Grenadiers with the 2d Battalion of the Sherwood Foresters who moved into the Factory the night of January 28.[33]

The capture of Campoleone was a vital feature of the forthcoming VI Corps offensive that Lucas intended to launch on January 30. In addition to fulfilling the wishes of both Clark and Alexander to expand the beachhead, there was now a second purpose, to complement a Fifth Army offensive that Clark intended to launch against Cassino on February 1.

The British were to seize Campoleone as the staging area for Harmon's newly arrived 1st Armored, which was to thrust toward Adrano and then turn and seize the Alban Hills from the west. The move on Campoleone was to be complemented by a fresh attack by the 3d Division to capture Cisterna and cut Highway 7. With Campoleone and Cisterna in Allied hands, Lucas would have severed an important part of the German resupply link to the Gustav Line. In theory, the capture of Cisterna and Campoleone was for the purpose of enabling VI Corps to continue on the offensive toward the elusive Alban Hills, which he intended to seize by means of a double envelopment.

The instrument of Lucas's offensive punch was the U.S. 1st Armored Division, one of the first formations to fight the Germans in North Africa and the victim of the first shocking American setback of the war at Kasserine Pass in February 1943. The arrival of the 1st Armored Division brought to Anzio one of the genuinely outstanding and colorful armored commanders produced by the U.S. Army in World War II: Major General Ernest Nason Harmon. Cut from the same cloth as Patton, and, like Patton, occasionally prone to putting his foot in his mouth, the outspoken Harmon became one of the U.S. Army's most audacious, fearless, and respected armored division commanders. By the end of the war in May 1945 Harmon had more command time as an armored division commander in combat than any other officer. Better known as "Old Gravel Voice" and built not unlike the turret of one of his tanks, the barrel-chested Harmon was a painfully blunt, profane, no-nonsense leader whose most outstanding trait was decisiveness.

Bradley later wrote that he possessed "the rare combination of sound tactical judgment and boldness that together make a great commander. More than any other division commander in North Africa, he was constantly and brilliantly aggressive; in Europe he was to become our most outstanding tank commander."[34] An incident during the later stages of the Tunisian campaign illustrates something of the flavor of his character. He told Bradley how he found himself and his tanks on an exposed hill during the Battle of Mateur, when German aircraft began a bombardment. There was no protection, no slit trenches, no shell holes to hide in. "There was only one thing I could do, Bradley, that was to pray. Goddammit, how I prayed!!"[35]

Orphaned at the age of ten, Harmon was a product of the hard-scrabble environment of rural New England at the turn of the century where hard work was the norm and few escaped poverty. Where others merely dreamed, Harmon succeeded in obtaining not only an education but an appointment to West Point, graduating in 1917. Within months he was serving with a horse cavalry unit on the battlefields of France, where, like so many officers who rose to high command in World War II, his experiences imbued him with an abhorrence for the needless loss of life that symbolized the war of the trenches. Later convinced that the era of horse cavalry was a relic of the past, Harmon was one of the first to embrace the concept of the new armored force whose future in the formative years of the late 1930s was anything but secure. By 1942 he was a major general in command of the 2d Armored Division when it landed in Morocco as part of Patton's Western Task Force during Operation Torch.

When it became evident that Fredendall had lost control of II Corps it was Harmon whom Eisenhower summoned from Morocco and ordered to the front to help reverse the situation by any means necessary. While Fredendall cowered in a massive concrete bunker sixty-five miles behind the front lines, Harmon took charge of the battle and was instrumental in restoring order to a chaotic and highly dangerous situation. Indeed, one of his first acts, when he countermanded an order from General Anderson, might have earned him a court-martial for insubordination. This occurred when Harmon visited a ragtag collection of Anglo-American units called Nickforce, which had already given some of Rommel's best a bloody nose and seemed capable of stemming a German thrust by the 10th Panzer Division that threatened to rupture the Allied line at Thala. There was no time for the niceties of a request to Anderson to cancel his order, which—given his distrust of his American ally—Anderson would certainly have disapproved. Harmon cancelled Anderson's order to the U.S. 9th Infantry Division artillery (three battalions) to withdraw to the rear. The unit was ordered to remain in support of Nickforce.

Harmon's rationale was typical: "I figured that if I won the battle I would be forgiven. If I lost, the hell with it anyway."[36] In his report to Eisenhower he bluntly referred to Fredendall as "a son-of-a-bitch" who was unfit to hold command. When Eisenhower offered Harmon the command of II Corps he refused, saying he could not accept the job after recommending the relief of its commander. Instead he returned to the 2d Armored Division. When Patton assumed command of II Corps Harmon was again summoned from Morocco, this time to assume command of the faltering 1st Armored Division.

Harmon's arrival triggered an unusual incident. He summoned the officers and senior NCOs of the division in groups to hear harsh words about their performance during the recent battles. In his usual candid language he told his officers that the casualties at Kasserine and Sidi Bou Zid had died unnecessarily. Some of those who did not, he remarked, were yellowbellies who were afraid to die. Harmon's aim was to shake up a division that was feeling sorry for itself, but his tactics backfired when someone in the back began to boo. Soon the booing spread like wildfire and quickly rose to such a crescendo of disapproval that Harmon was forced from the podium and into a humiliating retreat from his own officers and NCOs.[37]

A lesser officer might well have broken, but not Harmon—who refused to be cowed even by the boos of his own troops. (The men of the 1st Armored were angry that their popular commander, Major General Orlando Ward, had been relieved by Patton and replaced by this SOB who had the temerity to call them cowards.) It was the last time anyone ever booed Ernie Harmon.

He quickly began to restore confidence at every level of the division. One of his first acts was to sack Alexander's hand-picked British liaison officer at his first staff meeting.[38] By the time the Tunisian campaign ended Harmon had restored credibility to the 1st Armored, whose anger at their commander began to ebb when they began to win battles. He spent most of his time at the front, where he bullied, cajoled, lectured, and always led by example. (During the final decisive battle in Tunisia he came upon a group of tanks by the side of the road, pinned down by heavy German machine-gun and antitank fire. When the commander reported his dilemma, Harmon simply said, "All right, you follow my jeep forward." Seeing the division commander deliberately exposing himself to German fire, the embarrassed officer stirred his tanks into action.[39])

Harmon never denigrated the performance of his predecessor, but "he made it exquisitely plain that he was going to require of the division a much higher level of performance than it had thus far demonstrated. . . . I can tell you that quite a number of the officers of the division resented it and felt the division had not . . . didn't deserve the strong words that it received. But . . . the division started doing a good deal better right then."[40]

Harmon was one of the most aggressive commanders ever to command an armored unit in battle. One of his former officers has said of him:

The one quality that made him an outstanding soldier was an almost rabid love of battle. When his division was in action he was a picture of bounding energy. He delighted in throwing every bit of the great weight of the armored division into the fray. He once boasted to me that every gun in the division was firing. . . . I never knew a man so anxious to get in and get his feet wet.[41]

In the Vietnam War, GIs would coin the phrase "the meanest son-of-a-bitch in the valley." In the 1st Armored Division in World War II there was never any doubt about who merited that designation.

When he first arrived at Anzio the British commanders viewed Harmon with suspicion. Like Patton, he liked to wear two ivory-handled revolvers, only in shoulder holsters. Suspecting an imitation Patton, their first reaction was to question Harmon's gruff, profane image. Their impressions were not enhanced when at a commanders' conference on January 27 Lucas said to him, "Ernie, I reckon you got to go places," whereupon Harmon stood up, said, "Jesus, I'll go places," and abruptly left the meeting.[42] Those who saw Harmon in action soon realized that, as with Patton, his external posing masked a superb military leader.

Harmon's aggressive qualities were to be sorely needed at Anzio. When he first reported to the VI Corps command post in Nettuno, the sound of guns could be clearly heard in the distance. Harmon found his corps commander in an office adorned with maps, his trademark corncob pipe in his mouth. A somber Lucas laid down his pipe, arose, and, shaking hands with Harmon, said simply, "Glad to see you. You're needed here."[43] In the coming days Harmon's "Old Ironsides" would earn the well-deserved new nickname, Anzio Fire Brigade.

The first of Harmon's Shermans made its appearance at Carroceto on the afternoon of January 29, when a reconnaissance element of Combat Command A rumbled up the Via Anziate to the Flyover and then headed west for a mile before turning north along a track leading toward Buonriposo Ridge. Approximately two miles west of Carroceto, the ridge, which ran northeast from the Moletta River toward the Embankment, commanded the surrounding terrain. Before long they were rudely initiated into the pitfalls of Anzio, when a tank and half-track became mired in the mud of a field that had looked deceivingly able to support the weight of armored vehicles. Moments later a German observer called down a heavy volume of 88-mm fire that killed nine men.[44]

Harmon's intention was to employ Combat Command A in a flank attack to envelop Campoleone from the west, using the Embankment as a line of departure for the attack, which was to thrust up a secondary road leading from Ardea to Campoleone Station. As the American armor moved into position during the night, the Irish and Scots Guards completed preparations for the delayed thrust to the lateral road halfway between Dung Farm and Campoleone that the 3d Brigade was to use as its starting line.

One of the major problems confronting VI Corps during the early days of the campaign was insufficient battlefield intelligence about the German units opposing them. There were not, for example, supposed to have been any German paratroop units defending the beachhead, and even when the Irish Guards produced a POW the paper pushers in the rear balked at the evidence, which contradicted their premise.[45]

Reports from their front had convinced Brigadier A. S. P. Murray, the 24th Guards Brigade commander, that they were facing considerably tougher opposition than the intelligence officers were willing to concede, including what were believed to be at least three companies of parachute troops. As evidence Brigadier Murray paraded the German paratrooper before Penney, who had already made up his mind that the German "is not a parachutist; he may have been once, but now is just one of a scratch lot of troops that the Germans scraped up wherever they could."[46] Penney's intransigent attitude suggested he had fallen victim to the misconceptions of the corps and division intelligence officers.

Despite the evidence of three days' fighting at Carroceto and the Factory, the official view remained that the composition of the German formations defending the Campoleone salient were spread thin and that Campoleone itself was ripe for the taking. This delusion applied to the attack on January 29, which was to be supported by a creeping barrage that would drive off any German force resisting the advance of the Irish and Scots Guards.

> The H.Q. staff persisted in their belief that the ground was only lightly held and that there would be no serious opposition after this barrage had rolled over the Germans. At half-past ten the following morning, according to the corps plan, the 3d Brigade would capture Campoleone and then the [U.S.] armour would "pass through" to cut Routes 6 and 7 and end a crowded day by going to the top of the Colli Laziali.[47]

The attack commenced at 2300 hours the night of January 28, with the Irish Guards advancing to the left of the railway and the Scots Guards to the right. After a punishing barrage the entire salient was ominously quiet, and not even a single shot was fired until the Guards were halfway to their objective. Suddenly the sky was lit by Very lights and flares that enabled German automatic weapons, artillery, and mortar fire to engulf the surprised Guardsmen. Earlier that day a British officer from the 2d Brigade carrying a copy of the 1st Division plan for the night attack had wandered into German lines and been captured. The Germans not only knew where their enemy was but had laid an elaborate ambush and were difficult to detect in the dark.

Hardest hit were the Irish Guards, whose predicament along the railway line soon worsened with the arrival of several panzers. The night came alive with tracer fire, burning buildings, and the explosions of four trucks towing antitank guns and carrying ammunition forward to the Scots. The blackened corpses of the drivers were later found in the charred remains of their vehicles. In the olive groves that dotted the ridge running northwest from Dung Farm toward Campoleone, the Scots were held up by German machine gunners who threatened to annihilate the confused attackers. One company retreated in disarray until it ran into the battalion commander, Lieutenant Colonel David Wedderburn. After a stormy confrontation the young Scots quickly decided their better choice was to regroup and fight the Germans. They were only too glad to be led forward by the resolute Wedderburn, whose firm leadership prevented a panic that might easily have spread to nearby units.

The battle raged throughout the night as the embattled Guardsmen fought off attacks from the rear, where some Germans had cleverly let them pass before attacking. German artillery and mortar fire pulverized Dung Farm, which still served as the Irish Guards' command post. In the darkness the battle became a series of small unit actions, in which German and British soldiers fought each other at close quarters. Despite the confusion and stiff German resistance, two companies of Irish Guards managed to advance to the Brigade objective, the east-west lateral road that crossed the Via Anziate before passing under the railway line. However, as dawn neared it was clear that without assistance from friendly armor the infantry faced certain annihilation at first light. Both Wedderburn and Lieutenant Colonel C. A. Montagu-Douglas-Scott, the Irish Guards commander, pleaded with Brigade and Division for tank support. Very little was forthcoming, and the five remaining Shermans of the 46th Royal Tanks were sent to support the battered Scots, who had lost an entire company to a German tank-infantry assault near Dung Farm.

The two beleaguered companies at the lateral road had been promised tank support, but a dismayed Colonel Scott was told there simply was no more to be had. Two Tigers were attempting—so far without success—to eradicate the Irish Guards, who were machine-gunned as they attempted to dig protective foxholes. In the dark the two sides were at an impasse, but when dawn came the Guards would be forced to face the Tigers with only their small arms, grenades, and bare hands. To make matters worse the only radio link to the Battalion command post at Dung Farm went silent at a critical moment. Under heavy fire, the radio operator, Lance Corporal G. Holwell, calmly went about repairing his radio by moonlight and the aid of a small pencil light. At 0615 hours Holwell came back on the air—to the intense relief of Colonel Scott, who ordered the two companies to get out at once while there was still time. During the withdrawal under the cover of a less-than-effective smoke screen, the survivors suffered heavy losses. Among those killed during the withdrawal was the valiant Corporal Holwell, who was credited with saving the force.[48] Under the care of a medic the wounded were trapped for another eighteen hours in the shelter of the railway bridge before being rescued.

The only success came on the left flank, where No. 3 Company of the Irish Guards, supported by a platoon of tank destroyers of the U.S. 894th Tank Destroyer Battalion, was operating along Vallelata Ridge. During the morning of January 30 this small force captured fifty-five prisoners and literally removed any German obstacle in its path. One German position in a farmhouse was taken out by the simple expedient of demolishing it with a tank destroyer, which "went through the house like a dose of salts, driving 'Krauts' out in all directions."[49] There were no further threats from the left flank. During the chaotic night the Guards had no way of knowing that their attack had driven a wedge some two miles wide between the 3d Panzer Grenadier Division and the 65th Infantry Division, which was defending the Vallelata Ridge sector. Less than a platoon of Germans, two antitank guns, and a tank destroyer were all that stood between the Guards and Campoleone.[50]

The heated night battle had dealt the Guards other severe losses, the worst of which were to the Scots, who suffered the most crippling casualties of any of their battalions during the war: forty-five killed and several times that number wounded.[51] The light of day revealed the full extent of the previous night's carnage: broken and burning vehicles and the rubble of destroyed farmhouses. Worst hit was Dung Farm, which had received the brunt of German attention. The large farm was a shambles, its buildings reduced to rubble and the bodies of dead animals and unburied soldiers everywhere. Spandau machine guns continued to make life very uncomfortable outside the farm even as the Irish Guards began reforming within its confines. In the flower garden one platoon used fresh-dug graves (meant for the Scots) as foxholes.

As the British regrouped to renew their attack on Campoleone the following day, similar plans were being finalized in the U.S. sector for an attack on Cisterna, to be spearheaded by Darby's Rangers. During the next forty-eight hours heartbreaking setbacks would occur in both sectors of the Allied front.

10

Calamity at Cisterna and Campoleone

Of the 767 Rangers who had started toward Cisterna, only 6 returned; the rest were either dead or captured.

—OFFICIAL HISTORY[1]

I had never seen so many dead men in one place.

—MAJOR GENERAL ERNEST N. HARMON

As Lucas finalized his plan for the VI Corps offensive at the end of January, he was unaware that von Mackensen had massed thirty-six battalions of infantry in the Campoleone-Cisterna salient, supported by large numbers of tanks and artillery. Both Cisterna and Campoleone were obvious Allied objectives that the astute Kesselring intended to defend to the fullest. Kesselring would later remark: "The Allies had no liking for risks; that was very clear to me." His orders to von Mackensen were equally clear: Strengthen the defensive cordon around the Anzio beachhead and then eliminate it.[2]

Unknown to the corps and division intelligence officers was the fact that the Germans had brought up large numbers of reinforcements the night before the VI Corps offensive was scheduled to commence. Now filling the previous void around Cisterna were not only the battle-tested units of the Hermann Göring and 4th Parachute divisions but also substantial elements of a fresh unit, the 26th Panzer Division, that Kesselring had withdrawn from the Tenth Army front and sped to Anzio.

Had Lucas attacked a day earlier, on January 29, as originally intended, the VI Corps offensive might have turned out far different. However, Lucas elected to postpone the operation for twenty-four hours to provide time for the British 1st Division and Harmon's newly arrived Combat Command A to complete preparations for their attack. The plan called for the British to seize Campoleone, whereupon Harmon's armor would spearhead an attack on the Alban Hills from the direction of Albano. What seemed a simple one-day delay was to prove disastrous.

The main attack was to occur on the left flank, with the 1st Division followed by the massed armor of the 1st Armored Division. Truscott's role on the right flank was secondary: Capture Cisterna, cut Highway 7, be prepared to continue on to Velletri, and, if all went according to plan, interdict Highway 6 at Valmontone. Truscott had at his disposal the 3d Division, Darby's three-battalion Ranger force, and Tucker's 504th Parachute Infantry Regiment. He was well aware of how thin the Hermann Göring—attempting to defend the entire Cisterna sector by means of strongpoints and mobile reserves—was spread. His plan was for a three-pronged attack to take full advantage of the German defensive liabilities.

He and Darby believed that two Ranger battalions could successfully infiltrate at night between the German strongpoints and literally sneak into Cisterna, where they would capture and hold the town while wreaking havoc behind the German lines, easing the way for the main attack an hour later by the 15th Infantry Regiment, supported by Darby's other Ranger battalion. To aid these attacks Truscott ordered Tucker's paratroopers to carry out a diversion along the eastern fork of the Mussolini Canal by attacking the German left flank. On the left flank the 7th Infantry Regiment was to attack west of Cisterna, cut Highway 7 to the north, and continue on to seize Cori, a small ancient Roman town nestled in the Alban Hills five miles northeast of Cisterna. The entire operation was to be supported by tanks, tank destroyers, and the 3d Division artillery, which was to be massed to provide rapid direct support wherever needed.[3] To protect the right flank a portion of the 179th Regimental Combat Team was to take over the positions occupied by the 504th Parachute Infantry along the Mussolini Canal.

The Rangers were withdrawn from the British sector during the night of January 28–29 and shifted to assembly points near the Mussolini Canal to prepare for their new mission. Darby and his three battalion commanders met to review the plan for Cisterna. Worked out between Darby and Truscott, the general outlines called for the 1st and 3d battalions to lead the attack on Cisterna while the 4th Battalion cleared the road leading from Isola Bella to Cisterna for the 15th Infantry Regiment and its supporting tanks, which were to spearhead the main attack and relieve the Ranger force before the Germans could react to overwhelm it.

The 767 men of the 1st and 3d battalions were to advance to Cisterna under the cover of darkness by infiltrating along the Pantano Ditch, which ran between two strongpoints manned by the Hermann Göring Division. The Fosso di Pantano was a partially dry extension of the Mussolini Canal that provided cover for the Rangers to get within approximately one and one-half miles of Cisterna without being detected. The remainder of the Ranger foray would be across mostly open terrain to the outskirts of the town. Both Truscott and Darby believed that the Ranger force could create sufficient confusion and panic to ease the main attack by the 15th Infantry and the 4th Ranger Battalion along the Isola Bella–Cisterna road. Once clear of the Pantano Ditch, the Rangers would infiltrate Cisterna before dawn, led by the 1st Battalion. If trouble arose, the 3d Battalion was to cover the 1st Battalion, whose orders were to avoid combat at all costs until it reached Cisterna. Once inside Cisterna the 1st Battalion was to clear the town, assisted by the 3d Battalion if needed. Otherwise the 3d Battalion was to occupy terrain northeast of Cisterna to block and repel any attempted enemy counterattack.

There were mixed opinions about the operation. A 3d Division reconnaissance report indicated that the road to Cisterna was only lightly held by outposts of the Hermann Göring Division, and Darby himself considered his mission an acceptable risk.[4] Truscott's G-2 was "optimistic and suggested that Ranger Force would accomplish its mission without undue difficulty."[5] Major Jack Dobson, the commander of the 1st Battalion, which was to lead the attack on Cisterna, remembered that there were no accurate maps of the route of advance and no aerial photographs: "G-2, as I was told, felt that there was little enemy out there because our air had received little or no flack from the area."[6] However, at Ranger headquarters there seemed to have been less optimism when the keeper of the daily journal entered a comment that the German defense of Cisterna might be "considerable."[7]

There was no time for more than brief observations of the terrain by company commanders, and these revealed no unusual German activity. To have attempted a more detailed reconnaissance behind enemy lines would have compromised the operation. Instead the Rangers were obliged to rely on intelligence that indicated that the German defenses were still spread thin and in places manned by mixed forces of Germans, conscripted Poles, and other non-Germanic soldiers who had been integrated into Wehrmacht units as a means of compensating for Germany's growing manpower shortages. Dobson was not particularly happy with the mission and expressed doubts concerning the attack, but as Darby told him: " 'We've been ordered.' Off we went with no doubts about our ability to get to the objective if other attacking elements of the attacking force accomplished their assigned missions. . . . Brigadier General John ('Iron Mike') O'Daniel was at our Line of Departure as we crossed that night and his last words to me were not to worry, that the 3d [Div] would be there on their objective."[8]

With Darby controlling the operation from an isolated farmhouse off the Isola Bella–Cisterna road, the 1st and 3d battalions entered the Pantano Ditch at 0100 hours the morning of January 30 in single file and quickly disappeared into the darkness. Once behind German lines there could be no resupply, and the Rangers had shed all but essential gear and were laden with extra ammunition and grenades. Exactly one hour later the 4th Battalion began moving along ditches on both sides of the road toward Isola Bella. There was an ominous silence across the battlefield as the Ranger force passed the point of no return.

From the outset, signs did not augur well for the operation. The first occurred when several radio operators attached to the 3d Battalion broke radio silence to inform Darby that they were "lost." A seriously worried Ranger commander was heard to grumble that it was "the goddamndest thing he ever heard of." Not long afterward the 1st and 3d battalions lost contact with each other, and as a result the 1st Battalion commander decided to split his force by sending three companies ahead while the other three remained in place in an attempt to reestablish contact with the 3d Battalion.[9] There was far worse to come. A 1st Battalion runner brought the disturbing news back to the battalion rear element that the 3d Battalion had encountered a German tank that spotted the Ranger force in the drainage ditch and killed the battalion commander, Major Alvah M. Miller. Even though the Germans now clearly knew of the presence of an enemy force behind their lines there seemed to be no indication that a general alarm had been raised and the Rangers thus believed the intent of their operation had not been compromised.[10]

Soon after crossing the line of departure,[11] the 4th Battalion ran into heavy German resistance where none had been expected. The Rangers had advanced barely half a mile when the night was turned into a similar version of what had befallen the Irish and Scots Guards the previous night:

Out of the black night, coming from far out into the fields on both sides of the road, machine-gun tracers suddenly magnified into a solid wall of flaming steel. Swiftly the leading company attacked at close quarters with grenades and bayonets. Two machine-gun nests were wiped out, but others seemed to rise out of the ground to take their places. After two ferocious assaults failed to penetrate the solid line, the company with many killed and wounded, including the commander, was forced to hold up in a shallow ditch. Every inch of ground seemed covered by deadly grazing fire . . . throughout the night the battle raged with growing intensity. Suspecting that Allied tanks would follow on the road, the Germans began registering on the road with artillery, plastering the area as far back as the canal.[12]

The advance of the two assault battalions continued into the night, but another major problem soon became evident. The presence of German positions and patrols close to the ditch forced innumerable delays. Twice sentries found guarding the ditch were surprised and silently killed with knives. Several Germans joined the Rangers in the mistaken belief that they were a friendly force. They, too, were quickly and silently dispatched.[13] Dobson remembers one incident in which a German sentry stood over him as he crouched in the ditch and asked for his identification. His executive officer's bodyguard immediately killed the soldier with his knife.[14] Numerous lucrative German targets in the form of strongpoints and artillery positions had to be bypassed quietly. The knowledge that an American force of unknown size was behind their lines as a spearhead for an impending major attack against Cisterna resulted in the constant firing of flares across the front to illuminate the night. Each time a flare appeared, the Rangers were forced to lie low to avoid detection.

The success of Darby's plan hinged on advancing to Cisterna while it was still dark. At about 0400 hours the point company of the 1st Battalion arrived at a road running perpendicular from Isola Bella to Highway 7. What Major Dobson observed was clearly not what he had been briefed to expect:

> To our right about 200 yards away were at least two batteries of German self-propelled artillery firing away merrily. Traffic was moving in both directions along the road, all German except for one U.S. jeep containing the CO of the 3d Division Provisional Reconnaissance Squadron who was captured forthwith. . . . We moved the point company across the road by infiltration between German vehicles and at this point I decided we must be running into at least one division and perhaps more, so I set up my radio and broke radio silence in order to contact Darby and recommend that we turn here with both battalions, eliminate the artillery and sweep everything else before us, keeping the Mussolini Canal on our right flank. . . . Unfortunately, after ten minutes of trying we could not raise Darby's HQ, so we had no alternative but to proceed to the objective, which we did.[15]

The outcome of what transpired later that morning might have been dramatically altered, but not for the first time in this war a radio malfunctioned at a critical moment. Dobson faced a difficult choice: alter the mission and risk early detection, which might fatally compromise the Ranger mission, or continue in the hope that they could infiltrate into Cisterna before being detected. With first light imminent, to have unilaterally changed the mission and alerted and briefed the 1st Battalion would have consumed precious time. Still unable to raise Ranger HQ, Dobson elected to carry on. In retrospect he had no other choice.

The Pantano Ditch provided cover, but it ended approximately one and one-half miles below Cisterna. The remainder of the Ranger foray was the most dangerous part of their mission as they moved across exposed, open fields. First light found the Rangers still some eight hundred yards south of the town, when deadly trouble began.

The Rangers were detected as they attempted to bypass a German bivouac area, and a violent battle began. It was close combat and nearly a hundred Germans were killed by knives and bayonets. Within minutes German troops began firing from every farmhouse; from the town itself; and from haystacks, ditches, and foxholes. Instead of the expected gap in front of Cisterna the entire sector was infested with German troops, all of whom seemed intent on making it their business to annihilate the Ranger force who had literally stumbled into a deadly ambush. An attempt was made by the advance element of the 1st Battalion to storm Cisterna, but they were unable even to gain the temporary safety of some high ground outside town and were forced to fight from a ditch and a nearby road, neither of which offered much protection.

The remainder of the two battalions were strung out in a long column, either in the ditch or in the open. Battles cannot be effectively fought from a column and it was from this awkward formation that the Rangers had to defend against the deadly attacks that were now directed their way. The operation had hinged on moving to Cisterna undetected; however, the same ditch that had served as the key to their success became a death trap as the Germans surrounded the Rangers and sealed off their escape route back to U.S. lines. The 4th Battalion, which was to have been nearby to assist in just such a situation, was still pinned down outside Isola Bella at dawn.

As the morning wore on the plight of the Rangers deteriorated from dangerous to desperate as casualties mounted. Finally, at 0730 hours the Rangers broke radio silence to advise their anxious commander of their plight. Several Ranger companies attacked nearby farmhouses and managed to oust the Germans but the majority remained trapped in ditches from which movement was suicidal. At 0835 the War Room journal of the 3d Division recorded the following:

Call received from 1st and 3d Battalions, in south edge of Cisterna completely surrounded. Both battalion COs out, one killed, one wounded. Can't adjust fire; enemy in buildings; town strongly held.[16]

The most serious German counterattack occurred when a large armored force attacked the Ranger positions from the rear. At first the Rangers thought this was an American relief column and they began cheering. The cheers soon turned to dismay and curses when they came under heavy fire. Major Dobson later wrote a moving account of the desperate battles fought by his unit outside Cisterna:

> The Germans' first counterattack came from the rear—from the direction of our own lines—in the form of seventeen tanks and armored, self-propelled guns. They overran our position, but we knocked out fifteen of them with bazookas, grenades and about everything else we could lay our hands on. I saw one of our sergeants trying to plaster a sticky bomb on a German tank turret when a bazooka shot hit it on the opposite side. It knocked him into the air and he did a complete somersault but landed running. All these tanks and guns were burning and exploding in the middle of our position at one time—a beautiful sight.[17]

What Dobson modestly neglected to mention was his own bravery. When a German Mark IV rumbled into the Ranger position, halted nearby and began firing, he shot the tank commander dead with his .45 caliber pistol and then mounted the tank, pulled the pin on a phosphorous grenade, and dropped it down the open hatch. "The tank blew as I leapt from it and while in the air I got hit by something in my left hip." After being captured he was taken to a nearby German casualty station. "I was operated on at a German MASH [mobile army surgical hospital] that night without benefit of anesthetic and was given the hunk of metal by the surgeon. Unfortunately I passed out at that point and dropped my souvenir."[18]

Several other Rangers also daringly mounted two moving tanks and after killing their crews made a dash toward Cisterna in an attempt to break through the German positions that were tormenting the 1st Battalion. They failed when other Rangers, unaware the tanks were manned by their comrades, destroyed them with bazooka fire. "No quarter was given or asked for by either side. For the Rangers it was a battle to the finish."[19]

The situation grew steadily more grave. For the remainder of the morning the Germans launched a series of infantry attacks that were beaten off as "all the time the entire position was swept by point-blank artillery fire, two batteries of Nebelwerfers [multiple rocket launchers] and fire from German anti-aircraft batteries nearby."[20] Two companies of the 3d Battalion managed to fight their way to a point outside Cisterna near the 1st Battalion. But time was rapidly running out and ammunition was dangerously low.

The Germans had better success against the beleaguered remnants of the 3d Battalion, who were trapped in the ditch. "The Germans just ran tanks up to the edge of the ditch, lowered their guns and began slaughtering our troops. It was a dreadful way to die," wrote a British journalist who covered the Italian campaign.[21] "Casualties were extreme and finally those still alive were overpowered." Some Rangers were deliberately spared, pulled from the ditch, and formed into a ragged column, closely surrounded by some one hundred German infantrymen (later identified as paratroopers), two tanks, and an armored car. Here is Major Dobson's chilling description of what happened next:

> They started about eight hundred yards away and moved toward us. The column built up as it moved along and they pulled more of the Rangers out of the ditch. As they approached our position, we arranged ourselves to dispose of the armored vehicles with the last remaining rounds of bazooka ammunition and the last two or three rounds of mortar ammunition. Riflemen were stationed to pick off the German infantry.
>
> We opened fire when they were three hundred yards away. What was left of the Third Ranger Battalion came toward us with their hands over their heads. Nevertheless, we opened fire. We killed several German infantry, and we killed or wounded some of our own men in an attempt to stop the column. The Germans machine-gunned and bayonetted some of the helpless prisoners in the column. They had already shot the wounded men left in the ditch. Then they got behind those who remained and forced them to march right into our position. Our ammunition was finished and we had no way of stopping it.[22]

As the German paratroopers herded their hostages within shouting distance of the 1st and 3d Battalion positions, an ultimatum in English came from an officer. One Ranger witnessed seven or eight POWs killed to drive home the message that they must surrender or the remainder would be shot. Having nothing left to fight with except knives and bare hands, the survivors were compelled to surrender.

T/5 James P. O'Reilly of Company B, 3d Battalion, exemplified the courage of the Rangers. He survived and became a POW for a short time before escaping to fight with Italian partisans for some months before returning to Allied lines. He recounts how his small group attacked a flak wagon (a self-propelled antiaircraft gun) with sticky grenades. One "landed right on the gun platform. The flak-wagon kept going for about 100 yards before the explosion. It was an awful mess. The road was splattered with the gnarled wreckage of twisted steel and broken bodies."[23] O'Reilly praised one of his company officers, Lieutenant Newman, who led an attack on a German machine-gun position:

> He sure had a lot of guts. He was a little fellow with big thick glasses. But boy he loved a fight. . . . He broke his glasses when he jumped [the]

machine-gun nest with only his pistol. With his glasses broken he couldn't
see worth a damn. That's how he was captured. He never would send his
men where he wouldn't go. And there was never a place, however hot,
that he would hesitate at going.[24]

One company commander and a lieutenant prepared to take on the
Germans single-handedly. The commander ordered eight of his men to
try to escape. "It's too late now. That direction is south. Take out [sic]
and God bless you."[25] O'Reilly's description of the final moments of the
3d Battalion was typical of the agony of Darby's Rangers at Cisterna:

> The Germans were attacking from all sides; from the front, the flanks and
> the rear. It was hopeless. We could hear more tanks coming from the
> Appian Way. We only had a few shots left apiece, and a lot of our boys were
> out there in front of the Germans with their hands up, not even asking us
> to surrender and save them. I guess they wanted the decision to be ours
> and ours alone. Again a German Officer who spoke perfect English yelled
> to us to come out or your comrades die. . . . We came out.[26]

Despite the urgent radio requests received by Ranger HQ, there was
nothing Darby or Truscott could do to help the two lost battalions. The
4th Battalion was engaged in its own battle for survival south of Isola
Bella. A few of the newer 1st Battalion Rangers panicked during the
third German attempt to march the 3d Battalion hostages into their
positions. These "got hysterical and started to leave their positions and
surrender." Orders from some of the veteran Rangers were to no avail,
and men continued to surrender in small groups. Other old-time Rangers threatened to shoot those who gave up, but even this could not stop
the surrenders.[27]

Although few of the survivors of the savage attacks that morning
actually gave up hope of relief, most sensed there would be no dramatic, last-minute rescue and they broke into small groups and attempted to escape the German trap. Virtually all were detected and
either killed on the spot or captured. Only 6 Rangers managed to return
to U.S. lines. The remaining 761 were either killed or captured, a staggering loss rate of 99 percent. The last known Ranger to contact Darby
was Sergeant Major Robert Ehalt of the 1st Battalion, only moments
before his position was overrun by German tanks and infantry. In a very
emotional exchange for both men, Ehalt told his commander, "So long,
Colonel. Maybe when it's all over I'll see you again."[28] Fortunately,
there exists a record of Darby's final words to Ehalt at 12:15 P.M.,
January 30 and his helplessness as the Ranger ordeal neared its nadir:

> Issue some orders but don't let the boys give up! . . . Who's walking
> in with their hands up? Don't let them do it! Get some officers to

shoot! . . . Don't let them do it! . . . Do that before you give up! . . . Get the old men together and lam for it. . . . We're coming through. Hang onto this radio until the last minute . . . Stick together. . . . Use your head and do what's best. . . . You're there and I'm here, unfortunately, and I can't help you but whatever happens, God bless you![29]

Across the battlefield similar poignant scenes were played out as the end came for the Rangers. Calls for help were received at Ranger HQ. Most were defiant. One 1st Battalion sergeant told Darby, "Some of the fellows are giving up, Colonel, we are awfully sorry. They can't help it, because we're running out of ammunition. But I ain't surrendering. They are coming into the building now." Then the radio went dead.[30] In ditches, in farmhouses, wherever there were Rangers, the Germans attacked relentlessly with everything in their arsenal. Snipers attempted to pick them off as others used machine guns, rifles, automatic weapons, tanks, mortars—including the dreaded "Moaning Minnies" fired from the *Nebelwerfer* flak wagons—and artillery. Long since out of bazooka ammo, the Rangers were down to a few rounds of ammunition each. Time had run out on the Rangers whose exemplary bravery was no longer enough to resist an enemy force many times their size.

Among those captured was the 3d Battalion medical officer and the many wounded men in his care. When his protests at being separated from his men went unheeded, the doctor shot one of his captors with his own pistol and was immediately killed by another German as he attempted to return to his men.[31]

The German after-action reports stated that most of the Rangers were captured by the Hermann Göring Division, which claimed to have taken 680 prisoners.[32] Few accurate statistics have been kept on the Cisterna operation, but Major Dobson believes that approximately 450 enlisted men of the two Ranger battalions were captured that terrible day. No one seems to have determined how many Rangers perished in the first battle for Cisterna, but 250–300 is a reasonable estimate. What is certain is that only 6 Rangers returned to Allied lines, thus ending one of the most ill-fated small-unit operations of World War II.

The Germans paid their own butcher's bill on January 30. Statistics show that over a two-day period across the entire front they reported losses of 188 killed, 465 wounded, and 443 missing, most of which were from the Hermann Göring Division and the parachute regiments.[33] While in captivity Dobson was told by an interrogation officer that 400 dead Germans were later found on the battlefield at Cisterna.[34]

Darby was devastated by the loss of his beloved Ranger force, and an already ailing Truscott was reported by his aides as "very disturbed."[35] When he learned the full extent of the Ranger losses,

Darby blamed himself and then "put his head down on his arm and cried . . . he broke down. Darby had always put the safety of his men first and he couldn't stand the thought of what was happening to them."[36] Nevertheless, he was mistaken in his belief that his presence at the head of his men that day could have averted the tragedy. Even for the valiant Bill Darby it would have meant either death or capture, for the truth was that the Rangers were simply outgunned and overwhelmed by a vastly superior force. From the first moment when the alarm was spread outside Cisterna at dawn on January 30, the Ranger force was doomed. Their brilliant fight against overwhelming odds was a tribute to the strong heart of the fighting force that Truscott had helped create and Darby had trained and led. The following day Darby went to the Ranger bivouac area near the Mussolini Canal, "his eyes rimmed with red and a two day's growth of beard on his face. He stood silently looking at the pile of bedroll and barracks bags, studying the stenciled names and serial numbers of his men. Then he went away."[37] For some time Darby was despondent, and many believe he was never the same again.

In the aftermath of the Cisterna debacle the surviving 4th Ranger Battalion, which itself had suffered 50 percent losses, was assigned first to the 3d Division and subsequently to the 504th Parachute Infantry Regiment. Darby's agony was compounded when he learned that many of the captured Rangers were paraded as trophies through the streets of Rome by their captors, who took full advantage of the propaganda coup of having annihilated the most elite force in the U.S. Army. Axis Sally, the sultry propaganda voice that daily taunted and cajoled Allied soldiers over German radio, gleefully trumpeted: "The Rangers have at last entered Rome, but they have come not as conquerors but as our prisoners." Propaganda leaflets claimed that "over 1000 American soldiers were made prisoner at one blow near Cisterna." Some of the sting of this bitter defeat might have been removed if Darby had known that the Germans ended up with considerably fewer Ranger POWs than they had captured. A number managed to escape and these men later formed the Ranger Houdini Club.[38]

Cisterna was the most tragic day in the brief but heroic saga of the U.S. Army Rangers of World War II, created in the spring of 1942 as an elite American version of the British Commandos. Its architects were Marshall and Truscott, then a colonel sent by the chief of staff to London to organize a force he called Rangers, both to differentiate them from the British Commandos and because there had been several such units dating to before the Revolutionary War (the best known of which was Rogers' Rangers). The officer chosen to form and train the first Ranger battalion in Northern Ireland and Scotland was a young artillery officer,

Captain William Orlando Darby, a West Pointer, class of 1933. Restless performing the duties of a general's aide, Darby found his appointment to train and lead a Ranger force to be precisely the challenge he sought, and he made the most of it.

Darby trained the Rangers to perform unconventional military operations that required not only the basic skills of an infantryman but the ability to operate with speed and daring behind enemy lines under the most dangerous conditions. Modest and unassuming, Darby endeared himself to his men by practicing what he preached: No officer should ever ask a soldier to do anything in combat he was unwilling to do himself. Despite the old Army maxim about never volunteering for anything, Darby found no shortage of men willing to risk their lives for what he promised would be the toughest training they would ever endure. "There would be no privileged characters, Darby said; the Rangers would judge men by what they could do, and not by their rank or the shape of their faces or the color of their hair. What they would do would be tough; no outfit would have it tougher. They would spearhead actions; there would be no one ahead of them but the enemy." More than 2,000 men volunteered, 700 were selected, and 520 completed the first training course.[39]

Within ten weeks of his nomination to command the first Ranger unit Darby was a lieutenant colonel. In 1943 in Tunisia, Darby's 1st Battalion fought with such distinction at El Guettar that they were awarded one of the first Presidential Unit Citations and later were cited a second time. He then organized two additional battalions and commanded "the Ranger Force," which soon became simply "Darby's Rangers." In Sicily and Salerno the Rangers distinguished themselves, and Darby's reputation soared. At Gela he personally held off an attack by Italian light tanks with a machine gun. Then, with the help of a Ranger captain, Darby manned a captured antitank gun and destroyed a tank as it bore down on his Ranger command post. Patton personally decorated Darby with the Distinguished Service Cross, but the Ranger commander turned down a promotion to full colonel and command of an infantry regiment in order to stay with his beloved Rangers. In his diary Patton noted that "this is the first time I ever saw a man turn down a promotion. Darby is really a great soldier." One of his NCOs later said of Darby, "He made us an outfit that would do what he wanted. We were like sons to him. So he wouldn't leave us."[40]

Shortly before Anzio Darby was promoted to full colonel and provided a command and control HQ that was designated the 6615th Ranger Force (Provisional). Although the 1st and 3d Ranger Battalions had won Distinguished Unit Citations at Salerno, there had already been several disturbing examples of Clark's misuse of the Rangers. Their role at Salerno had been expected to last two days and instead stretched into two weeks, during which they were forced to fight as conventional infantry—a fact that was responsible for most of the Ranger casualties at Salerno. For about forty-five days thereafter they were given another conventional role and again suffered heavy losses. Because of their training it was difficult to replace such losses. The result was that Ranger units were unavailable for periods of a month or more in order to train replacements to Ranger standards. There was a noticeable decline in the quality of replacement Ranger personnel after Salerno.[41] The tragedy of Cisterna had little to do with this problem, however, and was "virtually inevitable given the faulty intelligence developed by the Third Infantry Division, and should be blamed neither upon Darby nor the Ranger concept."[42]

Within weeks of Cisterna the Ranger force was formally disbanded. Some of its surviving members returned to the United States, their war over; others were reassigned to another unconventional force, the First Special Service Force, which arrived for duty at Anzio on February 1.

When Truscott called Clark with the news there was "quite a flap." The loss of the Rangers alarmed Clark, who seems to have feared unfavorable publicity and implied that Truscott had used them improperly. He demanded an investigation to affix responsibility—and blame. Lucas came to his defense and assumed full responsibility when the three commanders met on January 31. "The disaster . . . he apparently blames on Lucian. He says they were used foolishly as infantry which they were not equipped to do. . . . Neither I nor Truscott knew of the organized defensive position they would run into. I told Clark the fault was mine as I had seen the plan of attack and had OK'd it."[43]

An angry Truscott bluntly reminded the Fifth Army commander that he had "been responsible for organizing the original Ranger battalion and that Colonel Darby and I perhaps understood their capabilities better than other American officers," a pointed reference to Clark himself. There was no need for an investigation when "the responsibility was entirely my own," and both he and Darby had believed the Rangers' mission could have been successfully carried out. "That ended the matter."[44]

Clark was also beginning to show increasing signs of concern over Lucas's performance and a sense that Lucas had squandered opportunities that were now lost. "I have been disappointed for several days by the lack of aggressiveness on the part of the VI Corps," Clark wrote in his diary on January 31. "Although it would have been wrong, in my opinion, to attack to capture our final objective on this front, reconnaissance in force with tanks should have been more aggressive to capture CISTERNA and CAMPOLEONE. Repeatedly I have told Lucas to push vigorously to get those local objectives. He has not insisted on this with the Division Commanders. . . . I have been harsh with Lucas today, much to my regret, but in an effort to energize him to greater effort."[45]

Across the 3d Division front on January 30 there was savage fighting as Truscott's infantry ran headlong into the newly reinforced German defenses in front of Cisterna. The Rangers were not the only force to be trapped. A forty-three-man platoon of the 3d Reconnaissance Troop that had been sent to outpost the Ranger rear during the advance along the Pantano ditch tried to escape by jeep but could not evade a German roadblock. Only one GI made it back to friendly lines.[46]

The 3d Division attack had also begun at 0200 hours but soon ran into obstacles from both the Germans and the terrain, which consisted of numerous drainage ditches overgrown with wild briar bushes that made movement by the supporting Shermans at night impossible and left the advancing infantry without a vital source of fire support. It took until the afternoon of January 30 before Isola Bella fell to the 3d Battalion, 15th Infantry Regiment, after a stiff fight that required tanks and tank destroyers to pry the Germans from the rubble of the village.

A diversionary attack across the Mussolini Canal by the 504th Parachute Infantry fared little better when the paratroopers encountered the 7th Luftwaffe Jaegers, who literally fought for their lives defending against the airborne advance. German losses were heavy at the intersection of the Mussolini Canal and the Fosso di Cisterna, where two bridges were blown up. There was little the paratroopers could do against the array of German artillery and weapons blocking their way. For the next eight weeks there was a standoff in the northeastern corner of the beachhead as the 504th were forced into trenches that for sheer misery had nothing on their World War I counterparts. During that time they alternated with the 4th Ranger Battalion, and until both units were relieved in the last week of March, they were subjected to heavy attacks and "the most intense artillery and point-blank flak-wagon barrages ever experienced."[47]

The 1st Battalion, 7th Infantry, was caught in the open the night of January 29–30, when the Germans fired illuminating flares and began to rain automatic weapons fire on the Americans from the protection of nearby knolls. Unable either to advance or retreat, the men of the 1st Battalion were trapped as the Rangers would be later the same morning. Throughout the remainder of the night they were subjected to continued heavy fire. Daylight revealed the full extent of their plight, of which the Germans promptly took full advantage. The battalion suffered 150 casualties and was nearly destroyed.

Attempts to break out of the trap failed, but control of one of the knolls was wrested from the Germans and turned into an American strongpoint. Finally, during the afternoon of January 30 the shattered remnants of the 1st Battalion struck back, and when they were at last able to withdraw, they left an estimated 200 dead Germans behind. One 1st Battalion infantryman described the savage clash:

> Hollywood would have paid five million dollars to have had that on film. Here we were, *walking* in on the enemy and he had every weapon from machine guns on up zeroed in on us. Small arms and artillery were intense. Men were dropping all around . . . the men never even hesitated, just kept walking forward, only stopping to shoot. The tanks and TDs were moving right along with us, shooting hell out of houses and haystacks. When we got in on the Jerry positions they couldn't take it. They poured out of those foxholes . . . rifles, BARs and the TDs and tanks with their .30 and .50 caliber machine guns went to work on them. . . . In the orchard they were practically piled one on top of each other. The Marines at Tarawa had nothing on the 3d Division at Cisterna that day.[48]

This small unit action was typical of the many, seemingly endless, bloody battles of Anzio where both sides fought each other to a standstill and, almost always, to little or no tactical gain.

The ordeal of the Rangers was far from over. The 4th Ranger Battalion fought bravely but without success—enduring fearful losses—in a vain attempt to break through to Cisterna, but they were thwarted time and again south of the tiny farm hamlet of Isola Bella, also known as Femmina Morta (the Dead Woman). There were still pockets of German defenders between Isola Bella and the 4th Rangers, and German snipers were particularly effective. One company commander who had tried four times to carry out Darby's orders to flank Isola Bella and reach Cisterna with half-tracks returned in tears to report that he could not get through. As he left Ranger headquarters he was shot dead when a sniper's bullet shattered his head.[49]

Truscott reorganized his forces in an attempt to renew the attack on Cisterna but after two days of bloodletting could only get within a mile of the town. The second attempt to capture Cisterna took place on January 31, when two battalions (the 2d Battalion, 15th Infantry, and the 1st Battalion, 30th Infantry) managed to struggle forward against fierce resistance to new positions only two thousand yards south of the town before running out of steam. Again on February 1 there was a final attempt to crack the German defense of Cisterna, and although one battalion gained another five hundred yards, by midday Truscott had seen enough and called off the offensive. There was no momentum left in his battered units, some of which, like the 1st Battalion, 15th Infantry, had been reduced to about twenty men per company.

During World War II thirty-one members of the 3d Division won the Medal of Honor for conspicuous valor on the battlefield. Four of them were earned during the first battle for Cisterna, three of them posthumously. One of them was T/5 Eric G. Gibson, a twenty-four-year-old Swedish immigrant whose courage at Isola Bella earned him renown as the "fightin'est man" in the entire division. A cook who was far more comfortable wielding a submachine gun than a spatula—although his friends claimed he was one of the best cooks in the Army—Gibson often volunteered for combat duty, and during the first of the many vicious engagements at Isola Bella he single-handedly wiped out four German machine-gun nests, killed five Germans, and captured two more before being fatally struck by bullets from a Schmeisser machine pistol.[50]

What had gone wrong at Cisterna? The answer lies in the twenty-four-hour delay imposed by Lucas to permit Penney and Harmon to prepare for their offensive on the left flank at Carroceto. The loss of the Grenadier commanders on January 28 triggered a twenty-four-hour delay in the attack on Campoleone, and that, combined with the late arrival of the 1st Armored Division, was the key factor in Lucas's fateful decision to postpone the offensive by one day. Had the Ranger operation begun the previous night as originally scheduled, they would have met scant resistance and more than likely would have captured Cisterna. However, on January 29 the Germans began moving heavy reinforcements into the Cisterna sector, both in anticipation of the Allied offensive and also in preparation for their own counterstroke against the beachhead. On January 29 the strength of the Fourteenth Army increased by 25 percent when 14,100 German reinforcements, most of whom were immediately dispersed around Cisterna, arrived in the Anzio beachhead.[51]

Kesselring ordered the LXXVI Panzer Corps, the most experienced corps headquarters then in Italy, to take over the defense of the German left flank at Anzio. This unit had previously been responsible for the defense of the Adriatic end of the Gustav Line and was commanded by General der Panzertruppen Traugott Herr, yet another of the veteran tank commanders whose skills had been honed on the Eastern Front. Other reinforcements sent to Anzio were the 26th Panzer Division and the 1st Parachute Regiment, consisting of three battalions of veteran paratroopers of Heidrich's 1st Parachute Division. Several infantry divisions were en route from northern Italy to plug gaps in both corps. The Germans had now redrawn their chain of command to deal with both Anzio and the defense of Cassino. I Parachute Corps and LXXVI Panzer Corps would form the Fourteenth Army under von Mackensen, while von Vietinghoff's reorganized Tenth Army continued its resistance along the Gustav Line. The Fourteenth Army was organized to cope with both an Allied attack and their own counteroffensive to eliminate the Allied beachhead. At the end of

January, there were 83,600 Germans at Anzio, representing nine divisions, some of them at full strength and others only partially represented, such as the 1st Parachute Division.[52]

Where there had once been great gaps in front of Cisterna, there were now a regiment of Heidrich's veteran paratroopers, the Machine-Gun Battalion of the 4th Parachute Regiment, the entire Hermann Göring Division, and substantial elements of the 26th Panzer Division.

Once again Kesselring had outgeneraled his opponent. Cisterna and Campoleone were obvious objectives, and the German commander reasoned that sooner or later Lucas would attempt to capture both towns. Determined that Cisterna and Campoleone remain in German hands, Kesselring, when he ordered the gaps plugged at Cisterna, was not only anticipating the obvious but also realigning his forces for the forthcoming counterstroke.

It was the Rangers' misfortune that the push to Cisterna had been delayed for twenty-four hours. A report by the VI Corps G-1 called the disaster at Cisterna "an incident of campaign contributed to by so many factors that it can be ascribed only to chance." However, a postwar study of Ranger operations notes that the "G-1 would have placed the blame more squarely if he had laid it on poor intelligence. Although sufficient information had been collected to correctly determine the enemy's capabilities and probable courses of action, they had been sorely misjudged."[53]

The bad luck that dogged the operation was exacerbated when it was later learned that a Polish soldier named Stempkofski had deserted the German unit he was serving with near Cisterna the day before and attempted to warn the Americans of the German presence there. However, no one could understand Polish and he was sent to the rear to be routinely interrogated at Fifth Army after the battle.[54]

With his reserves fully committed and his losses since January 22 now more than three thousand plus a third of his tanks and tank destroyers, Truscott recognized he had no chance of breaking the German defense of Cisterna. More ominous was the fact that the 3d Division now occupied terrain unsuitable for stopping a strong counterattack and Truscott had to begin preparing to resist the long-awaited German counteroffensive. The first battle of Cisterna was over and the Germans were the victors.

Six miles to the west the British and the 1st Armored Division were about to undergo their own ordeal. During the morning of January 30 the tanks of Harmon's 1st Armored began their left hook aimed at capturing Campoleone from the west. There had been no time for a reconnaissance, and the operation had been planned from maps and aerial photographs. Unfortunately, what turned out to be minor indentations on the map were in reality the fifty-foot-deep gullies that criss-crossed the wadi or gully country north of Anzio. A powerful armored-infantry force attempted to break free by moving northwest along the Embankment toward the secondary road leading from Vallelata to Campoleone but was soon halted in its tracks by heavy fire from Val-lelata Ridge. When the tanks were unable to maneuver in the boggy soil, this avenue of approach became checkmated. The 1st Armored had driven into a natural tank trap of its own making.

Without room to maneuver the tank has little effectiveness as a fighting vehicle. During the winter months at Anzio tanks were virtu-ally useless except on roads, which the Germans took great pains to defend. The knowledge that his armored forces had lost a considerable portion of their mobility was Harmon's harsh introduction to the Anzio beachhead, and he was candid about the lessons it taught him. One particular incident on January 30 illustrates the perils of attempting to maneuver armor away from the solid footing of a road. Harmon relates that when four tanks became mired in the mud, "I ordered an armored wrecker to pull them out. The wrecker was ambushed by the Germans. I sent four more tanks to rescue the wrecker. Then I sent more tanks after them. Apparently I could learn my first Anzio lesson only the hard way—and the lesson, subsequently very important, was not to send good money after bad. Because I was stubborn, I lost twenty-four tanks while trying to succor four."[55]

Harmon's abortive attempt at a left hook northwest of Carroceto had the full approval of Penney, who recorded the problems both commanders faced in this account of a conference at VI Corps the morning of January 29:

> I pointed out the difficulties of bottleneck roads and lack of troops and of width of front. After a lot of palaver persuaded them at least to start recce out on the left with view to a turning movement north. Corps commander insisted that armour must go through on [the] 30th but I pointed out that it was quite impossible on our one road. . . . Still a lot of waffle and HILL [the VI Corps G-3, who did not rank high on Penney's list of favorite U.S. officers] again demonstrated his stupidity and ignorance. It is *not* a corps battle in a close co-ordinated sense and plans are made by each division for everything.[56]

The British had better success on January 30 as Penney realized that the work of the Guards had opened the way for the 3d Brigade to com-mence their long-delayed attack. The morning was spent clearing a German force blocking the approach to the start line along the lateral road, and it was midafternoon before the two assault battalions could begin their attack with the 1st Battalion, Duke of Wellington's Regiment (DWR), on the left and the 1st Battalion, King's Shropshire Light Infantry (KSLI), on the right. The KSLI advance was successful and within two hours the battalion had captured 118 Germans and established positions astride the railway bank at Point 131 overlooking the Rome-Naples railway, several hundred yards southeast of Campoleone Station. The Dukes had a considerably more difficult time, coming under heavy fire and taking a number of casualties, but nevertheless managed to end the day in fresh positions along the south side of the rail line opposite the station.[57]

After a series of sharp engagements the morning of January 31 the Sherwood Foresters and C squadron of the 46th Royal Tank Regiment managed to advance through to the railway line opposite Campoleone Station. But even with additional support from one of Harmon's tank battalions, they could not gain control of either the station or its important road net.

War histories are prone to describe military campaigns in terms of armies, corps, and divisions maneuvering against one another. At the sharp end, where those battles are won or lost, the maneuvering and fighting is carried out by small groups of men in battalions, companies, platoons, and sections pitted against one another in the most elemental and brutal form of combat.

On the last day of January 1944 in the British sector of the Anzio beachhead there occurred what is known as a small-unit action. It pitted the Sherwood Foresters and a squadron of Shermans against a battalion of infantry, thought to be from the 29th Panzer Grenadier Regiment of the 3d Panzer Grenadier Division, which had moved into positions north of the railway line the previous day. The Germans had commandeered every building between the railway embankment and the station and had established strongpoints in the protection of these sturdy stone houses, some of which concealed tanks that had been driven through the rear, awaiting the expected attack. As the Sherwood Foresters began their advance with fixed bayonets at 1030 hours, across several hundred yards of vineyards that lay between their start line and the railway embankment, the German gunners poured fire on them. The most deadly fire came from machine-gun positions on the British right flank. Losses were heavy, but the Foresters managed to reach the relative safety of a small bluff overlooking Campoleone Station. However, when they left the protection of the bluff and attempted to attack across the railway embankment, they were literally mowed down by an incredible storm of fire. Most of those who managed to cross the railway soon met the same fate, and the survivors eventually were forced to retreat to the bluff. The heaviest fire came from machine guns cleverly mounted in rail wagons in the Campoleone yards that delivered withering sheets of enfilading fire on the hapless Foresters, whose toll of wounded and dead steadily mounted.

The battalion commander pulled his troops back three hundred yards to safety while artillery pounded the Germans north of the railway line. After the Foresters reoccupied their former positions the attack resumed, this time with the Sherwood Forester reserves attempting to advance beyond the embankment. Despite American tank support the Foresters were again cut down mercilessly as the Germans poured fire as intense as before. The artillery bombardment had failed even to soften up the defenders of Campoleone, who had not ceded a single foot of ground.

To support the second Forester attack, Harmon employed the 2d Battalion, 1st Armored Regiment, in a supporting thrust along the Via Anziate in an attempt to punch through the Campoleone overpass. The attack failed as heavy German tank and antitank fire made further progress impossible. An attempt to attack Campoleone Station from the west also failed. By now Harmon was seething with frustration. The left hook the previous day had been an unmitigated fiasco, convincing him that the only chance for his armor to punch through to Albano lay with a thrust through Campoleone, where—according to his latest reports— his tanks were again stalled. For the second time in two days Harmon came forward, this time to see for himself what could be done to assist the Sherwood Foresters. He came in a tank; "a jeep wouldn't have lived long there," he later recalled. What he found appalled him:

> There were dead bodies everywhere. I had never seen so many dead men in one place. They lay so close together that I had to step with care. I shouted for the commanding officer. From a foxhole there arose a mud-covered corporal with a handle-bar mustache. He was the highest-ranking officer still alive. He stood stiffly at attention. "How is it going?" I asked. "Well, sir," the corporal said, "there were a hundred and sixteen of us when we first came up, and there are sixteen of us left. We're ordered to hold out until sundown, and I think, with a little good fortune, we can manage to do so."[58]

Harmon, who knew good soldiering when he saw it, later wrote: "I think my great respect for the stubbornness and fighting ability of the British enlisted man was born that afternoon."[59] One survivor remembered that there was no cover in the vineyards and that "shells [were] screaming and whirring like mad. . . . Sprays of fire all over the place. Shrapnel like hail. Bullets whizzing from nowhere. And on top of that the bloody rain. We were so cold. Half the soldiers disappeared—mown down, captured, or just fucked off."[60]

By late afternoon the 3d Brigade commander, Brigadier J. G.

James, had seen enough and ordered the decimated Foresters to pull back into reserve positions in the rear. The battle to open the way for the 1st Armored to exploit toward Albano had begun far too late and, as will be seen, had no hope of success even if Campoleone had fallen. The attack had driven into the teeth of the German units massing for Kesselring's counterstroke. Later claims that it had served some useful purpose by driving a deep wedge into the German front were false. The reality was that the battles of January 31 were fought in vain and merely created what would shortly turn into a defensive nightmare for the 1st Division. The battle for Campoleone was over, and it was a solid victory for the Germans.

The Foresters suffered grievous losses that dreadful day. In 1944 the standard British infantry rifle battalion consisted of 35 officers and 786 enlisted men (called "Other Ranks" by the British). After the battle for Campoleone Station on January 31 the Foresters could only muster eight officers and 250 other ranks. What was left of what had been nearly a full-strength battalion that morning "presented a heartbreaking sight. The strongest company had some 40 men left; the weakest 20. The Battalion CO and every company commander was either killed or wounded. Even the Medical Officer was lost when he was captured when he went too far forward in an attempt to reach the wounded."[61]

That night several replacement officers from the Black Watch regiment reported to the adjutant: "We had to send them out on patrol that night because we had no one else to go out, and they were killed in the night. And none of us saw them in daylight. It was tragic. Can you imagine? Probably they had never had battle experience. It was awful, awful. I heard the Spandaus hitting them."[62]

The Germans offered a somewhat different version, which suggests that they considered their positions west of Campoleone station more vulnerable than originally believed. "It is not understood why the enemy tanks halted their attacks, when they had advanced at several points within 50 yards of our main line of resistance. . . . A breakthrough of tanks could not have been stopped."[63] Despite this German claim it seems doubtful that the smaller attack from the west could have succeeded in negotiating the minefield, which was swept by machine-gun and antitank fire. The hazards of cross-country maneuver had been amply demonstrated the previous day.

The British immediately went into defensive positions around Campoleone in what became known to both sides as the "Thumb" (some gave it a very rude nickname), a narrow, pencil-like salient that protruded nearly two and a half miles into the German lines from just south of Campoleone Station into the U.S. 3d Division sector several thousand yards above Padiglione. Although the British 1st Division had driven a wedge some two miles wide between the German 65th Infan-

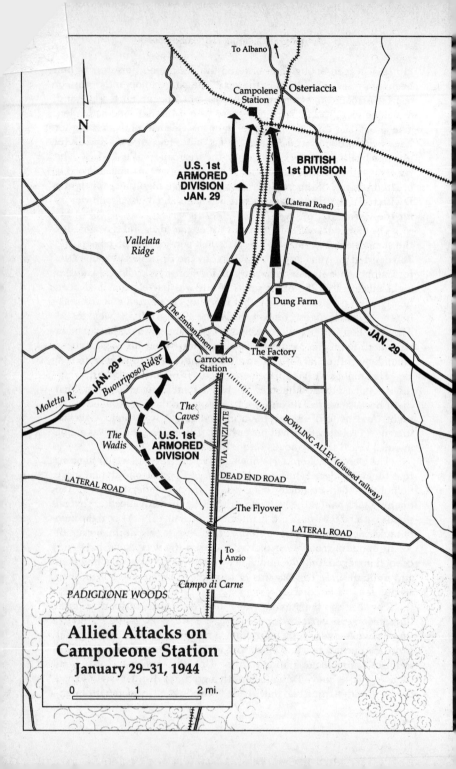

To Albano

Campolene
Station   Osteriaccia

U.S. 1st
ARMORED
DIVISION
JAN. 29

BRITISH
1st DIVISION

(Lateral Road)

N

Vallelata
Ridge

The Embankment

Dung Farm

JAN. 29

JAN. 29
Buonriposo Ridge

Moletta R.

Carroceto
Station

The Factory

The
Caves

The
Wadis

U.S. 1st
ARMORED
DIVISION

VIA ANZIATE

BOWLING ALLEY (disused railway)

LATERAL ROAD

DEAD END ROAD

The Flyover

LATERAL ROAD

To
Anzio

PADIGLIONE WOODS

Campo di Carne

**Allied Attacks on
Campoleone Station**
January 29–31, 1944

0   1   2 mi.

try and 3d Panzer Grenadier divisions, the protrusion between Aprilia and Campoleone posed an immediate and serious defensive problem for General Penney. The net result was that despite modest gains VI Corps was actually worse off than before the offensive. Without control of Campoleone the VI Corps left flank had become dangerously overextended. As they would soon learn, the Thumb would prove impossible to defend. At Cisterna the 3d Division was not quite as vulnerable, but its new positions were hardly ideal.

The failure of the left flank to capture Campoleone did not please Alexander, who viewed both Cisterna and Campoleone as vital objectives for the eventual occupation of the Alban Hills. Clark, however, supported Lucas's decision to call off the offensive. When Clark and Alexander conferred on January 31 there was open disagreement. "Alexander brought up the Anzio situation and indicated that he did not agree with my order to Lucas. . . . He urged me to be prepared to attack with the 3d Division again in an all-out effort to get Cisterna, and expressed the opinion that the enemy would not counter-attack in force."[64] That night Alexander reversed himself when fresh intelligence warned of the dangers of an imminent German counteroffensive.

Clark was nevertheless "disappointed by the lack of aggressiveness on the part of VI Corps, although it would have been wrong in my opinion to attack to capture our final objective [the Alban Hills] on this front . . . reconnaissance in force with tanks should have been more aggressive to capture Cisterna and Campoleone."[65]

Lucas had squandered his only opportunity to capture Cisterna and Campoleone, and the dilemma he now faced was that his corps was overmatched by a superior German force. It was, in short, a no-win situation. "All my eggs are in one basket," he lamented. "We are engaged in a hell of a struggle."[66]

The decision by Clark and Lucas to go on the defensive to prepare for von Mackensen's counteroffensive brought to a close the first phase of the Anzio campaign. The abortive VI Corps offensive was Lucas's one and only attempt to capture the Alban Hills. It was also a decisive turning point of the war in Italy. Not only was the stalemate at Cassino unbroken, but Anzio was shortly to become an extension of the same stalemate and a colossal liability for the Allies who, like Kesselring, were obliged to rush reinforcements from the south to meet the threat of the massive German buildup opposite VI Corps. Instead of a stalemate on one front, the Allies now found themselves with the problem of how to extricate themselves from a deadlock on two widely dispersed fronts. At Anzio, only seven days after the successful Allied landings, the initiative had passed to the Germans.

11

The Battle for
the Thumb

In the next few days the "Battle for Rome" will break
out. . . . It must be fought in holy wrath.

—ADOLF HITLER

The struggle for Anzio entered a
new and lethal phase in the opening days of February 1944. The unsuccessful VI Corps offensive of January 30–31 ended once and for all the
illusion that Shingle was to be a ten-day operation without further
major logistic support or additional reinforcements other than Harmon's 1st Armored Division. The Germans had massed well over ninety
thousand troops in a tight ring across the VI Corps front, and by the
second week of the Anzio operation the Allies were forced onto the
defensive. Not only must Lucas counter the coming German counteroffensive, but without a major infusion of additional combat strength
there was little likelihood of regaining the initiative in the foreseeable
future.

For the Germans the first week at Anzio had been, in Kesselring's
words, a "higgledy-piggledy jumble—units of numerous divisions fighting confusedly side by side." However, it was with growing confidence
that he had taken the measure of his enemy's intentions and could now
tell the new Fourteenth Army commander that "we no longer had to
reckon with any major reverses."[1] Now it was von Mackensen's turn to
lead the German Army at Anzio on the attack.

Hitler's usual bluster was contained in his messages to the high
command in Italy, exhorting German soldiers to fight with special fury

"against an enemy who wages a ruthless war of annihilation against the German people" in order to lance what he termed "the abscess south of Rome."[2] Although he would have been pleased to annihilate the Allied force at Anzio, "Hitler's sixth sense urged caution on him too, telling him that Anzio was less a Battle for Rome—whatever the dramatic purple prose he used in his messages to Kesselring—than a sly enemy attempt to lure the high-grade German reserves . . . away from France and into a peripheral war of attrition in Italy."[3]

Kesselring's counterattack against the beachhead had been delayed primarily due to heavy Allied air interdiction of his reserves moving to Anzio from northern Italy and the Gustav Line. Canaris's false assurances to Kesselring seemed to take the heat off the German commander in chief, whose enemies—among them Field Marshal Wolfram von Richthofen, the Luftwaffe commander in Italy—nevertheless continued to snipe at him privately. In his diary von Richthofen complained: "We violate the cardinal rule of war accepted for many millennia—to lay into enemy beachheads with everything you've got immediately, so as to exploit the disorder always reigning in the first few days."[4] Von Richthofen was guilty of second-guessing Kesselring, who needed no reminding of what he could have done if adequate forces had been defending the Anzio sector the morning of January 22.

Kesselring's orders to von Mackensen were crystal clear: "The main mission of Fourteenth Army is to annihilate the beachhead, which the enemy is reinforcing."[5] The main attack was to be delivered by formations attached to I Parachute Corps that were to thrust straight down the Via Anziate toward Anzio, "with the main concentration on either side of Aprilia." General Schlemm, the parachute corps commander, dispersed his forces into three combat groups and a corps reserve. The main force was Group Gräser, consisting of seventeen battalions of infantry, supported by 144 long-range artillery guns, howitzers, and rocket launchers and a tank battalion of the 26th Panzer Division. In further support were another 169 anti-aircraft guns. Subsidiary attacks west of Cisterna by a small battle group and west of Campoleone by Group Pfeiffer's nine infantry battalions were to complete the operation.[6]

The opening of the German counteroffensive was originally slated for February 1; however, Kesselring correctly surmised it might well be postponed if the 715th Infantry Division, two reinforcement panzer grenadier regiments, and a number of other artillery, panzer, and jaeger units did not arrive in time to be in position to support operations.[7] Thus, between the late arrival of these reinforcements and the abortive VI Corps attacks to seize Cisterna and Campoleone at the end of January, the German counteroffensive was delayed by seventy-two hours.

In response to the threat posed by the German Fourteenth Army,

Lucas was sent two infantry regiments of the 45th Division, the 168th Brigade of Major General Gerald Templer's 56th British Division, and Frederick's First Special Service Force.

An Ultra intercept of Kesselring's orders to von Mackensen of January 28, although not received until February 3, clearly outlined the German plan of attack. Regarded as one of the most important Ultra intercepts of the entire war, it spelled out not only Kesselring's intentions but also the complete order of battle of the Fourteenth Army, to include its tank strength as of January 25. As a result, as Ultra historian Ralph Bennett notes, "It was possible to gain a good idea of the scale of the coming attack. At least 25 Mark III tanks, 20 VIs (Tigers), 25 assault guns, and 90 heavy antitank guns were to be employed, and probably many more."[8] Moreover, it was this intercept which at least seemed to have convinced Clark of the value of Ultra and other forms of signal intelligence. Heretofore, Clark had not only been sceptical of such intelligence but had openly disparaged its value.[9]

Penney hardly needed Ultra to perceive that his division was literally out on a limb. As the 1st Division history explains, "The enemy gave ample evidence, if evidence were required, that he was preparing to launch a major drive against our new positions. By night [of February 1–2] his patrols were reported on either flank of the salient probing to establish the locations of our troops; by day and night his artillery and mortars pounded away at 3 Brigade in the tip of the salient."[10] Feverish preparations were undertaken to prepare for the German attack and on February 1 Lucas made one of his rare ventures from the VI Corps command post in Nettuno to visit the front.

Lucas found his worst fears confirmed. His left flank was in dire peril. According to Penney, "Lucas expressed his general misgivings about the vulnerability to counter attack on the 1st Division stretched out as it was." Lucas himself wrote that he was "much more disturbed about my left flank than my right. I thought the British situation was very serious."[11] It was one of the few times the two commanders ever agreed on anything.

Neither Lucas nor Penney were reassured by Alexander's presence for an extended visit to the front. Although Penney and Alexander were close, the 1st Division commander was troubled by the latter's apparent lack of concern for his tenuous position when he and Clark visited the front separately on February 3. When Penney mentioned Lucas's anxiety, both Alexander and Clark exhorted him not to withdraw so much as a single foot.[12] The vast disparity between Alexander and Clark was never more evident than on that day. Clark supported Lucas's fears that Penney was likely to lose his division unless he drew in his horns; Alexander never saw it as a problem worthy of action.

Two days earlier Clark and Alexander had clashed over the situation and Lucas's culpability. Clark's diary records that he "had a serious conversation with General Alexander about the latter's supposition that SHINGLE had not been exploited as rapidly as might have been the case. General Clark pointed out that there was no valid ground for dissatisfaction with the progress made."[13]

Clark used the occasion to propose to Alexander and Harding an alternate solution: a second amphibious operation with two divisions, no later than mid-February at Civitavecchia. Although Clark knew there would be powerful resistance from the naval commanders, he believed the Germans could not mount sufficient forces to defend against the landings and the dire threat to Rome from a pincer movement. Despite the further dispersion of Allied ground forces and the obvious logistic problems inherent in such an operation, there was considerable merit to Clark's proposal. Moreover, "the results," said Clark, "would greatly enhance General Alexander's reputation as a military commander."[14] But, as Clark recorded in his diary, "General Alexander and General Harding appeared to be taken aback by the suggestion and could only state that it presented logistical difficulties." Clark's reply was blunt: " 'Overcome them!' This would require Alexander to press Cunningham and 'rub his nose' until he agreed to locate the necessary landing craft to carry out the operation." Although both British officers said the matter would have to be studied "very seriously," the idea soon died when it was decided instead to concentrate on victory at Anzio.[15]

As for Lucas, he already sensed that his days as the beachhead commander were likely to be numbered. His diary for February 1 reads:

> General Alexander is here. He was kind enough but I am afraid is not pleased. My head will probably fall in the basket but I have done my best. There were just too many Germans here for me to lick. . . . As I told Clark yesterday, I was sent on a desperate mission, one where the odds were greatly against success, and I went without saying anything because I was given an order and my opinion was not asked. . . . Before going [Clark] apologized for having harassed me as much as he has. I am glad he did as I really like him very much.[16]

As for Alexander, Lucas confessed that he "is not easy to talk to as he really knows very little of tactics as Americans understand it and I still have trouble because I don't understand the British very well." An example of their disparity lay in Lucas's contention that Alexander failed to appreciate that German combat strength had reached 95,000 versus about 76,000 Allied troops in the beachhead, an estimate that Alexander ought to have known but was obviously not aware of, possibly due to his absence from Caserta for forty-eight hours.[17] Alexander's apparent ignorance of the true situation in the beachhead led Lucas to remark in his diary that his superior "failed to realize this as he told me emphatically that the Germans could not possibly supply as many as five divisions in opposition to me. He insisted that Cisterna was the key to the situation and also insisted that an advance of the 3d Division through Cisterna to the northeast would not materially extend the line I had to hold. This was foolish of course. My contention was that for any large scale effort I had to have more troops. General Alexander apparently could not see that any major effort on my part could only be with my left because it must cover the port as well as driving into the enemy."[18]

Alexander correctly asserted in his postwar interview that the Cisterna attack would have succeeded without any appreciable cost to VI Corps if it had been made soon after the beachhead was established,[19] but by the date of his visit to the beachhead on February 1, Truscott's division was a spent force. He was equally correct in asserting that "until we had captured Cisterna and Campoleone it would be impossible to undertake any important offensive operations."[20] However, with the German buildup proceeding despite the heavy harassment from Eaker's airmen, all bets were now off. Unless there was a significant increase in Allied troops, further offensive operations were an invitation to annihilation.

On January 29 von Mackensen's HQ journal left no doubt of German aims: "The main mission of the Fourteenth Army is to annihilate the beachhead which the enemy is reinforcing." Nevertheless, when it finally came, the German attack fell with stunning force, as both ground forces and the Luftwaffe responded to Hitler's January 28 order of the day to, as the Führer so crudely put it, fight "with bitter hatred . . . an enemy who wages a ruthless war of annihilation against the German people . . . it must be driven home to the enemy that the fighting power of Germany is unbroken and that the invasion of the year 1944 . . . will be crushed in the blood of British soldiers."

The key to a successful German counteroffensive was Carroceto and the Factory. For the attacking force to concentrate its massive striking power it was crucial that the British salient between Campoleone and Carroceto be eliminated so that Group Gräser could deploy. Thus, von Mackensen's intermediate objectives were the exact reverse of Lucas's several days earlier: first Campoleone and then the twin obstacles of the Carroceto and the Factory. Once firmly in control of these two key objectives von Mackensen could mass his forces for a devastating main thrust toward Anzio and the beaches.

In anticipation of slicing off the Thumb on February 3, von Mackensen ordered a series of preliminary advances to realign the Fourteenth Army front lines. He was particularly concerned about the failure of the Hermann Göring Division to advance to their assigned jumping-off positions west of Cisterna. Allied artillery and aerial attacks had begun to take a serious toll and on February 2 Allied fighter bombers destroyed the Group Grässer artillery-fire direction center and with it the carefully prepared charts for the attack on the Thumb, causing a twenty-four-hour delay. Von Mackensen had decided to see for himself the condition of his troops and what he learned was not reassuring. That evening he told Kesselring that Allied artillery bombardments were taking their toll on both younger, inexperienced troops as well as some of the veterans. Even though he believed his men would eventually regain their composure, the Fourteenth Army commander was clearly worried. German concerns were not limited to the obvious difficult battle ahead but embodied the continuing belief that the Allies still intended to carry out a second attack, at Civitavecchia. Von Mackensen's fears of the threat this posed to Rome and to the Fourteenth Army were clear proof of the validity of Clark's proposal and the seriousness with which the Germans viewed a second landing.[21]

There was little love lost between the outgoing Kesselring and the stiff Prussian aristocrat, von Mackensen. Tensions between the two, which seem to have begun virtually with von Mackensen's arrival, within a week led him to offer his resignation. According to von Mackensen, there were "long-standing and deep rooted differences of opinion between Field Marshal Kesselring and myself [which] led me to ask him twice within a short time at the beginning of February to transmit my request for a transfer to higher authorities. As I was unable to convince him that my less optimistic appraisal of the situation was correct, I felt I should be betraying the trust the troops placed in me if I did not tender my resignation. Unfortunately, at that time Kesselring refused my request."[22]

According to General Westphal their differences were entirely professional and arose from widely divergent operational and tactical conceptions. Von Mackensen was not the first to complain that Kesselring's assessments were far too optimistic, while the German c in c "took the view that Generaloberst von Mackensen had too little confidence in what could be done by the troops the latter had at his disposal. As time went on, this inevitably gave rise to a certain discounting by the Field Marshal of the anxieties (e.g., about the lack of strength) put forward by 14th Army."[23] Westphal was in fact suggesting that von Mackensen lacked the backbone that Kesselring demanded of his subordinate commanders.

Nevertheless, in one of the few criticisms of his chief, Westphal noted that "the 14th Army was not worse off numerically than the 10th

Army, but it was qualitatively. The 14th had mainly young infantry divisions, whereas 10th Army had at its disposal for the most part seasoned formations. I am of the opinion that this was not always taken sufficiently into account at the time."[24]

What Kesselring and von Mackensen did agree on was the broad strategy of the counteroffensive. Both had "discarded the obvious idea of trying to unhinge the bridgehead by a flanking attack along the coast to the north of Anzio, as we should have had to assemble and attack under the flanking fire of all the naval guns without being able to make fully effective use of our own artillery; furthermore the co-operation of strong German panzer forces would be prejudiced by the densely wooded and mine-sown country."[25] The two German commanders had also ruled out an attack from the direction of Cisterna because of the heavy marshland, which made the employment of armor equally impossible. By a process of elimination this left only the Campoleone sector, and Kesselring approved von Mackensen's plan to launch the main attack along the Via Anziate, supported by secondary attacks to the east and west.

German retaliation began on February 3 when enemy troops infested the Campoleone sector in an effort to cut the Thumb off at its base, along the line of Carroceto and the Factory. Of the two, the Factory was the more important. In British hands it remained a major fortified obstacle that would prevent the second phase of the counteroffensive from being carried out. In the process Group Gräser hoped to isolate and destroy the 3d Brigade, thus eliminating a major fighting element of the 1st Division. Lucas had ordered the 1st Armored withdrawn to the rear as the corps reserve, leaving the British on their own to defend what was essentially an indefensible salient. Early on February 3 the 1st Division issued a warning order to the three brigades: "Strong counterattacks to be expected." Penney pleaded for reinforcements but could only pry loose from VI Corps the 3d Battalion of the 504th Parachute Infantry Regiment, which became part of the division reserve positioned south of the Embankment. Heavy skirmishes took place throughout the day around Campoleone Station, involving the Duke of Wellingtons and the KSLI, who beat off a large German force in the positions occupied by the Sherwood Foresters during their ordeal three days earlier.

The Irish Guards now occupied positions near the railway line facing Vallelata Ridge, approximately halfway between Carroceto and Campoleone Station. Their otherwise peaceful day was broken by the unexpected arrival of some thousand sheep whose bleating shattered the afternoon calm. "Like a dirty, ragged wave a huge flock surged over the crest of the Vallelata ridges and scampered crazily through No. 3

Company. Those wise after the event later said that it was a typical German trick to use poor dumb animals as mine-detectors, but at the time no one felt anything but gratitude."[26]

It remained quiet that evening until precisely 1100 hours, when the long-awaited German attack began with a violent five-minute artillery barrage, followed by a short ominous silence before resuming, as the German ground forces began their attack. One of the first mistakes made that night was committed by the Germans whose white phosphorous mortar rounds set haystacks afire near the positions occupied by the Irish Guards. As the German infantry emerged from the darkness in regimental strength into the illumination from the fires, "in a mass, very hard, thick and fast . . . the machine-gunners mowed them down but they came on just the same." One machine gun blasted off eight thousand rounds, but "nothing seemed to stop them, they came on shouting and gesticulating wildly as if doped." Cries of *"Sieg Heil!"* and *"Gott mit Uns!"* could be distinctly heard over the roar of the guns. Out of ammunition, the three Guardsmen manning the machine gun were assaulted by three Germans who demanded, "Hands up, Englishmen!" This only seemed to anger the Guardsmen, who retaliated by attacking their enemy with fists and escaping into the night.[27] Only later was it learned that No. 3 Company of the Irish Guards had been assaulted by more than two battalions, which continued their human-wave attacks despite hideous casualties.

Throughout the night of February 3–4 it became increasingly clear that Group Gräser had managed to infiltrate troops between the units defending the Thumb. Some were detected and suffered heavy losses from the accuracy of the Royal Artillery gunners. One attack group forming on the railway line south of Campoleone Station, in the KSLI sector, was shattered. Although there were problems in every sector of the Carroceto-Campoleone salient, as dawn came the morning of February 4 the three battalions defending its extreme tip around Campoleone Station had not only restored their perimeters but were confident they could repel any German attack.

On the left flank of the Thumb, the Germans had managed to drive a wedge between the positions of the Irish and Scots Guards. No. 3 Company of the Irish Guards was overwhelmed as the fighting spread furiously into chaotic small-unit actions across the Irish front, where the company HQ was overrun and the company commander captured. A lance corporal who was twice captured and twice escaped said, "I had never seen so many people killed round me before in my life." Similar scenes were occurring everywhere in the Thumb that night. The loss of No. 3 Company heightened the problems facing the British commanders, as their loss left a mile-wide gap between the two Guards battalions. The Irish Guards acting commander, Major D. M. L. Gordon-

Watson, warned that tanks and infantry reinforcements would be needed at dawn if the battalion was to hold its tenuous positions. He was promised six self-propelled antitank guns but only two arrived; the other four refused to move forward even though an officer and an NCO of the Irish Guards risked their lives by infiltrating back to Carroceto to guide them forward.[28]

The most insecure portion of the 1st Division salient was the sector along the right flank and shoulders of the Thumb, which was defended by the 2d Brigade. The 1st Reconnaissance Regiment and the 1st Battalion, the Loyal Regiment, were astride the shoulders to the northeast between the Factory and Dung Farm. Defending the right flank of the Thumb was the 6th Battalion of the Gordon Highlanders, which was spread over a very large area that ran from Dung Farm, where the commander, Lieutenant Colonel James Peddie, had established the battalion command post, to the overpass at the lateral road (Milestone 23), opposite the Irish Guards. Three companies, A, C, and D, were tenuously concentrated in this narrow area to defend against expected German attacks along the tracks leading to the Via Anziate and the railway line. Unfortunately, however, the terrain occupied by the Gordons was exposed to German observation, and their positions had little depth nor were they capable of mutual support.[29] In the middle, approximately halfway between Dung Farm and Milestone 23, was B Company. One-half mile to the southwest were the Scots Guards defending the southern approaches of Vallelata Ridge and the railway line. The remaining portion of the shoulders of the salient were defended by the Grenadiers, who occupied the sector along the Embankment northwest of Carroceto. It was this glaring weakness, where three infantry battalions were disposed across an eight-thousand-yard front, that the Germans chose to attack in force.

February 4 was a typically nasty winter day at Anzio, with fog and a drizzling rain that soaked and numbed the combatants. Throughout the night the Gordons had been pelted by equally miserable doses of artillery and rain, which reduced visibility and gave the Germans an opportunity to slip two companies between B and D companies. This enemy force now occupied the high ground that looked down on both positions. After the battle it was learned that the Germans had also managed to move nearly a battalion of infantry forward under the cover of the darkness and rain into positions behind a ridgeline to the east. The battalion war diary and various other documents record the progress of the battle and the increasingly dire straits of the Gordons.

One of the few comprehensive accounts of what occurred on February 4 was written shortly after the event by Lieutenant Edward Grace of B Company. It reflects the ordeal of the Gordons, which began when the silence across the front was broken the night of February 3.

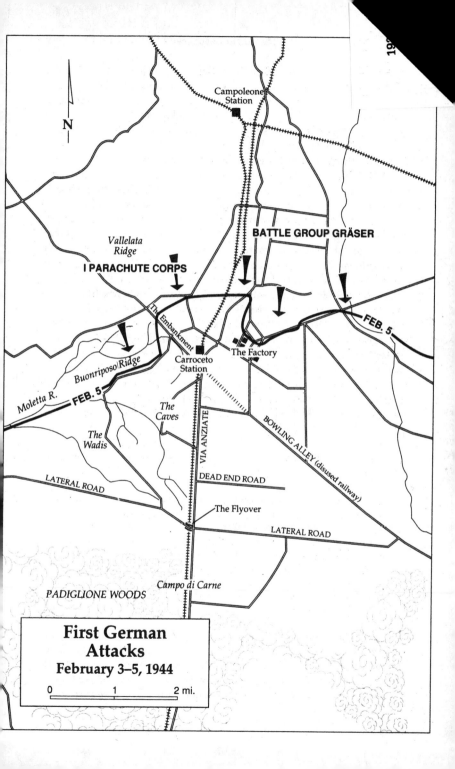

N

Campoleone
Station

BATTLE GROUP GRÄSER

Vallelata Ridge
I PARACHUTE CORPS

FEB. 5

The Embankment

Buonriposo Ridge
Carroceto
Station

The Factory

Moletta R. — FEB. 5

The Caves

The Wadis

VIA ANZIATE

BOWLING ALLEY (disused railway)

LATERAL ROAD

DEAD END ROAD

The Flyover

LATERAL ROAD

PADIGLIONE WOODS

Campo di Carne

First German Attacks
February 3–5, 1944

0   1   2 mi.

"Suddenly looking in the direction of Rome, I saw a jagged line of flames flash up into the darkness. . . . Two seconds of complete silence. Then a shriek in the air above us, and a tremendous explosion which seemed only a few yards away. . . . Shells were falling all around with such frequency that they merged together like the rolling of a drum. One could do nothing but crouch down as far as possible into the slit trench and listen to the spiteful hiss and crash of each shell."[30]

The silence marking the end of the opening barrage was the calm before the storm: "We knew the barrage must have been the prelude to an attack but could never have imagined the intensity of machine gun fire which suddenly shattered the waiting darkness. From both our flanks bullets swept over our heads with the fierceness of a great hailstorm. They hit the ground all around. . . . Tracers were flashing and spitting like sparks from a volcano."[31] The Germans remained unseen and all around. Though the men of Lieutenant Grace's platoon did not give their positions away by firing back, fire from other nearby positions brought groans in German of, *"Otto, Otto! Hilfe! Ich sterbe! Otto!* [Otto . . . Help! I'm dying! . . .]" Otto, however, never appeared and soon the plaintive cries for help ceased. Several attempts to penetrate the B Company positions were repulsed, and all around them the Gordons could hear Germans digging in. Then came orders from Colonel Peddie to launch a counterattack in the morning to drive the Germans off their hill. "We can get no support," the commanding officer, Major R. L. H. Bridgman, was told. "The other three companies are completely out of touch."

The severity of the situation was not immediately understood. Lieutenant Grace recalls that the sounds of German digging were unmistakable.

> As I strained my ears listening it seemed as though a large number of picks and shovels were being plied only a very short distance from our own positions. Suddenly I heard a German voice louder than the other confusing sounds. It was probably an officer attempting to make himself heard on the wireless. Twice he repeated in German, "Yes, my company is in position here beside No. 1 Coy. Two more companies are behind us." Not for some moments did I realise the significance of this message. My platoon, now about twenty-five men, were opposed by two German companies of two hundred men each![32]

As the night ebbed into the gray dawn the remnants of B Company made plans to attack a much larger German force at first light. Grace remembered that Major Bridgman treated the whole affair "quietly and casually as though this were an everyday occurrence." He told his platoon leaders the battalion commander's order would be carried out as directed, even though all understood the task was suicidal. "There's nothing left for us to do but drive the enemy off this ridge. Each platoon will attack at first light."

Moments later came the welcome news that Peddie was sending some Shermans of the 46th Royal Tanks to support the attack. "Thank God for that!" remarked Bridgman. "There's hope for us once again."[33] Elation soon turned to despair as there was no sign of the tanks and the word went out that the attack would commence in thirty minutes with or without the tanks. At about 0630 hours, with barely ten minutes left, there came a message that brought a hint of a smile to the poker-faced Bridgman. "Five Shermans are on the way! They'll be here in fifteen minutes. We are to follow them up, clear the enemy from their trenches and collect the prisoners."

As the rumble of the tanks was heard, the Germans opened their attack on B Company. Here is Lieutenant Grace's graphic account of what followed:

> The leading Sherman tank lumbered slowly out of the orchards behind us. The two attacks were beginning so simultaneously that one might have thought a referee had blown a whistle for the battle to begin. The appearance of the first tank must have caused great consternation, for the Germans hectically fired off belts of machine gun bullets over our heads. A shell landed just beside the tank, which rumbled onwards in a scornful manner.

A second tank made its appearance, and in his slit trench Grace heard a tremendous bang from just above his head.

> Some two hundred yards away a German anti-tank gun . . . was completely destroyed together with the tree that had been camouflaging it. With added confidence the two tanks slowly advanced on the enemy while three more approached from behind. Thundering up to the enemy trenches they poured a hail of machine gun bullets onto the helpless enemy. Further on the right other Germans jumped out of their trenches and began to run away down the hill . . . waiting excitedly in our trenches, [we] opened up with all the weapons we had.

NCOs began to lead the attack as the tanks continued to pour fire on their hapless enemies, who quickly disintegrated much as the Rangers had five days earlier at Cisterna. Many tried to run to safety, one at a time, but few managed to get far before being cut down. As they rumbled forward, German troops "began to run out to the tanks, throwing away their weapons, . . . their hands above their heads." More than one hundred prisoners were taken in a short time, most of them terrified of the Shermans. A captain, one of the four officers captured, turned out to be the officer Lieutenant Grace had heard the night before.[34] As quickly as they had arrived, the Shermans moved to new hull-down positions a half mile north in an attempt to deal with a deadly new threat in the form of Tiger tanks, the leading one of which was knocked out and began spewing thick black smoke. As the battle faded into the distance there was a momentary lull for the men of Company B. They had survived when a modern version of the cavalry had come to their rescue in the most dramatic manner possible. They were the lucky ones. The fate of the remainder of the 6th Gordons the morning of February 4 was tragic.

During the early hours of February 4 Companies A, C, and D simply disappeared, virtually without a trace. An indication that all was not well came shortly after the unexpected success of B Company, when Peddie ordered the three companies to join the Shermans and mop up the Germans inside the pocket. Wire communications had long since been lost and the Gordons' commander was obliged to depend on wireless, which proved none too reliable. Peddie's orders had to be relayed to C Company via A Company. At 0645 A Company reported the approach of six Tigers, and moments later all communications with the unit stopped.[35]

A conversation with D Company brought the sudden and shocking news that A and C companies were leaving their positions and withdrawing. Frantic efforts to restore communications with the two units failed, and a furious Peddie directed D Company to relay an order for them to return to their positions at once. "Very shortly afterwards 'D' Coy went off the air and no communications with them was possible."[36] A thoroughly perplexed and worried Peddie sent his adjutant, Captain James C. Williamson, forward on foot in an effort to learn the fate of his three companies.

Lieutenant Grace takes up the account. "What's the latest news?" queried Major Bridgman, whose inspired leadership on February 3–4 was to earn him the Military Cross. "No one knows anything," replied Williamson. "I'm just going to find our three companies. Meanwhile the C.O. wants you to hang on here."

Williamson "strode on beyond our lines all alone, armed only with a pistol. Nearly an hour later he returned, his legs covered with mud. He had no time to stop except to give us the brief but alarming news that the three companies were no longer there. Apparently they had been completely wiped out. Of the whole battalion ours was the only company left! . . . the battle ground in front of us was still constantly swept by machine gun fire. In spite of this, he swung left to where our companies should have been. No trace of them were [sic] to be seen."[37]

To this day there is no coherent version of what occurred that grim morning, except that three companies of Gordons simply disappeared into the rain and mist. There are some clues to their fate. It is known that the area was infested with German infantry, that between 0640 and 0700, six Tiger tanks were reported in the vicinity of the Via Anziate, and that they turned east and then south toward A Company. One of the survivors, Lieutenant Harry Garioch, states that "soon after midnight a strong enemy force came up behind the ridge to my right and rear and started to dig in." At 0620 Garioch spotted seventeen tanks rumbling down the track from the east, which then stopped at the German infantry positions before attacking A Company from the rear. With all communications now severed, the company commander, Major David Hutcheon, ordered Garioch to report the situation to Colonel Peddie in person. Garioch had not even reached B Company when he was taken prisoner but managed to escape during an artillery barrage and return to A Company.

Major Hutcheon decided to attempt to reach battalion headquarters himself to report the plight of A Company, but as he attempted to leave the safety of a ditch he was killed by a burst of machine-gun fire.[38] At about this time Colonel Peddie received a report of their withdrawal:

> Between 0615 and 0645 hrs . . . a large number of Germans were killed and taken prisoner by 'B' Coy [supported by the tanks of the 46th RTR]. While the German infantry were still being swept out, however, a message came from 'A' Coy to say that six German tanks could be seen . . . at 0630 hours. A few minutes later 'A' Coy reported that they urgently required tank support and were told that it was even then in action north of 'B' Coy's area. At 0645 a message was received from 'D' Coy to say that 'A' and 'C' coys were withdrawing and asking why. I was dumb-founded and ordered a message to be sent to 'D' Coy to hold their ground at all costs. As soon as 'D' Coy opened up on the wireless they reported 'We are now withdrawing' and went off the air. Nothing more was heard from the forward Coys.[39]

One of the survivors, Corporal George Wilson, a member of an antitank crew, ignored the withdrawal order until he and a sergeant had knocked out a Tiger approaching his position. According to Peddie's report:

> At this stage . . . Major Hutcheon gave the order for his Coy to withdraw to Bn. H.Q. I have no knowledge of the reasons that caused him to issue this order, which was of course contrary to my orders and issued without reference to me. The decision to withdraw was not reported to Bn. H.Q. Survivors are unanimous in stating that the order was given at this particular stage, but they cannot say whether the [German] tanks had opened fire. None of the Coy left the position until the order to withdraw was given. . . . Survivors agree that there was a good deal of M[a-

chine]. G[un]. fire now from the [enemy] tanks. . . . There are no survivors from 'C' Coy and only two from 'D' Coy, who shed little light on the matter.[40]

Peddie was unable to reconcile the loss of three companies with what had been reported to him. What Peddie did understand was that the sudden withdrawal of A Company was the key to the potential collapse of the entire right flank of 1st Division:

> The initial withdrawal of 'A' Coy is to me quite inexplicable. Two of the Pl[atoon]s had not apparently even seen enemy tanks when the order to withdraw was given. I am unable to establish whether 'A' Coy was fired on from the west of the road *before* they withdrew. 'C' and 'D' Coys positions would have been virtually untenable once they were dominated from 'A' Coy's position and from the west of the road by M[achine]. G[un] fire. Remarks about being 'surrounded' made by some stragglers are a little difficult to understand as by the time 'A' Coy had withdrawn through 'C' and 'D' Coys, the enemy between 'B' Coy and 'C' and 'D' had been ejected and this was the route by which the stragglers escaped. Some stragglers from 'A' Coy in fact, escorted some prisoners back, who had been mopped up by 'B' Coy and the tanks.[41]

An obviously troubled Peddie wrote that "while 'A' Coy's withdrawal remains unexplained, I feel sure that 'C' and 'D' Coys were placed in a weak position . . . and the calibre of the officers and W[arrant]. O[fficer].s and N.C.O.s was such that I feel a stout resistance was put up." This included the fact that "none of the survivors mention seeing any enemy infantry, apart from dead or those taken prisoner by us."[42]

Fortunately there were other witnesses to the fate of the Gordons. One was Major A. T. Jones, the commander of Company C, of the support group of the 2/7th Middlesex Regiment, whose report read:

> 0700—Enemy tanks observed moving North [toward the A Company positions astride the lateral road].
> 0800—Enemy tanks had now overrun area of leading coys of GORDONS. . . . Leading coys of GORDONS seen to be surrendering.

In his written report, Major Jones noted that at 0800 "many other enemy tanks were milling around the area and I saw several knocked out from fire which appeared to come from the KSLI area. I then saw that the whole of the left coy [A Company] were being rounded up and taken back under escort."[43]

The surrender of the Gordons perplexed another eyewitness, an officer of the Irish Guards, whose report after the battle questioned why the Gordons had found it necessary to surrender when there did not appear to be a compelling reason to do so. The Irish Guards were also aware of the presence of the Tigers and some Mark IV medium tanks that posed a strong threat to both themselves and the Gordons. The two antitank guns that had moved forward during the night were "tucked in under the railway bridge . . . [and] in perfect position and any tank that moved to menace the Gordons was immediately knocked out by this magnificent 3" Naval gun. As far as we could see they accounted for three Mark VI and one Mark IV."[44]

Captain Williamson's attempt to reach the three companies left him in no doubt as to their fate:

> The positions of the three forward companies were definitely in the hands of the enemy at 0800 hours. . . . I was unable to get over the ridge between them and B Company because of the enemy fire which had earlier knocked out several of our tanks. Because of this I continued down behind the ridge westwards towards the main road [the Via Anziate] in order to try and get along the ditch which ran alongside the road and I can confirm that the enemy were in complete control of the ground to the west of the road and were happily advancing south from what had been the Irish Guards position. . . . [There] I was hit by several bullets (fortunately spent) from across the road by a very large German Warrant Officer who was firing what appeared to be the equivalent of a Tommy Gun.[45]

It seems likely that Williamson is correct when he asserts: "The enemy force which had dug itself in during the night to the rear of A Company and those who had infiltrated during the night between B and D Companies, once they were supported by tanks, simply overwhelmed our people once daylight came. Dug in as they were in slit trenches on the forward slopes facing northwest they would have been sitting ducks for armoured vehicles bearing down on them from behind. The manner in which Major Hutcheon was killed bears this out."[46] The unfortunate loss of the Gordons left many unanswered questions, and after the war neither the War Office nor the regiment was able to compile statistics that matched liberated POWs with their former regiments, thus revealing the fate of the men lost the morning of February 4.[47] Like the Rangers, most of the Gordons became prisoners of war but, with minor exceptions, their ultimate fate remains as much of a mystery today as it was to Peddie at Anzio in 1944.

The sudden collapse of the right flank put the entire defense of the Thumb in serious jeopardy. Fortunately, at that moment the Germans were unprepared to take advantage of it. Both the Irish Guards account and Major Jones's report specifically commented on the confusion and uncertainty exhibited by the Germans they encountered. It seemed to the Guards that "the Germans would have been only too delighted to have been taken prisoners themselves," while Jones observed that most seemed more frightened than the British. Most were very young and believed to belong to several panzer grenadier units that, in fact, were part of the Group Gräser strike force.

The loss of three companies decimated the 6th Gordons. The casualty report showed 7 killed, 18 wounded, and from the forward companies 10 officers and 319 enlisted men missing in action, along with four mortars, four antitank guns, and the complete fighting equipment of three companies.[48]

The battle for the Thumb raged throughout the day and spared no one in the 1st Division. Chaos reigned in the Irish Guards sector, where dozens of battles ebbed and flowed. In gullies, along ridgelines, wherever there were combatants there were ambushes and skirmishes. The battle lines had long since become a shambles, and the German infantry and tanks that had successfully infiltrated from both east and west were now freely roaming the area. Men fought in groups, and the miserable weather added to the confusion. The experience of Major Jones was typical. At 1030 hours he was part of a group of Irish Guards attempting to escape entrapment when they were ambushed and captured by a thirty- to forty-man German force. The new POWs were marched north toward the railway bridge and the sector defended by the Sherwood Foresters. "Many men were forced over the railway embankment with hands up, the enemy calling on the Foresters to surrender, many of whom did. The enemy were obviously very frightened and several had been shot. In the confusion some of the British POWs escaped, got hold of arms and counterattacks were staged which proved successful."[49]

Another group of Guardsmen of the battalion HQ captured a small group of Germans and were marching toward Dung Farm when they were captured by a group of some thirty German soldiers who began marching them back in the direction from which they had just come. The party was led by the HQ company commander, Captain Simon Combe, who politely muttered to his guard escort that he was going to kill him at the first opportunity. When their captors became distracted, Combe soon found an opportunity to suit actions to words and led a sudden and deadly counterattack on the Germans. In the ensuing melee the angry Guardsmen slaughtered twenty of their captors, took another nine prisoner, and successfully escaped to the safety of British lines at Carroceto bearing a number of wounded, found in several still-intact Bren carriers near where the railway bridge crossed the lateral road.[50]

The key to the fragile British defense became a single company of beleaguered Irish Guards and the remaining company of the Gordons. Despite being outnumbered and outgunned, they managed to prevent the Germans from isolating and destroying the 3d Brigade. No. 4 Company of the Guards had somehow managed to remain mostly intact and, before withdrawing to Dung Farm, captured over a hundred Germans. To its right B Company of the Gordons clung grimly to its positions throughout the day, and it was this tenacity that kept the entire right flank from collapsing.

During the morning the Guards commander, Brigadier Murray, reported: "The situation was very serious, and something had to be done at once. The enemy were showing signs of activity on the Grenadiers' front, and I told the Divisional Commander that I expected an attack on Carroceto might develop which, if successful, would involve the encirclement of the best part of the Division."[51] Fortunately, the chaos that reigned in the Irish Guards–Gordons sector included the Germans, who seemed unable, and possibly unwilling, to mount any serious effort to punch through to Carroceto and the Factory.

Penney was desperate for reinforcements and wanted Harmon's 1st Armored committed, but Lucas was convinced that the German threat was merely the opening skirmish and that it was too early to employ his only reserve. Instead, by yet another stroke of good fortune, the first units of the British 56th Division were ashore, and the 168th brigade was sent to Penney's rescue.[52] Lucas intended to retain the brigade to strengthen his reserve but was finally persuaded by Penney that its presence was essential to the survival of his division. By midafternoon the 1st Battalion, the London Scottish Rifles, was counterattacking toward the lateral road in an attempt to win back the positions lost when the three forward companies of the Gordons had been wiped out.

Aided by tanks of the 46th Royal Tank Regiment, whose men by this time were intimately familiar with the terrain, the London Scottish fought their way forward over sodden ground under heavy German fire in a driving rain to a point some four hundred yards short of the lateral road. The object of their counterattack was to shore up the right flank long enough to enable Brigadier James to extract the 3d Brigade from its precarious positions between the lateral road and Campoleone Station. From a farmhouse north of the Factory the brigadier coolly directed his men's retreat to safety. BBC correspondent Wynford Vaughan-Thomas witnessed in the gloom of early evening what he later described in his book as a classic in a long line of "triumphant retreats":

> The weary men stumbled through the rain, the wounded supported by their comrades or flung over the Bren-carriers and the antitank guns. The one road was choked with marching columns. . . . There were dead everywhere, with tanks on fire and smoke rolling over the shell-torn fields. . . . The battalions had to leave sorely needed equipment behind;

tanks and anti-tank guns were abandoned and lorries left to burn, but the
brigade was still intact as a fighting organization. . . . This was the reward
that had been torn from the jaws of almost certain defeat.[53]

British losses during the twenty-four hours of the opening battle were
very high. The Irish Guards, who fought brilliantly, could muster only
140 men that night at Dung Farm. The Duke of Wellingtons had lost
260 men, and the newly arrived London Scottish suffered more than
100 casualties in a few short hours of combat. In all, 1st Division casualties were about 1,400 men.[54] Three regiments had been gutted by
losses, leaving the Irish Guards and the Sherwood Foresters with a
fraction of their men still intact. Worst off were the proud Gordons,
whose commander was left with more questions than answers to explain the loss of three entire companies.[55] During the first twenty-four
hours of the German counteroffensive (and forever afterward), Dung
Farm became known to the Gordons as Horror Farm.

The Germans reported 74 killed, 161 wounded, and 498 missing,
of whom 80 percent were believed killed. German data later confirmed
that 19 officers and approximately 900 enlisted men became prisoners
of war on February 3–4.[56]

For the moment von Mackensen was thwarted in his objective of gaining control of Carroceto and the Factory. The large bag of POWs and
the capture of approximately one-half of the Thumb was hardly cause
for elation within the German high command. Indeed, for the British,
the virtually indefensible salient had now been reduced to far-more-
manageable proportions. Among those who were least surprised by the
German failure to take the entire Thumb on February 3–4 was Kesselring, who expressed the opinion that he had not expected von Mackensen to succeed in the first place. Kesselring believed that the Fourteenth Army had overestimated the strength of VI Corps and that the
attack should have commenced at least twenty-four hours earlier,
before the arrival of the 168th Brigade.[57]

The wretched weather grounded the air forces of both sides but it
did not impede the artillery and among the unsung heroes of the first
day of the German counteroffensive were the gunners of the Royal
Artillery and the U.S. Army, whose accurate salvos insured the Germans could not mass Group Gräser for a killing thrust that might have
broken the 1st Division's back.

Penney and Lucas were rarely in agreement and the events of
February 3–4 were no exception. According to Lucas: "General Penney
objected strenuously to any retrograde movement and I had the greatest sympathy for his point of view. I could, however, see no alternative
and, therefore, gave him a direct order to pull out. He probably never

forgave me but I am sure that another 24 hours would have caused the death of many brave men with nothing gained for us." Although it galled Penney to cede terrain that his men had paid for in blood, Lucas was right when he wrote in midafternoon: "News very bad. The British are in serious trouble and I am greatly disturbed about them. I ordered General Penney this morning to withdraw but, due to enemy pressure, he has been unable to do so. I hope it is not too late."[58] To have done otherwise would have played directly into von Mackensen's hands and resulted in the needless loss of the 1st Division and possibly the Anzio beachhead itself.

Lucas had correctly sensed that VI Corps had only begun to experience the wrath of the German attacks and that the worst was yet to come. Artillery ammunition was growing short and replenishment dangerously out of sync with consumption. As a veteran gunner himself, Lucas was only too conscious that it would likely be artillery that would spell the difference between German success or failure. The motto of the U.S. infantry may have been Queen of Battle, but at Anzio artillery was proving that it was king. During the six days of the 3d Brigade Campoleone offensive and withdrawal, the 1st Division gunners fired more than 23,000 rounds, which was more than twenty-seven tons of ammunition.[59] In the days to come the artillery would time and again provide the means for the infantry to survive during the savage German counterattacks.

British morale remained generally high even after the ordeal most had endured during the previous twenty-four hours. There were, however, some exceptions. The following day correspondent Vaughan-Thomas recorded an interview with a 3d Brigade soldier who described seeing a group of British POWs being herded north into captivity. Some shouted: "It's hopeless. You'd better join us." Some of his comrades began doing so until they were ordered back into their slit trenches by the company commander, who was fully prepared to shoot the first soldier to surrender. Others shouted at the POWs to run as they opened fire on the column, killing Germans and British alike.

So ended the first phase of the German counteroffensive. As costly as the battle for the Thumb had been, it was, as Lucas had predicted, merely von Mackensen's opening gambit. On February 7 there began the bloodiest battles yet fought for the Anzio beachhead.

PART III

"Lancing the Abscess"

The German Counteroffensive

If we can wipe them out down there, then there won't *be* an invasion anywhere else.

HITLER

12

The German
Onslaught

There are not enough Huns anywhere to drive us off
this beach.

—LUCAS

The Germans could claim only partial success in the first phase of their counteroffensive. The I Parachute Corps attack failed to advance anywhere near its objective of the Flyover, and although the 1st Division was badly battered from the battles of February 3 and 4, it nevertheless remained intact as a fighting force. Three of the five German battalions participating in the main attack had themselves suffered heavy losses and were obliged to reorganize before von Mackensen could launch the first phase of his counteroffensive.[1]

Lucas's mood swung from cautious optimism that VI Corps could withstand an all-out German counteroffensive to deep concern over casualties, which were now averaging nearly eight hundred per day. Although Allied losses were being replaced, it was at a rate of only some five hundred per day, leaving a shortfall of nearly nine thousand men per month, most of whom were infantry.[2]

The artillery duels continued unabated as the focus of German attention became the Factory, and shells continued to rain down all over the beachhead. On the night of February 6 a 90-mm shell tore through the roof of Lucas's Nettuno command post during his absence but failed to explode.[3] Another German shell found one of the main ammunition dumps outside Nettuno and set off a chain of explosions that made it difficult to differentiate between incoming rounds and those exploding in the nearby dump. Allied gunners retaliated by heavily shelling enemy rear areas where German troops and tanks were concentrating. Even so, after the initial German attacks, there was a slight lull on the ground as both sides made feverish last-minute preparations for the inevitable bloodletting that was certain to characterize the counteroffensive. VI Corps scrambled to prepare as best it could an in-depth defense that would prevent a breakthrough by the Fourteenth Army to the Allied rear areas.

Captured enemy documents soon revealed German intentions, and they were ominous. The main attack was again to be launched by I Parachute Corps, which had orders to seize Carroceto and the Factory. Nine battalions of the 65th Infantry Division, heavily supported by tanks, were to attack across Buonriposo Ridge and along their left flank toward the Factory. On their left, in the LXXVI Panzer Corps sector, another twelve battalions of Battle Group Gräser were to assist in capturing the Factory and exploit down the Via Anziate, south of the Flyover, toward Anzio.

To counter this massive force, the frontline defense of VI Corps remained Penney's beleaguered 1st British Division, whose four understrength brigades were deployed along the outlines of the Campoleone salient, now in the shape of a stubby thumb. The Guards Brigade anchored the left flank from a point along the Embankment, approximately a mile northwest of Carroceto (1st Scots Guards), to Buonriposo Ridge (5th Grenadier Guards and 2d North Staffordshires). Defending the upper right portion of the Thumb, southwest of Dung Farm, was the newly arrived 168th Brigade of the 56th Division, augmented by Colonel Reuben Tucker's U.S. 504th Parachute Infantry Regiment, which was placed astride the Via Anziate. Two battalions (1st London Irish and 10th Royal Berkshires) guarded the Factory, while on the right flank was the 2d Brigade (1st Loyals), a squadron of the 1st Reconnaissance Regiment, and the remnants of the battered 6th Gordons. In reserve was the 3d Brigade, late of the battles for Campoleone Station.

The lull was made all the more miserable by pelting rains, which turned the ground into sticky mud that had the consistency of grease, overflowed ditches and foxholes, and made off-road travel by vehicle all but impossible. Except for the enterprising Irish Guards, who (as part of the division reserve) had found warmth and shelter in the Cava di Pozzolana, a series of caves north of the Flyover, the misery of the troops was lessened only by the absence of heavy fighting.

The first probing attacks came on February 6: short, sharp, and quite brutal small-unit actions generally of platoon size or smaller. It soon became clear that the main German focus was the defenses of the Factory. The 10th Royal Berkshires and 1st London Irish became the recipients of one probe after the other, as the German infantry attacked under the cover of smoke and heavy supporting artillery fire. One of the London Irish companies was in a precarious position by nightfall, but managed to remain in place. The order had gone throughout VI Corps that no ground would be voluntarily given up to the enemy.

Captured documents and prisoners pinpointed the German attack to commence at 0400 the morning of February 7.[4] The moment passed without incident, and the dawn brought sun and clear skies for the first time in days. "There was a deathly stillness throughout the morning . . . the dearth of artillery fire . . . gave portent of something terrible about to happen."[5]

During the afternoon Germany artillery and the Luftwaffe became very active, particularly over Anzio, where the accidental bombing of the U.S. 95th Evacuation Hospital earned it the disparaging designation of Hell's Half Acre.[6] It was obvious to the anxious soldiers manning the frontline positions that the long-awaited attack was not far off. If evidence was needed, it came in the form of larger-than-expected numbers of German prisoners, some of whom were deliberately surrendering to escape the forthcoming battle.

On German maps circles appeared around Aprilia. Badly battered by days of shelling, the Factory was the prize that had to be seized before the counteroffensive could get into high gear. Its outlying defenses were thinly held, for not only was the 1st Division woefully understrength from nearly two weeks of savage combat, but the ebb and flow of the battle for the Thumb had left the division in an impossible position from which to withstand a massive attack. Dung Farm—the hellhole others had dubbed Smelly Farm and Horror Farm—was back in German hands and one of the many places from which the attack against the Factory was expected.

As before, there was no front line in the usual sense, but rather a series of scattered features of terrain defended only by sorely understrength infantrymen, supported here and there by tanks and antitank guns. There was absolutely no continuity. Each unit was expected to fight its own battles in small pockets against an enemy who might attack from any direction. For days the Germans had been infiltrating troops into the British sector, and from hour to hour no one could say with certainty where they were. Some could be observed digging in behind nearby knolls and in the dozens of gullies that crisscrossed the area. Others could only be heard, as could the rumble of diesel engines and the unique squeaking noise made only by the treads of tanks on the move.

As the British official history describes it, the battlefield "presented a deceitful air of openness from the few vantage points, but was very blind to men who were dug-in at ground level or who were moving about at night. . . . The ground was admirably suited to the tactics of infiltration and counter-infiltration and both sides used them."[7] The problems facing the commanders made command and control virtually impossible. Because there was simply no cohesion to the battles fought in the Anzio beachhead, one unit might actually be advancing while another on the flank was withdrawing; a unit might be overrun while others were not even engaged.[8]

These problems were compounded by the fact that most of the fighting inevitably took place at night. Thus, "at the headquarters of battalions commanding officers and others had to read the battle as best they could from the sound of firing, from faint voices conjured out of the air by wireless sets, and from the reports of officers and other messengers sent in from the dark."[9]

Of all the units defending the British sector, the most dangerously positioned was the 2d Battalion of the North Staffordshire Regiment, whose mission was to protect the left flank of the division along Buonriposo Ridge. Rising like an ungainly lump from the plain northwest of the Flyover, the mile-long ridge was the most vulnerable point of the British defenses. If it fell to the Germans the entire Allied left flank would be in danger of collapsing. Small wonder, then, that the Germans began infiltrating wo battalions of the 65th Infantry Division through the southwest portion of the ridge, while other formations attacked along the northeast corner held by the Grenadier Guards. At least two companies managed to penetrate the North Staffordshires, and part of the enemy force advanced undetected as far as the Via Anziate.

At 2100 the night of February 7 the long-awaited attack began with heavy mortar and artillery attacks. The infantry assaults came from all directions, while to the east the LXXVI Panzer Corps launched diversionary attacks against 3d Division positions in the Cisterna sector. Two battalions fell upon the North Staffordshires two hours later. "Hordes of yelling fanatical infantry swamped up onto the ridge, and enemy tanks and self-propelled guns closed in and poured shells into the company area and supply routes. Within an hour 'A,' 'B' and 'C' Companies were almost surrounded, and the battle had resolved itself into a confused pattern of fierce individual hand-to-hand struggles among the slit trenches on the scrub-covered hill top."[10] A and B Companies took heavy losses, and C Company was completely surrounded and eventually ceased to exist when German infantrymen overran their positions.

On the northern end of the ridge the Grenadier Guards were on the receiving end of an equally strong assault, part of which came from behind them, by the same German troops that had penetrated the North Staffordshires and now had No. 3 Company trapped on the forward slopes, where it was impossible to repel an attack from the rear. The Grenadiers suffered heavy losses, and when about fifty men—all that was left of No. 1 and No. 3 companies—attempted to cross German lines to the safety of the Embankment, they found themselves in the jaws of a trap, compelled to surrender. During a chaotic night the Grenadier Guards lost most of No. 4 Company, and its few survivors were pushed into a tiny salient between Buonriposo Ridge and the Via Anziate called the Gully—a quarry that had created an ugly gash in the earth. A normally dry watercourse that began as a track near the Embankment and ran parallel to the highway for six hundred yards before dipping deeply into the ground, the Gully was honeycombed with small caves that harbored Italian civilians who had sought shelter to escape the carnage. On the higher ground near the entrance to the Gully runs Carroceto Creek, nicknamed the Ditch, whose waters were deeper than normal from the heavy winter rains. The Ditch was also covered with a natural obstacle in the form of impenetrable bramble bushes sharp enough to tear a man's clothes to shreds.

> The Gully was the last undefended line west of the road, and if the enemy had broken through at this point they would have cut off not only remnants of the Grenadiers but the American parachutists, the Scots Guards in Carroceto, and the London Irish Rifles in the Factory, as well as opening up a passage to the tanks, which had been heard moving up in readiness behind the German infantry. There never was a more critical moment. The fate of the whole beach-head was about to be fought out in a narrow strip of ground between the Ditch and the Gully.[11]

All that was left to defend against the German onslaught was No. 2 Company, the battalion headquarters and support company, and a company of U.S. paratroopers (Company H, 504th Parachute Infantry) who were part of the division reserve and the only troops that could be sent to assist the Grenadiers. When the Germans on Buonriposo Ridge attempted to exploit their advantage by attacking across the Ditch into the mouth of the Gully, they had every reason to expect success. This sector was held by Major W. P. Sidney's support company, and it was then, as Wynford Vaughan-Thomas writes, at a crucial point in the battle, that the fighting seemed, "for a few brief minutes, to concentrate in a way rare in modern war onto one place and one man."[12]

Guarding the only crossing point over the Ditch, Major Sidney and his tiny group of Grenadiers all that stood between the Germans and the Via Anziate. If the Germans successfully overran this final defensive position, they would control the vital Anzio highway and isolate Carroceto and the Factory, whose defenders would be entirely surrounded. Above Sidney and his men on the slopes of Buonriposo Ridge were the infantrymen of Lieutenant Heinrich Wunn's No. 7 Company, 147th Regiment, of the German 65th Infantry Division.

They began their assault by charging en masse down the slope toward the Grenadiers with the by-now-familiar screaming and shouting that characterized German night attacks. The Germans fully expected to charge across the Ditch, but their attack quickly broke down as they attempted to find a way through the natural defenses of the brambles. The shouting became hysterical as the guns of the Gully's defenders began to cut them down with surgical precision.

Major Sidney—a descendant of Sir Philip Sidney, the Elizabethan soldier, poet, and statesman—was defending with two other Guardsmen the focus of the German assault, a makeshift crossing hacked through the brambles by one of the local farmers, probably to move sheep. The brambles were as effective an aid to the British and American defenders of the Gully as barbed wire, and it was the determined Major Sidney who kept Wunn's infantrymen from driving through the crossing. By the light of a rising moon, he delivered a hail of fire from his tommy gun until the weapon jammed. Sidney then hurled grenade after grenade at the Germans. One Guardsman was killed when he pulled the pin of his grenade prematurely, wounding Sidney in the posterior, where "I bled like a pig."[13]

As Lieutenant Wunn's men made attempt after futile attempt to overrun the British, Sidney kept throwing grenades their way until he himself was finally hit in the face with a stick grenade. About 0330 some of the American paratroopers moved in to assist and by dawn the worst was over. The German attack had failed and would not be repeated during daylight. For the moment the most critical point in the British front continued to hold by the slenderest of threads. The area around the Ditch was littered with German corpses, which served as mute testimony to the ferocity of the engagement. Throughout the following day Wunn could hear the cries for help of the wounded, who were stranded and in great pain on the battlefield.[14] Other than No. 2 Company, which continued to hold its positions along the Embankment near the northeast corner of Buonriposo Ridge, the Grenadiers could muster a mere twenty-nine men and about forty-five U.S. paratroopers.

One officer and his courageous men had held off an entire German infantry company. For his exploits the night of February 7–8, Major Sidney was awarded Britain's highest decoration for valor, the coveted Victoria Cross. Appropriately, the medal was pinned on Sidney's uniform by another Guardsman—Harold Alexander.[15]

The fresh German attacks left the already battered infantry battalions of the British 1st Division slowly bleeding to death in the rain, mud, and scrub of Carroceto and Aprilia. The existence of these men was confined to a few yards around their position. Sometimes it took in another hill, a culvert, perhaps a part of the highway, or one of the landmarks such as the Factory tower or the Embankment. When the torrential rains resumed, the visibility often narrowed to mere feet. Here they fought and bled and very often died in the most miserable of circumstances.

And with each passing hour, as the German attacks increased, so too did British losses. Companies were reduced to platoon size or less, and a growing number of battalions could muster scarcely more than handfuls of men that were re-formed into a company or a small task force. There was little hope of relief, and all fought with the certain knowledge that they were likely to be the next to die.

Throughout the day on February 8 the Germans kept hammering away at the British flanks in an effort to collapse the 1st Division salient. The most-threatened sector remained Buonriposo Ridge. To stem the German advance General Penney sent the remainder of the U.S. parachute battalion to reinforce the 24th Guards Brigade on the left flank. A counterattack in midafternoon by the reserve 3d Brigade against Buonriposo Ridge was led by the Sherwood Foresters, who paid a heavy price to regain a slender hold on the southern slopes of the ridge, well short of the former positions held by the North Staffordshires. Other units of the 3d Brigade were less successful, and the British front line looked like something drawn by a man with a terminal case of the shakes.

Even before these latest losses, the Foresters had been a mere shadow of the unit nearly bled to death at Campoleone a week earlier. The present attack to retake Buonriposo Ridge left A Company with only thirty-five men; other units were scarcely better off. By nightfall the drenching rains had returned, "which froze hands round the handles of picks and shovels, filled boots with water and soaked the Foresters to their skins and compelled them to eat their first issue of bread on the Beach-head in sodden handfuls."[16] Nonetheless mercifully, the Foresters spent the next four days fighting the miserable weather more than they did the Germans, whose attention was focused elsewhere.

Other attacks across the front failed to dislodge the Scots Guards or the London Irish, although an element of the 29th Panzer Grenadier Regiment managed to gain a small toehold along the eastern side of the Factory until three tank destroyers of the 894th Tank Destroyer Battalion, led by First Lieutenant Bernard T. Schaefer, intervened. Schaefer's tank destroyer raked the house where the Germans were holed up with .50 caliber machine-gun fire and shells from its 90-mm gun. Forty Germans died, and the remaining thirty immediately surrendered.[17]

As the battle entered the second night an uneasy calm reigned before the next phase. The attacks had further sapped the already badly weakened British 1st Division. Casualties to the North Staffordshires were nearly 50 percent: Of the 40 officers and 664 men who had been defending Buonriposo Ridge the previous night, only 17 officers and 364 men remained.[18]

The 5th Grenadiers were in far worse shape. What had once been a rifle battalion of more than 800 officers and men was reduced to less than 25 percent of its original strength and, at the front, to less than 10 percent.[19] As the Grenadiers faced a second night defending the Gully, the Germans again attempted to find a way across the Ditch and were again repelled. But the rains had turned the Gully into a river, whose waters were now more than a foot deep, making it impossible to defend any farther. The handful of exhausted surviving defenders were ordered withdrawn, and the remnants were able to re-form along the Embankment, near the Via Anziate, in the early morning hours of February 9. During what turned out to be their final day in the line in support of the nearby Scots Guards in Carroceto, the Grenadiers' ordeal continued as the Germans renewed their attacks and killed the new battalion commander, Lieutenant Colonel A. C. Huntington, who had taken command only that day. His replacement was the fourth commanding officer in the three weeks the battalion had fought at Anzio. By February 11 what little was left of this proud battalion was not enough to muster a fighting force, and the battalion was relieved, its job at Anzio done and its losses staggering: 9 officers killed, 12 wounded, and 8 captured; 52 enlisted men killed, 222 wounded, and another 303 missing in action.[20]

Another unit near the end of its rope was the Irish Guards. When the Germans attacked Buonriposo Ridge, the Guards' brief respite from combat was ended. No. 1 Company was sent to the aid of the North Staffordshires the night of February 8 over the objections of Colonel Scott, who, in a tense, emotional wireless confrontation, told Brigadier Murray that the situation was too confused to commit nearly half of what remained of the battalion. "We have not the men to spare for gestures. It is throwing good men away," he pleaded. "This is now the position to hold and we can do it if you will cut your losses. Some of the North Staffords are trickling back. . . . By the morning you will have enough survivors to put in a proper counterattack."[21]

Murray's order stood, and Scott sat silently by the radio before ordering No. 1 Company off into the night. For awhile the unit (in reality it was only two platoons) remained in radio contact with battalion HQ until its terse, final transmission—"We've hit the Germans"— was followed by deathly silence. The following morning twenty men who had become separated in the dark returned with no idea of what had happened to their comrades. It was only some days later, when Radio Rome blared the names of some of the men of No. 1 Company, that its fate became clear.[22]

The Germans finally succeeded in capturing the Factory the afternoon of February 9, leaving the British hanging on to the Carroceto railway station and the nearby overpass, where the Embankment spanned the Via Anziate. The ordeal of the London Irish defending the Factory was now entering a third day of "very hard, bitter and almost continuous fighting." The previous thirty-six hours' battles now paled next to the size and ferocity of the German attacks. During the night of February 8–9 regimental-size attacks fell on the defenders of the Factory. The London Irish and Royal Berkshires bore the brunt of German fury. During the night, when attacks came from left and right, parts of the Irish simply disappeared as communications were severed.

By dawn it was increasingly evident that the German tide could not be stemmed much longer. Tanks, artillery, mortars, and a gray tide of German infantrymen slowly began to strangle the defenders of the Factory. Typical of the urgent wireless exchanges the morning of February 9 were these entries in the Royal Berkshires' war diary:

> 0638 hours—Enemy tanks approach from the north-east.
> 0652 hours—Enemy tanks approach from the east.
> 0704 hours—More enemy tanks.[23]

The Royal Berkshires, defending the division right flank east and north-east of the Factory, were overwhelmed a short time later. By 0830 hours the battalion commander had little left to command except his own small headquarters element, two sections of Charlie Company, and a handful of other troops; in all only about forty men remained of a battalion that had arrived at Anzio at full strength. As they calmly awaited the final German attack, the regimental history records: "Then came a miracle. . . . No further attacks. No advance. The Germans, depleted and exhausted, could not—or did not—walk on, but halted in the forward company's positions and remained there for some days."[24] Later that afternoon the survivors quietly disengaged and were sent to the rear, where the battalion ordeal was over for the time being.

So too for the London Irish. Their main tormentors were para-troopers attached to Battle Group Gräser, whose mission was to capture the Factory. The Irish were chewed up unit by unit. D Company vanished in the gray tide and A and B companies could barely muster a third of their normal strength. A radio message from the B Company commander told of their plight: "I am doing all I can but it looks as if this is our last fight." When an A Company counterattack eased the pressure, this message came: "I must apologise for my earlier despondency."[25] The survivors—about two companies—were pulled back to new positions along the lateral road south of the Factory, which ran east from Carroceto to the Fosso della Ficoccia, where the remnants of the

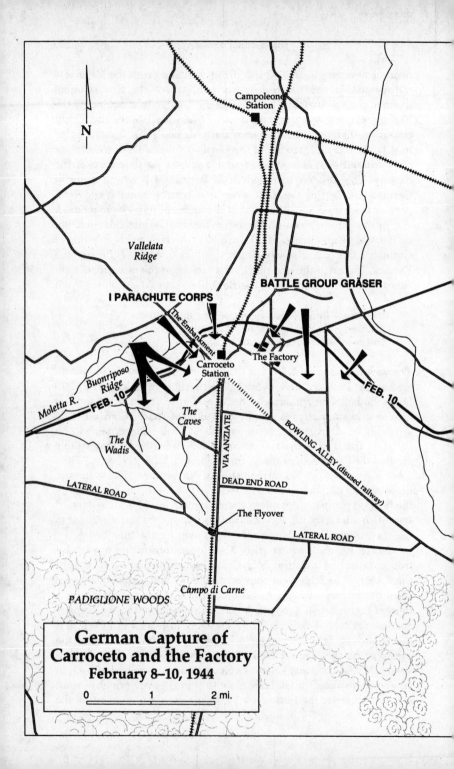

Campoleone
Station

*Vallelata
Ridge*

I PARACHUTE CORPS

BATTLE GROUP GRÄSER

The Embankment

Carroceto
Station

The Factory

*Buonriposo
Ridge*

Moletta R.   FEB. 10

FEB. 10

*The
Caves*

*The
Wadis*

VIA ANZIATE

LATERAL ROAD

DEAD END ROAD

BOWLING ALLEY (disused railway)

The Flyover

LATERAL ROAD

Campo di Carne

PADIGLIONE WOODS

German Capture of
Carroceto and the Factory
February 8–10, 1944

0   1   2 mi.

Royal Berkshires were defending the extreme right flank of the 1st Division.

By midday the Germans had taken control of most of the Factory but remained thwarted in their attempts to capture Carroceto. All that remained of the left flank of the Thumb was a small bulge in and around Carroceto, manned by what was left of the Irish Guards and by the sorely depleted 1st Battalion, Scots Guards. They had stood firm against local attacks, but by the time the 168th Brigade had completely withdrawn from the Factory and were in fresh positions along and below the lateral road, the Scots Guards were the only British unit defending a position north of the Embankment. Their only escape route to the south was guarded by the pitiful remains of the Grenadiers and the American paratroopers. The Germans reported the capture of 420 British troops and a lone American that day.[26]

An attempt by tanks of the U.S. 1st Armored Division to retake the southwest end of Buonriposo Ridge bogged down at once in the mud and a minefield and succeeded mainly in annoying the British troops they had come to assist, by attracting huge volumes of unwelcome German artillery fire.[27] Seven tanks of Company B, 3d Battalion, 1st Armored Regiment, were lost. Once again the unsuitability of armor at Anzio anywhere but on a solid highway had been graphically demonstrated.

The afternoon of February 9, the entire focus of the Allied defensive effort in the Anzio beachhead was concentrated on the left flank, as Allied cruisers offshore and the massed fires of the VI Corps artillery pounded the Germans. Two hundred twenty-four Allied aircraft joined in the attempt to stem the German advance. The colossal Allied artillery concentrations apparently had little effect, however, and, according to Penney's personal diary, were aimed at targets northwest of the British front. When Lucas called at 1400 hours to inform Penney of the impending bombardments, the 1st Division commander asked for a reason, inasmuch as such an attack was not needed in that sector. Lucas was unable to respond, except to note that the corps artillery officer had spotted German targets there.[28]

In the early morning hours of February 10 the Germans turned their attention to the last of their objectives and launched heavy attacks against Carroceto. Carroceto was defended by the 24th Guards Brigade, at full strength well over 2,500. This day its three battalions were at less than one-third strength. Those Grenadiers who had survived Buonriposo Ridge and the Gully were bolstered by the arrival of a hundred hastily assembled replacements, but the Irish Guards were split, with No. 4 Company forward to assist the Scots Guards defense of Carroceto, while the rest of the battalion remained in reserve in the Caves.

The Scots Guards had shortened their lines and were defending from the stone buildings of the Carroceto railway station. From plans found on a captured German warrant officer, they knew an attack by three regiment-size formations was imminent. While the 29th Panzer Grenadier Regiment attacked east from the Factory, the 65th Infantry Division would attack along the Embankment and a regiment of the 4th Parachute Division from the direction of Vallelata Ridge.

Shortly after midnight the German attack from the direction of the Factory signaled the beginning of the end for the Scots Guards. A German infantry force of undetermined size was spearheaded by tanks, which had easily bypassed the exposed British right flank. One of the tanks, a Mark IV,[29] rumbled to a halt about forty yards from the railway station. The rains had stopped again, and by the light of a full moon the tank began to destroy the railway station. Rounds from its 75-mm gun tore gaping holes in the building and its machine gun delivered a hail of fire through the holes. The station began to fall down on the heads of its trapped defenders, who had retreated to the cellar that now began to fill with dead and wounded men. By wireless the adjutant reported to Brigade HQ: "There is a [bloody] great German tank sitting outside my door demolishing my house brick by brick."[30]

As the scene of desolation around Carroceto Station worsened, the battalion commander, Lieutenant Colonel Wedderburn, realized that something had to be done to remove the obnoxious German intruder before what was left of the battalion bled to death. At great risk, Wedderburn and a captain ran a gauntlet of fire to the rear, where several U.S. M-10 tank destroyers and a troop of Shermans had sought the protective cover of the Embankment. The next few hours were among the most frustrating of Wedderburn's life. Although the German tank was barely more than two hundred yards away, to his amazement and disgust Wedderburn learned that no one would come to his aid. He argued, pleaded, cajoled, threatened, and raged for *four hours* in a futile attempt to enlist one of the tanks or tank destroyers to his cause. None would respond, and his own brigade headquarters refused to order the armor forward. As a surviving Irish Guards officer later observed, "Our tanks, which were waiting behind the embankment for just such an occasion, seemed to think this was none of their business."[31] Throughout the night pleas over the wireless for help went unheeded. At 0430 Wedderburn returned empty-handed and justifiably embittered.[32]

A postwar American monograph applauds the actions of the U.S. tank destroyers that night, noting that "the 'fighting tank busters,' as the British troops called them, appeared to be all over the battlefield. In addition to their normal role, they operated as tanks, as mobile pillboxes, as assault artillery, and even as infantry. The British troops, fighting against odds, needed their support."[33] The men of the Scots Guards might be forgiven for disbelieving such a claim. Even though the German Mark IV that was tormenting the railway station was a sitting duck in the open under the bright moon, no one was willing to engage it.

With dawn not far off, Wedderburn reluctantly ordered his HQ moved back to the safety of the Embankment. The withdrawal was covered by No. 4 Company of the Irish Guards, which remained in defense of Carroceto Station. In the Caves Colonel Scott became deeply worried when all communications were lost about dawn after this final message: "We must have a tank-destroyer up to settle this tank."[34] Scott's fears were fully justified: They were never heard from again. Only after the war was it learned that with the aid of the Mark IV tank, three companion tanks, and two self-propelled antitank guns, German paratroopers had stormed the station redoubt, captured its surviving occupants, and smashed the radios. The outlying elements of the Irish Guards had been no match for an overwhelming force and they too had either been killed or captured.

The Irish Guards found their captors "very korrect" and honorable soldiers. Those who were wounded remained in the cellar of the station for another day. Two surviving Guardsmen later told the tale of their German ambulance driver, who was

> either drunk or very stupid for he had no sense of direction, and at first drove into British lines. They passed a private of the Duke of Wellington's Regiment, who had cut his hand opening a bully-beef tin. . . . The "Duke" thumbed a lift, the Germans leapt out and bundled him into the back of the ambulance. To this day that "Duke" does not know what happened to him. All the way to Rome he repeated plaintively, "The platoon sergeant will have my life for being away so long."[35]

So ended the first phase of the German counteroffensive. A scratch force of Scots Guards and Grenadiers under the command of Colonel Wedderburn continued to cling to the Embankment pending the arrival of the Duke of Wellingtons to replace them. The rain was back, and the ugly carnage of war was everywhere to be seen.

> The embankment was a scene of peculiar desolation. The rain beat down on a litter of smashed equipment and burnt vehicles, shattered ammunition and derelict tanks. Lying on his back was a Gunner officer, shot through the head, and then run over by a tank. It was not a pretty sight. Up on the embankment the sodden, exhausted remnants of two battalions crouched in their slit trenches. Battalion H.Q. was in a culvert . . . knee-deep in water . . . looking tired, but unmoved in the babel was Colonel

> Wedderburn surrounded by Americans, Sappers, Gunners—all that could be scraped together to reinforce the Scots Guards and Grenadiers.[36]

The Germans had intended to capture the Carroceto-Aprilia salient the night of February 8. Instead, it took three days of some of the bitterest fighting anyone at Anzio would experience to complete the task. Although von Mackensen had achieved the objectives of the first phase of his counteroffensive, the price had been so high that he was obliged to call a halt while his forces regrouped to prepare for the second and decisive thrust that would crush VI Corps and "lance the abscess south of Rome" once and for all.

The three-day battle for Carroceto and the Factory typified the bad feeling and misunderstanding between Penney and Lucas. By the morning of February 11 Penney had reported that the ability of the 1st Division to hold out without reinforcements was near an end. Penney's dilemma was one of the catch-22s of war. He was ordered to hold positions that were essentially untenable with only token reinforcements from his corps commander, but when his division paid the price, was soundly criticized by Lucas for not making the most of his situation.

Nothing could have been farther from the truth. The defense of the indefensible by the gallant rifle battalions of the 1st Division was one of the outstanding feats of the war by any formation, Allied or German. And in the process the division was all but destroyed. The casualty rate estimated by the British official historians displays evidence of excessive conservatism:

EFFECTIVE STRENGTH OF 1ST DIVISION RIFLE BATTALIONS, FEBRUARY 10, 1944

	Official Estimate	Author's Estimate (Based on Casualty Rates)
5th Grenadier Guards	50%	26%[37]
1st Scots Guards	55%	20%[38]
1st Irish Guards	60%	30%[39]
2nd North Staffordshire	55%	insufficient data available
6th Gordons	65%	46%[40]
1st DWR	65%	insufficient data available
2nd Foresters	65%	30–35%[41]
1st KSLI	65%	insufficient data available
10th Royal Berkshires	30%	30%
1st London Scottish	40%	40%
1st London Irish	40%	insufficient data available

During the three days of the battle for Carroceto and the Factory British losses were appalling. On the first day of the battle the Germans reported capturing 791 British, most of whom were Grenadiers, North Staffordshires, and Irish Guards. The following day the Fourteenth Army reported another 420 British POWs and a lone American, while on February 10, 326 more British and 12 Americans were taken. During the seven-day period from February 4 to 11, 2,563 Allied soldiers, virtually 99 percent of whom were British, filled the German prisoner-of-war cages.[42] This equated to the capture of more than three full-strength infantry battalions. When the killed, wounded, and those lost for nonbattle reasons are added to this total, it becomes possible to visualize the dreadful losses incurred in the defense of Carroceto and the Factory during only one week of the Anzio campaign. And the main battles had yet to be fought!

Until the morning of February 11, when regiments of the 45th Division began arriving in force to take up the defense of the Carroceto-Factory salient, Lucas had consistently denied Penney the reinforcements he had sought for three days. On February 8, Lucas "reiterated [his] order to hold where we were and said that he could provide nothing from corps reserve to help." The following day Penney personally went to the VI Corps command post in Nettuno and informed Lucas that "I was getting so weak that I couldn't go on holding [the] present line unless [a] major counter attack [were] staged and [the] front shortened." That evening the VI Corps chief of staff replied to the latest grim report from Penney that "orders stood to fight it out."[43]

Finally, at 0530 the morning of February 10 came the final warning that his situation had become intolerable and that some decision must be reached on either the relief of his division or a counterattack. Half an hour later came the first positive decision from VI Corps in more than three days. The 45th Division would counterattack that day to restore the line and retake the Factory.[44] The 45th Division commanders had no sense of the battlefield or the conditions that faced them, and the attack was delayed until the following morning, much to the dismay of Penney, who believed the Germans were exceptionally vulnerable to a counterattack by fresh troops.

Despite the terrible toll taken of his division, Penney remained full of fight and after the war was incensed by a comment in an unofficial account that he had reported to Lucas "that his division could not hold without the help of a counter-attack by fresh troops who would have to take over much of his front."[45] The essence of Penney's report to Lucas was that the "situation cannot go on. S[cots] G[uards], I[rish] G[uards] and Gren Gds attacked all night and factory strongly held by Germans. Gds gradually fading out—attack by fresh tps necessary to reestablish the front and to hold it to allow 1 Div to reorganise and to biff the enemy a blow for which he is ripe."[46] In short, Penney needed reinforcements and did not get them until the situation became desperate.

Although Lucas himself rated the situation on the left flank "highly dangerous" on February 8, he never fully understood the problems facing Penney and the British. After the counterattack that same afternoon, Lucas complained that he wished he had an American division there. "It is probably my fault that I don't understand them any better. I think they suffer excessive losses. They are certainly brave men but ours are better trained, in my opinion, and I am sure that our officers are better educated in a military way." A day later came further criticism: "The British are badly disorganized and knocked to pieces. It seems to me they are in worse shape than they should be considering what they have done."[47]

Lucas rarely visited the front and seemed to have little appreciation for the problems facing Penney. By his own admission, it was essential to retain control of both Carroceto and the Factory, yet the attempt to do so resulted in a perilously unstable front that was indefensible against the massive attacks launched by von Mackensen.

What irked Penney was how out of touch the VI Corps commander and staff were with the situation. Writing in 1956, Penney noted: "I was not prepared to go on having my Division eaten away piecemeal while the Corps Commander and his staff sat in their cellars in Nettuno and never even came up to see what the situation was and who therefore required something in the nature of a sledgehammer to drive anything into their heads. The Boche and the time were both ripe for a vigorous counter stroke and the Corps Commander had the means to deliver it."[48]

Both protocol and good leadership demand that a senior officer visit his subordinates and personally assess the conduct of a battle. This Lucas conspicuously failed to do. Unfortunately, the bad blood between Lucas and Penney became part of a larger issue of nationality that only exacerbated a very dangerous military situation. Penney was correct when he asserted that at Anzio it was impossible to understand the situation at the front without personal contact with those doing the fighting. "No British Corps Commander or staff would have failed to realise that or to have acted upon it."[49]

Lucas was not happy with the obvious need to commit his only reserve, the U.S. 45th Division. The previous day he had asked Clark for an additional infantry division. The Fifth Army commander's reaction was one of irritation. His diary noted that Lucas "should know better than to demand another infantry division, realizing full well that I do not have the division, except those that are tired and committed to battle, nor do I have the shipping, nor could it be maintained logistically in the beachhead."[50] However, when the Factory fell the next day,

Clark and Alexander were persuaded that it was essential to send the other two brigades of Gerald Templer's 56th British Division.

Whereas Clark and Lucas were thinking defensively and only in terms of limited counterattacks to restore the British front line, Alexander seemed bent on resuming the offensive to carry out the beachhead mission of VI Corps. A February 11 cable from Alexander to Lucas directed him to "resume the offensive immediately the tactical situation permits." Lucas dismissed this latest entreaty as beyond his control until "considerably reinforced."[51]

Penney's relentless prodding finally brought Lucas out of his shell and to the British front the afternoon of February 10, where he held a conference to coordinate the counterattack by the 45th Division to recapture the Factory the following morning. Here is Penney's recollection of that meeting:

> Eventually Gerald Templer and myself persuaded the Corps that the counter-attack was necessary and the Corps Commander agreed to hold a conference at the Headquarters of the Guards Brigade (his first time out). It was a travesty, pathetic and tragic. I gave the situation and Lucas turned to General Eagles and said "O.K., you give them the works." No G-2 appreciation, no orders, no intention, no objective, no nothing. Lucas then left and I said to Eagles "I have got 6 Regiments of Artillery in action whose guns can all fire on the front of your attack. What do you want?" Eagles reasonably replied that he would send his Artillery Commander to see mine.
>
> The attack was to be made at first light the next day. The 45th Divisional Artillery Commander came to see Peter Paisley [the commander, Royal Artillery] after dark. Peter Paisley asked him what he wanted to do and the American replied, "Say General, you know more about this part of the country than I do and what to shoot at." Paisley thereupon asked him what the plan of attack was, Infantry, tanks, etc. The answer he got was "Say General, I am only the Artillery commander; I don't know anything about the Infantry."[52]

After the conference a British signals officer, Captain Nicholas Mansell, wrote sarcastically in his diary, "Would you believe it? Old Corncob Charlie has actually *been* near here to see Penney and the Guards HQ."[53] Yet Lucas never did see the battlefield itself and consequently failed to gain even the slightest appreciation of the desolate, gully-riddled country or the problems faced by Penney and his troops.

The decision for the 45th Division to counterattack the Factory on February 11 failed to reassure the British, who now more than ever were convinced that Lucas and his VI Corps staff were incapable of directing the battle. Even so, morale remained excellent, which was in itself a tribute to British grit and determination in the face of the most appalling conditions.

German losses were heavy, but considerably less than those inflicted on the 1st Division. Nevertheless, the three days taken to accomplish what had been anticipated as a one-day operation left von Mackensen's forces unable to continue the second and decisive phase of the counteroffensive without yet another period of consolidation and preparation. It had proved necessary to commit the German reserves to the battle, and eventually the equivalent of more than twenty battalions of infantry were involved in the battle for Carroceto and the Factory. Like their enemy the Germans were obliged to come to grips with the horror of the Anzio battlefield. When Lieutenant Wunn's panzer grenadiers finally took control of the Gully after capturing eighty British POWs, they were greeted by a scene of horror. As Raleigh Trevelyan writes, "The stench of death and cordite was incredible." Among the dead was a British soldier being eaten by three starving pigs that were running loose in the Gully. Staff sergeant Bernhard Luy became enraged and fired at the pigs to drive them away from the rotting, half-eaten corpse. "Is this what we are fighting for, to be eaten by pigs?" Luy and another soldier buried the dead Tommy.[54]

As was common throughout the campaigns in Sicily and Italy, German morale remained the highest among the men of the parachute corps. One cocky German major politely asked his British captor in heavily accented English, "Ver is der sea?" When told, he replied, "Tank you very much, I vanted to know for you vill soon be in it."[55]

13

"Deafening, Mad, Screaming Senseless Hatred"[1]

This battle must be won. . . . It may be the decisive battle of the Italian campaign.

—LUCAS

The struggle for the Factory was renewed on February 11 by the Thunderbirds of the U.S. 45th Division,[2] as American forces were baptized into the horror of Aprilia during some of the bitterest fighting of the campaign. Backed by heavy artillery fire a tank-infantry task force of the 1st Battalion, 179th Regiment, and two tank companies of the 191st Tank Battalion attacked the Factory from two directions. The fighting became hand-to-hand in the ruins, and despite being near the end of their tether the Germans inside the Factory managed to launch a counterattack that drove the Thunderbirds back to a point some five hundred yards to the south. After more than two weeks of pounding the Factory had been reduced to a rubble-strewn ruin. Although the Germans were the temporary tenants, Charon, the mythical boatman who ferried dead souls across the River Styx to Hades, was the real master of Aprilia.

The 1st Battalion, 179th Regiment, bore the brunt of the German fury. A Company suffered such heavy losses that only three officers and forty enlisted men were left unscathed. With considerable understatement an official U.S. Army monograph stated: "It appeared that a major effort would be required to retake the Factory."[3] The attack failed in part because of a breakdown in support between the infantry and the supporting 191st Tank Battalion of Harmon's 1st Armored. The regimental historian later wrote with considerable bitterness that the Germans

> dug in around the Factory spewed forth overpowering small arms, machine gun and tank fire. Then, from behind Carroceto tanks thundered out, straight at the U.S. riflemen. Behind the armor came counterattacking enemy infantry. And the 191st's tanks were nowhere to be found—they were two hours late! Unsupported and isolated, the attackers, what was left of them, fell back for fear of annihilation.[4]

With minor exceptions tanks at Anzio were roadbound and often a liability. An example occurred that morning when, in the gray light of dawn, some seventy U.S. tanks rumbled up the Via Anziate in single file. As the regimental history of the Irish Guards recounts:

> The column paused and the three leading tanks rolled under the bridge and out the other side. The Germans knew what to do—they brought their guns down on the road and turned mortars on the embankment. From the far side of the embankment came the clatter of Browning machine-guns and the thud of anti-tank guns. One more tank went through the bridge and then shot back again. The whole clanking column turned and slowly rumbled back towards the sea. "What good they did," said the Brigadier [Murray], "I never heard," and neither did anybody else.[5]

The first tank had run into trouble immediately after passing under the Embankment overpass, when it took a direct hit from a German artillery shell. A second Sherman attempting to gain the east-west lateral road leading to the Factory hit a mine two hundred yards beyond the overpass and the attack died. As a result the U.S. infantry found itself supported only by friendly artillery fire. The tank company in support of B Company, 1st Battalion, 179th Regiment, never advanced beyond the road junction southeast of the Factory and soon withdrew to the rear after running out of ammunition.

The division historian believed that two regiments could have retaken the Factory that day, but only one regiment and, in turn, only the 1st Battalion, was committed to attacking the Factory. In the end, it was undertaken by only two rifle companies, which, without tank support, were not sufficiently powerful to dislodge the Germans.[6] Truscott later criticized Eagles for failing to employ the entire regiment against the Factory. Even had he done so, however, it was later revealed that the attack had been compromised when the Germans intercepted a radio message two hours before, enabling General Gräser to reinforce the Factory in time.[7]

A second attempt by the entire 1st Battalion, supported by a tank company, began at 0200 hours on February 12 and failed when the German defenders again mounted a small but powerful counterattack at dawn. New American positions were established five hundred yards south of the Factory, and yet another battle for the ruins of Aprilia ended in failure.

While the 45th Division was attacking the Factory, the Duke of Wellingtons were catching hell in their new positions along the Embankment. Fierce fighting on February 12 forced the Dukes to withdraw to new positions some five hundred yards south of the Embankment.

Although both sides could claim at least a moral victory in the struggle for control of the Anzio beachhead, time was now on the Allies' side. If Kesselring and von Mackensen were to achieve their object of destroying the VI Corps beachhead, they would have to do so before the Allies could rush additional reinforcements to Anzio. The powerful Allied air interdiction effort was taking a toll of the German fuel supplies, which were beginning to run dangerously low.

Nevertheless, the Germans had captured important intermediate objectives from which to initiate their decisive thrust to crush the Allied expeditionary force. With each passing day the Fourteenth Army's strength was being increased by the arrival of numerous additional infantry, panzer grenadier, parachute, and panzer units, bringing their total numbers to a staggering 125,000 troops, of which 70,000 were combat forces.[8] These included the 114th Jäger Division from Yugoslavia and the 362nd Infantry Division from northern Italy. Three more independent infantry regiments and a tank battalion had also arrived, and German forces now numbered the equivalent of ten divisions versus less than five for VI Corps.[9] Lucas controlled approximately one hundred thousand Allied troops in the burgeoning Anzio beachhead.[10]

As savage as the fighting had been up to this point, the worst was yet to come, as von Mackensen prepared the long-awaited counteroffensive, which was assigned the code name Fischfang: "to catch fish." Other than its scope, the German plan varied little from their earlier tactics. Two corps would simultaneously attack both ends of the Allied beachhead line. I Parachute Corps was to carry out the main attack down the Albano-Carroceto-Anzio highway, while the LXXVI Panzer Corps launched a diversionary attack toward Anzio from Cisterna. Von Mackensen still believed he could crush the main Allied defenses with overwhelming infantry attacks along the narrow, four-thousand-yard-wide front and exploit the breach with his massed armor to Anzio and Nettuno.

At 0630 hours on February 16 the two corps would launch attacks toward Anzio, using the Via Anziate as the focal point. To the west of the highway, I Parachute Corps would also attack with two divisions to secure the flank and place added pressure on the Allied line. To the east of the highway the main attack was to be carried out in two waves. The first echelon would spearhead the attack with the 3d Panzer Grenadier Division, the 715th Infantry Division, and the Infantry Lehr Regiment, which had been sent personally by Hitler to Anzio. Exploiting directly behind them would come the second echelon, consisting of two veteran divisions, the 29th Panzer Grenadier and the 26th Panzer.

In an attempt to sow confusion and mask their true intentions, German forces were to commence simultaneous attacks across the entire front line of the beachhead. A heavy feint attack was to be aimed at Isola Bella, and the two exploiting divisions were to remain in the Cisterna area until the morning of February 16 to convince the Allied commanders that they were part of the attacks from Cisterna.

Tight security prevailed. No one was permitted to discuss the forthcoming attack over the telephone, and the movement of German tanks the night before the attack was to be drowned out by noise from nuisance attacks by the artillery and the Luftwaffe.

Up to now Hitler's influence in the operational conduct of the Italian campaign had been minimal. Unfortunately for Kesselring, the Führer's penchant for meddling in the tactics employed by his generals surfaced over Fischfang. On February 5 von Mackensen appeared personally before Hitler to present his plan for the counteroffensive. Hitler viewed success at Anzio as an essential factor in delaying or even forcing the cancellation of the expected cross-Channel attack. Von Mackensen's chief of staff, Major General Wolf Hauser, wrote after the war: "Hitler placed considerable political significance on the outcome of this battle. He believed that if it ended successfully the Allied invasion of western Europe would at least be postponed." Unfortunately for the front-line commanders, "Hitler and OKW interfered a great deal with the tactical direction of the attack. Thus, Hitler ordered the attack to be made on a front of scarcely more than six kilometers."[11]

Von Mackensen would later complain somewhat disingenuously that Hitler had reduced the front too severely,[12] but Kesselring believed that the Fourteenth Army commander was "generally pleased with the results and looked upon Hitler's excitement as a fait accompli."[13] When von Mackensen pressed for an additional division his request was refused, but Jodl persuaded Hitler to send to Anzio the Infantry Lehr, a highly regarded demonstration regiment stationed near Berlin. Neither commander was happy with Hitler's order that this prestigious formation was to be included in the main attack force, but neither was willing to incur the Führer's wrath by challenging his edict.

Although Kesselring was uneasy about the delay in launching Fischfang, he was confident that the offensive would be successful.

German morale was high, perhaps artificially so as a result of Hitler's recent order of the day to wipe out the "abscess" south of Rome. As with the earlier attacks on the left flank, the German commanders never seriously entertained any thought of an attack along the coast to roll up the beachhead from the northwest or from the northeast, along the Mussolini Canal.[14] It was to be the Via Anziate, and both sides knew it; the only question left was when the attack would begin. (It was hardly revealing when a German paratrooper from the 10th Parachute Regiment captured on February 15 by the Duke of Wellingtons blabbed that "big things" were soon to commence.)[15]

THE FIRST DAY: FEBRUARY 16

The second and decisive phase of the battle for Anzio began at dawn on one of the first sunny days in weeks. A massive German artillery barrage filled the sky over the front lines with heavy clouds of smoke and dust, from which emerged waves of infantry, in their field gray-green uniforms, heavily supported by tanks. Despite its initial intensity, which made it the heaviest concentration yet fired at Anzio, there were such growing shortages of artillery ammunition that the German gunners could not sustain the rate for long without seriously jeopardizing their needs for the remainder of the counteroffensive, and strict controls were imposed on its expenditure.*

The area south of the Factory again became the scene of the most intense fighting, as the 45th Division incurred the full wrath of the German break-in attacks. The 715th Infantry Division attacked from its ruins, while from the direction of Carroceto came attacks by the 3d Panzer Grenadier Division down the Via Anziate.

The attacks on the right flank of the 45th Division were easily contained by the 180th Regiment, but it was the 179th Regiment and the 2d Battalion, 157th Regiment, that bore the brunt of the German counteroffensive on February 16. The regimental historian described the attackers as "wave upon wave, a grey blur, a flesh and steel tide" that once unleashed seemed unstoppable. As the British had long since

---

*The supporting artillery fire came from the combined fires of 452 weapons, ranging from antiaircraft guns, rocket launchers, howitzers, and field guns to the two massive railway guns, "Anzio Annie" and "Anzio Express." These two weapons received the lion's share of postwar attention, and few may be aware that there were two other railway guns only slightly smaller (21-cm versus 24-cm) that also inflicted considerable damage and casualties at Anzio. One of these guns was destroyed and the second derailed during a series of heavy air attacks shortly before the German counteroffensive. The conservative von Mackensen was so concerned about these losses that he attempted to delay the start of the offensive, but he was firmly overruled.

learned, once begun, these battles quickly turned into a free-for-all as the front lines disintegrated into chaotic small-unit actions. "Time ceased, only 'Sturm and Drang' remained."[16]

German tanks, followed by a gray tide of infantry on foot, raced down the Via Anziate in an attempt to overwhelm Captain Felix L. Sparks's Company E, 2d Battalion, 157th Regiment, which had moved into blocking positions along the Via Anziate south of the Embankment only the previous night. The first attack succeeded in overrunning the left platoon and knocking out one of the two tank destroyers attached to the company, but not before losing two panzers and a large number of infantry, which were cut down by the machine guns from the surviving tank destroyer.

Two of the three attacking panzers were destroyed in the nick of time at a range of about 150 yards. The devastating fire of the three-inch tank destroyer gun blasted them to pieces. The third tank had seen enough and hastily withdrew, leaving the infantry unprotected. Captain Sparks describes what happened next:

> Following the tank attack, there was a lull of three or four minutes. Then the German infantry came pouring in, several hundred of them. As one group approached my command post, a sergeant in one of the tank destroyers strapped himself to a .50 caliber machine gun on the side of his tank destroyer. At a range of about forty feet, he scattered Germans around the landscape. Then I saw dust coming in spurts from the back of his field jacket as a burst from a machine pistol hit him squarely in the chest. His heroic action saved the command post from being overrun. He was a brave soldier. I never even knew his name.[17]

A few minutes later Captain Sparks was surprised when the Germans broke off their attack just as they were on the verge of overwhelming Company E. It was not to be the last time they failed to press their advantage at a critical moment of battle. On both sides the mournful cries of "Medic!" could be heard. After a considerable lull a German captain mounted in a half-track began moving forward waving a Red Cross flag. As it reached his position the German captain dismounted, and Captain Sparks went forward to meet him.

> He spoke in good English with words to this effect: "Captain, you have many wounded and we have many wounded. Would you agree to a thirty-minute truce, so that we can both evacuate our wounded?" I immediately agreed and ordered all firing stopped. . . . It was the only time during the entire battle that we were able to evacuate our wounded, except for the few walking wounded who were able to filter back. After the brief truce the battle raged on. . . . My one remaining tank destroyer exhausted its ammunition supply, and I ordered the commander to make a break for the

rear. I watched him as his vehicle made a miraculous escape under a hail of German tank fire. By nightfall, we still held our position, but less than a hundred men were left in the company.[18]

Undeterred, the Germans continued their relentless attacks across the front. Company E became an Allied oasis in a sea of Germans who now enveloped F and G companies of the 2d Battalion, 157th Regiment, farther to the rear. When one unit suffered heavy losses, another would immediately take its place and renew the attack. "The fury of the German assault was almost unbelievable," wrote the division historian. "All morning the German infantry moved across the open fields, into our interlocking fire. Hundreds died, but the assault waves never ceased." Troops of sixteen different regiments assigned to seven divisions were identified in these assaults.[19]

In order to avoid the relentless Allied artillery fire, small groups of four to eight tanks sallied forth from the ruins of the Factory to fire at point-blank range at Thunderbird positions. The attacks continued until their ammunition ran out, whereupon they returned to the safety of the Factory to rearm before the artillery forward observers could register fire upon them.

During the day both Companies F and G of the 179th Regiment suffered very heavy losses but managed to hold their positions. In some places the fighting was hand to hand; in others the Americans were killed or compelled to surrender when panzers rumbled up and fired point-blank into their foxholes.

On the left flank of the 2d Battalion, 157th Infantry, in the area of the Caves occupied by the Grenadier Guards the week before, elements of the German 4th Parachute Division and the 65th Infantry Division swarmed over Buonriposo Ridge in a series of attacks designed to gain a foothold along the Via Anziate and split the 45th Division regiments from one another and from the British 56th Division, which was defending the extreme left flank of the beachhead. 1st Lieutenant Joe Robertson's G Company was heavily attacked by tanks and hordes of infantry that continued to infiltrate his positions even after the tanks were stopped by artillery fire. As many as two hundred Germans died, and eventually Robertson ordered friendly artillery fire down on his own positions. "Though it brought casualties to Company G, it slaughtered the exposed enemy. Assaulting Germans plunged into foxholes to engage the men of the Company in hand-to-hand combat."[20] The survivors withdrew, and the Germans took over their positions.

The German attacks in the Cisterna sector were equally forceful but far less successful. To overcome the weakness of his main line of defense, Truscott ordered his tanks and tank destroyers forward to provide the fire support the infantry required to hold their positions.

He also massed his artillery so that the fire of seven battalions could be directed upon any target at a moment's notice.

The results of Truscott's foresight were immediate. The Germans began paying a heavy price for their diversionary attacks, which varied from platoon to battalion size. All were handily beaten off with the aid of the massed fires of the artillery. Near Ponte Rotto, the largest attack was along the seam between the 7th and 30th Infantry regiments by two companies of the Hermann Göring Division's Parachute Demonstration Battalion and nine Mark IV panzers. The German infantrymen were all killed or became POWs. A second attack managed to penetrate some three hundred yards into the seam before it, too, was stopped with heavy losses, including five panzers. By that night the front had been restored. The Germans reported 180 casualties and U.S. forces at least 200 more taken prisoner, many of whom were discovered to be suffering from dysentery.[21] An attempt to penetrate the Allied right flank via the Mussolini Canal was equally fruitless. In front of Company D of the 504th Parachute Infantry were at least 38 dead and a large number of wounded. That afternoon the Germans asked for and received a short truce to remove their wounded from the battlefield.[22]

Despite Truscott's earlier misgivings, the German attacks against the Cisterna sector never seriously threatened the division, and he modestly observed in his postwar memoirs: "Never again during the entire beachhead period was any German attack to endanger the front of the 3rd Infantry Division."[23]

After a day that marked the heaviest combat of the Anzio campaign to date, the Germans had very little to show for their massive effort. Gains averaged from a mere five hundred yards in front of the Factory, to a mile by the 3d Panzer Grenadier Division, and what was painfully obvious to the German commanders was that there was no cause whatsoever for elation. The Allied beachhead line was still intact and in no danger of breaking. Despite the terrific German pressure, Lucas had not yet been forced into committing his reserves, the U.S. 1st Armored and the battered British 1st Division. Both remained in positions behind the final beachhead line of defense, the Lateral Road that crossed the Via Anziate at the Flyover.

Von Mackensen was severely handicapped by his inability to commit his large and powerful armored reserves. Both sides had long since learned the hard way that their armored vehicles could only operate on the roads. The warm weather had worked against the attackers. The Germans found particular difficulty employing their tanks in support of the infantry. The ground had been frozen the previous night, but daylight brought a thaw and the newly arrived heavy Tigers and Panthers soon paid the penalty for leaving the roads. But to remain roadbound was to face the full fury of the Allied artillery and air strikes that

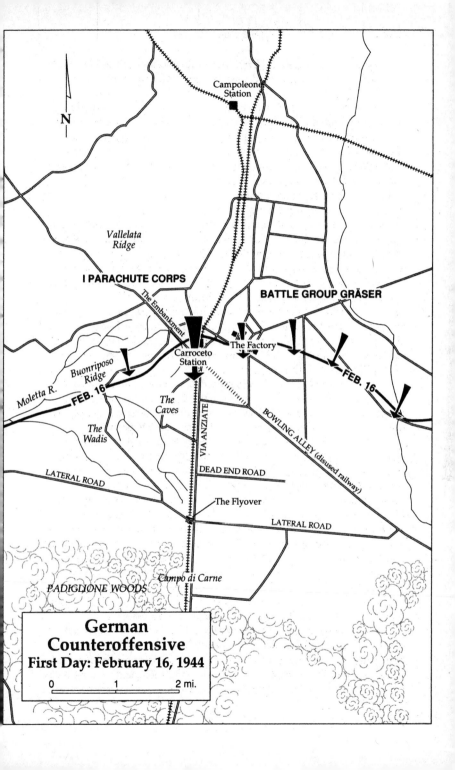

Campoleone
Station

Vallelata
Ridge

I PARACHUTE CORPS

BATTLE GROUP GRÄSER

The Embankment

The Factory

Carroceto
Station

Buonriposo
Ridge

Moletta R.

FEB. 16

FEB. 16

The
Caves

VIA ANZIATE

BOWLING ALLEY (disused railway)

The
Wadis

LATERAL ROAD

DEAD END ROAD

The Flyover

LATERAL ROAD

Campo di Carne

PADIGLIONE WOODS

German
Counteroffensive
First Day: February 16, 1944

0   1   2 mi.

concentrated on the limited number of approaches to the battlefield. Thus, even before they could be committed, German tank losses were exceptionally high.

The German performance that day ranged from methodical to pitiful. Among the latter was the dismal showing of Hitler's much-vaunted Infantry Lehr Regiment, which was attached to the 3d Panzer Grenadier Division and, as Hitler had ordered, given the key mission of attacking down the Via Anziate. During the afternoon the regiment broke under heavy fire after sustaining severe losses to its officers and NCOs and retreated some five hundred yards to its original line of departure that morning. Despite its inflated reputation and the fact that about half its troops had previous combat experience, the Lehr Regiment was essentially an inexperienced unit that had been rushed into combat before its officers and NCOs could gain an appreciation of the terrain they were to fight over. Kesselring called their performance "shameful," and von Mackensen ordered a full investigation after visiting the regiment that night. "I am firmly convinced that the 29th Panzer Grenadier Division or the 26th Panzer Division could have withstood the attack instead of the Lehr Regiment," Kesselring wrote after the war. The Lehr attack should have come much earlier that morning, but had to be delayed until dawn because of the regiment's unfamiliarity with the terrain.[24]

The greatest German success came to naught when elements of the 10th Parachute Regiment struck south from Buonriposo Ridge and penetrated to the lateral road west of the Flyover before being mopped up by tank and infantry units of the British 1st Division.[25]

On this first day of the fight to the death for Anzio, artillery was again the king of the battlefield. VI Corps did not have sufficient forces to defend in adequate depth against massed infantry and tanks, but it did possess the priceless advantage of greatly superior artillery support that again and again spelled the difference on the battlefield for the hard-pressed infantry. At Lucas's command were 432 guns, three companies of Harmon's Shermans, four batteries of 90-mm antiaircraft guns, and the fire of two Royal Navy cruisers offshore. In addition, he had the entire resources of the XII Air Support Command and the Desert Air Force. On February 16 alone, the battlefield and highways and railroads leading to Rome were plastered by 174 tons of bombs.[26] The Luftwaffe was active, flying 172 sorties, but did only slight harm and was not a factor during the German counteroffensive.

The 3d Panzer Grenadier Division had fought at Stalingrad, but even its veteran soldiers had never experienced anything resembling the intense fire the Allied gunners poured on them on February 16.[27] Some German POWs captured that day told their captors they would have preferred the Russian front to Anzio. German losses are impossible to calculate, but not including the 715th Infantry Division, which was known to have suffered serious casualties attacking from the Factory, 324 were reported killed, 1,207 wounded, and 146 missing. The corpses of the dead were piled into trucks and removed from the battlefield and buried at Ardea, a small town nearby.[28] Two hundred twenty-four Allied soldiers became prisoners of war.[29]

That evening von Mackensen summoned his two corps commanders, Traugott Herr and Alfred Schlemm, and ordered the attacks renewed later that night. The Allies were to be granted no reprieve to reinforce. Strong tank-infantry attacks down the Via Anziate were to expand the wedge between the two regiments of the 45th Division. Fresh troops and supplies were moved forward under the cover of darkness.

THE SECOND DAY: FEBRUARY 17

Shortly before midnight a rifle company of the 725th Grenadier Regiment (715th Infantry Division) began infiltrating the lines and methodically wiping out the forward positions of Company E of the 157th Regiment. Despite the support of two Shermans of the 191st Tank Battalion that poured machine-gun and 75-mm shells at point-blank range into the attackers, Company E lost the entire forward elements of its left flank.

The Germans had now created a dangerous gap between the 157th and 179th regiments, and they were quick to press their advantage. At about 0740 hours the assaults resumed when thirty-five Focke-Wulf and Messerschmitt fighter-bombers struck the Thunderbirds' front lines. The Luftwaffe strike was followed by powerful infantry attacks by six battalions of German infantry and an estimated sixty Tiger tanks operating in small groups that struck both regiments.

With Company E virtually annihilated, a group of panzers was able to cut in behind Company G, which was now under tank attack from both the front and rear. Tiger tanks and German infantry ran unchecked inside the 45th Division lines. The day before had been horrific, but the events of this morning were even worse. Units began to crumble and were cut off from one another. Company G suffered the same fate as Company E. At 1100 hours the Luftwaffe attacked again, and by midday the Germans had driven a wedge two and one-half miles deep and a mile wide to the east and west of the Via Anziate. Time and again the men of the 45th fought back against overwhelming odds. The Allied air forces went all out in their support, flying 724 sorties during the day and dropping 833 tons of bombs.[30] The main targets were the

Via Anziate, the Factory, Carroceto, Campoleone, and the Embankment overpass. It was one of the few times during the war that B-17 Flying Fortresses and B-24 Liberator bombers flew in direct support of an army on the ground.[31] Even their best efforts, however, could not stem the German advance. As the 179th Regiment attempted to withdraw and re-form a kilometer farther south, wrote a divisional historian: "the withdrawal turned into a slaughter. In the broad daylight and in full view of the German attackers, the men of the 179th were torn to shreds."[32]

Company E was again attacked at dawn, but the Germans never pressed their attacks, which were fended off with the aid of the two Shermans that had moved forward during the night.[33] By noon the German attacks against Company E had ceased entirely, as the main battle took place a mile farther south. Captain Sparks realized he would eventually have to withdraw to a defensible position and that to do so with the Shermans would invite unnecessary German attention. He made a critical decision to order them to withdraw as best they could. "This they did under a hail of fire . . . at full speed. They got out safely. About thirty minutes later I was to regret my decision," as a German Mark IV rumbled down the Via Anziate and then suddenly turned along the dirt road that led toward the Company E command post. "We were virtually helpless and I considered the end to be at hand. However, we had one final chance, the bazooka that we still had left."

As Captain Sparks relates:

> From Salerno to Anzio there was a Corporal George Holt in the company headquarters who carried a bazooka. He never once had a chance to fire his weapon during the entire campaign and was the subject of some ribbing by the other men. . . . When the German tank turned into our position, Corporal Holt was in his foxhole about ten feet away from mine. . . . I yelled to him: "Holt, here is your chance. Get that tank!" He immediately reared up from his foxhole, took a wavering aim and fired. He missed. However, the bazooka round landed squarely in front of the tank and exploded. This seemed to confuse the German crew and they wheeled the tank around and went back to the main highway.[34]

Fearing the tank's return, Sparks ordered Holt to reload, but the corporal did not appear to hear him. "I then went to his foxhole and found him slumped there and crying. His words were incoherent and he was in a complete state of shock. That night I told him to make a break to the rear and to report to the medics. I never saw him again."

That afternoon fourteen German battalions continued the attack. The Germans had shown the day before that their casualty rate was of secondary consideration, and when one flagged, another was thrown into the breach in battalion-size waves. One of the attacking forces was the Infantry Lehr Regiment, whose troops, stung by the previous day's failure, were back in action. The Lehr belatedly began to perform up to its inflated expectations. Elements of the regiment managed to advance to the corner of the Via Anziate and Dead End Road, where, with the aid of several tanks, they began attacking toward the Flyover. The two tanks achieved the deepest penetration of any German element in the battle for the beachhead. One was finally knocked out at the base of the Flyover, and the other was dealt with by the forces that Lucas had ordered to man what was designated the line of no retreat, the Flyover itself—the final line where VI Corps would triumph or perish.

With the 45th Division forced back to a point some six hundred yards above Dead End Road, Harmon was ordered to launch a battalion-size tank attack early that afternoon to assist the beleaguered Thunderbirds, who were ordered to retake some of the ground lost that morning. The attack along three roads fared poorly when the tanks could not operate cross-country. They became prime targets of the German antitank guns but did manage to stem any further advances by German armor. By sunset they were withdrawn.

It is on such occasions that men rise to unheard-of levels of performance. During the day the Germans encountered Private First Class William J. Johnson, a machine-gunner with Company G, 180th Regiment. When some eighty Germans attacked his machine-gun position, Johnson refused to be intimidated by such overwhelming odds and inflicted an estimated twenty-five losses on his attackers, who were forced to withdraw and regroup. Throughout the day the attacks against Johnson continued, and when two Germans got too close he killed them with his pistol. That night, though badly wounded in the chest by shrapnel—the company medic thought him near death and too seriously hurt to move—Johnson remained behind to cover the withdrawal of his platoon, vowing to make the Germans pay dearly for the privilege of killing him. By the next morning Johnson was not only alive but had killed seven more Germans who foolishly got too close to his gun pit.

Johnson was duly reported Missing in Action, but—in one of those inexplicable incidents of war—Johnson survived an ordeal that included capture, escape, and, two days later, a painful return to friendly lines. When his position was finally overrun, the German medic who treated him believed he would soon die, and he was left alone. Another German soldier stripped him of his boots, and when Johnson stumbled and crawled toward U.S. lines near dawn on February 19, he was barefoot. Although more dead than alive, the indestructible Johnson survived and had the presence of mind to bring with him valuable intelligence that helped pinpoint the location of German gun positions. Several months later in recognition of one of the outstanding feats of bravery in the Anzio beachhead, President Franklin Roosevelt personally draped the Medal of Honor around the neck of Private First Class Bill Johnson.[35]

One of the wounded on February 17 was the commander of the British 1st Division, Major General Penney. When a shell exploded in a tree outside his trailer, Penney was hit in the back by flying shrapnel but, with his clothes in tatters, managed to crawl from the debris.[36] Alexander was unwilling to lose Penney, whose wounds were reported as minor, and he ordered Major General Templer, commander of the newly arrived 56th Division, also to take temporary command of the 1st Division while Penney recuperated. Penney's injuries later proved so serious they would plague him to the end of his life. Although he resumed command of the 1st Division on February 23, Penney's days as its commander were numbered.

In an attempt to restore a more defensible front line, General Eagles ordered the 2d and 3d battalions of the 179th Regiment and the 3d Battalion, 157th Regiment, to counterattack that night to retake Dead End Road. In the darkness the badly understrength and weary battalions collided head-on with the Germans who were being heavily reinforced for their thrust to breach the final beachhead line the following day. There had never been much hope of success, and now the 179th was left in an exposed position near the eastern end of Dead End Road, and K Company in a trap from which it could not escape. The K and L company commanders and most of their troops were captured. Confusion and disillusionment reigned, and as the I Company commander later wrote, "Men trickled back in small groups hysterical and crying. This appeared to be the last bitter end to a day of reverse."[37]

A postwar account provides a brief glimpse of the ordeal of the 179th Regiment on February 17:

> For the first time in its history the 179th's companies and battalions were disorganized, scattered. . . . Communications cut. . . . The casualties were appalling. Men did trickle back in twos and threes . . . they came back crying, hysterical. Even veteran section leaders, ashen-grey and quaking broke under the strain: sleepless for days and pinned in their holes by artillery . . . only to find Brobdingnagian steel monsters charging them from all sides, pouring out a deadly fire as they came. . . . Those who lived were only half alive. One haggard, ragged squad leader who came back without a squad, squatted in front on his haunches outside the S-1 tent. . . . Not a sound escaped his lips but for two hours tears rolled down his cheeks unchecked.[38]

Except for the remnants of the 2d Battalion, 157th Regiment, which were holed up in the Caves west of the Via Anziate and surrounded by elements of two divisions, the Germans were less than a mile from the

Flyover. In a smaller version of what would occur later that year when the U.S. 101st Airborne Division was surrounded at Bastogne during the Battle of the Bulge, the gallant infantrymen of the 157th clung tenaciously to the Caves. On the right the 180th Regiment remained intact and in good shape, its losses comparatively light for the second day in a row.

Before the night counterattack, the 3d Battalion, 179th Regiment, could muster only 274 men. Now even these sparse numbers had been reduced to the breaking point. But despite their ordeal and some panic, the Thunderbirds had simply refused to crack. Their tenacity in the face of overwhelming enemy superiority on the ground, and the equally superior Allied air and artillery support, had combined to thwart the German counteroffensive for the second straight day.

To the dismay of their enemy, the Allied beachhead line remained very much intact. What these weary men, who had endured the battles for the Factory and were now fighting for their very existence, could not have known in the midst of their ordeal was that their valor was far from unavailing. To the contrary, they had badly disrupted the German timetable and brought about a crisis that required a major change of plan that night. Despite the deep wedge in the Allied front lines, the Fourteenth Army had not come close to attaining its objectives or to "skinning any fish." Even worse, there were growing indications that German morale was beginning to crumble under the endless shelling from Allied artillery.[39] One grenadier of the 715th Division wrote home: "It's really a wonder I am still alive. What I have seen is probably more than many saw in Russia. I've been lying night and day under artillery barrages like the world has never seen."[40] In an effort to inject new optimism, the German propaganda machine circulated stories that an Allied embarkation was already under way and that the forthcoming victory would culminate in a giant victory parade in Berlin featuring British POWs.[41] Thousands of propaganda leaflets were dropped behind Allied lines. Their content ranged from warnings of the immediate fate of all Allied soldiers in the beachhead to exceptionally crude anti-Semitism and suggestions that British wives and girlfriends were all cheating on them with American GIs in England while they bled and died in the mud of Anzio.

The German losses for February 17 were 222 killed, 635 wounded, and 35 missing in action.[42] In two days German losses totaled 2,569 men, mainly from Allied artillery fire, and had risen to the point where the average strength of the infantry battalions was rarely more than 120 to 150 men.[43]

Von Mackensen's chief of staff later recounted the German dilemma:

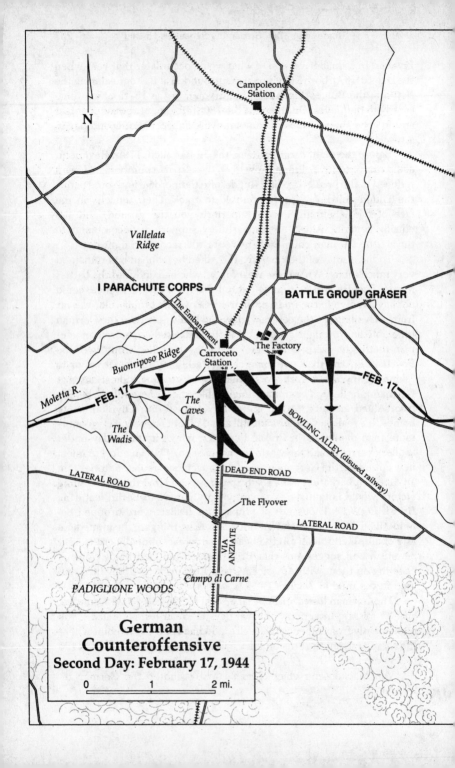

N

Campoleone
Station

*Vallelata
Ridge*

I PARACHUTE CORPS

BATTLE GROUP GRÄSER

The Embankment

Buonriposo Ridge

Carroceto
Station

The Factory

FEB. 17

Moletta R. FEB. 17

*The
Caves*

BOWLING ALLEY (disused railway)

*The
Wadis*

LATERAL ROAD

DEAD END ROAD

The Flyover

VIA
ANZIATE

LATERAL ROAD

Campo di Carne

PADIGLIONE WOODS

German
Counteroffensive
Second Day: February 17, 1944

0   1   2 mi.

The first wave of the German attacking forces had incurred [such] heavy losses . . . they could no longer be expected to make the breakthrough as had been planned . . . it had to be decided whether the attack should be discontinued altogether or whether it would be possible to achieve a success if the second wave were put into action. Apart from the fact that the higher authorities had ordered that the offensive be continued, the Army was also of the opinion that every possible means must be tried to force a decision favorable to the Germans. In spite of the enemy's unprecedented superiority in the supply of materials he had suffered heavy losses during the second day; if, as seemed possible, the battle was almost won, it would be folly to break off now.[44]

The decision was made to go for broke. While the first wave resumed its attacks throughout the night, at 0400 hours the following morning, the exploitation force—26th Panzer and 29th Panzer Grenadier Divisions—were to follow hard on their heels, while the I Parachute Corps continued to anchor the German right flank. The difference was significant. As the official U.S. historian writes: "[Von Mackensen] had hoped to use the two fresh divisions to exploit a breakthrough. But now he had to commit them to gain a penetration."[45]

The officer who took charge of the final Allied defensive line was the new British commander of the 1st and 56th divisions, Major General Gerald W. R. Templer, a strong and vigorous leader cut from the same mold as Ridgway and Harmon. As a field marshal in the postwar years he would earn the nickname Tiger of Malaya, a title that would have been equally applicable for Anzio during the desperate days of February 1944. Instead he earned the sobriquet the Scalded Cat, a reference to the emblem of the 56th (Black Cat) Division. (During his first address to his officers Templer had pointed to the emblem of a large, somewhat overweight black cat and announced that henceforth there would be some fundamental changes in the animal's physique: "When the tail is pointing left, then we are going to the left. When the tail is pointing to the right, then we are going to the right. And when the brute has a bright red arse-hole, then we are going straight up the middle.") A commander of boundless energy who suffered neither fools nor incompetents, Templer was like a breath of fresh air.[46] Where Penney had been stolid and somewhat uninspiring, Templer was dynamic, visible, and inspirational. More than a few have described him as breathing fire. At all times of the day and night the tall, thin figure of Gerald Templer could be seen restlessly prowling the front, dispensing orders and raising the morale of his men. Templer had cleverly disposed his forces and realigned every antitank and antiaircraft gun he could lay his hands on, so that each covered the avenues of approach the Germans would be forced to employ.

Lucas had reorganized the beachhead defenses into the hands of three very resolute men who had no intention of affording their enemy the spoils of a famous victory. The unassuming Eagles, whose actions spoke louder than his words, took control of the defenses west of the Via Anziate. To the east was the fresh 56th Division, while in reserve were the battered remnants of the 1st Division, both under Templer. In the area of the Padiglione Woods were the tanks of Harmon's 1st Armored Division not already in support of the 45th Division. In Templer, Harmon, and Eagles the fate of the beachhead was in good hands. Even when Harmon saw that some American officers were approaching the breaking point, his mind remained set on counterattacking. As he has candidly written: "Fortunately there were among my brother commanders some sturdy characters who realized that if we were near exhaustion, the Germans must be tuckered too."[47]

From all parts of the beachhead came men who were ordered to stand ready to participate. If the front line did crumble at the Flyover, all that remained were four stop lines hastily manned by support personnel. Men from ordnance, quartermaster, transportation, and even finance units were thrust into the rear lines with rifles in what was to be a kind of Custer's Last Stand.[48] Preparations included the sowing of thousands of mines in front of the Flyover and demolitions to blow giant craters in the highway. And, as Peter Verney tells us, "Lurking behind the Flyover itself were lorries loaded with concrete ready to drive under the bridges and plug them."[49]

As both sides geared for the showdown on February 18, it was obvious to one and all that it would determine the fate of the Anzio beachhead.

THE THIRD DAY: FEBRUARY 18

The single most important day of battle for the Anzio beachhead began the morning of February 18, when von Mackensen threw caution to the winds and launched his all-or-nothing attempt to break the Allied left flank. At first the bulge was enlarged at the expense of the 45th Division, when the armor of the 26th and 29th Panzer Grenadier Divisions, joined by the 715th Infantry Division, six battalions of the 114th Jäger Division, and the remnants of the 3d Panzer Grenadier Division, turned the battlefield into a cauldron.

From positions along Dead End Road the attack came at 0500 hours on a gray, foggy morning. Throughout the previous night troops and equipment flooded the front, while the leading wave continued its relentless pressure on the desperate 45th Division. The main battlefield was now reduced to a postage-stamp-size rectangle that resembled a grotesque playing field that might have been created by Dante himself. The bulk of the German attack forces were massed along and behind the start line of Dead End Road. On their right was the Via Anziate; their left boundary was the Fosso di Spaccasassi.

The stakes and the limits of the field of battle left absolutely no doubt where the showdown would occur. There were no options for a flanking movement either to the east or west. To the east of the Via Anziate lay the Caves and the unfriendly gullies, which offered no hope of a breakthrough, and to the west the terrain simply would not permit the employment of armor. Like two gladiators grappling for survival, both protagonists understood that the climactic act of the counteroffensive would be a life-and-death struggle for control of the Flyover and the east-west Lateral Road that marked the final beachhead line.

One of the few rifle battalions of the British 1st Division at full strength after the savage battles for the Thumb and Carroceto was the 1st Battalion, the Loyal Regiment, a North Lancashire unit that had been deployed for nearly a week in reserve along the final beachhead line. Although they had been in action since the first battles fought by the 1st Division, the Loyals had managed to escape the decimating losses that had crippled the other rifle battalions.[50] Their defensive sector ran east from the Flyover for a mile along the lateral road, which they called Wigan Street.[51] Three rifle companies were dug in along a mile-long front, with the remainder of the battalion in reserve behind the Flyover. To their immediate left, directly in front of the Flyover, was Company I of the 157th Regiment, while to their right the 1st battalions of the 179th and 180th regiments were deployed along Wigan Street to the Bowling Alley.

Their backs were literally up against the embankment along which ran Wigan Street. It was a dreadful place to defend. The terrain to their immediate front was flat, virtually treeless plain that offered little cover except for several small gullies, an occasional farmhouse, and a small depression three hundred yards north of the main Loyal positions that was sufficiently deep to shield advancing German infantry from direct fire. The slit trenches dug by the men of A, B, and C companies soon filled with water, and any movement outside them in daylight drew immediate German fire. All preparations for the battle had to be carried out at night.

After an all-night bombardment, the first probing attacks came from the Lehr Regiment, which attacked en masse with all three of its battalions across a minefield and through the barbed wire protecting the Loyals' front lines. A platoon of Loyals was annihilated, and throughout the day as the battle raged the sheer size of the German attack threatened to engulf them. Fierce hand-to-hand fighting took place as forward platoons of A Company, B Company, and the B Company command post were overrun during a savage two-hour battle. The remainder of B Company held firm and at 0730 hours a counterattack by C Company and tanks of the 46th Royal Tanks recaptured the B Company command post and drove off the Lehr Regiment, which withdrew to regroup.

Two hours later the Lehr was back, as a tidal wave of men surged across the plain, determined to carry through the final line.

> Waves of German infantry poured across the open ground below the Dead End Road, only to meet a veritable hail of artillery, mortar and machine gun fire. The enemy was suffering appalling casualties, yet there appeared to be no limit to his resources in manpower and wherever a German soldier fell, there seemed always to be another ready to take his place.[52]

In a campaign marked by carnage this engagement was, as British historian Peter Verney recounts, "a Charge of the Light Brigade without the horses. As soon as the enemy emerged from the dip in front of the companies they were deluged by a staggering weight of shell and caught by the machine guns of the Middlesex [Regiment] in enfilade fire. For every man who managed to get into the Loyals' positions at least six lay dead or dying. It was sheer slaughter," as the attackers were cut down time and again by machine-gun and shell fire.[53]

Little has been written about the battles for the gully-riddled country to the east of the Via Anziate, where British infantry and German paratroopers were locked in a similar desperate struggle. Although considered diversionary attacks in the larger scheme of maneuver, the series of battles along Buonriposo Ridge and in the Caves and gullies were nevertheless taking a deadly toll of the participants on both sides. The Germans had quickly adapted to gully warfare:

> [British] patrols would move forward from their company areas and vanish without a trace, while on other occasions our own troops would leave the cover of their wadis to assault one held by the enemy, and on return find Germans in occupation of their own positions. So, in the mud and pouring rain, among the deep, overgrown wadis to the west of the main road, this grim game of hide and seek was played out. "Be careful," was a more tense warning at the time, "these parachutists have a habit of eating a platoon for breakfast every morning."[54]

Many of the British troops referred to the gullies as the Lobster Claw; others called it the Boot. One of those who died in this godforsaken place was a signals captain named Nick Mansell, who had voluntarily taken over a Bren gun at the front. Mansell's diary survived but his body was one of hundreds that disappeared in the morass of the Anzio beachhead.[55]

With the weather marginal and Allied air attacks limited to 150 sorties on February 18, Allied artillery became the primary defender of the final beachhead line. The guns now began directing their fire with devastating results wherever the Germans attempted to advance. For every round fired by the German artillery, the Allied reply in kind was often 10 to 20. One British 4.2-inch mortar platoon fired an incredible 2,600 rounds during a two-hour period. When the massed artillery struck, men literally disappeared. In one instance shortly after 1100 hours, an aerial observer noticed an infantry force estimated to be 2,500 men accompanied by a tank force advancing south of Carroceto along the Via Anziate. Twelve minutes later the earth seemed to explode as if a volcano had erupted beneath their feet. As the Allied guns spewed forth their deadly venom, men simply disappeared, and others were wounded or deafened by the noise of the explosions. Units became disorganized, and even as fire was brought to bear on other targets, waves of Germans continued to hurl themselves against the 45th Division and the Loyals.[56] One company of the 6th Gordons and a company of Harmon's Shermans arrived in time to back up the Loyals, whose isolated pockets of defenders were fighting hand to hand.

German prisoners would later tell their captors just how effective and deadly the Allied artillery had been. Some formations had started out as battalions and had simply disintegrated from the fires and confusion on the battlefield. Others could barely muster a single company by the time they were committed. To a man the prisoners spoke of the confusion, disrupted communications, and the dreadful toll inflicted by the Allied gunners.

Nevertheless, across the front wave after wave of tanks and surviving infantry continued to hurl themselves on the British and American defenders in a furious and ultimately futile series of attacks. The 179th Regiment was almost crushed by the weight of the German attacks and by midmorning had been driven back to Wigan Street. The 180th Regiment on its right was coming under increasingly heavy pressure. Company G of the 2d Battalion was surrounded by tanks and infantry but somehow fought off repeated German assaults to remain an oasis in a sea of death and chaos. At the Flyover, Company I of the 157th found itself in a similar predicament as the corpses of German infantrymen began to pile up in the barbed wire in front of its positions. The company had absorbed terrible punishment in the previous forty-eight hours and was now the focus of both German artillery and infantry. "Enemy 170-mm and 210-mm guns, registered on the overpass, blasted huge craters out of the swampy ground into which oozed muddy water to cover the torn remnants of what had been a rifleman or a machine-gun crew." The taunts of their enemy to "Watch out, Company I, here we come," were no longer to be heard. Isolated, without food or water for two days, and low on both survivors and ammunition, Company I held.[57]

Another who was in dire straits that fateful morning was an artillery forward observer of the 160th Field Artillery Battalion, 1st Lieutenant James M. Sherrick, whose observation post became surrounded on three sides by onrushing tanks· and infantry. The surviving infantry began withdrawing, and he ordered his team to escape while there was still time. Lieutenant Sherrick did not need to be in such a dangerous position and had been dissuaded from doing so by his commanding officer. But Sherrick believed the outpost line offered the best observation point to adjust the fire of his battalion and ignored the obvious risks. His last known communication was, "I am destroying my code. Three hundred yards right." His final act had been to order the battalion fire control center to fire on the building he occupied. Moments later shells began raining down on the small building.[58]

The commander of the 179th Regiment had been without sleep for days and was out on his feet. General Eagles decided he was incapable of functioning and must be replaced. He summoned Colonel William Darby to take command of the 179th. The regimental history bitterly describes that their popular and humane former commander was abruptly relieved at 1415 hours.[59] It is now known that Clark instigated the change during his visit to the front that day. His diary for February 18 reads: "The situation was confused. The 179th Infantry had not performed well—Eagles admitted it. I suggested he relieve Kammerer and that I would put Colonel Darby in command. This was done."[60] An eyewitness describes Darby's arrival and his immediate positive impact on the men of the 179th Regiment. The commander of the 3d Battalion, which had been all but wiped out that morning, reported to Darby, fully expecting to be sacked:

> "Sir, I guess you will relieve me for losing my battalion?" With a friendly pat on the back, the intrepid ranger replied, "Cheer up son, I just lost three of them, but the war must go on." The remark was not at all flippant, but admirably achieved the desired effect of relieving tension and injecting new hope in the listeners. Colonel Darby then stepped outside and invited us to do the same. "Just look back of us," he said, pointing back at the artillery . . . "No one can continue to attack through that." He then invited us to get back to the business of fighting. His confidence, energy and enthusiasm were just the tonic for an exhausted, discouraged command. His subsequent visits to the front and good advice proved him to be a man without fear. . . . He actually seemed to enjoy fighting![61]

Although he delivered exactly the right infusion of leadership that Eagles desired at this critical moment in the battle, Bill Darby was sufficiently worried about the state of the regiment to recommend it be permitted to withdraw to the Padiglione Woods to reorganize. Eagles categorically refused. The 179th Regiment would stay and fight. Regardless of its condition there would be no retreat.

The fate of the beachhead was still in doubt as it began to grow dark. Crippling losses of tanks and antitank guns during the past two days of fighting had left the German tanks free to operate at will down the Via Anziate and the Bowling Alley. The Fifth Army history records: "It was questionable whether the final beachhead line could hold."[62] The gravest menace came from a tank attack by twelve panzers down the Bowling Alley that seemed unstoppable. Then fate took a kind hand, when the tanks were unable to cross Carroceto Creek because its bridge had been blown.

In the wine cellar VI Corps utilized as its command post in Nettuno the atmosphere was decidedly gloomy. At midday Lucas assembled his commanders, and under considerable prodding from Truscott, Harmon, and Clark, who was visiting the beachhead that day, Lucas reluctantly agreed that his only recourse was to attack, lest his left flank eventually be cut to pieces by the German juggernaut. According to Truscott, Lucas was reluctant to commit his only reserve force but changed his mind when Clark backed Truscott and Harmon.

The decision was made to strike back with a large tank-infantry force under the aggressive Harmon. The following morning the entire 30th Infantry Regiment (the reserve force of the 3d Division), the 6th Armored Infantry Regiment, and a battalion of tanks of the 1st Armored Division would attack the Germans from the southeastern corner of the salient, along the Bowling Alley. At the same time the 169th Infantry Brigade of the 56th Division (landed only that morning) would attack up the Via Anziate. The objective of both forces was to converge at Dead End Road.

In retrospect, the German commanders had erred in not continuing their attacks against the Flyover and the 1st Loyals. As terrible as the German losses had been, the Loyals were near the end of their rope, and even this gallant battalion probably could not have withstood another heavy attack that day. However, by switching the main weight of their attacks to the Allied right flank the Germans failed to crush the 180th Regiment, the only 45th Division unit left that was capable of defending against such an attack.[63]

Thus ended the most critical day of the battle for the Anzio beachhead. The Germans had all but shot their bolt and come up empty. To their dismay they discovered that the thumb-shaped wedge they had driven into Allied lines now left them in the same predicament as the British 1st Division two weeks earlier. The German thumb in the Allied lines was an invitation to a counterattack, and the following morning it was delivered.

German losses for February 18, have never been adequately documented, but they were exceptionally high. A German account claims that 364 Americans were taken prisoner, 293 of whom belonged to the 179th and 180th regiments. Their own losses were incomplete—63 killed and 350 wounded—and never clarified in any postwar account. These statistics inexplicably never included the three most heavily committed divisions, the 29th Panzer Grenadier, the 114th Jäger, and the 715th Infantry divisions.[64]

The mood of the Fourteenth Army was grim that evening. The great counteroffensive had failed and one and all knew it. General Hauser would later pay special tribute to the British infantry guarding Buonriposo Ridge, which prevented the I Parachute Corps from prying open the shoulders of the German right flank and expanding the attack down the Via Anziate. "By the evening of 18 February there was no doubt that the German attack must be considered a failure; the impetus of the attack was broken . . . all that was achieved during the hard fighting of the following day was the consolidation of both flanks of the wedge that had been driven into the enemy lines; but it was no longer possible to think of resuming the German offensive. . . . A new course of action had to be decided upon."[65] The result was a last futile attempt to crack the final beachhead line the following morning.

Little more than forty-eight hours earlier there had been nearly 190 men in Company E, plus a twenty-eight-man machine-gun platoon and two tank destroyers (ten men), and a five-man antitank squad—in all, approximately 230 troops were defending the most important Allied position on the left flank of the beachhead. The entire machine-gun platoon had been captured, five of the ten tank destroyermen were lost from a direct hit, and the others had escaped to the rear when the second destroyer ran out of ammunition and was ordered to make a break for safety by Captain Sparks.

By 0500 hours Company E had been reduced to a mere twenty-eight riflemen and two officers. Captain Sparks realized that his tiny force could no longer defend against a German attack. Although the battle now raged to the south at the Flyover, Company E had been a constant irritation to the Germans for two days and it would not be long before someone decided to eliminate it once and for all. Captain Sparks led his men to a new position, a small hill some four hundred yards to the rear, along the west side of the Via Anziate and several hundred yards from their eventual sanctuary in the Caves. The dead had to be left behind. Losses were 92 percent.[66]

Although the new position was occupied without incident, as Sparks relates:

The Germans noticed our digging in and greeted us with both artillery and tank fire. A lone German tank, in particular, gave us a lot of grief. This tank

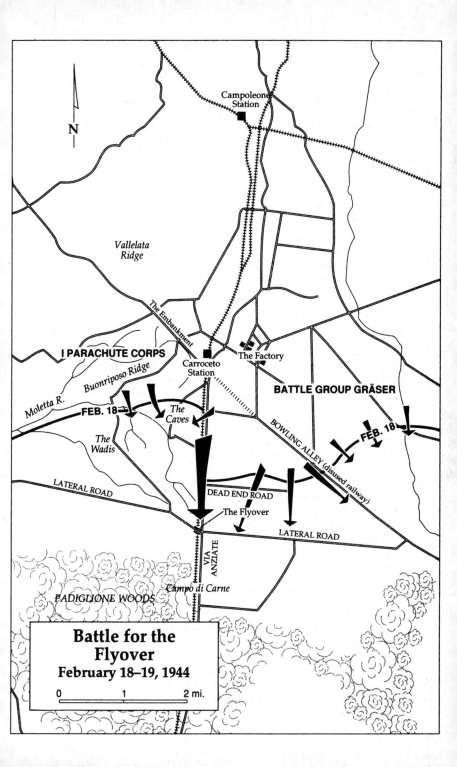

Campoleone
Station

*Vallelata
Ridge*

The Embankment

I PARACHUTE CORPS

Buonriposo Ridge

Carroceto
Station

The Factory

BATTLE GROUP GRÄSER

Moletta R.

FEB. 18

*The
Caves*

*The
Wadis*

BOWLING ALLEY (disused railway)

FEB. 18

LATERAL ROAD

DEAD END ROAD

The Flyover

VIA ANZIATE

LATERAL ROAD

Campo di Carne

PADIGLIONE WOODS

Battle for the
Flyover
February 18–19, 1944

0   1   2 mi.

was about 300 yards to our front at the side of an Italian farm house. He attempted to pick us out of our foxholes with his main gun. I retaliated with about fifty rounds of artillery fire, but to no avail. One German calmly dismounted from the tank, looked in our direction and lighted a cigarette. I desperately wanted a heavy calibre direct fire weapon at that time, but none were available. We had one man killed and several wounded by that tank on that day.[67]

THE FOURTH DAY: FEBRUARY 19

For the weary men of the 1st Loyals the fresh shelling and dive-bombing that began during the night were merely a continuation of the nonstop combat that had begun the previous morning. The only difference on this day was that the attacks came an hour earlier, at 0400 hours. Supported by tanks, two reinforced battalions of the 1st Panzer Grenadier Regiment fell upon Company C of the Loyals and overran most of this unit and portions of B Company. One isolated platoon was cut off for over twenty hours but managed to hold their positions. More than a hundred Germans perished in the attack.

A large number of German troops began moving forward to reinforce the 1st Panzer Grenadiers, which remained in force inside Company C's lines. It was yet another in a long list of large and small crises that confronted the beachhead defenders. If permitted to join forces, the resulting powerful enemy force threatened to drive a dangerous gap into the Allied line near the Flyover. The British brigade commander knew a bad situation when he saw one and ordered all rear area personnel to the front lines to aid the Loyals: "Storemen, cooks and drivers stood to arms, and even the Docks Operating Companies left their derricks to take up rifles and Brens."[68]

The British artillery laid down another massive barrage that drove off the German second echelon in disarray. At about 1100 hours the first of two counterattacks to restore the front was launched. The first failed but the second broke the Germans. Opposite C Company a white flag appeared, and the first of eight officers (one of them a battalion commander) and 192 dispirited soldiers shuffled into British lines. Some were dazed, others babbled. All seemed shocked to learn that they had been fed propaganda lies that their enemy was reembarking to flee the beachhead.[69]

The Allied counterattack had gotten off to a bad start that morning when Templer's 169th Brigade was unable to attack. Their supporting guns and equipment had not been unloaded at Anzio when the port was suddenly closed after the Luftwaffe had dropped mines into the harbor. The port officer's decision to close the harbor was taken without reference to Lucas, who was furious when informed four hours later. Although he immediately countermanded the order, it was already too late. The LSTs bearing the 169th Brigade's equipment had scattered to sea and could not be recalled in time.[70] Templer attempted to attack with only tanks, but without full infantry support the attack came to naught.

When the Germans began threatening the Flyover during the night, Lucas began to have second thoughts about Harmon's attack. Harmon was awakened at 0200 hours by a telephone call from Lucas, who attempted to dissuade him from carrying out his counterattack the following morning. Harmon refused and convinced Lucas that it was essential to carry out the original plan. Two hours later the 1st Armored Division Artillery Commander reported that a battalion of the 45th Division was occupying positions in front of the no-fire zone. Harmon was called upon to make one of the most difficult decisions of his life:

> If we laid down our barrage we would kill our own troops. There are times when the responsibilities of a military commander are, in the true meaning of the word, awful. To order the artillery attack might mean the death of many fine, brave American soldiers. To abandon the artillery attack would be to abandon the sortie upon which, I was convinced, the saving of the beachhead depended. The brutal, naked choice seemed to be between the loss of some hundreds of men and loss of many thousands. Backed up by [VI Corps] Headquarters, I gave the order to fire.[71]

A relieved Harmon later learned that in the confusion a platoon that was in no danger had been thought to be a battalion. It did "not change the reality of the decision I had to make. Looking back, it seems to me I could have made no other."[72] Supporting Force H (for Harmon) was the combined fire of eight British artillery regiments, which was to saturate the zone of attack. Another eight battalions of VI Corps artillery were to plaster German assembly areas around the Factory for forty-five minutes, while naval and antiaircraft guns concentrated on the Factory and Carroceto. Allied aircraft were once again active and the woods northeast of the Factory were pounded by 180 aircraft and a nearby assembly hit by another 48 medium bombers.[73]

Battles raged throughout the day as Force H encountered stiff opposition but managed to reach the junction of the Bowling Alley and Dead End Road by midafternoon. Evidence abounded of the low state of German morale. Promised an easy victory, even veteran formations like the 29th Panzer Grenadier Division had been dismayed to discover what one POW described as "carnage." Most believed they had been deceived, and their desire to continue the fight died. The German salient had become a death trap for both tanks and infantry.[74] More than four hundred Germans became prisoners on the fourth day, when

Allied artillery fired 30,000 rounds.[75] During their twenty-three days of combat in Sicily the 45th Division had fired 14,697 rounds of ammunition. In a three-day period from February 17 to 19 the division fired 62,486 rounds.[76]

The Germans were a spent force that could advance no further into the teeth of such savage resistance. By sheer grit on the part of the infantry and the masterly employment of massed artillery the beachhead was saved and the Germans had suffered a stunning reversal that dashed all hope of what would have been one of their greatest triumphs of the war. Instead, their casualties numbered 5,389 killed, wounded, and missing in action.[77] Over six hundred of the missing were captured during the four days of the battle.[78] Several German divisions that had borne the brunt of the offensive were shattered. The 3d Panzer Grenadier Division was in terrible shape, and the 65th Infantry Division could muster only 901 officers. Regiments, battalions, and companies were reduced to mere handfuls of men and had to be consolidated with other units.

Macabre evidence of their failure was to be seen in the piles of German dead that littered the battlefield. When the fighting died down on February 21 the men of the 179th Regiment counted five hundred German corpses in front of their positions. An escaped American artilleryman observed the extent of the carnage near the Carroceto overpass. "We saw a German bulldozer digging a trench for the German dead. There were several piles of bodies, with about 150 or more in each pile. There were also many hundreds [more] dead along the route we marched—killed by our artillery."[79]

In the aftermath of this chaotic battle even the statistics were erratic. Allied losses have never been properly tabulated. According to the *Fifth Army History* (Allied) losses during the four-day battle were 404 killed, 1,982 wounded, 1,025 captured or missing, and another 1,637 nonbattle casualties from exposure, exhaustion, and trench foot.[80] The lion's share of the casualties were in the 45th Division. The 179th Regiment lost 55 percent of its officers and men during the week of February 12–19 with 142 killed, 367 wounded, 728 missing* or cap-

---

*The statistics recorded by the *Fifth Army History* are clearly inaccurate. It records only 404 killed from February 16–20 even though it is known that there were 400 killed in the 45th Division alone. Apparently the Fifth Army historians failed to take into account any of the British losses (the Loyals suffered more than 200 casualties on February 19 alone) or those of the 1st Armored Division. None of the other official or unofficial British and American accounts provides statistics that adequately compare with or substantiate each other. For example, while the *Fifth Army History* reflects 1,637 nonbattle casualties, Blumenson in the U.S. official history puts the figure at 2,500. Unfortunately, it is impossible to determine what the correct figures ought to be, but we do know that Templer's 56th British Division (less the 169th Brigade, which was just arriving) was decimated. While some of the British casualties occurred in the days prior to February

tured, and 670 evacuated for psychiatric reasons or for battle exhaustion.[81] Total casualties in the 45th Division were 400 killed, 2,000 wounded, 1,000 missing and 2,500 nonbattle injuries.[82]

The most disconcerting aspect of the German failure was the disintegration of morale in the front-line units. The will to survive that had galvanized the Allied defenders of the beachhead had deserted a significant number of German troops, who had seen for themselves the futility of their attacks.

Although the fighting continued on February 20 it was clear that this was the final effort of a failed offensive that had turned the German penetration into a death trap. From February 21 to 25 the Germans demonstrated that while they had lost the initiative, they were still a very dangerous foe. Allied losses during this so-called lull in the fighting were 231 killed, 1,304 wounded, and 117 missing.[83]

For the Allied troops manning the foxholes in the front lines of the beachhead there was to be no respite. VI Corps was 20,000 below its authorized strength, and there was little opportunity for an escape from the miserable cold and wet conditions that were the lot of the infantryman at Anzio. Weariness, not elation, was the prevalent feeling among these men who had fought one of the most savage engagements of this or any other war. In the aftermath of the German attacks the survivors of the 2d Battalion, 157th Regiment, remained trapped behind enemy lines in the Caves. Their ordeal was only beginning as the Germans now started a determined effort to eradicate this unpleasant source of irritation.

The successful defense of the beachhead line by the Allied force at Anzio was a triumph of will over daunting obstacles. The hard-boiled Ernie Harmon was not a sentimental man. A veteran of two wars, Harmon understood better than most commanders that this battle had been won as much by determination as it had by the implements of war. "What a difference a will to win can make! The day before the enemy seemed to be infiltrating everywhere, Allied communications had broken down, whole companies and battalions were cut off. Now it was the Germans who were disorganized, disillusioned, and at the end of their offensive strength."[84]

The German counteroffensive of February 16–20 marked the turning point of the Anzio campaign, which had started a month earlier with lofty intentions and had now turned into the bloodiest stalemate on the western front of World War II.

16, a significant number were during the period of Fischfang. A reasonable estimate may by that overall Allied losses were at least 40 percent higher from February 16–20.

14

A House Divided

The idiots! They've done it after all.

GENERAL FRIDOLIN VON SENGER[1]

The stalemate at Anzio was merely part of the crisis that faced the Allies in early 1944. The atmosphere across the beachhead was of grim determination to avert another Dunkirk. As the situation in Italy grew more uncertain day by day, there was increasing evidence that nerves were becoming frayed. Reports appearing in the British press and on American radio were of a growing crisis at Anzio. Among these were reports by CBS correspondent John Charles Daly, who said on the night of February 11–12: "The situation in the bridgehead is grim: we have been forced to give ground . . . the Germans have massed strong forces against us." A typical headline appeared in the London *Daily Herald:* DESPERATE STRUGGLE AT ANZIO. What caused an uproar in Whitehall were references to Anzio as another Dunkirk in the making, and the word *desperate* was viewed with alarm by the British Government.[2]

Roosevelt himself had described Anzio at his weekly press conference as "a very tense situation" and before a revised statement was issued in Ottawa, Prime Minister MacKenzie King noted: "We are witnessing the possibility of terrible reverses in Italy that may prolong the war, not only for days or months, but for years."[3]

The pressures on Alexander and Clark were enormous and, as before, emanated mainly from Churchill. News reports flowing from Anzio told of a growing sense of despair, and when these began to appear in the British and American press an alarmed Churchill urgently cabled Alexander and Jumbo Wilson for an explanation. Even the normally mild-mannered Alexander finally boiled over with a rare public display of fury during a visit to Anzio on February 14, when he tongue-lashed the war correspondents for spreading false pessimism over the situation in the beachhead. Their "defeatist" attitude, he charged, was detrimental to the Allied effort in Italy. Lucas was shocked by the sarcastic tone of the diatribe, but Alexander at first refused to listen to his attempts to explain that the beachhead correspondents were not the source of the problem. Both Lucas and the correspondents were incensed by Alexander's attack.[4]

Later in February, Churchill was obliged to defend Alexander's decision to cut off transmission facilities and impose censorship on dispatches emanating from Italy.[5] A group of British newspaper editors expressed their deep concern over Alexander's actions to the secretary of state for war, Sir James Grigg, who minuted the prime minister that "this business is very much of a storm in a teacup . . . it looks as if General Alexander has hit the wrong head. The bridgehead correspondents have on the whole behaved pretty well. It is the Algiers correspondents, plus some distortions by the News Agencies plus the headlines of the London newspapers which have created most of the alarm and despondency."[6] Within days Alexander's actions were ordered revoked and the flap passed.

The burden of the Italian stalemate fell on the broad shoulders of Mark Clark, who could be forgiven for wondering if his British ally was an unnecessary cross to bear. Clark's diary reflects his growing isolation as the only major American ground commander in Italy, and his frustration that the British were running the campaign at the expense of the Fifth Army. On January 26 he attended a meeting with Jumbo Wilson, Alexander, Admiral Cunningham, and General Ira Eaker.

> They have two meetings a day. Every subject discussed pertained to the Fifth Army, whereas I am the first Fifth Army officer who has ever attended one of these meetings. Apparently none of these headquarters have any other mission in life than to interest themselves in affairs pertaining to Fifth Army. . . . My opinions were asked on none of [the] subjects [discussed]. I merely record this to show how several headquarters have moved in on top of Fifth Army and, having nothing else to do, are gradually taking over many of its functions. Again I repeat, never have so few been commanded by so many.[7]

Clark had been told he was to command the Anvil forces for the summer landings in southern France, and the prospect left him gloomy that he would be obliged to give up command of his beloved Fifth Army to take command of an operation in which he had little faith. Clark got

along with Jumbo Wilson far better than he did with Alexander and at
a meeting in late January he frankly told the Allied commander in chief
that "the Fifth Army had landed at Salerno, taken Naples and battled
its way to the north through hellish terrain and with bloody losses and
that it was entitled under my command to take Rome . . . [and if] ANVIL
should become a 'fart in the dark' of one division . . . I wanted no part
of it."[8] Although Wilson assured that if possible he would stay with the
Fifth Army, the prospect cannot have improved Clark's frustration that
only he could prevent the British from stealing the limelight from his
army.

Not only were things going nowhere on the ground at both Cassino
and Anzio, but the Fifth Army commander believed he was being let
down by the Navy. He clashed with the dour Admiral John Cunningham, who had restricted the resupply of Anzio to 2,500 tons per day.
Clark complained that this was insufficient and precluded an essential
buildup for a future offensive. The greatest problem was the expenditure of artillery ammunition, which was being fired in quantities unprecedented even by World War II standards, although Clark had an
artillery reserve in the form of naval gunfire from the supporting ships
offshore.

Virtually from the first days after the Shingle landings, Cunningham had been complaining about the Army. Writing to "ABC" Cunningham on January 27 he said:

> I'm afraid I have not so far had any reason to modify my opinion of the
> Army's dilatory methods. I am sure that had they had any guts at all they
> could have walked practically without opposition to secure any "feature"
> that they wanted—instead their obsession that they must always have
> weeks and weeks of "reserves" behind them caused them to sit down and
> wait for the Hun to scratch up an opposing force—now of course they say
> they need 4 divisions to do the job they previously were confident of
> accomplishing with two! And I foresee their wanting still more troops and
> this venture, which had all the makings of a brilliant success, is developing
> into another Tobruk so far as the Navy's part is concerned.[9]

Cunningham had conveniently forgotten or ignored his opposition to
Shingle. A signal to Churchill noted: "The situation as it now stands
bears little relation to the lightning thrust envisioned at Marrakesh."[10]
He also demonstrated an almost total ignorance of events ashore. In
another sour letter to the First Sea Lord on February 11, his observations were wildly wide of the mark:

> The position at Anzio continues to stagnate—The enemy has been allowed
> to collect round it a weird collection of odds and ends amounting to some
> 25,000 to 30,000 (sic) men, while inside the perimeter of the beachhead

the leaders of our 130,000 to 150,000 sailors, soldiers and airmen await, in a state of chronic and pitiful trepidation an attack which they expect today, tomorrow, the next day or some day! From the highest the false doctrine that our chaps are outnumbered anything up to 4 to 1 has in fact percolated down to lower formations with, presumably, lamentable potential effect upon morale Anyhow the idea that it might be a good idea for us to do the attacking seems to be quite lacking. It is Sulva [Bay] all over again, and has been from the beginning.[11]

Clark saw the problem in the far different light of the Navy's reluctance to do its job. In particular, he was annoyed by the Navy's habit of moving its ships safely out of range whenever Anzio Annie or Anzio Express delivered fire in the Army's direction. His frustration boiled over in his diary: "[Cunningham] does not come to me but insinuates to everyone he sees that he has been hoaxed into the position which makes it necessary for him to maintain my forces in the Anzio bridgehead. He not only does not cooperate in the supply setup but with his naval gunfire. He imposes so many restrictions and makes it so difficult that it is easier in most cases to do without."[12]

What Clark found equally frustrating, as his biographer writes, was that Cunningham ignored his requests and "neither Alexander nor Wilson was willing to speak with Cunningham on Clark's behalf. Frustrated, Clark threw up his hands over the British system of command. Unity was absent because the British Army, Air and Navy were independent entities."[13] In his diary Clark wrote that he had complained to Devers: "I want to record my definite feelings that Admiral Cunningham has been as uncooperative as possible in this SHINGLE operation. Yesterday Lucas asked for cruiser gunfire support and did not get it. Today he asked again. Admiral Cunningham will give it only if it comes from Lucas through his liaison officer, not honoring *my* request."[14]

Neither side seemed to have a clear picture of what the other was accomplishing. A total of 379 naval vessels had been committed to the Shingle landings,[15] and those that remained in support of operations ashore were in constant peril, not only from the German artillery in the Alban Hills but from radio-controlled glider bombs, torpedo attacks from marauding E-boats (motor torpedo-boats), and torpedo and dive-bomber attacks from the Luftwaffe. And always there was the threat of floating mines where physical contact generally meant heavy loss of life. Ships enroute to and from Naples were at risk of ambush from U-boats, with the most frequent victims being Liberty ships and LSTs. The bad weather and gale-force winds merely compounded the problems posed by the Germans.

After the landings, Rear Admiral J. M. Mansfield's 15th Cruiser Squadron provided the fire support for VI Corps.[16] From January 22 to the end of February, Mansfield's warships fired 8,400 rounds of 6-inch, 7,800 rounds of 5.25-inch, and 3,500 rounds of 4.7-inch ammunition at ground targets in the Anzio beachhead.[17]

Clark's negative impressions notwithstanding, the Allied navy acquitted itself well at Anzio, and by the end of February had, in fact, exceeded Clark's requirement of 2,500 tons per day by a substantial margin. According to the British official historian: "Between D-Day and the 20th of February 97,669 tons were discharged and, in spite of two severe gales and constant enemy shelling, bombing and minelaying, the average daily figure for the month was 3,441 tons."[18] Thus, Cunningham's limit of 2,500 tons per day proved meaningless. What did worry the British admiral was that his resources were stretched to the fullest and he doubted he could continue to maintain such a high level. Losses, breakdowns, and a lack of replacement craft were all problems over which there was no control. Nevertheless, he told Jumbo Wilson: "Every possible effort has been, is being, and will continue to be made by the Navies to support the Armies ashore." Barring circumstances beyond his control, Cunningham pledged to maintain a delivery rate of at least 2,500 tons per day.[19]

Another bone of contention between Clark and Cunningham was the exceptionally high number of vehicles in the beachhead. Cunningham was amazed by what he estimated were 25,000 vehicles ashore and wrote sarcastically: "What they do with them I cannot imagine since there are few roads in the area. I suppose they keep the engines running to give warmth and to ensure a worthwhile petrol consumption."[20] It was inevitable that Churchill would learn of the profligate numbers and react accordingly. Jumbo Wilson found himself bombarded by cables expressing the Prime Minister's indignation and insatiable demand for explanations. When told by Wilson on February 12 that the number of tanks, carriers, half-tracks, and vehicles totaled eighteen thousand, Churchill at once rejoined to inquire: "How many of our men are driving or looking after the 18,000 vehicles in this narrow space? We must have a great superiority of chauffeurs. I am shocked."[21]

After the Rapido disaster the Germans remained in full control of the critical heights overlooking the Liri Valley, and it was not until early February that Mark Clark turned his attention to the town of Cassino. Situated at the base of Monastery Hill, astride both the Rapido and the Via Casilina (Route 6), the town had to be captured before the Fifth Army could advance along Route 6 toward Rome. Cassino now became the target of a new Fifth Army offensive.

The Cassino Massif served as the western anchor of the Gustav Line and was the key to von Senger's defense of the Liri Valley. The ruins of a medieval castle lay directly above the town, and at the top of

Monastery Hill stood the ancient Abbey of Monte Cassino, one of the holiest shrines of Roman Catholicism and the cradle of the Benedectine Order, founded by Saint Benedict in the year 529. Von Senger had turned Monastery Hill into an integrated position that took full advantage of the terrain both in the valley and atop the heights. However, the German XIV Panzer Corps commander assiduously avoided occupying the abbey, in the hope that it would not become an Allied target. A lay Benedictine and a devout Catholic, von Senger was instrumental in first persuading and later helping the abbots to remove the abbey's priceless art and treasures to safety in the Vatican.

The approaches to Cassino lay in full view of the defenders, and the plains in front of the town had been flooded. Still, Clark had insisted on pressing the Rapido crossing even though his most promising option had been along the Garigliano River, with McCreery's 10th Corps.

After Kesselring was forced to begin shifting units from Cassino to Anzio, the German task became increasingly difficult as losses grew and replacements became scarce. Across the Gustav Line the Germans were forced into their usual hand-to-mouth existence. Von Senger's fortunes were bolstered when Lieutenant Colonel Ludwig Heilmann's veteran 3d Parachute Regiment was shifted from the Adriatic sector to replace Baade's hard-pressed 90th Panzer Grenadier Division, whose units had been decimated defending the Cassino Massif. A series of attacks in early February by the U.S. 34th Division threatened both the town and the heights of Monastery Hill. An excellent opportunity to win what historians have designated the First Battle of Cassino was lost when Clark made no effort to reinforce the 34th Division. Although the chronic shortage of replacement troops in the Italian theater would have made it necessary to employ British troops under U.S. command, neither Keyes nor Clark showed any inclination to seek help outside II Corps.

To the contrary, the notion of using British troops horrified Clark, who refused to countenance the possibility that another nationality might steal the limelight from the Fifth Army. When Alexander created a strategic reserve as his *corps de chasse,* called the New Zealand Corps, under Bernard Freyberg, whose ego Clark thought was as large as his Victoria Cross, "Well that scared me," Clark later told an interviewer, "because Freyberg was a prima donna, and he had to be handled with kid gloves, very adroitly, very carefully."[22] In his memoirs Clark admitted annoyance at Alexander's decision to place the independent-minded New Zealanders under his command without consulting him. "I got a definite impression that 15th Army Group and Freyberg were going to tell me what to do."[23] His diary was even more candid: "Freyberg may be an extremely courageous individual, but he has no brains . . . and altogether is most difficult to handle."[24]

Clark was not reassured when Geoffrey Keyes and the feisty Freyberg clashed during their first meeting on February 4. With more British and Dominion than American troops assigned to the Fifth Army, Clark also admitted that "I was about ready to agree with Napoleon's conclusions that it is better to fight Allies than to be one of them."[25]

Meanwhile, the Germans had rushed in reinforcements to fend off this dire threat. Like the battles being fought at Anzio, the ferocious engagements fought in the jagged mountains surrounding Cassino were among the worst horrors of the Italian campaign. Most of the battles of the heights were referred to simply by the number shown in meters on the participants' maps. The Germans cleverly established their defenses on reverse slopes, with mutually supporting fires to cover an attack from any direction.

The mastermind controlling the assignment of reserves to Anzio and Cassino was Kesselring, who managed like a chessmaster to balance the needs of each front by adroitly shifting units from place to place as the situation dictated. Allied tactics of piecemeal employment of divisions played directly into Kesselring's hands. This enabled the Germans to hold "the front with small kampfgruppen not divisions, but as they fought against single Allied divisions . . . these piecemeal defense methods into which [the Germans] were forced by necessity became a virtue."[26]

One of the keys to breaking the German grip of the Cassino heights was Point 593, which controlled Snakeshead Ridge, one of the anchors northeast of the abbey. Point 593 changed hands several times but ultimately ended back under German control after a series of bitter battles with Ryder's 34th Division. Although forced to endure unspeakable hardships in the cold and brutal mountains overlooking Cassino, this National Guard division, which Alexander a year earlier had pronounced unfit for combat in Tunisia, had long since come of age and was now one of the most battle-tested divisions in the entire U.S. Army. The performance of the 34th at Cassino was so outstanding that not only were a private first class and a lieutenant awarded the Medal of Honor, but a British historian later wrote that their exploits "must rank with the finest feats of arms carried out by any soldiers during the war."[27] After suffering enormous losses of nearly 80 percent in the infantry battalions, and with its troops at the very end of their endurance, the division was pulled from the line to rest and refit. Their respite was to be short-lived; in early March they were sent to bolster the defenses of VI Corps at Anzio.

II Corps had come exceedingly close to breaking the Gustav Line, and by mid-February Alexander and Clark decided to turn the task of finishing the job over to Freyberg's New Zealand Corps. However, the decision to commit the New Zealanders came far too late to take advantage of the gains made by II Corps. It turned out to be a fateful decision that shortly resulted in one of the most hotly debated incidents of the war—the destruction of the ancient Abbey of Monte Cassino.

As Graham and Bidwell record, "No better example could be found of the disadvantages of coalition warfare which handicapped the Fifth Army in Italy time and again." If Freyberg's force had been committed by February 9, "the battle for Cassino could have been won then and there. Instead an exhausted 2nd Corps held on too long . . . the momentum was lost and the new brooms resorted to the bombing and destruction of the Benedictine Monastery."[28]

At Anzio Clark did not have sufficient forces to carry out the Fifth Army mission; at Cassino in February 1944 he had ample forces to have won the battle, if they had not been employed piecemeal. In an unfortunate example of nationalism taking precedence over sound military sense, first McCreery's and later Freyberg's corps were left unused in critical situations in which their presence would have been decisive. Had Alexander acted to overrule Clark there would have been time and the immediate consequence was the bombing of the abbey.

Although Clark was opposed to bombing the abbey, the truth was that his own inaction was a major factor when, several days later, Freyberg requested that the monastery be attacked by Allied bombers. The New Zealanders had made little progress against the German strongpoints guarding the approaches to the abbey, and in the mistaken belief that the enemy was using it to direct artillery fire on his men, Freyberg insisted on its elimination. Alexander also did not favor the bombing of the abbey, but like Clark, he was on the cutting edge of Churchill's growing displeasure over the inability of the Allied armies to break the stalemate in Italy.

That the monastery had never been occupied by German troops was of little consequence, because it formed an essential component of the German defenses overlooking the Liri Valley. Von Senger had established and then violated a self-imposed 330-yard neutral zone around the monastery, and as long as it formed a key element in the German defense of Cassino, its eventual destruction was inevitable. The fact that the instrument of destruction turned out to be Allied bombs instead of Allied artillery shells is irrelevant.

The sequence of events and the individual actions and responsibilities of the major commanders are complex, involving the entire chain of command from Freyberg to Clark, Alexander, and, ultimately, Allied Commander in Chief Maitland Wilson. In the end, although adamantly opposed to Freyberg's request, Clark felt obligated to approve any recommendation whose purpose was the saving of lives. In doing so he unleashed a monumental controversy that more than forty years later is still the object of contentious debate.[29]

An unusual quiet hung over the Liri Valley on the clear, bright morning of February 15, when more than two hundred bombers of Major General Nathan Twining's Fifteenth Air Force smashed the Abbey of Monte Cassino to rubble. An almost festive atmosphere existed as spectators, who included combatants, rear-area personnel, reporters, and the senior generals of the Allied high command in Italy, watched from across the valley while waves of B-17 bombers dropped their deadly loads. The explosions shattered the morning calm as cheers erupted from the soldiers who witnessed the bombing. The monastery seemed to erupt in black-and-white smoke, flames, and flying debris. For the fourth time in history the abbey had been destroyed by force.[30]

Despite its considerable size, the Allied bombing of the abbey was, on the whole, highly inaccurate and did little harm to the thick foundation. Most of the bombers missed the abbey altogether, and it was only the final bombing runs that did any significant damage. What the bombs failed to accomplish, Allied artillery did, as the ruins were pounded into rubble. German troops of the 1st Parachute Division occupied the abbey that night and rapidly strengthened the defenses of Monastery Hill, using the ruins to full advantage.

Among the missing observers that morning was Clark, who saw no point in wasting time witnessing an act he personally deplored. On this day he and von Senger shared a common reaction: disgust. When he felt the blast emanating from the dying abbey, a distraught von Senger kept repeating, "The idiots! They've done it after all. All our efforts were in vain."[31] Although he personally deplored the bombing, von Senger cannot escape a share of the responsibility for making no effort to prevent German troops from occupying positions right up to the edge of the monastery. The day before the bombing, Lieutenant General Ira Eaker observed Cassino firsthand from a small aircraft, and noted: "I could have dropped my binoculars into machine-gun nests less than 50 feet from the walls."[32] After the war Clark offered a powerful defense of von Senger: "I said then that there was no evidence that the Germans were using the Abbey for military purposes. I say now that there is irrefutable evidence that no German soldier, except emissaries, was ever inside the monastery for purposes other than to take care of the sick or as sightseers."[33]

Eaker likewise had reservations, and his biographer, James Parton, notes that "he had no enthusiasm for bombing the Abbey, sharing the views of Clark and Alexander that the ruins would make an even stronger obstacle."[34] Equally unhelpful was the propaganda coup handed the Germans, who proclaimed that the Allies had perpetrated a brutal and wanton act of barbarism.

But the worst part of the Cassino fiasco was the unpreparedness of the 4th Indian Division to take advantage of the bombing until nearly three days later, by which time the Germans had strengthened their defenses and the Allies had lost the initiative. Several days earlier the 34th Division had been driven from the critical Point 593, and the Indians had been unable to retake it prior to the bombing. A series of misunderstandings and Freyberg's failure to inform his superiors of the truth for fear the bombing attack would be cancelled had all contributed to the premature bombing of the abbey. A series of attacks on Point 593 failed, and when the 4th Indian Division bypassed this strongpoint and attacked the abbey on February 17, they were severely repulsed by Heidrich's paratroopers, who inflicted more than six hundred casualties.[35]

The bombing of the abbey became a visible reminder of good intentions gone awry, and the ensuing controversy sullied the reputations of the Allied military commanders, particularly Freyberg and Clark. Even though American money contributed to the eventual rebuilding of the abbey, to this day the monks refuse to display English-language signs.

The bombing of the Abbey of Monte Cassino was the crowning example of the failure of Allied strategy in Italy in 1944. The Allies had not reaped a single tangible military benefit from it and had instead committed a major blunder. The justification had hinged on "military necessity," which was not served. The only people killed in the bombing were civilians. "There was never any evidence, then or later, that the bombs dropped that day killed a single German."[36] And, as British historian John Ellis writes: "The second battle of Cassino had ended in a bloody shambles . . . the battle represents one of the low points of Allied generalship during the Second World War . . . a willful failure at the highest level to take due account of the terrible problems involved in mounting a concerted attack across such appalling terrain."[37]

So ended the Second Battle of Cassino. Other attempts by Freyberg and Clark to capture the abbey and the town of Cassino came to naught in the weeks following the bombing. The Third Battle of Cassino began in mid-March with a two-pronged assault on Fortress Cassino that was preceded by a thunderous artillery barrage from nine hundred guns and a massive aerial bombardment of the town, which was pulverized by more than one thousand tons of bombs. The artillery fires began shortly after dawn on the Ides of March and continued hour after hour until some twelve hundred tons of shells had been hurled against the town and the Cassino Massif. Eaker reported in a speech later the same day: "Today we fumigated Cassino. . . . Let the German . . . well ponder that what we have done on the Ides of March to their fortress of Cassino, we shall do to every other stronghold where he elects to make a stand."[38]

Again the follow-up ground attacks ended in failure. The 2d New

Zealand Division, supported by the 4th New Zealand Armoured Brigade, moved against the town and Castle Hill, while the 4th Indian Division attacked Hangman's Hill some three hundred yards below the abbey. They also launched a tank attack from the vicinity of Albaneta Farm in the mountains to the northwest.

The defenders of all three levels of the Cassino defenses were Heidrich's tough paratroopers, whose tenacity was unsurpassed in the war. When the New Zealanders entered the ruins of Cassino town during the afternoon of March 15 they found its few surviving paratroop defenders groggy and dazed but miraculously still spoiling for a fight. Small pockets of infantry fought each other for control of the town, with the New Zealanders getting by far the worst of the casualties from snipers.

Some 160 of the 300 paratroopers defending Cassino were crushed to death beneath tons of rubble. An officer of the Gurkhas later described it as an inferno, and remembers thinking at the time, "Dear God, take pity on these men." A German panzer grenadier, who mercifully was only an observer that morning, wrote in his diary: "Today hell is let loose at Cassino. . . . We can see nothing but dust and smoke. The troops who are lying up there must be going mad. . . . The ground is shaking as if there was an earthquake." Survivors later spoke of half-crazed, filthy men stumbling from the shattered ruins only to be obliterated by bombs or shells. "It was," said one, "like the end of the world."[39]

Very heavy fighting took place for the town, Castle Hill above it, and the abbey itself. Huge mounds of rubble and deep craters made it impossible for the tanks to maneuver in support of the infantry, who often fought hand to hand with the hundred or so paratroopers of the 3d Parachute Regiment who had somehow survived the bombing in cellars and bunkers. Against a far larger Allied force the paratroopers managed to hold the town long enough for reinforcements to arrive that night.

Although Castle Hill fell to the New Zealanders late in the afternoon of the first day, there was little else to show for the five-day Third Battle of Cassino, which ended in more death and continued stalemate. It was later estimated that it had taken more than three tons of bombs for each German paratrooper killed during the battle. Von Vietinghoff paid tribute to Heidrich's men when he reported to Kesselring: "No troops but the 1st Parachute Division could have held Cassino."[40]

It was Alexander, however, who delivered the ultimate compliment when he wrote to Brooke to explain the latest failure. "Unfortunately we are fighting the best soldiers in the world—what men! I do not think any other troops could have stood up to it perhaps except these para boys."[41] There would have been little disagreement from the

Allied troops fighting at Anzio. The men of the 4th Parachute Division did not have anywhere near the combat experience of their 1st Parachute Division counterparts at Cassino, but even in the short period they had fought at Anzio they had already earned a reputation for toughness.

There was a terrible irony in the battles for Cassino that tied them irretrievably to the mess at Anzio. As British historian Fred Majdalany points out, by the time of the bombing the weather was so bad, and the first two battles so indecisive, that common sense dictated that no further attempts be made until spring. The First Battle of Cassino had been driven by the need to protect and draw off German forces from the Anzio landings and had been prematurely launched, and the Second even more prematurely so. Thus, having trapped themselves in a catch-22 of their own making, the Allied commanders were now in an even worse dilemma—one that became completely insoluble. With every clear sign that the German Fourteenth Army was about to launch an all-out counteroffensive to drive the Allies back into the sea, the pressure to break the Cassino deadlock became even more acute. As Majdalany writes: "Anzio had originally been designed to rescue the Cassino front from deadlock. Now it had become a liability, and was itself in need of rescue."[42]

As they had so many times in the past, the Germans benefited from the failure of the Allies to take advantage of situations that should have broken the back of the Cassino anchor once and for all. The result benefited Kesselring, who continued to plug the gaps successfully despite mounting losses he could ill afford.

Neither Cassino nor Anzio was of much help to the other. Anzio was showing no evidence of weakening the Cassino front. To the contrary, the drain on resources was taking a far higher toll on Allied units, which were being chewed to bits in both places. Allied forces that remained could have broken the Gustav Line if they had been better employed, but as long as Clark and Alexander continued to commit them in piecemeal fashion, prospects of ending the Cassino stalemate grew dimmer day by day.

The Changing of the Guard

Instead of hurling a wild cat on to the shore all we
got was a stranded whale and Suvla Bay over again.

—CHURCHILL

Legend has it that Nero fiddled at Anzio while Rome
burned. In 1944, it appears that General Lucas fiddled
at Anzio while Winston Churchill and General
Alexander burned.

—BRIGADIER GENERAL FELIX L. SPARKS

It's a thousand pities we didn't let Patton do the job.

—ADMIRAL SIR JOHN CUNNINGHAM

In the aftermath of the desperate
battles for the beachhead it was inevitable that Lucas would be replaced as the Allied ground commander. What had begun with false
promise one month earlier had turned into a monumental embarrassment. In such situations, whether political or military, it is an unwritten
axiom that someone must take the blame. Lucas was an ideal candidate.
He was distrusted by the British, held in near contempt by Alexander,
and generally held accountable for all that had gone wrong since the
invasion. Most serious of all, Lucas had earned the distrust of Winston
Churchill.

Churchill had begun to chafe within the first week of Shingle when
it became plain that VI Corps would not capture the Alban Hills. A
series of exchanges between the prime minister and Alexander ensued.

264

The early telegrams dealt mainly with the ways and means of improving the beachhead. Some were designed to reassure Alexander, while others were clearly meant as warnings of Churchill's growing dissatisfaction with the situation at Anzio. In turn, Alexander's replies were soothing reassurances that everything possible was being done to resolve the problems.

By the end of the first week Churchill began to display an edginess about the failure to advance to the Alban Hills. On January 28 he signaled Alexander that, "it will be unpleasant if you get sealed off there and cannot advance from the south." As the days followed he began bombarding Alexander with telegrams that by early February had not only grown more accusatory but inevitably raised the question of Lucas's fitness for command. "There is of course disappointment here that the brilliant surprise and landing of Shingle should have led so far to no good result. . . . No one understands why it was necessary for General Lucas to sit so long on the beach instead of pegging out claims well inland, if only to delay the enemy's deployment. You have not told me why the [U.S.] airborne troops were not used otherwise than as infantry. The operation has now changed its character completely from the lightning dash of two or three divisions which we contemplated at Marrackech [*sic*]."[1]

For once, Churchill and Brooke were of like mind regarding Anzio. That day his diary recorded that Churchill was "full of doubts as to whether Lucas was handling this landing efficiently. I had some job quieting him down again. Unfortunately this time I feel there are reasons for uneasiness."[2]

Anzio was an increasingly dominant subject of Churchill's weekly cabinet meetings. At the February 7 meeting the Australian high commissioner in London, Stanley Bruce, recorded that Churchill gave a long dissertation, "which was down the lines of a great opportunity having been lost." Brooke appeared to paint an even gloomier picture, and "it is quite clear that there is going to be, at some stage, a considerable controversy as to whether or not a great opportunity was lost by not thrusting on immediately after the surprise of the landing in the bridgehead."[3]

In ensuing weeks the inability of those in London to comprehend Anzio became more and more apparent. Churchill complained that he could not see "why, if we had superior numbers of fighting troops . . . some 15 to 20,000 more in the Bridgehead than those opposing us—a larger number of tanks; quality if not superiority in guns; and complete control of the air, it was not possible for us to attack." When Brooke replied that it was possible because "we had not got the necessary superiority forces . . . the Prime Minister quite pertinently replied that

[this] seemed a strange answer if the Germans with inferior forces were in a position to attack."[4]

What no one, not even Brooke, seemed to grasp was that the dreadful state of the enfeebled Allied infantry battalions, the ineffectiveness of armor, and the extremely rugged terrain made offensive action impossible. It was Brooke's responsibility to articulate the problems faced by VI Corps, and it seems clear that he was unable to convince Churchill and the other skeptics of the massive problems faced at Anzio. Instead, the reasons given left a false impression of excuses for inaction. Bruce seems to have been one of few to have understood that "our Bridgehead is so narrow that we cannot risk a reverse, whereas the Germans can without disastrous consequences."[5]

Somewhat wistfully, Churchill wondered if perhaps Clark would redeem the situation by succeeding at Cassino where Lucas had clearly failed at Anzio. On February 10 Churchill began gently prodding Alexander to take a more active role by suggesting that perhaps he had

> hesitated to assert your authority because you were dealing so largely with Americans and therefore urged an advance instead of ordering it. You are however quite entitled to give them orders, and I have it from the highest American authorities that it is their wish that their troops should receive direct orders.... Do not hesitate, therefore to give orders just as you would to our own men.

If Alexander was dissatisfied with Lucas's performance, "you should put someone there whom you can trust."[6] To Dill, Churchill privately expressed his disappointment in both Alexander and Clark, who should not "urge" but "order." From Shingle, "we should also learn a good many lessons about how not to do it which will be valuable in Overlord."[7]

Alexander agreed Anzio was "a great disappointment," but "we must face the facts" that the Germans had been able to assemble a powerful force that had put VI Corps on the defensive. "The battle has now reached the second phase in which we must now at all costs crush his counter attacks." Alexander also admitted that he would have preferred McCreery and a British corps headquarters, but when that was not possible Lucas was deemed acceptable. "Lucas was highly recommended by General Clark and had been specially selected by Eisenhower.... Amongst the American Corps Commanders he is probably their best but all the American higher commanders lack the years of practical battle experience we have had and this is an undoubted weakness when it comes to fighting difficult battles against veterans."[8] At no time did Alexander ever admit to anyone that Harding had voiced skepticism about Lucas well before the Anzio landings.

To Brooke he was somewhat more candid:

> I am disappointed with 6th Corps Headquarters. They are negative and lack the necessary drive and enthusiasm to get things done. They appear to have become depressed by events. I am sending [Major General Vivian] Evelegh late Commander of 78 Div and recently with 6 Armd Div to 6 Corps Headquarters to buck them up and to help them mount and lay on a properly staged offensive. General JUMBO [Wilson] arrives tonight and I am seeing him, Devers and Clark to find a solution to this problem. What we require is a thruster like George Patton with a capable staff behind him or to replace 6 Corps Headquarters by a British Corps Commander and staff. The latter solution is completely drastic. . . . Perhaps [Eisenhower] could advise on the best available American Commander. The trouble is the lack of battle experience. It is one thing to command a Corps when everything is going in the right direction and quite another to regain the initiative when lost.[9]

From England Eisenhower had been monitoring the situation in Italy with considerable interest. Late the night of February 15–16 his naval aide, Captain Harry C. Butcher, was awakened and informed there was an urgent message that Eisenhower must see at once. Eisenhower was startled that Alexander was placing the blame for Anzio squarely on Lucas and that he had not first consulted with either Clark or Devers, thus leaving the impression he was seeking a scapegoat for "what is publicly regarded as a failure in the beachhead." Eisenhower telephoned Brooke and made it clear that "for Alexander to change from an American to a British Corps headquarters, or to change from one nationality to another during a crisis would be unwise, to say the least." He offered Patton for one month but only if Devers would personally request him.[10]

Patton was alerted to prepare to depart for Italy on short notice, and an aircraft was placed on standby in London. Despite what seemed a certain return to a combat role, Patton had mixed feelings about Anzio. The months of inactivity and uncertainty since the slapping incidents in Sicily had been the most trying of his long military career. At first he was uncertain he wanted any part of the mess at Anzio: "I hope I don't have to go back and straighten things out." However, when he learned of Alexander's compliment, "I have been skipping like a gazell [sic] ever since," he wrote his wife. "I guess a real love of fighting belongs to but a few people." In his diary Patton wrote: "I told Ike that I was anxious to go. . . . I suppose I am the only person in the world who would be elated at the chance to commit personal and official suicide, but I am tickled to death and will make a go of it."[11]

The idea of employing Patton evaporated as quickly as it had arisen. Without explanation, he was told to return to his headquarters in northern England and never learned why he was not sent to Anzio. The principal reason was the presence of Truscott, whom Eisenhower had earlier attempted without success to have transferred to England and placed in command of one of the two American assault corps for the Normandy landings. Had Patton taken command at Anzio it would have pleased senior officers on both sides, among them Admiral Sir John Cunningham, who wrote to the First Sea Lord: "I am sure [Alex] should take a hand in this affair. The awful trouble is that nobody will ever interfere in 'Buggins' battle.' . . . It's a thousand pities we didn't let Patton do the job!"[12]

After the war Alexander told the official U.S. historians he first suggested Lucas be relieved when he failed to push to the Alban Hills soon after the landings. From Harding we now know that not only was Alexander dissatisfied with Lucas's performance, believing he was too tired and defeatist to continue in command of VI Corps, but that he had lacked confidence in him well before the Shingle landings. In mid-February, when he finally called for his dismissal, it was a tacit acknowledgment that he should have heeded Harding's warning that Lucas was the wrong man to command VI Corps. In their notes, the official U.S. historians wrote that Alexander said:

> A better man was needed for the post. . . . Alexander indicated he had lost confidence in Lucas. During his visits to Anzio Alexander had talked to Penney and Truscott . . . Penney had indicated a lack of confidence in Lucas's ability and pointed out to Alexander that Lucas was never up at the front and didn't seem to have any ideas about what to do about the situation. Alexander found out that Lucas stayed in the house that was his CP and didn't move out of it. Truscott never uttered a word to Alexander against Lucas or against his actions and therefore any ideas Alexander got about Lucas or against his actions came either from Alexander's own impressions or from Penney.[13]

At first Alexander found Clark very reluctant to relieve Lucas and that he was sure Alexander was wrong and that he was a good man:

> Alexander made the same suggestion a second time and Clark was still reluctant to relieve Lucas . . . [he then] broached the matter to Clark a third time. This time Alexander used an argument purposely which he thought would be effective with Clark, knowing Clark as he did as a man whose own ambition was a key to his actions. . . . Alexander thinks he said to Clark and this is almost verbatim: "I am very much dissatisfied with General Lucas. I have no confidence in him and in his ability to control the situation. I very much fear that there might be a disaster at Anzio with Lucas in command and you know what will happen to you and me if there is a disaster at Anzio." This was a clear statement to Clark [that they would

both] be blamed and "sacked" for such a disaster. The threat of what might happen . . . Alexander is sure was what brought Clark to agree to relieve Lucas.[14]

In his memoirs Clark admitted that he was inclined to agree with Alexander's dissatisfaction with Lucas and "had for some time been considering a change. My own feeling was that Johnny Lucas was ill—tired physically and mentally—from the long responsibilities of command in battle. . . . I said that I would not in any circumstances do anything to hurt the man who had contributed so greatly to our successes since Salerno . . . I told Alexander that for the time being I would put Truscott in as Lucas's deputy commander and later transfer Lucas to another job, making Truscott VI Corps commander."[15] Clark also told Alexander that "he had lacked some aggressiveness after the landing, although allegations that he could have gone to his objective or to Rome were ridiculous, for had he done so with any force he would have been cut off from his bridgehead."[16]

In a series of postwar interviews with official U.S. historians, Clark maintained that Lucas was relieved without prejudice and that the VI Corps commander had done all he could at Anzio. In an interview several days earlier, however, Clark had contradicted himself by stating that he had been putting pressure on Lucas, who had failed to respond. For example: "Clark told Lucas to put mines along the coast in the Anzio area. The next time Clark went up, no mines had been put up. On one occasion before his relief, General Clark had told Lucas he probably would be relieved if he did not buck up." According to Clark, the only candidates to replace Lucas were Truscott and Harmon. In reality, Truscott was Clark's first choice, and there is no evidence the outspoken Harmon was ever seriously considered.[17]

Much as Clark genuinely liked Lucas, he too had finally realized even without Alexander's blunt comments that what the troops in the Anzio beachhead needed was an inspiring and visible commander. Lucas had done little to help himself in Alexander's eyes by remaining in his bunker. One of Alexander's greatest virtues was his grasp of the absolute necessity for a senior commander to present himself regularly at the front. At Anzio he was appalled to learn that Lucas never did so and that he seemed to have no clear ideas of how to run the battle. It had been only a year since he had seen the disastrous effects of Fredendall's bunker mentality in Tunisia, and now Lucas had lost the confidence of his own commanders for much the same reason. As Truscott would later imply somewhat reluctantly in his own war memoirs, he too had lost confidence in Lucas, but he was too loyal a soldier ever to admit his feelings to Alexander.[18]

The problems of command at Anzio were further muddled by

Churchill, who believed that the best solution seemed to be for Alexander to take personal charge of the battle and for Jumbo Wilson to replace him as 15th Army Group commander. An exasperated Brooke challenged the prime minister to cease meddling in the affairs of his commanders.

> This was one of Winston's typical wild plans based on no clear thinking. Alex was at present commander of all Land Forces in Italy and Wilson Supreme Commander in the Mediterranean. . . . Now because Alex finds Lucas unsuitable in the Anzio Bridgehead, Winston wishes to put Alex in Anzio to serve under Clark and Wilson to leave his post and replace Alex! He could not appreciate that the matter must be left to Alex to replace Lucas if necessary from the many commanders at his disposal, and to go personally to the Bridgehead to reassure himself that all was well.[19]

Clark's main justification for replacing Lucas seems to have been that, in his judgment, he was "very tired." Although Lucas would have denied the charge, the perception of his superiors was that he clearly lacked the stamina to withstand the pressures of a battle he did not himself believe in. This was all secondary to the fact that Lucas had outlived his usefulness and had thus become a liability.[20]

The appointment of Truscott as his deputy the night of February 16 was a clear signal that his days were numbered. "I hope I am not to be relieved from command," he wrote the following day in his diary. "I knew when I came in here that I was jeopardizing my career because I knew the Germans would not fold up because of two divisions landing on their flank and, as the high command was convinced that they would, I saw what was in store for me. I have done my best. I have carried out my orders and my conscience is clear. I do not feel that I should have sacrificed my command."[21]

Although he met with Lucas, Clark apparently said nothing concerning the VI Corps commander's imminent relief. He did, however, inform Truscott of his intention, "to put him in command of the VI Corps and to bring Lucas into my Army as Deputy until something else developed."[22]

Four days later Lucas knew his fate was sealed: "Message from Clark. He arrives today with eight generals. What the hell." When summoned to Clark's command post that night, Lucas was told by the Fifth Army commander that pressure from Alexander and Devers had led to his removal and replacement by Truscott. "Alexander said I was defeated and Devers said I was tired. I was not surprised at General Alexander's attitude. He had been badly frightened, but what I heard about Devers was a great shock. All of us were tired. And I thought I was winning something of a victory [and] had been told so by the Army Commander after Harmon's counter-attack."[23]

Throughout his ordeal Lucas never lost his composure nor his dignity. "I left Anzio the following day. I left the finest soldiers in the world when I lost VI Corps and the honor of having commanded them in their hour of greatest travail cannot be taken from me."[24]

The most unforgiving was Gerald Templer who said of him: "Lucas was absolutely full of inertia, and couldn't make up his mind. He had no qualities of any sort as a commander, absolutely no presence; he was the antithesis of everything that a fighting soldier and general ought to be."[25]

The decision to promote forty-nine-year-old Major General Lucian King Truscott, Jr., to the command of VI Corps was universally applauded. Truscott's reputation as a combat commander had been hewn by more than twenty-six years of Army service that began in 1917, when he was commissioned a second lieutenant of cavalry. Born in Texas in 1895 of Irish and Cornish parents, Truscott was raised in rural Oklahoma. As a young man he became a schoolteacher but, anxious for something more stimulating, seized an opportunity to become an officer in the United States Army.

Truscott saw no action during World War I, but during the interwar years he came to the attention of George Marshall as a promising young officer. An expert polo player with a four-goal handicap, who exhibited a reckless disregard for his own physical safety, Truscott was a member of the Army polo team in the mid-1930s.

Truscott exhibited a fierce competitiveness on the polo field. His son recalls: "Polo was a big part of his life when he was growing up in the cavalry, and he was one of the best players in the army. He was absolutely fearless, which gave him an advantage over many opponents who would eventually back off a little when he pushed them too far. And he played to win. For sport and exercise, too, but mainly to *win*."[26]

This same philosophy carried over into the principles by which Truscott functioned as an officer. He once told his young son:

> Listen, son, goddamnit. Let me tell you something, and don't ever forget it. You play games to *win*, not lose. And you fight wars to win! That's spelled W-I-N! And every good player in a game and every good commander in a war, and I mean really *good* player or *good* commander, every damn one of them has to have some sonofabitch in him. If he doesn't, he isn't a good player or commander. And he never *will* be a good commander. Polo games aren't won by gentlemen. They're won by men who can be first-class sonsofbitches when they have to be. It's as simple as that. No sonofabitch, no commander.[27]

At the time of Pearl Harbor, Truscott was a lieutenant colonel. His raspy voice terrified subordinates and was said to be the result of a childhood mishap when he mistakenly swallowed carbolic acid, ruining his vocal cords.

As a newly promoted brigadier general, in 1942, Truscott was one of the first American officers sent to England, where he served on Mountbatten's Combined Operations staff and is credited, along with William O. Darby, as the father of the U.S. Rangers. An observer during the ill-fated Dieppe raid in August 1942, Truscott participated in several other hit-and-run operations and soon earned a reputation as the officer in the U.S. Army who was most knowledgeable about amphibious operations. He won a Distinguished Service Medal for helping to plan the Torch landings and leading a task force under Patton that liberated Port Lyautey, in French Morocco, from Vichy forces. As Eisenhower's deputy chief of staff in Tunisia, the recently promoted Major General Truscott was reunited with the colleague with whom he had previously served at Fort Lewis, Washington. In March 1943 he was given command of the 3d Infantry Division, then in French Morocco, taking it back to Tunisia for the finale of that campaign.

A hard-driving, harsh disciplinarian, Truscott's arrival shocked the 3d Division. "I had long felt that our standards for marching and fighting in the infantry were too low, not up to those of the Roman legions nor countless examples from our own frontier history, nor even to those of Stonewall Jackson's 'Foot Cavalry' of Civil War fame."[28] He summoned the operations and training officer (G-3), Lieutenant Colonel Ben Harrell, and announced that one of the division infantry battalions was to make a march at four miles per hour. Harrell replied, "But General, infantry marches at two and one-half miles per hour." After further futile protests Harrell got the message when Truscott ordered the training manual tossed in the wastebasket. In the months that followed the men of the 3d Division learned what became known as the "Truscott Trot" and developed countless blisters, while sweating and cursing their new commander. To his officers came the exhortation: "You can't lead your men from a command post in the rear," and henceforth they were required to march with their troops.[29] Officers who complained got little sympathy from their new commanding general. Truscott's response was usually, "What do you mean, it can't be done? Have you tried it? Go out and do it!"[30]

The results were immediate, and the 3d Division soon earned a reputation as the best trained and disciplined in Patton's new Seventh U.S. Army. Truscott's insistence on tough physical training eventually enabled most of the infantry battalions to march fully combat-loaded at up to five miles per hour. In Sicily this paid enormous dividends, as the 3d Division marched the length and breadth of the island, from Licata to Agrigento, to Palermo in record time across the harsh mountains in the central part of the island, and eventually to Messina, under the most grueling conditions.[31]

The square-jawed, rough-hewn Truscott was admired as much as he was feared. He commanded such fierce personal loyalty that more than one officer refused a promotion in order to stay with him. Somewhat superstitious about his dress, Truscott considered his ancient pink cavalry breeches and equally worn knee-high brown cavalry boots "lucky." The boots were so old and fragile they could not withstand the rigors of daily wear. However, whenever Truscott wore them under fire, enemy shelling seemed to stop as if by divine command. During the breakout from the Anzio beachhead, when things were going badly, Truscott was injured in a jeep accident. In his profile of Truscott in *Life,* reporter Will Lang wrote: "There was regret, of course, that the Old Man had broken a rib and that his legs had been injured. But there was also concern because of reports that he couldn't get his boots back on. Embarrassed, admitting that this was a silly way for grown men to act, his officers approached and asked him if he couldn't try just once more to get his lucky boots on. Truscott groaned into them. The offensive succeeded."[32]

Absolutely fearless, Truscott was once observed by a correspondent under fire. When German shells began raining down around him others dived for cover. Truscott, whom the reporter thought either crazy or brave, failed to break stride as he marched up the hill. On another occasion during the difficult Volturno River crossings in October 1943, German artillery shells were falling nearby as Truscott was decorating a colonel. "I can think of no finer way of presenting this decoration than under battle conditions," he said to the officer, who happened to be an old friend. Then Truscott growled in his raspy voice: "Now, what are you going to do about this goddamn situation on the river? Goddammit, your men will be in trouble if you don't get some armor over to help them."[33]

Another incident at the Volturno illustrates why Truscott was admired and feared. A regiment had crossed the river in rubber rafts and was under heavy German fire on the northern bank. As engineers were erecting a pontoon bridge for tanks and vehicles, Truscott suddenly turned up:

> "Hurry!" he urged. "Hurry!" He spotted his tanks sitting by idly, waiting behind trees for the bridge to be finished. Truscott bounded out of his jeep and began pounding on the steel sides of the tanks until the commanders' heads poked up through the turrets. "Goddammit, get up ahead and fire at some targets of opportunity. Fire at anything shooting our men, but goddammit, do some good for yourselves!" he shouted.
>
> He stopped and talked to several wounded men lying on the ground,

then turned to the others. He was wearing his lucky breeches and boots and, as could be expected, the shelling stopped at that moment. His carbolic voice rasped through the sudden silence. "You've only got picks and shovels, men, only your hands, but right now they're better than guns. For God's sake, let's get this job done. We've got a whole regiment of men over there. They'll get wiped out unless you get those tanks across!" Silently, like men offered new hope, the engineers went back to work. They finished the bridge that day and the Sherman tanks crossed the river in time to frustrate the German counterattack.[34]

In Sicily, Truscott won a Distinguished Service Cross under similar conditions near Licata. As usual, he had been under heavy fire rallying his officers and men.

Truscott's idiosyncracies included having four Chinese-American cooks and valets who served with him throughout the war—he refused meals prepared by anyone else—and during and after Sicily what became his trademark, a white scarf made from an airman's escape-kit map of the area being fought over. This custom began in Sicily, where someone had given him such a map as a present, which he later pulled out of his pocket to protect his nose, mouth, and ever-ailing throat, Texas cowboy style, from the all-pervasive dust on the roads. This worked so well that he adopted it as his trademark, substituting a new escape map for each new campaign through the rest of the war.[35] In addition to the scarf, Truscott habitually wore a beat-up brown leather jacket and an ordinary .45 caliber pistol strapped to his waist in a GI-issue holster. His tent was always decorated with fresh flowers taken from wherever they could be found.

By long habit, Truscott spent most of his time visiting his officers and men at the front where they toiled. The notion of remaining in his command post was anathema to him. As one of his former aides notes: "Truscott was a highly visible commander—deliberately—who was habitually out seeing what was happening and being seen. He was forceful and direct, inspiring a lot of confidence . . . [he] could be painfully blunt, but he also had a remarkable capacity for listening and appreciating other people's problems . . . [and] a lively sense of humor."[36]

The critical days of Fischfang had seen Lucian Truscott in a new role he clearly did not relish. Shortly before midnight on February 16 he had been abruptly awakened by his chief of staff, Colonel Don Carleton, who bore startling news. "Boss, I hate to do this, but you would give me hell if I held this until morning." It was a copy of a message from Clark to Lucas, appointing Truscott deputy commander of VI Corps. Truscott was dismayed and frustrated at being forced to leave his beloved 3d Division for an assignment where he would have no command authority. Not only had he not been warned of the decision, but he had no desire to give up his division to play second fiddle at VI Corps. Good soldier that he was, Truscott's bitterness was only momentary. He later wrote: "This was certainly no time to consider personal preferences. The order had no doubt been issued after all factors had been thoughtfully weighed. There was a job to be done, and I was a soldier. I could only carry the order out loyally. But it was not easy to leave the 3d Infantry Division."[37] His replacement to command the 3d Division was Brigadier General John W. O'Daniel, an equally tough and demanding officer whose determination on the beach at Salerno had earned him the nickname "Iron Mike."[38]

Truscott regarded Lucas as an old friend of long standing with whom he had always had an open and frank relationship that had seen both men offer and receive advice and recommendations with consideration and respect. However, as commanders the two men were cut from entirely different cloth. Tactfully, Truscott has described their differences:

> I was not blind to the fact that General Lucas lacked some of the qualities of positive leadership that engender confidence, and that he leaned heavily upon his staff and trusted subordinates in difficult decisions. His was a lovable personality, although his appearance invited the less respectful among his juniors to refer to him as "Foxy Grandpa." I was also aware that General Lucas had little confidence in the British troops of his command, and that his British commanders had even less confidence in him. There was even some feeling that perhaps I was being used to "pull someone else's chestnuts from the fire."[39]

Truscott thus faced two daunting tasks as the new beachhead commander. Not only must the beachhead remain secure but it was crucial that immediate steps be taken to reassure the British and eliminate the dreadful bunker mentality that prevailed in VI Corps headquarters. During a telephone conversation with Colonel Carleton the night of February 16 the VI Corps chief of staff, Brigadier General Lawrence B. ("Dutch") Keiser, had observed that he had no idea if there would even be a VI Corps headquarters in existence the following morning, "for they would probably be driven into the sea."[40] Keiser was one of several corps staff officers sent packing by Truscott.[41]

What Truscott found in the Nettuno bunker was a sense of desperation and gloom. He assured the staff that the situation on the ground rarely was as bad as it looked on a headquarters map. He did not mention that sitting in a bunker was no way to run a battle. Within a short time Truscott was off to the front to view the situation for himself.

Several key members of the 3d Division staff accompanied Truscott, who immediately began to stamp his imprint on a demoralized corps staff. Although they were permitted to remain in the bunker,

Truscott himself lived and worked aboveground in a converted wine-shop. In addition to the usual situation maps posted in the new corps war room, Truscott also hung an enlarged Bill Mauldin cartoon from the U.S. Army newspaper *Stars and Stripes*. The cartoon depicted the famous "Willie and Joe" GI characters reposing in a mud- and water-filled Anzio foxhole that was captioned: "The hell this ain't the best hole in the world. I'm in it."[42]

Even before Lucas was sacked, Truscott had already made his presence felt. Former aide James Wilson recalls that it was not accomplished without several applications of "corncob and turpentine to the corps staff." It was helpful that virtually every senior American officer in the beachhead enjoyed Truscott's confidence. The 3d Division had always been known for having "its tail up," and

> much of this same spirit was communicated in rapid order to the American units and their commanders, though Harmon needed little coaching in this regard, and Eagles at the 45th [Division], of course, had already absorbed much of the Truscott esprit, if not dash, as [a former] assistant Third Division commander. [Colonel Reuben] Tucker [504th Parachute Infantry Regiment] and Darby too were old Truscott pals, and he had got to know Bob Frederick and the 1st Special Service Force well in the mountains in front of Cassino.[43]

Fences were also mended with the British. Truscott visited their units frequently. Unlike Lucas and his staff, who were familiar with neither British organization, tactics, nor methods, Truscott fully understood their unique problems. "Few comprehended the effect that Britain's ordeal and British manpower shortages had upon their tactical methods."[44] Despite a severe case of laryngitis Truscott visited every unit in the beachhead front during the first twenty-four hours of his command.

Truscott also went out of his way to cultivate and effectively employ his new British deputy commander, Major General Vivian Evelegh, the amiable former commander of the 78th Division, who soon became a Truscott admirer. Evelegh carried the message to the British elements of VI Corps that the ineffective leadership of the old regime had been replaced by something quite different.

Wilson recounts an incident that exemplifies the success Truscott enjoyed. One day, in the company of Templer, Truscott visited a forward observation post. "The two generals crawled up the side of a fosso to have a look only to be met with heavy machine gun fire. As the beachhead and division commanders came tumbling down from the top they both lost their helmets (even Templer was wearing one, which was unusual). In the ensuing confusion each ended up with the other's helmet on his head, much to the merriment of the Tommies, who doubly appreciated the visit."[45]

Within a short time Truscott was able to reverse the long-standing antipathy to VI Corps. It was a marvelous example of inspirational leadership. Brigadier Charles Richardson remembers him as a commander who "had a real grip of operations and fully understood the problems of the front-line soldier. . . . A real tough guy with a 'feel' for the battle."[46] Even though he was not directly involved in the battles for the left flank as 3d Division commander, Truscott spent considerable time studying the situation there. The British appreciated his take-charge attitude and firm grasp of their plight. As his aide recalls, "The years at Leavenworth [as a student and instructor] certainly paid off, but he had [also] learned a lot of the British ways too at [Mountbatten's] COHQ and had a hearty respect for their 'appreciations.' Much of this had already been conveyed to the members of his own staff brought with him to corps. . . . The rest of the staff read the message in a hurry."[47]

It was common for British officers to spend informal evenings in Truscott's quarters over a drink. A good deal of serious business was conducted in a relaxed atmosphere so unlike that of his predecessor. Wynford Vaughan-Thomas was impressed with Truscott's first meeting with the correspondents and wrote in his diary that although the new commander made it clear the coming months would be difficult, " 'Gentlemen, we're going to hold this Beachhead come what may.' And he stuck out his jaw in a way that convinced you that any German attack would bounce off it."[48]

In many respects Truscott resembled Patton. Both were profane around their troops, both passionately despised the Germans and operated by the same aggressive principles. Truscott's all-consuming philosophy that he constantly drove home to his men was: "Be aggressive, be tough. When you strike the enemy, aim to kill and destroy. Take your objective at all costs. Be alert. Use your initiative. Take advantage of every opportunity. Give the enemy no pause. Destroy him!" However harsh his philosophy, Truscott was an unfailingly fair man who cherished democracy. Unlike Clark, who elevated press relations to an art form, Truscott was almost contemptuous of his personal image. To the correspondents in Germany during the Occupation in the autumn of 1945 he said, "You can go anywhere. You can see everything. Tell the way things are, just so long as you don't give information to the enemy. So far as I personally am concerned, you can call me a son-of-a-bitch if you want."[49]

Anzio had become a bitter pill for Winston Churchill, who immortalized the failure of Anzio by his often-quoted observation that, "instead of hurling a wild cat on to the shore all we got was a stranded whale and Suvla Bay over again."[50] These remarks were contained in a long telegram to Field Marshal Jan Smuts, the prime minister of South Africa, to whom Churchill often confided his problems and whose counsel he sought. He found the stalemate at Cassino disappointing but reserved his sharpest comments for Anzio:

> In my conferences at Carthage and Marrackech [sic] I managed to get this large Anzio amphibious operation soundly organized and to clear difficulties out of the way. My own personal efforts did not extend to the fighting of the battle which I naturally left entirely to the Commanders once they were put safely, as they were, at the right place. The essence of the battle as contemplated by Alexander in all his talks with me was the seizing of the Alban Hills with the utmost rapidity.

The problem, lamented Churchill, was:

> the American General Lucas . . . seems to have had in his mind the idea that he must at all costs prepare against a counter-attack. Therefore, although as soon as the landing was successful I sent injunctions to Alexander to peg out claims inland rather than dig in bridgeheads, the whole operation became stagnant. . . . Lucas has now been superceded by a young American Divisional Commander named Truscott, who is spoken of most highly on all sides. My confidence in Alexander is undiminished, though if I had been well enough to be at his side as I had hoped at the critical moment I believe I could have given the necessary stimulus. Alas for time, distance, illness and advancing years.[51]

Above all, Churchill remained blind to his own culpability. Oblivious to Alexander's leadership deficiencies, although the prime minister mildly complained that Alex should "order" instead of "urge," he never seems to have questioned how a mere major general, subject to the orders of an army and an army group commander, could bear sole responsibility for the mess at Anzio.

Nevertheless, even Churchill was unable to conceal his worry over what Anzio would do to the outcome of the war in Italy and the forthcoming cross-Channel invasion. In his diary the deputy under secretary of state at the Foreign Office, Sir Alexander Cadogan, observed how deeply Anzio was affecting the British leader. "P.M. v. despondent about the Anzio landing," he wrote on January 31. "Said this had now become an American operation, with no punch in it. We were clinging to a bridgehead and rendering it defensively fireproof. A bad prospect for this operation and a bad omen for greater ops. later."[52] Many years later, the only living survivor of Company E, 157th Regiment, from Fischfang and the battle for the Caves, retired Brigadier General Felix L. Sparks, wrote: "Legend has it that Nero fiddled at Anzio while Rome burned. In 1944, it appears that General Lucas fiddled at Anzio while

Winston Churchill and General Alexander burned."[53]

His disappointment notwithstanding, Churchill and the British chiefs of staff could at least take comfort from the knowledge that in Lucian King Truscott the Anzio beachhead was now commanded by a man respected for his leadership and toughness.

PART IV

Stalemate

Question most asked by new arrivals
at Anzio: "What's it like, mate?"
The inevitable reply: "Bloody awful!"

16

The Ordeal of the Caves

It was a savage, brutish troglodyte existence.
—IRISH GUARDS HISTORIAN

As the two sides continued to bloody each other after the great German counteroffensive, the nightmare of the men of the 2d Battalion, 157th Regiment, continued unabated. Although some supply parties managed to bring up food and ammunition, the men in the Caves along the base of Buonriposo Ridge remained surrounded. K rations were often shared by three men. The only source of water for one company was a nearby stream that ran red with the blood of several dead Germans. Even so, the water was boiled and drunk by the thirsty soldiers.[1]

Attempts to air-drop supplies more often than not resulted in resupply to the Germans, not always to their advantage. One case of explosives blew up in their faces.

The Germans managed to infiltrate their infantry between the companies of the 2d Battalion, making any excursion outside their perimeter a dangerous affair. Combat was close, intense, and deadly. Machine guns and grenades were the weapons of choice. The evening of February 18 a German rifle company that had managed to get between the outer battalion perimeter and the Caves attacked, and a furious battle ensued in which it was necessary to bring down waves of friendly artillery fire on the battalion position. Some of the fighting was hand to hand. Smoke, the explosions of artillery and grenades, and the deadly whine of bullets turned this unlikely battlefield into a raging inferno.

Somehow the Americans held, as had the Grenadiers in similar circumstances two weeks earlier.

At dawn the following morning the Germans launched company-
size human-wave attacks directly into the teeth of heavy automatic
weapons fire. There were two more attacks that day, and all were
repulsed. Some Germans got as far as the perimeter wire before being
cut down. Their bodies dotted the landscape, and some of the wounded
could be heard moaning in no-man's land.

It is fair to state that the capture or annihilation of the 2d Battalion
had become an obsession. The more the Germans tried and failed to
eradicate it, the greater their determination to do so. When the human-
wave attacks failed, they returned to infiltration tactics. Pairs of soldiers
would advance along gullies and ravines under the cover of artillery
barrages until they were able to build up a solid line. Sooner or later
they had to attack over open ground that was swept by fire. Another
attack against Company I failed when British and American artillery
fire broke up the attacks and rained death on their positions.[2]

During the ordeal of the 2d Battalion hope was kept alive by rumors that attempts were being made to break through to the lost battalion. Although the Guards Brigade managed to relieve the 3d Battalion,
the first attempt by the 56th Division to get through to the beleaguered
2d failed. Truscott and Templer were determined to relieve the 2d
Battalion at all costs, and the unit chosen to relieve them was the newly
arrived 2d/7th Battalion, the Queen's Royal Regiment, one of three
battalions that made up the 169th Infantry Brigade, which was also
known as the Queen's Regiment.[3] Templer's eighteen rifle battalions
had been decimated during the German counteroffensive, and many
were at or below company size. The Queen's were fresh, and during the
evening of February 21 the battalion fought its way forward to the
Caves, taking heavy casualties in the process from an air raid launched
in conjunction with a renewed enemy attack against the Allied left
flank. German antipersonnel ("butterfly") bombs accounted for most of
the seventy-six casualties. Many weapons and considerable ammunition
were lost during the treacherous infiltration to the Caves.

Earlier that day Templer had attempted to push an armored rescue
force up the Via Anziate to the Caves, but it never came close to
succeeding and three tanks and an antitank gun were lost in the process. Further attempts were deemed futile.

The Queen's got their first taste of the wicked nature of combat in
the Anzio beachhead when they found numerous Germans ensconced
inside friendly lines. In fact, the situation was so confused that the
Queen's battalion commander, Lieutenant Colonel D. C. Baynes, asked
the American survivors to remain for an additional twenty-four hours.
The immediate problem was ammunition. What little the small Allied

force had could only be brought up by sweating men who became ammunition coolies. Many of these troops were lost attempting to re-supply the men defending the Caves.

D Company was defending positions nearest the Via Anziate, and within hours of its arrival all contact was lost with this unit and was never restored. Despite repeated attempts to regain contact, it was later found that its sector was unoccupied and Colonel Baynes concluded that they had been overrun.[4] It was an ominous beginning for the Queen's, whose first day of heavy combat around the Caves was a portent of what was to follow. Had it not been for the presence of an American artillery forward observer the Germans might well have overrun both forces the night of February 21. A heavy artillery barrage broke up the attacks, after which the moans and screams of wounded German soldiers could be heard piercing the night.

The survivors of the 2d Battalion began a fighting withdrawal to friendly lines the night of February 22. Many never made it. During the day the Germans had tightened their grip around the Caves and had cut the Queen's supply lifeline to the rear. As the 45th Division history relates, "The Germans seemed to be in possession of all the ground except the caves."[5]

In the early morning hours of February 23 the 2d Battalion attempted to break out of the latest trap. The men split up into small groups. The most badly wounded remained behind in the Caves under the care of Captain (Dr.) Peter Graffagnino and his medics, who refused to abandon their patients. Led by the battalion commander, Lieutenant Colonel Lawrence C. Brown, the survivors began infiltrating south toward Allied lines. Just as it appeared the column would reach Allied lines, it was attacked by machine guns and rifles from a group of nearby houses. In the ensuing firefight the column was split. Colonel Brown and the first half made it to safety. The remainder were scattered in the confusion and darkness. Some eventually ended up with British units; others never made it to safety.

One of those who succeeded was the lone survivor of E Company, its commander, Captain Sparks. Two days later the only other survivor, an NCO, returned from a stint with a British unit. On February 16 there had been nearly 1,000 men in the 2d Battalion. When the survivors emerged from their ordeal a week later, a mere 225 men were left, and 90 of these were hospital cases from trench foot and other disorders ranging from loss of hearing to shattered nerves. Although overall battalion losses were 75 percent, those of E Company were 99 percent. In a tribute to their extraordinary bravery, the Army later noted "that any man returned is a tribute to the courage and stamina of the American infantry soldiers who have made the battle of the caves an epic of defensive fighting."[6]

The ordeal that was ending a solid week of hell for the Americans was only beginning for the men of the Queen's. The gray dawn of February 23 brought home to Colonel Baynes the grim reality of their situation. Ammunition in the forward platoons guarding the approaches to the Caves was nearly exhausted. Another attempt at resupply the previous night had ended in costly failure. There were no reserves to draw on and no prospect of resupply before that night. C Company found itself surrounded and under serious threat from German troops between the Caves and friendly lines. Cut off from the rest of the battalion, the survivors managed to hold out until late morning when they were attacked by flamethrowers. Out of ammunition and surrounded, like the U.S. Rangers at Cisterna three weeks earlier, there was nothing the men of C Company could do except surrender. Their only consolation was that their captors were taking heavy losses from British snipers firing the M-1 rifles of the 157th Regiment from the Caves.

With C and D companies gone, the remnants of the 2d/7th Queen's were forced into the Caves, where they were attacked by machine guns and hand grenades dropped into the entrances. Inside were scenes from a surrealistic nightmare. Pieces of the wall and roof were blasted loose, creating clouds of dust. The headquarters cave included British troops, American wounded, a growing number of British wounded, more than thirty Italian refugees, and a very large pig whose owners wailed in terror as the noise of the explosions reverberated through the Caves.[7]

Not only was ammunition critically low, but food was running out, and for a while all radio communications with the rear were knocked out. With the appearance of three German Mark IV tanks that began shooting high-explosive shells into the mouths of the caves the situation became even more desperate. Signalmen managed to repair one radio and a call for artillery support quickly brought a hail of fire down upon the attackers. Aid men from both sides managed to remove many of the wounded from the battlefield under a white flag, but one British stretcher party was taken prisoner and never returned.[8]

It was obvious to one and all that any prolonged attempt to hold the Caves would result in the complete annihilation of the 2d/7th Queen's, and as Colonel Baynes made plans for a breakout to the rear, the order came through late that afternoon to get out that night. Early that evening under the cover of yet another artillery barrage, the remnants of the 2d/7th Queen's began infiltrating to the south. The Germans soon discovered the ruse, and in the ensuing chaos the British column was shattered and splintered in all directions. "All hell broke loose . . . suddenly there were Germans everywhere and it was impossible to avoid completely their positions and patrols: the party led by

Lieutenant Colonel Baynes at one time lay flat on a wadi bank while Germans with automatic weapons walked up and down immediately behind them while another party was fortunate in being mistaken for Italian refugees and walked right through an enemy position without being fired at."[9]

Few made it. Only Colonel Baynes, who received the DSO for valor, three other officers, and seventeen troops managed to evade the Germans. Although many of the troops of the Queen's were later confirmed to be POWs, the losses to the battalion during its forty-eight hours in and around the Caves were a staggering 362 officers and men killed, wounded, and missing. During the weeklong battle two battalions had been all but annihilated. The 2d/7th Queen's had suffered losses approaching 85 percent.

The survivors of the Queen's were assured the following day by General Templer himself that they had held off five German battalions and had gained valuable time to shore up the defenses of the left flank. Templer argued that if the Germans had broken through to Shepherd's Bush, as the road west of the Flyover had been nicknamed by the British, they might have cut the main supply routes to the 36th Engineer Regiment holding the Moletta River line.

As the Fifth Army historian reminds us, "The battle of the caves did not end the fighting on the left shoulder of the salient. It was merely the most important and most costly action in a bloody war of attrition in which whole squads and platoons disappeared without leaving a trace."[10] There was to be yet more heavy fighting before both sides tacitly acknowledged that a stalemate existed on the Anzio front. British and American units alike were decimated from Fischfang and its bloody aftermath. The British 1st Division remained a patient on the critical list, and it was now joined by Templer's 56th Division. In the space of a single week it too had been stripped by fatigue and heavy casualties. Overall, the three brigades of the Black Cat division were at less than 43 percent of effective fighting strength.[11]

The hard-hit Irish Guards had already paid a fearsome price in casualties during the earlier battles for the Thumb, and as their final mission in the Anzio beachhead they were thrust into the breech once again to plug gaps in the Allied left flank. Now they were given one final taste of the hell of Anzio. From February 21 to 25 the 1st Battalion occupied positions in the gullies west of the Via Anziate and south of the Caves where the men of the 45th Division and the 2d/7th Queen's had held out. They had been led to believe that they were soon to quit Anzio for refitting in Naples. Instead they were told that they were to relieve an American infantry battalion in the gully country north of the Flyover. The newly assigned commander of the 24th Guards Brigade assured them: "The sector is very quiet, so you will have no trouble, and your weakness does not matter." The main Guards positions were along a long T-shaped gully nicknamed the Boot.

Contrary to their brigadier's assurances, from the moment they arrived they were subjected to repeated attacks by desperate Germans. During the three days and four nights the Irish Guards occupied the Boot they were under almost continuous attack. As bad as their earlier experiences had been, this one was even worse, a brutal, horrific existence that exceeded anything Dante might have conceived as a vision of hell. This was war at its absolute nadir, aptly described by the historian of the Irish Guards as "unremitting drudgery":

> It was a savage, brutish troglodyte existence, in which there could be no sleep for anyone and no rest for any commander. The weather was almost the worst enemy, and the same torrential rain, which sent an icy flood swirling around our knees as we lurked in the gullies, would at times sweep away the earth that covered the poor torn bodies of casualties hastily buried in the Boot. Wallowing in a network of gullies, isolated by day and erratically supplied by night, soaked to the skin, stupefied by exhaustion and bombardment, surrounded by new and old corpses and yet persistently cheerful, the Guardsmen dug trenches and manned them until they were blown in and then dug new ones., beat off attacks, changed their positions, launched local attacks, stalked snipers, broke up patrols, evacuated the wounded, buried the dead and carried supplies . . . a recurrent nightmare. Carrying parties got lost, jeeps got bogged and, as the swearing troops heaved at them, down came the shells.[12]

As one Guards officer recalled: "What I remember most is the long strain of hanging on all day to hear the list of casualties every evening, to see the stretcher-bearers livid with fatigue, staggering past with their load, a dirty Red Cross flag held aloft as a precarious appeal."[13]

Not only were the troops manning the Boot subjected to unremitting shelling and automatic weapons fire, but during the relief of a battalion of the 157th Regiment on February 21–22, two German fighter-bombers dropped an entire load of antipersonnel bombs directly on to a large concentration of troops and, as one Guardsman described it, turned the night "into a brilliant green mass, changing to orange and white as bomb after bomb hit the ground. . . . It was a cruel and crippling blow." Another reported to the adjutant: "Could we have a doctor please? The Company's very bad. The bombs hit us." More than seventy Americans and British were killed.[14] The only constant was death, and it came with increasing frequency.

After four of the bloodiest days of fighting in their tenure at Anzio, the Irish Guards had nothing left to give and were at last relieved by the 1st Battalion, the Duke of Wellington's Regiment, many of whom were frightened replacements who had had no experience of the horror

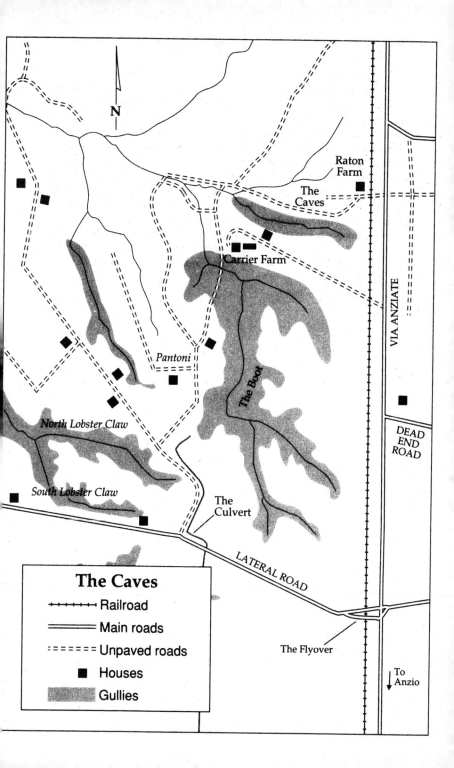

N

Raton
Farm

The
Caves

Carrier Farm

VIA ANZIATE

Pantoni

The Boot

North Lobster Claw

South Lobster Claw

The
Culvert

DEAD
END
ROAD

LATERAL ROAD

The Flyover

To
Anzio

The Caves

+++++++ Railroad

———— Main roads

====== Unpaved roads

■ Houses

▨ Gullies

of the Anzio beachhead. To the end, the gullies claimed victims, the most heartbreaking of whom was killed during the hand-over to the Dukes. A gallant sergeant named Jimmy Wylie had survived two previous campaigns only to die in the final moments of a third. It was a somber scene that was recorded by the commander of the Dukes, Lieutenant Colonel B. W. Webb-Carter: "As the tall Guardsmen filed out, leaving us the heritage of death and desolation they had borne so long, a peculiar sense of isolation struck us. In all the long-drawn-out crucifixion of the beach-head, no positions saw such sublime self-sacrifice and such hideous slaughter as were perpetrated in the over-grown foliage that sprouted in the deep gullies."[15]

This horror translated into a crushing casualty rate of 94 percent. In barely more than a single month of combat the 1st Battalion, the Irish Guards, lost 32 officers and 746 enlisted men, 414 of whom were missing in action.[16]

17

Impasse

German forces in Italy . . . were no longer capable of
assuming the initiative by attack.

—KESSELRING TO HITLER

The unit designations changed as
battalions were rotated in and out of the Boot, the Culvert, the Lobster
Claw, and other assorted hellish places that made up the gully country
on the left flank of the Allied beachhead defense line. But the killing
and misery were destined to continue until May as Germans, Americans, and British fought for some of the most miserable terrain on the
planet Earth in what had become a trench-warfare stalemate that bore
an obscene similarity to the Western Front of World War I. Another
division, the British 5th, made its appearance in early March to relieve
the exhausted and battered 1st and 56th divisions, but otherwise life
(and death) went on much as it had before.

Nor were the Germans about to accept the stalemate without one
final attempt to succeed where Fischfang had failed. As Fischfang
ended, plans were being drawn up for another large-scale counteroffensive. This time Kesselring and von Mackensen devised an attack
aimed at driving a wedge through the 3d Division west of Cisterna to
the vicinity of the northeastern edge of the Padiglione Woods. The plan
was predicated on the belief that VI Corps was so short of reserves that
it could not cope with these attacks in conjunction with secondary
attacks in the familiar Via Anziate sector.

This was wishful thinking on Kesselring's part. In fact, his decision
to attack the Allied right flank at Cisterna was tantamount to an open
admission that the Allies were not to be driven back into the sea.

Kesselring's postwar comments suggest that though he had little faith in this operation, he undertook it in the knowledge that Hitler would not have accepted a decision to go over to the defensive without a second counteroffensive. Up to now Kesselring had been reasonably free of Hitler's amateurish orders from the *Führerbunker.* However, as with Churchill, who at Anzio exerted his influence to a degree that could only be described as meddlesome, it had been only a matter of time before Hitler interfered with the direction of the campaign in Italy.

To no one's surprise, and for the second time in the battle for the Anzio beachhead, the Führer decreed the tactics to be employed by the Fourteenth Army. In disapproving Kesselring's scheme, Hitler ordered the main attack launched from Cisterna toward the Mussolini Canal in the belief that the Allies would be obliged to shift valuable defenders from the Flyover sector to the threatened right flank. Without protest "Kesselring and von Mackensen bowed to their master's tactical wisdom and revised their plans."[1]

The heavy rains that pelted the beachhead delayed the start for three days. When it commenced the morning of February 29 the German effort was halfhearted and stood little chance of success. It is difficult to discern what Kesselring hoped to accomplish—other than going through the motions of carrying out an attack—by an attack by three German divisions of the LXXVI Panzer Corps across the 3d Division front. The heaviest attacks were from the west of Cisterna and were directed against the paratroopers of Lieutenant Colonel Yarborough's 509th Parachute Infantry Battalion, which was defending the village of Carano. 1st Lieutenant John R. Martin's Company B was defending a low hill a mile northeast of the village when it was struck shortly before dawn by waves of German panzer grenadier troops advancing under the cover of a smokescreen.

The airborne had been manning an outpost line and were spread too thin to resist the sort of attack the Germans launched. German engineers had pried open gaps in the barbed wire strung along the Allied front line with bangalore torpedoes and wire cutters. Behind them came the infantry, singing and shouting. Although many were cut down by machine guns as they assaulted the American positions, the hill seemed to erupt in a mass of fire as Yarborough's paratroopers fought hand to hand, but they stood no chance against the overwhelming numbers of German infantry arrayed against them. The survivors were ordered to withdraw, but only a single officer and twenty-two of his men made it to the main U.S. defensive line farther to the rear. The majority of B Company was officially declared missing in action, although a great many were not missing but had been killed in the initial onslaught.

A similar attack against A Company was defeated when Yarborough was able to call in the 3d Division and VI Corps artillery to support his mortars. Although the attack had driven a small wedge some eight hundred yards deep, it was not enough to pose a threat of further serious penetration. Elsewhere German tank and infantry attacks were stopped dead in their tracks. Neither Hitler nor Kesselring and von Mackensen had reckoned with the awesome effect of the Allied artillery. Truscott had long since proved himself the master of the employment of artillery in support of his infantry, and what greeted the German attack stunned even the veteran artilleryman Albert Kesselring. For every shell the Germans expended, twenty came back. Even before the German attacks commenced, counterbattery fire was savaging assembly areas. Alerted by Ultra and intelligence reports from the front, Truscott decided to take the initiative and deliver a devastating preemptive artillery attack an hour before the German attack began. German reports later indicated that 66,500 rounds were fired against them on February 29, exceeding by more than twice the 30,000 rounds fired on February 19 during the height of Fischfang.[2] It took much of the sting out of the German attacks.

The German commanders had little to show for their efforts on February 29, and by the following day most of the ground lost to their penetrations had been regained. While Truscott's massed artillery pounded the attacking infantry, often breaking up formations, thoroughly disrupting communications, and terrifying many German troops, tanks and tank destroyers dealt with German panzer threats wherever they arose. To add to German woes, in midafternoon on February 29 the heavy overcast lifted sufficiently for 247 fighter-bombers and twenty-four light bombers to bomb and strafe the attackers. Early that evening a U.S. counterattack partially restored the front in Colonel Yarborough's sector. German tactics of company- and battalion-size attacks across a wide front not only failed but left the attacking units at the mercy of Truscott's artillery and the Allied air forces.

German losses that day foretold the failure of their counteroffensive: 143 killed, 429 wounded, and at least 361 Germans in the VI Corps prisoner-of-war cages.[3] The following day was even more futile for von Mackensen's troops. At Truscott's instigation the aggressive O'Daniel had ordered the 2d Battalion, 30th Infantry, to retake the 509th Parachute Infantry's outpost line around Carano. Supported by eighteen battalions of artillery, the American infantry fought a bloody battle during the night and again the morning of March 1. Battles raged throughout the day, but the outcome was never in doubt. The gains for which the Germans had paid a heavy price were wiped out and the entire front line restored to its previous configuration.

March 1 was the worst day of the campaign for the Germans, whose casualties swelled to 202 killed, 707 wounded, and 465 missing.[4] When the weather cleared the following day, Eaker's airmen unleashed the heaviest concentration of aerial attacks of the campaign. Supported by 176 fighters flying air cover, 241 B-24 Liberators and 110 B-17 Flying Fortresses hammered German gun positions and assembly areas, with special attention to those near the railway lines leading to Cisterna and Campoleone. The attack was witnessed by Truscott and his aide, Lieutenant Wilson, who observed the bombing with awe. "Christ, General, that's hitting a guy when he's down."[5] Their elation soon turned to dismay as a B-26 received a direct hit from German ack-ack and fell to the ground in flames. There were no parachutes.[6]

Although there were two more days of heavy fighting, Kesselring had already thrown in the towel and unofficially terminated the operation the night of March 1. Aggressive attacks by the 3d Division on March 3 put paid to the abortive German counteroffensive, which ended with no gain. Both sides had again bloodied themselves to exhaustion. The Anzio campaign was now six weeks old and neither side could pay the price of sustained combat on such a scale. German casualties were at least 16,192 and were undoubtedly considerably higher because of incomplete statistics to units known to have suffered heavy losses during the three counteroffensives.[7] Allied forces had lost nearly 21,000 (10,168 British and 10,775 American) in the Anzio meat grinder.[8]

Among the casualties was Lieutenant Colonel David Wedderburn, the commander of the Scots Guards, who was grievously wounded and his driver and four other officers (two of them company commanders) killed the afternoon of February 27, when a shell burst directly over the battalion bivouac in the Padiglione Woods (demonstrating once again that there was no safe place anywhere in the Anzio beachhead). The following day Wedderburn died of his wounds. He had led the Scots Guards during the most trying period of the 1st Division defense of the Thumb. "The whole division is absolutely miserable," wrote Lieutenant Colonel Montagu-Douglas-Scott of the Irish Guards. "He had done wonders for the battalion . . . it is so wicked to think that he got over all these dangers to catch it back here." Among those who paid their last respects at his burial in the new Anzio cemetery was General Penney, who had himself come close to death from a German shell.[9]

For the British the battle for the gullies was to continue unabated well into March. Here the Germans, as one regimental historian noted, continued "to gnaw the right shoulder of the salient." The area had many nicknames, one of which was coined by the Sherwood Foresters, who simply referred to the place as the "Bloody Boot."[10] The Foresters, who had suffered such heavy losses at Campoleone Station at the end of January, had been sent an infusion of replacements, and on February

27 the battalion was back in the thick of the fighting when it replaced another battalion of the Queen's Regiment (the battered 2d/6th) in the northern sector of the Boot.

The Foresters had scarcely arrived when a disheveled officer reported to the battalion commander with the grim news that C Company had been wiped out moments after taking over its positions adjacent to two small buildings situated near a track junction called Pantoni. The few survivors told a confusing tale of German troops occupying positions inside the company perimeter as they arrived to take over from the Queen's. Apparently the unsuspecting Foresters were ambushed by waiting Germans, some of whom were thought to have been dressed in British uniforms and spoke English, who had infiltrated the area under cover of the heavy rains. The last anyone had seen of the C Company commander, Captain C. Kilby, he was firing a tommy gun and attempting to rally his men. Three months after the battle Captain Kilby's body was recovered, along with those of seven of his men who perished with him and had been laid out beside him by the Germans.[11]

D Company fared little better when it, too, came under heavy attack. It was later established that a substantial part of a German infantry battalion supported by tanks had all but overwhelmed the company, of which "not many were left."[12] Their foe was a familiar one to the American and British infantry units that had fought in the gullies: the tough paratroopers of the 4th Parachute Division.

In little over twenty-four hours the fighting strength of the four infantry companies of the Foresters had been shattered. "The Battalion had seen some sorry scenes, but now it was in its worst plight of having one [combined] company of one hundred men left in the line. There was no relief for them and the days that followed for them are undoubtedly the ones of which the Divisional Commander was thinking later when he said: 'They experienced times and conditions which seemed to be almost beyond human endurance.' "[13]

The 56th Division was so badly decimated that despite its plight nothing could be done for some days to relieve the Foresters.

> Such was the lack of reserves within the Division at this time that the relief of this pitiful little band of Foresters was not at once possible . . . these hundred men were obliged for five days to hold their positions, while the enemy, who by day directed an almost ceaseless fire from his artillery and mortars into the Boot and the wadi to the North of it, by night sent his patrols—mostly parachutists from 4 Parachute Divison—to lob grenades from the edge of the gully down into the Foresters' slit trenches, before they could be driven off by automatic weapons covering a hopelessly inadequate field of fire.[14]

Captain P. A. Hewitt, the valiant officer commanding the remnants of the original four companies, was so exhausted by March 3 that he could not stand upright. When replacement officers and men were sent up the following day, the forty men they relieved had to be helped from the trenches. The new commander was so appalled at the sight that he reported to division that he could not answer for the consequences if they were attacked. The following night the Foresters were relieved by the 40th Royal Marine Commandos. The survivors of what had been a rifle battalion a week earlier had been reduced to little more than a platoon. The Foresters were in no doubt that they had just vacated "the worst half a mile in Italy at that time."[15]

The arrival of the 660 men of the 9th and 40 Royal Marine Commandos heralded a period of harassment and raids behind German lines by well-trained, fresh troops, who began giving the Germans a dose of their own medicine. The left flank was further stabilized by the arrival on March 5 of the 5th Division from the Garigliano sector. Although they had been in combat a mere three weeks, the spent force of the 56th Division was finally pulled from the front lines for an urgently needed rest and refit.

The Germans fared little better in these brutal encounters. Diversionary attacks in support of the abortive March offensive and nightly probing actions took a heavy toll. German after-action reports recited the toll of dead and wounded. An entire company of the 4th Parachute Division met the same fate as C Company of the Foresters. German POW cages continued to swell with Americans and British. During the final week of February the Germans reported losing 362 killed, 1,259 wounded, 221 missing, and the capture of 965 Allied troops, 402 of whom were identified as troops of the 2nd Battalion, 157th Infantry, and the 2d/7th Queen's. Most of the German casualties were from the gullies.[16]

When it became obvious to the senior German commanders that further attacks were futile, there began a painful reassessment of what had gone wrong. The reasons were not difficult to discern and were marked by poor morale, the use of some units that were ill-trained and -prepared for Anzio, a faulty plan, and, as the Germans candidly admitted, the tough resistance of the men of VI Corps. Most worrisome was that although German troops continued to attack with their customary aggressiveness, evidence was mounting that it could not be sustained. Morale was ebbing in the face of the steel curtains of artillery fire and the bombs falling from the sky.

Kesselring knew that Hitler would have to be told in person of the failure at Anzio. Neither Jodl nor Keitel could be trusted to represent the truth fairly. Kesselring believed that his able chief of staff, General

Siegfried Westphal, stood a better chance of making an impression on Hitler. "The duty of the Army Group," wrote Westphal after the war, "was to tell the unvarnished truth. A written report would have been useless, because it would have made no impression on Hitler. The only way was to speak to him in person [on behalf of Kesselring]. I was therefore sent to Berchtesgaden."

On March 6, 1944, it became Westphal's unpleasant task to report that although German forces in Italy could still fight defensively, Army Group C was no longer capable of going on the offensive. "General-oberst Jodl first received my views. He declined to take me personally to Hitler. He would, he said, tell Hitler himself and alone." What he told Hitler apparently so disturbed the Führer that he demanded to see the officer "who had been slandering his troops."[17]

Hitler's refusal to listen to the truth when it was reported by his field commanders was notorious, and even eminent generals and field marshals were often reduced to impotence in the face of the screaming and shouting that usually greeted them. On this day Westphal was spared, and for three grueling hours he disclosed how German troops had been decimated by five years of war and that those in Italy were now "exhausted to a frightening degree." Westphal's presentation was frequently interrupted by Hitler who remained uncharacteristically calm in response to the many unpalatable things told him about the dire situation in Italy. "At the end, he said, with obvious emotion, that he knew well how great was the war-weariness which afflicted the people and also the Wehrmacht." Hitler had hoped to alleviate this by a great victory at Anzio. Afterwards an astonished Keitel reminded Westphal that: "You were lucky. If we old fools had said even half as much the Führer would have had us hanged."[18]

As if to challenge Westphal's veracity, OKW summoned twenty front-line officers from company commanders to division commanders from the Italian theater to Hitler's mountaintop retreat, the Berghof. According to Westphal, for two days following his report, "they were questioned, sometimes singly, by Hitler about their experiences in the Anzio beachhead. . . . As I afterwards learned . . . their answers amounted to the same [things] I had reported on 6 March."[19] The delegation was led by Lieutenant General Walter Fries, the veteran commander of the 29th Panzer Grenadier Division. Fries told an angry Führer that the German failure had resulted from the devastating Allied artillery and naval gunfire, overwhelming Allied air superiority, and the roadbound panzers, which could never exploit the gains made at such heavy cost by the German infantry. Others spoke with equal eloquence of the rain of death that descended without warning from the sky.

Hitler trusted these men to be candid, and they told him of the horrors of Anzio, "of the crushing enemy artillery superiority, of the slime and the filth, of the inferior German radio gear and faulty hand-grenades. . . . Hitler ordered Kesselring to apply the lessons of 1918 trench warfare to Anzio; remorseless pressure must be put on the enemy by the long-forgotten techniques of storm-regiments and artillery bombardments."[20] As usual, Hitler's instructions bore scant relation to reality. Not only did Kesselring face a growing shortage of artillery ammunition as a result of an inability to move supplies to the front against the interdiction of the railroad lines in northern Italy by the Allied air forces, who daily pounded the German lines of communication, but he scarcely had manpower to spare for the type of costly forays that characterized warfare on the Western Front of 1918.

On both sides there was little enthusiasm for another large-scale battle. The dreadful battles of February and early March had taken an enormous toll and neither would be capable of mounting an offensive until spring. There followed a period of stalemate that lasted nearly three months. As if to remind each other that they were still at war, the daily casualty reports reflected the deadly effect of just what stalemate meant. Yet, as the killing went on, there were small but significant signs that the protagonists were wearying of the sacrifices being demanded of them. Soon, too, Axis Sally, the German propaganda mouthpiece, whose daily broadcasts from Berlin over German radio had become a fixture of the beachhead, began describing Anzio as "the largest self-supporting prisoner-of-war camp in the world."[21]

18

"Will I Be
All Right, Sir?"

The dirty bastards.
—LUCAS[1]

For those who served there, Anzio was quite simply a never-to-be-forgotten horror. For sheer misery, for danger, for the uncertainty of whether one would live or die, Anzio had few peers. What made Anzio different from other campaigns was the close proximity of every single Allied soldier and sailor to the fighting. The beachhead was so small that no one in it was safe. As Ernie Harmon later wrote, "It is true that all of us were in the same boat: we were there to stay or die. But it is not true that such a situation always creates brotherhood. I have never seen anything like it in the two World Wars of my experience. There was at Anzio a confidence in unity, an unselfish willingness among troops to help one another, that I never saw again."[2]

The Germans soon brought in the largest guns in their arsenal, including two notorious 218-ton monsters, each mounted on a railway car and capable of firing a 280-mm shell up to thirty-six miles. Allied shipping offshore was subjected to frequent bombardment, as were the support facilities located in and around Anzio-Nettuno. These giant guns (the aforementioned "Anzio Annie" and "Anzio Express")[3] were kept secure in caves in the Alban Hills and only rolled out to fire several rounds. They then retreated to the safety of their caves before the Allied air forces could react and attack them.

The two railway guns were merely the icing on the cake for the Germans, who employed 372 guns, of which 150 were of calibers over

105 mm. The beachhead was shelled around the clock by these guns or bombed and strafed by the Luftwaffe, which also introduced a deadly new weapon in the form of radio-controlled glider-bombs and anti-pesonnel "butterfly" bombs that claimed numerous victims. Men wounded in combat sometimes lost their lives in one of the field hospitals. Cooks, bakers, mechanics, medics, dentists, clerks, ordnance and signalmen, engineers, truck drivers, and chaplains—all shared a common peril that in the rear areas was sometimes so great that AWOLs and troops resting and recuperating voluntarily returned to the front where it was considered "safer."

These chaotic conditions produced a sense of total isolation among the infantry manning the slit trenches. What seemed like an eternity would often be only a matter of hours. "Rain, mud, shells, and mortar bombs, the arrival of food, ammunition, and water were the realities of an existence which fatigue sometimes made dream-like."[4]

We can only empathize with these men, facing such conditions day in and day out. The Sherwood Foresters, who eventually would earn the dubious honor of suffering the largest percentage of losses of any British rifle battalion on the beachhead (100 percent of its men and 200 percent of its officers), existed under unspeakable conditions in the gullies. The last hundred men, all that had survived the initial attacks by the Germans in the Bloody Boot after relieving the 2d/6th Queen's, were forced to defend a gully that ran north and south, directly into the teeth of the German guns several hundred yards away. How bad was it? Consider this description in the regimental history:

> The drenching rain, which never seemed to stop, had swollen the stream in the bottom of the gully to a deep flood and filled the trenches up on either side of the stream with water, which came up to the knees and stayed there . . . at night the venturous enemy parachutists crept up to near the edge of the gully and lobbed grenades into the trenches before they were thrown back by the fire of automatics sited in the most pitiful positions without the hope of more than a few hundred yards' field of fire. By day and night enemy artillery observers, sitting on Buonriposo Ridge . . . directed an unceasing battery of mortar and gun-fire right into the "Boot." Every night more shallow graves were dug into the lower slopes of the gully, and every day the swelling flood washed away the rough crosses of wood made from "compo" boxes and with them the earth from the tops of the graves, gruesomely revealing a khaki-covered arm.[5]

Some of the Foresters' tormentors were fresh troops sent from Germany and flung into the line against the bruised and battered British and American rifle battalions. Allied replacements were bewildered and totally unprepared for the shock of trench warfare. No amount of training could have prepared them for the horror of what awaited them in the front lines of Anzio. Some died or were captured within hours of arriving, and it was common for men to simply disappear without a trace and without anyone even knowing their names. During World War II the term *missing* generally meant that a man would eventually turn up in captivity. While this was also true of Anzio, it was here that the term took on an ominous meaning. Many whose names were on the rolls of the missing were never found, their bodies washed away by the rains and buried in the mud.

In one regiment of the 3d Division, a group of worried replacements was personally welcomed by the regimental commander who gathered the men around him and said:

> You're going up as replacements to the best damn regiment in the United States Army. You'll be expected to live up to the traditions of that regiment and that division. You're going to suffer. You came here to suffer. You're going to suffer in everything the Boche can throw at you and you're going to suffer everything that goes with this miserable damn climate. But you're going to take it like men. Listen to what the men up there tell you about how to kill Germans. You're new, but as far as we're concerned, you're every bit as good a man, each one of you, as the best man in the division—until or unless you show us otherwise.[6]

Supplies and ammunition had to be brought in on the backs of men. The closest anyone could get to the Foresters was about three hundred yards. After that everything had to be manhandled across open ground under the direct observation of the Germans, whose flares at night left the porters trapped like rats in a blaze of light. Their usual method of arrival was to slide down the muddy sides of the gully into the water below, the rations kept dry in packs on their backs. Although American troops usually received fresh socks every other day, they were generally soaking wet within five minutes, and as a result trench foot was the curse of the frontline troops. As Ernie Pyle reported: "The boys learned to change their socks very quickly, and get their shoes back on, because once feet were freed of shoes they swelled so much in five minutes a man couldn't get his shoes [back] on."[7]

As disgusting as the gullies were, it was infinitely better to endure the mud and water than to be so foolish as to stick one's head above the level of a trench or slope. Each side developed tricks to insure maximum harassment of the other. It was no coincidence that Allied artillery barrages happened to fall at German meal hours. Allied gunners kindly remembered Hitler's birthday (April 20) by sending a fifty-one-shell barrage into a sector where it was believed German soldiers had gathered to celebrate the occasion. A further barrage contained propaganda leaflets expressing appropriate wishes.[8]

The use of propaganda leaflets became an increasingly common practice both sides employed. German leaflets ranged from crude anti-Semitic slurs to a cartoon depicting a naked British woman in the embrace of a GI sergeant, captioned: "You Americans are soo different!" Another showed the grave of a soldier and the words: "British Soldiers! You are fighting and dying far away from your country while the Yanks are putting up their tents in Merry Old England. They've got lots of money and loads of time to chase after your women." Undoubtedly the best-known leaflet was a map of the beachhead on which was superimposed a grinning skull and the words: BEACH-HEAD DEATH'S HEAD!

On other battlefields it was usual for the graves-registration troops to recover the bodies of those killed in action. At Anzio it was seldom possible to return bodies from the gullies. To attempt to do so was to court a death sentence for the porters. By the time the bodies could be recovered they were often in a terrible state of decay and unidentifiable except through identification tags.

The troops manning the front lines turned themselves into moles. No method of protection was too bizarre. Major H. L. S. Young of the Irish Guards used his "brolly" to the envy of his comrades. He would dig a small, deep hole, lower himself into it, and place his umbrella down over himself "like a big, black mushroom."[9] Trenches, holes in the ground, bunkers, caves—in short, anything that provided cover from incoming shells—were employed. Foxholes were covered with groundsheets, reinforced with tree trunks, sandbags, brushwood, pieces of timber, even barrels. Where possible, barbed wire was laid and barricades were constructed to thwart German patrols or raiding parties that roamed no-man's land at night seeking targets of opportunity.

During the wet season it was impossible to dig more than six inches without hitting water. One Irish Guardsman made the mistake of falling asleep in his foxhole. He did not awaken when water began to seep over his body. The next morning he was found unconscious and near death, with his body a terrible slate gray color. One man described him as looking like a three-day-old corpse. Miraculously, the soldier survived what the medics described as the worst case of exposure they had yet seen.[10] A trooper of the British 5th Division who snored too loudly attracted a German patrol and was captured and never seen again.[11]

If the wet was not misery enough, another unwelcome creature that inhabited the warm bodies of the protagonists was the louse, the blood-sucking insect that all too frequently infested the hair and bodies of its principal victims, the front-line soldiers.

In a seemingly endless quest to keep dry and safe from German artillery, several enterprising troopers of the U.S. 1st Armored Division sunk large wine casks they had liberated from nearby caves deep into the ground and used them as underground bunkers. Tankers soon learned it was safer to sleep inside their steel vehicles than to risk death outside from a stray bullet or shell. A 45th Division NCO overcame the problem of water in the bottom of his foxhole by nailing together several empty C-ration wooden boxes to form a raft that was intended to float on top of the water. It was reputed to have been somewhat less than successful in keeping the man dry.[12]

Even in death, things were done differently at Anzio. Harmon tells the story of Lieutenant Colonel John W. McPheeters, who had commanded the 91st Armored Field Artillery Battalion since North Africa. Near Cassino late in 1943 McPheeters climbed a mountain slope to study the terrain for future artillery positions and was fired on by a nearby German sniper. Unarmed, McPheeters "picked up a stone and heaved it with an Indiana boy's accuracy. The German sniper ran." His battalion once fired 8,700 rounds in a single day at Anzio and nearly melted his guns. One day he was killed when a German shell struck the tree above him. As Harmon relates:

> McPheeters' troops loved him. They arranged the most impressive funeral I ever attended. The Anzio cemetery lay down by the seaside; indeed, most new recruits had to pass the expansive field of wooden crosses when they first reported for duty. It was a grim introduction to Anzio but I guess it was accurate enough. Most of McPheeters' men were still at the front, but they persuaded the Signal Corps into an unusual and elaborate use of battlefield communications. There was a loud-speaker at the graveside. When the time came to fire the farewell salute, the 91st Battalion piped into the loud-speaker a memorable one. It was eighteen guns in battery, shooting live ammunition at the enemy. It was, in fact, the "fire mission" that McPheeters had charted [when he was killed]. I can't think of a better requiem for a valiant fighting man.[13]

The casualty rate among artillerymen was high at Anzio. The guns were situated close to the front lines, and it became almost impossible to disguise the muzzle flash from German observers in the Alban Hills. As time passed, the Allied guns sank lower and lower into the ground in an attempt to make them safer from the inevitable counter-battery fire. There was a serious shortage of 105-mm ammunition in the beachhead, but 100,000 rounds of tank ammunition were available. Inasmuch as tanks were relatively ineffective in a stalemate situation, Harmon's tankers devised an ingenious solution. Trees were cut down and logs rolled underneath the front treads to raise the elevation of the Shermans' 75-mm guns, which increased their maximum range from 12,000 to 14,000 yards. Thus, some 250 Shermans became static artillery pieces and a new part of the Allied artillery repertoire.[14]

The day of his arrival at Anzio, Harmon moved his command post away from a nearby British field artillery unit in the Padiglione Woods, later writing: "I had no intention of dying my first night in Anzio." Harmon's command truck was moved into an open field. "The gravity of the battle could be charted by the height of that roof line. Every day the wheels were dug in a little deeper, until finally only a foot or two of the truck could be seen above ground—a prudent acknowledgment of the mathematical accuracy of the German artillery fire." Harmon was later reproved for locating his CP too close to German lines, and he replied that he felt safer where he was than in the rear. He was not alone. Two men of the First Special Service Force lived in a large dugout in the middle of an exposed field. When asked by an amazed visiting general if they actually lived there, one replied, "Sure, the Heinies know we are crazy, but they don't think that we are this crazy and leave us alone." The general walked away shaking his head and no doubt talking to himself.[15]

Electricity was drawn from a portable field generator that supplied light at night, when most of the division staff work was accomplished. Before long Harmon noticed that the lights seemed to get dimmer with each passing night. An electrician was called in and reported there was no problem; the generator was working at capacity. Then the lights dimmed so badly that Harmon could not even read a map. The electrician soon located the source of the problem. Harmon's troops had tapped his lines, and as many as 250 of them were being supplied with electricity in their underground bunkers.[16]

Among the unheralded men and women who risked their lives was a young operative in Rome named Peter Tompkins, who masterminded the clandestine efforts of the OSS in the Italian capital. A twenty-three-year-old American who spoke fluent Italian, Tompkins spent much of his youth in Italy and thus had many friends and contacts in Rome. After attending Harvard University he became a war correspondent and volunteered for service with the OSS in 1942.

A week before January 22, the OSS boss, Major General William J. "Wild Bill" Donovan, asked Tompkins to undertake a dangerous mission. He was to slip into Rome with a radio, false papers, and a large cache of gold coins to establish an intelligence network and coordinate the activities of the Italian resistance. With his knowledge of Rome and his many connections (which included high officials in the Italian government and the Vatican), Tompkins was the ideal operative to help the Allies keep track of the German reaction to the Anzio landings. Donovan's goals for the mission, however, were far loftier than a mere intelligence and resistance operation. He wanted Tompkins to take control of the intelligence and partisan operations on behalf of the OSS, which would have buried forever the subservience of the OSS to its more experienced British rival, the Special Operations Executive, better known as the SOE.[17]

Under the code name Pietro, Tompkins entered Rome the day before the invasion and immediately began to organize what soon became one of the most effective OSS intelligence operations of the war. His organization recruited watchers who were strategically placed around the clock along the twelve major highways leading from Rome. They observed and recorded all troop movements into and out of Rome and the movements of fuel and supplies. Nothing the Germans did escaped the attention of the watchers. Tompkins also obtained intelligence directly from a highly placed operative in Kesselring's HQ: "All this information was boiled down to the bare facts and brought to me daily at about noon. It then took me about two hours to check it all with past information, find localities on our maps, and draw up the cables of the most urgent information for transmission to the beachhead."[18]

Within days, the first of a steady stream of important intelligence messages began flowing from Tompkins's clandestine Radio Rome to the OSS section attached to Fifth Army HQ. Code-named Vittoria, the location of the clandestine station was moved frequently to avoid the ever-active German radio-detection finders that searched relentlessly to pinpoint its location. Tompkins composed his messages on thin tissue paper (which could be swallowed in an emergency) that was secretly conveyed by a series of couriers and eventually arrived in the hands of the trusted men who operated the station. By employing three couriers for each delivery, "the central messenger knew neither where the message came from nor where it went." Thus, if the Germans succeeded in finding Vittoria, "there would be absolutely no way they could trace the message back to us—or vice-versa."[19] Tompkins's insistence on tight security was to save his life. In early 1944 Rome was an exceptionally dangerous place, and some of those with whom Tompkins was obliged to deal were men of shifting allegiances who could be bought and were informers in the employ of either the Gestapo or the Abwehr. "Need to know" has become an overworked phrase in the postwar years, but for men like Tompkins, who operated behind enemy lines, with no safety net and with only their wits and experience to keep them alive, it was the key to survival or death at the hands of a firing squad or a Gestapo interrogator. Tompkins had found through harsh experience that the most difficult and unreliable people with whom he had to deal were professional spies, both those of the OSS and in Rome. Some were gangsters and many, he found, concocted false intelligence, inflated their claims, or gathered their intelligence "from the recesses of their boudoirs, their convents or the back corridors of the Vatican."[20] Loyalties were often as fleeting as the sums of cash offered by eager buyers for betrayal. It did not take Tompkins, an amateur himself, long to become a very careful spy. Soon after his arrival he found that the head of one of the main Roman underground groups, Clemente Menicante, who had been appointed by the OSS as "chief OSS clandestine agent in German occupied Italy," was not only an intriguer attempting to undermine Tompkins's mission, but that his organization had been thoroughly infiltrated by the Germans.

The OSS in Italy was rife with ambitious men, and many of their recruits, such as Menicante, were not noted for their high moral standards. Some were not above sacrificing one of their own if it enhanced their prospects of advancement and recognition. Unknown to Tompkins, his own boss, an OSS colonel named Huntington, had not bothered to inform him that he had also named the unreliable and greedy Menicante as Rome OSS chief. Menicante claimed to be Mark Clark's personal representative in Italy, a role that—though it obviously did not exist—caused confusion in the underground. To Tompkins's distress, he found yet another pretender claiming that the same title had been conferred on him by Clark.[21]

Radio Vittoria was in direct contact with both the beachhead and Fifth Army HQ at Caserta. The first message of substance was sent on January 29 and indicated that the German attack would come from the west in the sector known as the Practica di Mare, which included the area around the Via Anziate. The message was immediately disseminated to all units in the beachhead. Although the Germans were obliged to postpone the first phase of their counteroffensive until the night of February 3–4, this was the first of a series of messages emanating from Radio Vittoria that provided an accurate and exceptionally valuable picture of what was going on behind German lines. When Allied air attacks hit the HQ of the I Parachute Corps on January 30 and demolished the corps' artillery command post, a message sent on February 1 gleefully noted: "Nice going bombing Practica di Mare . . ."[22]

Moreover, Radio Vittoria's messages were not only independent confirmation of what Ultra was reporting, but they were generally received by Fifth Army well before Bletchley Park could decode and forward the same information through the top-secret Ultra network.[23]

Nevertheless, Tompkins's warning seemed to have been an important factor in convincing both Alexander and Clark to halt Lucas's Cisterna-Campoleone offensive to prepare for the German counterstroke. As is now known, Alexander was not fully convinced until later that night, but Clark did react and signaled Lucas the night of February 1 to call off his offensive and prepare to defend against a German attack.[24] As the U.S. official historian later wrote: "Intelligence from Rome seems to have played an important part in this belief, which is substantiated in Clark's personal war diary."[25]

In spite of tight security there would be extreme losses to Tompkins's organization in Rome. In March disaster struck when the Radio Vittoria operator was betrayed and under torture revealed the name of the man to whom he reported. This was Lieutenant Maurizio Giglio, a member of the Rome mounted police, who was Tompkins's trusted assistant and ran Radio Vittoria. Giglio was captured by Fascist agents working for the Sicherheitsdienst (SD), the secret intelligence service of Himmler's SS. For a week Giglio somehow withstood the tortures of his brutal interrogators without disclosing any information about either Tompkins or his secret radio operation. On March 25, 1944, in reprisal for the killing of thirty-two Germans in Rome whose truck was blown up by the Resistance, the SS executed with machine guns 320 Italians in what has come to be known as the Massacre of the Adreatine Caves. Among the members of the Italian underground slaughtered that day was Lieutenant Giglio, who took his secrets to the grave.

Until the liberation of Rome in June, Tompkins lived in mortal danger and was hounded by the German SD, who came close to catching the elusive American operative on several occasions.

As previously noted, superstition and intuition played a role in the behavior of soldiers in the beachhead. One American artillery gun crew had chalked a Christmas greeting to "Uncle Adolf" on the first shell ever fired in North Africa in December 1942. At once a German shell was fired back that wounded seven of the twelve-man crew that had signed the shell. At Anzio a photographer showed up one day to take pictures of the crew in action. He asked for a message to Hitler to be chalked on the shell. Although the crew agreed, what the photographer never learned was that they refused to fire the shell and instead buried it in a hillside.[26]

Small wonder that soldiers are a superstitious lot. U.S. artillery spotters flew unarmed Cub aircraft over the beachhead at considerable risk to their lives. The Germans knew they spelled trouble and took great pains to shoot them down, succeeding only rarely. One day an Allied 155-mm "Long Tom" gun fired only a single shell. The odds were probably about a billion to one of hitting an aircraft, yet on this day the shell somehow hit and destroyed a Cub aircraft taking off from the Anzio airfield. In another incident a U.S. regiment had acquired a police-dog mascot named Sergeant who was so well trained that he immediately jumped into the nearest foxhole whenever he heard planes. Yet he was so badly wounded in his foxhole by shrapnel from a German air burst that he could not be saved and had to be put down to prevent further suffering.[27]

Sergeant Jesse N. Bradley, the ball-turret gunner on a U.S. B-24 bomber, whose navigator had earlier judged Anzio to be of no particular value, would certainly subscribe to the belief that there are those upon whom the gods of war occasionally smile. His aircraft and many others were diverted from interdiction missions elsewhere in Italy to direct support of the beleaguered Anzio beachhead during the February German counteroffensive. After one bombing mission Bradley's brand new B-24, on its first (and last) mission, was crippled by German ack-ack, and the pilot knew it could not remain airborne long enough to return to its base. The only chance was to get as close to Anzio as possible and then bail out.

The crew managed to bail out over the water, but the winds blew Bradley and the others back onto land. Bradley missed landing directly in a trench latrine by a mere three feet. Two other crewmen landed between the lines near the Mussolini Canal and were rescued. For the airmen, who admittedly had previously given little thought to the plight of their comrades on the ground, Anzio came as a great shock. Bradley recalls the gnawing fear of the incessant German shelling and how his night in Anzio seemed like an eternity. As the crew boarded a Naples-bound LST they were accompanied by several hundred Allied wounded:

> In shocked silence we watched the medics herd them aboard, both walking and litter borne. There were bandaged heads and bodies with crusty red stains showing through, missing arms with flapping sleeves pinned over, chopped off legs, with blankets lying horribly flat, and stark, staring shock cases. The sight of these pathetic men made our troubles seem awfully small; in fact, I felt almost ashamed that I was still in one piece. "Did you notice that most of them are smiling? [observed the bombardier]." "Even minus an arm or leg, they are still happy to be leaving Anzio."[28]

Tales of miraculous survival at Anzio abound. An Irish Guardsman who ran to the aid of a mortally wounded colleague was himself hit by fragments from an artillery shell. The adjutant in turn ran to his aid and on turning him over found the young officer laughing. Small fragments had penetrated his thigh but several potentially lethal jagged chunks had imbedded themselves in a pornographic book the officer was carrying in his pocket.[29]

Captain Donald B. Williams was a surgeon attached to the U.S. 56th Evacuation Hospital. After the disastrous bombing of February 7 the staff was acutely aware that it could easily happen again. Anzio Annie and Anzio Express made a daily habit of shelling the rear of the beachhead in the early evening. The mess tent was not a place where anyone lingered after one of the cooks was killed by a shell. One evening Williams stopped momentarily to observe a soccer game being played in the gap between tents. Someone said to him, "Interesting game, isn't it?" "Not interesting enough for me to stay and watch," replied Williams. "I walked about fifty steps and heard a loud trajectory pop, hit the dirt, and a big shell struck in the area I had been standing [in]. All the players either hit the dirt or were knocked down by the blast but fortunately not one was wounded." The only casualty was the hospital CO, who was slightly wounded in a nearby latrine.[30]

Virtually every battalion reported instances of lives saved by shells failing to explode. The Grenadier Guards historian recounts one example when the Germans had pinpointed a small patch of the Padiglione Woods, where both the Grenadiers and the Guards Brigade had located their command posts. A deluge of shells fell all around, and 90 percent were duds. On another occasion several stretcher bearers were standing outside their aid station eating dinner when a German 88-mm shell struck two nearby trees before landing between two men. "It spun slowly round and round at their feet, steaming as it did so on the wet ground. They were not in the least perturbed."[31]

During the stalemate men longed for home and their loved ones. Lieutenant Colonel William P. Yarborough, the hard-nosed paratroop commander of the 509th Parachute Infantry Battalion, was one:

> The day is bright and beautiful. Spring is almost here. Already among the S mines and booby traps violets are pushing their way through the green sod. In the not-too-far distance I can see the snowy hills that mark the German's lines. He has just sent over a dozen large calibre shells, one of which hit Company 'A's supply trailer. Now the smoke and dust have drifted away. Everything is peaceful. My Signal Corps radio is pouring forth the poignantly beautiful strains of "Berceuse"—from Germany! God looks down on our lines and the enemy's—we are both listening to the universal language of the music—thinking of our loved ones at home.[32]

Such were the incongruities of Anzio that one minute men would be killing each other with savagery and the next sharing music or food with each other. A group of Sherwood Foresters was interviewed after the war for the British documentary series "The World at War." When they relieved another British battalion in the gullies, a sergeant warned that the following morning, " 'you'll have a German sergeant come up to you . . . it's quite all right, a friendly chap . . . he'll bring some rations to swap' . . . I just laughed it off . . . I thought he was pullin' me leg. Well, next morning . . . everybody stood to the guns till it got daylight . . . an Irish fellow named Tommy McGeogh . . . says 'bloody Jesus Christ' . . . I could see this fellow was ambling down the wire and he could speak very good English. 'Where's Fred,' and I says, 'he's gone,' and I says 'quite all right. What have you got?' " The two men swapped rations and stories about their lives and hometowns.

Each attempted to convince the other that his side would win. The German returned to his lines and was never seen again.[33]

Another German found the Irish Guards less accommodating. At dawn one morning soon after taking over positions in the gullies, the Guards' sentries noticed a German leisurely strolling toward their lines with a bottle clutched in his hand. He was permitted to come in and was then unceremoniously taken prisoner. "The German was most indignant; he had come, he explained, on the usual errand, to exchange brandy for tinned meat. Sergeant-Major Pestell explained that the trade agreement was cancelled 'as from now.'" The German spent an unhappy day digging Major Fitzgerald's trench and asking at intervals why Irishmen were in Italy at all. The failure of their agent's mission clearly annoyed his colleagues, for soon afterward they started lobbing mortar bombs into the gully.[34]

Other individual encounters between protagonists were not so peaceful. An Irish Guards officer won a duel with a particularly large German officer by blowing him away with a PIAT—the British version of the U.S. bazooka.

The toll on men's minds was particularly onerous at Anzio. The growing numbers of battle fatigue cases in turn led to a considerable number of AWOLs, desertions, and cases of self-inflicted wounds, a situation not enhanced by the experience of replacements, many of whom had been in the Army scarcely four months and had no combat experience. The 179th Regiment incurred more court-martial offenses in February 1944 than in the previous eight months combined. As the regimental historian writes, courts-martial had little effect in deterring others. Many offenders escaped court-martial, while others were never tried. Of those who were, harsh sentences ranging from twenty to eighty years were frequently imposed but generally commuted within several months. The troops knew that deserters were getting precisely what they wanted: "OUT OF COMBAT. The man who stuck it out proved to be the one who was really penalized. He got killed."[35]

There were similar examples on the British side. Attrition had removed most of the veterans, many of whom had served since the war began. Their replacements were green, "and then they were dropped straight into a mess like that and they just couldn't take it. . . . You'd be out on patrol with them and all of a sudden they'd start yelling and going off their rockers . . . and you just had to thump them one to keep them quiet because they were giving your position away."[36]

AWOL and desertion became serious problems. Morale had been sapped in some replacements by the comments of the LST and LCI crews, whose practice of telling lurid stories of conditions ashore while en route to Anzio so disturbed the Allied high command that Alexander

"Will I Be All Right, Sir?"   311

personally complained to the Navy that the practice must be curtailed immediately.

Equally worrisome was the quality of the replacements. General Penney noted the troubling decline in the quality of men sent to replace his battered battalions: In a letter to Alexander in mid-March, he noted that "our first problem is the literal rebirth of units with raw, inexperienced officers and men often already bewildered by their continual reposting to a succession of units . . . I daresay Gerald Templer will have told you of the RASC driver who has been in 16 units!"[37] The situation continued to worsen to the point where it became a matter of "grave anxiety" that so many were deliberately AWOL or deserting, despite the possible consequences. On any given day there were sixty to seventy deserters in the 1st Division, and the data available suggest that these figures were even higher for the recently arrived British 5th Division. Front-line commanders like Penney advocated harsh treatment for desertion, including the establishment of a penal colony in the beachhead. This idea was approved by Alexander's headquarters and ordered implemented in May 1944.[38]

A number of commanders also advocated the reintroduction of the death penalty for desertion. Although scrapped after World War I, the idea was considered but ultimately rejected by the British government on the grounds that it was not a sufficient deterrent. A War Office study revealed that the 1914–18 desertion rate was 10.26 men per thousand, per annum, and from 1939–45 the rate was 6.89. Desertions and AWOLs throughout the Mediterranean totaled 1,311 for the three-month period February through April 1944.[39] The American experience was comparable and solutions equally difficult to come by. What was certain was that stalemate had no effect in controlling the problem of AWOL and desertion.

For every AWOL or desertion there were countless examples of bravery above and beyond the call of duty. During the battle for the Caves the surgeon of the 2d Battalion, 157th Regiment, Captain Peter Graffagnino, and his team were captured after they refused to leave the wounded. The following day the regimental dentist, Captain Hugo Fielschmidt, volunteered to return to the Caves in an effort to bring the wounded to safety. He departed in a halftrack prominently displaying a Red Cross flag. Fielschmidt and his driver were never seen again.

The plight of the Italians living in the battle sector was typical of civilians caught in the middle of war. During the period when the Allies controlled the Factory sector a sergeant of the London Irish was approached one morning by an elderly Italian who by gesture indicated that he was in need of the assistance of several men. The group proceeded to a barn and in one corner the man pointed to a homemade coffin. Inside was his dead wife, the victim of a shell. The soldiers helped the grateful Italian to carry the coffin to a nearby grave where it was lowered into the ground with ropes.[40]

Despite the horror going on all around them, some Italians refused to leave their homes and farms and somehow managed to survive with only minor concessions to the war. One peasant and his wife refused to leave their homestead and washed Harmon's clothes to help make ends meet. The many caves in the beachhead were filled with civilians. At least twenty thousand displaced Italians were taken in LSTs from Anzio to Naples, where they joined the tide of refugees. In some instances those who did not leave found unwelcome German or Allied intruders. The stone farmhouses made ideal strongpoints and many concealed not only troops and various types of guns, but often the Sherman tanks of Ernie Harmon's 1st Armored Division. By knocking down the back wall, tanks could be installed inside the house and the windows used to shoot from. During the stalemate the tanks remained in place but the crews were changed periodically.[41]

Harmon and others have recorded scenes of cattle and mules grazing among the combatants, in minefields, and wherever there was precious grass to be found. Many died from bullets and shells and others at the hands of hungry soldiers. Fresh food was always difficult to come by in the beachhead, and the men quickly wearied of the monotonous canned rations on which most of them subsisted. Despite the incredible bombing and shelling a considerable number of cattle managed to survive. The Army attempted to protect them from being slaughtered for food but, as Harmon notes with tongue in cheek, "At Anzio, cattle seemed to have a habit of attacking soldiers. Anyway, the soldiers always maintained they shot in self-defense." Some GIs discovered the remnants of a pheasant preserve located about four hundred yards from German lines, and on at least one occasion Harmon crawled on his belly across open terrain into the thicket to bag dinner with a shotgun.[42]

Mules tended to fare better, and many were adopted as pets by various units and used to the amusement of the men in races. Wherever there were soldiers, means were devised to pass the time. Horseshoes, softball games, track meets, band concerts, films, cookouts (when beef was available; the cattle, of course, had died by mysteriously meeting an untimely demise), and USO entertainment.

Some enterprising GIs decided to stage their own Anzio Derby in mid-May. The considerable efforts of many resulted in an elaborately staged event that included a band, a public-address system, a wreath for the winner, a camera in the event of a photo finish, and an announcer to call the race. The "thoroughbreds" were another matter altogether. "If American bloodstock pundits could have seen that mass of hossflesh they would have wept in their beer." Some of the entrants suspiciously resembled donkeys, and one was a white jackass named George, ridden by a 240-pound jockey! The event was so successful another was held several days later. However, the judges ruled that future races could only be run by "horses" who weighed more than their jockeys.[43]

Harmon and other commanders were determined to get their men away from Anzio periodically for R & R (rest and recuperation), and the Fifth Army agreed that up to 10 percent could be away at any one time for a four-day R & R in Naples, where there were ample wine, women, and song. Business in the brothels of Naples boomed. However, when Harmon learned that his men were being arrested and jailed by the military police for improper uniforms he had to be dissuaded by his chief of staff from sending half his division to "clean up" the city.

The workhorses of the Anzio campaign were the LSTs, which plied back and forth endlessly between Naples and Anzio. Aboard one LST in April 1944 was a young officer of the 45th Division, 2d Lieutenant Ernest Childers, an Oklahoma Indian. To one of his companions he confided, "You know, that old combat makes me nervous." The following day he was presented the Congressional Medal of Honor for conspicuous gallantry the previous September during "one of his nervous states."[44] Another who was decorated for bravery was 1st Lieutenant Donald T. Knowlton, the 45th Division forward observer, who received the Distinguished Service Cross from Mark Clark as he recuperated in an evacuation hospital.[45]

Death and danger were by no means limited to those ashore. The brave men who manned the minesweepers and the landing craft that plied the perilous waters off Anzio were responsible for keeping open the lifeline between Naples and the beachhead. Perhaps the most dangerous occupation of all was aboard the minesweepers, whose unenviable function it was to keep the sea channels clear for the other ships and landing craft. In their profession there was no room for error. To strike one of the floating or undersea mines planted in their thousands by the Germans was to die.

Life aboard a minesweeper was fraught with peril. The endless exposure to the deadly mines simply decreased the odds of survival. Lieutenant Commander G. H. Dormer commanded a British minesweeper. After months of near misses sweeping the Anzio channels, Dormer recorded in his diary on April 13:

> We started sweeping again at 0800.... A few minutes later ... BANG ... the sweep just ahead of us is blown up. As we alter sharply to keep in swept water, someone looks over the side amidships.... There is a mine just under the water, about six feet away ... whew. And we had to go back again and

find it, to sink. . . . Finally we lost it, so presumed it had been holed and sunk
but I doubt it. I've hardly ever been so scared in my life.[46]

"No one ashore, or at home, can realise the strain of seafaring like
this. . . . It's like walking on rotten ice. Luckily we are hardened mentally to the extent of being unable to think or talk seriously of anything at all. We shall probably die joking just from habit."[47]

Occasionally the Luftwaffe scored a major success. Its most important victim was the cruiser HMS *Spartan*, which was sunk by German
bombs. Her death knell was observed by Commander Dormer. "Spartan lies on her side, the bilge just showing. . . . For miles the sea is full
of blackened, bloated corpses."

The landing-craft crews were also exposed to torpedoes, mines,
bombs, the long-range German artillery, and the sea itself. During
February 1944 there were thirty-three incidents of damaged or lost
landing craft. Three LSTs were torpedoed and sunk, another was a total
loss from storm damage, and a fifth was sunk from unknown causes.
Other LSTs and LCIs were hit by shells, bombed, grounded, or collided
with rocks or sunken wrecks. Like the men ashore, several simply
disappeared and were presumed sunk.[48]

The loss of LST 348 occurred the morning of February 20 at 0225
hours, when a German torpedo suddenly struck the 5,500-ton ship from
out of the blackness. Survivors later recalled it was like running into a
stone wall at full tilt. The forward half of the ship seemed to disappear,
and her skipper gave that saddest of orders to any sailor: "Abandon
Ship." The ship's engineer, a lieutenant jg, started below decks to attempt to set up ballast pumps to trim the ship when he encountered
Chief Motor Machinist's Mate John J. O'Brien, who insisted that, as the
older of the two, it was his task to go down. He was not seen again until
four hours later, when his stiff and swollen body was recovered by an
LCI.

Ten minutes after the first attack the ship was broken in two by a
second torpedo. During this time the crew had sighted a German
U-boat off the port side. "Shoot the son of a bitch," shouted the LST's
skipper, but just as a deck gun fired, the second torpedo hit the port fuel
tank and "wiped out the engine room like a welding torch set to tissue
paper." LST 348 died, and with her twenty-four of her crew. Another
thirty-four were eventually counted in one of the Anzio evacuation
hospitals. It was nearly two hours before help came in the form of an
LCI, and some died in the water. True to the naval creed, the last to
leave the dying ship was her skipper, Lieutenant jg Stephenson Jennings. Only one lifeboat was left intact, and inside huddled forty men,
many of whom were badly burned. The ship was consumed as flames
roared

like a forest fire. The diesel oil came down just like rain, rain on fire. Barrels were flying around in the air. Ventilators were blown off, Everything seemed to come apart. Said skipper Jennings: "It was like an oven with turkeys roasting inside. We were the turkeys. You could see men on fire just standing there, sort of like they were naked and their red bodies aflame with oil fire, standing out like torches against the black sky." Charles M. Ward, motor machinist's mate third class, New York, and one of the quietest men on the ship, rushed up to one of the burning men and started beating out the fire with his bare hands. After getting the fire out on this man he ran over to a second burning man, now a veritable flaming torch, and threw him overboard. The water extinguished the fire and the man now lives.[49]

LST 348 was a veteran of three invasions: Sicily, Salerno, and now Anzio. During the first sixteen days of the battle the ship had seen only a single day off and had survived between twenty and twenty-five near misses from German bombs and the heavy guns in the Alban Hills. "She had enough shrapnel holes to make her look like a smallpox case."[50] This time her luck had finally run out.

That hoary maxim "the fog of war" was never more true than at Anzio. There is no more dismaying feeling than to be isolated and cut off from your comrades. When Captain Sparks and his small Company E task force were sent to plug the dike against the flood of Germans attacking down the Via Anziate the night of February 15, they were "quite alone," wrote Sparks forty-six years later. "I never at any time had any idea where units of the 179th Infantry were located, except that they were somewhere off to my right. To my left were no friendly troops at all, although I knew that somewhere and several hundred yards to my left rear Companies 'G' and 'F' of my battalion were dug in. My position was completely untenable from the very beginning."[51]

The front lines were a terrifying place. As we have already seen, entire squads, platoons, and companies simply disappeared, very often in the winter fog of the Anzio beachhead. At night it was suicidal to use any form of light. It was common for men to move around with the aid of white engineer tape, which would be strung from one point to another for men to follow. On numerous occasions German patrols would discover the tape and "rearrange" it so it led straight into the nearby German lines and captivity. More than one British patrol or ammunition or supply party followed the white tape and was never seen again. "Soon as it's daylight, they used to be shouting to you just over the hill—'have you got your water Johnny? Have you got your rations?' You'd just peep over [your foxholes] and you'd see all your mates there lined up getting into lorries."[52]

Danger, physical discomfort, and boredom were the curses of duty in the front lines during the stalemate. Historian Raleigh Trevelyan served with the British 5th Division, which was sent to Anzio in mid-March to plug the gaps in the gullies. Trevelyan served in a place nicknamed the Fortress, and in a bitter postwar memoir he records: "We do nothing but watch and wait. . . . Twice a day we expect the attack that never materializes. Our weapons are cocked, our eyes strain into the twilight; the slightest gust of wind causes palpitations. It will be a relief to be in danger again."[53] To stay alive meant to learn the nuances that sometimes spelled the difference between death and survival. For instance, frogs became the watchdogs of the front. The absence of their croaking was a certain sign of the presence of humans nearby. As Trevelyan recounts, "On a number of occasions they have warned us of Jerry marauders."[54]

An eight- to ten-day stint at the front was common. Movement during daytime was suicidal, and night offered the only opportunity to escape the squalid conditions of the trenches. To protect themselves from the mud and incessant water the British Tommies were furnished tins of smelly black grease. "It was terrible," recalled one. For those like the Sherwood Foresters, who had been in and out of the line for three months, life at Anzio was wretched.

> We used to pick up the rations at night and then bring any dead out and then they were buried the next day in the cemetery . . . You could smell them a mile away. You couldn't put no washing out [to dry]. . . . Jerry used to train his machine-guns on it . . . After three months it was demoralising. . . . It was every night, every night everybody was hunting Germans, everybody was out to kill anybody. You used to go out . . . creeping to kill . . . we was insane. (Another): We did become like animals in the end. . . . Yes, just like rats. . . . It was far worse than the desert. You were stuck in the same place. You had nowhere to go. You didn't get no rest, like in the desert. No sleep . . . You never expected to see the end of it. You just forgot why you were there.[55]

When one of his friends was shot by a sniper, one Forester grabbed his rifle and went charging into no-man's land. "The Jerries stuffed about fifty bullets in him before he dropped. Everybody just stood there looking at him and he just went crazy. A young chap. This is the kind of thing that people would never believe if you tell them, but we've seen these things happening."[56]

It was not only men who became crazed by Anzio. Raleigh Trevelyan writes that one of his companions in the gullies was "a starved tabby, so thin and covered with bald patches that it look[ed] like the reincarnation of one of the mummified Egyptian cats in the British Museum . . . [was] absolutely crazed by the noise." Later, the cat was savaged and blinded when it attacked an owl.[57]

Inevitably, men began to weary of needlessly dying to achieve some vague military aim. Night patrolling was a feature of life at the front and it became a sure way to get oneself killed. On both sides of the lines, patrols sent out to capture prisoners or obtain information would crawl to a protected spot and then deliberately make their presence known to the other side. After the usual flurry of fire the leader would bring his patrol back and report their "unfortunate" detection by the enemy. In this way no one got hurt and military honor was satisfied. Presumably the intelligence and operations personnel grumbled, but to the infantryman, this was merely another way of staying alive for yet another day.

Even in the always-dangerous rear areas it was necessary to develop unique methods of accomplishing even the simplest activities. Among the most hazardous endeavors was driving a vehicle. They kicked up dust and could be spotted in daylight anywhere in the beachhead by the ever-vigilant German spotters. German gunners focused their efforts on the heavily traveled roads, with particular attention to road junctions. One popular target was Truscott Boulevard, a new road connecting the Via Anziate and the Anzio-Cisterna highway. In addition to fighting as infantry on the extreme left flank of the beachhead, and later in a similar role guarding the right flank along the Mussolini Canal, the intrepid men of the U.S. 36th Engineer Combat Regiment built and maintained roads, ammunition dumps, and anything else that required their special skills.

Drivers became adept at devising means of not making themselves targets by varying their speeds. Military police devised a traffic pattern for crossing Truscott Boulevard that permitted only one vehicle at a time at varying intervals. With only two major roads to service the beachhead, it was inevitable that a senior officer would be charged with solving the burgeoning traffic problem. This particular general found a simple solution: Establish a priority system for traffic by means of a sticker affixed to the windshield of each vehicle that would permit the military police to effectively control traffic. What the general failed to take into account was that the reflections from windshields were open invitations to the German gunners. So, all windshields were covered and folded down, thus concealing the priority stickers and rendering the system useless.[58]

It generally took the ordinary soldier to devise the most effective use of even the simplest item. Correspondent Fred Sheehan writes that a certain brand of tooth powder was equally effective for cleaning the barrels of a rifle. American periodicals sported advertisements for Lucky Strike cigarettes that announced: "Lucky Strike green has gone to war." When the red circles on the package were fitted to the lenses of GI-issue flashlights, they became effective blackout devices that kept the Germans from spotting the lights. Another popular item was the recoil oil used in howitzers, which, "when used as a shortening in preparing French fried potatoes produced an extraordinary cathartic effect." When the supply of wine to be pilfered from the wine cellars of Anzio and Nettuno dried up, enterprising GI moonshiners turned to copper tubing liberated from German planes that had crashed within the beachhead. According to Sheehan, they were able to produce "an especially virulent brand of raisin-jack" that was always in demand because the supply of German airplanes was far outstripped by the large number of thirsty customers.[59]

The unit that adapted to the Anzio beachhead better than any other was Brigadier General Robert T. Frederick's maverick Canadian-American First Special Service Force. Formed in 1942 under the command of a young, unknown American lieutenant colonel named Frederick (West Point, class of 1928), the 2,500-man brigade, one-third of whom were Canadians, was created as an elite guerrilla force that would be employed to tie up large numbers of German combat troops and perform impossible missions no other unit was trained to carry out. When he specified that his enlisted men be "rough, tough and unafraid of anybody or anything," what Frederick got from Canada were some of its best soldiers. American commanders followed the practice of dumping their misfits and emptied their stockades of ne'er-do-wells, who joined a good many volunteers. Nevertheless, one later said "he hadn't been sure of his acceptance by Frederick because 'I didn't have a criminal record.'"[60]

One of the myths that grew about the Force was that it was composed entirely of cutthroats, when in fact a great many were volunteers looking for something more interesting than their present circumstances. The name Special Service Force was conceived by Frederick to conceal its mission and fool outsiders into believing it had something to do with GI entertainment. Eventually every branch and service of the U.S. military was represented. The weak and the inept were soon weeded out, and those who withstood Frederick's tough regimen eventually were turned into the toughest collection of soldiers ever to wear a military uniform in World War II.

Like Darby with his Rangers, the no-nonsense Frederick turned the Force into an image of himself. His men soon learned that their commander shared their training and their hardships. On more than one occasion a soldier found himself next to Frederick in a boiling surf or a mountain top. In Italy a Force battalion once arrived behind enemy lines at its objective only to find its commander already there. Frederick had infiltrated behind enemy lines alone several hours earlier in order to be able to evaluate how well his officers were performing.

During the breakout from the Anzio beachhead a patrol whose members thought they were the leading element were suddenly surprised when they observed Frederick in a jeep coming toward them herding fourteen German POWs.[61] Needless to say, those who showed even the slightest traits of weakness or lack of leadership were ruthlessly replaced.[62]

The tales of Frederick's toughness were no exaggeration. Once, after the war, he was in a bar in uniform, wearing the two stars of a major general, when an obnoxious policeman loudly questioned that one so young could not possibly be a general in the U.S. Army. Demanding his ID, the policeman looked it over and dropped it on the floor. After refusing a request to pick up the ID card, the officer was knocked out by a single punch by the soft-spoken Frederick.[63]

Outfitted with red berets and needle-sharp sheathknives, which they were trained to use with deadly efficiency, the Special Servicemen also became parachute qualified. Disdaining the usual three-month period the Army took for airborne training, Frederick's men learned in six days. "Frederick himself made his first jump after only 10 minutes of instruction in which cords to pull to do what and how to land without breaking his neck (doing it in his bedroom slippers because their jumpboots hadn't arrived)."[64]

By early 1944 the Force was a veteran unit that had fought in southern Italy and earned from the tough Hermann Göring Division the nickname "The Devil's Brigade." Fifth Army had suffered heavy losses for two weeks attempting to capture two key mountain fortresses guarding the approaches to the Gustav Line. Frederick's men climbed the razorlike ridges at night and caught the Germans flatfooted. In the furious battles that followed the Force lost nearly one-third of its fighting strength, but the southern jaws of the forward defenses of the Gustav Line were now in Allied hands and in the process both Frederick and his men had become instant legends.

The Force moved into Anzio at the end of January and took over the defense of the Mussolini Canal, on the extreme right flank of the beachhead along an eight-mile front. The Germans provided a rude greeting by killing several Force officers. The Forcemen found their enemy "too close, too brassy, and too obnoxious for their own good."[65] In short order the Germans were made painfully aware that something very different was occurring. Their faces blackened, Force patrols suddenly became vigorous and pushed deep into German lines at night. They seemed to be everywhere and would appear with lethal suddenness in strange uniforms, often consisting of fur-lined parkas, baggy trousers, and all manner of weapons.

The most visible result was that they brought back valuable intelligence of German positions. Artillery fire soon began crashing down into heretofore safe locations, and by the end of their first week in the bridgehead the Germans prudently elected to pull back their lines nearly a half mile, leaving the void a deadly no-man's land.

The occupancy of the small farms and villages became a matter of considerable dispute between the Forcemen and the Germans. The Germans would occupy them by day, and by night there would be vicious firefights as Frederick's men ejected them. Finally tiring of this, Frederick ordered the dwellings blown up. That ended German occupancy but not the exploits of the Forcemen, who were accorded another nickname—"Black Devils"—by the Hermann Göring Division. Clear evidence of just how badly the Germans were unnerved by these deadly nightly forays into their lines was found in the diary of a dead German officer: "The Black Devils are all around us every time we come into the line, and we never hear them come."[66]

Perhaps escapades would be a cleaner definition than forays. The men of the 2d Company, First Regiment, decided they very much liked the tiny village of Borgo Sabotino and after driving out the Germans elected to remain. These men had seen enough of Anzio to decide it was foolish to endure unnecessary hardship. They renamed the place Gusville, in honor of Lieutenant Gus Heilman, a former University of Virginia football player who had become notorious in Charlottesville for the tavern he ran for the benefit of himself and his fellow students. Heilman was not pleased that the war had interrupted a lucrative business and even less elated when his draft notice arrived in 1941. Unimpressed with Gus's attempts to gain a draft deferment, the local draft board unleashed him on an unsuspecting Army. Gus fared so badly at officer candidate school that to avoid being sent overseas as an infantry replacement he was recruited into the Special Service Force and given an immediate commission.[67]

Heilman was an irreverent and well-liked officer, and it was no surprise that a town should be named after him. What made Gusville unique was that it was about a quarter of a mile behind German lines. Such minor obstacles never deterred Gus or his platoon, and to no one's surprise, among the new mayor's first acts was the appointment of men to various positions, such as chief of police. And of course, the opening of a bar. While others might consider opening such an establishment behind enemy lines in the midst of one of the most desperate battles of World War II something of an impossibility, it was for the Forcemen of Gusville merely a challenge. The main street of the village was renamed Tank Street, for the numerous German tank shells that flew down its length with regularity. Another street was named Prostitute Avenue because, as one correspondent wrote: "A man walking down it a little ways will find himself without visible means of support."[68]

Taxes were levied on other units passing through Gusville and of course, the new occupants proved their mastery of scrounging, begging, borrowing, and, most often, stealing. There were almost nightly raids behind German lines to obtain the necessary food and drink with which to live the good life. Garden plots were begun and tenderly cared for by the same men who gleefully killed Germans at night. Cabbage and potatoes flourished and were the crops of choice in Gusville. While their fellow soldiers elsewhere in the beachhead lived off GI rations, Gusville's occupants dined on fresh eggs, fresh meat, fowl, and fresh vegetables. When wine supplies ran low, the wine cellars of Nettuno became prime targets and it was reputed that a group of Forcemen invaded Truscott's command post and made off with casks of wine after disarming the military police guarding the place. Truscott is alleged to have made only a token complaint to Frederick about this impudence.[69]

Weekly church services were held in a small chapel in Gusville by the Protestant and Catholic chaplains each Sunday, until they became so popular that the increased attendance drew heavy German artillery fire and had to be moved to foxholes and fortified farmhouses. The Catholic chaplain performed christenings for which he was paid in eggs, and the Second Regiment medical officer delivered five *bambini* of several large Italian families that had remained in the battle area.[70]

Word of the Forcemen's activities soon spread throughout the beachhead, and rather than cause resentment among their less fortunate comrades, their enterprise became a considerable morale booster. Inevitably, however, the enterprising Forcemen soon drew the unwelcome attention of cattle and chicken rustlers who operated in jeeps by night and were widely suspected of belonging to the 3d Division.

The press soon learned of Gusville, and stories about it began appearing in editions of the *Stars and Stripes*. It became something of an accomplishment for correspondents to dateline their stories Gusville. One piece that gained national attention in the United States told of a patrol returning not only with captured Germans but a cow and a sewing machine.[71] Not to be outdone by the outside press, the men of Gusville began publishing a newspaper of their own called the Gusville *Herald Tribune*. The Force also soon began publishing its own daily newspaper, *The Braves' Bulletin*, which was filled with news of the beachhead and the outside world. This included a gossip column that would do credit to the best of today's purveyors of trivia. Typical entries read:

From First [Regiment]: Sergeant Jack W. Stallings of Cerreto Alto outpost blasting fame, is taking over the Victory Garden section of Gusville Farm Projects, Inc., and plans to start spring plowing in the near future.

From Service [Battalion]: Since the Christian twins bought that cow they are having trouble finding room for her in their foxhole.

From Second [Regiment]: After reading home-town clippings Sergeant Arky Cameron was heard to exclaim: "My God, I'm another Sergeant York!"[72]

Gardening became such a major craze that one officer complained, "I can't do a thing with those sons of bitches. They patrol all night and they farm all day."[73] Gusville was not the only place to enjoy a higher degree of creature comforts. It was common for units swapping positions at the front to argue, and sometimes fight, over the ownership of the livestock or egg rights in henhouses. When the 36th Engineers took over the Force sector during the breakout battles in May, they found the roads leading to the rear clogged not only with Forcemen but with "horses, cattle, chickens, household goods, pens of rabbits, sheep—a noisy cross section of Pontine live stock [that] went back with the companies." Two of the more enterprising Forcemen were seen with a horse and surrey. Unlike what happened at Gusville, most of these animals had been legitimately purchased and receipts were produced to prove it.[74]

However, not all was fun and games. At night the deadly serious business of war was carried out by the Special Service Force, whose patrols behind German lines became feared. Frederick made a specialty of demolishing houses being used by the Germans. Usually a bazooka would be used to attack the structure and divert the attention of its occupants, while a demolition crew quietly moved in and laid explosive charges. Up would go one or more houses at a time, usually with their unsuspecting occupants still inside. As one Forceman recalled, "The most enjoyable patrols were . . . when we went out to blow up a house or some other structure used for outpost or observation. We always got a kick out of driving the jerries upstairs and then blowing the building out from beneath them."[75]

In late February, as the Germans prepared for their final counteroffensive, they displayed unusual interest in an outpost near a bridge outside Borgo Sabotino. The Forcemen attacked and, after a fierce firefight, took control of the strongpoint and captured thirty-five Germans. For the next hour groups of Germans walked unsuspecting into a trap and were captured. By 0800 hours the next morning the bag totaled 108 POWs, but the final three to approach detected danger and fled to the rear. Determined not to spoil his perfect record, the Force commander, Lieutenant George Krasvac, took two men and pursued the fleeing Germans two kilometers. An hour later the lieutenant returned with his prisoners and considerable booty: "The three Germans were burdened down. One was pushing a baby carriage full of potatoes.

Another bore a bed and mattress on his back while the third carried a large crate of live chickens."[76]

Frederick also devised a nasty calling card in the form of paper stickers containing the symbol of the Special Service Force (two crossed lightning bolts with a dagger pointing upward through the middle) and a phrase in German that translated into: "The worst is yet to come." Whenever a German was killed behind their lines, one of these stickers would be left on his helmet or forehead. Other calling cards in the form of red stickers emblazoned with the Force spearhead symbol were left on buildings and fenceposts behind German lines.[77] The word soon spread within German ranks that these fearsome men whose faces were darkened with black grease took no prisoners.

During their three-month stint guarding the Allied right flank the First Special Service Force earned immortality for their exploits. More than one senior officer came away from a visit to the front believing these troops were lunatics in uniform. Frederick, of course, knew that idleness bred problems and was content to see his men gainfully occupied, no matter how wacky their endeavors. There was nothing humorous about the number of losses to the Special Service Force during those three months: Eighty-nine men died or were reported missing in action or known to have been captured.[78]

Perhaps the saddest places in the beachhead were the casualty clearing stations, where the wounded were first brought and where the medics fought to save the lives of their patients who were receiving their first treatment since being evacuated from the front line. The British facility near the Via Anziate was taxed almost beyond endurance during the February battles. The tents were unable to contain the heavy rains, and their floors became a sea of mud as the icy winds howled outside, while inside gravely ill men clung to life. Doctors, nurses, and orderlies worked frantically as cases piled up. At the height of the battle there was no such thing as catching up. The average time between when a Tommy was wounded and his appearance on the operating-room table was about seven hours.[79] An average day for a surgeon might entail operating all night, a few hours' sleep, followed by another eight-hour session. One surgeon did fourteen major cases overnight and twelve more during his second session the following afternoon.

The most difficult aspect was triage: sorting out the casualties and determining who would be treated at the clearing station and in what order. The worst were the abdominal cases, which were usually given about a fifty-fifty chance of survival and had to be treated at once. Yet such wounds took inordinately longer to treat in the operating room than wounds to the limbs. Though it could have been argued that it was wasteful to spend a longer time treating men who were of no further

military value even if they made a complete recovery, the temptation
was resisted by the medical officers.

Here is one British surgeon's description of the charnel-house atmosphere of a clearing station:

> The wounded lay in two rows, mostly British but some Americans as well,
> in their sodden filthy clothes . . . soaked, caked, buried in mud and blood;
> with ghastly pale faces, shuddering, shivering with the cold of the Febru-
> ary nights and their great wounds. . . . Most men had their first field
> dressings or shell dressings on. I grew to hate that combination of yellow
> pad, bloody, dirty brown bandage and mud-darkened skin . . . head wounds
> [were distinguished by] loud snoring breathing.
>
> . . . some (too many; far too many) were carried in dying, with gross
> combinations of shattered limbs, protrusions of intestines and brain from
> great holes in their poor frames torn by 88-millimeter shells, mortars and
> anti-personnel bombs. Some lay quiet and still, with legs drawn up—pene-
> trating wounds of the abdomen. Some were carried in sitting up on the
> stretchers, gasping and coughing, shot through the lungs. . . . All were
> exhausted after being under continuous fire, and after lying in the mud for
> hours or days.[80]

As if the conditions were not already bad enough, the hospitals and
clearing stations were subjected to frequent artillery and mortar attacks. During one such attack the chief clerk of a clearing station was
horribly wounded. Within minutes he was attended by a medical officer. "Will I be all right, sir?" he asked. "Of course," assured the doctor,
whose lie was an attempt to make the sergeant's final moments as
humane as possible, for "he was only half a man—What were these I
saw, feebly moving? They were once his legs, but now, mere bloody
stumps. He was only a frightful, legless, bleeding fragment, beating
feebly in the mire. . . . He kept trying to clasp my busy hands, muttering
as if very cold, 'Major, sir, will I be all right?' That fine, tall, handsome
fellow! Just a monstrous bit of tangled flesh! . . . I could not help thinking . . . 'It might have been me, it might have been me!' "[81]

Among the unsung heroes of the beachhead were the men of the
American Field Service. Consisting mostly of conscientious objectors,
these were civilians whose religious and moral convictions precluded
bearing arms, but who willingly carried out alternative service as ambulance drivers. Some were veterans of the Western Desert campaigns of
the British Eighth Army. The fact that they were technically noncombatants made little difference in the hellish environment of Anzio. Like
their comrades who bore arms, some of these men died in the line of
duty in an attempt to save lives.

The men and women who served at Anzio dreamed of the day they
would leave that dreadful place. Among the first units to leave Anzio

were the battered remnants of the proud Guards Brigade. Its three battalions had been at the apex of the deadly battles for the Thumb from the beginning, and they had paid an awful price in casualties. It was decided to send them south to recuperate and refit for battles yet to come. For others, the dreary, endless days made them feel as if the stalemate would go on forever. One lieutenant wrote his family, "One gets inured to a 20 hour day but I get rather tired of the blood and tears, toil and sweat. Like Monty, I am getting rather tired of war, like Churchill I think there's too much optimism."[82]

Another unit that left Anzio at about the same time was the 1st Battalion, the London Irish Rifles. In six weeks the battalion lost thirty-two officers and 550 men. Only twelve officers and 300 men embarked, and many of these had only just returned from the hospital.[83]

For some relief was merely a blessed few days out of the hateful frontline trenches and foxholes. Fusilier Gilbert Alnutt later wrote:

> I well remember the night we left our front line position. Packed and ready to go we heard the relief party splashing its way through the water. Heard them cursing as they stumbled up the rain soaked slippery slopes to our position at the top of the wadi. The usual exchange of greetings "What's it like, mate?" The inevitable reply "Bloody awful!" Shakespeare's words would have been much better.
>
> "For this relief much thanks."[84]

Plans and
Controversies

I am thoroughly disgusted with [Alexander] and his
attitude.

—CLARK

Rome was obviously a magnet and Mark Clark . . .
was obviously determined to be the first there.

LIEUTENANT GENERAL SIR JOHN HARDING

On both fronts the stalemate
dragged on into the spring of 1944, with neither belligerent posing a
serious threat to the other. Across the Anzio front the Allies turned the
battle into a holding action. Harmon recalls the "haunting unreality" of
the World War I atmosphere of the front lines of the beachhead. During
the final counteroffensive, the German Fourteenth Army had paid
dearly for its latest failure with the loss of thirty tanks and more than
3,500 men. Henceforth the Germans would return to the defensive to
await the inevitable Allied breakout offensive. In fact, six weeks of what
must rank as the bitterest combat of World War II had left both sides
utterly incapable of carrying out further offensive operations.

Both sides of the beachhead were swarming with troops even
though Kesselring had stripped the Fourteenth Army of four divisions
to army group reserve, including three of the best in Italy, to counter
perceived Allied threats of another amphibious landing in his rear north
of Rome. This significant decline during March and April changed the
character of the army to that of a defensive force. Nevertheless, Hitler

was impressed by the similarities at Anzio to the positional warfare he had observed on the Western Front in World War I. He ordered attacks to claim small but important portions of the beachhead from the Allies in March. However, these plans never got beyond the planning stage, and the only offensive operations carried out by the Fourteenth Army consisted of sporadic raids of battalion size or less. The Fourteenth Army's assigned strength in early May was approximately 100,000 German troops of two corps and five divisions, with a fighting strength of approximately 51,600. A sixth division was held in reserve directly under von Mackensen's control.[1]

Kesselring and von Mackensen explored the possibility of a new offensive at the end of March but called it off in early April when it became obvious there was little to be gained against what were now the heaviest defenses yet devised by the Allies. Truscott's staff was likewise busy drawing up plans for new offensive operations by VI Corps to enlarge the beachhead, but these, too, never progressed beyond the planning stage. Nothing would happen at Anzio until spring, when the Allies attacked Cassino for the fourth time.

Even the ever-optimistic Kesselring now understood that it was pointless to continue decimating his units in futile attacks, particularly with replacements and resupply increasingly serious problems. In fact, Anzio now ranked a distant third on his list of problems, as the focus shifted to the Cassino front and the new threat of another Allied amphibious landing behind German lines. As a postwar American study later revealed, Hitler "concurred in Kesselring's judgment. Only General Jodl seems to have realized the disastrous potentialities in the Anzio situation: on May 2 he once more suspended orders for the transfer of the Hermann Göring Division to France because he feared that an attack from the beachhead could not be stopped without its strength and mobility."[2]

Except for local probes, each side spent the remainder of the winter and early spring fortifying itself against the other. As it had been on the Western Front thirty years earlier, the greatest danger lay in death from artillery fire. Despite the relative inactivity the casualty rate for VI Corps continued to exceed one hundred per day.

In preparation for the anticipated breakout, priority was given to a buildup of supplies and the replenishment of VI Corps' battered units. Local skirmishing was carried out only to keep the other side from gaining an advantage. As a result of inadequate aerial reconnaissance and inability of the front-line units to capture prisoners, the Germans were starved for intelligence pointing to future Allied intentions. Commanders up and down the chain of command were reduced to pleading for prisoners. In a fit of frustration, the normally calm von Vietinghoff became so desperate for information that he admonished his two corps commanders for the lack of sufficient POWs.[3]

An example of how desperately the Germans would grasp at any straw concerned the case of a Spanish-Moroccan deserter captured by the Tenth Army, who predicted a major Allied offensive starting on April 25 aimed at Monte Cassino and Monte Cairo. The most gullible German to accept the truth of this prediction was Hitler, who alerted both Kesselring and von Vietinghoff to the impending attack. The deserter became the subject of a telephone conversation between Kesselring and von Vietinghoff shortly before midnight on April 23. Immediately orders were flashed by XIV Panzer Corps: "Enemy large-scale offensive seems to be directly imminent. Highest degree of readiness as of 2400 hrs, 24 Apr."[4] A postwar Canadian study notes: "When the big attack . . . failed to materialize, the high ranking officers who had packed their belongings in the evening and had arisen at an early hour 'in order to be ready' felt rather sheepish." The Tenth Army chief of staff, Major General Fritz Wentzell, complained to a colleague: "Whenever you are well prepared—nothing happens."[5] The sorry state of German intelligence was evident when the presence of the 10th Indian Division was detected in Italy. General Wentzell lamented:

> The appearance of 10 Ind Div gave me quite a jolt because no intelligence source had noticed either their departure from the Orient or their arrival here. Great gaps in the intelligence services are apparent![6]

Liberty ships and LSTs from Naples continued to be the lifeblood of the Anzio beachhead and the sole source of resupply, which had grown to an average of more than four thousand tons a day. On any given day the waters off Anzio were filled with Liberty ships, serviced by a fleet of more than five hundred DUKWs and LCTs. The excellent work of the engineers had resulted in the creation of considerable dock space in the port of Anzio, which could now accommodate eight LSTs, eight LCIs, and fifteen LCTs at the same time. There were daily convoys from Naples to Anzio by six LSTs, loaded to capacity with fifty trucks, each of which carried an average of fifteen hundred tons of cargo and ammunition.[7] On their return runs these workhorses became taxis that ferried POWs and the sick and wounded to Naples.

Supplies of ammunition, spare parts, and other essential supplies began filling the supply dumps in the rear of the beachhead to capacity in preparation for the breakout operation, which would consume them rapidly. The 34th and 36th U.S. Infantry divisions were pulled from the Cassino sector and sent to Anzio to participate in the breakout, as was Combat Command B of Harmon's 1st Armored, which originally had been intended as the exploitation force up the Liri Valley after the

Rapido defenses were breached. Truscott's forces were still building, but in early May there were an estimated ninety thousand troops in the Anzio beachhead, with many more to come.

The dilemma facing the Allied commanders in Italy was by what means they would break the two-front stalemate. Alexander came to the conclusion that there could be no breakout from the Anzio beachhead until the Gustav Line was successfully cracked. The piecemeal tactics employed by Alexander and Clark against the Rapido defenses and to capture the Abbey of Monte Cassino and the town had been bloody and dismal failures. Martin Blumenson points out that Alexander and Clark had never seen Anzio and Cassino in the same light:

> Originally, Alexander had expected the Anzio force to be the compelling instrument in forcing the Germans to withdraw from Cassino, whereas Clark had seen the Anzio force as making an important assist to the decisive action at Cassino. Now, in the spring of 1944, they reversed their positions, Alexander coming to anticipate the important battle at Cassino, while Clark envisaged the significant action at Anzio. To these divergent ends, each commander applied his energy and intelligence.[8]

That the two rarely agreed on anything is well established and is critical to an understanding of the events leading to the capture of Rome. These fundamental differences, which left the two commanders once again at loggerheads regarding the basic strategy of the campaign, not only poisoned the atmosphere but had a fatal impact on the end of the Anzio story. It also set the stage for one of the great battlefield controversies of World War II and a lingering legacy of bitterness over the capture of Rome.

With three significant failures at Cassino already behind them, it was clear that there could be no fourth setback. This time the long-awaited Allied spring offensive would have to be decisive or doom the entire campaign in Italy to permanent stalemate south of Rome. Alexander remained under intense pressure to break the stalemate at the earliest possible opportunity. The original target date of April soon proved impossible. With few exceptions, most of the Allied divisions were tired and in need of rest, reorganization, and refitting. Moreover, the ground was still far too wet for a major offensive in which armor would play a key role.

When Alexander traveled to London in early April, the news he brought Churchill was that there would be no Allied offensive in Italy until May. With Overlord still many weeks off, there was little to bolster war-weary spirits in Britain. Churchill himself was demonstrating unmistakable evidence of being desperately fatigued by the crushing weight of his responsibilities. Brooke's diary for this period reflects the weariness that had begun to take its toll on everyone. One such entry describes a meeting of the Chiefs of Staff Committee in late March in which, "We found him in a desperately tired mood. I am afraid that he is losing ground rapidly. He seems quite incapable of concentrating for a few minutes on end, and keeps wandering continuously. He kept yawning and said he was feeling desperately tired."[9]

The problems of planning Overlord and Alexander's reports of one failure after another in Italy had done little to relieve the constant pressures on Churchill. In March, as if the news from the Anzio beachhead were not sufficiently pessimistic, a depressing cable from Alexander revealed the latest setback during the Third Battle of Cassino, when a handful of resolute German paratroopers held the rubble of the town in the face of apparently overwhelming superiority.

Sir Alexander Cadogan wrote of the malaise: "We are bogged down in Cassino and, indeed, in Italy. It looks to me like a Passchendaele, beloved of Generals." Even Churchill made no effort to conceal his feelings when he cabled Alexander on March 21 that "the war weighs heavily on us all just now."[10] And, as Churchill's official biographer writes, "After nearly four years as Prime Minister, three serious illnesses, and many setbacks, there seemed to be no end to the intractable problems and difficult decisions."[11]

When he briefed Churchill and the Chiefs of Staff Committee on the situation in Italy, Alexander "made it clear that the offensive in Italy could not be launched before the middle of May and the hoped-for junction between the main attacking forces and the bridgehead before the first week in June."[12] *Delay* and *postponement* were never acceptable words to Churchill but, as he cabled Roosevelt two weeks later, Alexander "defended his actions or inactions with much force, pointing out the small plurality of his army, its mixed character, there being no fewer than seven separate nationalities against the homogeneous Germans, the vileness of the weather and the extremely awkward nature of the ground."[13]

Alexander based his case on the presence of an estimated twenty-three German divisions in Italy, eighteen of which were deployed south of Rome. Most had been reinforced at an average rate of fifteen thousand per month and were generally up to full strength. "They still held the Gustav Line . . . and had constructed two more fortified positions in its rear, the Adolf Hitler and Caesar Lines, the first running east from the River Liri to the slopes of Monte Cairo north of Cassino, the second across routes 6 and 7 between Anzio and Rome . . . through Avezzano, to positions west of Pescara. Alexander would thus encounter three defended positions."[14]

Alexander believed he would need a three-to-one infantry superiority, which was the accepted norm in World War II,[15] to successfully break the Gustav Line. The Allies could only muster a maximum of twenty-eight divisions in central Italy, leaving their numerical superiority over the Germans at a slender one and one-quarter to one. Only four Allied divisions in the entire Mediterranean were left uncommitted to the Italian campaign.

Alexander's primary responsibility was to insure that the Italian offensive be launched in sufficient time to benefit Overlord.[16] Like a sword of Damocles over the Italian campaign hung the prospect of losing a significant number of ships and combat divisions to Anvil, the proposed Allied landings in southern France in support of Overlord. In the opinion of Churchill and the British chiefs of staff, Anvil would cripple the Italian campaign by stripping Alexander of shipping and key formations at the very moment when a decisive military operation was likely to be launched to break the long stalemate. Like no other military operation of World War II, Anvil was a bone in Churchill's throat. The more he complained and argued for its cancellation, the more it seemed to harden American insistence on what the British considered a major operation of dubious value. However, in Marshall— and later in Eisenhower—the prime minister encountered an implacable advocate of the landings in southern France.

To Marshall he wrote in mid-April: "We should above all defeat the German army south of Rome and join our own armies. Nothing should be grudged for this. We cannot tell how either the Allied or enemy armies will emerge from the battle until the battle has been fought. It may be that the enemy will be thrown into disorder and that great opportunities of exploitation may be open. Or we may be checked and the enemy may continue to hold his positions south of Rome against us with existing forces."

Pleading for relief from Anvil, Churchill argued with considerable merit:

I believe that whatever happens on the mainland of Italy, the enemy forces now detached to the Riviera can be fastened there by feints and threats. One thing that alarms me, however, is lest our Directive to General Wilson should make him fall between two stools. This would mean that we should be denied the exploitation of any victory gained south of Rome (and victories are wonderful things) or the power to pin down German Divisions in Italy, and yet on the other hand not be able to make a major operation out of "Anvil."[17]

Roosevelt and Marshall were unmoved, and Marshall replied: "We appear to be agreed in principle, but quite evidently not as to method. If we are to have any option as to what we can do when the time comes, preparations for 'Anvil' must be made now even though they may be at the partial expense of future operations in Italy after the beach-head has been joined to the main line."[18]

The only concession the British could wring from the reluctant American leadership was a postponement of Anvil from July 10 to a later date, and it probably had less to do with Churchill's persuasiveness than it did to the fact that Alexander's May offensive simply could not be carried out if the July date remained.

Despite the gloomy long-term outlook, for perhaps the first time in the Italian campaign there emerged a clear definition of what Alexander was expected to accomplish, and this came in the form of a directive from the Combined Chiefs of Staff to Jumbo Wilson that read:

> OBJECT: to give the greatest possible assistance to Overlord by destroying or containing the maximum number of German formations in the Mediterranean.[19]

There was no mention of Rome in the Combined Chiefs' directive. Although it satisfied hardly anyone in London, it was in fact a victory of sorts for the British, who at least gained a respite from Anvil and a clear mandate to Alexander. In Washington, even though Dill continued to negotiate with Marshall, there was no resolution of Anglo-American differences. The parties remained poles apart, and at one point Marshall informed Dill that "only over my dead body will you get a change of outlook."[20]

While his superiors fought over Anvil, Alexander had outlined the fundamental strategy to be employed by Allied forces in Italy and its basis was soon to be the focus of the split between himself and Mark Clark. No longer content merely to gain ground, Alexander intended "to destroy enemy formations in Italy to such an extent that they must be replaced from elsewhere to avoid a rout. Tactical plans should therefore be designed to bring about [such] situations."[21]

In addition Alexander asked for stepped-up attacks against German road, rail, and sea communications by the Allied air forces, and the result was Operation Strangle, an aptly named aerial offensive designed to so cripple everything south of the Apennines that the Germans would be compelled to withdraw from central Italy. Most of Strangle was carried out by Major General John K. Cannon's Mediterranean Allied Tactical Air Force (MATAF), whose all-weather fighter-bombers flew 9,263 sorties against railway targets (marshaling yards, bridges, trains, motor transport, and rail lines) in central and northern Italy.[22]

From mid-March to mid-May Cannon's airmen carried out the most relentless aerial offensive ever carried out in the Mediterranean.

Some targets out of fighter-bomber range were attacked by the heavy bombers of Nathan Twining's Mediterranean Allied Strategic Air Force. By early April Kesselring reported that his two armies were receiving only 60 percent of the minimum daily requirement of 2,261 tons of supplies. No longer could supplies be moved south of Florence except by road. Although Strangle was never able to achieve the overly ambitious objective of compelling a German withdrawal, it all but paralyzed rail traffic in central Italy and greatly reduced the resupply of von Vietinghoff's and von Mackensen's armies. It also forced the Germans to allocate considerable manpower to the task of emergency repairs and put "almost impossible" strains, which included the consumption of huge quantities of fuel, on their motor transport system. Convoys were obliged to run a two-hundred-mile gauntlet that included mountain roads and attacks by partisans.

A German movements control officer in Italy, Colonel Klaus Stange, would later write that "the dreaded period began on 20 March . . . new, intensive . . . [and] extremely unpleasant." He continued:

> All lines south of the Apennines were threatened all day long by fighter-bomber attacks. Stationary and moving trains were shot up; electrical conductor-cables and standards were machine-gunned at many places . . . bombs were dropped on small bridges and on open stretches of the lines; the railway telephone network was cut and destroyed at many places and over considerable lengths . . . the labor forces were under the perpetual menace of air attacks . . . damage was caused at many different and at an ever-increasing number of new places . . . the demand for repair gangs steadily increased . . . power stations failed . . . more and more locomotives and rolling stock were . . . also causing lines to be blocked . . . the difficulties multiplied and seemed to become insurmountable.[23]

On March 25 Alexander's new chief of staff, Lieutenant General Sir John Harding, submitted an appreciation that called for the main breakout attack to come first at Anzio, followed by the southern attack. Alexander changed his mind when Ultra and other intelligence began to indicate that the Germans expected the main effort to emanate from Anzio. Thus, Alexander's change of heart left him convinced that an Anzio offensive launched first might exhaust itself before the Allies could attain what he believed was the principal objective of cutting Highway 6. Later events would validate Alexander's thinking:

> Alexander said he always believed in a one-two punch—the first punch to be delivered to the main [Cassino] front, suck in German reserves, but breakthrough there. Then after the enemy had withdrawn his reserves to the main southern front [which] should have the Germans on the run,

Alexander expected he would have the Anzio beachhead force strike out and cut the German line of communication in the rear of Tenth Army. Although . . . the Mediterranean Tactical Air Force promised that [it] could support both operations at the same time . . . Alexander felt that . . . a simultaneous attack would leave no flexibility in the plan—[would] remove the element of surprise and show our hand to the Germans from the start.[24]

Although Alexander is properly credited with creating the overall strategy for the breakout offensives, it was Harding who masterminded the plan that was at long last to end the stalemates at Cassino and Anzio. When Brooke sent Harding to Italy, it was because he had little faith in Alexander's ability to direct the Italian campaign without a strong, experienced chief of staff.

Graham and Bidwell have described Harding as "a man of ruthless logic," who brought to Alexander's headquarters not only experience as a fine combat commander but the traits of a superb staff officer who understood the dictates of the battlefield and could figure out how to develop a sound plan to achieve an end.[25] An officer of humble origins, Harding had none of the usual ties to the upper-class caste of the British Army and none of the vain ambition sometimes found in such men.

Harding created the strategy for a plan, code-named Diadem, to break the Gustav Line. Its crux was to annul once and for all the penny-packet tactics and mentality that had characterized the first three battles of Cassino. Instead Harding opted to apply a huge concentration of force at a decisive point. He proposed a sweeping realignment of forces that would concentrate Leese's Eighth Army opposite Cassino for the main attack. With three corps (13th British, 1st Canadian, and 2d Polish), Leese's mission was to unleash a massive force against Cassino. The Fifth Army was to be shifted to the Garigliano sector and would be joined there by General Alphonse Juin's Corps Expéditionnaire Français, while the Polish II Corps took over the former French sector on the Eighth Army right flank. The Adriatic end of the Gustav Line was to be stripped of virtually all its troops. After four failures—the Rapido and the first three battles of Cassino—Harding intended Diadem to be a battle of annihilation, not attrition.

Harding's appreciation was prepared in February and sent to AFHQ where, as his biographer, Field Marshal Lord Carver, writes, "It was coolly received . . . as it contained some suggestions which would clearly cause difficulties."[26] While there was no quarrel over the aim of forcing the Germans to become fully committed in Italy while Overlord was carried out, Harding was not content merely to break a long stalemate. His plan was to wipe out German ground forces in Italy. "Harding, with ruthless logic, pointed out that neither pushing back the German line nor the capture of Rome would help achieve the aim" of drawing off formations from France and the Eastern Front. What the Allies must do was "to destroy German formations in Italy to such an extent that they had to be replaced from elsewhere in order to prevent a disastrous collapse. . . . If his criteria were met, there would be a good chance that an attack by three or four divisions from Anzio, combined with a major offensive up the line of the Liri valley, would stand a reasonable chance of encircling and destroying a considerable part of Kesselring's forces."[27]

What made Harding's proposal unpopular was its conclusion that Operation Anvil ought to be scrapped in favor of a decisive offensive in Italy. There were not enough troops and landing craft to do both, and Anvil should be reduced to a deception operation to tie down even more German forces on the southern coast of France. Although Harding's plan was accepted, his recommendation that Anvil be cancelled never had a chance against American intransigence. Nevertheless:

> For the first time since the invasion of Sicily a clear, penetrating, overall examination had been made of what the allies were trying to do in Italy and how they should achieve their aim. All Harding's clarity of mind . . . straight-forward, realistic commonsense, practical military experience, determination and courage to put forth an unpopular view shone through this example of what a military appreciation, as taught him by Montgomery at the staff college sixteen years before, was designed to achieve.[28]

Disdaining the piecemeal tactics so unsuccessfully employed by Clark, Diadem called for the Eighth Army to concentrate its vast array of firepower, supported by the full weight of the Allied air forces, on simultaneous attacks on key points in the German defenses. A major feature of the plan was the concentration of armor at the mouth of the Liri Valley, where Harding intended the breakthrough to occur. Once the Allies were in control of Highway 6, the Gustav Line would be effectively cut and the German Tenth Army would be fighting for its life and unable to reinforce the Anzio front. Meanwhile, with a similar operation taking place at Anzio, there would be no reinforcements available to send south to Cassino. Moreover, with the Gustav Line broken, Kesselring and von Vietinghoff would lose the capability to plug gaps by the timely shifting of their forces across the Gustav Line, a tactic so successfully employed during the first three battles for Cassino.

Leese would have at his disposal six infantry divisions, three armored divisions, and three independent armored brigades, while on the Garigliano front Clark would have the two divisions of Geoffrey Keyes's II Corps plus Juin's four divisions. At Anzio VI Corps was likewise to be reinforced by Walker's 36th (Texas) Division. With the arrival of Ryder's 34th Division in March, Truscott had a total of six infantry divisions (British 1st and 56th; U.S. 3d, 34th, 36th, and 45th); Harmon's 1st Armored Division, complete for the first time since the previous year; and Frederick's Canadian-American First Special Service Force.

Harding's plan for DIADEM included a powerful breakout offensive from the Anzio beachhead aimed not at Rome, but northeast through the Alban Hills to cut Highway 6 at the mountain town of Valmontone. If VI Corps could slice through the Valmontone gap and block Highway 6, both Harding and Alexander believed the bulk of the German Tenth Army would be trapped between VI Corps and the Diadem force driving them up the Liri Valley. In addition, by selecting Valmontone, Harding ensured that the VI Corps offensive would enable Truscott's forces to control all road and rail lines between Rome and Cassino.

To add to the German uncertainties, Harding also conceived what proved to be an exceptionally successful deception designed to convince and worry the German commanders that the Allies were about to initiate another attack from their rear.[29]

So successful was this deception that Kesselring now found it necessary to protect his coastal flank at the expense of reducing his forces at both Anzio and Cassino. The Hermann Göring Division was withdrawn from its positions along the Mussolini Canal (no doubt to the intense relief of many of its troops, who would no longer have to contend with Frederick's Forcemen) and sent to Livorno (Leghorn), where it was under the direct control of OKW. The 26th Panzer Division had been pulled from the Anzio front and assigned a coastal sector from Ostia north to Orbetello; the 29th Panzer Grenadier Division was now northwest of Rome to reinforce either along the coast or again at Anzio.[30] Ernst-Günther Baade's 90th Panzer Grenadier Division, the Tenth Army reserve, had been sent to Ostia, southwest of Rome, at the mouth of the Tiber River. War games held by Kesselring and his commanders on May 3 stressed fresh Allied landings in their rear in connection with an attack of some kind along the Cassino front.[31]

Truscott had independently come to the same conclusion as Harding on the merits of a thrust to block the Valmontone gap. Although his VI Corps staff devised four separate planning scenarios, the one that offered the most promise was called Operation Buffalo, a thrust by VI Corps via Cisterna and Cori to cut Highway 6 at Valmontone. The other three plans and their aims were:

- Operation Turtle—the main breakout attack was to be a thrust along the Via Anziate to Campoleone and the junction of Highway 7, near Lake Albano in the Alban Hills.

- Operation Crawdad—an offensive aimed at the village of Ardea near the coast, twelve miles northwest of Anzio. Although this was the shortest route to Rome, it not only lacked a favorable road net, but the terrain was unsuitable for the employment of armor. Known as the Practica di Mare, this was the sector that Kesselring had briefly considered using for his counteroffensive but had ruled out because of its proximity to the sea and Allied naval gunfire.
- Operation Grasshopper—an attack eastward from the vicinity of Littoria on the right flank of the beachhead. It was never considered anything more than an emergency operation to achieve a linkup in the event the Fifth Army units advancing from the Liri Valley ran into trouble and a breakthrough was required.[32]

Buffalo became the focal point of the renewed controversy between Alexander and his two army commanders. Both Leese and Clark began acting like prima donnas more interested in their own personal agendas than what was good for the Allied effort. Leese was proving a disappointment as Eighth Army commander, and during the planning for Diadem the two quarreled over the boundary line between their armies along the Liri Valley and north of Rome, each maintaining they had been allotted insufficient space in which to deploy their forces.[33]

Clark's fixation with capturing Rome had by this point turned into an obsession, and it was to color his thinking badly during the planning for the May offensives. What Alexander, Harding, and now Truscott had cooked up was the very antithesis of what Clark had in mind. As the U.S. official history records:

> General Clark, no longer considering the beachhead a holding action as he had during the winter, saw Truscott's corps as the potential spearhead of a Fifth Army drive on Rome. The Alban Hills had become in Clark's eyes a gateway rather than a barrier to Rome. Moreover, as long as the enemy held the hills in strength a threat remained to the flank of any thrust from the beachhead in the direction of Valmontone and Highway 6. Clark believed that his forces should secure the Alban Hills before attempting to cut off the Tenth Army's right wing at Valmontone.[34]

Valmontone and Operation Buffalo had absolutely no place in Clark's priorities. Not only would it take the main force he intended to use to seize Rome away from the city, but he maintained then and after the war that there were too many other escape routes open to the Tenth Army, and the result would be that the Allies would be unable to bag a significant number of German troops. "Alexander's desire for the thrust on Valmontone had, in Clark's view, been dictated mainly by an expectation that it would help to loosen up German resistance opposite the Eighth Army and enable the latter to accelerate its advance up the Liri-Sacco Valley. For Clark that was insufficient to justify the risks to his Fifth Army inherent in Alexander's plan."[35]

The intentions of Alexander and Harding went way beyond whatever help the attack might have been to Leese and were known to Clark, whose public reasons for objecting to the Valmontone attack masked the true purpose of his opposition: Rome. Any operation that took VI Corps away from winning the race for Rome was to be resisted. The thought of Oliver Leese and the British Eighth Army robbing Clark of the liberation of Rome was abhorrent and as long as he remained Fifth Army commander would be opposed by every means at his disposal.

Clark could cite the desires of George Marshall as ample justification for placing the capture of Rome above all else. The American chief of staff considered the Eternal City a great prize and saw in the British proposal to scrap Anvil a threat to reduce its capture to a low priority. And, as the official history notes, Clark believed that Diadem placed Leese in a better position to win a race for Rome, unless VI Corps concentrated its breakout offensive north into the Alban Hills and then directly into Rome along the axis of Highway 7. Then, and only then, Fifth Army might win the "race." "Moreover, in addition to winning the race Clark was very much concerned about reaching Rome before the beginning of Operation OVERLORD, as George Marshall had frequently and pointedly urged him to do."[36]

Thus, at least in Clark's mind, the forthcoming operations had been reduced to a simple circumstance: how to win the race for Rome. All else he considered secondary. After Clark learned of Alexander's intent to attack Valmontone, his diary entries for May 5 reflected his intense commitment to becoming the first into Rome: "I know factually that there are interests brewing for the Eighth Army to take Rome, and I might as well let Alexander know now that if he attempts any thing of that kind he will have another all-out battle on his hands; namely, with me."[37]

When Alexander at one point told Clark that he wanted the Eighth Army at least to take part in the capture of Rome, the Fifth Army commander was irate. In an astonishing admission in his postwar interview with official historian Sidney T. Mathews: "[Clark said] he told Alexander if he [Alexander] gave him [Clark] such an order he would refuse to obey it and if Eighth Army tried to advance on Rome, Clark said he would have his troops fire on the Eighth Army." According to Clark, Alexander backed down and never pressed the issue again. After the war Alexander denied Clark's version.[38]

Truscott, on the other hand, was delighted when Alexander fully backed Operation Buffalo when he was briefed at Truscott's HQ on May 5. According to Truscott: "General Alexander, charming gentleman and magnificent soldier that he was, let me know very quietly and firmly that there was only one direction in which the attack should or would be launched, and that was from Cisterna to cut Highway 6 in the vicinity of Valmontone in the rear of the German main forces."[39]

His feelings notwithstanding, Truscott was duty bound to report his conversation to Clark, and his message to the Fifth Army commander that night noted that Alexander had made it abundantly clear, "when I informed him of the four plans on which I am working, . . . that I was paying too much attention to alternate plans. He said the only attack he envisaged from the beachhead is the Cisterna-Cori-[Valmontone] attack. He does not consider that any other attacks will attain worthwhile results. He advised me to concentrate on plans for the [Buffalo] attack and said that if and when he ordered the attack, he would give me every support that I considered necessary. . . . He [also] informed me he had reserved to himself the decision as to the time of launching the attack from the [Anzio] bridgehead."[40]

When Clark learned of Alexander's visit he was irate. According to his diary:

> I phoned Lemnitzer [Alexander's U.S. deputy chief of staff] and told him how deeply I resented Alexander's issuing instructions to my subordinate commanders, particularly those that are in conflict with mine. . . . When Alexander came on the phone I told him I had received a radio [message] from Truscott which thoroughly astounded me because Truscott reported that he had issued instructions to him which were contrary to mine, and Truscott, being confused, asked me for clarification. I told Alexander that if Truscott's report was correct I resented deeply his issuing any instructions to my subordinates; that if he did not like the manner in which I was carrying on the functions of the VI Corps he should issue any orders to the contrary through me and that under no circumstances would I tolerate his direct dealings with subordinates.[41]

This was the perfect opportunity for Alexander to have asserted himself in a situation in which his authority was being openly challenged by a subordinate. Clark had cleverly avoided directly challenging the Buffalo plan and limited his complaint to one of military protocol. Alexander certainly ought to have recognized Clark's protestations as a ploy to discredit Buffalo and acted accordingly. While it was Clark's prerogative to complain that Alexander should not have bypassed him, it was equally within the Fifteenth Army Group commander's purview to issue orders and guidance. In fact, it was his duty to have done so. Nevertheless, instead of reiterating his earlier instructions to Truscott that the Valmontone attack was to take priority, Alexander backed down in the face of Clark's wrath. A more forceful general would long since have brought Clark into line, but Alexander was not about to change his modus operandi at this late stage of the war. Instead of answering this blatant challenge to his authority, Alexander hedged and in doing so left Clark with the whip hand.

Throughout the planning for the two offensives Clark had again and again expressed his uncertainty (and his displeasure) over the direction of an exploitation until the enemy reaction to Diadem could be determined. He was equally aware that "Alexander held an almost single-minded devotion to a drive from the beachhead through the German stronghold of Cisterna to Valmontone. Throughout the planning period, Clark's freedom to consider alternative plans had been facilitated by the failure of Alexander to issue a direct written order, even though he had expounded the general concept of the Valmontone maneuver at several [command] conferences. Clark himself had expressed no opinion at these conferences about Alexander's concept."[42] Even when the written order did come, in the form of Alexander's operations order for Diadem and Buffalo, Clark had laid the foundation for implementing his own plan and that plan had nothing to do with Valmontone.

At a planning conference held during the first week of April Alexander had clearly outlined his intentions in writing[43] to the army commanders. Diadem was to commence on May 10, and VI Corps was to be prepared to launch its breakout offensive on as little as twenty-four hours' notice. The offensive was to be aimed in the direction of Cisterna-Cori-Valmontone. Its object was the destruction of the German Tenth Army and the withdrawal of the remnants of the Tenth and Fourteenth armies north of Rome.

From the outset Alexander had made it explicitly clear that although Diadem and Buffalo were separate plans, the aims of each were closely linked. As the U.S. official historian notes: "General Alexander described the coming offensive in terms of a one-two punch, with the Eighth and Fifth Armies throwing the first punch on the southern front and the Fifth Army's VI Corps the second punch—a left hook from the Anzio beachhead."[44] The attack from the Anzio beachhead was to be Alexander and Harding's "most important weapon of opportunity, to be launched when the situation was fluid."[45] When the 15th Army Group operations order was issued on May 5—the same day Alexander verbally confirmed his intentions to Truscott—it explicitly directed that VI Corps was to cut Highway 6 at Valmontone.[46]

Nevertheless, the following day Clark made his displeasure with Alexander and Buffalo known in person when he informed Truscott that "the capture of Rome is the only important objective." To Truscott it seemed that Clark "was fearful that the British were laying devious plans to be first in Rome."[47] Clark made it clear that no matter what Alexander wanted, Truscott was to be prepared to undertake any of the four existing plans. Under the cloak of flexibility there was to be no commitment to any plan, regardless of Alexander's wishes.

In the days that followed Clark's shrill criticism of Alexander continued. The final command briefing on May 1 was "marked by bickering and mounting tension."[48] At another meeting on May 6, Clark complained of "being embarrassed" by Alexander when he told Truscott that except for Buffalo the other plans were a "sheer waste of time." Clark also argued that the VI Corps attack could not begin with less than forty-eight-hour notice. "Alexander immediately jumped to the conclusion that I was not all out for the attack; that I did not approve of his plans. I assured him the Fifth Army attack would be as aggressive as any plan or attack he had ever been in or read of." According to Clark:

> I told Alexander that I wanted to attack out of the beachhead with everything I had; that if conditions were right I wanted to attack towards Cori but that what I was guarding against was pre-conceived ideas as to what exactly was to be done and that I felt that he and Harding had such pre-conceived ideas. I told him that there was a chance for a great victory if we played our cards right and did not attack prematurely. He kept pulling on me the idea that we were to annihilate the entire German Army and did it so many times that I told him that I did not believe that we had too many chances to do that; that the Boche were too smart. He again seized the opportunity to accuse the Americans of lack of aggressiveness. I was disgusted and disappointed with my conference. . . . I told him that I had directed Truscott to give first priority to the Cori attack but that he would continue plans for the attack to the west of the Colli Laziali. . . . I am thoroughly disgusted with him and his attitude.[49]

Thus were sown the seeds of one of the great unresolved controversies of the war. Nothing Alexander said or did swayed Clark's adamant belief that he should resist what was to his mind a British plot to deny him the glittering prize of the liberation of Rome. From Clark's diaries the full extent of this determination can now be fully understood for the first time.

Clark's shrill opposition was nothing less than insubordination, and, as Graham and Bidwell accurately point out: "Valmontone was not open for bargaining, for it was integral to the whole plan . . . at that moment Alexander should have dropped on Clark like the proverbial leopard from a tree, but alas, though Alexander was a lion, he was no leopard. As usual he soothed and temporised."[50]

Alexander had been given fair warning that Clark would do everything in his power to thwart the Buffalo plan, including outright disobedience of the Fifteenth Army Group commander's orders. Yet Alexander did nothing to head off what seemed certain to be a major crisis when Diadem began a few days hence.

During April and early May, in one of the most complex maneuvers of its kind ever undertaken, the Fifth and Eighth armies completed the difficult task of realigning themselves for Diadem without revealing their intentions. The Fifth Army was shifted to the Allied left flank, north of the Garigliano River, and given the mission of turning Kesselring's right flank. The main effort was assigned to Leese's Eighth Army, which was to launch a massive break-in offensive into the heart of the Liri Valley. It was to be a classic military operation, with the break-in attack to be carried out by the infantry and the exploitation of their success by the massed armor lurking in the rear, which would ram through the opened breech. Once this gigantic battering ram was able to rupture the Gustav Line, the damage to the German Tenth Army would be fatal.[51]

The full measure of the success of the Allied preparations was that despite numerous potential sources of intelligence, the Germans never detected Allied intentions. Thanks largely to the realism of the deception operation, Kesselring became convinced that the Allies were done attacking the Gustav Line and would settle for another Anzio-type attack near Rome or in the north near Livorno.

As the date for Diadem approached, German intelligence remained ignorant of the timing and scope of the Allied offensive, even though on May 3 observers in the Tenth Army noted the presence behind the Garigliano River of white engineer tape to guide the infantry forward and the even more ominous presence of bridging equipment being unloaded. Three days later German patrols took note of the fact that Allied outposts in both the Fifth and Eighth Army sectors were no longer being manned. During the first ten days of May a mere fifteen Allied soldiers were captured on the Cassino front, and what little information they were able to give proved inconclusive and misleading.[52] "The day before the Allied offensive began, the two corps commanders blandly predicted that nothing would happen in the immediate future."[53]

The success of the Allied deception was borne out by the disposition of von Senger's XIV Panzer Corps. Still believing that the main Allied effort would come along the vulnerable Tyrrhenian Coast, the German commanders had shifted one-fifth of the corps infantry, one-fourth of the artillery, and all of its tanks to protect against a landing behind their lines and a thrust north along Highway 7.[54]

Up to the final moment the Germans remained almost completely unaware of the great offensive to begin the night of May 11. To the contrary, the German mood was one of utter complacency. Von Vietinghoff was so unconcerned that he left his headquarters early that evening and flew to Germany to be personally decorated by Hitler with the Oak Leaf Cluster to the Knight's Cross. Von Senger was still in Germany on a thirty-day leave; General Westphal, Kesselring's chief of staff, and Colonel von Altenstadt, von Senger's chief of staff, were both on leave and unavailable. "Thus, the Fifth Army attack was destined to strike a corps minus its regular commander and chief of staff, an army minus its commanding general, and an army group minus its chief of staff. This extraordinary situation . . . was the fruit of their painstaking cover plan."[55]

Allied preparations included the most massive buildup of artillery ever undertaken in the war. Some seventy-five thousand artillerymen of 124 battalions, consisting of more than fifteen hundred guns, were preparing to fire several million rounds of ammunition in support of Diadem. On May 11, 1944, Kesselring was shocked to learn the inaccuracy of his estimate of Allied intentions when this colossal artillery announced the start of the great Diadem offensive with thunderous bombardments that one German survivor described as "a blaze of flame down the valley . . . ear-splitting, screaming" that made the ground tremble under its sheer force.[56]

PART V

Breakout

There is always an easy solution to every human problem—neat, plausible and wrong.

—H. L. MENCKEN

Forward, always forward. The hour of LIBERATION IS NEAR.

—GENERAL ALPHONSE JUIN

20

The Great Allied Offensive

The decisive battle is imminent. We must and we
will succeed.

GENERAL EBERHARD VON MACKENSEN

Even for the Germans, who had
grown used to everything but the kitchen sink being thrown at them,
Diadem came as a terrific shock. The opening barrage had been timed
to coincide with the nightly relief of the German forward positions. In
his superb account of the Cassino battles, historian John Ellis quotes a
Canadian officer who described its intensity as:

> hard to believe. In those few miles between the hills, a thousand guns
> suddenly let go as one, and then they kept on firing. We'd never seen or
> heard or imagined anything quite like this. You could see the flashes of
> nearby guns and you could hear the thunder of dozens and hundreds more
> on every side and you could only imagine what sort of Hell was falling on
> the German lines. It damn near deafened you.[1]

During the first six days of Diadem, the artillery supporting the British
13th Corps fired an incredible total of 476,413 rounds of artillery in
support of its operations to rupture German defenses at the mouth of
the Liri Valley.[2] Despite the great surprise and the vast edge in Allied
firepower, however, the first three days of Diadem were ominously
reminiscent of previous failed operations. General Wladislaw Anders's
2d Polish Corps was the first to feel the sting still left in the German
tail. Exceptionally well led and highly motivated, the Free Poles, like the

Free French, were among the most effective members of the Allied contingent in Italy. Von Vietinghoff had concentrated the LI Mountain Corps to repel their expected attack, which was once again aimed at capturing the abbey. The Poles fought valiantly against Heidrich's equally determined paratroopers along the rocky slopes of Monastery Hill around the abbey but took heavy losses in yet another ill-fated attempt to succeed where others before them had failed.

However, it was in the Liri Valley that the operation was most threatened. Here, Lieutenant General Sidney Kirkman's 13th British Corps spent three hellish days establishing a bridgehead across the Rapido and Gari rivers.[3] The Germans fought with fury, aided by a thick fog that caused utter chaos as the leading assault units of the 8th Indian Division became lost and confused. Even the white tape normally so effective in guiding men forward at night became useless; units were forced to creep forward with each soldier grasping the belt of the man ahead of him to avoid getting lost.

The opening phase of Diadem thus had all the trappings of another "bloody river," as the Germans took full advantage of the weather and confusion to make life difficult for the 13th Corps. The Indians found, as the Texans of the U.S. 36th Division had before them, that their greatest problem was emplacing bridges across the Rapido under heavy German fire. Plans quickly broke down in the fog, and one 8th Indian Division beachmaster actually lost his river and had to be shown where it flowed.[4] In other instances some of the mines previously laid by the Texans and their British replacements in the front line were not located and removed, with deadly results.

Despite the obstacles, many men rose to the occasion. One in particular was Private H. W. Grainger of the 2d/4th Battalion, the Hampshire Regiment, who swam naked across the swiftly flowing river three times to carry lines across and then assisted men ashore from their boats and rafts. Although Grainger survived the German fire the night of May 11–12, he was killed on May 12.[5]

Although the British managed to establish a slender toehold across the river, there could be no exploitation until there were bridges for the armor and supporting artillery to cross. Until then the 13th Corps bridgehead remained tenuous at best. It took three days of tough fighting to gain a firm foothold in the Liri Valley north of the Rapido, but by May 13 the British 4th Division had managed to move five battalions of infantry and two tank battalions across the Rapido and had enlarged the bridgehead nearly a mile. There were signs that the German defenders were beginning to crack under the new and unpleasant presence of tanks, which for the first time in the Italian campaign were able to operate on firm, dry ground in the Liri Valley in support of the infantry.[6] The 13th Corps was now poised to join hands with the Poles, provided their second attempt against the abbey and its surrounding heights was successful. The Germans continued to view the Cassino offensive as merely a prelude to a breakout offensive from Anzio in conjunction with another amphibious assault elsewhere to the north by forces standing by in Naples and North Africa.[7]

On May 16 the 13th Corps had suffered nearly four thousand casualties but had driven a wedge nearly three miles deep into the German defenses of the Liri Valley. Even though the Germans still held the Cassino heights overlooking the valley, the British were able to operate effectively in the valley by deluging the heights with smoke. That night Alexander felt sufficiently confident of the outcome of Diadem to signal Brooke: "The battle is progressing steadily forward . . . we can now claim that we have definitely broken the Gustav Line."[8] Equally sanguine was Leese, who ordered the commitment of the Canadian 1st Corps the following morning. The Canadians were to pass through the Indian positions and begin attacking up the southern portion of the Liri Valley.

Kesselring, on the other hand, was at the point where irrevocable decisions that would effect the outcome of the campaign had to be made at once. Several hours earlier Kesselring and von Vietinghoff had this telephone conversation:

KESSELRING: I consider withdrawal to the Senger [Line] position as necessary.
VIETINGHOFF: Then it will be necessary to begin the withdrawal north of the Liri. Tanks have broken through there.
KESSELRING: And how is the situation further north [the sector north of the Abbey, along Highway 6]?
VIETINGHOFF: There were about one hundred tanks in Schulz's area [a battle group defending Highway 6 around Aquino].
KESSELRING: Then we shall have to give up Cassino.
VIETINGHOFF: Yes.[9]

Within the hour the war diary of the Tenth Army recorded the issuance of directives for a general withdrawal to the Hitler Line.[10]* LI Corps, which was defending the left flank of the Gustav Line (that is, the sector north of the Liri River through the Cassino positions), was ordered to withdraw to the Hitler Line the following night. The XIV Panzer Corps sector remained Kesselring's principal worry, and his worst fears became reality as the news of a breakthrough by the French became known.

*Originally called the Hitler Line, the defensive positions running across the Liri Valley near Pontecorvo and Aquino had been renamed the Senger Line in January 1944 for the commander of the XIV Panzer Corps responsible for its defense, Fridolin von Senger. Even so, most accounts refer to it as the Hitler Line.

The U.S. II Corps was assigned to penetrate the extreme left flank near the mouth of the Garigliano, where McCreery's corps had come so close to success in January, only to be denied it by Clark's failure to take advantage of the bridgehead north of the river. Although a regiment of the 88th Division succeeded in capturing an important hill mass north of the Garigliano, the main corps attack farther east met bitter resistance from XIV Panzer Corps and stalled.

On the II Corps right flank, Juin's French corps faced formidable terrain north of the Garigliano, but by dint of a bold plan and highly imaginative maneuvering the French accomplished precisely what Harding intended. In a series of hard-fought battles they not only took the heights dominating the western slopes of the Liri Valley, but by May 21 had driven as far as Pontecorvo on the valley's northwestern rim.

The Germans had vastly underrated both the combat strength and the ingenuity of the French, with disastrous results. Of all the senior Allied commanders, there was no more daring or imaginative tactician than Alphonse Juin, who grew up in Algeria, graduated first in his class at the French military academy at St. Cyr, and honed his talents in command not of elite French regiments but of the Algerian Light Infantry. Badly wounded in the right arm in World War I, Juin was noted for his left-handed salute.[11]

Among the more memorable mistakes of the Allied high command in the Mediterranean was its paranoiac distrust of the French in Italy, who were regarded mainly as reserve troops of questionable ability. Among those holding to this faulty judgment were a number of senior officers within AFHQ, who cynically viewed the French as little better than expendable cannon fodder. Three of the four divisions of the Corps Expéditionnaire Français consisted of colonial troops plus the equivalent of a brigade of Goumiers, hardy soldiers who found themselves fighting in terrain ideally suited to the talents of men from the Atlas Mountains of Morocco.[12]

Juin's career had been marked by brilliance, and among the senior Allied field commanders his combat experience was unexcelled except perhaps by that of Freyberg and Alexander. During the battle of France in 1940 Juin's division had fought without letup until it ran out of ammunition. Although released by the Germans after Pétain's personal intervention, Juin declined an offer to join the Vichy government and instead replaced Weygand as commander in chief of the French Army in North Africa. He was among those who enthusiastically joined the Allies after Torch. Both Rommel and Kesselring held Juin in the highest esteem, as did Mark Clark, who warmed to the French general in a way he never did with any of the British commanders. Even so, in Italy Juin was obliged to overcome Alexander's resistance to his pleas that his

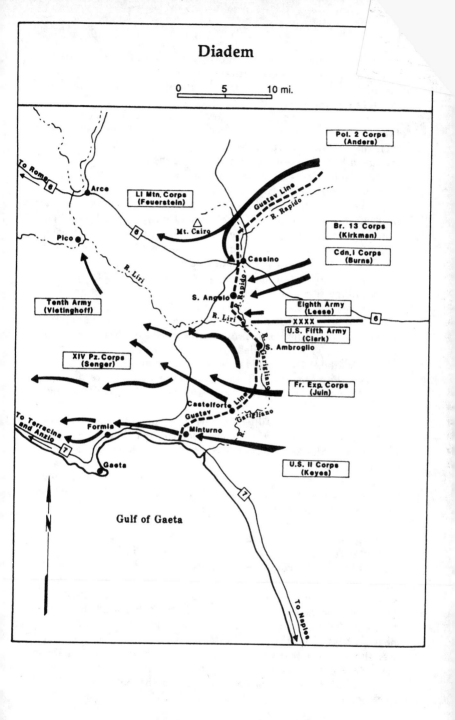

Diadem

0   5   10 mi.

To Rome

Arce

LI Mtn. Corps
(Feuerstein)

Pol. 2 Corps
(Anders)

Gustav Line

R. Rapido

Mt. Cairo

Pico

R. Liri

Cassino

Br. 13 Corps
(Kirkman)

Cdn. I Corps
(Burns)

S. Angelo

R. Rapido

R. Liri

Tenth Army
(Vietinghoff)

XXXX

Eighth Army
(Leese)

U.S. Fifth Army
(Clark)

S. Ambroglio

XIV Pz. Corps
(Senger)

R. Garigliano

Fr. Exp. Corps
(Juin)

Castelforte

Gustav Line

R. Garigliano

To Terracina
and Anzio

Formia

Minturno

U.S. II Corps
(Keyes)

Gaeta

Gulf of Gaeta

N

To Naples

corps fight as a unified force.[13] And, as Graham and Bidwell observe, "Juin had a profound aversion [to] bull-headed frontal attacks against strength . . . and a preference for surprise, the attack on the unexpected line and rapid maneuver."[14]

Juin's superbly executed thrust tore a gaping hole in the right flank of the Gustav Line. With the loss of this vital anchor, the line collapsed when the Poles finally succeeded in capturing the Abbey of Monte Cassino on May 17. With the 13th Corps and the Canadians at last on the move into the heart of the Liri Valley, the long-sought breakthrough was realized.

Moreover, with Monte Cassino in Polish hands, his right flank in shreds after Juin's attacks, and Leese's armor threatening to thrust clear to Rome along Highway 6, Kesselring was left with few options and scant hope of containing the rupture of the Gustav Line. He was forced to rush the 26th Panzer and the 29th Panzer Grenadier Divisions from army group reserve, but these proved to be too little and far too late to redeem the situation at Cassino.

The capture of the abbey by the valiant Poles was the final chapter in the bloody saga of Monte Cassino. During the final seven days of combat to capture this heap of rubble, the terrible cost was 860 Polish dead and nearly 3,000 wounded. After the battle 900 German corpses were recovered.[15] There could be little joy at the sight of the Polish flag flying over the gutted abbey. The carnage of war was truly dreadful, yet across the mountain battlefield masses of red poppies had emerged across the now-silent battlefield.

The defenses of the Hitler Line were bolstered by the arrival of forces withdrawing from the Cassino sector of the Gustav Line, and Leese reported to Alexander on May 19 that it would require a major assault to breach it and that such an attack could not be mounted until the night of May 21–22 by the Canadian 1st Corps.[16] Even though they were aided by the fires of nearly seven hundred guns, which opened the assault by delivering 3,509 shells (some ninety-two tons) of artillery fire in a mere thirty-three minutes the afternoon of May 22,[17] the Canadians fought a brutal series of battles over a three-day period from May 22 to 25 around Pontecorvo and Aquino before finally breaking the Hitler Line at a considerable cost in lives. There was unusually heavy aerial activity, with more than two thousand sorties flown by Allied tactical aircraft on May 24 alone. Two days earlier B-17 Flying Fortress heavy bombers had flown missions in both the Anzio and Cassino sectors. On May 25 the Luftwaffe came out fighting during one of the heaviest days of aerial combat in the Italian campaign. The Germans went home losers after Allied airmen and gunners destroyed thirty-two Luftwaffe fighters in the air and on the ground.[18]

Juin and the French solved the problem of the southern end of the

Hitler Line during the fierce battles following their capture of the heights overlooking the Liri Valley. The details of the French triumph are too lengthy for this account, except to note that it was "one of the most remarkable feats of a war more remarkable for bloody attrition than skill, and deserves to be better known. . . . It was orchestrated with extraordinary skill."[19] Both Clark and Juin were critical of the slowness of the Eighth Army in attacking the defenses of the Hitler Line, and in his postwar memoirs Juin argued that the Eighth Army had squandered a chance to outflank and envelope the right wing of the Tenth Army on May 17 by not pressing harder to crack its defenses while the line was relatively vulnerable.[20]

Well before breaching the Hitler Line Alexander had decided the time had come to implement the second phase of the great Allied offensive, the breakout by VI Corps from the Anzio beachhead toward Valmontone. Brigadier General Lemnitzer delivered Alexander's order to Clark:

> The C-in-C directs that the attack from the Anzio bridgehead on CORI and VALMONTONE is to be launched on the night of 21/22 May or on the morning of 22 May according to whether you have decided on a night or day attack.[21]

Clark wrote that he was outraged. "I was shocked . . . to think that a decision of this importance would have been made without reference to me. I sent that word back to General Alexander who made the weak excuse that he felt that we had discussed it for the past three days."[22] Clark's complaint was partly on military grounds (that the attack was premature until more German reserves were committed to defending the Hitler Line), but mainly the result of pique with Alexander. The implications in his diary that he had been cut out of the planning process are without foundation. He had known of Alexander's intentions for the better part of two months, and the confrontation with Alexander two weeks earlier had changed nothing other than to suggest that Clark would reluctantly comply but felt free to alter his orders if, in his opinion, Buffalo failed to trap the German Tenth Army. His instructions to Truscott the previous day had been a repetition of his earlier guidance: Carry out Buffalo as instructed but be prepared to shift to another axis of attack on short notice if so ordered.

Clark met with Alexander and Harding the next day (May 20) and the discussion centered on Diadem. "He has always been opposed to my southern effort," complained Clark immediately afterward in his diary, "and he apologized today, stating that he never dreamed that we could make the progress we have through the mountains. . . . I believe that if the Eighth Army will attack the Hitler Line in the Pontecorvo region in the next two days, we hit it north from Pico all-out with all our forces and [from] the [Anzio] bridgehead the next morning, [we] will fold up the German Army in Italy."[23] In light of Clark's contradictory actions in the ensuing days, this was an amazing admission. If Clark is to be believed, for once he was thinking not of Rome, but of ending this frustrating campaign then and there by destroying Army Group C.

Nonetheless, it is important to keep in mind that whenever Clark received an order from Alexander with which he did not agree, he would often term it a "suggestion," thus rationalizing that he was free to ignore it. Graham and Bidwell believe that Clark was suspicious that a quick penetration of the Hitler Line might result in a sudden dash to Rome by the Eighth Army. "He had no intention of taking any action that might accelerate the dogged but slow advance of the Canadians and the 13th Corps, whose lack of progress he continually decried."[24] Moreover, Clark had been ordered by Alexander on May 18 to be prepared to outflank LI Corps by attacking north with II Corps and the Corps Expéditionnaire Français and could easily have pressed Alexander harder for this option.

Clark need not have worried, for Leese was no Patton or Juin, and his reaction was as predictable as it was ponderous. The attack on the Hitler Line would be planned like any other set-piece battle. Since assuming command of the Eighth Army six months earlier, he had shown no inclination to either audacity or initiative, and in failing to press his advantage as early as May 17 he had ensured that the battle for the Hitler Line would be unimaginative and bloody. It was the first of several opportunities that were lost during the drive for Rome.

At Anzio, despite Clark's earlier complaints, Truscott was anxious to open the Buffalo offensive. His preparations to carry out any of the four plans had been meticulous. The logistic aspects alone were colossal. In great secrecy hundreds of emplacements were dug for the supporting artillery and from six hundred to one thousand rounds per gun were moved into concealed positions without the Germans detecting what was afoot. Some were emplaced within five hundred yards of the front and cleverly camouflaged. More than one thousand truckloads of ammunition had to be moved forward merely to supply the initial requirements of the U.S. 1st Armored Division.[25]

Success depended as much on concealment and deception as it did upon a sound tactical plan. As Truscott writes, not only were thousands of rounds of ammunition moved forward but "miles of telephone lines were laid. Assembly areas were selected, routes reconnoitered and orders were in readiness for the movement of troops, tanks and supporting weapons over our congested road net. This would have been a difficult problem under any circumstances; but in the confined area of the beachhead with its restricted road net it was a staggering one."[26]

Traffic control alone required the oversight of an orchestra conductor and would have been difficult enough in daylight. For the two nights preceding the opening of the offensive, massive troop and vehicle movements took place as the U.S. 3d Infantry and 1st Armored Divisions got into position to open their attacks.

An important aspect of the preparations for Buffalo was the successful deception that hoodwinked the Germans as to Allied intentions. For weeks Truscott had been conditioning the Germans to believe that Allied artillery fire in the early hours of each day was nothing more than harassment. Gradually, instead of replying in kind, the Germans began to treat these daily displays as typical examples of Allied prolifigacy.

Another operation involved lulling the Germans into believing that the movement of Harmon's tanks was routine. Every evening and morning for several weeks a number of tanks would suddenly dash forward to the front lines, fire off a load of ammunition, then beat a hasty retreat. At first this drew fire, but the Germans soon found that doing so exposed their gun positions to counter fire from Allied guns, and they began contemptuously to ignore these forays as another wasteful American idiosyncrasy. It was precisely what Harmon wanted them to believe. During the days prior to the attack, more and more tanks would appear at the front, but the Germans never seemed to notice that not all returned. Over a period of days Harmon was able to emplace a large number of tanks under camouflage nets in gullies and depressions. His men ate cold rations and remained motionless, some for several days, awaiting zero hour.[27]

After one postponement the operation was set for the predawn of May 23. The night of May 22–23 was starlit and showed promise of a fine, clear day to come. The guns had fallen silent as 150,000 men tensely awaited the opening salvos that would mark the start of the long-awaited breakout from the despised Anzio beachhead. As it always does before such battles, time passed at a snail-like pace. Finally, when the clock read 0545 hours, it began. After months of stalemate the Allies were at last set to take the initiative and win the battle for Rome.

As at Cassino, the early morning calm was shattered by the thunder of more than a thousand Allied guns, tanks, and mortars, most of which were aimed at the ruins of Cisterna, the key jumping-off position for the Buffalo offensive. Truscott later described how "the ground quivered and trembled . . . towering clouds of smoke and dust broke through the pall about Cisterna as bombs [from Allied aircraft] crashed into the town and enemy positions . . . [then] the artillery began anew. H hour had come and the battle was on."[28]

Ernie Harmon was from the school of commanders who believed that Tennyson's "theirs not to reason why" was an anachronism. He went to extraordinary lengths to prepare his 1st Armored troops. Every man in every unit had been thoroughly briefed. "We did more than tell the troops the plan of attack; we made them study it." Platoon and company commanders were taken aloft over the beachhead in small aircraft to enable them to study the route of advance from the air. Harmon also had a fifty-foot-square terrain model constructed that contained every road, bridge, river, and village. Above it was a boardwalk and his men came in shifts to study it in detail: "Day after day I would see them, using sticks and twigs as pointers tracing the routes their units were to pursue."[29]

As the artillery preparations slackened the ground attack began. Along the Moletta River sector two British infantry divisions, the 1st and 5th Infantry, mounted limited offensives. The mission of both divisions was essentially to anchor the Allied left flank while the U.S. 45th Division drove northwest across familiar terrain toward the Factory and Campoleone. Although the two divisions launched diversionary attacks during the night of May 22 and into the next day, they were to contribute little else to the offensive or the capture of Rome.

The breakout from the Anzio beachhead was essentially an American operation. Alexander had ordered Truscott to assign the two British divisions the task of protecting the VI Corps left flank and, if at all possible, to avoid committing it to heavy combat. The battered 1st Division was a spent force, and the performance of the 5th Division, which had arrived in March, had never earned Clark's respect. As the offensive progressed, Clark's disenchantment grew. "The 5th Division is poorly led . . . [and] I have continually talked with my British commanders in an effort to energize them into an attack. There is no attack left in them . . . the 5th Division is poorly led by [Major] General Gregson-Ellis. He has no offensive spirit . . . [even though] I believe there is only a shell in front of them."[30] Not for the first time did Truscott disagree with Clark's judgment, later writing of Gregson-Ellis, whom he had known previously in England: "He had a first-class mind and was one of the ablest staff officers I knew. He was fearless."[31]

After months of fighting at Anzio, Clark was displaying evidence that he had yet to grasp the full extent of the British experience. Nor was he prepared to accept what the postwar testimony of Kesselring and other German commanders would establish—namely that the British did what was asked of them by successfully tying down several German formations that were badly needed elsewhere.

Between the 45th and 3d divisions was Harmon's 1st Armored, whose mission was to rupture the German defenses and drive toward Valmontone, while at the same time protecting the left flank of the 3d Division advance on Cisterna. The division attacked along a very narrow two-thousand-yard front with two combat commands (eight com-

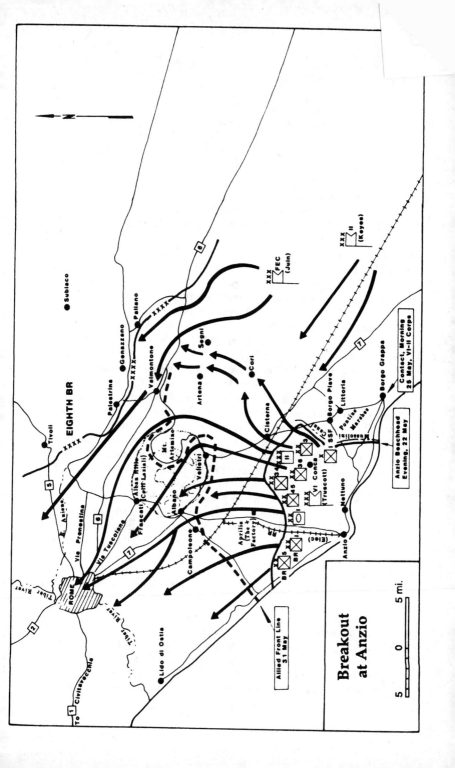

Breakout at Anzio

Allied Front Line 31 May

Anzio Beachhead Evening, 22 May

Contact, Morning 25 May, VI-II Corps

5   0   5 mi.

panies of Shermans) rumbling forward abreast across relatively open terrain well suited for the employment of armor. Behind them came four battalions of infantry supported by light tanks to eradicate pockets of resistance in the event it became necessary to—in one of the favorite sayings of American tankers—"haul ass and bypass." Once the initial objective of the Rome-Campoleone-Cisterna rail line was secured, Harmon's mission was to advance to the base of the Alban Hills around Highway 7, followed by a drive into the Velletri gap toward the town of Artena, a mountain village located only three miles south of Valmontone and Highway 6.

The most difficult task was given to "Iron Mike" O'Daniel's veteran 3d Division. The plan was a classic double envelopment. While the 7th Infantry Regiment advanced in a frontal attack to fix the attention of Cisterna's defenders (elements of two infantry divisions, the 362d and 715th), the other two regiments (the 30th on the left and the 15th on the right) were to attack the town. Once Cisterna fell, the 3d Division was to advance and capture Cori, then turn north and complete the drive into the Valmontone gap and Highway 6. On the extreme right flank of the beachhead, Frederick's Special Service Force was charged with securing the 3d Division's right flank throughout the advance.[32]

Harmon had vehemently objected to Truscott's plan, arguing that his armor could be best employed in its more conventional role of a reserve force to exploit a breakthrough and that its use as the breakthrough force would result in the loss of a hundred tanks in the first half hour of the offensive. It was "a crazy idea," said the outspoken Harmon.[33] Truscott well understood that this was an unusual mission for an armored division, but Cisterna worried him—and for good reason. The Germans had turned its narrow streets and stone ruins into a formidable strongpoint, and any delay in seizing Cisterna would threaten a successful thrust into the Valmontone gap. Truscott had no illusions as to the difficulty faced by his former division. "We knew its strength from bitter experience." Moreover, the VI Corps commander knew only too well that Clark was actively seeking any plausible excuse to kill Buffalo in favor of Operation Turtle, the offensive toward Rome via the Via Anziate and Highway 7.

Although artillery and antitank guns were always a problem, the gravest menace facing the attackers was the destructive force of the German minefields. During the stalemate thousands of mines had been placed across every possible avenue of approach by both the Allies and the Germans, and they quickly began to take a toll. Harmon's lead tanks had a strange-looking homemade device attached to the front called a "snake." This was a four-hundred-foot-long series of unwieldy steel pipes filled with explosives. They were towed to the front and then pushed by a tank into a minefield, where they were detonated by machine-gun fire. In practice tests the snakes had cleared gaps fifteen feet wide and exploded mines as deep as five feet in the ground.[34]

On the first day of the offensive, the 1st Armored managed to advance only as far as the railway line and a low-lying ridge to the north before being halted by fresh minefields and the fire from nearby German antitank guns. German resistance and the minefields had proved difficult. By noon Combat Command B alone had lost twenty-three tanks and seven tank destroyers. At day's end a young second lieutenant had won a Medal of Honor, but 35 men had been killed and another 137 wounded.[35] Total tank losses for the first day of Buffalo were eighty-six tanks and tank destroyers.[36]

German losses were heavy. The worst hit was the LXXVI Panzer Corps. The 362d Infantry Division lost 50 percent of its fighting strength the first day and two of the regiments of the 715th Infantry Division were severely mauled. Von Mackensen pleaded to no avail with Kesselring to shorten his right flank by withdrawing troops from the Moletta River–Factory sector and shifting them to the LXXVI Panzer Corps front around Cisterna. The holding attacks by the British had done their job, and Kesselring's refusal reopened the long-standing rift between the two German commanders. Kesselring did order the veteran Hermann Göring Division to return to Anzio from Livorno with all possible speed.[37]

Cisterna was the key to Buffalo and like angry bees whose hive has been disturbed, the Germans furiously resisted the attacks of the 3d Division. On the left the 30th Regiment encountered a hail of fire from well-entrenched enemy troops firing from strongpoints, gullies, creekbeds, the ruins of farm buildings, and from inside Cisterna itself. The fighting was a violent and bitterly fought series of small-unit engagements. German resistance seemed endless. The crews of 88-mm guns lowered their barrels and fired directly at the infantry; machine guns, mortars, rifles, the ever-present minefields, and concertina wire all contributed to the immensely difficult task of capturing Cisterna.

On the extreme right flank, after successfully advancing to the rail line north of Highway 7, Frederick's First Special Service Force fought off a tank-supported counterattack and was pushed back some seven hundred yards, losing an entire company in the process, most of which were captured. German losses were high, and a captured Forceman later told of German dead piled in long rows near the Mussolini Canal.

At Ponte Rotto the 3d Battalion, 30th Regiment, was pinned down by fire from three machine guns and a mobile 88-mm gun. After enduring half an hour of murderous fire Private First Class John W. Dutko, a BAR (Browning Automatic Rifle) man, had seen enough. "I'm going to get that 88 with my heater [the nickname Dutko gave his BAR]!" he told his squad leader, who witnessed an incredible display of valor during the next few moments.

> Before I could say a word he took off like a ruptured duck. He made the first hundred yards in a dead run. Machine-gun bullets were striking the ground only a foot or two behind him but he was running faster than the krauts could traverse. The kraut 88 crew let a couple of fast shells go at him, but . . . he dived into a shell hole which one of our own guns had conveniently made a split second before he got there. The enemy fire, coupled with our own artillery was the heaviest that I had ever seen in such a small area. The enemy machine gunners converged their fire on the shellhole occupied by PFC Dutko.
>
> After a short rest Dutko jumped from his hole and ran in a wide circle toward the 88-mm gun. . . . By flanking the gun Dutko had succeeded in aligning the machine guns so that only one could fire at him, which it continued to do with long, murderous bursts. After running about 175 yards Dutko hit the dirt and threw a hand grenade into the machine gun pit, killing the two-man crew.

Another eyewitness, Private Charles R. Kelley, who had attempted to follow Dutko, takes up the tale:

> Pfc. Dutko was a madman now. He jumped to his feet and walked toward the 88-mm firing his BAR from his hip. He had apparently forgotten the other two machine guns. . . . When he had gone about halfway to the 88-mm he reached a point within ten yards of the weapon and wiped out the five-man crew with a long burst of fire. Pfc. Dutko then wheeled on the second German machine gun and killed its two man crew with his BAR. The third machine gun opened fire . . . [from] twenty yards away and its first burst wounded him, making him stagger, but like a wounded lion he charged this gun in half run . . . [killing the two-man crew] with a single burst.[38]

Mortally wounded, Dutko staggered and fell across the two dead German gunners. By the time Kelley reached him, Dutko was dead from his wounds. He was later awarded a posthumous Medal of Honor.

Cisterna did not fall on May 23, and the following day the Germans continued to demonstrate that the rubble-strewn town would not be taken without considerably more bloodshed. The 3d Division had drawn the noose tighter around Cisterna, but the 362d Division fought with continued fury even though they were doomed. Meanwhile, as the 3d Division and the First Special Service Force were encircling Cisterna, 1st Armored Division spearheads had thrust nearly to Velletri and Cori.

On the afternoon of May 25 Cisterna finally fell to the 3d Division after nearly three days of brutal combat. The Germans still alive inside the town held out to the bitter end and had to be neutralized building by building. On May 24 another 3d Division soldier, Private James H. Mills of Company F, 15th Infantry, a replacement in only his second day of combat, also won a Medal of Honor. Mills single-handedly captured six German soldiers and then enabled his unit to capture its objective without a single loss by repeatedly exposing himself to enemy fire to create a diversion.[39] In all, there would be four Medals of Honor awarded to soldiers of the 3d Division during what became officially known as the Second Battle of Cisterna.

Nearly sixteen hundred German prisoners were captured by the 3d Division during the three-day battle for Cisterna, most from the 362d Division, which ceased to exist.[40] An equal number were thought to have been killed or wounded. The division had performed poorly when it first arrived at Anzio some months before, but whatever the stain on their reputation, it was erased by their performance in the defense of Cisterna. Despite appalling casualties, the 362d Division had held the shattered town of Cisterna for three grueling days against the hammering of the 3d Division, inflicting heavy losses of 1,400 killed and wounded.[41] Overall American casualties during the first three days of Buffalo were 2,872, including 476 killed. At midday on May 25, 2,640 Germans had been processed into the VI Corps POW cages at Anzio.[42]

Eric Sevareid entered Cisterna soon after the town fell, and he compared its shattered appearance to that of Ypres in World War I. It was difficult even to tell where there had been streets and the military vehicles that passed through the town kicked up great clouds of thick caramel-colored dust on what passed for a main thoroughfare:

> The ruins had the stillness of ancient ruins, but without their dignity. There was a temple, whose roof had fallen in. . . . Across the front was a legend that read: "The Quietness of Christ." A dust cloud drifted away to reveal a buggyload of old men in what had been the central square. They said nothing. They did nothing. They merely sat there and stared with unbelieving eyes. In the little park the palm trees lay blackened and uprooted. Over them a shining white victory statue stood erect on a pedestal. It was the figure of a woman holding aloft a torch in a gesture of triumph. Though her marble head and her torch were gone, in its present attitude of shocked surprise the statue seemed the only vital, living thing within the city.[43]

At virtually the same moment as the long, bloody siege of Cisterna ended, the 1st Armored captured the key town of Cori. With Harmon's tanks at the mouth of the Velletri gap, its reconnaissance units already outside Artena, and the 3d Division and First Special Service Force at the base of the Lepini Mountains outside Cori, the threat posed by Buffalo had become acute. Ryder's 34th Division had secured the Cisterna sector, leaving the 3d Division and the First Special Service Force free to begin exploiting the virtual collapse of the German front.

The prescient Harmon was prepared to do just that. As the division historian writes: "By the end of the second day, the Division had cut off Cisterna, forced the evacuation of Cori, taken 850 prisoners, and reached a good position to exploit the penetration toward the Velletri Gap. Two mine free routes . . . to Highway No. 7 were cleared and marked. . . . The attack was really rolling."[44] Harmon was now ready to commit his reserve, a powerful tank-armored infantry task force under the division reserve commander, Colonel Hamilton H. Howze, to take advantage of what gave evidence of being a wide-open path to Valmontone.[45]

Task Force Howze was to spearhead the division thrust through the Velletri Gap to Valmontone. In the aggressive Howze, Ernie Harmon had picked the right man. Howze, a former cavalry officer and a graduate of West Point (Class of 1930)[46] and a future four-star general, was personally given his orders by Harmon the evening of May 24. At 0640 hours the morning of May 25 Task Force Howze was on the move into the Velletri Gap. The only opposition came from ten or twelve German tanks that were falling back in front of the lead tank battalion. The two sides engaged in occasional long-range duels, which did little damage to either side and proved no impediment to Howze's progress. On his right flank Howze had sent a battalion of tanks across a series of long ridges running perpendicular to the front. Although it was less than ideal tank country, Howze believed it could be negotiated and that the results might prove rewarding.

Howze was right. Along the road running from Cori to Giulianello an enormous column of German vehicles was fleeing northwest. In a postwar speech, Howze described this event:

It had been stopped by the attacks of our aircraft. . . . [Lt. Col. Bogardus S. Cairn's 3d Battalion, 13th Armored Regiment] completed the job, chewing up the vehicles in his immediate vicinity and then putting enfilade fire down to his right rear. There were 15 Mark VI [Tiger] tanks on that road when I drove down it a day or so later, as well as great quantities of guns and half tracks. At the head of our column, which was all mixed up with the destroyed German column . . . there was carnage indeed: bodies and pieces of bodies strewn about among the wrecked and burning vehicles. The air force added further excitement by straffing the entire area, without taint of discrimination, spraying German troops as well as American.[47]

By early afternoon Task Force Howze had advanced deep into the Velletri Gap and had blocked one of the two German escape routes to the northwest of Cisterna, the Cori-Giulianello road. That evening the town was occupied, and Howze recognized that he had struck a soft spot in the German flank that was wide for further exploitation. Howze went personally to the CCB command post, informed his superior, Brigadier General Frank Allen, "and begged that the whole division be diverted into our area. This conclusion seemed obvious. . . . General Allen agreed and relayed the opinion to Division; Division relayed it, approved, to VI Corps."[48] Having isolated the outer links to Rome—Highway 7 and the coastal railway line—the 1st Armored Division was thus poised to cut the most vital link—Highway 6, Valmontone, and the inland railway line—connecting the Tenth with the Fourteenth Army.

To appreciate the extent of the carnage wrought in the Velletri gap on May 25 is to understand just how close VI Corps was to an uncontainable breakout. Air force reports that morning estimated at least six hundred German vehicles were moving through the gap toward Valmontone. Throughout the afternoon the forward ground controller of the XII Tactical Air Command diverted missions to attack these lucrative targets. *"By dusk the air force had scored one of its most resounding triumphs in direct support of ground operations thus far in the Italian campaign* [italics added]."[49]

Reports of the stunning success began flowing through air channels, and by day's end claims were made of 645 tanks and vehicles destroyed and 446 more damaged. For once air force claims were not exaggerated. Reports from ground elements of VI Corps confirmed the extent of the devastation on the few roads leading north from Cisterna-Cori toward Valmontone. "The essential accuracy of these figures was proved in the next week as our troops moved up to Valmontone, for the roads were littered with the burned, twisted wrecks of tanks, self-propelled guns, trucks, command cars, personnel carriers—a vast graveyard of all types of German transport. One company alone of the 10th Engineer Battalion pushed 150 wrecks off the road from a point 1½ miles southwest of Cori around through Cori to Giulianello."[50]

Another significant event took place when, after 123 days, the siege of Anzio officially ended the morning of May 25 when the two fronts linked up on the edge of the flooded Pontine Marshes southeast of the tiny coastal village of Borgo Grappa, nicknamed "Borgocrappa" by the Anzio men. Here troops of the 36th Engineer Regiment greeted advance elements of the U.S. II Corps, the 48th Engineer Regiment, and the 91st Reconnaissance Regiment. In his memoirs, Clark leaves the impression it was all spontaneous: Driving nearby in his jeep, "Our radio picked up word that [these] elements . . . were close to a junction . . . I drove hurriedly to the sector, arriving as the two groups were meeting."[51] What Clark fails to mention is that he was actually at the Fifth Army command post awaiting notice of the linkup and that he was accompanied by twenty-five photographers and correspondents.[52] His presence was a cleverly orchestrated public

relations operation that would today be defined as a "media event"
and the most prominent figure in the photographs that preserve the
historic event is the tall figure of Mark Clark.

The event had in fact taken place with such swiftness that Clark
was caught flat-footed. Contact had actually been made at 0730 hours
the morning of May 25 when Francis X. Buckley, an engineer lieutenant assigned to II Corps, stopped his jeep at a blown bridge north of
Terracina. There he met a platoon marching south from the beachhead,
led by Captain Ben Souza, who did not think Buckley was part of the
beachhead force. " 'Where the hell do you think you're going?' 'I'm
trying to make contact with Anzio forces,' answered Buckley. 'Boy,' said
Captain Souza, 'you've made it!' " When Clark finally arrived some
three hours later the event was restaged for the benefit of both the
correspondents, photographers, and the Fifth Army commander. As he
posed for the cameras, Clark kept repeating, "It's a great day for the
Fifth Army."[53] And so it was, except for the forgotten citizens of Terracina. Eric Sevareid writes that the town was "an awesome shambles,
its buildings spewn into the roadways, its whole skyline ripped away.
There were still dead mules and bodies along the curbs, and a terrible
stench issued from the ruins. . . . These little places were meaningless
names to the outside world. But to us who had followed the fighting
from hill to crossroad, from hedgerow to street corner, they were areas
of the most intense intimacy. . . . Part of our lives was left there forever."[54]

The pivotal day in the drive for Rome was May 25. Despite the bitter
fighting for Cisterna and the delay in its capture, plan Buffalo was
succeeding beyond the wildest dreams of its architects. The German
defense in the center of Fourteenth Army had collapsed like a house
of cards. The Fifth Army history summed up the triumph:

> By the morning of 25 May the enemy situation in the Cisterna area was
> chaotic . . . everywhere else on the German left flank the scene was
> one of hurried retreat, partly toward Velletri, partly toward Valmon-
> tone. . . . At Cisterna and Velletri alone did the enemy resist strong-
> ly. . . . Cisterna, Cori and Mount Arrestino—the first objectives of Opera-
> tion Buffalo were all in our hands by the evening of 25 May. Here as on
> the southern front our victory had been quicker, less expensive, and
> more devastating to the enemy than had been hoped. . . . It had not even
> been necessary to commit our [VI Corps] reserves as planned. Enemy
> resistance in the Cisterna-Valmontone corridor had collapsed. . . . Thus
> far our attack was a superb success.[55]

The Fifth Army was on the verge of a historic victory. The scenes
recorded on May 25 were a prelude to what would occur in August 1944

in the Falaise gap of Normandy. The cutting of the German lines of communication at Valmontone was a foregone conclusion as Alexander and Harding had envisioned. Moreover, the back door to Rome had been left virtually undefended. Harmon was galvanized to do what he did best: exploit with his entire division and use the cutting and slashing power of his armor to tear what was left of the German flank to shreds.

The long stalemate at Anzio may have ended, but on the memorable day May 25 Clark delivered a bombshell that was to affect the outcome of the Italian campaign. Unknown to Howze, Harmon and the other battlefield commanders, Mark Clark, the commander who had made the capture of Rome his *raison d'être,* had earlier that afternoon deliberately committed what must rank as one of the most misguided blunders made by any Allied commander during World War II. About to win a stunning victory that would not only have gained him the glittering prize of Rome virtually without a fight but have earned him immortality as a great battlefield commander, Mark Clark suddenly dismembered Operation Buffalo and in the process sparked a controversy that continues to this day.

21

The Battle for Valmontone Gap

Never attack a position in front which you can gain
by turning.

—NAPOLEON

The First Armored could—and should—have rolled
onto Highway 6 and been in Rome in an hour and a
half.

—ERNIE HARMON

Although it seemed sudden and precipitous to the senior commanders of VI Corps, Clark's decision on May 25 was a calculated act that was to prove as militarily stupid as it was insubordinate. The evidence, most of it supplied by Clark himself, is overwhelming that his intention all along was to obey Alexander only briefly, then switch the main attack from Buffalo to Turtle and thus capture Rome from the northwest. When Truscott and Clark conferred at 0900 the previous morning (May 24) at the 1st Armored command post, the Fifth Army commander had asked, "Have you considered changing the direction of your attack to the northwest—toward Rome?"

Truscott replied that he had, but only if the Germans managed to concentrate all their available reserves in the Valmontone gap, thus so weakening the western part of the Anzio beachhead that an attack to the northwest would produce worthwhile results by cutting off a withdrawal north of the Alban Hills. "My staff was already preparing plans to meet this contingency," Truscott told Clark. "Clark agreed with my analysis and asked that I keep the plans up to date."[1] Although Truscott did not ascribe an ulterior motive to Clark's remarks, the conversation nevertheless left Truscott uneasy. Why was Clark still talking about cancelling Buffalo when VI Corps was on the verge of a stunning success?[2] The following afternoon he was to learn the reason.

We turn now to the events of the fateful day of May 25, 1944. Clark's diary records that his first order of business that morning was to visit the VI Corps command post at 0830 hours,

> where he conferred briefly with General Truscott concerning the progress of the VI Corps attack and the possibility of diverting the 45th, 34th and 36th Divisions to attack in a northwesterly (sic) direction toward Velletri and to its south, while at the same time the 3d Division [and the 1st] Special Service Force [to] continue north to Valmontone, the 1st Armored Division to support both attacks with its bulk going to the attack toward Velletri. He [Clark] returned to the Fifth Army Advance command post where he conferred briefly with General Brann and left immediately for the vicinity of Borgo Grappa where he was to see the overland junction of II Corps [and the] bridgehead forces.[3]

Not only was there no mention of switching the main attack from Buffalo to Turtle, but Clark actually seemed prepared to reinforce the success of Buffalo. However, if Truscott thought Turtle was a dead issue, he was shocked when he returned to the VI Corps command post in midafternoon to find the Fifth Army G-3, Brigadier General Brann, awaiting him. Brann was the bearer of bad news and he got straight to the point: "The Boss wants you to leave the 3rd Infantry Division and the Special Service Force to block Highway 6 and mount that assault you discussed with him to the northwest as soon as you can." Truscott could hardly believe what he was being told. Clark had said nothing whatsoever that morning about switching the attack. Now, here was Brann with orders that in effect emasculated Buffalo at the very moment when the air forces were tearing German convoys to shreds and the 1st Armored was on the march toward Valmontone.

In his memoirs Truscott was to write bitterly:

> I was dumbfounded. I protested that the conditions were not right. There was no evidence of any withdrawal from the western part of the beachhead, nor was there evidence of any concentration in the Valmontone area except light reconnaissance elements of the Hermann Goering Division. This was no time to drive to the northwest where the enemy was still strong; we should pour our maximum power into the Valmontone Gap to insure the destruction of the retreating German [Tenth] army.[4]

Truscott insisted: "I would not comply with the order without first talking to General Clark in person. Brann informed me that he was not in the beachhead and could not be reached even by radio, and that General Clark ordered the attack to the northwest."[5] His protests fell upon deaf ears, and although he later told Clark personally the change of plan was a mistake, Truscott loyally carried out an order he personally deplored.

The evidence clearly suggests that Clark's actions the morning of May 25 were a ploy to avoid having to face Truscott personally. Clark's diary does not support Brann's contention that the Fifth Army commander was out of touch in the afternoon. In fact, at one point that afternoon Clark was at the Fifth Army main command post conferring with his chief of staff, Alfred Gruenther. Moreover, as the official historian wrote in a postwar essay, "At 3:55 P.M. on 25 May General Brann radioed General Clark that Truscott was 'entirely in accord' with the Army commander's plan."[6] If Brann's version is to be believed, it is certain that Truscott would have insisted on personally speaking with Clark.

What is rather more clear is that Clark's brief midmorning conference with Brann was for the purpose of ordering the Fifth Army G-3 to carry the change of plan to Truscott that afternoon. Until his diaries were opened in 1989, no one knew of Clark's actions on the pivotal day of May 25, 1944. After the war he freely and graciously gave interviews to the official historians and even agreed to make his diaries available for their use. However, what Clark loaned the official historians turned out to be an edited and highly selective version of his diaries. He gave them only what he wanted them to see, and in the case of the May 25 incident, it is clear that he chose not to reveal that he had visited Truscott only moments before returning to his CP and instructing Brann to become his messenger.[7]

The official historians never knew that they had been deceived. Ernest F. Fisher, Jr., and another official historian, Sidney T. Mathews, interviewed Truscott many years apart. In both instances and in his memoirs, Truscott states that his first knowledge of Clark's decision was Brann's sudden and unwelcome presence on the afternoon of May 25.[8]

Official historian Mathews also writes: "At 5:55 [P.M.] Truscott telephoned Brann, saying, 'I feel very strongly we should do this thing [the attack to the northwest]. We should do it tomorrow.' "[9] Whether the meaning of what Truscott said to Brann was misinterpreted by Mathews or his source (the VI Corps journal) was faulty, there is no other known evidence to support the notion that Truscott ever agreed with Clark and Brann. To the contrary, Truscott's diary and the recollections of his aide-de-camp point to precisely the opposite conclusion. According to James Wilson:

I was on hand a couple of days before when Clark and Truscott discussed the possibility of doing TURTLE. Truscott had said it was feasible only if the Krauts weakened their positions west of Velletri, and Clark had not disagreed.

I was also aboard when Don Brann appeared on the beachhead on the afternoon of May 25 to convey Clark's new decision. Truscott very much disagreed and made no bones about saying so loudly and forcefully, telling Brann he would have to talk to Clark personally about it before complying. But Clark wasn't immediately available at the beachhead or on the phone. . . . Why he [Clark] chose this particular time or this method to spring this on his corps commander I have never understood. Truscott did call in the staff and start the wheels turning to put the complex execution of TURTLE in motion. But he managed to see Clark that evening (something neither mentions in their books) in a session I did not attend.[10]

Truscott's diary for May 25 also contains a cryptic entry that: "Gen. Brann in re: plans to attack Carroceto," and a subsequent entry that night reading: "to 5th Army to see Clark." Later Truscott underlined the latter entry in pen and wrote underneath the day's typed entries: "Protested to Clark then."[11]

It was not until 2300 hours the night of May 25 that Truscott met with his division commanders to announce the change of plan. None of the participants has left a record of that meeting, but as Wilson writes, "As I remember, it was a fairly stormy session, and both Iron Mike and Ernie Harmon, who were not known for their reticence, protested loudly, as did a couple of others, but to no avail. Truscott continued to disagree with the decision personally afterwards, as he said several times later on; but he carried out his orders notwithstanding."[12] Like it or not, Clark's orders would be carried out despite the fact his corps commander and the division commanders believed they were based on a terrible decision.

Clark's subsequent defense of his actions was similar to his plan for the Rapido crossings in January: He adjusted his operations to fit a preconceived notion, even though the decision contradicted the military maxim that a commander should always exploit success. After the war Clark told Sidney Mathews that even before Buffalo he did not believe the attack would reach its ultimate objectives of Highway 6 with the troops at the disposal of VI Corps and that merely cutting Highway 6 was no guarantee of cutting off the German Tenth Army because there were too many alternate routes. "The VI Corps was not strong [enough] even if it got to Valmontone to push on and cut those alternate routes—this was absolutely impossible, Clark says. The attack on this axis was bad because VI Corps would be attacking on an axis parallel to the main German positions, the Alban Hill line."[13]

Clark's most astounding claim was that the really important objective was the Colli Laziali hill mass, that "that was what would make the enemy unable to stand on the Alban Hill line or south of Rome. If we took Colli Laziali . . . the Germans around the beachhead and on the southern front would have to pull back."[14] Clark's defense of his decision ignored the obvious fact that if VI Corps had severed the links between the beachhead and the Tenth Army, the road to Rome was wide open and the German forces left at Anzio were doomed. However, to have captured and held the entire Alban Hill mass would indeed have been an impossible task for a force the size of VI Corps. To defeat the Fourteenth Army and crack the Caesar Line would eventually require the combined efforts of three U.S. corps. Moreover, to capture the Alban Hills meant an attack into the strength of von Mackensen's defenses which were stacked against an attack along the very axis of advance that Clark had now ordered Truscott to carry out. In short, Clark had ordered his corps commander to abandon a successful exploitation and attack in a northwesterly direction precisely where the Germans hoped he would.

Clark's pride in the Fifth Army and his desire to focus attention on the American contribution to the campaign were one thing, but at a stroke his order to Truscott—an order based more upon vanity than military necessity—destroyed any hope of trapping von Vietinghoff's retreating army.

There was overwhelming evidence that Clark would act as he did. Alexander's order to launch Buffalo led Clark to write in his memoirs:

> We had massed all our strength to take Rome. We were keyed up. . . . We not only wanted the honor of capturing Rome, but we felt that we more than deserved it; that it would make up to a certain extent for the buffeting and the frustration we had undergone in keeping up the winter pressure against the Germans. My own feeling was that nothing was going to stop us on our push towards the Italian capital. Not only did we intend to become the first army in fifteen centuries to seize Rome from the south, but we intended to see that the people at home knew that it was the Fifth Army that did the job and knew the price that had been paid to do it."[15]

Other accounts also describe Clark's obsession with Rome. The night of May 21 Clark briefed the correspondents in front of a large map in his Anzio command post. With sweeping gestures he assured the correspondents more than once that "We're going to take Rome."[16] Among the skeptics was Eric Sevareid, whose CBS broadcast script was censored for including this statement: "There is a question whether the aims [of getting Rome and of destroying the enemy] are mutually exclusive." Clark personally reviewed all press and radio material of significance and, according to Sevareid: "Before all the correspondents, he referred to 'a broadcast' that suggested that we might be able to capture the bulk of the Germans. 'That is sheer nonsense,' he asserted with vigor, and with his pointer he indicated various side roads to the north by which, he said, the Germans could easily escape. No amateur could prove otherwise."[17]

When the 36th Division arrived in the beachhead, an eyewitness to Clark's first visit to Fred Walker's command post noted that he was accompanied by his photographer, who recorded the event on film. "The army commander was determined to be the first to get to Rome. He seemed tense and excited . . . he pulled out of the camp in a rush, again leaving clouds of dust behind him."[18] And, to a former British officer, Clark revealed after the war that his passionate defense of his actions had not diminished:

> The facts are that everybody agreed including Churchill and Alexander months before the event, that Rome was the primary objective. Alexander never gave me orders not to take Rome. . . . I know he was concerned about my maintaining my thrust to Valmonte (sic), but hell when we were knocking on its door we had already destroyed as much of the German Tenth Army as we could have ever expected. By this time I learnt that Alexander was questioning my intentions . . . and it looked as if he wanted to run my own Goddam army without ever talking to me man to man. One thing I knew was that I had to take Rome and that my American army was going to do it. So in all the circumstances I had to go for it before the British loused it up. . . . I did not want any accident of planning or interference from Alexander's staff to stop me from taking Rome. We Americans had slogged all the way up from Salerno and I was not going to have this great prize, the honor of taking Rome denied to me and my GIs by anyone. We had earned it, you understand.[19]

How, then, did Clark go about explaining to Alexander that he no longer intended to follow superiors' orders? He did so by deceiving Alexander. Clark radioed Gruenther with instructions specifying what Alexander was to be told. After describing his intention to make an aggressive follow-up the following day toward Valmontone with the 3d Division and the First Special Service Force, Clark said: "I am launching this new attack with all speed possible in order to take advantage of impetus of our advance and in order to overwhelm the enemy in what may be a demoralized condition at the present time. You can assure General Alexander that this is an all-out attack. We are shooting the works."[20]

Clark deliberately withheld informing Alexander for nearly twenty-four hours, and when it was finally revealed at 1115 the morning of May 26 by the Fifth Army chief of staff, it was for all practical purposes too late for Alexander to reverse the decision. Gruenther informed Alexander that Clark was in fact mounting two thrusts, one toward Valmontone and the other toward Rome. His "new" offensive

(Operation Turtle), Alexander was told, would overwhelm an already demoralized enemy in "an all-out attack." VI Corps was also pressing forward with "powerful forces" against Valmontone. Gruenther assured Alexander that Clark was not abandoning Buffalo, but rather was extending the offensive to include both operations. Alexander asked somewhat wistfully, "I am sure the army commander will continue to push toward Valmontone, won't he? I know that he appreciates the importance of gaining the high ground just south of Artena. As soon as he captures that he will be absolutely safe!" Gruenther replied that Clark had exactly that in mind and could be relied on "to execute a vigorous plan with all the push in the world." According to Gruenther, Alexander seemed satisfied and had left "with no mental reservations as to the wisdom" of the change of plan.[21]

Gruenther was dead wrong. Alexander understood perfectly well that he had been hoodwinked by Clark and he was furious. Shortly afterwards Harold Macmillan met Alexander. Macmillan "knew there was trouble because Alex's eye was twitching as it would do before a big battle. He asked what was wrong. 'What is right?' Alex snapped back, and told him. Macmillan asked him why he had not put his foot down. 'Why do you talk such nonsense?' Alex replied. 'How can I give orders?' This was the only time Macmillan had ever seen him lose his temper."[22]

Alexander's publicly placid acceptance of Clark's fait accompli suggests that he was not well briefed on the situation in the Velletri-Valmontone gap. Had he been fully aware of the stunning success of the previous day he could hardly have accepted Clark's and Gruenther's deceptive statements that the reason for switching to Turtle was that the thrust toward Valmontone was being stopped by German reinforcements and that Clark was shifting the axis to break through to the northwest quickly. In his postwar interview with the official U.S. historians, Alexander declined to admit he had been duped by Clark. Instead, he told them that he had accepted at face value what Clark said, only that "if the Germans hadn't blocked us at the time the axis of attack was changed [then] it was a mistake to shift the axis of attack, for it ended the chance of cutting off the 10th Army on the southern front. But Alexander did not know at the time that the Germans had insufficient strength in the Valmontone area and in the Velletri gap to have stopped VI Corps."[23]

Clark's deception and half truths regarding the situation in the Velletri-Valmontone sector were accepted at face value at AFHQ, where Wilson cabled the British chiefs of staff on June 2 that, "Our offensive north-eastwards from the bridgehead sector gave early promise of cutting Highway 6 at Valmontone. . . . Unfortunately we were forestalled in this, by a matter of hours, by the arrival of strong elements of the Hermann Goering Division reinforced."[24] One of Alexander's senior staff officers, Sir David Hunt, accepted Clark's version without complaint. In his war memoirs, Sir David noted that Clark's change of direction "meant that such chance as there was of a really decisive battle was lost," because Clark "had been meeting very stiff resistance in his original drive on Valmontone on the vital route 6."[25]

Clark's justifications varied widely. When Alexander's biographer bluntly suggested that the Fifth Army commander had willfully violated his commander in chief's orders, Clark vehemently replied:

> No, no. I never violated his orders. I told him, and he agreed, that I would simultaneously advance on Rome and send a task force to Valmontone. He wanted it. He never overruled me. Can you find any place where he said that I directly violated his orders?. . .I did send a column [to Valmontone]. If I had taken the entire army and pushed it against Route 6, the Germans would have had the opportunity to debouch from the mountains and attack my left flank. That is why I attacked the Alban Hills. To censure me for thinking only of the glory of capturing Rome is sheer nonsense. I know Alex didn't like the way I was doing it, but he issued no ultimatum to me to make me do it differently. . . . I told him exactly what I was going to do, and he acquiesced.[26]

The threat to the Tenth Army posed by the Buffalo force was menacingly clear and on May 25 Kesselring issued an order of the day demanding that his troops hold their positions and forbidding any further withdrawal without his personal permission. The following day, in a last-ditch effort to keep the cork in the bottle and prevent an unhindered exploitation into the Velletri and Valmontone gaps by VI Corps, Kesselring ordered reinforcements flung into the breach. Just as he did so, Kesselring became the beneficiary of Clark's blunder.

The worsening of the tactical situation was mirrored by the continued deterioration of relations between Kesselring and von Mackensen. Each later blamed the other for mishandling the defense of Rome. The greatest schism between the two commanders lay in their differing concepts of the Allied breakout offensive. As far back as mid-March, von Mackensen had adopted a defensive posture that assumed the main offensive would be up the Albano road, with only a secondary attack in the Cisterna sector. The best formations still remaining in the Fourteenth Army were assigned the defense of the Via Anziate sector where the bitter battles for the beachhead had been fought in January and February.

Kesselring later contended that he expected the main effort to be directed at Cisterna, but a postwar study by an American official historian states that there is no contemporary evidence to support this allegation. "The fact that Kesselring permitted von Mackensen to keep the weak 362d Division in that vital sector seems to refute it."[27] Thus, whether or not he agreed, Kesselring permitted von Mackensen to concentrate his main defense against what was now Operation Turtle. The Germans had constructed a deep system of defensive belts ten kilometers deep along the Albano highway. In the event these defenses failed to hold the Germans had begun work in early April on a secondary defensive line that ran across the southern edge of the Alban Hills to Highway 6 in the Valmontone gap. Formally named the Caesar Line, it was referred to by the Germans simply as the C-position. Its construction by German engineers and ten thousand Italian laborers had been completed to Labico, a village two miles north of Valmontone on Highway 6. Its final link north to the Avellino highway was a hollow shell. If used, von Mackensen considered it little more than a delaying position.[28] In the Velletri and Valmontone gaps north of Cisterna, the Germans had only weak delaying positions,[29] most of which had already been shredded by the successful drives of the Buffalo forces on May 25.

A major bone of contention between the two senior German commanders centered on the employment of the Hermann Göring Division and von Mackensen's failure to release the 29th Panzer Grenadier Division to the Tenth Army front on May 20, when ordered by Kesselring. When the division belatedly engaged Fifth Army units without the time to prepare its defenses, it was badly mauled. Kesselring blamed von Mackensen for the "calamitous consequences." Thus, "an excellent defensive zone had been thrown away and the enemy handed an almost impregnable position between Terracina and Fondi, the loss of which gave the Americans the victory."[30] A later incident at the end of May, when von Mackensen belatedly notified Kesselring of the presence of elements of the U.S. 36th Division on Monte Artemisio, northwest of Velletri, was the final straw in a relationship that had been sour from the first.

For his part, von Mackensen believed that Kesselring's orders to transfer valuable Fourteenth Army reserves, and the expansion of the interarmy boundary with the Tenth Army to as far south as Frosinone, were a fundamental error that led to the serious situation faced by Army Group C. Kesselring argued that von Mackensen never understood the big picture and the consequences if he had not acted. Both commanders were right, but the shortage of reserves to plug the ever-widening gaps forced Kesselring into stripping the Fourteenth Army. There is a discernible pattern in Kesselring's actions. Always the pragmatist, he virtually always decided where the most serious threat lay and acted accordingly to commit his reserves against that threat, even if it meant creating problems elsewhere. There is little evidence that von Mackensen understood this, and the result was that within days Kesselring decided to relieve him of command. He had wearied of von Mackensen's constant carping and was convinced that the Fourteenth

Field Marshal Albert Kesselring, Commander-in-Chief, South. (*Imperial War Museum*)

General Heinrich von Vietinghoff, the German Tenth Army commander. (*U.S. Army Military History Institute*)

Lieutenant General Fridolin von Senger und Etterlin, XIV Panzer Corps commander and the defender of Cassino. (*Imperial War Museum*)

The town of Cassino and the abbey under artillery attack, February 1944. (*Official U.S. Army photograph, National Archives*)

British troops in the ruins of Cassino, May 1944. (*National Archives*)

The terrible gullies.

British troops under fire in the gully country northwest of the Flyover. (*Imperial War Museum*)

Stretcher bearers evacuating wounded of the 2d Battalion, Sherwood Foresters, under a white flag. (*Imperial War Museum*)

The lifeline of the beachhead: LSTs in the port of Anzio. (*Imperial War Museum*)

British troops battling "General Mud," Anzio beachhead. (*Imperial War Museum*)

The new beachhead commander, Lucian Truscott, and Alexander. (*Imperial War Museum*)

Lieutenant General A. F. Harding, 15th Army Group chief of staff and the architect of Diadem. (*Imperial War Museum*)

The British Eighth Army commander, Lieutenant General Sir Oliver Leese, with Clark. (*Imperial War Museum*)

A rare scene of joy as Allied troops celebrate the linkup of the southern front with the Anzio beachhead, May 25, 1944. (*Imperial War Museum*)

Contrasts of war: Italian sheep share the battlefield with Allied tanks. (*Imperial War Museum*)

Allied airfield in Italy, 1944. (*Imperial War Museum*)

American self-propelled howitzer crew, Anzio beachhead, March 1944. (*National Archives*)

A GI shares his rations with a young Italian refugee, January 1944. (*Official U.S. Army photograph, National Archives*)

First Special Service Force patrol blasting a German-held farmhouse, April 1944. (*Official U.S. Army photograph, National Archives*)

Crude German propaganda leaflets. (*Official U.S. Army photograph, National Archives*)

A British patrol in the Anzio beachhead. (*Imperial War Museum*)

Captured German paratroopers assisting a wounded Tommy whose foot has just been blown off by a mine. (*Imperial War Museum*)

U.S. armor spearheading the breakout from the Anzio beachhead, May 1944.
(*Official U.S. Coast Guard photograph, National Archives*)

After months of combat, the Factory
shortly before its recapture by the British
on May 28, 1944. (*Imperial War Museum*)

Wrecked German vehicles near Velletri,
May 1944. (*Imperial War Museum*)

Troops of the U.S. 36th Division moving up near Cisterna, May 1944. (*Official U.S. Army photograph, National Archives*)

Aerial view of Valmontone and Highway 6, the objectives of Operation Buffalo. (*Official U.S. Army photograph, National Archives*)

Private First Class Earl H. Brendell covers the bodies of two 3d Division GIs killed by German fire during the battle for Cisterna. (*Official U.S. Army photograph, National Archives*)

A 3d Division patrol in the ruins of Cisterna, May 25, 1944. (*Official U.S. Army photograph, National Archives*)

Allied tanks in the Liri Valley during Operation Diadem, May 1944. (*Imperial War Museum*)

U.S. troops under fire outside Artena, May 27, 1944. (*Imperial War Museum*)

Major General Geoffrey Keyes (*left*) and Brigadier General Robert T. Frederick (*right*) confer with Clark outside Rome, June 4, 1944. (*Imperial War Museum*)

Troops of the First Special Service Force and 88th Division during mopping-up operations in Rome, June 4, 1944. (*Official U.S. Army photograph, National Archives*)

An American GI sharing his coffee with an Italian girl in Rome, June 5, 1944. (*Official U.S. Army photograph, National Archives*)

Generals Clark, Keyes, and Truscott climbing the steps of Rome's city hall, June 5, 1944. (*Imperial War Museum*)

The citizens of Rome celebrating their liberation, June 5, 1944. (*Imperial War Museum*)

Americans who died at Anzio and elsewhere in Italy are honored at Memorial Day ceremonies, 1946. (*Official U.S. Army photograph, National Archives*)

A bittersweet reunion of Ranger survivors of Cisterna in May 1945 after liberation from German POW camps. (*Official U.S. Army photograph, National Archives*)

Army commander was not prepared to carry out his orders faithfully, no matter how disagreeable or necessary. Kesselring had Hitler's authority to sack the Fourteenth Army commander, but, apparently aware of his fate, von Mackensen elected instead to resign. He was immediately replaced by General der Panzertruppen Joachim Lemelsen.[31]

German troop strength in the Valmontone gap on May 25 and 26 simply could not have stopped a sustained drive by VI Corps. Had the full-strength Task Force Howze and a full combat command of 1st Armored gained control of the Lariano-Artena-Valmontone-Labico sectors, all of which controlled access to either Highway 6 or the roads feeding into it from the Velletri gap, they would have cut the vital link between the two German armies. On the basis of what occurred in the Valmontone Gap during the final week of May, there is sufficient evidence to suggest that such a force in control of Artena-Valmontone–Highway 6 could never have been dislodged by the Hermann Göring Division.

Clark may not have given Valmontone top priority, but Kesselring was so concerned by this threat on May 25 that he retained control of the Hermann Göring Division. Although originally thinking of committing the division to the Tenth Army, Kesselring elected to keep his options open and decided to release only the reconnaissance battalion, which von Mackensen was to employ at Valmontone. According to German records this battalion had not yet arrived to defend against the advance of Task Force Howze and the other VI Corps units then in the Artena sector.

Although the situation had worsened at Valmontone by the next morning, Kesselring still refused to commit the entire division. On his own initiative, Major General Wilhelm Schmalz, the commander of the Hermann Göring Division, began sending reinforcements to the outgunned reconnaissance battalion on May 26 as they trickled in from the north. Many units had been decimated during their long run through the gauntlet of Allied air attacks. When Kesselring learned what Schmalz was doing he ordered the division to disengage at once and await his orders. Schmalz was convinced that American armor would soon cut Highway 6 unless he acted. The order was ignored in the belief that if Kesselring knew of the situation he would fully endorse Schmalz's action—which in fact he did late on the morning of May 27.[32]

Von Vietinghoff was keenly aware of the events unfolding in the Valmontone gap and its implications for his Tenth Army. If the entrance to the valley were to be blocked by Allied armor and infantry and Highway 6 cut off, "the whole southern wing of Tenth Army and some elements of Fourteenth Army would then be forced to retreat to the Caesar line over the road from Frosinone to Subaico with some forces using the secondary road via Fiuggi to Genazzano. A difficult traffic problem was bound to arise in the three mile stretch north of Alatri where only one road existed; a rapid advance of Eighth Army would lead to the encirclement of 14 Pz Corps."[33]

A telephone conversation between Major General Wentzell, the Tenth Army chief of staff, and Colonel Dietrich Beelitz, the Army Group C chief of operations, the evening of May 26 indicated the concern felt in both headquarters:

> WENTZELL: We have to get out of here as fast as possible or we will lose the whole Fourteenth Panzer Corps.
> BEELITZ: Everything is being upset . . . [the recorder at this point dared not make a verbatim report and merely entered words indicating that OKW was the source of the trouble.]

During a conversation with the XIV Panzer Corps chief of staff forty-five minutes later, Wentzell called the situation faced by Tenth Army "a catastrophe . . . the disaster will begin tomorrow."[34] The reference was both to OKW and Hitler, who had intervened with a futile order that Army Group C not only destroy the fighting potential of the Allied armies but that the Caesar Line be held at all costs. That night Kesselring made it clear to his two army commanders that they were to carry out the Führer's orders. The focal point of his directive was that the Valmontone escape route was to be kept open for the Tenth Army.[35]

By May 27 the dominant German concern was the effect of Allied air power upon their lines of communication. The Tenth Army war diary revealed that

> Serious difficulties are being experienced as a result of the systematic destruction of all supply routes and traffic centers by continuous heavy bombing and the disruption of traffic by ceaseless fighter-bomber attacks. During the last few nights serious traffic blocks occurred in the mountains where there are virtually no alternative routes or detours, and where the immediate repair of destroyed roads is most difficult. Due to the air attacks the Italian workers engaged in this task have fled to the mountains.[36]

As a result, von Vietinghoff was anxious to shorten his front and thus reduce his vulnerability, but OKW had forbidden a proposal by von Senger that had been previously approved by von Vietinghoff to withdraw both corps to new positions in the Frosinone sector, thus positioning the Tenth Army for an escape through the mountains northeast of Valmontone should Highway 6 become impassable. The German commanders were disgusted with what they regarded as a typical lack of understanding of the situation in the field by headquarters staff officers in Berlin who were making decisions they regarded as catastrophic. Nor was von Vietinghoff encouraged by Kesselring's naive insistence that Alexander's armies must be "bled white with hard fighting," to which the Tenth Army commander retorted that to do this required more troops than he had. It would shortly become evident that Kesselring was merely biding his time before seeking Hitler's permission to save Army Group C. As their fate remained uncertain, none of the senior officers of the Tenth Army had much confidence in their sister Fourteenth Army and even less in this latest fantasy dictated by Berlin.[37]

An examination of Allied activity in the Velletri-Valmontone sectors during the final week of May reveals that there was ample justification for German concern over the Allied thrust into the gap. The key to the success of the VI Corps drive during the first three days of Buffalo had been the capture of Cisterna. With its removal as an obstacle, the disintegration of the German front in the LXXVI Panzer Corps sector on May 25 became the worst of all possible situations.

So it was that when the weary Howze was awakened and summoned to the 1st Armored Division command post at 0200 the morning of May 26, he believed it was to receive orders to carry out his recommendation for an all-out thrust into the gap. Instead, to his shock and intense dismay, he was informed by Harmon of the change of plan. Task Force Howze was being stripped of two tank battalions and a reconnaissance company, and the remainder of his force was to be attached to the 3d Division. "I was sick about these orders, being very anxious to continue the deal of the day before." Now an incomprehensible decision to split VI Corps at the very moment when success beckoned was to nullify at a stroke the hard-won advantage.

When Howze reported to General O'Daniel he was ordered to lead the advance to Artena. Once again on the move the morning of May 26, a greatly diminished Task Force Howze encountered little organized resistance en route to Artena. Many Germans descended from the hills and surrendered, and the narrow road between Giulianello and Artena was littered with the still-burning hulks of German vehicles, guns, and tanks. As Howze's force neared Artena he received urgent orders from Truscott to cut the Velletri-Valmontone highway northwest of Artena, which was reported to be infested with enemy vehicles. Task Force Howze soon reached the highway but found no evidence of German vehicles. Howze himself led an advance to reach Highway 6 at Valmontone via the Artena-Valmontone section of the highway, but was blocked by heavy artillery fire, not from the Germans but from Allied guns.[38]

Two tank companies advanced to within six hundred yards of Highway 6 on May 26 and might have seized the highway had not the battalion commander been convinced he had met heavy opposition and ordered a withdrawal based on orders allegedly coming from Howze, which were relayed by a nearby artillery forward observer. In fact, at about that same time Howze's tank engine suddenly coughed and went dead, which meant he could not operate his radio. A frustrated Howze was out of contact with his troops for several hours. By the time he caught up it was too late, and his tanks had withdrawn. Mistakenly believing he had encountered "powerful" opposition, the commander had made repeated attempts to contact Howze and then pulled back to the railway line on his own initiative. The observer was killed in action the next day before he could be questioned, and the source of the mysterious order was never resolved.[39]

Kesselring's most important priority now became regaining German control of the critical Valmontone sector. The first German counter-move came the night of May 26, when Kesselring ordered the Tenth Army to transfer to the LXXVI Panzer Corps two battalions of a regimental infantry group, one regiment and two additional battalions of artillery, and antiaircraft artillery. The Hermann Göring Division was ordered to attack on May 27 to regain Artena and drive U.S. forces back to a new German defensive line to be established across the Velletri gap, southeast of that town. Infantry and artillery units of the 29th Panzer Grenadier Division were also ordered into the Velletri sector to bolster what remained of the battered 715th Infantry Division, which was thought to be in the Cori sector.[40] The mission of the Hermann Göring and the other German reinforcements was to establish blocking positions and keep Highway 6 open until the retreating Tenth Army cleared Valmontone.

The first serious German opposition was not mounted until shortly after dark on May, 26, the same evening that both the 3d Division and the First Special Service Force moved into the Valmontone gap. At 1930 that evening friendly 155-mm artillery fire mistakenly struck Howze's 1st Battalion, 6th Armored Infantry Regiment, causing grievous losses. The battalion was in the process of receiving an estimated 160 replacements, and at least half became casualties, along with many others, including the battalion commander, who was killed. The artillery barrage coincided with a planned counterattack by elements of the Hermann Göring that Schmalz had postponed from that afternoon until dark.[41]

Throughout Operation Buffalo, Frederick's Special Service Force guarded the Allied right flank and on May 26 had advanced unmolested across the Lepini Mountains from Cori to Monte Illiri overlooking Artena and the Valmontone plain. The next morning the entire Force had reached the hills outside Artena.[42] That night O'Daniel reported to Truscott that "the area is very soft . . . I'm convinced we could go into Rome, if we had more stuff up here." Truscott agreed and committed an additional tank battalion. O'Daniel was told: "Highway 6 must be . . . cut and the gap between Artena and the Alban Hills must be kept closed."[43]

On May 27 the 15th Infantry Regiment attacked and captured Artena from the Hermann Göring at a cost of seventy casualties. By nightfall the 7th and 15th regiments of the 3d Division and the Special Service Force were in control of Artena and its approaches. To the southwest the 30th Regiment was protecting the division left flank in the Giulianello sector.

Frederick established his command post in the ancient palace situated on a cliff with a commanding view of the countryside from the hill town of Artena. From the windows of the palace the night sky over the Valmontone gap was illuminated like the Fourth of July by tracers and artillery bursts. An officer from II Corps spent several days with Frederick and has described the palace and Artena as "the hottest spot I've ever seen." The forest-lined railway north of town, halfway between Artena and Valmontone, originally held by Task Force Howze, was now under the control of the Hermann Göring. From there German tanks could fire directly into Artena, and between the panzers and the fire from nearby artillery, the town was turned into a shooting gallery for the German gunners. Most had moved into position the night of May 27, and by the following morning they were continuing to torment U.S. troops in and around Artena so badly that General O'Daniel ordered the 7th Infantry, an attached tank battalion, and the Special Service Force to advance to the railway, capture this vital position, and destroy the tanks and 88s. A demolition patrol was to infiltrate behind German lines and blow the bridges across Highway 6.

The attack the afternoon of May 28 was furiously resisted by the Hermann Göring during a five-hour battle. In what the Special Service Force historian describes as the heaviest resistance a Force attack ever faced, the combined forces of the 3d Division and the Special Service Force captured the railway line but were unable to advance any further toward Highway 6. "At least 12 tanks and self-propelled 88s dug in along the bank were firing at point-blank range. There was a maze of high-volume 20mm flakwagons raking the flat wheat fields over which the uncovered advance was made. Every house had its complement of snipers . . . this heavy fire power was being wielded by troops of the Hermann Goering Reconnaissance Battalion."[44] The attempt to blow the bridges along Highway 6 failed when they were found to be heavily protected, and the vital link to the north remained open.

As German reinforcements continued to arrive, the battle for the Valmontone gap became a standoff, as neither side could gain the upper hand. The railway line became the anchor of the American defense of

Artena. The Germans attempted to retake Artena during the early
morning hours of May 30 and were decisively repulsed during a vicious
four-hour battle. By dawn it was over, and the large numbers of German dead that were found along the approaches to the railway line
were stark testimony to the futility of the attack. Although Kesselring's
orders to restore a defensive line much farther south in the Cori-
Velletri sector could not be carried out, the Germans could take satisfaction at being able to keep Highway 6 open for their comrades of the
retreating Tenth Army. As May passed into June the Germans took full
advantage of the Allied failure to cut Highway 6.

From London Churchill was closely observing the events unfolding in
Italy, and with increasing irritation he took rapid note of the opportunity being squandered at Valmontone. The night of May 28 he cabled
Alexander that "At this distance it seems much more important to cut
their line of retreat than anything else. . . . A cop is much more important than Rome, which would anyhow come as a consequence."[45] As the
hours passed Churchill began examining the tank strength of the Allied
force and several hours later sent a second cable to Alexander asking
why one-half of the reported 2,500 serviceable tanks could not be used

> in making a Scythe movement cutting off the enemy's retreat. . . . I should
> be wanting in comradeship if I did not let you know that the Glory of this
> battle, already great, will be measured not by the capture of Rome or
> juncture with the bridgehead but by the number of German divisions cut
> off. I am sure you will have revolved all this in your mind, and you have
> already acted in this way. Nevertheless, I feel that I ought to tell you that
> "It is the COP that counts."[46]

What neither Alexander nor Churchill knew was that until the night of
May 25 Ernest Harmon was preparing to carry out such an operation
before ordered to withdraw most of his division for Operation Turtle.
For two critically important days—May 26 and 27—the Valmontone
gap was relatively undefended. On May 25 U.S. armored columns and
Allied air power had shattered any possible defense of the Velletri gap
and had opened the way to Valmontone—which, as Task Force Howze
discovered on May 26, was there for the taking.

Among the sources that revealed the deteriorating German situation in Italy during the final days of May was Ultra, which intercepted
a series of signals from Kesselring to OKW. In considerable detail these
chronicled the deterioration of the Fourteenth Army. Antitank guns
were in desperately short supply, with only 80 of 520 guns still in action.
Three divisions had already been badly mauled by VI Corps, and the
morale and fighting power of the infantry were rapidly declining as
casualties reached crisis proportions.[47]

Even if the information gleaned by Ultra had reached Clark promptly there is little to suggest that it would have made any appreciable difference in his thinking. Unlike Patton and Bradley, Clark had little faith in Ultra and would certainly not have permitted himself to be influenced by anything contrary to his preconceived bias for Turtle.[48] Ultra historian Ronald Lewin writes that Clark "must have known with great clarity the condition of Germans retreating ahead of him. Apart from abundant air reconnaissance and 'Y' service, there was Ultra. Even at Bletchley people observed the German dispositions on their map and could not understand the 5th Army's behavior."[49] Moreover, it was not until May 28 that Kesselring began to doubt that Valmontone represented the main Allied attack. But it was not until May 29, when the 1st Armored Division was positively identified in the Albano sector, that the German commander in chief knew for certain that the Valmontone gap had become secondary to the recent attacks aimed at Albano, Lanuvio, and Velletri.[50]

Clark's own diary for May 27 reiterates his oft-repeated remarks about Alexander and Valmontone and suggests that either he was being badly informed by his own intelligence staff or simply misinterpreting what he was being told:

> All German troops withdrawing from the Cisterna area have taken a position between Velletri and Valmontone. This area has been reinforced from the British west flank and by Hermann Goering [sic] Division. Once we advanced to Valmontone it would be difficult to turn west . . . via Route No. 6. Communications alone would make this impracticable.[51]

Not only were Clark's remarks wildly inaccurate, but the Fifth Army staff could hardly have been ignorant of the fact that the German formations that survived the breakthrough at Cisterna had been savaged by both the Buffalo forces and Allied fighter-bombers.

An entry in the G-3 journal of the 1st Armored Division on May 26 tersely passed sentence on Clark's controversial decision: "It was a definite mistake not to continue to press along the CISTERNA-VALMONTONE axis."[52]

The impact of Mark Clark's unilateral action on May 25 was immediate and negative. As Sidney Mathews writes, "Clark's decision neither unlocked the door to Rome nor cut the enemy's rear at Valmontone."[53] To halt a major offensive operation of war, regroup, and turn it in an entirely different direction is among the most difficult challenges of the art of conducting war. Clark had again demonstrated that he had yet to learn this lesson. Aside from its tactical implications, what Clark had ordered Truscott to do was halt the 1st Armored Division and move it back to the rear and across the 34th and 45th Divisions to new assembly areas back in the Padiglione sector preparatory to launching a fresh attack down the Via Anziate corridor toward Campoleone and Albano. It was May 29 before the 1st Armored was committed. Nearly all the corps and divisional artillery, the command posts, and the communications links had to be relocated. "A more complicated plan would have been difficult to conceive," observed Truscott.[54]

After a day of unsuccessful attacks by two combat commands of the 1st Armored Division against the mountain city of Velletri on May 26, the task was turned over to the newly arrived 36th Division, and Harmon's division was relieved and sent back to the Anzio beachhead.

The difficulty of capturing Velletri seems to have been at the center of Clark's rationale for Turtle. However, with other routes leading to Valmontone open, Velletri was in fact irrelevant and should have been bypassed. The German force holding the city was no threat to cut these routes, and the left flank of the gap could easily have been held open by a tank-infantry force, while the remainder of the 1st Armored poured into the Valmontone gap. This force would then have been replaced by Walker's 36th Infantry Division on May 26 or 27.

After spearheading the breakout from the beachhead by means of an aggressive and highly successful offensive thrust that had come within sight of its objectives, the Buffalo force was emasculated at the very moment the operation verged on becoming one of the great achievements of the Italian campaign. The greatest irony of all was that instead of seizing the terrain Kesselring and the German commanders most feared they would, Harmon and his 1st Armored found themselves back in the Padiglione Woods, where they had first assembled upon their arrival at Anzio in late January.

22

All Roads Lead to Rome

Questions of prestige are shaping events, each one
wanting to make entry into Rome. History will not
fail to pass severe sentence.

—JUIN

To be first in Rome was poor compensation for this
lost opportunity.

LUCIAN K. TRUSCOTT

When Operation Turtle commenced along the northwesterly axis ordered by Mark Clark, the attacks ran headlong into the heart of the German defense of the Anzio beachhead. The offensive was spearheaded by the 45th and 34th divisions, which attacked abreast of one another toward Campoleone and Lanuvio, while on the right flank the 36th Division assumed responsibility for the capture of the mountain city of Velletri. On May 26 they advanced nearly a mile and a half. Not surprisingly, the heaviest fighting occurred in the 45th Division sector northeast of the Factory. On May 27 there was some progress but thus far the offensive had only made contact with von Mackensen's outpost lines. Blown bridges, long-range German artillery, and harassment from enemy tanks operating in the woods northeast of the Factory all combined to delay the Allies for as long as possible. Even against the thinly held outer shell of the Fourteenth Army, it was obvious that the attacks lacked the necessary strength to break the more heavily fortified German defenses of Campoleone and Lanuvio. Truscott decided the time had come to commit his only reserve and the 1st Armored was alerted to spearhead the attack on May 29.

After praising Clark's decision to initiate Turtle, the Fifth Army history records that "during the next three days [May 28–30] a breakthrough was not achieved." The authors praised German ingenuity in improvising their defenses without a solid base of troop units, as "rarely better demonstrated than in the battle of Lanuvio." While the 34th butted against the German defenses at Villa Crocetta in their attempt to gain the railway line and the town of Lanuvio, the Germans had given ground on the left. By midday on May 29 the leading elements of the 1st Armored cleared the last remnants of opposition from Campoleone Station. That afternoon Combat Command A reached the Albano road and began advancing north. It soon outdistanced its supporting infantry and artillery began taking heavy losses from German antitank guns. Twenty-one Shermans and sixteen M5 tank destroyers were lost, and among those killed that afternoon was 1st Lieutenant Allen T. Brown, George Marshall's stepson.[1] On the left flank the two British divisions attempted to match the advance of the main attack. On the twenty-eighth the Factory finally fell to an Allied unit for the first time since mid-February during the great German counteroffensive, and this hellish place which had changed hands so many times over the course of the campaign had seen its final combat. Although 5,156 Germans had been taken prisoner by the evening of May 28 and the original beachhead line established in January had at last been passed, there was no sign the Germans would break. To the contrary, the historian of the 1st Armored wrote that "the Division considered that the day's attack had been 'costly and fruitless.' "[2]

May 30 was equally deadly as another twenty-three tanks and tank destroyers were lost to virtually no gain. The utter bankruptcy of the Turtle plan was that after four of the bitterest days of combat during the entire Anzio campaign, VI Corps had managed to capture only Ardea on the extreme left flank, Campoleone Station, and Artena. The important objectives of Campoleone, Lanuvio, and Velletri remained firmly in German hands.[3]

Equally frustrated was the 34th Division, which could make little headway toward overcoming two German strongpoints in the center of the Caesar Line, the San Gennaro ridgeline and the Villa Crocetta. By the afternoon of May 29 Truscott had lost his patience and telephoned the 34th Division command post personally to convey his displeasure to the commanding general. Ryder was away, but Truscott sent a thinly veiled warning by growling at a staff officer to "tell him to crack this Lanuvio. It's holding up the whole thing."[4] Although both strongpoints were captured by the 34th Division on May 29, German counterattacks soon drove the attackers out and restored the Caesar Line positions.

After four days of Clark's great offensive, the Fifth Army had little to show for its efforts. Most of the gains were insignificant and generally resulted from German decisions to withdraw voluntarily to new positions along the Caesar Line. The 3d Panzer Grenadier, the 65th Division, and elements from the 4th Parachute Division had thoroughly shattered any hope of a rapid dash to Rome via Albano and Highway 7. The American official history paints a gloomy picture of the situation at the end of May:

> As Allied pressure mounted I Parachute Corps, pivoting on Velletri, had swung slowly back like a great gate toward high ground and the prepared positions of the Caesar Line. It appeared to Truscott at this point that the gate had been slammed shut against the Alban Hills. As night fell on the 29th the VI Corps' attempt to break through the Caesar Line on the most direct route to Rome seemed halted at every point.[5]

Harmon's 1st Armored became Truscott's battering ram to break through the Caesar Line, but on May 30 a renewed series of attacks across the VI Corps front produced few tangible results during one of the bloodiest days of the Anzio beachhead. As of midnight the 5,116 battle casualties suffered by U.S. forces in the Anzio sector since the morning of May 23 now matched those of the great German counteroffensive of February 16–20. Although Clark could hardly have failed to grasp that he had a tiger by the tail, his reaction was to blame his subordinate commanders for not being sufficiently aggressive. "I just phoned to Truscott, Harmon, Eagles and to Ryder to tell them I am disappointed with their efforts today—that one or two more days of all-out attack . . . may crack this whole German position in the Colli Laziali area. . . . I am throwing everything I have into this battle, hoping to crack this key position which will make it necessary for Kesselring to withdraw both of his armies to the north of Rome," Clark wrote in his diary the night of May 30.[6]

There is no evidence that Clark ever understood that the reason lay not with his commanders but rather with his insistence on attacking directly into the most strongly defended sector of the Caesar Line. He had, however, clearly come to the conclusion that success might yet elude him. "The German is making a determined effort to save Rome. There are indications that he is pouring in reinforcements from the north. If I do not crack this position in three or four days I may have to re-organize, wait for the Eighth Army and go at it with a coordinated attack by both armies, but I fear the same results from Eighth Army. It will not put in its full effort, for it never has."[7]

Moreover, Clark's obsession with Rome remained so deep that he still fantasized a British conspiracy existed to deny him the Eternal City. For his diary on May 30 he dictated the following:

> Most of my worries have nothing to do with the immediate battle. They are political in nature. I will name them in order of the trouble they cause me.
>
> First, the British have their eye on Rome, not withstanding Alexander's constant assurance to me that Rome is in the sector of the Fifth Army. They have drawn the Army boundary south of Route No. 6 just to the outskirts of Rome and then veered it to the north. The Eighth Army has done little fighting. It has lacked aggressiveness and failed in its part in this combined Allied effort. Yet, my effort to switch their boundary east met with a reply indicating that the Eighth Army must participate in the battle for Rome.[8]

Clark's other major concern was considerably more valid. Juin's French corps was being pinched out due to the nature of the converging corps boundaries of the Fifth Army in and around the Anzio beachhead. While the Eighth Army was still struggling up Highway 6 toward Frosinone, the French had made excellent progress along the Mediterranean flank of the Tenth Army and on May 28 were approaching the southern entrance to the Velletri-Valmontone gap. The French advance could not progress much farther without violating the II Corps boundary, which ran from south to north along the eastern slopes of the gap. About to become boxed in without a significant mission, Juin presented a plan to Clark that recommended shifting the Eighth Army into the area north of Highway 6 to encircle Rome via the axis Subiaco-Rieti-Terni, while the French drove up the highway parallel to the British toward Valmontone and Tivoli. At Valmontone the Germans would be crushed between the French and Keyes's U.S. II Corps.

The problem with Juin's proposal, which Clark endorsed, was it required that the French be given Highway 6. Even so, Alexander seemed prepared to grant Clark's request until persuaded otherwise by his chief logistician, Major General Sir Brian Robertson, who argued that the Eighth Army required Highway 6 to meet its resupply needs.[9] Alexander was not bold enough to grasp the potential of employing the French in a hooking movement across the Sacco River and Highway 6, which would have put them behind LI Mountain Corps and left von Senger's XIV Panzer Corps in the very difficult position of either retreating quickly or leaving a force behind to deal with the Eighth Army and risking encirclement. At the very least it would have forced von Vietinghoff into some difficult choices and, as Graham and Bidwell write, have taken the cork out of the Liri Valley bottle and enabled the Eighth Army to break loose.[10]

Juin's proposal was particularly propitious in light of the Eighth Army's ponderous advance up the Liri Valley. The Germans had blocked Highway 6 behind them at every bridge and culvert with mines and demolitions. They had been obligingly assisted by the Allied air forces, whose destruction of towns along the highway such as Frosinone, Ceprano, and Ferentino impeded the advance of Leese's army. The side roads were so steep and narrow that only one vehicle at a time could move forward. In short, it was poor terrain for the employment of armor. Yet this is precisely what was attempted. Major W. G. F. Jackson, a Royal Engineer officer and in the postwar years a full general and eminent historian, was a participant, and he writes:

> Eighth Army tried to advance, at first, with five divisions up. Even when this proved impracticable, there were rarely less than three divisions jostling for space as they struggled forward over roads quite unfit for the weight of traffic . . . [they] seemed to have a propensity for passing formations through each other at just the wrong moment, thereby doubling the confusion and congestion behind the leading troops, while at the same time allowing von Senger to break contact and slip back to his next delaying line almost unmolested.[11]

Once again a golden opportunity was wasted, and the French were relegated to a secondary advance that avoided Highway 6. With Clark's vaunted Turtle offensive at a virtual standstill, it was no small irony that it was Major General Fred Walker and the 36th Texas Division who saved the day. After the bloody Rapido battles, the division had reverted to Fifth Army reserve to rest and refit. Once Diadem was certain of succeeding, Alexander had decided, and Clark agreed, to shift the 36th Division to Anzio as the VI Corps reserve. On May 22 the division had begun arriving by ship and was committed to the Velletri sector three days later. Despite their somewhat stormy relationship, Clark was glad to have Walker's division at Anzio and thought it would perform well in any role assigned to it. Truscott was skeptical and believed the division was still shaky and might not be able to withstand a hard fight.[12]

Since May 27 Walker had been eyeing a possible breakthrough along the steep slopes of Monte Artemisio, whose lofty heights dominated the steep, heavily wooded eastern edge of the Alban Hills. This sector was thinly held, and the major German concerns lay farther north at Valmontone and west at Lanuvio. Walker's suspicions were confirmed when 36th Division reconnaissance units found a gap in the German lines behind Velletri. There was no sign of German troops defending the mountain.

Walker spent a sleepless night on May 28–29, but at corps commanders' conference early the next morning, Truscott issued orders that his division was to replace the ineffective 34th Division two days hence. Truscott seemed in no mood to listen to a proposed change of mission from Walker. When Truscott visited the 36th Division on May 30 Walker put it to him that his troops could drive a wedge through the Caesar Line over Monte Artemisio. Truscott conceded, "You may have something there. I'll call you back within the hour." After a hurried conference with Clark, who was enthusiastic, the plan was approved and Walker's mission changed. Truscott ended his telephone conversation with the words, "AND YOU HAD BETTER GET THROUGH," which Walker interpreted as a thinly veiled threat that he could expect to be relieved if he failed.[13] It was with confidence rather than hope that an undaunted Walker wrote in his diary the night of May 30 that the Monte Artemisio venture held promise of being spectacular. "We are taking chances, but we should succeed in a big way."[14]

That night two regiments silently climbed Monte Artemisio and captured a small (three-man) German artillery-spotting post without firing a single shot. One German was rudely interrupted in the act of taking his morning bath. The gap in the German lines was conveniently situated on the boundary line separating the I Parachute and LXXVI Panzer Corps, but by the time von Mackensen learned of the situation the afternoon of May 31, it was already too late. The Fourteenth Army commander directed his two corps commanders to do whatever was necessary to restore the situation, no matter what the cost. "In a situation of this kind, corps boundaries no longer have any meaning," he told them.[15] Von Mackensen seems to have been so distracted by the sudden turn of events on Monte Artemisio that he failed to inform Kesselring until that night. Kesselring was livid, believing that prompt notification by von Mackensen would have given him precious time to take countermeasures. As the official U.S. historian records, the disagreements between the two that had begun in early February had become a void as large as that on Monte Artemisio.[16]

A counterattack by the only Hermann Göring panzer grenadier battalion still uncommitted was firmly repulsed. Walker's engineers were assisted by the incredibly versatile 36th Engineer Regiment, which seemed to have had a hand in virtually every important battle fought at Anzio. Bulldozers worked at a dizzying forty-degree angle to turn a cart track into a passable road for tanks and vehicles. Eric Sevareid observed their feat. "This was all madly impossible," he wrote, "and yet it was being done. The men themselves, silent with fatigue, swung their shovels through the loose dirt and pitched it over the banks." Occasionally a sniper fired on them, and the shovelers would stop their work and, carbines in hand, crawl over their manmade embankment in search of the German.[17]

Velletri fell to the 141st Regiment on June 1 and, with the other two regiments now behind the Caesar Line on Monte Artemisio, Walker jubilantly noted in his diary that "we are having success everywhere. This is wonderful. I am proud of the 36th."[18] Walker had ample reason to praise his troops. The 36th had gained a reputation as the poorest division in the Fifth Army and, as a U.S. engineer officer assigned to the 15th Army Group recalls, it was during their brilliant coup on Monte Artemisio that the division was thought at last to have "found itself." The success of Monte Artemisio was no fluke, for despite the unhappy legacy of the Rapido, the 36th Division had gained valuable experience in mountain operations during the Battle of San Pietro fought in January 1944, and it was now proving the point by acquitting itself brilliantly. As Sevareid would write: "Rome must now fall. Generals Alexander and Clark would soon receive the key to the city, but surely it was General Walker who turned the key. From him they were receiving it."[19]

For Clark and Truscott the news that Monte Artemisio was in American hands relieved the frustration of the five dreadful days of stalemate along the Caesar Line. An excited Gruenther reported to his chief that the news "caused all of us to turn handsprings." For Truscott it was quite simply "the turning point in our drive to the northwest."[20]

With the successful break-in on Monte Artemisio, Clark belatedly seems to have decided to rethink how he would capture Rome. Two days earlier, on May 29, he had assigned the Valmontone sector to the U.S. II Corps, and he now ordered the 85th Infantry Division into the Lariano sector to protect the right flank of the 36th Division. Thus, five days after aborting Buffalo, Clark had come to the conclusion that the quickest way to Rome apparently lay via Valmontone after all. He created a powerful force by assigning the U.S. 88th Division from army reserve to fill the gap between the 85th Division at Lariano and the 3d Division at Artena, and directed that Frederick command a task force, "a fast hard-hitting, mobile unit with his Special Service Force, T[ank] D[estroyer]s and tanks to proceed east along Route No. 6. . . . Its mission is to destroy, discourage, disrupt, disorganize, and any other d's you can think of, any enemy forces in that area opposing Eighth Army or the FEC."

A formal directive was issued to II and VI Corps "to destroy the Fourteenth Army in our front . . . that is our mission, rather than busting into Rome." Clark confirmed his intentions at a press conference the same day. "General Clark made it clear that this attack does not have Rome as its primary objective but to kill and annihilate as many of the Germans as possible on our front."[21] This sudden change of plan can only be explained by the supposition that Clark finally realized that although the 36th Division had driven a wedge into the Caesar Line, there was no guarantee that VI Corps could successfully drive into

Rome for some days yet. Moreover, if a major effort were not made to
seize Valmontone and drive into Rome along Highway 6, Leese's
Eighth Army might well get to Rome first via the same road. Most
important, however, was the fact that a successful drive up Highway 6
toward Rome would collapse von Mackensen's left flank, making retention of the remaining Caesar Line positions virtually impossible.[22]

If ever there was vindication for having continued Operation Buffalo on May 26, it was Clark's tardy decision that the way to Rome
indeed led through Valmontone. The tragedy was that the decision
came nearly five days too late. Clark's plan required shifting the inter-
army boundary farther north, thus placing Highway 6 under Fifth
Army control and blocking Leese from entering Rome. Alexander's
reluctant approval was a tacit acknowledgment that there was no further possibility of trapping the Tenth Army. When Leese sent a liaison
officer to inform Clark that his army would advance north of Highway
6 toward Tivoli and pass east of Rome, the question of who would
capture the Eternal City was at last resolved. Rome would belong to
Mark Clark and the Fifth Army. The only unanswered question was
when the city would fall and to which American unit, Truscott's VI
Corps or Keyes's II Corps.

When Keyes opened his offensive on June 1 the Germans fought
furiously even as they prepared to abandon the Valmontone gap. In an
attempt to prevent this from occurring, Kesselring ordered the Tenth
Army to speed the 90th Panzer Grenadier Division to Valmontone, to
be followed by the remainder of XIV Panzer Corps. There a final stand
would be made. However, for Kesselring's plan to work the German
defenders had to buy time by holding Valmontone.

This proved impossible, and late on the afternoon of June 1 a white
flag appeared over the town, followed by the noise of heavy vehicular
traffic moving westward along Highway 6. The following day the 3d
Division entered Valmontone and by that night had captured the high
ground four miles further west at Palestrina. There was no sign of the
Germans, and although the vital Via Casilina belonged to the Fifth
Army, it was too little, too late.

The difficult and bitter final days of the Allied drive on Rome were
characterized by the same bloodletting that had hallmarked the entire
Italian campaign. Even as the 36th Division began to exploit the new-
found gap into the Alban Hills, elsewhere the Germans continued to
withdraw only grudgingly and after inflicting heavy casualties on the
advancing American infantry and armor. By the night of June 2–3 the
Germans had reached the limits of their ability to delay the Allied
advance on Rome. Those elements of the Tenth Army using Highway
6 had passed the Valmontone bottleneck and made good their escape,

and now it was the turn of the Fourteenth Army and they began retreating to the north, leaving only scattered units behind to harass and
delay the enemy and protect the German rear. Anzio Express, the
monster railway gun that had tormented the Allies for months, was
found in a tunnel near Nemi. The companion gun, Anzio Annie, was
successfully evacuated but was eventually captured in the port city of
Civitavecchia later in June.

Despite the serious problems faced by VI Corps, Kesselring for
some days had gradually been obliged to admit that the battle for Rome
could not last much longer. The important decisions of war are usually
made only after considerable thought and a series of appraisals of the
options. And so it was with Kesselring. The decision to abandon Rome
to the Allies was perhaps the most agonizing made by Kesselring during
the Italian campaign. Since the opening of the Allied offensive three
weeks earlier, he had used every means at his disposal to plug gaps,
delay, harass, and avoid the inevitable point where he simply ran out
of options. The morning of June 2 von Vietinghoff telephoned Kesselring to implore that permission be given to withdraw von Senger's XIV
Panzer Corps to the Caesar Line. "Kesselring changed the subject, and
for the time being evaded a definite answer. This was the beginning of
a series of interminable telephone conversations in which the Marshal
turned and twisted, and explored every conceivable possibility of re-
tarding the Allied tide. Throughout the critical days before the fall of
Rome he was in frequent consultation with the German High Command."[23]

With the Eighth Army finally beginning to pick up momentum and
the situation on Monte Artemisio and in the Valmontone gap worsening
by the hour, the time had come when nothing further was to be gained
by defending the approaches to Rome. Nor was there any advantage in
fighting for the city which would result in appalling losses and the
certain destruction of Rome's precious landmarks. On June 3 Kesselring
declared Rome an "open city" and left only minimal rearguard forces
to cover the German escape, as the remnants of Army Group C
bypassed the city and began the long journey toward the distant Gothic
Line.

For once Hitler had not insisted on a fight to the death or a pro-
tracted battle for Rome. Both Hitler and Kesselring considered that
Rome was no longer of strategic or tactical value. In February the two
had discussed what must be done when the inevitable day came when
Army Group C was forced to give up Rome to the Allies. Contrary to
Kesselring's recommendation, Hitler had ordered the bridges over the
Tiber to be left intact and on June 3 directed OKW to signal Kesselring:
"Führer decision. There must not be a battle of Rome. If necessary, the
Army Group must swing back far enough to the north-west to insure

that the city in no circumstances becomes a battlefield."[24] As much as it pained Hitler to cede anything to the Allies without a fight, even he recognized the extremely negative propaganda value that would ensue if Rome were destroyed. According to David Irving, "While [Hitler] could jest to Mussolini: 'You and I are the most reviled men in the world,' he did not want to go into history as the man who caused Rome to be destroyed."[25] Thus, for political rather than humane reasons the city was ordered spared.

On the eve of the great dash for Rome, Clark continued to display clear signs of unease. VI Corps was still encountering stiff opposition and taking heavy losses. Schlemm's I Parachute Corps fought with such fury that Truscott considered pulling the 45th Division out of the line and swinging it behind the corps front to the Velletri sector. Clark was furious with Truscott's progress and called the proposal "fantastic." Instead he ordered the 1st Armored to be prepared to exploit any breakthrough on one hour's notice. "This is a race against time, with my subordinates failing to appreciate how close the decision will be. Two German divisions are on the way down, which will, of course, sway the tide if they come in before we take the Colli Laziali."[26] To Gruenther he signaled, "Pray hard tonight." Clark's intelligence was wrong; Kesselring had no more divisions to pour into the battle and at this late date could not have committed them even if they had existed.[27]

The final drive on Rome by II Corps was appropriately led by Task Force Howze. Augmented by additional tanks, tank destroyers, and an infantry battalion of the 88th Division, Task Force Howze began leap-frogging up Highway 6 the morning of June 3. Rome was twenty-five miles away. At first there was gridlock as tanks and infantry competed for the limited space. Finally Howze worked out an arrangement whereby the tanks had exclusive use of Highway 6, with the infantry behind and to the south along parallel secondary roads. Progress was rapid despite the presence of a delaying force of some forty German panzers, there to ensure that Rome was not captured that day. When a German strongpoint was encountered, the infantry was brought in to clean it up with the aid of the tanks.

Howze placed a single tank platoon in the lead, and it would barrel down the road at ten miles an hour until the lead Sherman was invariably hit. Howze understood that speed was of the essence if the German rear guard was to be prevented from establishing an effective defense along the hilly terrain of the Via Casilina. "It was difficult and unpleasant to dispatch an element on what amounted to a suicide mission, but on the other hand such a maneuver frequently resulted in our gaining one or two thousand yards in ten minutes, at the cost of a single tank."[28] Before long Howze's tanks had outrun the infantry. "Haul ass and bypass" became the watchword, as pockets of resistance were left for the troops in the rear to clear out." Even though Howze's flanks were wide open there was little the Germans could do about it, and he knew that the forces behind him could take care of themselves.

Nevertheless, on more than one occasion that day there were several nasty engagements as Howze's tanks literally drove into the rear of fleeing German columns. On one occasion Howze was forced into a ditch with the commander of his leading tank battalion, Lieutenant Colonel Glenn Rogers, an avid student of literature. As bullets and shell fragments flew overhead, Rogers quipped, "You know, I wonder what would Walter Mitty do in a case like this?"[29]

Task Force Howze gained fifteen miles on June 3 and was now ten miles southeast of Rome. Behind them were Frederick's Special Service Force and three U.S. infantry divisions (the 3d, 85th, and 88th), all of which were desperately attempting to maneuver their forces into position to be the first into Rome. All day there had been "something akin to gold-rush fever in the air. . . . The 3d Division wanted to get some of its troops into Rome first. With that notion in mind a battalion of infantry had been held in mobile reserve on trucks for the last few days, waiting for a chance to sprint into the Eternal City. Nor were the 85th and 88th being backward about wanting to put foot into Rome first."[30]

A sense of impending victory began to pervade the command posts of every American unit involved in the drive on Rome. At Fifth Army Gruenther reported to Clark that "the Command Post has gone to hell. No one is doing any work here this afternoon. All semblance of discipline has broken down. Although the G-3 War Room purposely shows only a moderately conservative picture, every pilot—everyone in fact— who has come from Anzio . . . has brought back a pair of pants full of ants, with the result that this insuppressible wave of optimism and expectancy has swept through the headquarters. My picture to Harding has been: 'The condition is favorable. General Clark is quite happy with the situation but he will make no predictions. His big ambition is to kill Germans and then more Germans.'"[31]

Not to be outdone, Frederick sent two regiments at midnight to seize the western suburb of Tor Sapienza by dawn. Then, at 0106 hours, Keyes signaled Frederick: "Secure bridges over the Tiber above 68 Northing within the City of Rome."[32] The rush was on. Kesselring had ordered that the main bridges over the Tiber within Rome were to be left intact. Only those leading into the city were to be demolished. Teams of tanks, infantry, and engineers with bridging equipment were prepared to dash forward the following morning in an attempt to seize as many bridges intact as possible.[33] A message from Clark to all Fifth Army troops decreed that no unnecessary damage be inflicted on the city, but in the event of resistance commanders were to take whatever

measures necessary. On June 4 the German rear guard made it plain
there was still a price to be paid for entry to Rome.

Although many units have claimed to have been the first into
Rome, one account of the fall of Rome describes "Sunday, June 4, [as]
a day so crammed with confusion, drama, and historic high-water marks
that even now there is no one source which can accurately state, 'This
is the way it happened and this is the order of events.' "[34]

Most of the fighting took place in the suburbs of Rome, where Task
Force Howze and the Special Service Force encountered the stiffest
opposition of any unit on June 4. A heavy battle took place just past the
Roma sign on Highway 6 that marked the city limits. A steel curtain of
antitank and automatic weapons and artillery fire from Germans concealed in buildings and behind stone walls greeted the would-be captors of Rome. The battle raged for nearly nine hours as Frederick
withheld ordering artillery fire for fear of killing civilians caught in the
cross fire. Several tanks were knocked out and it became an infantry
battle. For the moment the Germans were delaying Allied entry to
Rome and doing a good job of it. These rearguard units were elements
of the 4th Parachute and Hermann Göring Divisions. Kesselring and
von Mackensen had left behind elements of two of the best German
divisions in Italy to protect the rear of the Fourteenth Army.

During the afternoon the Third Regiment of the Special Service
Force began moving into the city proper. There was no strong opposition, but the Hermann Göring and Fascist supporters turned every
streetcorner and piazza into traps that were sprung on the unwary.
Several Fascists, in the guise of assisting the liberators, led them instead
into captivity. Street warfare is among the deadliest endeavors to be
performed by infantrymen, and Rome this day was no exception. Snipers, scattered tanks, flak wagons, and antitank guns made up pockets of
resistance that had to be eliminated.[35]

As other II Corps units began probing the outskirts of Rome, Truscott's four divisions were still encountering stubborn resistance from
determined rear guard units. The 34th and 45th Divisions were busily
engaged in clearing the remaining Germans from Lanuvio and Albano,
Harmon's 1st Armored was loose on Highway 7, and Truscott fully
expected it would be the first VI Corps unit to enter Rome. Fred
Walker, however, had other ideas. He was angry that Clark had
reneged on a promise to give the 36th Division public credit for the
breakthrough of the Caesar Line and determined that by hook or crook
the 36th Division would be the first into Rome.

As his three regiments descended from the heights of the Alban
Hills toward Highway 7, Walker encountered Lieutenant Colonel Louis
V. Hightower at the head of a column of 1st Armored tanks. Although
outranked, Hightower made it clear to Walker that he had no business

there. The 1st Armored had priority. Walker, in turn, insisted the road would be shared by both units at the same time and there was nothing Hightower could do about it. The result was sheer chaos as tanks and infantry jockeyed for position along a highway that could barely accommodate one unit at a time, much less two. Not only was the bottleneck impeding progress to Rome, but the presence nearby of a II Corps infantry unit might soon cost VI Corps the use of its own highway. An angry Truscott soon learned of the mess on Highway 7 and roared up in his jeep to confront the 36th Division commander. " 'Fred,' he gruffly asked Walker, 'what are you doing outside your sector boundary?' " Walker had been caught redhanded violating his left boundary and was forced to move his troops north onto secondary roads. As they approached Rome they were greeted by artillery, tank, and machine-gun fire that necessitated a house-to-house advance. The artillery fire turned out to be from a battery of the 1st Armored Division; the rest came from the German rear guard.[36]

Truscott then turned to Hightower and asked if he knew his orders. "He assured me he was to secure the bridges over the Tiber. I asked: 'Well what are you waiting for?' He saluted and without a word turned and signalled 'Forward, march,' then ran for his own vehicle. There was a grinding of gears, a roar of motors, and clouds of dust and smoke and the column roared off down the street toward the Tiber."[37] A short while later Harmon joined Truscott on the outskirts of Rome, and as the two men began to confer over a map, a German machine gun opened fire from a nearby stone outhouse.

> This, I thought, was the ultimate anticlimax. The two of us, who had gone through so much together, were to be killed by fire from an Italian privy. As we crouched there, a Sherman tank came up the highway. I shouted and pointed. The Sherman tank didn't bother with its guns. It just turned at right angles and charged across the field and butted squarely into the building. When the tank had finished, there was neither machine gun, outhouse nor German.
>
> The tank commander saluted from his turret and rolled on. Truscott and I picked ourselves up, resumed the tattered vestments of our dignity, and went back to being generals again.[38]

Another who courted death on June 4 was Geoffrey Keyes. An engineer colonel named Andersson found Keyes sitting exposed on rock. " 'General, you know better than to sit out here where snipers are shooting,' and Keyes answered, 'Go away, Andersson, this is the first quiet spot I've seen in weeks. If I go back anywhere, they'll get me on the telephone.' "[39]

Robert Frederick was wounded twice on June 4, his eighth and ninth Purple Hearts of the Italian campaign, "thereby easily establishing himself as the most shot-at-and-hit general in American military history."[40]

Chaos reigned in the VI Corps sector as tanks and infantry competed for the roads. The situation was not helped by the VI Corps chief of staff, Brigadier General Don Carleton, whose calls to the various command posts urged all-out pursuit and suggested that speed was of the essence if VI Corps were to beat Crittenberger's U.S. IV Corps into Rome. The result was more delays from traffic jams than from German resistance.

Late that afternoon on the other side of Rome, Frederick's troops were still being held up along Highway 6 by heavy resistance from the Hermann Göring near the blue-and-white Roma sign. Several of Howze's tanks had been knocked out, and it was clear there would be no easy passage into the heart of the Eternal City for the next few hours. Frederick was directing his men when Clark and Keyes arrived in a jeep and inquired what was holding up the advance into the city. The heavy firing continued as Frederick explained the problem and what he was doing about it. During a lull, the three generals left the cover of a nearby ditch and approached the Roma sign to pose for photographers. "Golly, Bob," said Clark, "I'd like to have that sign in my command post." At that moment a German sniper opened fire with a Schmeisser. One of the bullets smashed through the sign, uncomfortably close to the Fifth Army commander's head, unceremoniously hastening the return of the three generals to the safety of the ditch. Frederick told Clark: "That is what's holding up the First Special Service Force." As anxious as he was to enter Rome, Clark realized there was to be no triumphal entry that day. After Clark departed, Frederick had the Roma sign removed and sent to the Fifth Army commander as a souvenir.[41]

The night of June 4 both the 1st Armored and 36th divisions penetrated the city limits. Harmon's division entered first and secured a number of bridges across the Tiber. About midnight Walker's infantrymen entered the city and began to pick their way through the maze of dark and deserted streets. With only moonlight to guide them, it was an eerie procession. At first there was only the sound of boots echoing from the pavement and, for those lucky enough to ride, the clashing of gears as the trucks followed. Walker had authorized his troops to ride on anything that moved, and they did. Some rode on the tubes of 155-mm howitzers, and sixteen men somehow managed to hitch a ride on a jeep and its trailer.

There were no Italian policemen, no directional signs, no street lights, and no lights in any of the buildings . . . as we moved along the dark streets, we could hear people clapping their hands at the windows of the buildings, but we could not see them. Later, when it became evident that the Germans had abandoned the city, men, women and children, in night dress and slippers, came into the dark streets to welcome the Americans. Some ran up and down the columns offering wine to the soldiers. . . . After daylight the Italians appeared on the streets dressed for a holiday; women and children threw flowers at the passing soldiers.[42]

It was another of the many ironies of this long, bitter campaign that by the time the citizens of Rome emerged into the streets to wildly celebrate their liberation the morning of June 5, most of the American units that had done the liberating had long since left the city in pursuit of the Germans. The recipients of Roman hospitality were mostly formations that had entered the city that morning. No British unit entered Rome until early on June 5, and it was not until early the following morning that the South African 6th Armored Division passed through en route to the northwest.[43]

On the other side of Rome the First Special Service Force was still cleaning out pockets of resistance and completing its task of seizing eight of the key bridges, including the Ponte Angelo, which led into the Castel Sant'Angelo. The streets were absolute bedlam as Romans shouted, paraded, and sang. Competition between American units for occupancy of the choicest hotels and villas was a sidelight that was pursued with considerable ingenuity and initiative. Not everyone was amused. Peter Tompkins, who had survived life on the run since January, arrived to find that his apartment had been requisitioned by a pompous American brigadier general. Tompkins soon found that even liberation brought with it the spoils of war. "The mentality of some of these senior [Allied] officers was incredible. The *first* thing they wanted us to do was to provide women for them. I had this apartment which I used in my work, and by God, if I didn't come home that night and there is this fancy young American general who wanted to know what *I* was doing there." As Tompkins watched with mounting anger and astonishment, "His aide appeared with some girls and he was something you will not believe. This one was a prize—you know, riding boots and breeches and so forth."[44]

Mark Clark entered Rome at the head of a small procession of jeeps with Gruenther and another general. They soon became lost but eventually found their way to St. Peter's Square. As Clark later described it:

As we stopped to look up at the great dome of St. Peter's a priest walking along the street paused by my jeep and said in English, "Welcome to Rome. It there any way I can help you?"

"Well," I replied, "we'd like to get to [the] Capitoline Hill."

He gave us directions, and added, "We are certainly proud of the

American 5th Army. May I introduce myself?" And he told me his name.
He came from Detroit.

"My name's Clark," I replied.

We both expressed pleasure at the meeting, and the priest started to
move on. Then he stopped and took another look and said, "What did you
say your name is?" A number of Italians had gathered round by this time
and were listening to our conversation. When the priest told them that I
was the commander of the 5th Army a youth on a bicycle shouted that he
would lead us to the Capitoline Hill. He did, pedalling along in front of our
jeep and shouting to everybody on the street to get out of the way because
General Clark was trying to get to the Capitoline Hill.[45]

One of Clark's first acts was to hold a press conference on the balustrade
of the city hall, overlooking the Piazza del Campidoglio. A horde of
photographers and newsreel cameramen were capturing the moment
as Clark posed against the backdrop of ancient Rome below. Juin, Truscott, Crittenberger, and Keyes all arrived. Clark shook hands with each
as the correspondents crowded around him. "Well, gentlemen, I didn't
really expect to have a press conference here—I just called a little
meeting with my corps commanders to discuss the situation. However,
I'll be glad to answer your questions. This is a great day for Fifth
Army."[46] Juin flushed with embarrassment, and the other corps commanders chafed at their role in this contrived *opéra bouffe*.

Eric Sevareid was among many of the correspondents profoundly
offended by Clark's insensitive remarks, which pointedly failed to mention British or French participation in the bloody battles to liberate
Rome. In his memoirs he wrote with considerable bitterness:

> That was the immortal remark of Rome's modern-day conqueror. It was
> not, apparently, a great day for the world, for the Allies, for all the suffering
> people who had desperately looked toward the time of peace. It was a
> great day for the Fifth Army. (Men of the Eighth Army, whose sector did
> not happen to include Rome but without whose efforts this day could not
> have occurred, did not soon forget the remark.) Then Clark spread a map
> on the balustrade, and with the whole mob pressing close proceeded to
> point out something or other to his commanders. The cameras ground, the
> corps commanders, red with embarrassment, looked back and forth from
> us to the map. We pushed down the steps. A colleague commented: "On
> this historic occasion I feel like vomiting."[47]

While Mark Clark was making his triumphal entry into Rome, most of
the weary men who had fought the bloody battles of Cassino and Anzio
were content merely to see a brief lull in the fighting. Some were on
the march northwest of Rome attempting to catch Kesselring's fleeing
forces before they reached the safety of the Gothic Line north of Florence; others were given temporary respite in encampments near

Rome. One was a British infantry lieutenant named David Cole, of the 2d Royal Inniskilling Fusiliers, who had marched on foot across Sicily, endured a winter on the Gustav Line, and had seen many of his comrades die during the stalemate at Anzio. Like his men, Cole was weary. Suddenly, the morning of June 4 became blissfully silent, almost unnervingly so. "No enemy shells or bullets; just the grass shimmering in the warm breeze; a bird hopping round cheerfully on a dead [German] paratrooper: butterflies flitting here and there: and the scent of wild flowers. The Germans had gone."

That evening Lieutenant Cole played no part in the wild celebrations taking place in Rome. His battalion was bivouacked some five miles west of the city, near the Tiber, and he observed the liberation of Rome by seating himself under a tree and trying "with a lighted cigarette, to put an end to some lice that had invaded my person."

The next day Cole wrote home: "Today I had my hair cut in Rome and drank gin and vermouth in the Excelsior." As his jeep moved slowly through the streets of the Eternal City, Cole heard the same thing over and over: "We are so happy to see you at last. Why did it take you so long?"[48]

Epilogue

I can only assume that the immediate lure of Rome
for its publicity value persuaded Mark Clark to
switch the direction of his advance.

—ALEXANDER

The unfortunate legacy of Anzio has
been controversy over what might have been and considerable but
misguided criticism that the fault lay with Lucas. The evidence has
revealed a far more complex picture than Lucas's mere failure to seize
the Alban Hills. In *Tug of War*, British historians Dominick Graham and
Shelford Bidwell argue that the Italian campaign was not only inevitable from the moment of the first Allied landings in North Africa, but
that, once begun, the war in Italy "demonstrated the self-generating
momentum of military operations. . . . The invasion of mainland Italy
was launched in the hope that a brief and limited effort could bring
about large gains. As so often seen in history of warfare, this had proved
a delusion."[1] Anzio was a prime example of what they meant. Until
Winston Churchill intervened to seize control of Shingle, the operation
had been headed for the scrap heap. However, once embraced by the
British prime minister, Shingle took on the force of a juggernaut at
the same moment that there were important changes of command in
the Mediterranean theater of operations.

Churchill never acknowledged his culpability over Shingle and,
indeed, publicly disavowed it with his now-famous complaint about the
wildcat turning into a stranded whale. During the planning for Overlord Churchill frequently used Anzio as a negative example. In one
instance the prime minister wrote to Eisenhower, "Let me remind you
of the figures of Anzio, viz., 125,000 men with 23,000 vehicles, all so

painfully landed to carry them, and they only got twelve miles."[2] Despite his public stance, Churchill privately seems to have been haunted by Anzio and feared that the same result might occur with Overlord. Churchill was never able to relate the boldness of an attack on the German rear to the hazards of an operation that made assumptions that had no basis in fact. Blinded by the prospect of seizing Rome and ousting the Germans from southern Italy by one magnificent military stroke, Churchill never heeded the warnings that the Shingle force was insufficient to accomplish the lofty aims set for it.[3]

Despite Churchill's public disavowal of Anzio, it seems clear from Lord Moran's diary that the prime minister fully understood his responsibility when he told him in September 1944 that "Anzio was my worst moment in the war. I had most to do with it. I didn't want two Suvla Bays in one lifetime."[4]

Only Alexander or Clark could have derailed Shingle and, although they might have succeeded, the inevitable result would have been their replacement with someone who would carry out the operation. However, as we have seen, it was unthinkable that Alexander would have taken such a position, even if he had opposed Shingle.

In the forty-six years since Anzio, John Porter Lucas has been the target of the critics who have complained that Shingle was a unique opportunity that was unnecessarily squandered by a timid American general. In recent years the focus of attention has begun to shift to the roles of Alexander and Clark, and what has emerged is the sorry tale of an operation that was doomed to failure from the moment of its inception.

There was nothing wrong with the basic conception of Shingle. In fact, if the operation had been carried out with a sufficiently large force, Kesselring might well have been forced to abandon the Cassino front in favor of a stand along the Gothic Line. The main flaw of Shingle was its logistical restrictions, which severely reduced its scope to a size far too small to achieve its basic aim of cutting the German lines of communication with Cassino.

Alexander's understanding of his enemy was at times shockingly deficient. Despite daily examples of German defensive intransigence, Alexander never seems to have grasped that his German counterpart was not the sort of commander to be intimidated. After the war Alexander told the official U.S. historians that he had expected the VI Corps landings to be followed by the immediate thrust of small mobile forces to the Alban Hills, which would cause the German Tenth Army to pull back from the Cassino front. "It was a bluff," he said, "to scare the Germans into pulling back . . . all would depend on whether or not the Germans were fooled by our bluff. If the Germans on the southern front felt that their rear was threatened and exposed, they might pull back."

Alexander qualified his remarks by stating that he had wanted three divisions in the assault, and looking back now, he felt the landings were made too soon, "before we had enough strength to make sure of its success. . . . The idea of an end-run was good, but as Alexander pointed out, this was a bluff which didn't work. He thinks it might have if Lucas had pushed out immediately after the landing." The notes of the official historians confirm their belief that Alexander sincerely anticipated success at Anzio. *"It seems clear from what Alexander said, that he never expected the Allies would have to fight to hold a line based on the Alban Hills. He felt the bluff would work.* [italics added]"[5]

Alexander's argument that Lucas's failure to advance to the Alban Hills was a major factor contributing to the Allied dilemma in early 1944 ignores the fact that Clark, too, had misgivings that were clearly expressed in the Fifth Army operational order, which he and Brann had deliberately modified to provide Lucas with a vague mission at Anzio. Moreover, although his own chief of staff had openly questioned Lucas's leadership abilities before the operation ever commenced, Alexander declined to replace him. Only when Lucas failed to live up to Alexander's fanciful expectations did the Allied ground commander decide he was unfit to command the beachhead forces.

We now know that Anzio managed to shake Churchill's faith in Alexander. By early February his anxiety had reached its zenith, and, as Sir John Colville noted in his diary: "The P.M. is suffering from indigestion and also very perturbed by Shingle's lack of success. It was strategically sound and it had a perfect beginning. He cannot understand the failure to push inland from the beach-head. While the battle still rages he is refraining from asking Alexander the questions to which the P.M. can find no answer, but his great faith in A., though not dissipated, is a little shaken."[6]

The Allied high command in Italy failed to address the all-important question of Kesselring's response to the landings. The intelligence estimates proved exceptionally accurate by predicting that the Germans could move twenty thousand troops into the Anzio sector within twenty-four hours, which is precisely what they did.[7] But would the presence of the Shingle force have compelled Kesselring to abandon the Gustav Line even if it had sent spearheads into the Alban Hills soon after the landings?

The unwarranted optimism within the Allied high command that the threat posed by VI Corps would be a sufficient threat for the German c-in-c to move Army Group C to the Pisa-Rimini Line never had any factual basis. To the contrary, Kesselring had consistently demonstrated that he was not one to panic, no matter how dire the circumstances. Moreover, the bluff that Alexander expected Lucas to carry out was only valid if Lucas moved VI Corps into the Alban Hills and was able to isolate the Tenth Army. Lucas never had any intention of doing so and Alexander should have known this. Even if he had done so, Alexander's premise neglected to take into account that Lucas would somehow have to keep open his logistical lifeline to the vital port of Anzio.

Without an adequate force to defend both the Alban Hills and his line of communication, Lucas could do one or the other but not both. Valmontone was the only place where a military force could have cut Highway 6 and the main railway line to Cassino. The notion that Lucas could have done so with the forces at his disposal and maintained a link to Anzio is ludicrous in the extreme.

Colonel (later General Sir) Desmond Fitzpatrick served on the 15th Army Group staff, and he has written: "To my mind, the most curious feature of the whole business was the fact that Fifth Army and 15 Army Group did nothing, anyway nothing effective, to ensure that VI Corps planned to carry out its allotted task. Brigadier Richardson (Alexander's liaison officer to Clark) certainly knew that there were no plans for exploitation."[8] If the intent was for Lucas to move into the Alban Hills, where was the additional armor necessary to man the spearhead force? Until the first elements of the U.S. 1st Armored Division began moving ashore late in January the composition of the Shingle force was simply never geared for exploitation operations.

In Sicily the Germans had held a force of nearly 500,000 Allied troops with 60,000 troops; at Salerno they had reacted violently to Avalanche, and since then had made the Allies pay dearly for virtually every yard of ground. Why Kesselring would suddenly abandon Cassino without a better reason never seems to have been seriously considered by the Allied commanders in Italy.

The case for Kesselring was well put by Alexander's chief intelligence officer, Major General Terence Airey.

> The Germans in our African and Italian campaign, were *invariably* surprised from Alamein onwards to the end. But they were *never* panicked and Kesselring's reaction was always to fight back hard with what reserves he could muster in the hope of restoring the situation before ordering a withdrawal . . . as soon as he saw he was being surprised [along the Garigliano and at Anzio], Kesselring deliberately set out to seal off the threatened area, thin out where he could to build up a reserve, and be ready to use the latter as soon as he was sure what we were really up to. He was never stampeded into a withdrawal.[9]

Although Lucas could be faulted for failing to seize Campoleone and Cisterna and for his inability to relate to the British commanders, his role as the scapegoat for Anzio was inevitable. Yet every commander

who served under Lucas at Anzio, including those who severely criticized his leadership, later made it clear that to have attempted to hold
the Alban Hills would have been military folly. Here is what Major
General Lucian K. Truscott has said:

> The initial strategic concept erred in two respects: overestimating the
> effect that the landings would have upon the German high command;
> and underrating the German capacity for countering this move. Our
> own high command expected—or at least hoped—the landings would
> cause a hasty German withdrawal from the southern Front. None of the
> commanders who landed at Anzio held any such belief, and we had
> learned through experience to respect the resourcefulness of our Ger-
> man opponent. Any reckless advance to the Colli Laziali without first
> establishing a firm base to protect our beaches would have been sheer
> madness and would almost certainly have resulted in the eventual de-
> struction of the landing forces. . . . I suppose that armchair strategists will
> always labor under the delusion that there was a "fleeting opportunity"
> at Anzio during which some Napoleonic figure would have charged over
> the Colli Laziali, played havoc with the German line of communications,
> and galloped on into Rome. Any such concept betrays a lack of compre-
> hension of the military problem involved.[10]

And Major General Ernest N. Harmon:

> Persistent people . . . maintain that the VI Corps, immediately after the
> Anzio landing, should have swept up through the mountain passes and on
> to Rome. To be sure, it could have been done, and, in staff meetings at
> Naples, I proposed it. I am glad now I was overruled. Armor could have
> been in the mountains by sunset and in Rome the next day, but the
> fast-assembling Germans would have sliced our supply lines and chewed
> us up at their leisure. The Allies would have had Rome for twenty-four
> hours. After that the Germans would have had us.[11]

And Major General G. W. R. Templer:

> I never understood how Anzio could possibly work. I am absolutely con-
> vinced that if Lucas had gone on (which he could have) he could have got
> to Rome, but within a week or a fortnight there wouldn't have been a
> single British soldier left in the bridge-head. They would all have been
> killed or wounded or prisoners. We would have had a line of communica-
> tions forty-five miles long from Anzio to Rome with absolutely open flanks.
> The Germans produced seven divisions in ten days, with plenty of armour,
> and we wouldn't have had a chance.[12]

And Major General W. R. C. Penney:

> Lucian Truscott was under no illusions. He was the original chap chosen
> to carry out the operation on a one division basis. His language describing

what would have been their fate was picturesque. . . . We could have had one night in Rome and 18 months in P.W. camps.[13]

Truscott, Templer, and Harmon were three of the most offensive-minded commanders of World War II and proved it on the field of battle. Nevertheless, each has thoroughly debunked the notion that a great opportunity had been missed.

Finally, Mark Clark himself clearly exhibited his misgivings when he deliberately let Lucas off the hook by modifying his orders. Although he accepted the premise that Lucas could have advanced to the Alban Hills, he was equally clear that they could not have been held, and later wrote:

> It was not possible that upon landing we could just move in and occupy the Alban Hills. The German reaction to our landing was swift. We had broken the German [Enigma] code and could read the message from Hitler 'to drive us into the sea and drown us.' . . . Knowing of the impending onslaught, it was necessary to dig in, for had we advanced, we would have surely been defeated. . . . Various armchair strategists in the United States and elsewhere are now criticizing the Fifth Army for failure to seize the Alban Hills and take Rome immediately. Such a course would have been reckless in the extreme.[14]

Among those who believed that Lucas had acted prudently was George Marshall, who noted: "We could have advanced to the Alban Hills, but . . . for every mile of advance there were seven or more miles added to the perimeter. We did not have enough men in the expedition to advance on the Alban Hills, hold them and also hold Anzio which was what was required."[15]

These pronouncements were substantiated by Kesselring, who told an American correspondent in 1946: "It would have been the Anglo-American doom to over-extend themselves. The landing force was initially weak, only a division or so of infantry, and without armor. It was a half-way measure as an offensive that was your basic error."[16]

After the war Lucas complained to Keyes: "If they wanted me to read beyond their instructions, or if they changed their points of view and wanted to do something else, they could have told me. Alexander, Clark, Devers—they were all there breathing down my neck and not one of them said to keep going, or to do this, that or the other thing until it was all over. Then they said, 'Oh my, Lucas hasn't done a thing.' "[17]

Finally, there is this assessment of Lucas by two American historians:

> By the time a man arrives at the rank of general, his capabilities and weaknesses are no strangers to the record. He becomes a readily identifiable piece of equipment. . . . General Lucas was a well known commodity.

He was a methodical and careful man, and when he was picked to lead the Anzio landing, a methodical and careful operation should have been expected. His role as the historical scapegoat for this key move in the march on Rome is unfairly awarded. If there is any blame, it should not be placed upon Lucas, who acted scrupulously within his own frame of reference in the execution of the orders given him. . . . Alexander was the superior officer on the scene. There was no reason for Sir Harold to "request" Clark to make the dismissal; he was at the beachhead during the time of the confusion and indecision and, as commanding officer, it was incumbent upon him to *order* the changes he felt necessary in order to achieve the victory in the size he wanted.[18]

No one can answer the question of what the Germans would have done had Lucas attempted the bluff Alexander seemed to think would work. Despite the assertion of Kesselring's able chief of staff, General Siegfried Westphal, that "the road to Rome was open, and an audacious flying column could have penetrated the city . . . for two days after the landing,"[19] the evidence strongly suggests that it would have ended very badly. Alexander was never prone to dwell on what might have been. However, in the case of Anzio, even Alexander was left wondering if perhaps there had been a more aggressive commander at Anzio, such as Patton, it might have turned out differently. And, as Martin Blumenson concludes: "For not having tried, Lucas could not altogether, nor would he ever, be forgiven."[20]

Another unresolved question is whether or not Anzio was even necessary. It has been generally accepted that, despite its dreadful price, Operation Shingle was an indispensable ingredient to the eventual breaking of the Cassino stalemate. Three years after the Anzio landings Kesselring was quoted as saying: "I can say this, if you had never pitted your divisions in the Mediterranean, as at Anzio-Nettuno, you would not have won the victory in the West."[21]

The challenge to those who believe Anzio was necessary comes from recent reappraisals of the Italian campaign. Both John Ellis and Graham and Bidwell have made a compelling case that at the Rapido and later during the assaults of the town and heights of Monte Cassino, Alexander and Clark repeatedly failed to make effective use of their forces and it was this, combined with poor tactics, that permitted the Germans to retain control of the Gustav Line for so long. As Ellis reminds us:

On the whole, both Fifth and Eighth Armies were poorly led during the Cassino battles, where operations were consistently marred by a lack of strategic vision and slipshod staff work. Again and again these two factors combined to produce attacks that were doomed from the start, directed as they were against the strongest and least accessible portions of the German line and against an enemy who resolutely refused to begin the withdrawal so often predicted by the Allies. Monte Cassino and the Liri Valley seemed to completely dominate the minds of Clark, Leese and Alexander as they pondered ways to rupture the Gustav Line. And so, month after month, they squandered fine divisions in isolated attacks mounted in quite inadequate strength.[22]

The Shingle force could have been better employed in support of a decisive operation to break the Gustav Line or in a shorter end run. " 'A correct strategic move' Anzio certainly was not," writes Morison. "By splitting the Fifth Army and landing part of it outside mutually supporting distance, the smaller part was exposed to destruction in detail; and that is probably just what would have happened, but for General Lucas's much criticized caution. If a 'left hook' was wanted to employ Allied amphibious forces, a short one to Gaeta or Terracina would have been wiser than the long one to Anzio. Unfortunately both were too far from Rome and the Alban Hills to interest Mr. Churchill."[23]

On the German side, Kesselring was not immune from criticism and his strongest detractor had from the outset been Erwin Rommel, who believed that Italy could not be held against major Allied attacks. Rommel had instead advocated a deliberate fighting withdrawal, which would inflict heavy losses to Allied forces, to the Gothic Line positions in the northern Apennines. Although Hitler initially wavered, he was sufficiently impressed by Kesselring's defense of southern Italy that he approved a strategy of holding the Cassino positions for as long as possible.

Another critic of Kesselring was Colonel Alexis Freiherr von Roenne, chief of the Western Intelligence Branch of OKW, the Army high command in Berlin. Writing to Kesselring's operations officer in March 1944, Roenne argued that the German army was defending the wrong place.

> The final decision of all western European operations, and presumably of the whole war, will be made at that point where the enemy high command commits the bulk of its forces. That point is not in Italy. It is the task of the German command therefore to meet the decisive enemy blow with all of the strength at its disposal. . . . If the western invasion [i.e., France] can be decisively repelled, even the complete loss of Italy will diminish in importance. And if the invasion succeeds, then a successful defense of Italy will have lost all meaning.[24]

Although Colonel Roenne's views never prevailed with either Hitler or Kesselring, his assessment of defending Italy instead of France was shared by none other than the U.S. chief of staff, George Marshall, who, it will be recalled, rendered the same opinion after the war.[25]

Equally controversial was the final offensive that led to the capture of Rome in early June. To his death, Mark Clark defended his decision to break off the attack against Valmontone in favor of an attack northwest of the Anzio beachhead to capture Rome.

One of his critics is Raleigh Trevelyan, who asserts that the lure of Rome became such a magnet that Clark literally "ran himself into a stalemate."[26] Clark never doubted he would overcome Alexander's misgivings for the simplest of reasons: He knew Alexander would not use his authority to overturn his decision. It was the most blatant challenge to Alexander's authority since Sicily, when Montgomery and Patton had run their own independent campaigns. A more audacious commander would have exploited his success as Clark should have in driving for Valmontone; and a more forceful commander than Alexander would have ordered him to do so. Graham and Bidwell argue that "a Patton or a Guderian might have dared to do it. It would be wrong to argue that any or all of these were certain to succeed, but it can be stated positively that to do nothing, to risk nothing, was absolutely wrong. That nothing was done was the consequence of the fatal conjunction of two such men as Clark and Alexander; the one with iron determination to pursue a false aim, the other with the worthiest of intentions but lacking in backbone."[27]

Although there is no evidence that Alexander was taken in by Clark's deception, he again declined to exert his authority. To have done so at this stage of the war would likely have been in vain, for, as Martin Blumenson writes: "He had no ground for questioning Clark's judgment on the best course of action in Clark's own zone of responsibility."[28]

Did Clark squander an opportunity to end the frustrating Italian campaign sooner? There are varying opinions about whether VI Corps could have trapped the Tenth Army, but there is every reason to believe that Truscott's Buffalo force would at least have taken a heavier toll on the retreating German army than it did. Nor could the Germans have prevented VI Corps from seizing the Valmontone Gap. As official historian Sidney T. Mathews writes: "The greatest irony was that if the VI Corps' main effort had continued on the Valmontone axis on May 26 and the days following, Clark could undoubtedly have reached Rome more quickly than he was able to do by the route northwest from Cisterna. The VI Corps also could have cut Highway 6 and put far greater pressure on the Tenth Army than it did."[29]

Truscott never wavered in his belief that Clark was dead wrong when he emasculated plan Buffalo in favor of a direct thrust on Rome.

"There has never been any doubt in my mind that had General Clark held loyally to General Alexander's instructions, had he not changed the direction of my attack to the northwest on May 26th, the strategic objective of Anzio would have been accomplished in full. To be first in Rome was poor compensation for this lost opportunity."[30]

Alexander's tepid public criticism of Clark's decision failed to mask his resentment over one of the great lost opportunities of the war. Typically, his feelings remained private except for these pointed remarks in his memoirs:

> When the final battle for Rome was launched, the role of the Anzio force was to break out and at Valmontone get across the German main line of supply to their troops in Cassino. But for some inexplicable reason General Clark's Anglo-American forces never reached their objectives, though, according to my information later, there was nothing to prevent their being gained. Instead, Mark Clark switched the point of attack north to the Alban Hills, in the direction of Rome. If he had succeeded in carrying out my plan the disaster to the enemy would have been much greater; indeed, most of the German forces south of Rome would have been destroyed. . . . I had always assured General Clark in conversation that Rome would be entered by his army; and I can only assume that the immediate lure of Rome for its publicity value persuaded him to switch the direction of his advance.[31]

Alexander discussed Valmontone at length during his interview with the U.S. official historians, and he reiterated that he believed that an attack by a reinforced VI Corps along the Cori-Valmontone axis was the only one that offered the opportunity to cut the German line of communications and threaten the rear of the Tenth Army on the southern front. Alexander believed that if

> VI Corps could get to Valmontone, it could exploit quickly up Highway 6 and get in behind the "C" positions based in the Alban Hills. . . . If the Albano road attack were made, the main point of the 'two punch' in his 'one-two punch' scheme would be directed at a place which would not be decisive. It would involve a frontal assault at a point where the German defenses were expected to be strong. . . . At the AAI conference in conversations with Clark in April, Alexander had made it plain that the Cori-Valmontone attack was the only one he thought worthwhile. Clark never told Alexander, as far as Alexander remembers, before the May 1944 attack began, that he was opposed to the Cori-Valmontone attack, even after Alexander visited the beachhead on 5 May.[32]

The evidence supports Alexander's assertion that Clark and Gruenther misrepresented to him the reason for switching the main attack to the northwest. "Alexander was told by Clark that the thrust towards Val-

montone was being stopped by German reinforcements and that he
was shifting the axis to break through quickly. . . . Alexander did not
know at the time that the Germans had insufficient strength in the
Valmontone area and in the Velletri Gap to have stopped VI Corps."[33]

The British official history covering this period of the war in Italy
was not published until 1986, and it delivered a stinging criticism of
Clark:

> On 25th May Clark did not face a new situation or new factors and he could
> very easily communicate with Alexander. He knew that Alexander's or-
> ders stood because Alexander had ordered 6th U.S. Corps to strike at
> Valmontone on 23rd May. In short he had no reason to depart from Alexan-
> der's orders except his ambition that 5th Army should be the first to enter
> Rome. Clark's determination to achieve his ambition spoiled his judge-
> ment and led him to disregard the principle of war which is termed
> maintenance of the objective.[34]

The most powerful evidence of Clark's blunder comes from the German commanders themselves. In a postwar report von Vietinghoff
wrote: "If the Allies, as in previous days, had directed their [main]
attack in the direction of Valmontone, the initially weak forces of the
Hermann Göring Panzer Division would not have been able to prevent
a breakthrough. The fall of Rome, the separation of both German armies, and the bottling up of the bulk of their units would have been
unavoidable."[35]

Not only was Clark's decision made at the precise moment when
the Fifth Army was on the verge of the greatest Allied triumph of the
Italian campaign, but it also coincided with the time of gravest peril for
Army Group C thus far in the Italian campaign. By changing horses in
midstream Clark was ignoring one of Napoleon's basic tenets:

> It is an approved maxim of war, never to do what the enemy wishes you
> to do, for this reason alone, that he desires it. A field of battle, therefore,
> which he has previously studied and reconnoitered should be avoided, and
> double care should be taken where he has had time to fortify or entrench.
> One consequence deductible from this principle is, *never to attack a posi-
> tion in front which you can gain by turning.* [italics added][36]

Fridolin von Senger fully agreed with Alexander that Valmontone was
the weak point to be exploited by the two Allied offensives:

> On May 26th, when the enemy had established a junction with his forces
> in the Nettuno bridgehead, I felt I should advise the 10th Army com-
> mander to take the mobile divisions out of the [XIV Panzer Corps] as
> quickly as possible and to employ them to screen its deep right flank at

Valmontone. This was the point of greatest threat to all German divisions standing [to the] south. . . . If the enemy should succeed in firmly securing the key position at Valmontone, the withdrawal of these forces would be jeopardized. The remaining available mountain roads east of the Via Casilina were now of doubtful and limited value in view of the enemy's overwhelming air superiority. Moreover . . . the enemy could use fast troops to block even these mountain roads.[37]

Kesselring was never in any doubt as to how his two armies managed to escape. "In my opinion," he wrote after the war, "the tardy drive from the [Anzio] beachhead allowed the withdrawal of the most powerful German forces over the Aniene [River] (while a few heroically fighting divisions of the 14th Army covered their right wing) and made possible a new stand north of Rome. By pivoting the FEC and later the American VI Corps they might have encircled 10th Army."[38]

Ultra historian Ronald Lewin agrees, noting:

When Clark decided to abandon the mission given to 5th Army and to make for Rome (which, from the beginning, had been agreed as his prize in due course), he must have known with great clarity the condition of the Germans retreating ahead of him. Apart from the abundant air reconnaissance and "Y" service, there was Ultra. Even at Bletchley people observed the German dispositions on their map and could not understand the 5th Army's behavior. Clark was fed . . . Ultra which, as has been seen, was coming quickly and copiously from the cryptanalysts. From the very start of Diadem constant decrypts from Bletchley and reports from the recce aircraft had provided a vivid picture of the 10th Army's deterioration. It must therefore be assumed that it was not for fear of the unknown that Clark turned aside from a broken enemy, but for personal reasons which have been scarcely disguised. And that was unfortunate.[39]

Lewin's judgment is affirmed by the British official intelligence history:

From the beginning of the battle on 12 May to 4 June, when the Allies entered Rome, Sigint [signal intelligence] in large quantities was available with little delay. No less than one-third of the high-grade decrypts of enemy traffic at and above divisional level were forwarded by GC and CS [the Government Code and Cypher School, that is, Bletchley Park] to the front in emergency signals. Army Y was still more valuable as a source of tactical intelligence, performing as well as it had ever done in north Africa, and it provided a detailed running commentary on the fighting while the Germans continued to resist south of Rome. The interrogation of POW, who were taken in fair numbers from the outset, made an important contribution to tactical and order of battle intelligence. . . . Photographic reconnaissance had provided thorough coverage of the terrain before the battle and it kept a close watch on the enemy's development of the Hitler and Caesar lines as the advance proceeded.[40]

The verdict on the performance of the Allied air forces was mixed. Clearly, it had improved dramatically after the problems encountered in Sicily, but Anzio and later campaigns and wars would reveal the limitations of air power. According to the official U.S. air historians, some of the senior air commanders were less than pleased with the air support of Shingle. Among them was the chief of the U.S. Army Air Forces, General H. H. ("Hap") Arnold, who criticized the air performance at Anzio, saying that "the air forces did not always concentrate their available air power so as to hit selected target areas with sustained mass attacks. He also noted that no systematic, complete, and enduring isolation of the battlefield was possible without more night operations than had been employed. But neither he nor anyone else suggested that MAAFs planes and crews had not done a fine job."[41]

Perhaps the ultimate irony of Mark Clark's obsession with becoming the first modern-day conqueror of Rome was that his triumph lasted less than forty-eight hours in the world's newspaper headlines. On the morning of June 6, 1944, the fall of Rome was all but forgotten as the greatest amphibious operation in history, Operation Overlord, the long-delayed, long-debated cross-Channel invasion of Normandy, took center stage.

It was the outspoken Juin who may have best summed up the folly of Clark's fixation with Rome. On May 30 Juin observed: "Once again we have run into one of the stumbling blocks of coalition warfare: the Allies cannot come to an agreement and co-ordinate their efforts. Questions of prestige are shaping events, each one wanting to make the entry into Rome. History will not fail to pass severe sentence."[42]

The legacy of Anzio has borne out Juin's judgment. In the years since this dreadful campaign, the speculation about what might have been continues unabated. What is certain is that when at last the Allies broke free of the stalemate at Anzio and Cassino, they had won a victory, but at a dreadful price.

Postscript

After forty-five years Anzio-Nettuno is like a bad dream.

PFC. MANNY RAMOS, 36TH ENGINEER COMBAT REGIMENT

> Death called my name,
> Then hesitated.
> Once more his theme
> Rang—understated.
> For one long thought
> He probed and stared—
> Thank you, grim friend,
> That I was spared.
>
> —PFC. HANS JUERGENSEN[1]

During the desperate months of the Anzio beachhead the Allies lost 7,000 killed, and 36,000 more were wounded or reported as missing in action. In addition another 44,000 were hospitalized from various nonbattle injuries and sickness.

Among the British losses were the grievous casualties suffered by the gallant men of the 1st Division, who bore not only the brunt of the early battles but also unfair criticism of their performance under nearly impossible conditions. During the nearly six months it served at Anzio, the 1st Division lost 100 officers and 1,030 enlisted men killed in action. A staggering total of 295 officers and 4,653 enlisted men were wounded and another 104 officers and 3,014 enlisted men missing in action. Officer losses were nearly 60 percent and those of the enlisted men 50 percent, but of the total casualties, 80 percent were suffered by the line infantry battalions.[2]

413

Fifth Army losses on both fronts from January 1 to June 4, 1944 were:[3]

	Killed in Action	Wounded in Action	Missing	Total
United States	8,678	34,298	4,369	47,345
British	3,348	16,045	7,744	27,137
French (Cassino front)	3,763	14,678	1,564	20,005
	15,789	65,021	13,677	94,487

During Diadem the combined Tenth and Fourteenth Army casualty figures were 38,024, which did not include 15,600 Germans taken prisoner. Of these, 25,000 were believed to have been killed, captured, or missing in action.[4] Total German losses for Anzio are impossible to calculate, but overall German casualties at Anzio from January to June 1944 were later estimated by Kesselring to be approximately 40,000, of which 5,000 were killed in action and another 4,500 captured.[5]

The horror that was Anzio did not end with the breakout from the beachhead in May 1944. Only then could the grim task of recovering the bodies left in no-man's land, some since January, be undertaken. Lance Corporal Hans Paul Joachim Liebschner was an eighteen-year-old paratrooper from Silesia who served at Anzio during the entire campaign, mostly as a runner with the 4th Parachute Division. Liebschner recalls that many of the German wounded could not be recovered at night and had to be left in no-man's land. Some screamed and shouted, some cried for their mothers. At times Liebschner found it so unbearable that he had to plug his ears.

Liebschner survived the entire Anzio campaign, but his luck ran out when he was taken prisoner on June 3 along the Appian Way, where he was part of a German machine-gun team attempting to delay the Allied advance into Rome. Of the two others captured with Liebschner, one was badly wounded and the other shot dead in the back of a jeep soon after being taken prisoner. Liebschner was kept blindfolded and told he had not been reported as a POW. If he did not answer the questions of his interrogators, he could be shot without anyone knowing. After three days without food or water Liebschner talked. He was then sent to the Allied war cemetery at Anzio where for several days he was placed on a detail to clean up no-man's land. Here is Liebschner's chilling description of his experience:

I dug single graves and was guarded by [Americans] who had shorthandled leather thonged whips with tails 12–15 feet in length. Anyone who dared to stretch was whipped. It created open wounds. I only stretched when the guards had their backs turned. There was no means of washing up to eat. We were working with badly decomposed bodies. The worst was climbing on lorries packed with bodies and unloading them in piles. They arrived every two hours. Some were dead anywhere between days and six months. Many were full of maggots. It was appalling. We had no gloves and had to put our hands into these ghoulish messes. The stench was indescribable. The weather was so hot it was a real nightmare. The bodies were any or all: American, British, German. One Allied soldier stretched out in death and a dead German paratrooper also dumped off the truck ended up arm-in-arm with one another in death. I thought what they couldn't do in their lifetime, now that they were dead they were able to do. It was on that occasion I think when I swore I would never take up arms again for anybody. It seemed to me quite, quite senseless what we had been doing the last six months. There it was all laid before us in that churchyard.[6]

The visitor to Anzio today will find little evidence of the brutal battles fought in 1944. The most visible reminder that something unusual happened there are the two Allied military cemeteries. The British cemetery is outside Anzio, while the American cemetery is at Nettuno.[7] In 1944 both were crude, with temporary white wood crosses over raw mounds of earth, as befitted the need to inter the recovered bodies as quickly as possible. Eventually, both evolved into permanent memorials, with well-tended, deep green lawns shaded by trees and white marble headstones that mark the final resting place of 2,300 British and 7,862 Americans. A marble memorial commemorates the 3,094 Americans missing in action who were never found.

On Memorial Day 1989, the American cemetery had an unusual visitor, newly elected President George Bush, who had come to honor the dead of the Italian and Sicilian campaigns. It was the first-ever visit by an American president to Anzio.

Forty-four years earlier the cemetery drew other distinguished visitors to celebrate Memorial Day 1945. The main speaker at the ceremony was Lucian Knight Truscott, now the Fifth Army commander. Also in attendance that day was famed GI cartoonist Bill Mauldin, who admitted that he had mixed emotions about even being there. "I am allergic to Veterans Days and Armistice Days and the like, but Truscott was somebody special." At the time Anzio was still a collecting point, and there were about twenty thousand U.S. graves. The cemetery was filled with visitors, VIPs (including several American senators), and a military honor guard. As Mauldin relates, this ceremony was very different indeed:

Truscott spoke, he turned away from the visitors and addressed
elf to the corpses he had commanded there. It was the most moving
re I ever saw. It came from a hard-boiled old man who was incapable
of planned dramatics. The general's remarks were brief and extemporane-
ous. He apologized to the dead men for their presence here. He said
everybody tells leaders it is not their fault that men get killed in war, but
that every leader knows in his heart this is not altogether true. He said he
hoped anybody here through any mistake of his would forgive him, but he
realized that was asking a hell of a lot under the circumstances. One of the
Senators cigars went out; he bent over to relight it, then thought better
of it. Truscott said he would not speak of the glorious dead because he
didn't see much glory in getting killed in your late teens or early twenties.
He promised that if in the future he ran into anybody, especially old men,
who thought death in battle was glorious, he would straighten them out.
He said he thought it was the least he could do.[8]

After the combatants had moved on, local farmers dug holes and buried
some of the dead who had lain in the Pantano Ditch and elsewhere in
the fields outside Cisterna since the end of January. Many German and
GI corpses were buried in mass graves and covered by a bulldozer in
the Pantano Ditch, which has since been renamed the Ditch of Holy
Souls. The Italians have renamed the Isola Bella–Cisterna highway the
Via Ranger, and the area around the ditch has been officially designated
as a battlefield.

The scene of the worst battles around Carroceto and the Factory
has been erased with the rebuilding of Aprilia into a modern city of
some eighty thousand, which is now part of the Roma-Latina industrial
zone.[9] The tower that had given the town the nickname of the Factory
was demolished in the fighting and never rebuilt after the war. The
disused railway line known as the Bowling Alley is likewise gone. In its
place is a new four-lane superhighway, the Via Pontina (the N148),
which connects Rome with Latina and Highway 7. The stone pillars of
the ruined Flyover bridge survived until 1976, when they were demolished to make room for a new bridge. North of the Flyover, where the
Allies made their final stand during the furious battles fought in February, there are now factories that comprise a part of this modern indus-
trialized section of Latium. Underneath the Flyover runs a new Via
Anziate—official designation, Highway 207—a modern two-lane road
that follows the old road north from Anzio toward Campoleone Station
and eventual junction with Highway 7 northwest of Lake Albano.

Both Anzio and Nettuno have been rebuilt and bear few scars of
war. Lorries and tanks have been replaced by the interminable urban
problems of too many cars clogging the narrow streets and too few
places to park them. Where once LSTs unloaded their lifesaving supplies are now berthed fishing and pleasure boats. Via Santa Maria 39 in

Nettuno, the site of the first VI Corps command post, is today a run-down building. Its successor, established in a nearby café and used by Truscott, is now a food shop called the OK USA. Anzio and Nettuno remain summer retreats for Romans and their combined population rises from 30,000 in winter (almost precisely the prewar figure) to more than 130,000 in the vacation months of July and August.[10]

Nearby the Mussolini Canal still exists but is now known as the Canale di Moscarello. X-Ray Beach, southeast of Nettuno, where the U.S. 3d Division landed is part of an artillery firing range used by the Italian army and is closed to tourists. The British beaches north of Anzio are open to anyone wishing to visit them.[11]

Cisterna is virtually unrecognizable from its pre-1944 form. Some of the Rangers who were taken prisoner outside the town returned in 1945 for a brief bittersweet reunion after being liberated from a POW camp in Poland. The headless statue that symbolized the destruction wrought in Cisterna has been restored and now sits in a piazza in the center of the town. Since the war many of the Rangers have returned for reunions with the citizens of Cisterna, with whom they have formed a powerful bond. Although the Rangers' attempt to liberate the town was a military disaster, the citizens of this ancient city have never forgotten the sacrifice of these men. In the era of the 1980s when excess and self-aggrandizement prevailed, the Italians continued to demonstrate simple gratitude for these aging men of the Ranger force.[12]

For some, the transition to peacetime was difficult. Lieutenant Commander G. H. Dormer, who had commanded a minesweeper in the waters off Anzio, found that living on the thin edge of danger had been like a drug. In 1946 he returned to Trinity College, Cambridge, to complete a degree interrupted by the war. "My first meal in the hall was strange . . . the surroundings so unchanged . . . the people so different . . . more than ever I felt like a ghost or time traveller. I don't like being a civilian and I don't much like peace. Give me a ship at war. . . . There is no future in being a tweed-jacketed nonentity."[13]

Lieutenant Colonel William P. Yarborough, the tough paratrooper who commanded the 509th Parachute Infantry Battalion during some of the grimmest days at Anzio, remained in the U.S. Army and eventually became a lieutenant general. He commanded the famed Green Beret Special Forces at Fort Bragg, North Carolina, during the period of their resurgence under President John F. Kennedy, and later the XVIII Airborne Corps. As is true of so many who fought there, Anzio retains a special place in his memory. In a speech to a group of beach-head veterans, he reminded them that they shared a common experience few could claim. Yarborough also spoke of the raw wound that was Anzio:

I remember the wrenching grief of seeing the young officers and men I had sent out on patrol brought back stiff and cold, to be laid out like cordwood waiting to be sent back to Naples for burial. This happened so many times—we learned to live with death all around us—to tolerate its grim presence but never really to get used to it.

I remember feeling a new appreciation and reverence for life—I had the feeling that any kind of a loving human being—a leper, a derelict sleeping in the gutter was a thing of beauty when compared to the pale, cold dead who we had not hours before laughed and joked with about the misery of Anzio. . . . Anzio was a place where many of us ceased to be young—where we became wise in the ways of human behavior. We recognized true courage—we forgave human weaknesses. We saw both the nobility and baseness of men. The lasting impressions of Anzio did not stem from rank but from the character of our comrades. . . . Nor was human suffering the only tragedy at Anzio. . . . I remember a flock of sheep among which a mortar round had fallen, killing all except a tiny lamb which continued to seek safety next to the corpse of its mother. The tragedy of Anzio was everywhere—even the toughest and most hardened of us felt it keenly and there was no escape.[14]

Yarborough's battalion left Anzio after seventy-three days of nearly continuous combat. It had shrunk from almost six hundred officers and men to less than two hundred. "But we left with honor," he told the Anzio veterans. "American soldiers had taken everything the German professionals could dish out and had frustrated every attempt to push us off the beachhead." Quoting airman Jesse Bradley, the B-17 crewman who had bailed out over Anzio and been rescued, Yarborough reminded one and all that: "Anzio was closely akin to Yorktown, Gettysburg, the Little Big Horn and Belleau Wood: small, remote, insignificant places all, until American fighting men had lifted them out of obscurity into history."[15]

General Sir Harold Alexander, about whom so much of the Anzio story revolved, continued to command the 15th Army Group until the autumn of 1944, when he was promoted to field marshal and succeeded Jumbo Wilson as the Supreme Allied Commander in the Mediterranean when the latter moved to Washington after the untimely death of Field Marshal Sir John Dill. After the war, from 1946 to 1952, the courtly Alexander served in Canada as governor-general, a position that required tact and diplomacy but few decisions. When Churchill returned to office briefly as prime minister in 1952, he summoned Alexander from retirement to be his minister of defense. As Sir John Colville has described it, his tenure from March 1952 to October 1954 was "inadequate and far from happy."[16] Alexander abhorred political intrigue, and "he thought politics, compared to soldiering, dirty."[17]

Throughout his life Alexander was fascinated by art and demonstrated considerable flair for it although he had had no formal training. He had won a drawing prize while at Harrow, and during World War I he filled several sketchbooks with drawings. Both before and after World War II he painted whenever there was time for leisure. During the postwar years Alexander became a close friend of artist William Seago and the two often embarked on painting holidays. In 1973 a collection of Alexander's paintings was published in a limited edition. Seago's introduction seems to capture the essence of Alexander. "What strikes me particularly about his paintings is the sense of enthusiasm and enjoyment. There is no sign of struggle or despair and there is nothing pretentious about them. They have no formula, no contrived style, no gimmick. . . . They are the completely honest product of someone with a passion for painting, and probably gave him some of the happiest hours of his life."[18]

In 1962 Alexander published his memoirs, which both his admirers and detractors found disconcerting. "The book appeared to have been written primarily to entertain, not as his considered contribution to history, and it was thought unworthy of Alexander, as if he had not really wanted to take the trouble."[19] To his death in 1969 at the age of seventy-seven, the complex man behind the public mask remained largely hidden.

Alexander's able chief of staff, Lieutenant General Sir John Harding, continued his distinguished career in the postwar years. By 1953 Harding was a field marshal and from 1952 to 1955 the chief of the Imperial General Staff. In 1958 he entered the House of Lords as Field Marshal Lord Harding of Petherton. Until his death in 1989 at the age of ninety-three, Harding remained an exceptionally popular and respected figure.

Mark Clark succeeded Alexander as the commander of the Allied armies in Italy and was promoted to four-star general. Whatever satisfaction he derived from the capture of Rome was soon lost as the Germans retreated north of Florence to the Gothic Line, where the Allies were held off in yet another bloody stalemate until the spring of 1945.

The war had barely ended when Clark became the commander of U.S. occupation forces and American High Commissioner in Austria. In 1946 the 36th Division veterans association demanded that Congress investigate Clark's handling of the Rapido offensive. Clark was vindicated by both Congress and the War Department, but the acrimonious affair reopened the entire question of whether the Rapido had been a wasted opportunity. Although the secretary of war ruled that the Rapido attack had been a military necessity, what remains unanswered is if the operation would even have been necessary had Clark been willing to exploit McCreery's earlier success along the lower Garigliano River.

In May 1952 Clark became the commander in chief of the United Nations Command in Korea and directed the final months of that war until July 1953, when he signed the armistice with North Korea on behalf of the UN forces. Clark found the Korean War as frustrating as he had the Italian campaign. In his memoirs Clark deplored becoming the first commander in U.S. history obliged to sign an armistice without being the victor. In October 1953 Clark retired from the U.S. Army after a career that spanned thirty-six years. From 1954 to 1965 he served as president of the Citadel, the military college of South Carolina. Mark Clark died in 1984, shortly before what would have been his eighty-eighth birthday.[20]

Lucian Truscott continued in command of the U.S. VI Corps during the Dragoon landings in southern France in August 1944 but soon returned to Italy as Clark's successor in command of the Fifth Army. In early 1945 Eisenhower rated Truscott as second only to George S. Patton as his most able army commander. By the time he succeeded Patton as the commander of the Third Army in Bavaria in the autumn of 1945, Truscott was a four-star general. When his health began to fail in 1948, Truscott was obliged to retire.

His son would later write: "I know of no other American officer who has successively commanded a regiment . . . a division, a corps and an army in the same war."[21] Of his 1954 memoirs, *Command Missions*, historian Edward M. Coffman writes: "This book is one of the best (some might argue the very best) of the American generals' memoirs to come out of World War II."[22] Truscott was seventy when he died in 1965.

Clark's nemesis, Lieutenant General Sir Richard McCreery, succeeded Oliver Leese as the commander of the Eighth Army in early October 1944 and performed with a distinction wholly lacking during the tenure of Leese, who soon self-destructed as the new commander of Allied Land Forces in Southeast Asia. (Leese foolishly attempted to relieve General [later Field Marshal] Sir William Slim, the British Fourteenth Army commander, and was himself relieved of command.) McCreery served as the British representative on the Allied Commission for Austria and later in the United Nations before retiring in 1949 with the rank of full general. He died in 1967.

Major General John P. Lucas remained as Clark's deputy for several weeks before returning to the United States via England, where he briefed Eisenhower's staff on Shingle. Marshall was normally unforgiving of failed commanders, but in Lucas's case he believed the former VI Corps commander had performed as well as possible under the circumstances he faced. Two days before his relief Marshall wrote to

Lieutenant General Lesley J. McNair, the commander of Army Ground Forces in the United States:

> This brings up the matter of Lucas. He has had a wealth of experience and quite evidently is tired out. I want to save his pride, I want to protect his reputation and at the same time get the best benefit of his service. Would you have a place for him? It might be that Eisenhower would like to have him in England to check with them on the various plans and training they are now in the process of carrying out.[23]

Eisenhower declined, but McNair replied at once that, "I should be very glad to have Lucas."[24] He was assigned to Fort Sam Houston, Texas, as the deputy and later as Fourth U.S. Army commander. According to his aide, Lucas was effectively muzzled from speaking out about Anzio or his relief when he attempted to publish his diary. The War Department objected to Lucas's candid criticisms of the British, particularly Churchill and Alexander, and ordered them deleted before permission to publish would be granted.[25] If Lucas held any bitter feelings over his relief they were mainly for Churchill, although his son observes that he had little respect for Alexander.[26]

From 1946 to 1948 Lucas headed the U.S. Army military advisory group in China. His final assignment was in Chicago as the deputy Fifth Army commander. In 1949 Lucas died very suddenly. Many mistakenly believed that Anzio was in some way responsible for his untimely death at age fifty-nine; however, according to his son, Lucas died from a blood clot brought about by injections he received to control the aftereffects of the amoebic dysentery he contracted while in China.[27]

His postwar aide, Colonel G. Gordon Bartlett, believes that Lucas could not see any fault in his conduct of operations at Anzio, and this was confirmed by Lucas himself in a 1948 interview in which he emphasized that he never intended to take the Alban Hills with the force he was given. On the contrary, to his death Lucas believed he had saved VI Corps from certain annihilation.[28] Although it was Mark Clark who formally relieved Lucas at Anzio, it should be noted that it was also Clark who saw to it that he was awarded the Distinguished Service Medal (DSM) as the VI Corps commander from Salerno to December 1, 1943, and a Silver Star for gallantry at Anzio. In 1946 the United States Navy awarded Lucas the Navy DSM for Operation Shingle.[29]

At Clark's instigation Major General Fred L. Walker was reassigned to the United States shortly after the fall of Rome. Despite his extreme dislike of Clark, Fred Walker never let his feelings interfere with his duty, and it was his testimony that largely demolished the case of the 36th Division veterans against Clark. In 1968 his opponent during the breakthrough at Velletri, Lieutenant General Heinz Greiner, commander of the 362d Infantry Division, wrote to praise "your bold decision to strike through the inter-army gap east of Velletri. . . . May I—23 years after the war's end—personally express to you my high regard for this deed . . . as your former opponent, [I] express to you my high regards and send you my best greetings."[30] In the aftermath of the Rapido affair, Greiner's tribute was clear evidence that the much-maligned 36th Division had come full circle at Velletri. It is one of the oddities of the miltary profession that men who are enemies in war can become united as comrades in arms.*

Major General Ernest N. Harmon credited the maintenance of the Anzio beachhead to the outstanding performance of the Allied fighting men in the front line and the effectiveness of the artillery. "I think they saved the beachhead," he later remarked.[31] Harmon led the 1st Armored Division until July 1944 and then was briefly assigned to the United States. Eisenhower soon asked Marshall to send him to northwest Europe to command his former unit, the 2d Armored Division.† During the Battle of the Bulge, Harmon earned immortality when he

---

*There have been numerous examples during the postwar years. For example, one of the heroes of the Battle of the Bulge, U.S. General Bruce C. Clarke, conducted battlefield tours in the Ardennes with the commander of the German Fifth Panzer Army, General der Panzertruppen Hasso von Manteuffel. Even the bitter Vietnam War produced subsequent reunions of old enemies. In 1965 Lieutenant Colonel Harold G. Moore commanded the 1st Battalion of the 7th Cavalry Regiment, 1st Cavalry Division (Airmobile) during the battle for the Ia Drang Valley, one of the bloodiest engagements of that war. Moore achieved renown as one of the finest battlefield commanders ever to wear U.S. Army uniform. In 1990, a retired lieutenant general, Moore journeyed to Hanoi to meet with General Vo Nguyen Giap, the legendary soldier who had successfully led revolutionary armies against Japan, France, and the United States. As their interview ended, "Moore slipped off his wristwatch and presented it to Giap, calling it a small gift 'from one old soldier to another.' Giap cupped the watch in both hands, visibly moved. Then he turned and embraced an old enemy who, suddenly, was as surprised and moved as Giap was" (*U.S. News & World Report,* October 29, 1990, p. 48).

†Marshall required little persuasion to comply with Eisenhower's request. In July 1944, Harmon wrote to Marshall that he was "a little depressed" about being reassigned to the U.S.A. "I hope that the action is not based on any erroneous assumption of battle weariness on my part. . . . As a soldier I desire to do what is for the best interests of my country at all times, but I feel that my greatest strength in service lies in my combat experience and natural ability to lead men in battle and have them willing to fight for me. . . . I feel that I ought to be back in the battle line where I am in my natural element. I have been reasonably successful in battle chiefly because I spare no personal effort to be at the front and thoroughly understand the situation. . . . My personal desire would be to stay not more than ten days or two weeks in the United States and then go to the French front or to the Pacific front. I would like to operate tanks against the Japs for I believe that I could make Ghengis Khan or Attila the Hun look like school boys in the job I would do on those people." In May 1945, Harmon again wrote to Marshall for a combat assignment. "I am terribly anxious to get into battle in the Pacific . . . I feel that I am qualified by battle experience to command a division of armor against the Japs, and, in my own mind, can command an infantry or an armored corps as good as anyone in the business. I am young, rested and want to get into combat. . . . I would be perfectly willing to give up my Corps and command an armored division, and if necessary, will step down

marched his division nearly one hundred miles by night and then engaged and annihilated the German 2d Panzer Division in late December 1944.‡ He briefly commanded XXII Corps and, when the war ended, became the U.S. Army Occupation commander in Czechoslovakia and later commander of the elite U.S. Constabulary in Germany.

Like Patton, Harmon was a true warrior who was restless in a peacetime role, and he retired in 1948. Two years later Harmon took up an entirely new challenge when he became president of Norwich University, the distinguished military college in Vermont that he had attended many years earlier. From 1950 to 1965 Harmon worked tirelessly in his new role, and to the surprise of his detractors, who questioned how a profane combat officer like Ernie Harmon could possibly function effectively in such an unlikely environment, the university grew and prospered under him. Prior to his arrival, Norwich was in severe straits both academically and financially, was losing qualified teachers, and the morale of students and faculty was poor. When Harmon retired again after fifteen years, the university had regained academic stature and dramatically improved its facilities. Enrollment had risen from 574 to more than 1,200.

What made Harmon so effective, whether commanding troops in battle or running a university, was his leadership. He became as adept at twisting the arm of a potential donor or telling the Norwich cadets what he expected of them as he had been at commanding troops. When he died at age eighty-five in 1979, Harmon left a legacy as one of the outstanding commanders of World War II.

Major General William W. Eagles commanded the 45th Division until December 1944, and the outspoken Major General "Iron Mike" O'Daniel commanded the 3d Division until the end of the war. Like Patton and Harmon, O'Daniel was not afraid to speak his mind in public. From 1948 to 1950 he served as the U.S. Army attaché in Moscow. He remained on active service until 1956, when he retired in the grade of lieutenant general. O'Daniel died in 1975 at the age of eighty-one.

Major General Ronald Penney was so badly wounded at Anzio that his military career was cut short. He retired in 1949 and was knighted in 1958. It is clear from his papers that Anzio haunted Penney the remainder of his life. He believed his men had fought well but had

---

and take a combat command." (Letters, Harmon to Marshall, July 15, 1944, and May 11, 1945, Box 70, Folders 4 and 5, Marshall Papers. See also *Combat Commander,* p. 206.)

‡Harmon's movement of his division in the middle of winter across hostile terrain to engage von Rundstedt's spearhead forces which were threatening to break loose across the River Meuse was perhaps the classic example of blitzkrieg warfare by an armored division. The motto of the 2d Armored Division is "Hell on Wheels" and Harmon turned this into reality during the memorable battle with the 2d Panzer.

|een given the credit they deserved for their sacrifice at Anzio.
proud to have been their commander but remained bitter over
what ne considered Lucas's failure to have supported him properly.
Penney died in 1964.

After giving up command of the 56th Division, Major General G.
W. R. Templer commanded the 6th Armoured Division for a brief
period before being invalided home after a traffic accident. After the
war Templer earned fame as the "Tiger of Malaya" for his highly successful campaign against the Communist insurgents there. From 1955
to 1958 he was the chief of the Imperial General Staff and in 1956
became a field marshal. Templer died in 1979 at the age of eighty-one.

Robert T. Frederick left the First Special Service Force in late June
1944 to organize and train an airborne force for the Dragoon landings
and was promoted to major general. In December 1944 he took command of the veteran 45th Division for the remainder of the war. By
1952 his many wounds forced him to retire from the U.S. Army with
a disability. When the exploits of the First Special Service Force were
immortalized in the postwar film *The Devil's Brigade,* Frederick was
portrayed by actor William Holden. Frederick was only sixty-three
when he died in 1970.

It was the outstanding leadership of men like Frederick that prevented the Germans from annihilating the Anzio beachhead. He was
one of the most respected and fearless American commanders, and his
accomplishments in organizing and commanding the Anglo-Canadian
First Special Service Force were unparalleled. Like Darby with the
Rangers, Frederick was the heart and soul of his unit and the right man
for the very difficult task of creating and training the most successful
unconventional unit ever fielded by the United States Army in World
War II.

Captain Felix L. Sparks, the lone survivor of Company E, 2d Battalion, 157th Regiment, served with distinction with the 45th Division
until the end of the war as a battalion commander and later as a full
colonel. Sparks was the commander of the troops that liberated the
Dachau concentration camp in April 1945. A highly decorated infantryman, Sparks, as a brigadier general, helped to reorganize the postwar
Colorado National Guard. He later became a lawyer and eventually a
justice of the Colorado Supreme Court. Now retired, he resides in
Colorado, where he continues to serve as the longtime secretary of the
157th Regimental Association.

Major Philip Sidney, VC, held a number of high-level positions in
the government after the war and in 1956 became Viscount De L'Isle.
He lives in Kent, England.

Major Jack Dobson was wounded twice on January 30 and spent six
months in a German military hospital before joining his comrades in

captivity. He escaped from a German POW camp near Shubin, Poland, along with several other Ranger officers, and after wading through the winter snows for several days they made contact with the Polish Underground near Warsaw. They were turned over to the Red Army and, after a lengthy odyssey, Dobson was among those who returned to Italy in January 1945. He later received a Silver Star for gallantry during the Cisterna operation and a Bronze Star for his activities while a POW. After the war Dobson remained in the Army, and among his assignments was that of aide to "Iron Mike" O'Daniel, whom he had last seen the morning of January 30 as the Rangers disappeared into the Pantano Ditch. After a varied career, Dobson retired in 1967 as a brigadier general. Now retired from a second career as the superintendent of the Culver Military Academy, Dobson lives in North Carolina.

In the aftermath of the capture of Rome, the outstanding courage and accomplishments of spy Peter Tompkins were conveniently forgotten when several of his OSS brethren disgracefully attempted to claim credit for his daring and dangerous exploits during the five months he spent behind enemy lines. For the remainder of the Italian campaign Tompkins organized and trained partisans to oppose the German armies defending northern Italy. Since the war Tompkins has written a number of books, including an account of his experience in Rome as an OSS agent. He lives in West Virginia.

Colonel William O. Darby did not survive the war. After two months in command of the 179th Regiment, Darby was ordered back to the United States where he chafed in a staff assignment. In 1945 Darby seized an opportunity to get back into combat when the assistant division commander of the 10th Mountain Division was wounded and he was appointed to fill the vacancy shortly before the war ended. On April 30, two days before the Germans surrendered in Italy, Darby was killed when an 88-mm shell landed outside his command post. Darby was only thirty-four, and in a rare recognition of his outstanding achievements he was posthumously promoted to brigadier general—an honor accorded no other officer in World War II. Truscott provided the most fitting epitaph: "Never have I known a more gallant soldier."

Another who did not survive was Captain John Strick of the 1st London Irish Rifles. Previously wounded several times, Strick was a gallant and well-respected soldier whose death near the Factory in February snuffed out the life of one of the most promising young poets of his generation. His final letter home reflected the anxiety all soldiers feel with death as their constant companion:

Yesterday after lunch and some wine, I sat alone feeling sentimental and looking at the small collection of photos I carry with me. They glowed suddenly with life and the all too distant past—and a spasm of fire shook me as I thought how far we had all travelled since they were taken.

Strick's body was not recovered until May by several friends who had great difficulty locating it among the tall grass and mines. An American friend later dedicated a book:

> To Captain John Strick, 1st London Irish Rifles, who fell on the road to Rome, that youth of all nations might become brothers.[32]

Field Marshal Albert Kesselring continued to frustrate the Allied advance into northern Italy despite losing divisions to other fronts where the Germans were in even worse trouble. After the German surrender Kesselring was imprisoned and, in 1946, tried by the British for war crimes in connection with the execution of 335 Italian civilians by the Gestapo in the Massacre of the Ardeatine Caves, and for allegedly ordering the shooting of civilians in reprisal for partisan activities. He was convicted and sentenced to death. Many, however, were appalled by the verdict, among them Winston Churchill and Sir Harold Alexander. Both thought the sentence too harsh. Alexander sent a cable in defense of Kesselring to the new British prime minister, Clement Attlee, in which he indicated his distress at the death sentence handed down by the court. "I hope it will be commuted. Personally, as his old opponent on the battlefield, I have no complaint against him. Kesselring and his soldiers fought hard but clean."[33]

Alexander's intervention apparently helped, for Kesselring's sentence was commuted to life imprisonment by the Reviewing Authority, General Sir John Harding, Alexander's erstwhile chief of staff in Italy. In 1952 Kesselring, a rather broken man in declining health, was released as an "act of clemency." His allegiance to Hitler and his regime were genuine, however misguided. Despite the stamp of "war criminal" that came with his conviction, history will certainly judge Kesselring as an honorable and able soldier.

Kesselring never second-guessed his actions and remained convinced he had done his best with what he had. Kesselring's British biographer, Kenneth Macksey, has written that he was a master of prolonged defensive warfare. "Of what other general can it be said that, over a period of two and a half years, he fought a virtually incessant delaying action against desperate odds, managed to impose his will upon strong-minded and skeptical subordinates, and yet emerged unscathed by serious rout, leading his men in fighting to the last gasp."[34]

In postwar Germany Kesselring became an immensely popular figure among war veterans. He was seventy-four when he died on July 20, 1960.

Lieutenant General Fridolin von Senger und Etterlin also survived the war, in no small part thanks to his attempts to save the Abbey of Monte Cassino, which earned him the respect of the Italians, including the partisans who never attacked him during his many trips through the Italian countryside. When Mark Clark and the other senior Allied commanders in Italy accepted the surrender of Army Group C in May 1945, it was von Senger who represented the German Army. It is fair to conclude that von Senger's military successes were the only reason he escaped OKW retribution for his repeated defiance of orders he considered illegal and immoral. Imprisoned by the British at the end of the war, he was eventually released and later wrote his memoirs, which were published in English. When he died in Freiburg in 1963 von Senger was seventy-two.

Heinrich von Vietinghoff succeeded Kesselring as OB West when the latter was summoned by Hitler to assume command of the crumbling western front in March 1945. It was the pragmatic von Vietinghoff who refused to carry out Hitler's insane orders to fight to the death. Instead he sought to end the fighting on honorable terms and for his temerity was immediately relieved of command and ordered arrested by none other than Kesselring himself, in what amounted to a meaningless gesture.

Eberhard von Mackensen's career effectively ended with his resignation/relief as the Fourteenth Army commander. Like Kesselring, von Mackensen was accused and tried by the British for complicity in the Ardeatine Caves massacre, although he had no direct connection with the atrocity and had merely signed a statement that the executions had been carried out. At his trial his old adversary Kesselring came to his defense by stating: "If General von Mackensen is found guilty, then I am guilty too." Nevertheless, von Mackensen was judged guilty and was sentenced to death in November 1945. Like Kesselring's, his sentence was subsequently commuted to life imprisonment in the wake of widespread belief that the military court had failed to understand that the SS in Italy acted independently from the military chain of command. Von Mackensen was released in 1952 and died in 1969.

The other senior German commanders who fought at Anzio all survived and included Traugott Herr, Alfred Schlemm, and Wilhelm Schmalz. Many of the German dead were lost in the morass of Anzio and never accounted for. Most of those who died at Anzio are buried in the German military cemetery at Pomezia, not far from the battlefield where they fought. The Pomezia cemetery contains the remains of 27,432 soldiers. Near Cassino lie the remains of another 20,043 German dead.[35]

The U.S. VI Corps participated in the invasion of southern France under Truscott's command and later under his successor in the final battles of the war in France and southern Germany. The two principal U.S. divisions at Anzio, the 3d and 45th, received no respite and fought in France and Germany until the end of the war. The record of the 3d Division was unparalleled. It participated in six amphibious landings and fought from Casablanca to Berchtesgaden. Its members won forty Congressional Medals of Honor, more than any other division. The 3d Division also suffered the heaviest battle casualties of any U.S. infantry division: 27,450, of which 4,922 were killed in action. Since the war the 3d Division has been stationed in Würzburg, Germany, as part of the U.S. commitment in Europe.

The 45th Division likewise distinguished itself during eight campaigns that took it from Sicily to Italy, France, and Germany. During those eight campaigns the division suffered 62,563 battle and nonbattle losses, more than 54 percent of which occurred in Italy.[36] The 45th Division returned to the United States shortly after the war ended and was deactivated in December 1945.

"Old Ironsides," the U.S. 1st Armored Division, fought for the remainder of the Italian campaign, including the battle for Bologna in 1945. The division liberated Milan and drove to Como during the final days of the war. It has remained on active service and took part in the Gulf War of 1991 as part of the allied Desert Storm force.

The British 1st Division fought in the battles in northern Italy for the Gothic Line, but the 56th Division was so badly battered at Anzio that it was sent to the Middle East to rest and refit before returning to the fray in Italy in the late summer of 1944. Once again the division bled heavily and by mid-October had ceased to be operational because of a lack of infantry replacements. When it did return to action the division could only muster two of its three authorized brigades.

The German formations of the Tenth and Fourteenth armies were badly battered by Diadem but nevertheless continued to give ground only grudgingly during their fighting retreat north to the Gothic Line. None of the Allied troops who had fought them needed reminding that they had engaged a worthy foe. Extraordinary above all, as John Ellis notes, was the manner in which "the most heterogeneous assortments of units, from a multiplicity of different divisions, could be brought together and within a few hours be welded into a perfectly effective fighting formation."* Alexander was in no doubt that this was a major factor in the battle for Anzio, when he wrote to Clark and Leese in February 1944 that German commanders and troops were: "quicker than we are: quicker at regrouping [their] forces, quicker at thinning

---

*Ellis, *Cassino: The Hollow Victory*, p. 465. Ellis cites the example of the 377 German POWs captured at Velletri, who were found to be members of fifty different companies.

out on a defensive front to provide troops to close gaps at decisive points, quicker in effecting reliefs, quicker at mounting attacks and counter-attacks, and above all quicker at reaching decisions on the battlefield. By comparison our methods [both British and American] are often slow and cumbersome."[37]

One of the unfortunate consequences of Anzio is the suspicion in some American minds that the performance of British troops was somehow lacking. As we have seen, nothing could be further from the truth. The British soldier earned the unqualified respect of veteran American commanders such as Ernie Harmon and Lucian Truscott, who said of them:

> The British soldier was the product of a far more rigorous discipline, of the Prussian type, than was the American soldier. This was due to British military traditions and in part to the social structure of British life. This stricter discipline may have made the British soldier appear more phlegmatic than his American comrade, lacking the American's ingenuity and resourcefulness. British soldiers always seemed to me more suited for defense than attack, while with American soldiers the reverse was true. Although the American could distinguish himself on defense when the occasion required, the British soldier could always be expected to hold to the last man whenever he was told to do so. British and American soldiers invariably got on well together, and it was only among the high echelons that friction developed between the Allies. All in all, British and Americans held each other in mutual respect; they were worthy Allies who fought well together.[38]

The legacy of Anzio can be viewed in microcosm from the testimony of the men and women who contributed to the making of this book. For a great many, Anzio remains a haunting memory. One is former Private First Class Manny Ramos, who has written: "After forty-five years Anzio-Nettuno is like a bad dream."[39]

The torment and suffering of those who fought there is beyond the comprehension of ordinary mortals who have not themselves been subjected to a journey through the hell of war. This seems an inadequate description of the Italian campaign, but as historian James L. Stokesbury has noted: "Few soldiers of World War II experienced the kind of deadening, soul-destroying fighting that characterized the earlier war, but most of those who did experience it fought in Italy."[40]

My British colleague John Ellis has described a similar journey through hell in his eloquent account *Cassino: The Hollow Victory,* which he describes as a victory of the human spirit over extreme adversity. But, as Ellis reminds us, "one should above all beware of letting this victory of the human spirit persuade one that war is therefore enobling, and so feed a mood that can only beckon us towards the precipice."[41]

Clearly, there was nothing even remotely ennobling about Anzio. To the contrary, the nearly half century since Anzio has shown that such battles remain the norm rather than the exception. The savage seven-year war of attrition between Iran and Iraq is but one case in point. Nevertheless, the example of Anzio still offers stark testimony to the need for finding other means of resolving conflicting national aims. Unfortunately, it was in the nature of World War II that peaceful solutions to German and Italian aggression made battles such as Anzio and Cassino inevitable. If some sense is to be made of the suffering that occurred at Anzio, it is to be profoundly hoped that perhaps it will serve as a reminder of the price of war and of its ultimate folly.

Many have returned to Anzio-Nettuno since the war, some in an attempt to purge their memories of a brutal campaign that had forever changed their lives, others to celebrate the unique bond of men in war and to mourn their lost comrades. For some, returning to Anzio was the only way to come to terms with their memories of what now seems merely a small chapter in a very large war. One of those who returned to Anzio twenty-five years later was former British lieutenant Raleigh Trevelyan, whose pilgrimage to the battlefield was both necessary and painful. "My return," he wrote in 1969, "was an exorcism. I was freed of Anzio forever."[42]

Some things never change, for, as Trevelyan learned, his impression of Anzio in 1969 varied little from that of 1944:

The place was still a horrible one in which to die.[43]

APPENDIX A

Order of Battle Allied Ground Forces (January 22, 1944)

ALLIED FORCE HEADQUARTERS (AFHQ)

Commander in Chief, Mediterranean Theater[1]

General Dwight D. Eisenhower
General Sir Henry Maitland Wilson (from 1/8/44)

Deputy Allied Commander in Chief

General Sir Harold R. L. G. Alexander
Lieutenant General Jacob L. Devers (from 1/8/44)

Chief of Staff

Lieutenant General Walter Bedell Smith
Lieutenant General Sir James Gammel (from 1/8/44)

15TH ARMY GROUP[2]

Commander in Chief

General Sir Harold R. L. G. Alexander

[1]The title changed on March 6, 1944, to Supreme Allied Commander, Mediterranean Theater.
[2]The 15th Army Group underwent several changes of designation during the Italian campaign. On January 11, 1944, 15th Army Group was changed to Allied Forces in Italy (AFI). A week later it was again changed to become Allied Central Mediterranean Force (ACMF). On March 9, 1944, it became Allied Armies in Italy (AAI). As previously noted, for ease of identification, it has been referred to throughout the book as 15th Army Group.

Appendix A

... of Staff

Lieutenant General A. F. Harding

EIGHTH ARMY

General Sir Bernard Montgomery
Lieutenant General Sir Oliver Leese (from 1/1/44)

Chief of Staff

Major General Francis de Guingand
Major General G. P. Walsh (from January 1944)

5TH BRITISH CORPS

Lieutenant General C. W. Allfrey

13TH (BRITISH) CORPS

Lieutenant General M. C. Dempsey
Lieutenant General Sidney C. Kirkman (from January 1944)

1ST CANADIAN CORPS

Lieutenant General H. D. G. Crerar
Lieutenant General E. L. M. Burns (from 3/19/44)

NEW ZEALAND[3]

Lieutenant General Sir Bernard Freyberg

2D POLISH CORPS

Lieutenant General Wladisaw Anders

FRENCH CORPS EXPEDITIONNAIRE

General Alphonse Juin

[3]Created by Alexander on February 2, 1944.

FIFTH UNITED STATES ARMY

Lieutenant General Mark W. Clark

Chief of Staff

Major General Alfred M. Gruenther

II (U.S.) CORPS

Major General Geoffrey T. Keyes

VI (U.S.) CORPS

Major General John P. Lucas
Major General Lucian K. Truscott (from 2/22/44)

10TH (BRITISH) CORPS

Lieutenant General Sir Richard McCreery

APPENDIX B

Organization of the Allied Air Forces

MEDITERRANEAN ALLIED AIR FORCES

Air Commander in Chief
Lieutenant General Ira C. Eaker, USAAF

Deputy Air Commander in Chief
Air Marshal Sir John Slessor, RAF

MEDITERRANEAN ALLIED STRATEGIC AIR FORCE

Commanding General
Major General Nathan F. Twining, USAAF

UNITED STATES FIFTEENTH AIR FORCE

Major General James H. Doolittle, USAAF

MEDITERRANEAN ALLIED COASTAL AIR FORCE

Air Vice Marshal Sir Hugh Lloyd, RAF

MEDITERRANEAN ALLIED TACTICAL AIR FORCE

Air Marshal Sir Arthur Coningham, RAF
Major General John K. Cannon, USAAF (from January 1944)

UNITED STATES TWELFTH AIR FORCE

Major General John K. Cannon, USAAF

UNITED STATES XII AIR SUPPORT COMMAND

Major General Edwin J. House, USAAF
Brigadier General Gordon P. Saville, USAAF (from February 2, 1944)

ALLIED TACTICAL AIR FORCE[a]

Formation	No. of Squadrons	Type of Aircraft	Base
U.S. XII Air Support Command[b]			
U.S. 31st Group	3	Spitfires	Naples
U.S. 33d Group	3	Kittyhawks	Naples
No. 324 Wing, RAF	4	Spitfires	Naples
U.S. 324th Group	3	Kittyhawks	Naples
U.S. 27th Group	3	Mustangs	Naples
U.S. 86th Group	3	Mustangs	Naples
U.S. 111th Squadron	1	Tactical Reconnaissance Mustangs	Naples
No. 600 Squadron, RAF	1	Beaufighters	Naples[c]
U.S. 415th Squadron	1	Beaufighters	Naples
No. 225 Squadron, RAF	1	Tactical Reconnaissance Spitfires	Naples
U.S. 79th Group	4	Kittyhawks	Naples[d]
No. 244 Wing, RAF	4	Spitfires	Naples[e]
No. 255 Squadron, RAF	(½)	Beaufighters	Naples
U.S. 47th Group	4	Bostons	Naples
Mediterranean Allied Tactical Bomber Force (MATBF)			
U.S. 12th Group	4	Mitchells	Naples
U.S. 340th Group	4	Mitchells	Naples
U.S. 321st Group	4	Mitchells	Foggia
U.S. 17th Group	4	Marauders	Sardinia
U.S. 319th Group	4	Marauders	Sardinia
U.S. 320th Group	4	Marauders	Sardinia
No. 241 Squadron, RAF	(½)	Strategic Reconnaissance Spitfires	Naples

ALLIED TACTICAL AIR FORCE[a] (*continued*)

Formation	No. of Squadrons	Type of Aircraft	Base
Desert Air Force			
No. 239 Wing,	5	Kittyhawks	Termoli
RAF	1	Kittyhawks	Foggia
No. 7 Wing, SAAF[f]	3	Spitfires	Termoli
No. 40 Squadron, SAAF	1	Tactical Reconnaissance Spitfires	Foggia
No. 232 Wing,	2	Bostons	Foggia
RAF	1	Baltimores	Foggia
No. 3 Wing, SAAF	1	Baltimores	Foggia
No. 600 Squadron, RAF	Det.	Beaufighters	Foggia
No. 241 Squadron, RAF	(½)	Strategic Reconnaissance Spitfires	Termoli
No. 80 Squadron, RAF	1	Fighter-Bomber Spitfires	Termoli
No. 274 Squadron, RAF	1	Fighter-Bomber Spitfires	Termoli
No. 682 Squadron, RAF	1	Photo Reconnaissance Spitfires	Termoli
U.S. 57th Group	3	Kittyhawks/ Thunderbolts	Foggia
Air Observation Post Squadrons			
With Main 8th Army	No. 651 (AOP) Squadron		Auster
With 5th Army, 10th Corps	No. 654 (AOP) Squadron		Auster
With U.S. VI Corps	No. 655 (AOP) Squadron[g]		Auster

SOURCE: Molony, *The Mediterranean and Middle East*, vol. 5, pp. 687–88.
   [a]HQ located at Caserta.
   [b]Advance and rear HQ at Caserta.
   [c]Detachment in Foggia area.
   [d]Detached from the Desert Air Force.
   [e]Same.
   [f]South African Air Force (SAAF).
   [g]Landed at Anzio on January 22, 1944.

APPENDIX C

Order of Battle VI (U.S.) Corps (January 22– March 31, 1944) Operation Shingle

HQ U.S. VI CORPS

Major General John P. Lucas
Major General Lucian K. Truscott (from 2/22/44)

1ST (BRITISH) DIVISION

Major General W. R. C. Penney

24th Guards Brigade

1st Battalion, Irish Guards
1st Battalion, Scots Guards
5th Battalion, Grenadier Guards

2d Infantry Brigade

1st Battalion, Loyal Regiment
2d Battalion, North Staffordshire
  Regiment
6th Battalion, Gordon Highlanders

3d Infantry Brigade

2d Battalion, Sherwood Foresters
1st Battalion, Duke of Wellington's Regiment
1st Battalion, King's Shropshire Light Infantry

Regiment   90th Light AA Regiment, RA
egiment, MG   2d, 19th, 24th, and 67th regiments,
th field   RA
                                      80th Medium Regiment, RA

giment

3D (U.S.) INFANTRY DIVISION

Major General Lucian K. Truscott
Brigadier General John W. O'Daniel[1] (from 2/22/44)

7th Infantry Regiment   703d Ordnance Company
15th Infantry Regiment   10th, 39th, and 41st Field Artillery
30th Infantry Regiment   Battalions
3d Reconnaissance Troop   69th Armored Field Artillery
441st AAA Battalion   Battalion
84th Chemical Battalion (Mortar)   3d Quartermaster Company
751st Tank Battalion (less than full   601st Tank Destroyer Battalion
    strength)   (less than full strength)
3d Medical Battalion   10th Engineer Battalion
3d Signal Company

56TH (BRITISH) DIVISION

Major General G. W. R. Templer

167th Brigade

8th Battalion, Royal Fusiliers
9th Battalion, Royal Fusiliers
7th Battalion, Oxfordshire and
    Buckinghamshire Light Infantry

169th Brigade

2d/5th, 2d/6th, and 2d/7th
    Battalions, Queen's Royal
    Regiment (West Surrey)

168th Brigade

10th Battalion, Royal Berkshire Regiment
1st Battalion, London Scottish
1st Battalion, London Irish Rifles

18th Brigade[2]

1st Battalion, Buffs
14th Battalion, Sherwood Foresters
9th Battalion, King's Own Yorkshire Light Infantry

[1]Promoted to major general on May 30, 1944.
[2]Detached from the British 1st Armoured Division and sent to Anzio on February 24, 1944.

Division Troops

44th Reconnaissance Regiment
67th Antitank Regiment, RA
69th Medium Regiment, RA
57th Heavy AA Regiment, RA
563d Field Park Company, RE
64th, 65th, and 113th Regiments, RA
100th Light Regiment, RA

42d, 220th, and 221st Companies, RE
6th Battalion, Cheshire Regiment, MG

45TH (U.S.) INFANTRY DIVISION

Major General William W. Eagles

157th Infantry Regiment
179th Infantry Regiment
180th Infantry Regiment
120th Engineer Combat Battalion
45th Reconnaissance Troop (Mech)
45th Signal Company
158th, 160th, 171st, and 189th Field Artillery Battalions

645th Tank Destroyer Battalion
120th Medical Battalion
45th Quartermaster Company
700th Ordnance Light Maintenance Company

1ST (U.S.) ARMORED DIVISION

Major General Ernest N. Harmon

Combat Command A
Combat Command B
Combat Command C
27th, 68th, and 91st Armored Field Artillery Battalions
47th Medical Battalion
47th Signal Company
19th Ordnance Company
16th Armored Engineer Battalion

6th Armored Infantry Regiment
1st Armored Regiment
13th Armored Regiment
67th Armored Regiment
601st Tank Destroyer Battalion (att'd)
81st Reconnaissance Regiment
13th Quartermaster Battalion

5TH (BRITISH) DIVISION

Major General P. G. S. Gregson-Ellis

13th Infantry Brigade

2d Battalion, Cameronians (Scottish Rifles)
2d Battalion, Royal Inniskilling Fusiliers
2d Battalion, Wiltshire Regiment

15th Infantry Brigade

1st Battalion, Green Howards
1st Battalion, York and Lancaster Regiment
1st Battalion, King's Own Yorkshire Light Infantry

17th Infantry Brigade

2d Battalion, Royal Scots Fusiliers
2d Battalion, Northamptonshire Regiment
6th Battalion, Seaforth Highlanders

DIVISIONAL TROOPS

5th Reconnaissance Regiment
50th Battalion Royal Tank
  Regiment (-)
91st, 92d, 98th, and 156th Field
  Regiments, RA
18th Light AA Regiment, RA

Belgian Troop, 10th Commando
7th Battalion, Cheshire Regiment,
  MG
102d Medium Regiment, RA
52d Antitank Regiment
215th Heavy AA Battery, RA

CORPS TROOP UNITS[3]

First Special Service Force

Brigadier General Robert T. Frederick

First Regiment[4]
Second Regiment
Third Regiment
456th Parachute Field Artillery (less than full strength)

Ranger Force[5]

Colonel William O. Darby
First, Third, and Fourth Ranger Battalions
83d Chemical Battalion
Cannon Company
Force Headquarters

[3]The units depicted were under the direct control of the VI Corps commander and operated independently, such as the First Special Service Force, or were at times attached to various units in the Anzio beachhead.
[4]Each regiment consisted of three numbered battalions.
[5]King, *Rangers: Selected Combat Operations in World War II.*

2d (British) Special Service Brigade

9th Commando
43d Royal Marine Commando

504th Parachute Infantry Regiment[6]

Colonel Reuben H. Tucker

36th Engineer Combat Regiment[7]

Colonel T. H. Stanley

509th Parachute Infantry Battalion

Lieutenant Colonel William P. Yarborough

---

[6]Assigned to the 82d Airborne Division and detached for service with VI Corps. The remainder of the division had long since been sent to England to prepare for Overlord. The 504th consisted of three parachute infantry battalions.

[7]An independent unit assigned to VI Corps, the 36th Engineers consisted of three numbered engineer battalions. An amazingly versatile unit, the 36th Engineers fought at Salerno; participated in the assault crossing of the Volturno River in the support of the 34th Division; and built roads, bridges, and restored rail lines during the Allied advance to the Gustav Line in 1943. During World War II, the regiment participated in five amphibious assault landings during the course of nine separate campaigns, fought for six months as infantry (most of it at Anzio), and earned eight battle stars in campaigns that began in North Africa and in addition to Salerno and Anzio included Sicily, southern France, Alsace, and the Rhineland.

APPENDIX D

Organization of the Allied Naval Forces

Commander in Chief

Admiral Sir John Cunningham

Chief of Staff

Commodore R. M. Dick
Rear Admiral J. G. L. Dundas (from March 1944)

SHINGLE NAVAL FORCES

TASK FORCE 81

Rear Admiral Frank J. Lowrey, USN

X-RAY FORCE

Rear Admiral Frank J. Lowrey, USN
HQ, U.S. VI Corps

3d (U.S.) Infantry Division
U.S. Ranger Force

PETER FORCE

Rear Admiral Thomas H. Troubridge, RN

1st (British) Division

NAVAL FORCES ENGAGED IN OPERATION SHINGLE[a]

Class	Northern Assault (Peter Force)	Southern Assault (X-Ray Force)
HQ ships	1	1
LSIs	3 (1 Polish)	5
Cruisers	2	2 (1 U.S.)
AA ships	1	1
Destroyers	11	13 (10 U.S./2 Greek)
Gunboats	—	2 (Dutch)
Minesweepers	16 (4 U.S.)	23 (U.S.)
Large LSTs (*boxer* class)	3	—
LSTs	30 (4 U.S./2 Greek)	51 (10 U.S.)
LCGs and LCFs	4	4
LCIs	29	60 (54 U.S.)
LCTs	18	34 (7 U.S.)
Salvage and repair craft (for LCTs and LCIs)	5 (3 U.S.)	6 (U.S.)
Antisubmarine-minesweeping trawlers	4	—
Beacon submarines	1	1
Tugs	3 (2 U.S.)	2 (1 U.S.)
Minelayers and scout craft	17 (9 U.S.)	23 (U.S.)
Miscellaneous	1	2
Totals	149	230

SOURCE: Roskill, *The War at Sea,* vol. 3, part 1, p. 304; and Samuel Eliot Morison, *Sicily–Salerno–Anzio,* appendix III.
    [a]British, unless otherwise identified.

APPENDIX E

German Order
of Battle

Note to the reader: An attempt has been made to re-create the German order of battle as it existed at approximately the time of the counteroffensive that commenced in early February 1944. Divisions, regiments, and battalions were constantly being shifted to meet the tactical needs of the moment. Some were attached to another corps; others to specially created battle groups *(Kampfgruppen)* or other divisions. For example, during the period of this account, the 15th Panzer Grenadier Division was assigned to both the Tenth and Fourteenth armies. Only combat units (including engineers who frequently fought as infantry) are shown below. Combat service support units, such as signals, military police, etc., have been omitted.[1]

ARMY GROUP C

Generalfeldmarschall Albert Kesselring

TENTH ARMY

Generaloberst Heinrich von Vietinghoff

XIV Panzer Corps

General der Panzertruppen Fridolin von Senger und Etterlin

[1] Unless shown otherwise, the principal sources for this appendix are Mitcham, *Hitler's Legions*, Bailey, OCMH Ms. R-50, "The German Situation in Italy," chap. 4: The Drive on Rome. "The German Operation at Anzio" and "Operations of British, Indian and Dominion Forces in Italy," part 1, The Conquest of Southern Italy, September 3, 1943, to March 26, 1944, Section F, German Strategy, USAMHI Library.

15TH PANZER GRENADIER DIVISION
104th Panzer Grenadier Regiment
115th Panzer Battalion
115th Panzer Reconnaissance Battalion
33d Engineer Battalion
33d Artillery Regiment
315th AAA Battalion
33d Antitank Battalion

94TH INFANTRY DIVISION
267th, 274th, and 276th Infantry regiments
194th Engineer Battalion
194th Artillery Regiment
194th Antitank Battalion
194th Field Deployment Battalion

71ST INFANTRY DIVISION
191st, 194th, and 211th Infantry regiments
171st Fusilier Battalion
171st Engineer Battalion
171st Artillery Regiment
171st Antitank Battalion
171st Field Deployment Battalion

LI Mountain Corps

General der Gebirgstruppen Valentin Feuerstein

44TH INFANTRY DIVISION
131st, 132d, and 134th Infantry regiments
44th Reconnaissance Battalion
46th Antitank Battalion (SP)
96th Artillery Regiment

1ST PARACHUTE DIVISION
1st, 3d, and 4th Parachute Infantry regiments
1st Parachute Machine-Gun Battalion
1st Parachute Antitank Battalion
1st Parachute Artillery Regiment

5TH MOUNTAIN DIVISION
85th and 100th Mountain Infantry regiments
85th Reconnaissance Battalion
85th Antitank Battalion
95th Mountain Artillery Regiment

114TH LIGHT DIVISION
721st and 741st Light regiments
114th Reconnaissance Battalion

114th Antitank Battalion
661st Artillery Regiment

Group Hauck

Generalleutnant Friedrich Wilhelm Hauck

334TH INFANTRY DIVISION
754th, 755th, and 756th Infantry regiments
334th Fusilier Battalion
334th Antitank Battalion (self-propelled)
334th Artillery Regiment

305TH INFANTRY DIVISION
576th, 577th, and 578th Infantry regiments
305th Fusilier Battalion
305th Antitank Battalion (self-propelled)
305th Artillery Regiment

FOURTEENTH ARMY[2]

Generaloberst Eberhard von Mackensen

I Parachute Corps

General der Fallschirmtruppen Alfred Schlemm

4TH PARACHUTE DIVISION
10th, 11th, and 12th Parachute Infantry regiments
4th Parachute AAA Battalion (motorized)

29TH PANZER GRENADIER DIVISION
15th Panzer Grenadier Regiment (3 motorized battalions)
71st Panzer Grenadier Regiment (3 motorized battalions)
129th Panzer Assault Battalion (assault guns)
129th Panzer Reconnaissance Battalion

[2]Operational approximately January 29, 1944. By February 16, the Fourteenth Army consisted of

Armored divisions	2
Motorized divisions	1
Parachute divisions	1
Infantry divisions	4
Total	8

With the addition of the independent regiments, an SS battle group, and a number of miscellaneous units, such as Luftwaffe ground troops, the actual total of German forces operating within the Anzio beachhead by February 16 was the equivalent of nine full divisions.

313th AAA Battalion (motorized)
29th Artillery Regiment (3 motorized battalions)

65TH INFANTRY DIVISION[3]

145th, 146th, and 147th Infantry regiments
165th Fusilier Battalion
165th Antitank Battalion (motorized)
165th Artillery Regiment (4 battalions, including 1 motorized)

715TH INFANTRY DIVISION (MOTORIZED)[4]

725th and 735th Infantry regiments
671st Artillery Regiment

114TH JÄGER DIVISION[5]

721st & 741st Jäger regiments
661st Artillery Regiment
114th Reconnaissance Battalion
114th Antitank Battalion
114th Engineer Battalion
114th Signal Battalion

LXXVI Panzer Corps[6]

General der Panzertruppen Traugott Herr

3D PANZER GRENADIER DIVISION[7]

8th Panzer Grenadier Regiment (3 motorized battalions)
29th Panzer Grenadier Regiment (3 motorized battalions)
103d Panzer Battalion (assault guns)
103d Panzer Reconnaissance Battalion
312th AAA Battalion (motorized)
3d Artillery Regiment (2 motorized battalions, 1 self-propelled battalion)

26TH PANZER DIVISION[8]

9th Panzer Grenadier Regiment·
67th Regiment
26th Panzer Regiment
26th Panzer Reconnaissance Battalion
304th AAA Battalion (self-propelled)
93rd Panzer Artillery Regiment (2 motorized battalions, 1 self-propelled battalion)

[3]Arrived from northern Italy prior to January 30, 1944.
[4]Arrived from southern France prior to February 4.
[5]Formerly the 714th Infantry Division, this unit arrived from Yugoslavia prior to February 10 (Mitcham, *Hitler's Legions*, pp. 327–28).
[6]Arrived from Adriatic sector prior to February 1.
[7]Elements arrived with a regiment of the 15th Panzer Grenadier Division on January 22–23.
[8]Most of the division in position in the Cisterna sector on January 30.

HERMANN GÖRING PARACHUTE PANZER DIVISION[9]

1st Parachute Panzer Grenadier Regiment (2 motorized battalions, 1 mechanized battalion)
2nd Parachute Panzer Grenadier Regiment (3 motorized battalions)
Parachute Panzer Regiment H.G. (1 tank battalion, 1 assault gun battalion)
Parachute Panzer Reconnaissance Battalion H.G.
Parachute AAA Regiment H.G. (3 motorized battalions)

Battle Group of the 16th SS Panzer Grenadier Division[10]

362D INFANTRY DIVISION[11]

954th, 955th, and 966th Infantry Regiments
362d Fusilier Battalion
362d Antitank Battalion
362d Artillery Regiment (4 battalions)

INDEPENDENT REGIMENTS[12]

Infantry Lehr Regiment
1027th Reinforced Panzer Grenadier Regiment (2 battalions)
1028th Reinforced Panzer Grenadier Regiment (2 battalions)

---

[9]Entire division in line in the Cisterna sector prior to January 30, with elements of the 1st Parachute Division.
[10]Attached to the Hermann Göring Division.
[11]In Army reserve by January 30. First elements committed on February 16.
[12]All arrived prior to February 16.

APPENDIX F

The German Reinforcement of Anzio (D day to D plus 10) January 22– February 1, 1944

Date	Formation	Number	Subtotal
D day	2d Battalion, 71st Panzer Grenadier Regiment	400	
(January 22)	No. 14 Co, 71st Panzer Grenadier Regiment	100	
	129th Reconnaissance Battalion	700	
	2d Battalion, 200th Panzer Grenadier Regiment	900	
	29th Quartermaster Battalion	300	
	Messina Battalion	300	
	Harbor Company	100	
	Artillery Untergruppe	100	
	Army coast artillery	100	
	H.G. tank regiment (-)	1,600	
	3d Battalion, 1st Parachute Regiment	500	
	Parachute M.G. Battalion	500	
	450th Artillery Battalion	800	
	1st Company, 29th Engineer Battalion	200	

Date	Formation	Number	Subtotal
	3d Panzer Grenadier Division (8th Panzer Grenadier Regiment and 1st Battalion, 29th Regiment)	6,200	
	H.G. AA Regiment	2,000	
	H.G. Engineer Battalion	500	
	4th Battalion, 171st Artillery Regiment	800	
	11th Parachute Regiment	1,500	
	Parachute Training Regiment	1,500	
	26th Reconnaissance Battalion	1,000	
		20,100	20,100
D plus 1 (January 23)	194th Infantry Regiment	1,800	
	104th Panzer Grenadier Regiment	1,500	
	1st Battalion, H.G. Panzer Grenadier Regiment	1,000	
		4,300	24,400
D plus 2 (January 24)	165th Reconnaissance Battalion	600	
	356th Reconnaissance Battalion	600	
	Elements H.G. Division	5,100	
	1st Battalion, 26th Tank Regiment	600	
	4 Antitank battalions	3,200	
	5 Artillery battalions	2,400	
	35th SS Regiment	3,000	
	Luftwaffe Jäger Battalion No. 2	500	
		16,000	40,400
D plus 3 (January 25)	3 Co, 71st Panzer Grenadier Regiment	100	
	165th Engineer Battalion	600	
		700	41,100
D plus 4 (January 26)	145th Infantry Regiment	2,000	
	1st Battalion, 49th AA Regiment	600	
		2,600	43,700
D plus 5 (January 27)	171st Reconnaissance Regiment	600	
	147th Infantry Regiment	2,000	
	114th Engineer Battalion	600	
	2d Battalion, 1st Parachute Regiment	500	
	764th Artillery Battalion	800	

Date	Formation	Number	Subtotal
	1st Battalion, 171st Artillery Regiment	600	
		5,100	48,800
D plus 6 (January 28)	715th Reconnaissance Battalion	600	
	67th Panzer Grenadier Regiment	1,500	
	26th Tank Regiment (-)	1,400	
	2d Battalion, 93d Artillery Regiment	600	
	Remainder 65th Division	4,500	
		8,600	57,400
D plus 7 (January 29)	Elements 26th Panzer Division	7,000	
	735th Infantry Regiment	3,000	
	1st Battalion, 1st Parachute Regiment	500	
	1st Battalion, 4th Parachute Regiment	500	
	2d Battalion, 36th SS Regiment	1,000	
	114th Reconnaissance Battalion	600	
	7th Jäger Battalion	500	
	56th Nebelwerfer Regiment	1,000	
		14,100	71,500
D plus 8 (January 30)	10th Parachute Regiment	2,500	
	60th Engineer Battalion	600	
		3,100	74,600
D plus 9 (January 31)	721st Infantry Regiment	3,000	
	Remainder 715th Division	6,000	
		9,000	83,600
D plus 10 (February 1)	Sturm Parachute Regiment	1,500	
	2d Battalion, 33d Artillery Regiment	800	
	4th Battalion, 13th Tank Regiment	600	
	9 Artillery battalions	7,000	
	2 HQ, AA battalions	1,500	
		11,400	95,000

SOURCE: Statistics for January 22; Lucas Papers, USAMHI; remainder: Anzio correspondence, box 47/5, Samuel Eliot Morison Papers, U.S. Navy Historical Center.

APPENDIX G

"Ammo Joe" at Anzio (January 22–May 31, 1944)[1]

At Anzio-Nettuno there were six Ammunitions Supply Points (ASPs) in operation by the end of May 1944. An estimated 40,000 tons of ammunition were stored under direct enemy observation and were continuously exposed to enemy fire. Over the 121 days of the siege of the Anzio beachhead there were sixty-five fires (an average of one every two days), and 3,807 tons were lost, or 31.5 tons per day. Four ordnance ammunition personnel were killed in action and 46 Purple Hearts were awarded, three with Oak Leaf Clusters.

The ordnance mission at Anzio was especially difficult. Conventional storage methods could not be used and Fifth Army was required to keep two widely separated fronts supplied simultaneously. New types of shells were created by the Fifth Army ammo men to meet the urgent new needs of the troops in the field.

Resupply at Anzio was maintained by use of 1,500 2½ ton trucks reserved for this purpose, a great majority of which were dedicated to carrying ammunition. These trucks embarked fully laden with approximately five tons at Naples and were unloaded and driven to the appropriate ASP where they were discharged. By employing a four-day turnaround system, 350–400 trucks per day carried 1,750–2,000 tons of stores and ammunition to Anzio. Others in the fleet were either en route to or from Anzio or being loaded at supply facilities in the south for shipment by LST to Anzio. It was the first mass employment of the roll-on, roll-off concept and was on a far more advanced scale than that employed by Captain von Liebenstein, who devised the German system for resupplying the island of Sicily during the German campaign in July–August 1943.

---

[1] Extracted from "Ammo Joe at Anzio," a document prepared by the Fifth Army Ordnance Officer, Brigadier General Urban Niblo, copy in USAMHI Library.

Listed below are types of guns fired by the Allies at Anzio, the average number in action, and the tonnages expended, by type of gun.

Weapon	Average Guns in Action	Total (rounds)[a] expenditures
155-mm gun	36	180,486
8-inch gun	1	1,286
8-inch howitzer	12	30,789
240-mm howitzer	2	3,601
37-mm AA gun	121	132,765
40-mm AA gun	96	263,565
3-inch gun	166	229,928
90-mm AA gun	42	188,620
37-mm gun	413	149,689
57-mm AT gun	749	57,628
75-mm gun	254	347,622
75-mm howitzer	79	406,114
76-mm gun	3	3,749
105-mm howitzer M-2	200	1,633,402
155-mm howitzer, M1917–18	16	119,079
155-mm howitzer, M-1	52	316,453
60-mm mortar	336	433,667
81-mm mortar	234	63,075
grenades (all types)	—	577,653
pyrotechnics (all types)	—	79,715
2.36-inch rockets	—	71,390
.30-caliber cartridges	—	62,822,996
.50-caliber cartridges	—	6,441,240
.45-caliber cartridges	—	5,906,820

[a]Highest daily issues were between February 15–20, when just under 2,500 tons per day were dispensed and around May 10, during the preparations for the breakout, when an average of 3,500 tons per day were issued.

APPENDIX H

"Anzio Annie" and "Anzio Express"

The two monster long-range guns that plagued Allied troops at Anzio were the creation of the Krupp Works and were among the largest artillery weapons employed during World War II.[1] The nine great Paris railway guns employed by the Germans on the Western Front in 1918, measuring 240 mm across the bore, were the forerunners of the World War II version.

During the interwar period the Germans secretly continued to refine and research the perfection of long-range guns and their projectiles and powder. The original Paris railway guns fired shells from as far as seventy-five miles away, but they had been largely ineffective due to the lightness of the shells and their relatively small bursting charges.

Hitler's ascension to power led to accelerated development during the 1930s in anticipation of their need to attack the French Maginot Line. The result was the K5(E) [Kanone No. 5 Eisenbahn] series, which were direct descendants of the 1918 Paris guns. Although never required when the Germans simply bypassed the Maginot Line in 1940, these guns were transported to western France and emplaced on the Channel near Cape Gris Nez and were known to have fired shells into England. The K5 fired an unconventional shell with special rifling, and although the British soon determined that a new type of shell was being employed, nothing more was known of the guns that had fired them.

With the advent of the Italian campaign OKW determined that the guns could be best employed in support of German troops in Italy. The Shingle landings in January 1944 led to the movement of two guns to support the German defense of the Anzio beachhead. They arrived about February 2 and were first employed on February 7 to shell Allied shipping offshore. Although the two guns came to be nicknamed Anzio Annie and Anzio Express, the Germans called them Leopold (Anzio Annie) and Robert (Anzio Express).[2] It

---

[1]The Czechs had produced a 320-mm railroad gun and a battery of these would have been shipped to Anzio, but there were no tunnels in the Alban Hills capable of accommodating these guns.
[2]When later captured, these names were stenciled on the side of the guns.

has been generally believed that the Allies were unable to pinpoint the location of either gun. In fact, one of the major contributions of Peter Tompkins and his network was to accomplish precisely that. On February 12 and 13 Radio Vittoria informed Fifth Army that Anzio Annie was southeast of Rome near the Ciampino airfield. On March 5 a detailed message located Anzio Express several miles to the south near Frattocchie Station. Radio Vittoria also described how both guns operated during their brief forays from the safety of nearby railway tunnels.[3] Despite this invaluable intelligence from Rome the Allied air forces managed only occasionally to damage inbound ammunition trains but were never able to knock out the two guns. What is even more perplexing is that the guns could have been neutralized merely by destroying the tracks outside their tunnels.

Each gun was drawn by a diesel-electric locomotive and consisted of the gun carriage and four support cars. It took twenty-four railway wheels on the gun carriage to support and transport the gun. One of the four supporting cars was a turntable-platform on which the gun was mounted in order to gain traverse when fired. Another of the cars was air-conditioned and carried the powder for the shells. The other two were a flatcar used to transport a mobile generating unit and an electrically operated derrick for hoisting ammunition and a car for carrying turntable rail segments and an inclined rail section, with a hand-operated derrick for unloading. Under favorable conditions it was believed that a skilled crew was able to emplace and prepare the gun for firing in six to ten hours. The turntable track alone consisted of eighteen sections.[4]

The version used at Anzio had less than half the range (approximately thirty-one to thirty-three miles) of its World War I counterpart, but its shell was far more deadly. The guns were so vulnerable to air attack that, despite their reputation, they could only be employed sparingly, which was fortunate for the Allies. During daylight hours their firing was at best sporadic, except on days when the weather was overcast and the Allied air forces grounded. In fact, the most-used railway guns at Anzio were not Anzio Annie or Anzio Express but a battery of 210-mm guns kept in a tunnel west of Albano, near the Pope's summer palace at Castel Gandolfo. As the U.S. Army Ordnance official history notes:

> Every time a shell from a long-range gun hit the Anzio beachhead, and they continued to hit regularly until the breakout in May, the troops blamed it on Anzio Annie, but the Germans had a formidable array of heavy artillery in addition to the railroad guns: 220-mm howitzers, 210-mm howitzers, and 170-mm guns. The 170s on surrounding hills, possessing a range of about 30,000 yards, did more damage than the railroad guns. On 16 February when the Germans began their big counteroffensive, they fired 454 rounds from six 170-mm guns and only 50 rounds from the two 210-mm railroad guns. On 29 February they had eighteen 170-mm guns, from which they fired 600 rounds; and on that day they fired only 12 rounds from their 210-mm railroad guns. The railroad guns were freaks; but Anzio Annie symbolized a bitter truth—the Germans had in the 170-mm. a gun that outranged the best gun

the Allies had, the 155-mm Long Tom, with its maximum range of 25,700 yards. It was at Anzio that the clamor for heavier artillery began.[5]

For the most part Hitler's generals were singularly unimpressed by these super-weapons and during their postwar interrogations described them as costly mistakes and typical of the Führer's mania for large and powerful weapons. The vital statistics of the K5 guns reveal their gargantuan size:

Weights: gun and carriage 462,000 lbs.
        diesel power unit and carriage 50,116 lbs.
        turntable and its two transporter cars 200,000 lbs.
        turntable track & transport car 120,000 lbs.
        Total shipping weight 832,116 lbs. (416 tons)[6]
Movement: approximately 5–10 miles per hour by rail.
Range: approximately 34,000 yds.; with rocket-assisted shell, approximately 93,000
        yds. (highly inaccurate)
Shell: High explosive (HE), 550 lbs.
Muzzle velocity: 840 meters per sec.
Rate of fire: one round every 4–5 min.
Weight of breechblock: 3,425 lbs.
Length of powder chamber: 10 ft., 5 in.
Tube length: 67 ft., 5 in.
Overall barrel length: 70 ft., 8 in.
Weight of barrel: 187,880 lbs.
Length of gun carriage: 69 ft., 8 in.
Length of gun with trucks: 95 ft., 7 in.
Width of gun carriage: 8 ft., 8.5 in.
Turntable, length of platform: 120 ft., 8 in.
Length of track on platform: 103 ft., 6 in.
Gun elevation: 50 degrees
Traverse on turntable: 360 degrees
Traverse on gun carriage: .5 degree
Recoil: 46.8 in.[7]

Both guns were damaged by Allied aircraft sometime in February, but one was thought to have been back in operation in early April. The destruction of the Italian railway system by the Allied air forces ensured that the guns would not escape Italy. However, the Germans managed to remove them from the Anzio beachhead, and they were found on June 7 at a railroad siding in Civitavecchia.[8] Both had been badly damaged, not only by Allied air but also by German demolitions, and in the ensuing weeks became an object of curiosity to passing GIs, who covered both with their names. Although Robert was beyond salvage, Leopold (Anzio Annie) was recovered and began a long journey to the United States via Naples.

    Annie left Italy in March 1945 but did not arrive in the United States until

[5]Lida Mayo, *The Ordnance Department: On Beachhead and Battlefront* (Washington, D.C., 1968), pp. 200–201.

[6]Lt. Col. G. B. Barrett, "German Long-Range Guns," *The Coast Artillery Journal*, May–June 1946.

[7]Ibid., and "Tactical and Technical Trends," Military Intelligence Service, War Department, Bulletin no. 50.

[8]Mayo, *The Ordnance Department: On Beachhead and Battlefront*, p. 200.

the summer of 1946, after an epic engineering effort by the U.S. Army 540th Engineer Combat Group. Its final resting place was a rail siding at Aberdeen Proving Ground, Maryland, where it is now the showpiece of the U. S. Army Ordnance Museum.[9]

The judgment of Lieutenant Colonel Barrett in 1946 that the guns are "undoubtedly all amazing monsters of small military value, developed at the direction of the mad paper hanger of Austria in his bid for world Domination, and a monument to his failure," now seems beyond dispute.[10]

[9] Kenneth H. Powers, U.S. Army Ordnance Museum, Aberdeen Proving Ground, Maryland, provided the data cited above.

[10] Barrett, "German Long-Range Guns."

APPENDIX I

The Strange Story of Angelita of Anzio

Sixteen years after the war the mayor of Anzio received the following letter from a former British soldier living in Teddington, Middlesex, England:

February 15, 1961

Dear Sirs:

I trust you will forgive me writing to you, also for writing in English but I would like to know how Anzio and Nettuno are going on today.

You see, I was one of the British troops who landed on Anzio Beach head and our Head Quarters was in the Cork Factory. What I am most interested in is the fact and background of one little girl called Angelita Rossi then about 5 years of age.

We found her on the Beach crying and the only information we could get from her was her name and that she was on holiday: when we could we tried to find her Parents or Guardians but no one in Anzio or Nettuno could give us any information so we came to the conclusion that with all the Civilians killed her Parents or Guardian were among them; we cared for her and gave her all we had as regards comforts also with the help of the American Red Cross who were going to adopt her but unfortunately during one heavy bombardment of the Beach head she was in a trench with 3 British soldiers and an American Red Cross Nurse when a German 88-MM shell hit inside their trench, all were killed, our whole company was upset. We vowed to find her Parents or Guardians but again unfortunately my entire company was killed; later I was awarded the Military Medal. Our Regiment was the Royal Scots Fusiliers. I wonder if anyone has ever enquired about her, but I would not like to upset anyone now after all those years of silence.

I would like to visit Anzio and Nettuno again and possibly find little Angelita's grave along with other Civilians and troops who were also killed. But I am married now and have 5 children and I cannot afford to visit but I would appreciate any photo of the area and any information which you can give me. I am sure it is all changed now, let's hope there will never be another ANZIO through the world.

Thank you for reading this letter.

Yours faithfully,
C. C. HAYES[1]

[1]Quoted in Ennio Silvestri, *Dove è Max? (Angelita di Anzio)*, privately printed, n.d. Extracts of Silvestri's book in both English and Italian were kindly furnished the author by Silvano Casaldi, a journalist who lives in Nettuno.

The letter from former Royal Scots Fusilier Christopher C. Hayes became the fuse that lit a controversy that remains unresolved to this day. Ennio Silvestri and his mother were among the many refugees living in caves in the Padiglione woods and although he had never heard of Angelita Rossi, Silvestri, now the head of the Anzio Tourist Board, was touched by Hayes's letter and went to see him during a visit to England a short time later.

Silvestri describes Hayes as "an Irishman from Ulster . . . [who] has a kind face. . . . He is calm and gentle, a little shy; but even on this day he will, as always, get angry, stop talking and the expression on his face will harden if there is any hint that the interviewer might in some way be 'profaning' the memory of Angelita."[2] Even though he could not verify Hayes's claims, Silvestri believed the story.

The Italian press soon learned of Hayes's search for Angelita and appeals for information were broadcast on Italian TV. The result was a nationwide search for the parents or relatives of the little girl, whose story touched the hearts of Italians and even resulted in a song called "Angelita of Anzio," which was composed and recorded by a group named Los Marcellos Ferial. The song quickly became a top hit on the Italian pop music charts.[3]

In 1964 Hayes told his story to a British tabloid called *Weekend*. A poignant article described how Hayes had found little six-year-old *(sic)* Angelita wearing a torn black dress and screaming in terror, cringing in the bushes in the midst of a minefield. The little refugee girl who called herself Angelita lived with Hayes and his platoon for approximately ten days and even went on patrol with her British protectors. According to Hayes, his platoon leader, Captain W. E. Pettigrew, also loved the child and permitted her to remain in their custody. However, the start of the German counteroffensive at the end of January left Hayes:

> desperate to get poor Angelita out of the battle area. His chance seemed to come when, in the middle of a heavy German artillery barrage, a jeep was about to set off for a hospital which had been set up in the American sector. He lifted her on to the vehicle and a corporal gently took hold of her. The explosion that came next left Hayes dazed. It shattered his rifle and steel helmet. And then he saw the full horror. A shell had hit the jeep. He said: "I lifted Angelita out. She was dying. But her doll was still clutched tightly in her hand. . . . I cried." Angelita was dead but her memory lived on.[4]

After the war Hayes stated that he and Pettigrew were the only survivors of his platoon and that "Pettigrew said it was now his mission in life to trace the parents—if they were still by the remotest chance alive. . . . He made a return journey to Anzio to pursue his inquiries—but he discovered nothing. He [Pettigrew] died in 1947."[5]

In 1965 a twenty-seven-year-old housewife came forward claiming to be Angelita and told of surviving her ordeal in the beachhead. Her name, she said, was Signora Angelina De Luca and her maiden name was Rossi. There was

[2]Ibid.

[3]*After the Battle*, no. 44, Anzio, p. 41, and Ivor Smullen, "A Little Girl Called Angelita," *Weekend*, September 16–22, 1964, p. 10.

[4]Ibid., quoted in *Weekend*, September 16–22, 1964, pp. 8 and 10.

[5]Ibid, p. 10.

elation in Anzio, and arrangements were made by the Italian State Tourist Board to help defray the expenses of bringing Hayes to Anzio to meet and identify the woman whose life he had saved in 1944.

On February 2, 1965, Hayes arrived in Italy and was driven from Rome to Anzio by the Rome correspondent of *Weekend*, Ronald Singleton, to participate in a press conference in which he would meet Angelita for the first time since the war. During the thirty-mile drive to Anzio, Singleton noted:

> The ex-Fusilier was strangely tense. He said: "I didn't want to come at all. The only reason I am here is so I can put things right once and for all."
>
> "He just blew his top," said Singleton. . . . The following day . . . Hayes attended a press conference at the office of the mayor of Anzio.
>
> The mayors and officials of the towns, with dozens of Italian pressmen, listened in shocked silence as Hayes exploded: "This has been a beautiful story for 20 years. Angelita's short life with the Fusiliers and her death were true stories, and they symbolised for all of us the simple, terrifying tragedy of little children caught up in the deadly game of war. It was better to leave it like that. . . . Then letters from strange women started arriving, enclosing meaningless photographs of little girls. I am here to ask you to stop all this undignified commercialisation of a simple, touching story which holds so much meaning for many British ex-soldiers and their wives."
>
> Then Hayes dropped the bombshell he had nursed for 21 years. He said: "This little girl we called Angelita died in my arms and she didn't move for 10 minutes. She was soaked in blood, and her head wounds were so terrible that I had no doubt she was dead."[6]

When presented with photographs of "Angelita," Hayes angrily handed them back, stating, "How can she be our Angelita when I saw the child die?"[7] The woman who called herself Angelita had disappeared into seclusion, but both were persuaded to meet and a tense encounter ensued in which Signora De Luca said: "If it had not been for you, I should not be alive today," to which "Hayes shook his head and said: 'I am sorry, but you are not the girl I knew. You are not the Angelita of The Royal Scots Fusiliers.' "[8] To the acute embarrassment of the Italian officials who witnessed the encounter, the two stiffly parted company with a handshake.

The story and their meeting in Anzio drew worldwide press coverage.[9] The Angelita affair become a *cause célèbre* not only throughout Italy, but particularly in Anzio and Nettuno, where Italian officials scrambled to disassociate themselves from responsibility for what had suddenly turned into an ugly incident. There seemed little doubt that Signora De Luca was a pretender, one of literally hundreds, as it turned out, who had claimed to be Angelita of Anzio.[10] According to *Weekend*:

[6]Quoted in Perrott Phillips, "Find the Truth about Angelita," *Weekend,* March 24–30, 1965, pp. 12–13.

[7]Ibid., p. 13.

[8]Ibid.

[9]The story made the Associated Press newswire and in addition to being reported in the United States and Britain, was covered in Italy by *Il Messaggero, Avanti!, Roma, Il Tempo, Oggi, La Stampa, Il Giornale D'Italia, La Nazione,* and the Italian equivalent of *TV Guide.*

[10]A large commemorative paperback book produced in 1979 for the thirty-fifth anniversary of the Anzio battles contains reproduced copies of dozens of articles in both English and Italian of the ill-fated Hayes visit in 1965. My thanks to Silvano Casaldi who furnished me a copy in 1990.

Influential townsfolk were accused of putting pressure on Angelina Rossi to pose as the Angel of Anzio for the sake of tourist publicity. Other officials claimed they were duped. In Rome informed opinion has flatly condemned the whole affair as a tawdry, tasteless and disgraceful attempt to cash in on the memory of a dead child. But it is Hayes who has the last words . . . "Maybe little Angelita can now rest in peace."[11]

Despite the endorsement and efforts of Ennio Silvestri, whose book about Angelita kept the story in the public eye, no verifiable family members ever came forward to corroborate the girl's existence. There is no record of anyone named Angelita Rossi buried at any cemetery—military or civilian—at Anzio or Nettuno. Nor did extensive investigation by the carabinieri reveal any record of anyone named Angelita.

The 1965 incident did not deter Italian officials from erecting a statue in downtown Anzio to the memory of "Angelita of Anzio." Situated near the beachfront where Allied troops landed on January 22, 1944, the statue was formally dedicated in 1979, on the thirty-fifth anniversary of the landings, as part of the Italian contribution to International Children's Year. Among the honored guests at the ceremony was ex-Royal Scots Fusilier Christopher C. Hayes.[12] Although she had been widely discredited in 1965, Angelina Rossi De Luca renewed her claim that she was Angelita, casting a shadow over the ceremony.

The Angelita story might have passed into history were it not for the fact that some Italian journalists began to probe Hayes's role in the affair. They observed that in the British military cemetery at Nettuno there were no Royal Scots Fusiliers who had died prior to March 1944. Their tombstones all reflected dates well into March or later. How could this be if, as Hayes had repeatedly claimed, everyone in his platoon had been killed in action in late January or early February? Clearly they could not all have died in March or later.

Among those raising troublesome questions about Hayes and Angelita was Luciano Traietti, a Rome journalist, whose investigation into the affair brought no response from Hayes, who had moved to Perth, Australia, in 1969.[13] Among those Traietti was able to track down was retired Major W. E. Pettigrew, the same officer whom Hayes told *Weekend* had died in 1947. Not only was Major Pettigrew very much alive and living in Glasgow, Scotland, but he recalled that Hayes had indeed been a member of his unit and that "when he was under my command he was a good soldier."[14]

Corporal Christopher Hayes was assigned to the 2d Battalion, Royal Scots Fusiliers. Official British war records reflect that the commander of Company A was Captain W. E. Pettigrew.[15] What neither Traietti or anyone else realized was that at the time of the Shingle landings on January 22, 1944, the 2d Battal-

[11]Quoted in *Weekend*, March 24–30, 1965, p. 13.

[12]The latest chapter in the Angelita saga was again widely reported in the world press. One American correspondent reported that "the statue here at Anzio is so striking that the Italian Ministry of Foreign Affairs will use it as the symbol of Italy at the Stockholm exhibition for the International Children's Year" (article by Gary Grant, syndicated in fourteen Illinois newspapers, April 5, 1979).

[13]Silvestri, *Dove è Max? (Angelita di Anzio)*, p. 14.

[14]Letter, Major W. E. Pettigrew, M.B.E., M.C., to Luciano Traietti, May 20, 1986. A photocopy of this letter and Traietti's 1986 correspondence with the U.S. Army Military History Institute was furnished the author by USAMHI in 1988.

[15]War Diary, 2d Battalion, Royal Scots Fusiliers, PRO (WO 169/10290 [September–December 1943]). Another inconsistency in Hayes's story is that Pettigrew was his platoon leader, when in fact he was the commanding officer of Company A.

ion, Royal Scots Fusiliers, was *not* at Anzio but some eighty miles south engaged in the fighting along the Garigliano River as part of Mark Clark's abortive attempt to storm the Rapido River.[16] The battalion belonged not to the British 1st Division—the only British unit at Anzio during the period Hayes claimed to have found and cared for Angelita—but to the 5th Division. Moreover, according to the battalion war diary, Captain Pettigrew was wounded in action near the Garigliano and evacuated on January 17, five days *before* the Anzio landings.[17] As Pettigrew has attested in a letter to the author, his wounds kept him from ever serving at Anzio.[18] After the war the regimental history would record that in early April 1944 Captain W. A. Pettigrew was one of four battalion officers to receive the Military Cross "for gallantry during the crossing of the Garigliano in January."[19]

The war diary also confirms that the 2d Battalion, Royal Scots Fusiliers, did not arrive at Anzio until March 7, when the advance party disembarked. Two days later the remainder of the battalion arrived and was sent to plug gaps on the left flank of the beachhead.[20]

Upon examination, the tale Hayes told Silvestri and various journalists was full of inconsistencies. Even Silvestri admits that Hayes's claim that Angelita was "on holiday" in January 1944 "was quite out of the question."[21] If it is true that Hayes and his comrades did not understand Italian and were limited to learning Angelita's name (which was, according to what he told Silvestri, "sewn into her dress"), how then were they able to understand that she was on vacation?[22]

There is irrefutable documentary evidence that Hayes's battalion was never at Anzio until March 1944. How then could Angelita even have existed except as a product of his imagination? In the version given Silvestri and *Weekend*, Captain Pettigrew was deeply involved in protecting Angelita. The fact that Pettigrew was recovering from wounds in a military hospital destroys the credibility of Hayes's claim that he did so.

Virtually every other aspect of Hayes's story rings false as well:

> Some days later we left the woods. Our destination was a railway station called Carroceto and it was here that our battalion was to join up again. There in the square, alongside a beautiful asphalt road, was a Red Cross van and several wounded

[16]Ibid., WO 170/1471, war diary for January through April 1944. On January 22 the 2d Battalion was positioned on a hill west of Minturno, a town situated on Highway 7 along the Gulf of Gaeta, several miles northwest of the mouth of the Garigliano River.

[17]Ibid., field return for the week ending January 22, 1944.

[18]Letter to the author, April 10, 1989. Pettigrew states: "I was never at Anzio and know nothing of this so-called incident. I was wounded on the Garigliano River on 18 January 1944 and treated in various general hospitals before being evacuated by ship back to the United Kingdom. I can inform that my Battalion (2d Royal Scots Fusiliers) continued to fight in the Garigliano/Minturno area of Italy until I think late in February 1944 when they were withdrawn and reformed before being sent to Anzio *for the first time* in early March 1944."

[19]J. C. Kemp, *The History of the Royal Scots Fusiliers, 1919–59* (Glasgow, 1963), p. 223. This information was also recorded in the battalion war diary on April 10, 1944 (WO 170/1353). Pettigrew's hospitalization for wounds is further confirmed by his regimental association (letter, assistant regimental secretary, Royal Highland Fusiliers [name of the former Royal Scots Fusiliers] to the author, June 23, 1989).

[20]2d Battalion War Diary, WO 170/1353.

[21]*Dove è Max? (Angelita di Anzio)*, p. 10.

[22]Ibid., pp. 8, 10.

people waiting around. At last, we thought, the child will be safe. And so, sadly, but according to our agreement, we handed Angelita over to an American nurse who was giving first aid to the wounded. I can still see her, sitting in the cabin, her eyes filled with tears, waving goodbye to each one of us as we filed by on our way south.

Suddenly there was a terrific explosion behind us. I turned around. Horrified, I could see that the whole piazza, right where the Red Cross van had stood, had been struck. . . . Angelita had been thrown out of the vehicle. I picked her up and clasped her to me but she was already dead.[23]

During my research for this book I found no evidence that any Red Cross vehicles operated in the forward area. Indeed, any vehicle visible to the German gunners in the Alban Hills would have been the immediate target of artillery fire. Moreover, there is no piazza at Carroceto, which in 1944 was little more than the railway station for Aprilia. Nor could Hayes have been referring to the Factory, which by the end of January had turned into a rubble-strewn battleground. Other inconsistencies include the fact that nurses were employed in field hospitals, not at the front giving first aid to the wounded—a task performed not by nurses but by combat medical corpsmen—and that the Red Cross function in World War II was not one of medical support.

In his original letter to the mayor of Anzio, Hayes claimed that Angelita had been killed when an 88-mm shell landed in the foxhole where she and three members of his platoon and an American Red Cross nurse had sought cover. However, another version of Angelita's demise appears in Raleigh Trevelyan's *Rome '44*, in which Hayes hands over Angelita to two American nurses in a jeep, which is then struck by a shell, killing everyone inside.[24] Hayes indicated he was close enough to the explosion to have his helmet and rifle shattered, yet he apparently emerged unscathed. If Hayes was wearing his helmet and it was shattered, how did he escape death or serious injury? And how did he survive, apparently unwounded, when twenty-eight others in his platoon were allegedly killed at the same time and his entire company died in the course of the battle?[25]

Although the casualties at Anzio were exceptionally high, there was no known instance in which an entire company died, particularly one which could only have been there during the stalemate period from March to May 1944. Everyone connected with Hayes conveniently seems to have died, thus leaving no single living witness to corroborate (or refute) Hayes except Captain Pettigrew, who was likewise (falsely) killed off after the war in the version given *Weekend* in 1964.

Another major inconsistency occurs in Hayes's description of Angelita's death. To *Weekend* in 1964 he said: "She was soaked in blood, and her head wounds were so terrible that I had no doubt she was dead."[26] Thirteen years

---

[23]Hayes, quoted in ibid., p. 9.

[24]Trevelyan, *Rome '44*, pp. 82–83. It should also be pointed out that American nurses simply did not drive around the front in jeeps at Anzio or anywhere else. In a later version given the *Sunday Independent*, Hayes stated that at the time of the explosion he had dived to the ground and his helmet was against the rear tire of the jeep. The explosion was so powerful that it not only killed everyone above him but flung the steering column across the road along with part of the dismembered driver ("The Search for Angelita," *Sunday Independent*, October 9, 1977, p. 20).

[25]Ibid. According to Hayes: "I realised then that she was dead. So were 28 of my comrades who had helped me care for her."

[26]Quoted in *Weekend*, March 24–30, 1965, p. 13.

later the version given the *Sunday Independent* read: "Angelita was quite still. 'I picked her up and, as I saw no visible injuries, ran with her off the road and lay down, thinking I could revive her. But as she rolled over, I saw why she was so still—her hair had become soaked in blood flowing from a large hole in her temple. I realised then that Angelita was dead.' "[27] Unless Hayes carried her upside down to the side of the road, he could hardly have failed to observe a large head wound in her temple.

What can be established with certainty is that:

1. The 2d Battalion, Royal Scots Fusiliers, *never* landed at Anzio until March 1944.
2. Hayes's commanding officer, Captain W. E. Pettigrew, *never* served at Anzio.
3. Captain Pettigrew did *not* die in 1947 as reported in 1964 in *Weekend* and in 1977 by the *Sunday Independent.* [28]

[27]Quoted in "The Search for Angelita," *Sunday Independent*, October 9, 1977, p. 20.

[28]Ibid. In this version he met Pettigrew in a Manchester hotel after the war: "The only survivors from their platoon, they talked about the war, about Anzio and about Angelita. Pettigrew said he was returning to Italy to try to trace Angelita's parents. He made the trip but returned to England disturbed—the people of Carrocetta [*sic*] would say nothing. He sailed for South Africa a few days later and died in Nairobi in 1948" (ibid., p. 20).

Notes

Prologue

1. Report of bombing raid on 95th Evacuation Hospital, February 12, 1944. Copy furnished by Vera Lee Rieck, a former nurse and survivor of the bombing.
2. Letter, Lieutenant Howard D. Anderson, D Company, 157th Infantry, 45th Infantry Division, to the author, July 3, 1988.
3. Recollections of Anzio furnished by Lieutenant Colonel Arnold W. Hirsch, June 23, 1988. Hirsch was a platoon leader in F Company, 157th Infantry Regiment, 45th Infantry Division.
4. Cecil A. Hampshire, *The Beachhead Commandos* (London, 1983), pp. 128–29.
5. Quoted in letter, Jerome Lowrey, former 1st Sergeant and Lieutenant, G. Company, 1st Armored Regiment, 1st Armored Division, to the author, May 19, 1988.
6. Major D. J. L. Fitzgerald, MC, *History of the Irish Guards in the Second World War* (Aldershot, 1949), p. 223.
7. Major General Ernest N. Harmon, *Combat Commander: Autobiography of a Soldier* (Englewood Cliffs, N.J., 1970), p. 168.
8. Letter, Grace C. Newton to the author, June 14, 1988.
9. David Nichols, ed., *Ernie's War: The Best of Ernie Pyle's World War II Dispatches* (New York, 1986), passim.
10. Quoted in Wynford Vaughan-Thomas, *Anzio* (New York, 1962), p. 197.
11. Anderson letter.
12. Quoted in Donald G. Taggart, ed., *History of the Third Infantry Division in World War II* (Washington, 1947), pp. 125–26.
13. Kesselring's official title was Commander in Chief South (Oberbefehlshaber Süd; OB Süd).
14. Major General W. R. C. Penney to Lieutenant General Sir Terence Airey, February 5, 1956, Penney Papers.
15. Letter, Dr. William J. McAndrew to the author, June 22, 1990.

Chapter 1. Alamein to Messina

1. Quoted in Martin Gilbert, *Winston S. Churchill, Road to Victory 1941–1945* vol. 7 (London, 1986), p. 253.
2. Martin Blumenson, *Anzio: The Gamble That Failed* (New York, 1986), p. 12.
3. The great strategic bombing offensive against German industrial, war-producing targets was called Pointblank and was the result of a directive in June 1943 from the Combined Chiefs of Staff. The architect of the air strategy against Germany was Air Chief Marshal Sir Arthur Harris, the czar of Bomber Command, who was convinced that air action alone, if properly applied, could win the war. Harris initiated a policy of relentless attacks against industrial targets in Germany, Italy, and the Balkans, coupled with the systematic destruction of German cities. Eventually Pointblank was misused by Harris and his American counterpart, Lieutenant General Carl ("Tooey") Spaatz, as an around-the-clock strategic bombing effort that both were convinced would bring Germany to its knees without the necessity for a major ground campaign in Europe. A full account is contained in Max Hastings, *Bomber Command* (London and New York, 1979).
4. Winston S. Churchill, *The Hinge of Fate* (Boston, 1950), p. 603.
5. Operation Barbarossa was the greatest German offensive of the war. Without warning, in late June 1941, a massive air-ground force of three thousand tanks, two hundred aircraft, and more than three million German ground troops swarmed across a front extending from the Black Sea to the Baltic. Had Hitler not miscalculated and waited too long, Germany might well have won the war on the Eastern Front in 1941. Instead, the Red Army managed to hang on by a slender thread until winter closed down the campaign.
6. *Operation "Symbol,"* the diary of Brigadier (later Lieutenant General Sir) Ian Jacob (copy furnished by General Jacob).
7. For opposing points of view of Montgomery's conduct of post-Alamein operations, see Correlli Barnett, *The Desert Generals,* rev. ed. part 6 (London, 1983); and Nigel Hamilton, *Monty: Master of the Battlefield, 1942–1944* (London/New York, 1983/1984) part 1.
8. By the standards of World War II, the battle of El Guettar was a minor engagement, but for the United States Army it was a significant victory. Patton's corps had successfully carried out an important mission and had begun the process of redemption for Kasserine. The lesson for von Arnim and the German commanders was equally clear: The U.S. Army was no longer to be taken lightly as an adversary.
9. Quoted in part 13 of "The World at War" television series, presented by Thames Television, London, 1976.
10. Alexander to Brooke, April 3, 1943, Alanbrooke (his postwar title) Papers.
11. Rommel had been recalled to Germany by the time his Panzerarmee Afrika linked up with von Arnim's Fifth Panzer Army. This combined force was placed under the command of von Arnim and designated Army Group Afrika.
12. The exact number of Axis losses has long been in dispute. Alexander's official dispatch claimed the capture of 250,000 German and Italian troops,

while the British official history records a total of 238,243, and the U.S. official history about 275,000.

13. Omar N. Bradley and Clay Blair, *A General's Life* (New York, 1983), p. 159. The price of this experience for the fledgling U.S. Army did not come cheaply. American losses were 18,221, including 2,715 killed. Overall Allied losses were 70,341: French, 16,180; British First Army, 23,545; and British Eighth Army, 12,395, from November 12, 1942, to May 13, 1943.

14. Readers interested in a full account of this campaign may wish to consult the official histories: I. S. O. Playfair and C. J. C. Molony, *The Mediterranean and Middle East*, vol. 4 (London, 1966); and George F. Howe, *Northwest Africa: Seizing the Initiative in the West* (Washington, 1957). A useful unofficial account of combat operations is Kenneth Macksey, *Crucible of Power: The Fight for Tunisia, 1942–1943* (London, 1969).

15. For a full account of Churchill's Mediterranean strategy, see Gilbert, *Road to Victory*, passim.

16. The term *Combined Chiefs of Staff* (CCOS) was given to the U.S. and British chiefs of staff operating together to formulate strategic policy and issue command guidance to the Allied commanders in chief in the field, such as Eisenhower. In reality the Casablanca Conference was a series of informal meetings of the CCOS.

17. Soon to be given the code name Operation Overlord by Churchill. Overlord was the best known of the many code names given military operations in World War II. Churchill personally selected Overlord from a list given him in his capacity as minister of Defense. The list of some nine thousand potential code names was maintained by a group known as the Inter-Services Security Board, which operated under the jurisdiction of the Joint Intelligence Committee. (See Gilbert, *Winston S. Churchill*, vol. 6, *Finest Hour, 1939–1941* [London, 1983], p. 966. In vol. 7, *Road to Victory*, Gilbert gives no indication why Churchill selected the title Overlord.)

18. David Fraser, *Alanbrooke* (London/New York, 1982), p. 314.

19. *Operation Symbol*. With uncharacteristic patience Churchill remained in the background and refrained from imposing himself upon the negotiations of the Combined Chiefs.

20. Arthur Bryant, *The Turn of the Tide* (London, 1957), p. 559.

21. C. J. C. Molony, *The Mediterranean and Middle East*, vol. 5 (London, 1973), p. 6.

22. The practice of employing brigade-size combined arms teams of infantry, artillery, and armor that fought independently of one another. In practice, these so-called penny packets (also known as "jock columns" and "brigade groups") proved ruinous because they violated one of the fundamental principles of war: concentration of force. When Montgomery took command of the Eighth Army, one of his first acts was to disband these formations. (See C. E. Lucas Phillips, *Alamein* [London, 1962], pp. 50–52.)

23. At Casablanca, Brooke orchestrated a committee system of separate (all British) commanders in chief for air (Tedder), ground (Alexander), and sea (Cunningham). Brooke's ploy shrewdly insured that future military operations in the Mediterranean would be British dominated. Eisenhower became little more than a titular head of a committee, which exercised the real decision-making power.

24. Churchill also observed, "What Stalin would think of this when he has 185 German divisions on his front, I cannot imagine." (A full account of both the planning and the Sicily campaign is in *Bitter Victory: The Battle for Sicily, 1943* [New York and London, 1988].)

25. "Remarks Made at Conference at Algiers on 2 May 1943 by General Montgomery," diary of Captain Harry C. Butcher, Eisenhower Papers.

26. Quoted in Samuel Eliot Morison, *Sicily–Salerno–Anzio* (Boston, 1954), p. 20.

27. The original Hermann Göring Division was lost in Tunisia. A Luftwaffe unit directly under the control of its namesake, the Hermann Göring was commanded by the aggressive former commander of his personal bodyguard, Lieutenant General Paul Conrath, who impressed Kesselring with his fervor to engage the enemy. The 15th Panzer Grenadier Division was formed from disparate independent units based on the island and the remnants of the 15th Panzer Division, which had managed to escape from Tunisia.

28. The 15th Panzer Grenadier Division was split into three *Kampfgruppen* (battle groups) and scattered across the breadth of Sicily. One of these was sent to eastern Sicily to augment a battle group of the Hermann Göring, which arrived minus nearly a third of its combat strength. Although he, too, believed the Allies were likely to target southeastern Sicily, Kesselring felt obliged to cover a possible invasion of western Sicily with a portion of the 15th Panzer Grenadier, which arrived there shortly before the invasion. In the back of his mind was the dispersion of German forces in the (likely) event the Italian Army in Sicily defected to the Allies.

29. The Husky landings were the largest amphibious landings ever undertaken and historically second only to the Overlord landings in Normandy on June 6, 1944. Eighty thousand troops were landed on Sicily on July 10.

30. Major General David Belchem, *All in the Day's March* (London, 1978), p. 167.

31. Bradley later revealed that the Allied objectives were to establish secure bridgeheads and capture the vital airfields, then to cut Sicily in half, face east and drive to the east coast by rolling up all Axis forces trapped between them and Mount Etna. It was merely assumed that the overall Allied objective was Messina.

32. Patton replaced the 45th Division with Major General Lucian K. Truscott's 3d Division for the final drive on Messina. Later conceding that it was "an unfortunate decision," the British 30th Corps commander, Lieutenant General Sir Oliver Leese, said: "I have a feeling now that if they [the 45th Division] could have driven straight up this road, we might have had a chance to end this frustrating campaign sooner" (quoted in Hamilton, *Monty: Master of the Battlefield*, p. 308).

33. "Report of Operations of II Corps in the Sicilian Campaign," September 1, 1943, in Reel 2, *Outline History of II Corps, 1918–1945*, USAMHI. The new eastward offensive toward Messina by II Corps was across such mountainous terrain that the U.S. 1st and 3d divisions were required to fight completely separate battles without benefit of mutual support. The key was the 15th Panzer Grenadier Division, whose troops performed brilliantly by defending every successive hill mass, counterattacking frequently, and generally making the advance of the 1st Division a painful and costly

experience. For a full description of the battle for Troina, see *Bitter Victory,* and Albert N. Garland and Howard McGaw Smyth, *Sicily and the Surrender of Italy* (Washington, 1965).

34. Quoted in Hugh Pond, *Sicily* (London, 1962), p. 218. This officer was Captain Gustav von Liebenstein, and from the time he took over in May 1943, von Liebenstein turned a ragged and grossly inefficient ferry service in the Strait of Messina into a model operation, including what was probably the first roll-on, roll-off truck operation ever undertaken.

35. Hanson W. Baldwin, *Battles Lost and Won* (New York, 1966), p. 225.

36. Only 18 percent of the Allied fighter and fighter-bomber force was committed to operations in the Strait of Messina and a mere 5.5 percent of the heavy bomber forces.

37. Von Vietinghoff, quoted in Ms. No. D-116, German Report Series, USAMHI copy.

38. German losses are believed to have totalled nearly 29,000: 4,325 killed, 6,663 captured, and an estimated 17,944 wounded, while the Allied armies lost 11,843 British and 8,731 American killed, wounded, missing, and captured.

39. Christopher Buckley, *Road to Rome* (London, 1945), p. 107.

Chapter 2. The Path to Stalemate

1. Minutes of Führer Conference, Fragment No. 14, "Briefing Conference 25 July 1943, 2130 hours," S. L. A. Marshall Military History Collection.

2. The vast distances between northern and southern Italy made it impossible for Kesselring to exercise command over both sectors. Moreover, as will be seen in a later chapter, Hitler was vacillating between leaving Kesselring in command or replacing him with Rommel. The result was merely the latest example of Hitler's penchant for using his generals as unwitting pawns in his intrigues.

3. Maurice Matloff, *Strategic Planning for Coalition Warfare, 1943–1944* (Washington, 1959), p. 9.

4. Dwight D. Eisenhower, unpublished manuscript, copy furnished courtesy of John S. D. Eisenhower.

5. No formal agreement on post-Husky operations was ratified at Algiers, but Eisenhower did assure the British that he intended to exploit Husky's success by continuing military operations across the Strait of Messina into southern Italy, and that he would notify the Combined Chiefs of Staff in ample time for their concurrence, to ensure that there would be no break in military operations (minutes of meeting at AFHQ, May 31, 1943, Eisenhower Papers).

6. John Ehrman, *History of the Second World War,* vol. 5, *Grand Strategy* (London, 1956), pp. 115–16.

7. Diary of General Sir Bernard Montgomery, August 7, 1943. Copies of the diary were furnished to me by Montgomery's official biographer, Nigel Hamilton. The entire Montgomery collection is now in the Imperial War Museum, London and (subject to cataloging) is open for research.

8. Allied problems in Sicily were directly attributable to the failure of the three commanders in chief—Alexander, Tedder, and Cunningham—to es-

tablish a joint headquarters in North Africa or Malta, despite pleas from the British chiefs of staff that to do otherwise violated "one of the most important precepts of Combined operations." Each of the Allied commanders remained based in a different location, with a consequent lack of coordination and consultation.

9. Quoted in Hamilton, *Monty: Master of the Battlefield, 1942–1944,* p. 387. Montgomery cited a vague directive from Alexander charging the Eighth Army to follow the enemy north and engage them in order to assist Avalanche.

10. War diary, Eighth Army, minutes of planning conference, August 10, 1943, Public Record Office (hereafter cited as PRO), London (WO 169/8494).

11. Montgomery diary.

12. Interview of Lieutenant General Walter Bedell Smith by official U.S. Army historian Howard McGaw Smyth, May 13, 1947, OCMH Collection, USAMHI.

13. The Volturno operation was considered equally dangerous and absurd by the commander of the 82d Airborne Division, Major General Matthew B. Ridgway. Eventually the operation was downgraded to a regimental-size landing by sea, and when the division was ordered committed to Giant II, the entire idea was scrapped. For a full account see Clay Blair, *Ridgway's Paratroopers* (New York, 1985), chap. 17.

14. Bedell Smith's case for Giant II was built largely around the fact that in September 1943 the Germans were thought to have had a mere two battalions of combat troops based near Rome that might have intervened against an Allied raid. To the contrary, highly reliable Signal Intelligence (SIGINT) had by August 28 disclosed that the 2d Parachute and the 3d Panzer Grenadier divisions were known to be in the Rome area. Had either Bedell Smith or the other principal advocate of Giant II, the AFHQ G-2, Brigadier Kenneth Strong, bothered to analyze their own intelligence they ought to have immediately determined that Rome could not have been held against what would certainly have been a rapid and violent German reaction. In fact, the details of these German dispositions were included in Strong's own Weekly Intelligence Summary No. 53, published on August 30, 1943 (F. H. Hinsley et al., *British Intelligence in the Second World War,* vol. 3, part 1 [London, 1984], p. 108, and AFHQ Papers, PRO [WO 204/967]).

15. Some planes had already taken off for what would have been certain annihilation. Taylor and Ridgway, who was never deterred by criticism, were both the object of censure for their alleged timidity by Smith and certain other members of the AFHQ staff. In his postwar memoirs Ridgway wrote: "I shall go to my grave humbly proud of the fact that on at least four occasions I have stood up at the risk of my career and denounced what I considered to be ill-conceived tactical schemes." Giant II was clearly one of them (see *Soldier: The Memoirs of Matthew B. Ridgway* [New York, 1966], p. 29). Taylor's reward was to be branded a coward by Bedell Smith in his May 13, 1947, interview by Howard McGaw Smyth. A fuller account of this episode is in Hamilton, *Monty: Master of the Battlefield, 1942–1944,* part 4, chap. 2.

16. VI Corps was the unit originally scheduled to carry out the Gela landings in Sicily. In April 1943, Patton persuaded Eisenhower to shift VI Corps to

the Fifth Army and substitute Bradley's II Corps for the Gela landings. Patton knew little of Dawley and preferred a commander and a corps he had confidence in to carry out the invasion of Sicily.

17. In floating reserve were two regimental combat teams of the 45th Infantry Division. The shortage of landing craft was never more evident than in the limitation imposed on the VI Corps reserve. There were sufficient craft to employ less than two-thirds of the 45th Division: a full regimental combat team of three rifle battalions and a second with only two battalions of infantry.

18. Dominick Graham and Shelford Bidwell, *Tug of War: The Battle for Italy, 1943–45* (London/New York, 1986), p. 54.

19. Quoted in Hamilton, *Monty: Master of the Battlefield, 1942–1944,* p. 406. To his credit, Clark fought hard to avoid Salerno, but as with Sicily, the committee system was still firmly in place, only with Clark filling the slot as ground C in C. Clark did not favor Salerno because the mountains that encircled the beachhead strongly favored the defender. However, Tedder refused to approve any operation north of Naples, thus effectively killing Clark's plan for Gaeta.

20. Des Hickey and Gus Smith, *Operation Avalanche: The Salerno Landings, 1943* (London, 1983), p. 41.

21. Morison, *Sicily–Salerno–Anzio,* p. 249.

22. Based in Berlin, OKW was the high command of the German armed forces.

23. The announcements over the PA systems of the troop ships to the invasion force were, as the official naval historian notes, necessary but "singularly ill-timed with reference to [the] embarked troops . . . [who] . . . proceeded to relax, mentally and otherwise" (Morison, *Sicily–Salerno–Anzio,* p. 252).

24. Quoted in Hickey and Smith, *Operation Avalanche,* p. 46. Von Liebenstein, who masterminded the ferry operations in the Strait of Messina, repeated his feat in Sardinia, where the German garrison was successfully evacuated to mainland Italy.

25. The scenes in the 36th Division sector were among the worst, as panzers created havoc against the lightly armed American infantry and enemy machine guns and mortars added to the carnage of what one officer recorded as "just plain unadulterated hell." Attempts to attack the German tanks repeatedly met with failure as badly needed supporting artillery and troops were unable to land under the heavy fire that raked the beaches, turning them into death traps. Offshore were the burning hulks of LCTs and LSTs hit by the German gunners.

26. Harry C. Butcher, *Three Years with Eisenhower* (London, 1946), p. 359.

27. Morison, *Sicily–Salerno–Anzio,* p. 260. With the aid of the air and naval forces somehow the 36th Division survived the landings, despite the confusion and the vicious German resistance across the entire front at Paestum. Few would dispute the fact that without the Navy the situation would have been far different. The division artillery commander may have said it best in a message to his navy comrades: "Thank God for the fire of the blue-belly Navy ships."

28. Clark pushed his luck too far by ordering a third night parachute drop in the hills at Avellino. The operation was a complete fiasco, with most of an independent airborne battalion scattered over a wide area. Although the

paratroopers harassed and sabotaged the Germans, their presence in the beachhead would have been far more valuable. The failure of this operation may well have had an impact on Clark's thinking at Anzio (see chap. 7).

29. Admiral of the Fleet Viscount Cunningham, *A Sailor's Odyssey* (London, 1951), p. 570.

30. Allied casualties during the Fifth Army's baptism of fire at Salerno numbered well over 13,000: 2,149 killed (379 of whom were U.S. and Royal Navy personnel), 7,339 wounded, and 4,099 missing (3,000 of whom became POWs). German casualties were a comparatively small 3,472, of whom 630 were killed in action.

31. Mark Clark, *Calculated Risk* (New York, 1951), pp. 198–99.

32. Clark claimed that "after having worked with Dawley over a period of months, . . . he has hidden his lack of force behind a bold and blustering front," and indicated in considerable detail why he had never had confidence in the VI Corps commander from the start of Avalanche. Alexander likewise was never impressed with Dawley and after visiting him at the Salerno front called Clark to one side and said, "I do not want to interfere with your business, but I have had some ten years' experience in this game of sizing up commanders. I can tell you definitely that you have a broken reed on your hands and I suggest you replace him immediately." It did not help that Dawley was extremely nervous in the presence of Alexander and Clark. Other generals, including Matthew B. Ridgway, who was temporarily assigned as Dawley's deputy by Clark, also recommended Dawley's relief (General Mark W. Clark, diaries, The Citadel Archives, Charleston, S.C., hereafter referred to as Clark diary).

33. As the Italian campaign progressed, so Clark's disenchantment with McCreery grew. During the difficult advance to the Gustav Line, Clark told his aide Lieutenant Colonel Arthur Sutherland that "it was a cause of regret to him that General McCreery was not more aggressive and that had he been an American Corps Commander it would have been necessary to relieve him long before this" (Clark diary, November 22, 1943).

34. OCMH Collection, USAMHI. The Alexander interviews are in three parts and were given to several official U.S. Army historians in Ottawa in 1949 during his tenure as governor-general of Canada.

35. The Salerno mutiny had its roots in the failure of the participants to understand that they were being sent to the front to help alleviate a dire situation instead of as ordinary replacements. Most believed their leaders had broken a promise to rotate them home with their parent divisions. The situation was further exacerbated by the Scots, who resisted being assigned to any unit except a Scottish regiment. The NCOs who led the rebellion were sentenced to death, but all were soon given a chance to redeem themselves by returning to duty in Italy with suspended sentences. Despite its successful resolution, the incident became a permanent stain on the honor of the Army. The British official history fails even to mention the Salerno mutiny (see Molony, *The Mediterranean and Middle East*, vol. 5).

36. Hinsley et al., *British Intelligence in the Second World War*, p. 116. For those readers not otherwise familiar with it, Ultra was the enormously successful secret intelligence source that enabled Allied code-breakers to

intercept and decode German message traffic from their Enigma cipher machine. A useful history of Ultra is Ronald Lewin's *Ultra Goes to War* (London, 1978).

37. "British Military Planning and Aims in 1944," unpublished paper by Sir David Hunt.

38. Alexander dispatch, published as a supplement to the *London Gazette,* June 12, 1950. Copies can be found in most major archives and libraries.

39. Molony, *The Mediterranean and Middle East,* vol. 5, chaps. 9 and 11, passim.

40. General George C. Marshall, interview with a group of official historians, July 25, 1949, OCMH Collection, USAMHI.

41. Graham and Bidwell, *Tug of War,* p. 90.

42. Gilbert, *Road to Victory,* p. 483.

43. Clark diary, September 26, 1943.

44. Diary of Major General John P. Lucas (hereafter referred to as Lucas diary), Lucas Papers, USAMHI. The Lucas Papers contain several different versions of his diary, one of which includes postwar comments on his entries. His papers also contain a manuscript based on the original diary, titled "From Algiers to Anzio," which Lucas tried and failed to have cleared by the Army for publication after the war.

45. Piers Brendon, *Ike: His Life and Times* (New York, 1986), p. 122.

46. Among the critics of what was perceived as British overcaution on the battlefield was Marshall, whose opinion of their fighting ability was founded on this point. "In Italy," he noted in a postwar interview, "the fighting spirit and aggressive quality of British divisions began again to decline and for the reason of the sheer factor of exhaustion. The British simply could not keep their battalions up to strength and it was very depressing to their men. They had no replacements" (Marshall interview).

Chapter 3. The American Eagle and the Gentleman-General

1. Graham and Bidwell, *Tug of War,* p. 96.

2. Ibid., p. 99. Clark's version is that Montgomery told him that Alexander "may order you to carry out some crazy plan. If he does, just tell him to go to hell." Clark retorted, "I'll tell you about it if he does and you can tell him to go to hell" (Clark interviews with official historian Sidney T. Mathews, May 10–21, 1948, part 5, OCMH Collection, USAMHI).

3. Ibid.

4. See appendix A, "Order of Battle, Allied Ground Forces," and appendix B, "Organization of the Allied Air Forces."

5. See appendix C, "Organization of the Mediterranean Allied Air Forces."

6. Nigel Nicolson, *Alex: The Life of Field Marshal Earl Alexander of Tunis* (London, 1973), p. 21.

7. Harold Macmillan, *The Blast of War* (London, 1967), pp. 303–4.

8. "The 'HUSKY' Problem," a personal chronicle of events detailing the planning for Operation Husky, written in May 1943, Montgomery Papers.

9. Charles J. Rolo, "General Sir Harold Alexander," *Britain,* July 1943.

10. Nicolson, *Alex,* pp. 280–81.

11. C. L. Sulzberger, *A Long Row of Candles* (New York, 1969), p. 230.

12. Ibid., p. 280.

13. E. P. Danger, diary of service with the 5th Battalion, Grenadier Guards, Danger Papers.

14. Quoted in John Cloake, *Templer: Tiger of Malaya* (London, 1985), p. 132.

15. Lord Moran, *Winston Churchill: The Struggle for Survival, 1940–1965* (London, 1968), p. 194.

16. Ibid., p. 195.

17. Ibid., pp. 184–85.

18. Ibid., p. 191.

19. Ibid., pp. 191–92.

20. John Colville, *The Churchillians* (London, 1981), p. 152.

21. Bryant, *The Turn of the Tide* and *Triumph in the West* (1959).

22. Fraser, *Alanbrooke*, pp. 271–72.

23. Alanbrooke diary. Lieutenant General Sir Ian Jacob, who served both as one of Churchill's military assistants during the war and as Alexander's chief staff officer when the latter was the postwar minister of Defense (1952–54), believes that Sicily was an example of his lack of grip. Without malice, Sir Ian has observed that Alexander never produced a single original idea in the time he knew him (author interviews with Jacob, 1979–84).

24. Alanbrooke diary and "Notes on My Life," Alanbrooke Papers. Brooke was not the only senior British officer to express this opinion. When, late in 1944, Churchill grew frustrated with "Jumbo" Wilson and decided to replace him with Alexander, the First Sea Lord, Admiral of the Fleet Sir Andrew Browne Cunningham, recorded in his diary the opposition of the British chiefs of staff to Alexander, whom he described as "totally unfitted for the job." Alexander was an exceedingly difficult man to understand, and most who served under him did not pretend to do so. During my research over the past ten years, many senior officers have spoken privately about Alexander. Their comments ranged from "intellectually lazy" to a commonly held belief that the real brains behind Alexander were his able chiefs of staff, Lieutenant General Richard McCreery in the Middle East and, in Italy, Lieutenant General Sir John Harding, about whom more will be said later in this narrative.

25. Montgomery was in the habit of writing candid opinions either in his diary or in memorandums he retained in his personal papers. His disparaging remarks about Alexander were written about a friend of whom he was genuinely fond. The quote above appears in a document titled "Reflections on the Campaign in Italy, 1943," Montgomery Papers. Similar remarks appear in his papers for the Sicily period. Admiral Lord Louis Mountbatten once commented to Alexander's biographer, Nigel Nicolson: "He had almost every quality you could wish to have, except that he had the average brain of an average English gentleman. He lacked that little extra cubic centimeter which produces genius. If you recognize that, it's perhaps a greater tribute to what he did achieve by leadership, courage and inspiring devotion in those who served under him" (quoted in Nicolson, *Alex,* p. 280).

26. "Reflections on the Campaign in Italy, 1943," Montgomery Papers.

27. Ibid. Field Marshal Lord Harding has described one such incident in Italy, in which four British officers, two RAF and two Army commanders, could

not reach agreement and were sent to see Harding, who told them they would be sequestered incommunicado in Alexander's office until they settled their differences. The threat sufficed and an accommodation was reached without Alexander's intervention. (Oral history interview of Field Marshal Lord Harding of Petherton, 1984, Department of Sound Records, Imperial War Museum.)

28. General Dwight D. Eisenhower, "Memorandum for Personal File," June 11, 1943, Eisenhower Papers.
29. Harold Macmillan, *War Diaries* (London, 1984), p. 154.
30. Diary of Captain Harry C. Butcher, July 16, 1943.
31. Oral history interview of Field Marshal Lord Harding of Petherton.
32. Quoted in Nicolson, *Alex,* p. 97.
33. Colville, *The Churchillians,* p. 152. Colville was Churchill's private secretary and an intimate friend of the prime minister.
34. Oral history interview of Field Marshal Lord Harding of Petherton.
35. Nigel Nicolson, quoted in Hamilton, *Monty: Master of the Battlefield,* p. 472.
36. Quoted by Canadian historian William J. McAndrew in the *Toronto Globe & Mail,* August 30, 1986.
37. Churchill, *The Hinge of Fate,* p. 384.
38. Martin Blumenson and James L. Stokesbury, *Masters of the Art of Command* (Boston, 1975), p. 191.
39. Clark graduated 109th in a class of 135. His profile in the 1917 West Point *Howitzer* was less than flattering, noting that he was "an excellent purveyor of B.S. and of more or less interesting rumors." Among Clark's classmates were a number of later general officers, two of them future Army chiefs of staff: General J. Lawton Collins and General Matthew B. Ridgway. Two others commanded divisions at Anzio: Major General Ernest N. Harmon and Major General William W. Eagles.
40. Report by war correspondent Jack Foise in the *San Francisco Chronicle,* August 28, 1945.
41. Blumenson, *Anzio: The Gamble That Failed,* p. 41.
42. Eric Sevareid, *Not So Wild a Dream* (New York, 1968), p. 379. Sevareid found Alexander's HQ far more overbearing, where often they were "told by his staff what one *ought* to write. These men, who were in ultimate control of censorship, effectively stopped any slight suggestion that their chief might have made a mistake. . . . To many professional British officers the journalist was still a 'pressman,' a lower order of human being, who should be kept in his place" (ibid.).
43. Quoted in Sulzberger, *A Long Row of Candles,* p. 231.
44. Author interview with Colonel G. Gordon Bartlett (USA Ret.), April 18, 1987. Colonel Bartlett served as Lucas's aide after the war.
45. Lieutenant Colonel (later General) Robert W. Porter, Jr., quoted in Hickey and Smith, *Operation Avalanche,* p. 33.
46. Extracts from the Clark diary and Clark, *Calculated Risk,* chap. 11.
47. *Life,* January 3, 1944. Clark was also a stickler for detail. In early December 1943 he was dissatisfied with the traffic control being exercised on a key bridge at Capua. He issued instructions that traffic was to be better regulated, and his aide wrote in the general's diary that "the highways there,

General Clark said, should be run with same precision and efficiency as the Pennsylvania Railroad" (Clark diary, December 1, 1943).

48. Jacob diary, *Operation Symbol.*

49. Eisenhower, "Memorandum for Personal File," June 11, 1943, Eisenhower Papers.

50. Quoted in Joseph P. Hobbs, *Dear General: Eisenhower's Wartime Letters to Marshall* (Baltimore, 1971), p. 129. Eisenhower's letters to Marshall reflect revisions to his opinion of Clark. In August 1942 he had written that "I know of no one upon whom you can depend with greater confidence and assurance, no matter to what post you may eventually raise him" (Eisenhower to Marshall, August 17, 1942, *The Papers of Dwight D. Eisenhower: The War Years,* vol. 1 [Baltimore, 1970], p. 478, hereafter cited as *The Eisenhower Papers*).

51. "Observer's Report" of Brigadier General Albert C. Wedemeyer, Appendix B, undated, Eisenhower Papers.

52. Graham and Bidwell, *Tug of War,* p. 37.

53. Ever since Kasserine, Marshall had considered Alexander's attitude toward Americans patronizing. By 1945 he still hadn't changed his mind, and at Yalta Churchill had to intervene to defuse a flareup between the two. The British attitude was disturbingly widespread and included King George VI, who once remarked to Marshall how good it was to have Eisenhower in nominal supreme command with Monty at his side (Marshall interview, July 25, 1949).

54. Blumenson, *Mark Clark,* p. 197.

55. Ibid., p. 7. According to Blumenson, Clark received an average of thirty letters daily and was recognized wherever he went.

56. Karl von Clausewitz, *On War* (London/New York, 1968).

57. Major General Baron von Freytag-Loringhoven, *The Power of Personality in War,* originally published in 1911 and reproduced by the U.S. Army War College in September 1983. Although Clark's biographer, Martin Blumenson, has noted his ability to grasp immediately the essentials of a problem or situation, there is little evidence that this trait applied to his battlefield decisions (*Mark Clark,* p. 2).

58. Blumenson, *Mark Clark,* p. 3.

59. Clausewitz, *On War,* book 1, chap. 3. Clark also lacked the imagination that Clausewitz deemed so important: "The commander in war must work in a medium which his eyes cannot see; which the greatest zeal cannot always determine, and with which, by reason of the constant changes, he can rarely become familiar."

60. Graham and Bidwell, *Tug of War,* p. 37. According to the Fifth Army G-4, Brigadier General Ralph Tate, Clark's tactics with his staff were intimidating. Clark and his G-3, Brigadier General Brann, would work out the tactical plan and then summon Tate and with a determined look say, "You can do it, can't you?" Tate generally said yes, noting that "General Clark is not the kind of man you say 'no' to." In Fifth Army logistics almost always followed tactics; that is, if Clark decided on a particular tactical action, the logisticians were expected to support it, regardless of its feasibility (interview in OCMH Collection, USAMHI).

61. Alexander interviews, part 2.

62. General Lyman L. Lemnitzer, interview by Sidney T. Mathews, January 16, 1948, OCMH Collection, USAMHI. Lemnitzer's opinion of Clark's possible relief was very likely based on his experience as an American officer of when a commander would be relieved for insubordination.

63. Clark diary, January 8, 1944.

64. Clark interviews, part 1.

65. After the battle, Clark believed he had been let down by the air forces, which had failed to interdict the roads used by the XIV Panzer Corps during its retreat from Calabria and had not provided adequate close-air support on the Salerno battlefield until September 14 (see Graham and Bidwell, *Tug of War,* p. 100).

66. Quoted in Lemnitzer interview. When Dawley reported to Marshall in Washington to explain his side of the story, the chief of staff felt sorry for his former World War I assistant but told him bluntly that he ought to have been relieved even earlier (Marshall interview, part 2).

67. Alexander interviews, part 2.

68. In early 1945 Eisenhower rated Devers twenty-fourth in an assessment of the contributions made by senior American officers in the ETO, noting that Devers had not, "so far, produced among the seniors of the American organization here that feeling of trust and confidence that is so necessary to continued success." By comparison, Clark was rated fifth, behind Bradley, Spaatz, Bedell Smith, and Patton (memo, February 1, 1945, *The Eisenhower Papers,* vol. 4, pp. 2468–69).

69. Alexander interviews, part 2. A classmate of Patton, Devers graduated from the United States Military Academy in 1909. His classmates described him as "a wonderfully clever young man . . . [and] an exceedingly earnest youth with rather Puritanical views . . . always ready to part with knowledge to whoever is willing to listen" (1909 *Howitzer*). According to Patton, Eisenhower thoroughly disliked Devers. Alexander, apparently, wasn't far behind. Once during the summer of 1944, when Devers came to the 15th Army Group CP when Churchill was present, Alexander was deliberately rude, saying only, "Oh, hello Devers," and then refusing to speak further to him (see Martin Blumenson, ed., *The Patton Papers* [Boston, 1974], vol. 2, p. 552; Alexander interviews, part 2).

70. Clark interviews, part 1.

71. Lemnitzer interview.

72. Blumenson and Stokesbury, *Masters of the Art of Command,* p. 178.

73. An example was Montgomery's habit of handing out cigarettes to his troops. In Italy, Leese was reputed to have stopped a Scotsman one day and after a halting conversation thrust a packet of the best John Player cigarettes into his hand. The Scotsman looked up at the towering Leese and replied with disdain, "You must be new; there used to be a wee bugger in a black beret before you who did this." (One of several sources for this quote is Graham and Bidwell, *Tug of War,* p. 254.)

74. Strome Galloway, *The General Who Never Was* (Belleville, Ontario, 1981), p. 180.

75. During the battle to break the Gothic Line in September 1944, Leese's failure to provide for a reserve squandered the brilliant success of 1st Canadian Corps during Operation Olive. Even when presented with an

opportunity to improvise, Leese failed to seize the initiative in what Graham and Bidwell deplore as "criminal inertia. . . . A German or American general would have galvanized his staff into immediate action. . . . Leese did nothing" (*Tug of War*, pp. 357–58).

76. Air Vice Marshal Harry Broadhurst worked closely with Leese in North Africa, Sicily, and Italy and regarded him as a "bully" who often lost his temper and berated his staff by shouting and using "filthy language . . . beating hell out of his staff, calling them all the rude names under the sun" (extract from an interview with Air Chief Marshal Sir Harry Broadhurst, November 2, 1983).

Chapter 4. The Decision to Launch Shingle

1. Quoted in Hamilton, *Monty: Master of the Battlefield*, pp. 451–52.
2. This fact was not lost on Eisenhower, whose visit to Churchill at Marrakech on the final day of 1943 left him with the impression that the prime minister had "practically taken over tactical command in the Mediterranean" (Butcher, *Three Years with Eisenhower*, p. 399).
3. Martin Blumenson, *Salerno to Cassino* (Washington, 1969), p. 180.
4. Not only did the Allies capture the German plans for the evacuation, but every subordinate intelligence officer was providing incontrovertible evidence. Even the war correspondents were aware of the evacuation. Nevertheless, Strong continued to deny the obvious, and as late as August 14, when the evacuation was all but over, the AFHQ G-2 report insisted that "there is no evidence of any large-scale withdrawal of troops from Sicily." ("The Sicilian Campaign," RAF operational narrative by T. Milne, Air Historical Branch, December 1955, PRO [AIR 41/52]. A full account is in *Bitter Victory*, chaps. 30 and 31.)
5. Graham and Bidwell, *Tug of War*, p. 127.
6. Blumenson, *Salerno to Cassino*, p. 181.
7. According to Lemnitzer, the 15th Army Group staff was also developing plans for an end run near Rome (Lemnitzer interview).
8. Blumenson, *Salerno to Cassino*, p. 237.
9. Ibid., chap. 14, passim.
10. MA 728, Alexander to CIGS, November 9, 1943, Alanbrooke Papers. With the exception of one American unit, the 504th Parachute Infantry Regiment (82d Airborne Divison), all Allied airborne forces had been ordered to England for Overlord.
11. "Map to Illustrate MA 728 of 9 Nov." and Map "Shingle—Most Secret," Alanbrooke Papers.
12. *Fifth Army History*, part 4, 1946, PRO (CAB 106/477). Copies are also in numerous other British and U.S. archives and libraries. Originally written by the staff in 1945 and privately printed, the history is a surprisingly comprehensive and candid account of Fifth Army operations for the entire Italian campaign.
13. Ibid., based on 15th Army Group Operations Instruction no. 31.
14. Ibid.
15. Quoted in Clark, *Calculated Risk*, p. 230.
16. On November 18, 1943, Montgomery observed in a letter to Brooke that

he feared that "Fifth Army is absolutely whacked" (quoted in Bryant, *Victory in the West*, p. 120).

17. Ibid., p. 56.
18. Quoted in Gilbert, *Road to Victory*, p. 526.
19. "Notes on My Life," Alanbrooke Papers.
20. Prime Minister to Chiefs of Staff, Frozen No. 736, December 19, 1943, PRO (PREM 3, 248/1). All telegrams exchanged between Churchill and the various military bodies concerned with Shingle are in a War Cabinet document entitled "Operations in Italy," dated January 28, 1944.
21. Chiefs of Staff to Prime Minister, Grand No. 736, December 23, 1943, ibid.
22. Ibid.
23. Prime Minister to Chiefs of Staff, Frozen No. 835, December 23, 1943, ibid. Lemnitzer alludes to Alexander's desire for a five-division lift, with the additional divisions to come from Sicily-based formations prior to their return to the UK for Overlord. The idea was scrapped when delays over the availability of landing craft resulted in the withdrawal of these divisions to the United Kingdom (Lemnitzer interview).
24. Chiefs of Staff to Prime Minister, Grand 806, December 24, 1943, ibid. This was the substance of the argument for additional landing craft presented to the Combined Chiefs of Staff.
25. Churchill to Roosevelt, Frozen No. 893, December 26, 1943, ibid.
26. Roosevelt to Churchill, December 27, 1943, in Warren F. Kimball, ed., *Churchill and Roosevelt: The Complete Correspondence*, vol. 2 (Princeton, N.J., 1984/London, 1988), p. 636.
27. Forrest C. Pogue, *George C. Marshall: Organizer of Victory, 1943–1945* (New York, 1973), pp. 330–31.
28. Churchill to British Chiefs of Staff, Frozen No. 913, December 26, 1943, PRO (PREM 3, 248/1).
29. Ibid.
30. Alanbrooke diary, December 15, 1944, Alanbrooke Papers.
31. Churchill, *Closing the Ring*, p. 428.
32. Churchill to Roosevelt, Frozen No. 949, PRO (PREM 3, 248/1).
33. Lieutenant General Sir Richard McCreery (1898–1967) was one of Britain's outstanding World War II commanders and an officer whose reputation was founded on both outstanding staff work and command on the field of battle. A graduate of Eton and Sandhurst, McCreery was a cavalry officer who won the Military Cross in the First World War and, in 1940, served as Alexander's GSO-1 (operations officer) in France. By 1942 he was an unemployed acting major general with a reputation for speaking his mind whenever he encountered military folly. When Alexander replaced Auchinleck, McCreery became his chief of staff and achieved a solid reputation for honesty and efficiency. He was given command of 10th Corps in North Africa in June 1943 when his predecessor, Lieutenant General Sir Brian Horrocks, was badly wounded. McCreery and Clark first became associated when 10th Corps was selected for the invasion of Salerno.

The enmity between Clark and McCreery was one of the more unfortunate aspects of the Italian campaign. Clark's dislike of McCreery was more the result of his antipathy to the manner in which the British conducted military operations than it was to McCreery himself. Like virtually all senior American commanders, Clark never properly appreciated that British and American tactics were poles apart. The respective staff colleges taught their future generals differing philosophies. The British believed in the principle of concentration of force, and a classic example of its execution was Montgomery at El Alamein. American tactics, while not rejecting this valuable principle, also espoused finding and capitalizing on weak spots in an enemy line. Thus it was inevitable that McCreery and Clark would clash, and beginning at Salerno, they did.

After the war McCreery admitted that "I had continuous problems with him. . . . I had to be on my guard the whole time to prevent him giving orders or misinterpreting events which would inadvertently undermine Alexander's expressed objectives and overall strategy. . . . On occasions I had terrific arguments with Mark Clark on some of his battle plans because I thought they would cause quite unnecessary loss of life." (McCreery quotes are from Brian Harpur, *The Impossible Victory* [London, 1980], chap. 9, passim.)

34. Letter, James M. Wilson, Jr., to the author, March 27, 1989. Wilson served as Truscott's aide for two years.
35. Clark diary, January 20, 1944.
36. Graham and Bidwell, *Tug of War,* p. 145. As the authors explain, a *hasty* river crossing is usually employed across a wide front when an army's opponent is on the run and unable to erect proper defenses. A *deliberate* river crossing is normally necessary against well-prepared defenses and requires "a deliberate attack on the most promising *Schwerpunkt.*" In this instance, "Clark chose neither" (ibid.).
37. Ibid., pp. 145–46.
38. These figures do not include losses substained by engineers and other troops supporting the operation.
39. Fred L. Walker, *From Texas to Rome: A General's Journal* (Dallas, 1969), p. 316.
40. Clark diary, January 24, 1944.
41. The grim details of this disaster are fully chronicled in Martin Blumenson, *Bloody River: The Real Tragedy of the Rapido* (Boston, 1970).
42. Quoted in ibid., p. 130.
43. Report of interview with Major General Fred L. Walker, February 4, 1946, Clark Papers, box 39, folder 9, The Citadel Archives.
44. Quoted in Blumenson, *Salerno to Cassino,* p. 319.

Chapter 5. "Smiling Albert"

1. Shelford Bidwell, "Kesselring," in *Hitler's Generals,* Correlli Barnett, ed. (London, 1989), p. 288.
2. Ibid.
3. Hickey and Smith, *Operation Avalanche,* p. 192.
4. *The Memoirs of Field Marshal Kesselring* (Novato, 1989, reprint of 1953 British edition [original title: *Kesselring: A Soldier's Record*), p. 188.
5. B. H. Liddell Hart, ed., *The Rommel Papers* (London, 1953), p. 524.
6. Graham and Bidwell, *Tug of War,* p. 38.

7. Had Kesselring waited for Hitler's official order to withdraw, the entire German corps in Sicily would have been lost.

8. Kenneth Macksey, quoted in the new foreword of *The Memoirs of Field Marshal Kesselring*, p. 9.

9. Keitel headed OKW and was universally regarded as a vassal of Hitler and an officer whose main attribute was a willingness to carry out without question the orders of his Führer. Behind his back Keitel was sneeringly referred to as *der Lakaitel* (lackey). Jodl was Keitel's deputy and the real power within OKW, who either made or carried out most of the important policy decisions of the German armed forces.

10. Kesselring received considerable support from Grand Admiral Karl Dönitz, the commander in chief of the German Navy, whose influence on Hitler had been on the rise throughout 1943. Dönitz subscribed to the philosophy that the Allies should have to fight for every foot of ground in the Mediterranean.

11. Ralph Bennett, *Ultra and Mediterranean Strategy* (New York, 1989), pp. 255–257.

12. Hube lost an arm in the Battle of the Marne during World War I. Stern, stubborn, and purposeful, Hube reminded Guzzoni of a Teutonic warrior without his armor, helmet, and spear. Von Manstein regarded him as "fearless," and as he proved on numerous occasions on the Eastern Front, Hube spoke his mind and was certainly not afraid of Hitler.

13. Quoted in David Hapgood and David Richardson, *Monte Cassino* (New York, 1984), p. 41.

14. Ferdinand von Senger und Etterlin, "Senger," in Barnett, *Hitler's Generals*, p. 389. Ferdinand von Senger fought in World War II on both the Russian and Italian fronts, and in postwar Germany he rose to the rank of full general and the command of NATO's Central Region. Like his father before him, Ferdinand von Senger was a Rhodes scholar. When he died before completing revisions to the essay about his father, *his* son, Stefan, completed the task.

15. Bidwell, "Kesselring," in Barnett, *Hitler's Generals*, p. 281.

16. Fridolin von Senger und Etterlin, *Neither Fear Nor Hope* (New York, 1964), p. 196.

17. See *Bitter Victory*, part 5.

18. In North Africa Baade had once forced a British soldier to lead him through a mine field and then released him. He was also fond of completing a night raid behind British lines by announcing over their radio net in English to, "Stop firing. On my way back. Baade." In Italy his longtime friend von Senger had found it necessary to deny to OKW that Baade had dined on Christmas with his enemy, but was forced to admit that Baade had signaled New Year greetings in English to the British commanders against whom he had fought in North Africa. It was also his habit to signal the names of captured Allied soldiers as a favor to their wives, mothers, and fiancées.

19. Quoted in Richard Brett-Smith, *Hitler's Generals* (London, 1976), p. 179.

20. The two commanders had certainly been the backbone of the defense of Sicily during the second half of the campaign. Fries guarded the northern coast during the retreat to Messina while to the south Rodt's 15th Panzer

Grenadier Division fought tenaciously and delayed the U.S. 1st Division a series of bloody noses along Highway 120 and at Troina (see *Bitter Victory*, chap. 28, and Garland and Smyth, *Sicily and the Surrender of Italy*, chap. 17).

Chapter 6. Mr. Churchill Takes Charge

1. John Colville, *The Fringes of Power* (London, 1985), p. 126.
2. Quoted in Gilbert, *Road to Victory*, p. 526.
3. In recent years numerous British accounts and memoirs have stressed that Churchill and Brooke were indeed committed to Operation Overlord. An equal number of American participants were of the opposite view. In an unpublished memoir, Eisenhower described how Brooke privately expressed deep misgivings about the cross-Channel venture and spoke favorably of a "thrust and peck" strategy of hammering Axis flanks to the benefit of the Red Army, whose responsibility, he said, should be the destruction of Hitler's land forces. Brooke later claimed that Eisenhower had obviously misunderstood him.
4. Gilbert, *Road to Victory*, p. 523.
5. Stephen Roskill, *Churchill and the Admirals* (London, 1977), p. 222.
6. Alanbrooke diary, October 8, 1943, Alanbrooke Papers.
7. Only through another of Churchill's timely interventions was Alexander permitted to retain the 504th Parachute Infantry Regiment for Anzio. The prime minister appealed directly to Marshall through Field Marshal Sir John Dill, head of the British Joint Staff Mission in Washington, to let them "do this one fine and critical job before they come home for 'Overlord.' " Over the protests of Ridgway and others, the Combined Chiefs of Staff eventually approved (PRO [PREM 3, 248/1]).
8. Cable, Churchill to Alexander, December 26, 1943, Alexander Papers, PRO (WO 214/29).
9. Cable, Churchill to Wilson, T-66A/34, January 18, 1944, PRO (PREM 3, 248/2).
10. Among Shingle's detractors was Alexander's own chief logistician, Major General Sir Brian Robertson, the highly regarded son of the World War I field marshal. On January 5, 1944, he advised his chief to cancel the operation "unless there is a reasonable prospect of a successful junction between 'SHINGLE' and Fifth Army within one week." (Alexander Papers, PRO [WO 214/28]).
11. Clark diary, January 2, 1944. (Clark's diary was maintained by his staff with contributions from their boss. It contained a complete record of his activities for days on which entries were made and frequently contained copies of messages sent to and from the Fifth Army, Clark's own comments, and those of his staff recording what he thought and said. The entry quoted above was probably entered on January 2 either by his senior aide or his chief of staff, Major General Alfred Gruenther.)
12. Ibid., January 4, 1944.
13. Ibid.
14. Sir John Cunningham was a cousin of Admiral Sir Andrew Cunningham,

who had returned to London in October 1943 to become the First Sea Lord on the untimely death of Admiral Sir Dudley Pound.

15. Lucas, "From Algiers to Anzio," p. 292.

16. A cable from Alexander to Churchill on January 5, complaining that there would be a shortfall of eight LSTs and insufficient craft for maintaining the Shingle force, was one of the principal reasons for the Marrakech conference on January 7–8, 1944. Alexander's problem was that "the whole operation must depend on the provision of the necessary craft to get our forces there and keep them going. . . . Time is very short. Although planning is going ahead it is of vital importance to get an assurance that I shall get the craft I need to build up the force with its essential supporting weapons and to maintain it in action until a decision has been reached" (Alexander to Churchill, MA 961, January 5, 1944, PRO [PREM 3, 248/1].

17. "Report of Colonel William H. Hill and Colonel E. J. O'Neill on Conference held in Marrakech, French Morocco, 7–8 January 1944," WW II Misc. Collection, USAMHI.

18. Major General Sir Kenneth Strong, *Intelligence at the Top* (London, 1968), p. 125.

19. Interview with Strong by Sidney T. Mathews, October 30, 1947, USAMHI.

20. Michael Carver, *Harding of Petherton* (London, 1978), p. 123. What makes this biography remarkable is that it was written by one field marshal about another. The author is better known as Field Marshal Lord Carver.

21. Oral history interview of Field Marshal Lord Harding of Petherton (Department of Sound Records, Imperial War Museum). Harding "didn't think the landing force was either strong enough or [that] the follow up was sufficient to make sure that the operation maintained . . . momentum . . . [to] cut the main withdrawal routes for the German Army coming back from Cassino." To the contrary, Harding believed the idea was wishful thinking and that the Fifth Army had almost no hope of breaking the German defenses in the Liri Valley in January 1944.

22. Richard Hough, *The Greatest Crusade: Roosevelt, Churchill, and the Naval Wars* (New York, 1986), p. 216.

23. Roskill, *Churchill and the Admirals*, p. 217.

24. Morison, *Sicily–Salerno–Anzio*, p. 328.

25. Molony, *The Mediterranean and Middle East*, vol. 5, p. 644.

26. Gerald Pawle, *The War and Colonel Warden* (London, 1963), pp. 277–78. Pawle's book is based on the recollections of Commander C. R. Thompson, RN, a personal assistant to Churchill from 1940 to 1945. Colonel Warden was Churchill's code name.

27. A Royal Marine officer and one of two military assistants of General Sir Hastings Ismay, chief of staff to Churchill in his role as minister of defense. The other military assistant was Brigadier Ian Jacob.

28. Pawle, *The War and Colonel Warden*, p. 283.

29. Ibid., and Roskill, *Churchill and the Admirals*, p. 224. Churchill's mischievous side emerged at lunch when he "announced that the naval C-in-C was arriving and advised Power to meet him; on hearing which the latter said 'But he's not my C-in-C any longer since this morning!' Churchill then told General Hollis . . . to tear up the appointment" (p. 224). "As they rose from

the table Churchill said blandly, 'Now you had better go and make peace with your Commander-in-Chief' " (Pawle, *The War and Colonel Warden*, p. 283).

30. Roskill, *Churchill and the Admirals*, p. 223.
31. Quotes from Pawle, *The War and Colonel Warden*, p. 284. Beaverbrook was the former minister of aircraft production and, since the previous September, Lord Privy Seal.
32. Churchill, *Closing the Ring*, p. 435.
33. Churchill to Roosevelt, Frozen No. 1173, January 8, 1944, PRO (PREM 3, 248/1).
34. Churchill to Defence Committee and Chiefs of Staff, Frozen No. 1170, January 8, 1944 (ibid.).
35. Quoted in Gilbert, *Road to Victory*, p. 640.
36. Clark interviews, part 1.
37. William Manchester, *Winston Spencer Churchill: Visions of Glory, 1874–1932* (Boston, 1983), p. 379.
38. Quoted in Robert Rhodes James, *Churchill: A Study in Failure, 1900–1939* (London, 1970), pp. 49–50.
39. Ibid., p. 78.
40. Lord Moran, *Winston Churchill: The Struggle for Survival*, p. 180.
41. Ibid., p. 210.

Chapter 7. Final Preparations

1. Pogue, *George C. Marshall: Organizer of Victory*, p. 331.
2. James M. Gavin, *On to Berlin: Battles of an Airborne Commander, 1943–1946* (New York/London, 1978), p. 77.
3. Quoted in *The Eisenhower Papers*, vol. 2, p. 1354.
4. Eisenhower to Marshall, December 17, 1943, in Hobbs, *Dear General*, p. 131.
5. Lucas diary.
6. Ibid.
7. In addition to the two panzer grenadier divisions in reserve near Rome, it was believed that Kesselring could shift two or three divisions from the Cassino front to Anzio without undue danger.
8. Lucas, "From Algiers to Anzio," p. 287.
9. Lucas diary, January 10, 1944. Patton also told Lucas that, "of course, you might only be wounded. No one ever blames a wounded general for anything." After telling Lucas to "read the Bible when the going got tough," he took one of his aides aside and said, "Look here, if things get too bad, shoot the old man in the back end, but don't you dare kill the old b———d." After his aide reported Patton's remarks, Lucas found himself "afraid to turn my back on him from D-day on."
10. Major General W. R. C. Penney to Brigadier Douglas Renny, February 8, 1956, Penney Papers.
11. Lucas, "From Algiers to Anzio," p. 295.
12. Ibid., p. 296. In his diary Lucas wrote, "Rather puts it up to me. Pray for sunshine."
13. Ibid., January 10, 1944.

14. Oral history interview of Field Marshal Lord Harding of Petherton (Department of Sound Records, Imperial War Museum).

15. Quoted in Vaughan-Thomas, *Anzio,* p. 45.

16. Ibid.

17. *Fifth Army History,* part 4, p. 60.

18. Vaughan-Thomas, *Anzio,* p. 42.

19. Penney, "Notes on Anzio," Penney Papers.

20. Oral history of General Ben Harrell, 1972, OCN Collection, USAMHI. Harrell was one of the many brilliant officers who served under Truscott and later went on to become a general officer.

21. Quoted in Blumenson, *Salerno to Cassino,* p. 355.

22. Lucas diary.

23. Quoted in Lucian K. Truscott, *Command Missions* (New York, 1954), p. 304. The best that Clark could do was to promise replacements for Truscott's lost equipment, which had to be taken from other divisions.

24. Lucas, "From Algiers to Anzio," pp. 321–22. Obviously Cunningham shed his misgivings over Shingle, and it is reasonable to conclude that Ultra had something to do with his sudden change of heart. Later Cunningham would become one of the strongest critics of Lucas's performance at Anzio.

25. Hinsley et al., *British Intelligence in the Second World War,* vol. 3, part 1, p. 186.

26. Lewin, *Ultra Goes to War,* p. 281.

27. Bennett, *Ultra and Mediterranean Strategy,* p. 263.

28. Truscott, *Command Missions,* p. 292. Penney recalls that Truscott's "language describing what would have been their fate was picturesque" (Penney Papers).

29. Fifth Army G-2, "Shingle Intelligence Summary No. 4," December 30, 1943, PRO (WO 204/10263). In *Calculated Risk,* Clark complained that Alexander's intelligence officer, Major General Terence Airey, issued an overly optimistic estimate of the German reaction to Shingle: "I felt that their estimate of the Anzio situation was deliberately made optimistic because it was shaped to fit the decision already made at Tunis." But a senior British officer on Clark's staff, Brigadier Charles Richardson, called it a "remarkably accurate prediction." Airey, a very highly regarded officer who had served with SOE, would not have compromised his integrity to fit a preconceived idea. Clark's complaint appears to be an example of his tendency to see something sinister in anything British (*Calculated Risk,* pp. 261–62).

30. Ibid. Five days before the landings, a new Fifth Army Intelligence Summary offered an even more ominous forecast: one panzer grenadier division (including a tank battalion), four airborne battalions, one tank battalion of approximately sixty tanks, and naval, AA, and antitank units (Fifth Army Intelligence Summary No. 9, January 16, 1944 (PRO [WO 204/10263]).

31. Molony, *The Mediterranean and Middle East,* vol. 5, p. 773.

32. Lucas, "From Algiers to Anzio."

33. Clark diary, January 9, 1944.

34. Ibid., January 11, 1944.

35. Ibid., January 9, 1944.

36. Fifth Army Outline Plan, "Operation SHINGLE," January 12, 1944, PRO (WO 204/10263).
37. Lucas, "From Algiers to Anzio," pp. 307–8.
38. Lucas interview, May 24, 1948.
39. Blumenson, *Salerno to Cassino,* p. 357. The original plan was to drop the 504th along the Anzio-Albano highway, however, virtually everyone connected with Shingle complained about the operation. Penney foresaw a potential disaster because his troops might confuse the paratroopers with the enemy. The air and naval commanders likewise felt the airborne would be in great peril and without adequate protection or cover.
40. Description by Morison, in *Sicily–Salerno–Anzio,* chap. 15, passim.
41. Field Order No. 1, January 13, 1944, HQ, Beach Group, 540th Engineer Regiment. Copy in USAMHI archives.
42. Lucas diary, January 21, 1944, pp. 24–29.
43. The ball gunner was Jesse N. Bradley, whose recollections appear in "Beachhead Bailout at Anzio," *The Retired Officer,* September 1983.

Chapter 8. The Invasion

1. According to the war logs of the German Naval Command, Italy, the order to destroy Civitavecchia came directly from Kesselring at 1100 hours the morning of January 22. Before the day was out Group Captain F. W. Winterbotham, the RAF officer responsible for disseminating Ultra information from Bletchley Park to Churchill, delivered a note to this effect to the prime minister (Winterbotham to Churchill, minute of January 22, 1944, PRO [PREM 3, 248/3], and extract from German Naval Command, Italy, War Logs, January 19–February 15, 1944, Samuel Eliot Morison Papers, Naval Historical Center, Washington).
2. Lucas diary, January 22, 1944.
3. William Woodruff, *Vessel of Sadness* (Carbondale, Ill., 1978), pp. 44–45. Although published as a combination of history, fiction, poetry, and journalism, this moving account presents a disturbingly accurate re-creation of Anzio.
4. What few have ever known is that a great debt was owed to the men who had taken great risks to reconnoiter the beaches at Anzio. Some of the most dangerous operations of the war were carried out by what were known as Combined Operations Pilotage Parties, or COPPs. The acronym COPP was used to disguise their real and more descriptive title of Beach Reconnaissance and Assault Pilotage Parties. Originally formed toward the end of 1942 under the authority of Admiral Lord Louis Mountbatten, chief of Combined Operations, these were in reality beach reconnaissance parties whose task, in the case of Shingle, was to lay the groundwork for the Anzio landings. This small elite force recruited mainly from the Royal Navy and the Royal Engineers was given special training and equipment.

    Operating at night in collapsible canvas canoes called "folbots," two-man teams were launched from submarines, and while one would remain several hundred yards offshore, the other would swim ashore to reconnoiter enemy defenses and record important details such as the gradients and composition of the beaches. Often it was either impossible to locate the submarine again or the fragile folbots capsized in rough seas. In December 1943, during the preparations for Shingle, at least two two-man teams were lost off Anzio. Prior to the Sicily landings the COPPs suffered grievous losses to more than half the operational teams in the Mediterranean. In one instance it was believed that the two officers, whose boat probably capsized, deliberately swam out to sea where they were lost without a trace. Both men sacrificed their lives in order to preserve the security of Husky.

During the Shingle landings a folbot manned by a U.S. Navy ensign marked Yellow Beach for Darby's Ranger force and, at zero hour minus 10 minutes, turned on a yellow battle lamp that guided the Rangers to their target. (See Morison, *Sicily–Salerno–Anzio*, p. 338.)

Disbanded after the war, the COPPs and their secret remained virtually unknown until 1954, when several veterans wrote about them. Only then did the world learn of their unheralded work. In his autobiography Admiral Sir Andrew Browne Cunningham acknowledged the debt owed "these gallant young men." (See Cunningham, *A Sailor's Odyssey* [London, 1951], p. 557 [which makes only a brief mention of the role of the COPPs], the papers of Commander J. S. Townson, Department of Documents, Imperial War Museum, London, and reports in the AFHQ Papers in the PRO [WO 204/6742]. Readers interested in learning more about the COPPs should consult Hampshire, *The Beachhead Commandos*.)

5. "Operations of British, Indian and Dominion Forces in Italy, 3 September 1943 to 26 March 1945," part I, section F, German Strategy, USAMHI Library. Originally prepared immediately after the war by the British Historical Section, Central Mediterranean, this is one of a well-documented series of unpublished monographs about the Italian campaign. Had the invasion taken place twenty-four hours later the port of Anzio would have certainly been destroyed. When the town was liberated it was found that German engineers had already placed the explosive charges and were merely awaiting daylight to compete the task.

6. Fitzgerald, *A History of the Irish Guards in the Second World War*, p. 217. (This book is easily the most outstanding regimental history of the war.)

7. Danger diary.

8. Ibid., pp. 218–19.

9. Lucas, "From Algiers to Anzio." Lucas also reported, "A diligent search failed to disclose the hiding place of the remainder of the bottle."

10. AFHQ Intelligence Notes No. 45, February 8, 1944, PRO (WO 204/985). A 29th Division panzer grenadier lieutenant whose unit had been virtually wiped out in Sicily seemed pleased to have been captured by "his old friends" [*sic*] of the 3d Division.

11. "The Italian Campaign," vol. 1, Air Historical Branch narrative, PRO (AIR 41/34). The principal air support came from the fighters and fighter-bombers of Major General Edward J. House's (U.S.) XII Air Support Command. The command post of the XII ASC was colocated with that of the Fifth Army in order to facilitate direct air support to VI Corps. Unlike Sicily, where close air support was virtually nonexistent and badly coordinated, Shingle was proof that the lessons of Operation Husky had been learned.

12. Ira C. Eaker (1896–1988) was a poker-loving Texan and one of the pioneers

of American aviation. First sent to England as an observer during the Battle of Britain, Eaker returned in 1942 to create and build the Eighth Air Force into a powerful air machine that acted in concert with Air Chief Marshal Sir Arthur Harris's Bomber Command to carry out Pointblank, the Combined Chiefs of Staff directive of June 1943 for the combined bomber offensive against Germany's war industry. While the British bombed Germany at night, Eaker's Eighth Air Force perfected the technique of daylight bombing. A superb biography of Eaker is James Parton's *"Air Force Spoken Here": General Ira Eaker & the Command of the Air* (Bethesda, Md., 1986).

13. Wesley F. Craven and James L. Cate, eds., *The Army Air Forces in World War II*, vol. 3, *Europe: ARGUMENT to V-E Day, January 1944 to May 1945* (Chicago, 1951), pp. 340–1. Twining wore two command hats as the commander of the U.S. Fifteenth Air Force and the Allied commander of the Mediterranean Allied Strategic Air Force.

14. Ibid.

15. Morison, *Sicily–Salerno–Anzio*, p. 339.

16. The situation was not helped when a senior British officer drove his command car across a pontoon to the beach, where it became stuck in the sand. The pontoon was anchored to a tractor, which the officer commandeered to pull the vehicle loose. With its only means of anchorage gone, the pontoon broke loose, and it took the Navy several hours and "a lavish expenditure of energy and bad language" to render it usable (see *History of the First Division: Anzio Campaign*, privately printed in Palestine, 1946, p. 22).

17. Craven and Cate, *Europe: ARGUMENT to V-E Day*, p. 348; and Morison, *Sicily–Salerno–Anzio*, p. 342.

18. In June 1943 the 1st Division was landed on the island of Pantelleria, an important Axis listening post fifty miles off the Tunisian coast that the Allies needed for its airfield, to support the Husky landings in Sicily the following month. The island had been heavily bombed by naval and air forces for days prior to the invasion. The Italian garrison commander surrendered before a single shot was fired, and the only British casualty was a soldier bitten by a mule.

19. Quoted in Truscott, *Command Missions*, p. 310.

20. Letter from John T. Cummings to the author, June 20, 1988.

21. The military intelligence department of OKW.

22. Blumenson, *Salerno to Cassino*, p. 319, and Report No. 20, Historical Section (GS), National Defence Headquarters, Ottawa. Copy in USAMHI Library. Also known as the Steiger Ms. The Germans misinterpreted the absence of landing craft from Bizerte as a sign they had been dispersed to other theaters, thus lessening the possibility of any amphibious operation in Italy. Westphal's comments are based on the Tenth Army War Diary, January 11, 1944.

23. Quoted in Blumenson, *Salerno to Cassino*, pp. 318–19.

24. Extracts from the diary of Field Marshal Kesselring, copy in Lucas Papers. The document is less a diary than a series of observations on his war experiences written while he was held by the Allies for trial as a war criminal in 1946.

25. Ibid.
26. Kesselring is quoted in a monograph in the German Generals' Collection, Liddell Hart Papers, King's College, London.
27. "The Italian Campaign," vol. 1, Air Historical Branch narrative, PRO (AIR 41/34).
28. Anthony Cave Brown, *Bodyguard of Lies* (London, 1976), p. 419.
29. Molony, *The Mediterranean and Middle East*, vol. 5, p. 661.
30. Extracts, German Naval Command, Italy, War Logs.
31. Denis Richards and Hilary St. George Saunders, *The Royal Air Force, 1939–45*, vol. 2, *The Fight Avails* (London, 1975), p. 354.
32. Molony, *The Mediterranean and Middle East*, vol. 5, p. 662.
33. The 4th Parachute Division was first activated in the late autumn of 1943 at Perugia from cadres of the 2d Parachute Division, from Luftwaffe sources, and from members of two former Italian parachute divisions. Under the command of Generalmajor Heinrich Trettner, this new unit turned in a very creditable performance. Ever since the airborne operation in Crete in 1942, the German airborne force had fallen into disfavor with Hitler. However, the success of Otto Skorzeny's daring rescue of Mussolini led Hitler to approve a plan to expand General Kurt Student's command from a corps to a parachute army (see Roger Edwards, *German Parachute Troops, 1939–45* [New York, 1974], pp. 117–18; and Samuel W. Mitcham, Jr., *Hitler's Legions: The German Order of Battle, World War II* [New York, 1985], p. 419).
34. Under German doctrine in World War II, antiaircraft defense was a responsibility of the Luftwaffe, and all flak units were under its jurisdiction rather than the Army's, which exercised little or no control over them.
35. Kesselring "diary," Lucas Papers.
36. Quoted in "Operations of British, Indian and Dominion Forces in Italy, 3 September 1943 to 2 May 1945," part 1, section F, German Strategy.
37. Manuscript T-1a, German Report Series, British translation by the Air Ministry, 1950, in Microfilm Roll No. A-5422, Office of Air Force History, Washington. Copies of this document in the original German are in several U.S. archives, including USAMHI.
38. Kesselring, *The Memoirs of Field Marshal Kesselring*, p. 194.
39. Vaughan-Thomas, *Anzio*, p. 63.
40. Graham and Bidwell, *Tug of War*, p. 150.
41. "Army Group's Comments" by General Siegfried Westphal, in Ms. T-1a.
42. Kesselring "diary," Lucas Papers.
43. In the U.S. Army the engineers were trained to fight as infantry. Because of their versatility most nondivisional engineer units were under the direct control of a corps HQ. The 36th Engineers (an independent unit that had no connection with the 36th Infantry Division) had fought in North Africa and Sicily and was in the thick of the fighting for the Salerno beachhead. At Anzio, when the regiment was not busily repairing roads and bridges, it fought beside the infantry to defend the beachhead. Before the war ended the 36th Engineers had more combat time than any unit in the ETO except the 34th Infantry Division.
44. *Fifth Army History,* part 4.
45. Lucas diary, January 22, 1944.

46. Lemnitzer interview.
47. Lucas, "From Algiers to Anzio."
48. Morison, *Sicily–Salerno–Anzio*, p. 336.
49. Lucas Papers, USAMHI. Among the first troops to reach the Anzio sector on January 22 were 4,000 paratroopers, approximately 9,500 panzer grenadiers (6,200 of whom were assigned to units of the 3d Panzer Grenadier Division), and 3,800 artillerymen. See appendix F, "The German Reinforcement of Anzio," for a day-by-day accounting of the first twenty days of the German buildup.

Chapter 9. Missed Opportunities

1. *Fifth Army History*, part 4.
2. Fitzgerald, *A History of the Irish Guards in the Second World War*, p. 223.
3. Taggart, *History of the Third Infantry Division in World War II*, p. 110.
4. The present division was a new one recruited from various elements of the Luftwaffe. Its official designation was the Parachute Panzer Division Hermann Göring (Hermann Göring Panzer Fallschirmjäger Division), but in reality it was *neither* a parachute *nor* a panzer division but rather a panzer grenadier division. The designation "parachute" was honorary, and its organization made it merely another mechanized formation similar to other panzer grenadier formations fighting in Italy.
5. Lucas, "From Algiers to Anzio."
6. The second lift of the 1st Armored Division from Naples was late arriving due to a storm that forced the convoy to anchor off Anzio for two days (see George F. Howe, *The Battle History of the 1st Armored Division* [Washington, 1954], p. 282).
7. Blumenson, *Salerno to Cassino*, p. 387.
8. Clark diary, January 23, 1944.
9. Ibid., January 25, 1944.
10. Lucas, "From Algiers to Rome," January 25, 1944.
11. Alexander interview, part 2.
12. Clark diary, January 26, 1944.
13. Ibid. Clark's aide also recorded his chief's concern in a memo later appended to the diary. General Clark "felt for some time that the force at Anzio is not being pushed forward with sufficient aggressiveness and that opportunities to make progress northward while the German troops were as yet disorganized at the time are being lost. Accordingly, he determined to go at once to the Anzio front and urge General Lucas to initiate aggressive action at once" (January 28, 1944).
14. Quoted in Gilbert, *Road to Victory*, p. 663.
15. Bennett, *Ultra and Mediterranean Strategy*, p. 265.
16. Major Arthur F. Fournier, "Influence of Ultra Intelligence Upon General Clark at Anzio" (master's thesis written for the U.S. Army Command & General Staff College, 1983), pp. 105–6. Y service was the interception and breaking of low- and medium-grade enemy codes and ciphers, through intercepted wireless traffic, most of which was accomplished in the field by code-breakers assigned to theaters, army groups, or army HQs.
17. Bennett, *Ultra and the Mediterranean Strategy*, p. 265.

18. Bernard Fergusson, *The Watery Maze: The Story of Combined Operations* (New York, 1961), p. 313.

19. Fitzgerald, *A History of the Irish Guards in the Second World War*, p. 221.

20. Ibid, p. 223. CRA is Commander, Royal Artillery, the British equivalent of the Division Artillery (Div/Arty) commander in a U.S. division. Both formations were commanded by a one-star general. In a British division, brigades were commanded by a brigadier; in a U.S. division the regimental commander was a full colonel.

21. Quoted in Peter Verney, *Anzio 1944: An Unexpected Fury* (London, 1978), p. 59. This is a fine account of British operations at Anzio.

22. Very little has been written about this phase of Ranger operations at Anzio. A brief account appears in James J. Altieri, *Darby's Rangers* (Durham, 1945), pp. 70–72.

23. Verney, *Anzio 1944: An Unexpected Fury*, p. 63.

24. Fitzgerald, *A History of the Irish Guards in the Second World War*, p. 233.

25. *History of the First Division*, pp. 28–29.

26. Another characteristic of life in the Anzio beachhead was the mysterious frequency with which farm animals disappeared whenever farms were occupied by soldiers. Amazingly, some managed to survive in the midst of the carnage.

27. Fitzgerald, *A History of the Irish Guards in the Second World War*, pp. 238–39.

28. Ibid., p. 243.

29. Ibid., p. 237.

30. Ibid., p. 239.

31. Quoted in Harmon, *Combat Commander*, p. 160.

32. Nigel Nicholson, *The Grenadier Guards in the War of 1939–1945*, vol. 2 (Aldershot, 1949), p. 399. The four officers who managed to escape did so only because of the poor aim of the German machine gunner who killed their comrades. Had the Germans bothered to check they would have found the plans for the attack on their bodies which were recovered the following day.

33. Verney, *Anzio 1944: An Unexpected Fury*, p. 70. Dung Farm became a very dangerous place to visit. One victim was a cigar-smoking American in a jeep who was warned to be very careful: "It's easy to go too far and be killed." The following day he was found in his jeep outside the farm gate, "the cigar clamped in his teeth . . . dead as a doornail" (Fitzgerald, *A History of the Irish Guards in the Second World War*, p. 250).

34. Omar N. Bradley, *A Soldier's Story* (New York, 1951), p. 100.

35. Bradley commentaries, USAMHI.

36. Harmon, *Combat Commander*, p. 117. Several days later Harmon told Patton that Fredendall was a moral and physical coward (see Blumenson, *The Patton Papers*, vol. 2, p. 177).

37. Author interview with Colonel Jacob Shapiro, USA (Ret.), July 29, 1988.

38. Alexander had sent liaison officers to every U.S. division in an effort to provide them with the benefit of British experience. When a British officer rose to deliver the situation report at Harmon's first briefing, the new commander realized that his first step must be to force the division to begin believing in itself again. When Harmon brusquely asked him who the hell

he was, the British officer replied, "General Alexander's liaison officer from 18th Army Group." The officer was unceremoniously tossed out and ordered not to bother returning unless personally "invited" by Harmon himself. Harmon's action was very popular with the division staff and so amused Patton that he attempted without success to have Harmon relate the story to King George VI when he visited North Africa (interview with George F. Howe, September 15, 1952, Harmon Papers, USAMHI).

39. Quoted in Harmon, *Combat Commander*, p. 136.
40. Oral history interview of General Hamilton H. Howze, USA (Ret.), USAMHI.
41. General Hamilton H. Howze, "Armor in the Breakout from the Anzio Beachhead" (1952 lecture, Howze Papers, USAMHI). Two months before the Anzio landings Harmon was able to boast that "if the 1st Armored Division can't operate [in Italy], by God there is no armored division that will be able to operate; and if I can't fight the 1st Armored Division in the coming fight . . . I don't believe anybody can. This may sound cocky to you . . . but I believe I know as well as anybody how to do it" (Harmon to Major General E. S. Hughes, November 20, 1943, Harmon Papers).
42. Quoted in Raleigh Trevelyan, *Rome '44: The Battle for the Eternal City* (London, 1981), p. 73.
43. Quoted in Harmon, *Combat Commander*, p. 161.
44. Howe, *The Battle History of the 1st Armored Division*, p. 284.
45. Verney, *Anzio 1944: An Unexpected Fury*, p. 70.
46. Fitzgerald, *A History of the Irish Guards in the Second World War*, p. 246.
47. Ibid., p. 250.
48. The Irish Guards regimental history credits Corporal Holwell's "unshakable courage and skill," without which the companies would not have been ordered to withdraw "and would have remained where they were till they were destroyed" (Fitzgerald, *A History of the Irish Guards in the Second World War*, p. 263). It is all the more perplexing that Corporal Holwell was never decorated posthumously. According to the Irish Guards' history, Holwell did not even rate a "mention in despatches."
49. Ibid., p. 266.
50. Verney, *Anzio 1944: An Unexpected Fury*, pp. 84–85.
51. Ibid., p. 84, and D. Erskine, ed., *The Scots Guards, 1919–55* (London, 1956), p. 212.

Chapter 10. Calamity at Cisterna and Campoleone

1. Blumenson, *Salerno to Cassino*, p. 391.
2. Ms. T-1a/k-1.
3. Truscott, *Command Missions*, p. 313.
4. Altieri, *Darby's Rangers*, p. 74, and Dr. Michael J. King, *Rangers: Selected Combat Operations in World War II*, monograph No. 11, Leavenworth Papers, June 1985, p. 33. Dr. King's monograph, published by the U.S. Government Printing Office, is available in some libraries.
5. King, *Rangers: Selected Combat Operations in World War II*, p. 34.
6. Letter, Brigadier General John W. Dobson, USA (Ret.), to the author, April 23, 1990. Dobson, a 1939 graduate of the United States Military Academy

and a former cavalry officer, applied to join the Rangers in 1942 but his application became mired in bureaucratic red tape. "I got my application back with 39 endorsements about one year later while in Tunisia serving with the 766th Tank Destroyer Battalion in support of the [U.S.] 1st Armored Division." When the Italian campaign opened he contacted Darby and joined the Rangers shortly before the Anzio landings. At the time of the Cisterna operation he had been in command of the 1st Battalion for only a few weeks.

7. Ibid.
8. Letter, Dobson to the author, May 22, 1990.
9. Dobson letter, April 23, 1990.
10. King, *Rangers: Selected Combat Operations in World War II*, p. 35.
11. For the benefit of readers unfamiliar with British or American military terminology, a line of departure is the equivalent of a start line in British parlance. Both were usually a recognizable landmark along the forward edge of a battlefield (road, track, ridgeline, etc.), perpendicular to the route of advance.
12. Altieri, *Darby's Rangers*, p. 75.
13. Trevelyan, *Rome '44*, p. 75.
14. Dobson letter, May 22, 1990. As his battalion passed through the second echelon of German security, Dobson vividly recalls that "you could hear various security points calling off their numbers as a check, e.g., *'Drei— Alles Geht Gut.'* "
15. Dobson letter, April 23, 1990.
16. Taggart, *History of the Third Infantry Division in World War II*, p. 115.
17. Dobson, quoted in Altieri, *Darby's Rangers*, p. 83.
18. Dobson letters, April 23 and May 22, 1990.
19. Ibid., p. 77.
20. Ibid., p. 83.
21. Buckley, *Road to Rome*, p. 280.
22. Major Jack Dobson, quoted in Altieri, *Darby's Rangers*, p. 83.
23. T/5 James P. O'Reilly, Co. B, 3d Ranger Battalion, quoted in Altieri, *Darby's Rangers*, p. 81.
24. Ibid.
25. William O. Darby and William H. Baumer, *We Led the Way: Darby's Rangers* (San Rafael, Calif., 1980), p. 188. This book is based on stenographic notes of interviews of Darby in 1944 by his West Point classmate Baumer.
26. Quoted in Altieri, *Darby's Rangers*, p. 82.
27. King, *Rangers: Selected Combat Operations in World War II*, p. 39.
28. Quoted in ibid., p. 39. Ehalt was one of the original Ranger NCOs recruited by Darby and the two men shared a special rapport.
29. Darby quoted in Taggart, *History of the Third Division in World War II*, op. cit., p. 115.
30. Darby, quoted in Darby and Baumer, *We Led the Way*, p. 186.
31. Ibid., p. 188.
32. "The German Operation at Anzio," p. 21. The Germans reported that overall Allied POWs for January 30 were 786 men, including 29 officers. Although there could not have been 680 Rangers captured, the total may

well represent the combined losses by the Rangers, the 3d Division, and the British and U.S. 1st Armored divisions on January 30 and 31.

33. Ibid., pp. 21, 23.

34. Altieri, *Darby's Rangers*, p. 84.

35. Truscott diary, Truscott Papers, George C. Marshall Library, Lexington, Va. The diary was kept on a daily basis by his two aides, Captain Jack E. Bartash and 1st Lieutenant James M. Wilson, Jr.

36. Darby's driver, Sergeant Carlo Contrera, quoted in Darby and Baumer, *We Led the Way*, p. 192.

37. Milton Lehman, "The Rangers Fought Ahead of Everybody," *Saturday Evening Post*, June 15, 1946, p. 50.

38. Verney, *Anzio 1944: An Unexpected Fury*, p. 75.

39. Lehman, "The Rangers Fought Ahead of Everybody."

40. Quoted in ibid.

41. King, "Rangers: Selected Combat Operations in World War II," p. 30.

42. Michael J. King, *William Orlando Darby* (Hamden, Conn., 1981), p. 185.

43. Lucas, "From Algiers to Anzio," January 31, 1944.

44. Truscott, *Command Missions*, op. cit., p. 314.

45. Clark Diary, January 31, 1944.

46. John Bowditch III, *Anzio Beachhead* (Washington, D.C., 1947), p. 30. This was one of the "U.S. Forces in Action" postwar monographs written for the Historical Division, U. S. Army.

47. Altieri, *Darby's Rangers*, p. 79.

48. Quoted in Taggart, *History of the Third Division in World War II*, p. 119.

49. Darby and Baumer, *We Led the Way*, p. 189.

50. Taggart, *History of the Third Division in World War II*, p. 113; and press release/Medal of Honor citation in the John W. O'Daniel Papers, USAMHI.

51. A day-by-day breakdown of the German reinforcements from January 22 to February 1 is in Appendix F (See Anzio Correspondence, box 47/5, Samuel Eliot Morison Papers, U.S. Navy Historical Center, Washington, D.C.).

52. German units at Anzio included the 3d Panzer Grenadier Division, 4th Parachute Division, elements of the 15th Panzer Grenadier Division, 26th Panzer Division, 65th Infantry Division, 71st Panzer Division, 715th Infantry Division, Hermann Göring Division, 1st Parachute Regiment (1st Parachute Division), and the 7th Luftwaffe Jaeger Battalion.

53. King, *Rangers: Selected Combat Operations in World War II*, pp. 39–40.

54. Ibid., p. 37.

55. Harmon, *Combat Commander*, pp. 163–164.

56. Penney diary, January 29, 1944.

57. *History of the First Division*, p. 36.

58. Ernest N. Harmon and Milton MacKaye, "Our Bitter Days at Anzio," part 1, *Saturday Evening Post*, September 18, 1948, p. 147.

59. Ibid.

60. Quoted in Trevelyan, *Rome '44*, p. 76.

61. John W. A. Masters, *The Story of the 2nd Battalion, the Sherwood Foresters* (Aldershot, 1946), p. 28. A similar account is in C. N. Barclay, *The History of the Sherwood Foresters, 1919–57* (London, 1959). Late that afternoon, in the aftermath of the battle, the British front line was dotted with white

flags as the survivors went about their grim task of rescuing the wounded and evacuating the dead. In general the Germans tended to ignore the presence of vehicles and men clearly on missions of mercy. (An obvious exception was the Foresters' medical officer.)

62. Sir Henry Marking quoted in Trevelyan, *Rome '44*, p. 77.
63. "The German Operation at Anzio," p. 22. There exist only very brief accounts of 1st Armored Division operations at Campoleone on January 31 (see Howe, *The Battle History of the 1st Armored Division*, chap. 14).
64. Clark, *Calculated Risk*, p. 273.
65. Clark Diary, January 30, 1944.
66. Lucas, "From Algiers to Anzio," January 30, 1944.

Chapter 11. The Battle for the Thumb

1. *Kesselring: A Soldier's Record*, p. 233.
2. Hitler's messages to Kesselring appear in a variety of accounts, including Vaughan-Thomas, *Anzio*, p. 101.
3. Irving, *Hitler's War*, pp. 604–5.
4. Quoted in ibid., p. 604.
5. "The German Operation at Anzio," January 29, 1944. This mission was to be carried out "as soon as possible," with the date dependent upon the arrival of the necessary forces which were being delayed because "the railroad system in Italy has been crippled by enemy air raids."
6. Ibid. It was German practice to name their battle groups after the commander. In this instance Lieutenant General Fritz-Hubert Gräser was the commander of the 3d Panzer Grenadier Division, which was to spearhead the counteroffensive. Lieutenant General Dr. Georg Pfeiffer commanded the 65th Infantry Division.
7. Bennett, *Ultra and Mediterranean Strategy*, p. 267.
8. Ibid. The intercept also included details of the German employment of artillery and how the large railway guns were to be used to silence the supporting fires of the Allied fleet. The Fourteenth Army journal listed 169 heavy antitank guns as of February 1, and these figures were soon raised to 193 by February 4.
9. Hinsley et al., *British Intelligence in the Second World War*, vol. 3, part 1, p. 190, quoting a postwar document entitled *The History of the Special Liaison Units*, or SLUs, which were created solely to process and control the flow of Ultra information in the field. In a study of Ultra and how it was used by senior Allied commanders, historian Harold C. Deutsch notes that Mark Clark was reluctant to employ Ultra. From his first briefing on this important new source of intelligence in August 1942, Clark had "reacted to Ultra with something between indifference and distaste." (See Deutsch, "Commanding Generals and the Uses of Intelligence," *Intelligence and National Security* [vol. 3], July 1988.)
10. *History of the First Division*, p. 43.
11. Penney diary and Lucas diary, February 1, 1944.
12. Penney Papers.
13. Clark diary, February 1, 1944.
14. Ibid.

15. Blumenson, *Salerno to Cassino*, p. 393.
16. Lucas, "From Algiers to Anzio," February 1, 1944.
17. See Anzio Correspondence, Box 47/5, Morison Papers.
18. Lucas, "From Algiers to Anzio," February 1, 1944.
19. Alexander interviews, part 2.
20. Alexander dispatch.
21. "The German Operation at Anzio," February 2, 1944.
22. Comments by von Mackensen quoted in Ms. T-1a/K-1.
23. General Siegfried Westphal, quoted in the German Generals' Collection, file 9/24/117, Liddell Hart Papers.
24. Ibid.
25. *Kesselring: A Soldier's Record*, p. 235. In this statement Kesselring is referring to the plan for the second German counteroffensive in mid-February, which was a virtual carbon copy of the attacks launched on February 3–4. Harmon and the troops of the U.S. 1st Armored Division would readily have confirmed the unsuitability of the terrain for tank operations.
26. Fitzgerald, *A History of the Irish Guards in the Second World War*, p. 273.
27. Ibid., p. 274.
28. Ibid., chap. 6, passim.
29. Verney, *Anzio 1944: An Unexpected Fury*, pp. 100–101. The dispositions of the 6th Gordons will provide some idea of the exceptional peril of their position. B Company was four hundred yards north of the battalion CP; D Company was eight hundred yards north of B Company, and A and C companies were six hundred yards north of D Company. The nature of the ground was such that in some instances the companies not only could not even see one another but could provide no mutual support whatsoever. If ever an impossible scenario existed for an infantry battalion in the defense, it was the positions of the 6th Gordons on February 3 to 4. Infantry can survive only by mutual support from its own units and from tanks and artillery. On the morning of February 4, 1944, the Gordons had none of these.
30. "Horror Farm," unpublished account by Lieutenant (later Major) Edward Grace, MC; copy furnished by the late Major J. C. Williamson, MC, former adjutant of the 6th Gordons at Anzio. Major Grace's account was written in the summer of 1944, when he was recuperating from a leg wound received at Anzio.
31. Ibid.
32. Ibid.
33. Ibid.
34. Ibid.
35. War diary, 6th Battalion, the Gordon Highlanders, February 4, 1944, PRO (WO 170/1394).
36. Ibid.
37. Grace, "Horror Farm."
38. Account of Lieutenant Harry Garioch in *6th Gordons, 1939–1945* (Aberdeen, 1946), privately printed and authored by Major J. C. Williamson, the battalion adjutant, who earned a Military Cross for gallantry the morning of February 4.
39. Report of Lieutenant Colonel James Peddie to Major General W. R. C.

Penney on the action of the 6th Gordons on February 3/4, 1944, Penney Papers.

40. Ibid.
41. Ibid.
42. Ibid.
43. "Statement of Experience of Major A. T. Jones, MBE, Company C, Support Group, 2d/7th Middlesex," Penney Papers. The 2d/7th Middlesex was a machine-gun battalion, one of which was normally assigned to each British infantry division. These battalions were under the direct control of the division commander, who employed them wherever he deemed necessary.
44. "Account of the Action of the 1st Battalion Irish Guards, Feb 3/4, 1944" (prepared on February 7), Penney Papers. The report states that it was written at the specific request of General Penney. This eyewitness also saw many of the Gordons returning to their positions to retrieve personal possessions, thus creating the impression that they had surrendered without putting up a fight. Without mentioning the Gordons by name, the television series "The World at War" briefly alludes to an incident at Anzio in which a unit gave up, implying that its men had seen too much combat and could not continue fighting. This could not have been true of the 6th Gordons. The battalion had last fought in Tunisia from March to May 1943 and until Anzio had not been in combat for nearly nine months. The battalion's first days at Anzio involved relatively light contact with the enemy. Unlike some units that were untested in combat, the Gordon officers and NCOs were mostly veterans.

    One survivor who was badly wounded later stated that the German officer commanding the unit that captured A Company permitted their prisoners to return to their slit trenches to retrieve their kit, which may well account for the impression that some had simply given up without a fight.
45. Letter, Major J. C. Williamson to the author, November 1, 1988.
46. Ibid.
47. Since the end of World War II the substantial collection of records that comprised the files of the Army adjutant general has disappeared. Virtually all the various documents covering the period 1940–45 were eventually deposited in the Public Record Office, except for the adjutant general files. Despite repeated attempts by the author to trace these files, there has never been a satisfactory explanation from the responsible officials. Although it would require considerable cross-checking, a researcher armed with the names of the missing could very likely eventually determine the ultimate fate of the men of the 6th Gordons from these records.
48. War diary, 6th Battalion, the Gordon Highlanders.
49. Account of Major A. T. Jones.
50. Fitzgerald, *A History of the Irish Guards in the Second World War*, p. 284.
51. Quoted in ibid., p. 281.
52. The 168th Infantry Brigade fought in Sicily as part of the 50th Division, and its three infantry battalions were the 10th Battalion, Royal Berkshire Regiment, 1st Battalion, London Scottish, and the 1st Battalion, London Irish Rifles. Toward the end of October 1943 it was reassigned to the 56th Division during the battle for Mt. Camino. In January 1944 the Brigade was

fighting along the Garigliano River when it was ordered to Anzio by Clark as part of the general reinforcements sent in anticipation of the German counteroffensive. The brigade nearly arrived too late to participate in the battles of February 4 when five of the nine landing craft comprising the flotilla carrying them from Naples to Anzio became lost in the "fog" of war. The five vessels had become separated in the Bay of Naples and hadn't a clue how to get to Anzio. The three naval officers of each crew had been selected for their jobs at the conclusion of training school by the following simple expedient: "On passing out day [they] had been lined up in three ranks—those in the front were nominated 'Exec,' the centre rank 'Navigator' and the rear rank 'Engineer.' Their knowledge of navigation was sketchy to say the least and . . . they preferred to follow their leader" (quoted by Colonel Terrence Law, CO, 1st Battalion, London Scottish Rifles, *The London Scottish Regimental Gazette,* April 1959).

53. Vaughan-Thomas, *Anzio,* pp. 111–12.
54. Molony, *The Mediterranean and Middle East,* vol. 5, p. 729, and Fitzgerald, *A History of the Irish Guards in the Second World War,* p. 282.
55. A distinguished Scottish regiment, the Gordon Highlanders date to the mid-eighteenth century, when the fourth duke of Gordon raised the first of three regiments of militia. For the next 150 years there was at least one active regiment of Gordon Highlanders. The lineage of the Gordons reflects activity in virtually every corner of the British Empire during the colonial wars of the nineteenth century, including Corsica, Gibraltar, Ireland, Holland, Egypt, Denmark, India, Afghanistan, the Peninsular Campaign and Waterloo under Wellington, and the Boer War. During World War I the Gordons suffered appalling casualties beginning in August 1914 at Le Cateau, where more than 700 men of the 1st Gordons were captured by the Germans. During the remainder of World War I nine battalions of Gordons fought on the Western Front. One of these was the 6th Battalion, which fought at Loos in 1915 and at Ypres in 1917. The regiment lost a staggering 1,000 officers and 28,000 men killed in World War I. In World War II the tragedy of the Gordons continued, with the total loss in June 1940 of the 1st and 5th battalions, when the 51st (Highland) Division was surrounded at St. Valery-en-Caux and forced to surrender to Rommel's 7th Panzer Division. The 2d Battalion suffered a similar fate in early 1942, when the British Tenth Army surrendered to the Japanese Army after the siege of Singapore.

The 6th Gordons of World War II were a Territorial battalion (the equivalent of a U.S. Army Reserve or National Guard unit) that was first mobilized in 1939 and sent to France as part of Field Marshal Lord Gort's ill-fated British Expeditionary Force. Unlike their sister battalions, the 6th escaped via Dunkirk and later fought in Tunisia in Anderson's First British Army. In June 1943 the battalion was part of the 1st Division force that seized the Italian island of Pantelleria after an air and naval bombardment lasting more than a week. Lieutenant Colonel James Peddie was a longtime Gordon Territorial officer who had previously served with the London Scottish and had commanded the 6th Gordons since July 1941 (see Wilfrid Miles, *The Gordon Highlanders, 1919–1945* [London, 1961]; and Christopher Sinclair-Stevenson, *The Gordon Highlanders* [London, 1968]).

56. "The German Operation at Anzio," p. 32.
57. Ms. T-1a/K-1.
58. Lucas, "From Algiers to Anzio," February 4, 1944.
59. A. M. Cheetham, *Ubique* (Formby, England, 1987), p. 98. The book is a record of the experiences of a junior Royal Artillery officer whose regiment was a part of the 1st Division. Cheetham notes that during the critical moments of the battles of February 3 to 4 most guns fired constantly and became so hot they had to be periodically cooled off with cold water to avoid burning out their barrels.

Chapter 12. The German Onslaught

1. Monograph, British Historical Section, Central Mediterranean, "The Conquest of Southern Italy," section D, "British Forces at Anzio," p. 12, USAMHI Library.
2. Lucas, "From Algiers to Anzio."
3. Two days later the VI Corps surgeon was killed instantly when a shell exploded in front of Lucas's command post. Lucas himself had been in the same spot only two minutes before (see Lucas, "From Algiers to Anzio," p. 370).
4. One of these sources fell into the hands of the Scots Guards the night of February 6, when the commander of a Nebelwerfer battery strayed into British lines in a Volkswagen and was captured. "There was a large quantity of documents, and even marked maps showing proposed dispositions. The Germans had wonderful maps—very much better and more accurate than our own" (Erskine, *The Scots Guards, 1919–55*, p. 216).
5. Verney, *Anzio 1944: An Unexpected Fury,* p. 116.
6. Moments later the German pilot was downed by a British Spitfire and the same afternoon became a patient in the hospital he had just inadvertently bombed. "There he received the regular treatment accorded the wounded" before being evacuated by LST to Naples and incarceration. Sadly, "his one moment of panic, one flicker of his finger, added twenty-eight new grave markers to the growing military cemetery on the hill behind Nettuno" (Fred Sheehan, *Anzio: Epic of Bravery* [Norman, Okla., 1964], p. 102).
7. Molony, *The Mediterranean and Middle East,* vol. 5, p. 727.
8. Ibid. The official history is quite accurate in the observation that "though the battles are simple in outline, their innumerable details were confused and can be followed only in regimental records and in regimental histories."
9. Ibid., pp. 327–28.
10. *History of the First Division,* p. 56. The inexperienced 65th Infantry Division previously fought against Montgomery's Eighth Army in the battles along the Sangro River in late 1943 and had been so severely mauled that it was all but written off. It was reconstituted immediately thereafter and was part of the reinforcements sent from northern Italy after the Shingle landings under a new commander, Lieutenant General Pfeiffer (see Samuel W. Mitcham, Jr., *Hitler's Legions: The German Army Order of Battle, World War II* [New York, 1985], pp. 86–87).

11. Nicolson, *The Grenadier Guards in the War of 1939–1945,* vol. 2, p. 407.

12. Vaughan-Thomas, *Anzio,* p. 124.

13. Quoted in Trevelyan, *Rome '44,* p. 147.

14. Ibid., p. 151. A few of the wounded were rescued by British medics, but most were trapped and helpless despite several attempts to retrieve them under the truce of a German Red Cross flag that, according to Trevelyan, was ignored by the British, who refused to cease firing at their enemy.

15. Various accounts of Major Sidney's exploits appear in Nicolson, *The Grenadier Guards in the War of 1939–1945,* vol. 2, pp. 406–8; Trevelyan, *Rome '44,* pp. 146–47; Vaughan-Thomas, *Anzio,* pp. 125–27; Sheehan, *Anzio: Epic of Bravery,* pp. 104–6; and Verney, *Anzio 1944: An Unexpected Fury,* pp. 125–26.

16. Masters, *The Story of the 2nd Battalion the Sherwood Foresters,* p. 38.

17. Bowditch, *Anzio Beachhead,* p. 57; and monograph, "American Armor at Anzio," U.S. Army Armor School, Fort Knox, Ky., May 1949, pp. 24–25.

18. *History of the First Division,* p. 62.

19. On the basis of the data available, it is impossible to provide an exact figure or percentage. Some of the British losses had already been replaced, and in the case of the Grenadier Guards, apparently some were not at the front during February 7–9. What is certain is that British 1st Division losses were far higher than those cited after the war in the official history.

20. Nicolson, *The Grenadier Guards in the War of 1939–1945,* vol. 2, pp. 409–13, passim.

21. Quoted in Fitzgerald, *A History of the Irish Guards in the Second World War,* p. 295.

22. The circumstances surrounding the loss of No. 1 Company were not learned until after the war, when the company commander, Captain David O'Cocks, was repatriated from a German POW camp. Under orders to reach the North Staffordshires at all costs, O'Cocks and two of his three platoons had broken through German lines and made contact with the second in command of the North Staffordshires, who was almost immediately shot and "fell in his tracks." As Colonel Scott had feared, the scene was utter chaos: The Germans were everywhere and it was impossible to determine friend from foe along the slopes of Buonriposo Ridge. What was left of No. 1 Company was by now less than platoon-size and in an attempt to reach the North Staffordshires, the survivors found themselves under heavy attack and trapped in the open along a false crest of the ridge. Within minutes No. 1 Company passed into history. Captain O'Cocks escaped but was wounded and eventually recaptured attempting to find his way to friendly lines through the mud and torrential rain, his war now over for good (Fitzgerald, *A History of the Irish Guards in the Second World War,* chap. 7 and 8, passim).

23. G. Blight, *The History of the Royal Berkshire Regiment, 1920–1947* (Staples, England, 1953), p. 288. One of the new weapons employed in the German counteroffensive was aptly called Goliath. This was a deadly, miniature radio-controlled tracked vehicle packed with high explosives detonated by electrical impulse. Although this tactic was an abysmal failure at Anzio, it was not for lack of effort by the Germans. A larger version of Goliath contained 550 kilograms of TNT, and its dangerous potential was

never taken lightly (See Molony, *The Mediterranean and Middle East,* vol. 5, p. 726).

24. Ibid., p. 289.
25. *The London Irish at War,* privately printed by the London Irish Rifles regimental association (London, n. d.), p. 140.
26. "The German Operation at Anzio," February 9, 1944, p. 42.
27. *History of the First Division,* p. 64.
28. Penney diary, February 8, 1944, Penney Papers.
29. The Mark IV tank was roughly the German equivalent of the American Sherman tank.
30. Quoted in Fitzgerald, *A History of the Irish Guards in the Second World War,* p. 310. Because of the presence of their No. 4 Company at Carroceto Station, the Irish Guards were monitoring all communications between the Scots Guards and Brigade HQ.
31. Ibid., p. 309.
32. Erskine, *The Scots Guards, 1919–55,* pp. 221–22.
33. Bowditch, *Anzio Beachhead,* p. 62.
34. Quoted in Fitzgerald, *A History of the Irish Guards in the Second World War,* p. 311.
35. Ibid., p. 312.
36. Ibid., p. 299.
37. The British official history (Molony, *The Mediterranean and Middle East,* vol. 5, p. 735) bases its statistics on these units going into action at full war establishment, that is, full authorization, which for an infantry battalion was 35 officers and 786 enlisted, total strength 821 men. Estimate for the 5th Grenadier Guards is based on losses of 61 killed, 234 wounded, and 311 missing or known captured. Total losses were 606 through approximately March 8. The battalion saw little action after being pulled out of the line on February 10 and was forced to consolidate their four rifle companies into two (Nicolson, *The Grenadier Guards in the War of 1939–1945,* vol. 2, p. 413).
38. Like the Grenadiers, the Scots Guards were so decimated that they were replaced in the line on February 10 and thereafter saw little action prior to departing the Anzio beachhead in early March. Total losses were 137 killed, 312 wounded, and 217 missing or captured. Of these only eight were known to have occurred after February 10. The regimental history records that on February 10 approximately 120 men were left in the battalion (Erskine, *The Scots Guards, 1919–55,* pp. 224 and 227).
39. The Irish Guards landed at Anzio with a strength of 794 men and as of February 13, after being withdrawn from the front line on February 10, reported losses of 54 killed, 165 wounded, and 341 missing, total 553. At this point in the campaign the Irish Guards were one of the few battalions to have received replacements, which totaled 286 men. Their reported strength on February 13 was 520 men, or a total loss of 560 men since January 22. (Fitzgerald, *A History of the Irish Guards in the Second World War,* p. 321).
40. The regimental history records losses of 8 killed, 18 wounded, and 319 missing after the loss of A, C, and D companies on February 4. Before being shifted to a quiet sector on February 9, an entire platoon of B Company

was lost. Although the numbers are not specified, there were obviously other casualties to this unit during their time in the line. A reasonable estimate is a total of 430 casualties by February 9. From an informal account of the 6th Gordons it can be deduced that A, C, and D companies were not at full strength on February 3–4, thus reducing the fighting strength of the Gordons to approximately 55 percent (Miles, *The Gordon Highlanders, 1919–1945*, p. 231; and Major J. C. Williamson, *6th Gordons, 1939–1945* [Aberdeen, 1946], passim).

41. Although no precise data are available, the 2d Foresters suffered the heaviest casualties of any 1st Division infantry battalion at Anzio. The battalion had been savaged at Campoleone and in the bitter defense of Buonriposo Ridge, both of which had taken place by February 10. A and B companies could muster little more than 35 men each and C Company was virtually wiped out at Buonriposo (Masters, *The Story of the 2nd Battalion the Sherwood Foresters*, chap. 5, 6).

42. "The German Operation at Anzio," February 4–11, 1944.

43. Penney diary, February 8–9, 1944, Penney Papers.

44. Ibid., 0600 hours, February 10, 1944.

45. Eric Linklater, *The Campaign in Italy* (London, 1951), p. 199.

46. Penney diary, 0530 hours, February 10, 1944.

47. "From Algiers to Anzio," February 8 and 9, 1944.

48. Letter, Penney to Brigadier Douglas Penny, February 8, 1956, Penney Papers.

49. Ibid.

50. Clark diary, February 9, 1944.

51. Blumenson, *Salerno to Cassino*, p. 396.

52. Ibid. Penney had forgotten the first names of Lucas and Eagles, whose name he also misspelled in his letter. In the interests of clarity these have been corrected in the text of the quote above. At that time, Penney believed his criticism was too strong for it ever to be published. After the February 11 conference Penney overheard the 168th Brigade commander tell his intelligence officer that, "he had no doubt seen many American movies but that he had never seen one like that conference and that he wasn't to mention it until after the war."

53. Quoted in Trevelyan, *Rome '44*, p. 153.

54. Incident and quote from ibid., p. 150.

55. Quoted in Verney, *Anzio: An Unexpected Fury*, p. 142.

Chapter 13. "Deafening, Mad, Screaming Senseless Hatred"

1. From the diary of Captain Nick Mansell. Quoted in Trevelyan, *Rome '44*, p. 160.

2. The 45th Division was a National Guard unit whose troops came from Oklahoma, Colorado, New Mexico, and Arizona. Two of its three infantry regiments originally consisted of large numbers of Cherokee, Seminole, Choctaw, Apache, and Sioux Indians. The division shoulder patch emblem was the Thunderbird, a golden bird with outstretched wings, an Indian symbol representing a sacred bearer of unlimited happiness.

3. Bowditch, *Anzio Beachhead*, p. 65.

4. Warren P. Munsell, Jr., *The Story of a Regiment* (San Angelo, Tex., 1946), p. 54.

5. Fitzgerald, *The Irish Guards in the Second World War,* p. 301.

6. Guy Nelson, *Thunderbird—A History of the 45th Infantry Division* (Oklahoma City, 1970), pp. 58–59.

7. Truscott, *Command Missions,* p. 317; and Sheehan, *Anzio: Epic of Bravery,* p. 110.

8. In World War II the average "tooth-to-tail" ratio was 10 to 1; that is, for every combat soldier an average of ten men supported him logistically and administratively. The Wehrmacht rarely had such luxury and was forced to make do with a far lower ratio, as exemplified at Anzio and Cassino.

9. "Operations of British, Indian and Dominion Forces in Italy," part 1, The Conquest of Southern Italy, Section A—Allied Strategy, chap. 2, p. 31.

10. Blumenson, *Salerno to Cassino,* p. 420.

11. "The Campaign in Italy," chaps. 12–14, "The Fourteenth Army in Action," by Major General Wolf Hauser, microfilm copy in U.S. Air Force Historical Office, Bolling Air Force Base, Washington, D.C.

12. Ibid.

13. Kesselring in Ms. T-1a/K-1.

14. Ibid., and *The Memoirs of Field-Marshal Kesselring,* pp. 195–96.

15. Verney, *Anzio 1944: An Unexpected Fury,* p. 163; and *Fifth Army History,* part 4, chap. 8.

16. Munsell, *The Story of a Regiment,* pp. 54–55.

17. Letter, Brigadier General Felix L. Sparks to the author, March 12, 1990, and 157th Infantry Association newsletter, March 31, 1989.

18. Ibid.

19. *The Fighting Forty-Fifth* (Nashville, 1978), p. 75.

20. Ibid.

21. "The German Operation at Anzio," p. 53; and Truscott, *Command Missions,* p. 319.

22. Bowditch, *Anzio Beachhead,* p. 74.

23. Truscott, *Command Missions,* p. 317.

24. Kesselring in Ms. T-1a/K-1; and von Mackensen in "The Campaign in Italy," chap. 12–14, "The Fourteenth Army in Action," by Major General Wolf Hauser. The official designation of this unit was the 309th Panzer Grenadier Regiment.

25. Bowditch, *Anzio Beachhead,* pp. 74–75. Although the Germans had driven a slight wedge into the British front along the Moletta River, its diversionary nature soon became obvious when no further attacks were aimed at exploiting the breach. In 1947, Major General Wolf Hauser, the Fourteenth Army chief of staff, stated that they were unaware of the successes of the 4th Parachute Division on February 16. It is doubtful it would have changed the outcome, for it was far too late to have switched the necessary forces to exploit fully these surprising gains (see "The Fourteenth Army in Action").

26. As of January 1, 1944, XII Air Support Command, a USAAF unit commanded by Brigadier General Gordon P. Saville, and composed of both American and RAF units, had nearly eight hundred aircraft assigned, most

of which were fighters and fighter-bombers (see Molony, *The Mediterra-nean and Middle East*, vol. 5, appendix 4 and p. 746).

27. Verney, *Anzio 1944: An Unexpected Fury*, p. 164.

28. Trevelyan, *Rome '44*, p. 161.

29. "The German Operation at Anzio," p. 55. Even without the benefit of the 715th Division's statistics, German losses on the first day of Fischfang were at least two thousand men.

30. Molony, *The Mediterranean and Middle East*, vol. 5, p. 746.

31. *Fifth Army History*, part 4, chap. 8, p. 134. In terms of the total numbers of bombers employed and weight of ordnance dropped, Allied direct-support air operations on February 17 were the largest ever undertaken. From January 22 through February 15 the Allied air forces flew 27,204 sorties and dropped 13,035 tons of bombs in direct support of military operations at Anzio. Three hundred twenty-six Luftwaffe aircraft were destroyed at the high cost of 96 Allied bombers and 133 fighters. This represented an enormous commitment by Eaker's Mediterranean Allied Air Forces. During this period 54 percent of the sorties and 52 percent of the bombs expended were in support of Anzio. Likewise, 62 percent of the bomber losses and 61 percent of the fighter losses were over Anzio. Nearly 70 percent of the Luftwaffe losses in Italy (326 of 468) occurred at Anzio (see MAAF document, "Air Force Participation in Operation 'Shingle,'" PRO [AIR 8/1217]). During Fischfang the USAAF official history records that thirteen Allied and forty-one Luftwaffe aircraft were lost. Allied air-craft flew from seven to eight times as many sorties over the battlefield as the 150–85 flown by the Luftwaffe during these critical days. This is all the more remarkable because the heavy German attacks had rendered the Nettuno airfield unusable, necessitating that all Allied fighter support ema-nate from airbases in the vicinity of Naples (see Craven and Cate, *Europe: Argument to V-E Day*, pp. 356–57).

32. Nelson, *Thunderbird*, p. 60.

33. Both the 45th Division history and the official U.S. Army monograph (Bow-ditch, *Anzio Beachhead*) incorrectly state that three tanks were supporting Company E, but as the company commander, Captain Sparks, relates: "I was informed [the afternoon of February 16] by regiment that a platoon of tanks would be attached to me that night . . . to my dismay the platoon turned out to be only *two* tanks. The lieutenant told me that his other two tanks had broken down" (letter, Sparks to the author, February 24, 1990).

34. Ibid.

35. Account compiled from Sheehan, *Anzio: Epic of Bravery*, chap. 7, passim; and *The Fighting Forty-Fifth*, p. 10.

36. In a letter to his wife three days later, Penney observed that, "My face is not very attractive at the moment nor my hair" (letter of February 20, 1944, Penney Papers).

37. Major James H. Cook, Jr., "The Operations of Company I, 179th Infantry (45th Infantry Division) in the Vicinity of the Factory, Anzio Beachhead, from 16–18 February 1944: The Personal Experience of a Company Com-mander," monograph, Fort Benning, Ga., 1950. Copy furnished by USAMHI Library.

38. Munsell, *The Story of a Regiment*, p. 55.

39. "The German Operation at Anzio," p. 57. Among the factors that affected the German infantry was the large numbers of white phosphorous shells and high-explosive shells that seemed to rain from the sky with an endless ferocity. Under these terrible conditions few had reason to believe they would survive the counteroffensive.

40. Quoted in Cheetham, *Ubique*, p. 103.

41. Verney, *Anzio 1944: An Unexpected Fury*, p. 167.

42. Ibid. These figures are incomplete and do not include the 29th Panzer Grenadier Division, which was still in Army reserve awaiting the final offensive.

43. Molony, *The Mediterranean and Middle East*, vol. 5, p. 747, and "The German Operation at Anzio," p. 57. Allied losses have been poorly documented except for the 571 new prisoners, 326 of whom were British.

44. Major General Hauser, quoted in "The Fourteenth Army in Action."

45. Martin Blumenson, *Salerno to Cassino*, op. cit., p. 422.

46. Quoted in Verney, *Anzio 1944: An Unexpected Fury*, p. 166. Templer later commanded the British 6th Armoured Division, which Shelford Bidwell, the brigade major, Royal Artillery, describes as tired and bored. When Templer took command the division was near Florence and being looked down on by the enemy from the commanding heights of Vallombrosa. As Bidwell recalls, the division organization included an infantry brigade of Guards, three battalions of the Rifle Brigade, Lancers, the Derbyshire Yeomanry, and other famed regiments, in all "a pretty posh affair. . . . All the commanders were pretty laid back, had been to the best schools . . . the division had had a very good war but it did not, as it were, like being told off, especially by some outsider like Gerald Templer. G.T. was also a 'gentleman' but he was also a warrior who wouldn't stand for any la-di-da stuff from the Guards or anyone else . . . [and] he proceeded to make himself unpopular with the infantry by rising at first light and going for a stroll around the front line as reported at last light the previous evening. On one occasion he woke up a discomfited battalion commander and told him that his forward troops were at least 500 yards short of the reported line."

At the morning and evening staff meetings (known as "morning prayers" and "evening prayers"), a brigade commander protested Templer's order to keep pressure on the Germans, saying his "chaps" were tired and that it was time for one of the other brigades which was fresh to assume this responsibility. Bidwell was in the back of the room with other junior staff officers and notes that Templer was shocked by what this brigadier believed to be a perfectly normal exchange of views between "gentlemen." Templer's eyes flashed and his face hardened. "I don't care if I run your brigade into the ground! What I want is one brigade up to strength and fresh for when I begin a serious offensive operation. Sit down!"

On another occasion, when asked by Templer what German forces were astride the nearby ridge and receiving no suitable reply from his G-2, the commander of the reconnaissance regiment "very unwisely began to explain to this infantryman that an armoured recce regiment was not ideally suited for the exploitation of steep, well-wooded hillsides, in terms suitable for the understanding of a 2nd lieutenant. Templer: 'Is that so? Well, Colonel so-and-so [no Christian names for G.T. on formal occasions], get your men out of their tanks, and let me have a report on the location and strength of the enemy positions this evening.' "

Templer endeared himself to the junior officers by his habit of appearing unannounced in places most commanding generals were loath to visit. Shortly after his arrival at 6th Armoured Division Major Bidwell was in the artillery operations van when Templer suddenly appeared and introduced himself as the new division commander. Asking to meet Bidwell's men, he said to a Royal Signals corporal, "I bet you do all the work here." As he left, Templer turned to Bidwell and said, "Now, if you have any problems, just come and see me. Don't ask permission, just come and knock on the door of my caravan." An impressed Bidwell later recalled he hadn't ever spoken to the previous division commander (letter, Brigadier Shelford Bidwell to the author, February 5, 1990).

47. Harmon, *Combat Commander,* p. 170.
48. Verney, *Anzio 1944: An Unexpected Fury,* p. 168.
49. Ibid.
50. The 131 casualties of the 1st Loyals had all been replaced and the battalion was in excellent shape with 31 officers and 747 men assigned. Moreover, as Peter Verney points out, "their original team of officers and non-commissioned officers . . . tough Lancashire men, was still intact. The 1st Loyals was a hardened, experienced and supremely self-confident battalion" (*Anzio 1944: An Unexpected Fury,* pp. 169–70).
51. Named for the old industrial city of Wigan, Lancashire, from which many men of the regiment came.
52. *History of the First Division,* p. 82.
53. Verney, *Anzio 1944: An Unexpected Fury,* p. 174.
54. Quoted in Nicolson, *The Grenadier Guards in the War of 1939–1945,* vol. 2, pp. 412–3.
55. Trevelyan, *Rome '44,* p. 164.
56. *Fifth Army History,* part 4, chap. 8, p. 138.
57. Bowditch, *Anzio Beachhead,* p. 80.
58. Quoted in *The Fighting Forty-Fifth,* p. 78. See also Munsell, *The Story of a Regiment,* p. 55. According to another account Lieutenant Sherrick continued to adjust fire and managed to kill two Germans and wound another before being struck in the head by a bullet from a machine pistol. He was captured, left for dead when the fires he had called for arrived, and then recaptured when the Germans returned (see Bowditch, *Anzio Beachhead,* p. 72).
59. Munsell, *The Story of a Regiment,* p. 56.
60. Clark diary, February 18, 1944.
61. Cook, "The Operations of Company I."
62. *Fifth Army History,* part 4, chap. 8, p. 138.
63. Like all units on the cutting edge of the German attacks, the 180th Regiment had taken heavy losses, but as it proved on February 18, it remained a very tough nut for the Germans to crack. The commander of Company F later wrote: "The men were cold, wet and completely fatigued. They had not rested for eight days and nights. They had been under constant artillery, mortar and air bombardment. They had been attacked steadily for three days by enemy forces amounting to a battalion reinforced by tanks

and supported by worlds of artillery. They had forward exposed positions under constant observation of the Germans. Daylight movement invited instant death. . . . One hundred enlisted men and two officers had been killed, captured or wounded. Despite this, esprit de corps and morale remained high" (see Major Robert A. Guenthner, "The Operations of Company 'F,' 180th Infantry, Six Days Previous to and During the Major German Offensive, 16–20 February 1944 on the Anzio Beachhead," monograph, Fort Benning, Ga., 1949. Copy furnished by USAMHI Library).

64. "The German Operation at Anzio," p. 60.
65. "The Campaign in Italy," chaps. 12–14, "The Fourteenth Army in Action," by Major General Wolf Hauser.
66. Letters, Felix E. Sparks to the author, March 12 and 24, 1990. According to the *Fifth Army History*, part 4, chap. 8, p. 133, four of the twenty-eight survivors were from the machine-gun platoon, Company H, 2d Battalion, 157th Regiment. The 45th Division history and the official U.S. Army monograph (Bowditch, *Anzio Beachhead*) incorrectly reflect the withdrawal of Company E on the morning of February 17.
67. Ibid., letter of February 24, 1990.
68. *History of the First Division*, p. 84.
69. Ibid., p. 85, and Trevelyan, *Rome '44*, p. 167.
70. Lucas, "From Algiers to Anzio," pp. 389–90.
71. Harmon and MacKaye, "Our Bitter Days at Anzio," part 1.
72. Ibid.
73. Bowditch, *Anzio Beachhead*, p. 86.
74. *Fifth Army History*, part 4, chap. 8, p. 144. The German tanks never became a factor in the battles of February 16–20. They remained roadbound and lucrative targets for Allied air and artillery. Many were destroyed by the simple expedient of knocking out the first and last tanks, which left the remainder trapped.
75. Two hundred thirteen were captured in the Loyals sector and 200 by Force H. Harmon's claim in *Combat Commander* and "Our Bitter Days at Anzio" that "we took 1,700 prisoners" is wildly inaccurate (Bowditch, *Anzio Beachhead*, p. 86; and Howe, *The Battle History of the 1st Armored Division*, p. 299). The artillery statistic is from "The German Operation at Anzio," p. 61. Some of the German dead were cut down by their own troops as they tried to surrender.
76. *The Fighting Forty-Fifth*, p. 81.
77. "The German Operation at Anzio," p. 63.
78. Bowditch, *Anzio Beachhead*, p. 87.
79. *The Fighting Forty-Fifth*, p. 81. The total estimate of Germans buried in mass graves near Carroceto is over 1,500. The exact figures will never be known. A German veteran of Anzio wrote to Harmon after the war to challenge the claim that bulldozers were used to bury their dead. "Our army never had bulldozers, not even captured ones and dead were never piled up like wood" (Alexander Freiherr von Ungelter to Harmon, October 22, 1948, Harmon Papers, Norwich University Library).
80. *Fifth Army History*, part 4, chap. 8, p. 146. Losses to the 1st Loyals were 27 killed, 74 wounded, and 102 missing.
81. Munsell, *The Story of a Regiment*, p. 58. "These dread figures would have

been even higher but for the tireless efforts of stretcher bearers, aid men, field surgeons . . . and the beachhead's field hospital staffs . . . [who] saved hundreds from death, hundreds more from being permanently crippled."

82. Blumenson, *Salerno to Cassino*, p. 424. These losses compared with 13,129 during the 120 days of combat in Sicily, Salerno, and the advance to the Gustav Line. Thus, in less than two weeks of combat at Anzio the 45th Division suffered 43 percent of its entire losses during the previous four months of combat.

83. Ibid.

84. Harmon and MacKaye, "Our Bitter Days at Anzio," part 1.

Chapter 14. A House Divided

1. Von Senger's comment on hearing Allied bombs destroy the Abbey is quoted in Hapgood and Richardson, *Monte Cassino*, p. 203.

2. Quotes in memo by Lord Burnham, "Press Treatment of Situation at Bridgehead," n.d., in the Churchill Papers, PRO (PREM 3, 248/5). Only the venerable *Times* declined to publish the pessimistic reports, stating in a leader: "Though no serious danger can be said to exist, the situation remains uncomfortable so long as the beach-head force is exposed to the fire of artillery installed upon the commanding ground of the Alban Hills."

3. Ibid. The Canadian government later claimed that King was referring to future operations in Northwest Europe, not to Anzio.

4. Lucas, "From Algiers to Anzio," pp. 378–79.

5. Minutes of Parliament, February 22, 1944, Official Report: Vol. 397, No. 34, in PRO (PREM 3, 248/5).

6. Minute, Grigg to Churchill, February 17, 1944, PRO (PREM 3, 248/5).

7. Clark diary, January 26, 1944. Several days earlier Clark had complained to Alexander that he was being deluged with official visitors. "Every place I go, I find my subordinate commanders, mostly corps, are being bothered by 'brass hats' from AFHQ, Air, Hq. ACMF (15th Army Group), Navy, etc. There being no other battle in the Mediterranean area, all headquarters, including General Wilson's, Admiral Cunningham's, General Eaker's, General Devers', General Alexander's and many lesser lights have moved into Caserta on top of my headquarters" (Clark diary, January 22, 1944).

8. Ibid.

9. Admiral Sir John Cunningham to Admiral Sir Andrew Cunningham, January 27, 1944, Papers of Admiral of the Fleet Viscount Cunningham of Hyndhope ("ABC"), Department of Manuscripts, British Library.

10. Quoted in Gilbert, *Road to Victory*, pp. 666–67.

11. Cunningham's reference was to the Gallipoli Campaign of 1915, where an unopposed British amphibious force was landed north of the main force, at Sulva Bay. To everyone's surprise instead of advancing, this force stopped and dug in, thus providing the Turks with two crucial days in which to react (Cunningham to "ABC," February 11, 1944).

12. Clark diary, February 16, 1944. One restriction the Army refused to accept was the ban on shipping ammunition on roll-on, roll-off vehicles, which were driven fully loaded with ammunition onto LSTs and at Anzio driven directly to ammunition dumps. Why this was more dangerous than loading and unloading ammunition into and off an LST was never made clear.

13. Blumenson, *Mark Clark*, p. 194.

14. Clark diary, February 16, 1944.
15. S. W. Roskill, *The War at Sea*, vol. 3, *The Offensive*, part 1 (London, 1960), p. 304.
16. The squadron consisted of six British and U.S. cruisers, and a dozen destroyers, which were joined in February by a French cruiser and an A.A. ship. Two cruisers and two destroyers were always on station off Anzio, while the remainder were anchored in the Bay of Naples and available to respond on short notice (ibid., p. 319).
17. Roskill, *The War at Sea*, p. 319.
18. Ibid. A letter from Admiral John Cunningham to Wilson on February 20 cited the tonnage per day between January 22 and February 20 as 3,365 ("Maintenance of the Anzio Bridgehead," PRO [ADM 199/873]).
19. Ibid.
20. Admiral Sir John Cunningham to Admiral Sir Andrew Cunningham, February 11, 1944 ("ABC" Cunningham Papers, British Library).
21. Various cables in PRO (WO 248/4 and PREM 3 series). The figures were somewhat misleading because as many as four thousand vehicles were used to carry cargo to Anzio in accordance with the roll-on, roll-off concept, and were empty and awaiting backloading to Naples.
22. Clark interview with Colonel Forrest S. Rittgers, October 27, 1972, USAMHI.
23. Clark, *Calculated Risk*, p. 273.
24. Clark diary, February 4, 1944.
25. Clark, *Calculated Risk*, p. 274.
26. Graham and Bidwell, *Tug of War*, p. 166.
27. Fred Majdalany, *The Battle of Cassino* (London, 1975), p. 99. The U.S. edition is titled *Cassino, Portrait of a Battle*. Majdalany commanded a British rifle company that fought at Cassino. The condition of the few survivors of Point 593 was so desperate that when they were relieved by the 4th Indian Division, they were so numb with cold and fatigue they had to be taken out by stretchers.
28. Graham and Bidwell, *Tug of War*, p. 179.
29. Full accounts of the battles for Monte Cassino and the destruction of the abbey are in Hapgood and Richardson, *Monte Cassino;* Graham and Bidwell, *Tug of War;* Majdalany, *The Battle of Cassino;* John Ellis, *Cassino: The Hollow Victory* (New York, 1984); and Blumenson, *Salerno to Cassino*. Clark's version is in his memoirs, *Calculated Risk*.
30. The others were sackings in about 580 by the Lombards and in 883 by the Saracens, and in 1349, when an earthquake destroyed the monastery.
31. Quoted in Hapgood and Richardson, *Monte Cassino*, p. 203.
32. Quoted in Parton, *"Air Force Spoken Here,"* p. 364. As Eaker's deputy, Air Marshal (later Marshal of the Royal Air Force) Sir John Slessor, has written: "All the argument about whether or not the Germans were actually holding the Abbey itself is completely beside the point, as anyone will confirm who has seen the place . . . the whole Cassino feature was one great strong point guarding the entrance to the Liri valley and Highway 6 to Rome." Moreover, as Slessor points out, no Allied soldier obliged to fight for the Cassino heights would have believed for a single moment that the Abbey was not being used in some fashion to aid the German defense that was killing his comrades in ever growing numbers (see Sir John Slessor, *The Central Blue* [London, 1956], pp. 577–78).

33. Clark, *Calculated Risk,* p. 285.
34. Parton, *"Air Force Spoken Here,"* p. 364.
35. The details of this unfortunate episode are in Graham and Bidwell, *Tug of War,* chap. 12; and Ellis, *Cassino: The Hollow Victory,* chap. 9.
36. Hapgood and Richardson, *Monte Cassino,* p. 212.
37. Ellis, *Cassino: The Hollow Victory,* pp. 193–95.
38. Quoted in ibid., p. 222.
39. Quotes by German survivors in ibid., chap. 11, passim.
40. Quoted in "Report No. 20, Historical Section, Ottawa, 19 July 1948."
41. Quoted in Bryant, *Triumph in the West,* p. 141.
42. Majdalany, *The Battle of Cassino,* p. 104.

Chapter 15. The Changing of the Guard

1. Churchill to Alexander, February 1, 1944, PRO (PREM 3, 248/4).
2. Alanbrooke diary, January 28, 1944, Alanbrooke Papers.
3. Minutes of Cabinet meeting, February 7, 1944, by Stanley M. Bruce (Viscount Bruce of Melbourne), Monthly War Files, 1939–1945, Australian National Archives. Bruce seems to have been one of the few in London who recognized that as a result of a thrust toward Rome "we might have walked into a somewhat unpleasant reverse."
4. Ibid., February 28, 1944.
5. Ibid.
6. Quoted in Gilbert, *Road to Victory,* p. 679.
7. Churchill to Field Marshal Sir John Dill, February 8, 1944, George C. Marshall Papers, box 61, folder 5, Marshall Library, Lexington, Va.
8. Alexander to Churchill, February 11, 1944, Alexander Papers, PRO (WO 214/14).
9. Alexander to Brooke, February 15, 1944, PRO (PREM 3, 248/4).
10. Diary of Captain Harry C. Butcher, February 17, 1944, Eisenhower Papers. Brooke, of course, agreed with Alexander that Lucas was to blame for the growing stalemate. "I did not feel that Lucas could be much of a thruster" (Brooke, "Notes on My Life," Alanbrooke Papers, King's College, London). Eisenhower made it clear he considered that Churchill was "almost exclusively responsible for the decision to do the end run. . . . True, plans had been made by the staff, as had others, but on this particular project Ike had been conservative" (Butcher diary, February 22, 1944).
11. Quoted in Blumenson, *The Patton Papers,* vol. 2, pp. 415–16.
12. Admiral Sir John Cunningham to Admiral Sir Andrew Cunningham, February 11, 1944, the Papers of Admiral of the Fleet Viscount Cunningham of Hyndhope, Department of Manuscripts, the British Library. The exception may have been Devers. Patton and Devers despised one another. Even so, Eisenhower proposed to Marshall on January 18 that Patton remain in the Mediterranean to plan and command the Anvil invasion of southern France. Lieutenant General Courtney Hodges would command the U.S. Third Army instead of Patton. Noting his impression that Patton and Devers were "not, repeat, not congenial," Eisenhower nevertheless believed that "both of them are sufficiently good soldiers that possible personal antagonism should not repeat not interfere with either one doing

his full duty as a soldier" (Eisenhower to Marshall, "eyes-only" cable, copy in Butcher diary, p. 991).

13. Alexander interview, part 2.

14. Ibid. In a postwar interview, General Lyman L. Lemnitzer, Alexander's deputy chief of staff, told the official historians he believed the principal reason for Lucas's relief was that he "was not equal to the physical strain of the critical Anzio situation. . . . Alexander on visits to Anzio sensed that General Lucas, harried looking and under tremendous strain, would not be able to stand up physically to the hard, long struggle . . . and was visibly affected, physically, by what had already taken place. . . . Alexander was impressed with the vigor and the good physical condition of General Truscott" (interview of January 16, 1948, USAMHI). While Lucas's fatigue was clearly a factor in Alexander's mind, his postwar interview made it clear that his dissatisfaction with Lucas ran far deeper.

Clark's version, recorded in his diary, is that Alexander "told me that Lucas was older than his age, he was old physically and mentally, was tired, had no flash and was not at all familiar with the details of the situation. I had found Lucas, on my many trips there, unfamiliar with many details, and I had urged him to send out members of his staff and to go out himself and satisfy himself with conditions as they were.

"Alexander had to admit to me that most of his information came from General Penny [sic]. . . . I told Alexander that as long as we were discussing personalities and being perfectly frank, that my trip up there a few days ago had revealed from Lucas, Truscott, Harmon and Eagles that none of them had any confidence in Penny. This shocked Alexander, and he replied that he had confidence in him, to which I replied, 'Naturally, for you appointed him.' I told him I was making no request for Penny's relief but that I did believe that a change in Lucas would be advisable, but under no circumstances would I hurt Lucas, for he had performed well as Commanding General of the VI Corps from Salerno north and in the initial landing at Anzio" (Clark diary, February 16, 1944).

15. Clark, *Calculated Risk,* p. 280.

16. Clark diary, February 16, 1944.

17. Clark interviews with Dr. Sidney T. Mathews, parts 4 and 5, May 1948.

18. Truscott, *Command Missions,* pp. 320, 329.

19. Alanbrooke diary, February 16, 1944; and "Notes on My Life," same date, Alanbrooke Papers.

20. During the height of the German counteroffensive Clark saw for himself that "Lucas is tired—very tired—but I did not take him out because it was in the middle of a battle and although Truscott had reported the night before he was not sufficiently into the western sector picture to take over. It would have been a great mistake, in my opinion, to have made the change in the middle of this particular fight" (Clark diary, February 18, 1944).

21. Lucas diary, February 17, 1944.

22. Clark diary, February 18, 1944.

23. Lucas, "From Algiers to Anzio," p. 394.

24. Ibid., p. 396.

25. Quoted in Nicolson, *Alex,* p. 275. Templer had warned Alexander: "We'll

lose the beachhead unless Lucas goes." At best, the British thought Lucas an oddity. Before the invasion the Irish Guards were visited by their new corps commander. "They saw a pleasant, mild elderly gentleman being helped out of layers of overcoats. The Corps Commander remarked that they were big men . . . [who were] 'mighty fine,' drank a cup of tea and drove away, leaving the Battalion slightly puzzled" (Fitzgerald, *A History of the Irish Guards in the Second World War*, p. 201).

26. Colonel Lucian K. Truscott III, in the preface to Lucian K. Truscott, Jr., *The Twilight of the U.S. Cavalry: Life in the Old Army, 1917–1942* (Lawrence, Kans., 1989), p. xiv. This book, which Truscott wrote in the later years of his life, is a superb memoir of life in the United States Army during the interwar period.

27. Ibid., p. xv.

28. *Command Missions*, pp. 175–76.

29. Will Lang, "Lucian King Truscott, Jr.," *Life*, October 2, 1944. The "Truscott Trot" required five miles the first hour, four miles per hour during the ensuing two hours, and three and a half miles per hour for all other distances up to a maximum of thirty miles.

30. Ibid.

31. The distance from Agrigento to Palermo is more than one hundred miles across some of the most treacherous terrain on earth. The 3d Division infantrymen accomplished this incredible feat in three days. One general observed: "What Truscott did in Sicily was to turn his infantry into cavalry."

32. Lang, "Lucian King Truscott, Jr." The boots were not always lucky. On January 24 a small German shell exploded near his left foot, and the boots failed to keep him from getting several shell fragments in his leg which necessitated a trip to the hospital to have them removed. As his aide recalls, "I remember it well because if I had not just turned back for a forgotten map in the war room the shell would have landed squarely on me" (letter from James M. Wilson, Jr., to the author, February 4, 1990). Lieutenant Colonel Wilson served for two years as Truscott's aide, from shortly before the Anzio landings until early 1946.

33. Robert W. White, *New York Herald Tribune*, September 16, 1965.

34. Lang, "Lucian King Truscott, Jr."

35. One of Truscott's cooks, Lee, had obtained a doll and had it in his hand one morning while standing in the garden outside the kitchen of Truscott's quarters in Nettuno. A German shell exploded nearby and a jagged fragment cleanly severed the head of the doll without scratching him. Lee's interest in Italian dolls ended with this incident (Truscott, *Command Missions*, p. 334).

36. Letter from James M. Wilson, Jr., to the author, March 27, 1989.

37. Truscott, *Command Missions*, p. 320.

38. "Iron Mike" O'Daniel first joined the Army in 1913 and served with Pershing during the punitive expedition against Pancho Villa in Mexico. A no-nonsense infantryman, O'Daniel bore a deep scar in his cheek from a German machine-gun bullet in World War I in 1917. He had fought on for twelve hours despite his serious wound. The following year as a lieutenant at St. Mihiel his bravery earned the young officer the Distinguished Service

Cross. As blunt and profane as Harmon, O'Daniel once replied to Alexander, who had asked if it was true that the 3d Division had not given an inch in a battle, "Not a ——— inch." General Paul D. Adams, then a lieutenant colonel, recalls an incident that occurred in the hills overlooking Salerno, which was related to him by a tank company commander. "I saw him on the mountain when things were bad. We had some tankers up there that had pulled back behind the crest. I saw 'Old Iron Mike' go up to one tank commander and heard him say this with his pistol in his hand, 'Listen, you get that tank back up there and get it in action or I'm going to shoot you. Now, you take your choice.' This fellow went back up and he [O'Daniel] went from tank to tank and ran them back up on that hill and helped save the day right there. . . . If it hadn't been for 'Old Iron Mike' we wouldn't have stayed there." The place was later called "Iron Mike's Mountain" (oral history interview of Gen. Paul D. Adams, USAMHI).

One 3d Division veteran has said of him: "If there was anyone who gave the Third Division its pride, its sense of identity, its personality, it was this short man with the huge scar on his cheek. He looked ferocious and could be ferocious, yet every man in the Division was proud of him. . . . He exemplified toughness and determination" (John H. Toole, *Battle Diary* [Missoula, Mont., 1978], p. xxvi).

An exacting taskmaster who believed performance was more important than form, O'Daniel had no mercy for those who failed to measure up to his exacting standards. He once told his officers that officers "are *never* tired. Any indication by an officer that he is tired is epidemic with the men he commands. Therefore that word is taboo." O'Daniel favored the carrying out of death sentences for desertion in the face of the enemy. When his paratrooper son was killed later that year in Holland he said, "The God of War is not choosy and such things have to be expected as hard to take as they sometimes are." During the fighting in France in the autumn of 1944 he told the men of the 3d Division that "the war will be won when *we*, by our actions, defeat the German Army. Let's have no more Anzios." When Truscott left the 3d Division under the command of "Iron Mike" O'Daniel, he left it in very capable hands.

39. Truscott, *Command Missions*, p. 320.
40. Ibid.
41. Although Keiser was apparently given the option of remaining on the corps staff in some diminished capacity, he was not wanted and elected to leave. Truscott did retain three key members of the Corps staff: the G-2, Colonel Joseph L. Langevin; the G-3, Colonel William B. Hill, and the G-4, Colonel Edward J. O'Neill, all of whom performed well under their new commander (see Truscott diary, February 25, 1944, Truscott Papers, Marshall Library; the diary was kept by Wilson and recorded the major events and actions taken each day by Truscott).
42. Ibid., p. 333. Truscott's living quarters were also above ground in a nearby house that was hit numerous times by German shells but never destroyed.
43. Wilson letter, March 27, 1989.
44. Ibid.
45. Ibid.
46. Letter from General Sir Charles Richardson to the author, August 5, 1988.

47. Wilson letter, March 27, 1989. Truscott was a student at the U.S. Army Command & General Staff College from 1934 to 36 and, after graduation, an instructor until 1940.
48. Vaughan-Thomas, *Anzio*, p. 190.
49. Pat Frank, *Philadelphia Record*, October 7, 1945, copy in Truscott Papers, box 22, folder 3, Marshall Library.
50. Churchill to Smuts, February 27, 1944, No. T. 413/4, PRO (PREM 3, 248/7). There are several versions of this quote, the major variation of which was coined by Churchill himself and omitted the reference to Sulva Bay during the Gallipoli campaign, the failure of which was blamed on Churchill. Brooke's diary records the prime minister telling the chiefs of staff at a meeting on February 29, 1944, that: "We hoped to land a wild cat that would tear the bowels of the Boche. Instead we have stranded a vast whale with its tail flopping around in the water!" (quoted in the Alanbrooke diary and in Bryant, *Triumph in the West*, p. 160).
51. Ibid.
52. David Dilks, ed., *The Diaries of Sir Alexander Cadogan, 1938–1945* (London, 1971), p. 601.
53. "Anzio," a short account written in 1985 by General Sparks for the 157th Infantry Association newsletter.

Chapter 16. The Ordeal of the Caves

1. *History of the 157th Regiment* (Baton Rouge, La., 1946), p. 66.
2. Ibid., p. 69.
3. The three battalions of the Queen's Royal Regiment (West Surrey) were Territorial units formed in 1939. Under the British regimental system, the Queen's Royal Regiment was originally "the Queen's (Second) Royal Regiment of Foot." During the two world wars there were a number of rifle battalions within the regiment. Many were deactivated after World War I, but with the advent of World War II it was necessary to greatly expand the Territorial Army. Thus the original battalions were split to form other battalions of the same regiment. For example, the 2d/7th was in reality the new 2d Battalion formed from the original 7th Battalion, the Queen's Royal Regiment.
4. Major R. C. G. Foster, *History of the Queen's Royal Regiment*, vol. 3 (Aldershot, 1953), p. 290.
5. *The Fighting Forty-Fifth*, p. 76.
6. *Fifth Army History*, part 4, chap. 8, p. 149. Also quoted in Bowditch, *Anzio Beachhead*, p. 94.
7. R. E. Bullen, *History of the 2/7th Battalion, The Queen's Royal Regiment* (Exeter, 1958), pp. 100–101.
8. Ibid., p. 102. The regimental historian notes that even though authorization was given to eat half of the emergency ration reserve, "those of us who had previously tried this obnoxious mixture tasting like desiccated ammunition boots, sawdust and dried mud preferred to remain hungry—those whose first experience of it this was, were not long in hoping it would be their last."

9. Ibid.
10. *Fifth Army History,* part 4, chap. 8, p. 150.
11. Collectively the figures were 167th Brigade, 35 percent; 168th Brigade, 50 percent; and the 169th (Queen's) Brigade, 45 percent—*not* counting the heavy losses to the 2d/7th Queen's (ibid).
12. Fitzgerald, *A History of the Irish Guards in the Second World War,* p. 335.
13. Ibid.
14. Quoted in ibid., p. 334.
15. Ibid., p. 356.
16. *History of the First Division,* appendix B, p. 172.

Chapter 17. Impasse

1. Molony, *The Mediterranean and Middle East,* vol. 5, p. 752.
2. "The German Operation at Anzio," p. 74.
3. Ibid.; and *Fifth Army History,* part 4, chap. 8, p. 153. The German casualty rate does not include the 362d Infantry Division.
4. "The German Operation at Anzio," p. 77.
5. Quoted in Trevelyan, *Rome '44,* p. 192.
6. Truscott, *Command Missions,* p. 346.
7. "The German Operation at Anzio," for the period January 22 through March 4, 1944. During critical phases of the various German attacks, key units such as the 3d Panzer Grenadier Division and Group Gräser are omitted from the daily casualty reports. The losses during Fischfang originally showed 670 killed, 2,403 wounded, and 210 missing, but these were later amended to a total of 5,389, with no breakdown of killed, wounded, or missing. A reasonable estimate is that German losses for the first six weeks totalled approximately 20,000 or almost exactly those of VI Corps.
8. Trevelyan, *Rome '44,* p. 194.
9. Erskine, *The Scots Guards, 1919–55,* p. 226. Wedderburn was posthumously awarded the Distinguished Service Order (DSO).
10. Masters, *The Story of the 2nd Battalion the Sherwood Foresters,* chap. 7, passim.
11. Ibid., p. 45; and Barclay, *The History of the Sherwood Foresters,* p. 111.
12. Masters, *The Story of the 2nd Battalion the Sherwood Foresters,* p. 46.
13. Ibid., p. 47.
14. *The History of the First Division,* p. 113.
15. Masters, *The Story of the 2nd Battalion the Sherwood Foresters,* p. 50. Even the withdrawal was hellish. "It took four hours before the last man of the company reached the Lateral Road, only half a mile behind, this only being achieved by the stronger men, who were nearly out themselves, helping their weaker comrades over trenches and up muddy slopes" (p. 49).
16. "The German Operation at Anzio," passim.
17. Quoted in Siegfried Westphal, *The German Army in the West* (London, 1951), p. 160, and the German Generals' Collection, Ref. 9/24/117, Liddell Hart Papers.
18. Ibid., p. 161. Westphal left the meeting convinced Hitler fully understood the problems of Army Group C. Only later did he conclude that "the logical

conclusions were not drawn. I had deceived myself if I believed that my report had made a lasting impression." Westphal quote is from the German Generals' Collection, Ref. 9/24/117.

19. Ibid.

20. Irving, *Hitler's War,* pp. 609–10.

21. Quoted in Robert H. Adleman and George Walton, *Rome Fell Today* (Boston, 1968), p. 168.

Chapter 18. "Will I Be All Right, Sir?"

1. Lucas's words on learning of the bombing of the 95th Evacuation Hospital, February 7, 1944.

2. Harmon and MacKaye, "Our Bitter Days at Anzio."

3. Some of the British referred to both guns as "Anzio Archie."

4. Molony, *The Mediterranean and Middle East,* vol. 5, p. 728.

5. Masters, *The Story of the 2nd Battalion the Sherwood Foresters,* p. 47.

6. Quoted in Collie Small, "The Third: Tops in Honors," *Saturday Evening Post,* August 11, 1945, p. 29.

7. Ernie Pyle, *Brave Men* (New York, 1944), p. 252.

8. Verney, *Anzio 1944: An Unexpected Fury,* p. 212.

9. Fitzgerald, *A History of the Irish Guards in the Second World War,* p. 326.

10. Ibid., p. 327.

11. Trevelyan, *The Fortress: A Diary of Anzio and After,* London, 1956 (1985 reprint edition), p. 46.

12. Pyle, *Brave Men,* p. 254.

13. Ernest N. Harmon, "We Break Out at Anzio," *Saturday Evening Post,* September 25, 1948.

14. Verney, *Anzio 1944: An Unexpected Fury,* p. 212; and Harmon, *Combat Commander,* pp. 174–75.

15. Robert H. Adleman and George Walton, *The Devil's Brigade* (New York, 1966), pp. 176–77.

16. Ernest N. Harmon, "Our Bitter Days at Anzio."

17. As one of Donovan's biographers has written, his aim was nothing less than "to bring the Roman resistance under OSS control and then, at a moment suitable to Allied military operations, to capture the Italian capital in the name of the OSS and the Grand Alliance" (Anthony Cave Brown, *Wild Bill Donovan: The Last Hero* [New York, 1982], p. 485).

18. Ibid., p. 490. Peter Tompkins recounts his activities in *A Spy in Rome* (New York, 1962). Tompkins had more than one hundred men who worked eight-hour shifts watching German movements along the twelve main highways in and out of Rome.

19. Ibid.

20. Ibid.

21. Ibid., p. 487. This same individual had previously been sacked by Tompkins as unfit.

22. Rome Clandestine Radio Station to Fifth Army, January 29 and February 1, 1944. Tompkins was obliged to burn the original messages in the spring of 1944 to avoid compromise in the event of capture. Copies of these messages from Fifth Army records were obtained by Tompkins in the U.S.

Army archives then located in Alexandria, Virginia. Copies were furnished the author by Tompkins in 1988.

23. See Bennett, *Ultra and Mediterranean Strategy,* p. 267. Both Ultra and Radio Vittoria provided strong indications of the strengths of the German forces massed along the Albano-Campoleone-Practica di Mare sector and thus of the probable scale of the forthcoming counteroffensive. Tompkins's message of January 29 also included a warning that the Germans had massed two to three hundred antitank guns in the beachhead, and later messages reported the arrivals of troops, tanks, and guns from southern Italy.

24. Although Clark's diary for February 1, 1944, refers only to "certain intelligence I had received the night before on enemy intentions in the Fifth Army Anzio bridgehead," this was a clear reference to Tompkins's message of January 29. Moreover, "last night additional corroborating enemy intelligence indicated strong likelihood of an enemy attack in force against my bridgehead position." Clark also reveals that initially Alexander had "contrary views" and was "greatly disturbed" by Clark's decision to call off the Cisterna offensive. It was not until late on February 1 that Alexander and Harding (who had received the same intelligence) came to the conclusion that Clark was right and had Harding telephone Clark personally at midnight. The following morning Clark spoke with Alexander. "He was delighted that I had taken the defensive attitude temporarily, and had changed his whole opinion."

25. Blumenson, *Salerno to Cassino,* p. 393n.

26. Pyle, *Brave Men,* p. 256.

27. Ibid., p. 240.

28. Bradley, "Beachhead Bailout at Anzio," *The Retired Officer.* In February the ten-man crew of a disabled B-24 parachuted into the area east of the Mussolini Canal. The pilot and copilot landed in no-man's land, half a mile from a company of the Special Service Force, and it became a race as to which side would reach them first. The Forcemen won and it turned out that the pilot was from Brooklyn and lived two blocks away from one of his rescuers (Robert D. Burhans, *The First Special Service Force* [Washington, 1947] p. 181).

29. Fitzgerald, *A History of the Irish Guards in the Second World War,* p. 326.

30. Captain Donald B. Williams, MC, "Experiences on Anzio Beachhead," unpublished monograph, USAMHI.

31. Nicolson, *The Grenadier Guards in the War of 1939–1945,* vol. 2, p. 413.

32. From "Vignettes from Anzio, 1944," the papers of Lieutenant General William P. Yarborough, Special Collections Division, Mugar Library, Boston University.

33. Extracted from transcript of group of veterans, 2d Battalion the Sherwood Foresters, interviewed for "The World at War," Department of Sound Records, Imperial War Museum, London.

34. Fitzgerald, *A History of the Irish Guards in the Second World War,* p. 339.

35. Munsell, *The Story of a Regiment,* p. 59.

36. Collective comments of a group of Sherwood Forester veterans interviewed for "The World at War," transcript in the Department of Sound Records, Imperial War Museum.

37. Penney to Alexander, March 14, 1944, Penney Papers.
38. Memo, "Absentees and Deserters," HQ, Allied Armies in Italy, May 8, 1944, copy in Penney papers. The 15th Army Group endured a number of changes of title, the latest of which occurred on March 9, 1944, when it became known as the Allied Armies in Italy, or AAI. It is not known whether a penal camp at Anzio was ever set up. Source of AWOL and desertion data is Monograph No. 5, "The Problem of Desertion," April 31, 1946, prepared by the British Historical Section, Central Mediterranean. Copy furnished by Dr. William J. McAndrew, Directorate of History, Ottawa.
39. "Wastage of Manpower," in the papers of the wartime adjutant general, Sir Ronald Adam, Liddell Hart Centre, King's College, London. The desertion total of 1,311 is for the entire Mediterranean, but according to a postwar study, the vast majority took place in Italy. During the same period there were 788 convictions in Italy by field general courts-martial for desertion in Italy.
40. Trevelyan, *Rome '44*, p. 155.
41. Harmon, *Combat Commander*, pp. 177–78.
42. Harmon, "We Break Out at Anzio."
43. Bill Harr, *Combat Boots* (New York, 1952), pp. 87–94. Fortunately there was no photo finish. The camera was found to have been set at the wrong angle.
44. Letter, Dr. C. L. Oglesbee to the author, November 21, 1988. Childers later became a full colonel of infantry.
45. Clark diary, February 23, 1944.
46. Diary of Lieutenant Commander G. H. Dormer, RNVR, Department of Documents, Imperial War Museum. Dormer also records that on May 1 a cheeky German broke in on his radio wavelength and said: "Two young Fascists in Rome were arguing about their grandfathers. 'My grandfather is one hundred', sez one. 'That's nothing,' replies the other. 'My grandfather was born on the day the Allies landed at Nettuno.' "
47. Ibid.
48. Data from the papers of Commander G. B. B. Richey, Department of Documents, Imperial War Museum.
49. Account of the loss of LST 348, in the Papers of Samuel Eliot Morison, U.S. Navy Archives, Washington Navy Yard. The normal crew for an LST was approximately 103 men.
50. Ibid.
51. Letter, Felix E. Sparks to the author, March 12, 1990.
52. Sherwood Forester veterans, loc. cit.
53. Trevelyan, *The Fortress: A Diary of Anzio and After*, p. 54.
54. Ibid., p. 55. One night when the frogs were silent an ammunition party was ambushed and suffered three wounded and one killed. The dead man's corpse was never recovered.
55. Sherwood Forester veterans.
56. Ibid.
57. Trevelyan, *The Fortress: A Diary of Anzio and After*, p. 40.
58. Sheehan, *Anzio: Epic of Bravery*, pp. x, xi, and 167–68.
59. Ibid., chap. 9, passim.

60. Lieutenant Commander Maxwell Hamilton, "The Greatest Fighting General of All Time," *The Retired Officer,* October 1981, pp. 24–25.

61. So loyal and devoted were the men of the First Special Service Force to their commander that on one occasion after Anzio, when Frederick took command of the 45th Infantry Division, a Forceman overheard a GI make a derogatory remark in a public lavatory. "Without bothering to introduce himself, the Forceman punched the speaker in the mouth, sending him headlong into the urinal" (Adleman and Walton, *The Devil's Brigade,* pp. 21 and 191).

62. Ibid.

63. Adleman and Walton, *The Devil's Brigade,* p. 20. Truscott described Frederick as "slight in build, with an almost unhealthy pallor, but rather dignified in appearance. He wore a somewhat inconsequential mustache and this combined with a gentle manner, gave him more the look of a haberdashery clerk than the first-class fighting man he was" (*Command Missions,* p. 548).

64. Ibid. The Force training was set up so that a newly recruited soldier would make his first parachute jump within forty-eight hours and his second jump a day later. As the force historian has written, this early parachute training served to separate "the sheep from the goats" (Burhans, *The First Special Service Force,* p. 21).

65. Ibid., p. 171.

66. Adleman and Walton, *The Devil's Brigade,* chap. 8, passim. The Germans also vastly overrated the strength of the First Special Service Force, believing them to be a full division by the vast frontage they held on the Allied right flank.

67. According to Adleman and Walton, Heilman "became known as one of the most complete foul-ups who ever wangled his way into officer training" at Fort Benning, Georgia (ibid., p. 76).

68. Quoted in Adleman and Walton, *The Devil's Brigade,* p. 164.

69. Ibid., p. 181.

70. Burhans, *The First Special Service Force,* pp. 195–96. Two of the children were named Roberto in honor of Frederick and Lieutenant Colonel Robert S. Moore, the CO of the Second Regiment. The coin of the realm was fresh eggs, and the medic, Major George Evashwick, soon found that his fee of two eggs from the Italians was three less than the chaplain was receiving for his baptismal services. It is not recorded whether or not his fee subsequently rose.

71. Adleman and Walton, *The Devil's Brigade,* op. cit., p. 177.

72. Quoted in Burhans, *The First Special Service Force,* p. 195. It was not uncommon for Forcemen to dig foxholes large enough to accommodate both themselves and a cow!

73. Quoted in Adleman and Walton, *The Devil's Brigade,* p. 177.

74. Burhans, *The First Special Service Force,* pp. 207, 209.

75. Adleman and Walton, *The Devil's Brigade,* p. 171.

76. Burhans, *The First Special Service Force,* p. 185.

77. Ibid., p. 194.

78. Ibid., pp. 303–4. Figures are from the arrival of the Special Service Force at the end of January to approximately mid-May 1944.

79. "With a Casualty Clearing Station at Anzio," *K.S.L.I. & Herefordshire Light Infantry Chronicle*, no. 92, January 1948. This article was written by an anonymous Royal Army Medical Officer who was a surgeon at Anzio in one of the casualty clearing stations, the British equivalent of a U.S. Army M*A*S*H facility. The surgeon, J. A. Ross, later published his memoirs as *Memoirs of an Army Surgeon.* In an article about Anzio in the *British Army Review*, no. 89, August 1988, "Cassino and Anzio: A Sketch of the Battles with some Personal Observations," Major C. W. Deayton-Groom quite rightly describes Ross's memoir as "without equal for unemotional, factual reporting."

80. Ibid.

81. Ibid.

82. Lieutenant Richard Sutton, Royal Artillery, letter of February 8, 1944, Sutton Papers, Department of Documents, Imperial War Museum. By the end of March Sutton's letters were reflecting the bitterness of duty at Anzio. "It makes you realize how much Churchill's little ideas in strategy cost. Don't know why you should think we should come home. That only happens to Divisions whose Generals have the time to write about 'my wonderful troops'—inferring 'a D.S.O. would be appreciated' " (letter of March 30, 1944). And a month later: "These generals have their careers to consider; they don't have to pick up dead bodies or talk to dying people and pretend that they're all right or write to their relatives" (letter of April 20, 1944).

83. *The London Irish at War*, p. 152.

84. Gilbert Allnutt, "A Fusilier Remembers Italy," unpublished manuscript, Allnutt Papers, Department of Documents, Imperial War Museum. Allnutt describes how his battalion relieved the U.S. 36th Engineers on the extreme left flank of the beachhead, in the heart of the gully country. "They told us that two of their buddies were out there—would we bury them if we had the chance? We promised to do so but through no fault of our own, failed to keep the promise."

Chapter 19. Plans and Controversies

1. The Fourteenth Army consisted of I Parachute Corps: 4th Parachute, 65th Infantry, and 3d Panzer Grenadier divisions; and LXXVI Panzer Corps: 362d and 715th Infantry divisions. There were also numerous independent infantry regiments and a hodgepodge of other nondivisional units that included antitank, artillery and rockets, armored, and two battalions of SS Police troops specially trained for guerrilla warfare (Ms. R-50, "The German Situation in Italy," chap. 4: "The Drive on Rome," by Britt Bailey, Center of Military History, U.S. Army. Previously the Fourteenth Army strength had been: assigned, 144,982; fighting strength, 76,873.

2. Ibid.

3. Ibid.; and Martin Blumenson, *Anzio: The Gamble that Failed*, p. 150.

4. XIV Panzer Corps war diary, April 25, 1944, extracted from Report No. 20, Historical Section (G.S.), Army Headquarters, Ottawa, July 19, 1948, USAMHI Library; and Bailey, Ms. R-50.

5. Ibid.

6. War diary, Tenth Army, May 10, 1944, quoted in ibid.

7. Blumenson, *Anzio: The Gamble that Failed,* pp. 148–49. The allocation carried in each of the trucks was ammunition: 60 percent, fuel: 20 percent, and rations: 20 percent.

8. Ibid., p. 152.

9. Alanbrooke diary, March 28, 1944, Alanbrooke Papers.

10. Cadogan quote from Dilks, *The Diaries of Sir Alexander Cadogan, 1938–1945,* p. 613. Churchill telegram quoted in Gilbert, *Road to Victory,* p. 714. The burden of the long war had begun to tell on many key members of the British war establishment. In his diaries, Cadogan refers not only to his own exhaustion after six grueling years, but to others, such as his own chief, Anthony Eden, who was on the verge of a breakdown. Others like Brooke were living on their nerves in the face of pressures and workloads that would have killed ordinary men.

11. Gilbert, *Road to Victory,* p. 739.

12. Bryant, *Triumph in the West,* p. 183.

13. Churchill to Roosevelt, April 24, 1944, in Kimball, *Churchill & Roosevelt: The Complete Correspondence,* vol. 3, p. 111. In his war memoirs, Brooke's director of military operations, Major General Sir John Kennedy, notes that Churchill described the news as "desolating delay" (*The Business of War* [London, 1957], p. 323).

14. Ehrman, *History of the Second World War,* vol. 5, *Grand Strategy,* p. 256. Both the Hitler and Gustav Lines were based on Mt. Cairo Massif and designed to block any Allied movement up the Liri Valley along Highway 6. Of the two, the Hitler Line was far more elaborate and featured permanent concrete works and the 75-mm guns and turrets of Panther tanks emplaced in the ground at key points where they could engage Allied armor. During the months of stalemate at Anzio work had begun on the Caesar Line, but as the final battles unfolded, it would play little part in the battles for Rome ("Operations of British, Indian and Dominion Forces in Italy," September 3, 1943, to May 2, 1945: part 2, "The Campaign in Central Italy," section F, German Strategy, prepared by the British Historical Section, Central Mediterranean, 1946. Copy in USAMHI Library, Carlisle Barracks, Pa.).

15. By contrast, some World War I commanders in France and Flanders believed it was necessary to have a six-to-one edge in infantry before an offensive stood a reasonable chance of success.

16. Alexander defined his goal as one of forcing the Germans to commit "the maximum number of divisions to operations in Italy at the time Overlord is launched" (Molony, *The Mediterranean and Middle East,* vol. 6, part 1, p. 5).

17. Churchill, quoted in ibid., April 12, 1944, p. 257.

18. Marshall, quoted in ibid., April 14, 1944, p. 258.

19. Bryant, *Triumph in the West,* p. 183; and Ehrman, p. 259. In a minute to Roosevelt on April 29, Churchill had made it clear that "I do not consider that the objective of the forthcoming battle in Italy called Diadem is the taking of Rome good though that would be or even the joining of the bridgehead which is indispensable. Its prime purpose is the destruction of the armed forces of the enemy, and if by mid-May we find the enemy

before us in its present strength I have every hope we shall be so closely engaged and entangled with them, we being the superior force, that much of the life may be struck out of this German Army" (Churchill to Roosevelt, No. 668, April 29, 1944, PRO [PREM 3/472]).

20. Ehrman, *History of the Second World War,* vol. 5, *Grand Strategy,* p. 255.
21. Quoted in Molony, *The Mediterranean and Middle East,* vol. 6, part 1, p. 6.
22. Ibid., pp. 36–37.
23. "The Campaign in Italy: The Transport Situation," unpublished manuscript by Colonel Klaus Stange, December 1947. Originally written for the U.S. Army Historical Division, this is one of a series of postwar documents by captured German officers that became known collectively as the U.S. Army Europe, German Report Series. Colonel Stange's account is in Ms. D-049.
24. Alexander interview, part 3. Alexander repeatedly stressed in his postwar interview with the U.S. Army official historians that German expectations governed his decision. Their notes reflect that "the most important factor in his decision to launch the [Cassino] attack first was . . . surprise—the intelligence estimates indicated that the Germans expected the attack to be made first at Anzio rather than on the southern front."
25. Graham and Bidwell, *Tug of War,* chap. 15.
26. Carver, *Harding of Petherton,* p. 126.
27. Ibid., pp. 126–27.
28. Ibid., pp. 127–28. Montgomery taught at the British Army staff college at Camberley from 1926 to early 1929.
29. This was in the form of a cover and deception operation code-named Nunton. This entailed planting information designed to convince the Germans that the main Allied effort in the spring of 1944 would be in the form of another amphibious operation at Civitavecchia and that what appeared to be offensive operations along the Rapido and Garigliano rivers were in reality merely demonstrations designed to draw German attention to this sector. The Allied deception staff of "A" Force (attached to AFHQ) created a fake wireless network that helped plant rumors of another coastal end-run and ran equally phony simulated practice landings in the Naples area (see Ernest F. Fisher, Jr., *Cassino to the Alps* [Washington, 1984], pp. 22–23; and Bennett, *Ultra and Mediterranean Strategy,* p. 273). As Graham and Bidwell write, "all this helped to strengthen Kesselring's conviction that the Allied commanders were too intelligent to continue bashing their heads against the Gustav Line, and that they would try to outflank it by sea" (*Tug of War,* p. 257).
30. No better example exists of the effectiveness of Allied deception activities than the transfer of the 29th Panzer Grenadier Division on March 29 on the orders of Army Group C, in the belief that landings at Civitavecchia sector were "imminent" ("The German Operation at Anzio," p. 90).
31. "The German Operation at Anzio," p. 99.
32. Fisher, *Cassino to the Alps,* pp. 105–6.
33. Carver, *Harding of Petherton,* p. 133.
34. Fisher, *Cassino to the Alps,* pp. 104–5. This statement is based on Clark's comments on the draft manuscript.

35. Ibid., p. 105.

36. Ibid., p. 104.

37. Clark diary, May 5, 1944.

38. Clark interviews with Sidney T. Mathews, May 10–21, 1948; and Alexander interview, part 3.

39. Truscott, *Command Missions*, p. 368.

40. Ibid.

41. Ibid. In *Calculated Risk* (p. 312), Clark implies a more tepid response to Alexander's visit to Truscott. His diary suggests a response bordering on insubordination. The truth is likely somewhere between these two extremes.

42. Sidney T. Mathews, "General Clark's Decision to Drive on Rome," in Kent Roberts Greenfield, ed., *Command Decisions* (Washington, 1959), pp. 274–75.

43. "Notes by General Alexander for Conference Held at HQ AAI on 2 April 1944," "Operations of British, Indian and Dominion Forces in Italy" (September 3, 1943–May 2, 1945), part 2, The Campaign in Central Italy (March 26 to August 10, 1944), Section A, Allied Strategy, USAMHI Library. This document clearly spells out precisely what Alexander intended. "I have called this high level conference," said Alexander, "to settle and fix important points connected with our forthcoming full scale offensive. I propose to start by giving you a broad picture of operations. . . . Phase I, Fifth Army . . . to break out of the Anzio bridgehead and advance on VALMONTONE." Alexander went on to lay out, step by step, the missions of the Fifth and Eighth armies. Part F was "the advance to secure the VALMONTONE area, astride the enemy's L of C to the east." On the day following the conference (April 3), copies of the minutes were forwarded by Harding to each attendee. Harding's letter directed that "a Commander or Staff Officer, who considers that his view has not been correctly represented, will please inform this H.Q. and an amendment will be issued." These minutes do not record any comments or dissent by Clark with respect to Valmontone.

44. Fisher, *Cassino to the Alps*, p. 27.

45. Ibid., p. 37.

46. Ibid., p. 38, and A.A.I. (15th Army Group) Operation Order No. 1, dated May 5, 1944, in *Fifth Army History*, chap. 6, p. 106, and appendix 1, p. 171.

47. Truscott, *Command Missions*, p. 369.

48. Fisher, *Cassino to the Alps*, p. 36.

49. Clark diary, May 6, 1944.

50. Graham and Bidwell, *Tug of War*, pp. 251–52.

51. Ibid., p. 247.

52. Molony, *The Mediterranean and Middle East*, vol. 6, part I, p. 97.

53. Bailey, Ms. R-50.

54. Ibid.

55. Ibid.

56. Quoted in Ellis, *Cassino: The Hollow Victory*, p. 293.

Chapter 20. The Great Allied Offensive

1. Quoted in John Ellis, *Cassino: The Hollow Victory*, p. 292.
2. Molony, *The Mediterranean and Middle East*, vol. 6, part 1, p. 99.
3. Below Sant'Angelo the Rapido flows into the Gari River, which in turn flows into the Liri River and within a short distance becomes the Garigliano River. In some accounts, including the British official history, the Gari is incorrectly depicted. On other maps it is not even shown and is referred to as the Rapido. During Diadem the 4th British Division assaulted the Rapido approximately one thousand yards north of Sant'Angelo, and the 8th Indian Division assaulted north and south of the village.
4. Ellis, *Cassino: The Hollow Victory*, p. 296.
5. Molony, *The Mediterranean and Middle East*, vol. 6, part 1, p. 105. The 2d/4th Hampshires were part of the 28th Infantry Brigade, 4th Division.
6. Ibid., chap. 3, passim.
7. Ibid., p. 128.
8. Ibid., p. 126.
9. Quoted in Report No. 20, Canadian Historical Section, July 19, 1948.
10. Ibid.
11. Graham and Bidwell, *Tug of War*, pp. 300–301. (Among Juin's classmates at St. Cyr was Charles de Gaulle.)
12. The Goumiers, native Moroccan irregulars, were mostly recruited from the fierce Berber tribes of the Atlas Mountains and were generally under the command of French officers and NCOs. The Goumiers relied not on tanks or vehicles, but on mules.
13. Ellis, *Cassino: The Hollow Victory*, chap. 3, passim.
14. Graham and Bidwell, *Tug of War*, p. 301.
15. By May 25 the Poles had suffered 3,779 casualties during their fight to capture the Abbey of Monte Cassino (Molony, *The Mediterranean and Middle East*, vol. 6, part 1, p. 134).
16. Ellis, *Cassino: The Hollow Victory*, p. 389. At first the Germans were not even aware they were battling Canadians. During one engagement a German parachute officer of the 1st Parachute Division came forward under a white flag and, apparently believing he had the upper hand, demanded: "Surrender, you English gentlemen—you are surrounded and will only die." From the cover of a nearby fortification, a voice shouted, "We ain't English. We ain't gentlemen—and be goddamned if we'll surrender" (quoted in Kurzman, *The Race for Rome*, p. 371).
17. Thirty-one artillery battalions and eight separate batteries fired this massive barrage, with guns ranging in size from 75-mm to 8-inch howitzers (Molony, *The Mediterranean and Middle East*, vol. 6, part 1, p. 193n.).
18. Ibid., pp. 206–7.
19. Graham and Bidwell, *Tug of War*, p. 318.
20. For full accounts of the actions and controversy surrounding this aspect of Diadem, the reader may wish to consult Juin's *Mémoires*, vol. 1 (Paris, 1959); Ellis, *Cassino: The Hollow Victory*, chaps. 15 and 16; and the British official history, Molony, *The Mediterranean and Middle East*, vol. 6, part 1, chap. 4. The northern sector of the Hitler Line was the most difficult to crack. The Germans had been given time to emplace Panther tank turrets

into concrete blockhouses, dig bunkers and antitank ditches, and lay mines and barbed wire obstacles (Kurzman, *The Race for Rome*, p. 372).

21. Quoted in Clark diary, May 20, 1944.

22. Ibid. Clark also noted: "He told me that General Leese would not be able to attack [the Hitler Line] until probably the night of the 23/24th [May] and then with one division—the Canadians. He asked me hesitatingly if I could attack and outflank the Germans making it unnecessary for the Eighth Army to attack. He said he desired to conserve losses. I told him to conserve losses in one place we would have them in another; mainly, the Fifth Army sector and that I strongly recommended that Leese speed up his attack. . . . I am convinced that the Eighth Army will hold their attack and let the French carry the ball for them as they have done so far in this battle" (Clark diary, May 20, 1944).

23. Ibid.

24. Graham and Bidwell, *Tug of War*, p. 337.

25. Harmon, *Combat Commander*, p. 187. The 1st Armored Division was equipped with 232 tanks and had 14,260 officers and men assigned. It was one of three armored divisions that were created earlier in the war as "heavy," before the U.S. Army decided to reduce its tank and personnel strength. In addition, the 1st Armored had a tank destroyer battalion and an antiaircraft battalion attached and its three assigned battalions of 105-mm self-propelled howitzers were augmented by the attachment of a fourth battalion. Truscott also attached the 135th Infantry Regiment of the 34th Infantry Division, a chemical battalion equipped with 4.2-inch mortars and several other specialized units that included a mine-clearing company. In all, the 1st Armored constituted a very formidable force (Fisher, *Cassino to the Alps*, pp. 112–13).

26. Truscott, *Command Missions*, p. 367.

27. Harmon, *Combat Commander*, pp. 186–87.

28. Truscott, *Command Missions*, p. 371.

29. Harmon, *Combat Commander*, pp. 184–85.

30. Clark diary, May 26 and 27, 1944. From the autumn of 1943 the British faced the same replacement crisis that was soon to plague their comrades in Normandy. British manpower was nearing its lowest ebb of the war, and with the priority given to Montgomery's 21st Army Group for Overlord, there were insufficient replacements for the Italian theater (see *Decision in Normandy* [New York and London, 1983], chap. 15).

31. Truscott, *Command Missions*, p. 548.

32. Fisher, *Cassino to the Alps*, chap. 6, passim.

33. Quoted in ibid., p. 113.

34. Ibid., p. 121.

35. Ibid., pp. 126–27. Although most were later recovered, their loss weakened CCB sufficiently that Harmon immediately replaced them with a similar number from his reserve.

36. "American Armor at Anzio," monograph prepared in May 1949 at the U.S. Army Armored School, Fort Knox, Ky. (USAMHI Library). Tank losses included those assigned and attached to the 3d Division.

37. "The German Operation at Anzio," pp. 105–7.

38. Quoted in Taggart, *History of the Third Infantry Division in World War*

II, p. 157. Dutko was assigned to Company A, 1st Battalion, 30th Infantry Regiment, which on May 23 was attached to the 3d Battalion.

39. Ibid., p. 170.
40. Later in the summer of 1944 the 362d Division was re-created and fought during the battles for the Gothic Line before its destruction a second time during the final battles fought in Italy (Samuel W. Mitcham, Jr., *Hitler's Legions: The German Army Order of Battle, World War II,* p. 245). A subsequent report by Army Group C to OKW was intercepted by Ultra, which assessed the fighting strength of the 362d Division at 5 percent. (Bennett, *Ultra and Mediterranean Strategy,* p. 286.)
41. Taggart, *History of the Third Infantry Division in World War II,* p. 171.
42. Fisher, *Cassino to the Alps,* p. 153.
43. Sevareid, *Not So Wild a Dream,* p. 401.
44. Howe, *The Battle History of the 1st Armored Division,* p. 326.
45. Task Force Howze consisted of a tank battalion of Shermans plus two additional tank companies from another armored unit, an armored infantry battalion, an infantry battalion attached from the 34th Division and two companies of tank destroyers.
46. Hamilton Howze was the latest in a long line of Army officers who had distinguished themselves by their service to the nation. His father earned a Congressional Medal of Honor fighting Apaches and during World War I commanded the 38th Division, and his grandfather and great-grandfather had been high-ranking officers (Kurzman, *The Race for Rome,* p. 387).
47. General Hamilton H. Howze, "Armor in the Breakout from the Anzio Beachhead," Howze Papers, USAMHI.
48. Ibid.
49. *Fifth Army History,* chap. 6, p. 115.
50. Ibid.
51. Clark, *Calculated Risk,* pp. 325–26.
52. Clark diary, May 25, 1944.
53. Quoted in Adleman and Walton, *Rome Fell Today,* pp. 218–19.
54. Sevareid, *Not So Wild a Dream,* p. 400.
55. *Fifth Army History,* chap. 6, passim.

Chapter 21. The Battle for Valmontone Gap

1. Truscott, *Command Missions,* p. 374. Truscott's diary contains a cursory entry that he had met Clark that morning. However, after the entry had been typed, Truscott appended a handwritten comment that read: "Clark asked if I had thought of possibility of changing my dir. [of] att to NW—had staff working on one—only to be used in case Germans moved HG & Para Div in to Artena Gap" (Truscott diary, May 24, 1944, Truscott Papers, Marshall Library).
2. Fisher, *Cassino to the Alps,* p. 163.
3. Clark diary, May 25, 1944. Clark's presence at Truscott's command post that morning is confirmed by Truscott's diary entry for May 25, 1944. Although Clark's diary refers to Velletri being northwest of the axis of attack of the 34th, 36th, and 45th divisions, it was northeast, and the overall

diary entry makes it clear that this was the intent conveyed by Clark to Truscott. It is assumed that there was an error in transcription by the diarist, who was usually Clark's senior aide, Lieutenant Colonel Arthur Sutherland.

4. Truscott, *Command Missions*, p. 375. In a postwar interview with official historian Sidney T. Mathews on April 5, 1948 (copy in OCMH collection, USAMHI archives, and in the USAMHI Library), Truscott's comments were precisely what later appeared in his 1954 memoirs. Truscott's interview shows far more circumspection than the depth of emotion he displayed in *Command Missions* six years later.

5. Ibid.

6. Mathews, "General Clark's Decision to Drive on Rome," in Greenfield, *Command Decisions*, p. 281.

7. Clark diary, May 25, 1944.

8. Interview with Truscott by Sidney T. Mathews, April 5, 1948, USAMHI Library; and Fisher, *Cassino to the Alps*, p. 163, which refers to correspondence in 1961 and an interview with Truscott in 1962.

9. Sidney T. Mathews, "General Clark's Decision to Drive on Rome," in *Command Decisions*, p. 281. On the basis of Mathews's statement, Robert H. Adleman and George Walton erroneously concluded in *Rome Fell Today* (p. 232) that Truscott was enthusiastic over Clark's decision. Whatever enthusiasm Truscott may have displayed was the result of his belief that a commander has a duty to carry out the orders of his superior even if he believes them to be wrong. His protests to Clark had not been accepted and now the distasteful order must be obeyed. It was for this reason that when he briefed his division commanders the night of May 25, he presented the plan "as if it were his own."

10. Letter, James M. Wilson, Jr., to the author, March 27, 1989.

11. Truscott diary, May 25, 1944. Although Clark's diary contains explicit accounts of virtually everything he did, the entry for May 25 unfortunately provides no clues to the substance of his meeting with Truscott: "At 2030 [hours] General Truscott and his Chief of Staff, Colonel Carleton, came to confer with General Clark, General Brann and Colonel Howard concerning the VI Corps attack tomorrow morning."

12. Wilson letter, March 27, 1989.

13. Clark interview with Mathews, part 4, May 19, 1948.

14. Ibid. The otherwise well-written *Fifth Army History* contains the self-serving statement: "The brilliance and daring of this order, which shifted the axis of [the] main attack, are equalled only by the speed in its execution" (chap. 6, p. 117).

15. Clark, *Calculated Risk*, p. 321.

16. Quoted in Adleman and Walton, *Rome Fell Today*, p. 228.

17. Sevareid, *Not So Wild a Dream*, p. 401.

18. Harold L. Bond, *Return to Cassino* (New York, 1964), pp. 184–85.

19. Quoted in Harpur, *The Impossible Victory*, pp. 121–22.

20. Clark to Gruenther, May 25, 1944, Clark diary.

21. Sidney T. Mathews, "General Clark's Decision to Drive on Rome," in *Command Decisions*, p. 282.

22. Quoted in Trevelyan, *Rome '44*, p. 292. After the war Lieutenant General

Sir Richard McCreery confirmed that Alexander was "livid and it has ran-
kled him ever since" (quoted in Harpur, *Impossible Victory*, p. 77).

23. Alexander interview, part 3.

24. Quoted in Ellis, *Cassino: The Hollow Victory*, p. 451n.

25. Hunt, *A Don at War*, pp. 258–59.

26. Quoted in Nicolson, *Alex*, p. 294.

27. Bailey, Ms. R-50, "The German Situation in Italy," chap. 4, "The Drive on
Rome."

28. Fisher, *Cassino to the Alps*, p. 156

29. Bailey, Ms. R-50, "The German Situation in Italy," chap. 4, "The Drive on
Rome."

30. Kesselring, *The Memoirs of Field Marshal Kesselring*, p. 202.

31. Ibid., pp. 202–3; and "The Campaign in Italy: The Fourteenth Army in
Action at Anzio-Nettuno up to 11 May 1944"; and Fisher, *Cassino to the
Alps*, pp. 189–90. This was the third occasion since he assumed command
of the Fourteenth Army in January when von Mackensen had offered his
resignation to Kesselring. This time it was accepted at once. By the end,
neither commander had any confidence left in the other.

32. Postwar account of Schmalz in Fisher, *Cassino to the Alps*, p. 169.

33. Report No. 20, Historical Section, Ottawa.

34. Ibid. Many of the subordinate German commanders and staff officers in the
Tenth Army were unhappy over what they perceived as Kesselring's unwillingness to e..tricate von Vietinghoff's army before it was too late. One
such example occurred at 2323 the same night, when Wentzell complained
to the LI Mountain Corps chief of staff that "Tenth Army has had a run-in
with the Field Marshal and the High Command."

35. Army Group C Ops. Order No. 5673/44, May 27, 1944, reproduced verba-
tim in Report No 20.

36. Extract from Tenth Army war diary, May 27, 1944, quoted in ibid.

37. Molony, *The Mediterranean and Middle East*, vol. 6, part 1, pp. 239–40.

38. Howze, "Armor in the Breakout from the Anzio Beachhead." Howze was
never able to learn where the artillery fire was coming from. His supporting artillery battalion could not determine the source, and no other unit
would admit responsibility. Near Velletri another unfortunate incident
took place at midafternoon in the 1st Armored Division sector, when Allied
tactical aircraft bombed and strafed friendly troops, prompting this message to VI Corps: "Friendly planes have strafed our troops three times in
the last two hours. Tell the Air Corps to get the hell out of the air, we can
get along better without them. If they don't stop strafing our troops we are
going to shoot hell out of them." According to Howze, the message wasn't
signed but "sounds a bit as though it might have been dictated by General
Harmon." This problem plagued the Allies throughout the war, and every
campaign recorded instances where friendly troops were bombed and
strafed by the Allied air forces. In Sicily, for example, the U.S. 2d Armored
Division was hit so many times by friendly air that one day, despite orders
not to fire on friendly aircraft, a P-38 fighter was shot down after a 2d
Armored column was shot up. The pilot safely baled out and, as the division
history records, "the Air Corps got the message." Both Oliver Leese and

Omar Bradley were nearly killed by friendly air attacks during the Sicily campaign (see *Bitter Victory: The Battle for Sicily, 1943*, p. 465n).

39. Ibid.; and Howe, *The Battle History of the 1st Armored Division*, p. 331. The irony of this unfortunate incident was that the battalion was mauled as it pulled back to the railway line as the result of a nonexistent order. It will never be known if Task Force Howze could have been sufficiently reinforced the night of May 26 or the morning of May 27 to have held Highway 6. What is certain, however, is that the battle for Artena would have been very different without the Hermann Göring Division occupying the railway line the night of May 27–28.

40. "The German Operation at Anzio," pp. 111–12. Among the problems facing the Germans the night of May 26 was a lack of communications with the 715th Division, which had lost all of its signal communications equipment during the battle for Cisterna and subsequent rout in the Velletri gap.

41. Howe, *The Battle History of the 1st Armored Division*, p. 331. It was of small consolation that these misplaced artillery fires may have convinced the Germans to break off their attack.

42. Burhans, *The First Special Service Force*, chap. 8.

43. VI Corps G-3 journal, quoted in Fisher, *Cassino to the Alps*, p. 168.

44. Ibid., p. 227. In the town of Artena it was suicidal to appear on the street. An Italian collaborator was signaling the Germans with a blinker light and provided the Germans with valuable assistance until caught and executed on the spot by members of the Special Service Force.

45. Quoted in Gilbert, *Road to Victory*, p. 784.

46. Churchill to Alexander, May 28, 1944, Alexander Papers, PRO (WO 214/15).

47. Bennett, *Ultra and Mediterranean Strategy*, p. 285.

48. Harold C. Deutsch, "Commanding Generals and the Uses of Intelligence," *Intelligence and National Security*, July 1988, pp. 218–19, reveals that Clark was never a fan of Ultra.

49. Lewin, *Ultra Goes to War*, p. 290. "Y" stood for the interception and breaking of German wireless traffic at the tactical level, in this case, within Army Group C. Examples would be messages between various elements of the Army Group C chain of command.

50. Fisher, *Cassino to the Alps*, p. 177, citing various Fourteenth Army reports and documents.

51. Clark diary, May 27, 1944.

52. Howze account. The *Fifth Army History* again whitewashes Clark's decision by claiming that the "Fifth Army again caught the enemy flatfooted by its swift exploitation of his weaknesses" (chap. 6, p. 118).

53. Ibid., p. 283.

54. Truscott, *Command Missions*, pp. 375–76.

Chapter 22. All Roads Lead to Rome

1. Howe, *The Battle History of the 1st Armored Division*, pp. 332–33. Lieutenant Brown was killed instantly by a German sniper when he stood up in the turret of his Sherman tank. His death was the bitterest moment of the war for Marshall, who had raised him as if he were his own. For a full

description of Lieutenant Brown's death, see *George C. Marshall: Organizer of Victory, 1943–1945*, pp. 344–47.

2. Ibid., p. 333; and *Fifth Army History*, chap. 6.

3. It would not have been necessary for VI Corps to capture Velletri if Buffalo had been carried out as intended. However, once Clark switched to Turtle, its capture became obligatory in order to drive the Germans from the Alban Hills. From an irrelevant objective, Velletri now became one of the few anchors of the German Caesar Line and a detriment to the success of Operation Turtle.

4. Quoted in Fisher, *Cassino to the Alps*, p. 179.

5. Ibid., p. 180. Although he was shortly to be replaced, von Mackensen took comfort in being vindicated by his decision to concentrate his defenses against an attack in a northwesterly direction. What the German commander did not know was that Clark's actions were contrary to the wishes of Alexander and every senior commander in VI Corps.

6. Clark diary, May 30, 1944. To bolster Truscott, Clark ordered the British 1st Division to be attached to VI Corps. "I believe [they] will help, for it seems to have its tail up." Clark never considered the British 5th Division for this role, writing that "to attach the 5th British Division to the VI Corps would be like giving a poor man a dirty shirt. They have no offensive inclinations."

7. Ibid.

8. Ibid.

9. Alexander interview, part 3. Alexander had the highest respect for Robertson and his knowledge of logistics. According to Alexander, if the French crossed Highway 6 there would have been a terrific traffic snarl when the Eighth Army moved closer to a point southeast of Valmontone where the crossings would likely have taken place.

10. Graham and Bidwell, *Tug of War*, p. 340. Von Senger confirms the threat in his war memoirs, *Neither Fear Nor Hope*, p. 249.

11. W. G. F. Jackson, *The Battle for Rome* (New York, 1969), p. 271.

12. Clark interview with Sidney T. Mathews, part 3. Walker was not without his problems. After the Rapido it was decided the division required replacements for its heavy losses and an infusion of Regular Army officers, who, it was reasoned, would provide the leadership allegedly lacking in the National Guard officers who had occupied the key positions. One such officer, a West Pointer, was given command of the 1st Battalion, 141st Regiment. On May 28 when he visited the battalion, Walker found the new commander drunk, "unable to think intelligently, ignorant of the location of his own troops and the location of the enemy. . . . It is a sorry situation when the government educates an officer . . . in order to have a competent officer ready to lead troops in battle, only to have him incapacitate himself by getting drunk, especially when his command is deployed for battle." Another recent replacement tank company commander was also found drunk, and a tank destroyer company commander refused the orders of the commander to whose unit he had been attached. "What kind of an organization do you suppose these inebriates came from?" Walker wrote in his diary (Walker, *From Texas to Rome: A General's Journal*, p. 373).

13. Walker diary, May 30, 1944, in ibid., p. 375.

14. Ibid.
15. Quoted in Fisher, *Cassino to the Alps,* p. 189.
16. Ibid., pp. 189–90.
17. Sevareid, *Not So Wild a Dream,* pp. 405–6. Another German sniper was captured by a 36th Division infantry battalion and, in revenge for shooting two American medics, was ordered to run for it. Outside a farmhouse that served as the battalion headquarters he was gunned down by thirteen bullets from a tommy gun. A short time later the four who had shot the German were themselves killed by a machine-gun burst a short distance away.
18. Walker diary, June 2, 1944. Walker was also exceptionally lucky to be alive. Unaware that a portion of the highway near his CP had been heavily mined, his jeep had miraculously passed over twenty-seven of them without triggering what would have been a fatal blast. As he was about to make a second trip over the deadly strip of macadam he was stopped by an engineer officer in charge of a demolition team, whom Walker thanked for saving his life.
19. Sevareid, *Not So Wild a Dream,* p. 408.
20. Clark diary, May 31, 1944; and Truscott, *Command Missions,* p. 377.
21. Clark diary, May 31, 1944.
22. Clark's biographer, Martin Blumenson, believes that this unexpected order may well have been a concession to Alexander (*Mark Clark,* p. 212). The assignment of the 85th Division freed Task Force Howze from its defensive mission at Lariano and permitted its transfer to Frederick's Force, where it became the spearhead.
23. Report No. 20, "The Italian Campaign, 4 Jan–4 June 1944," based on the Tenth Army war diary, June 2, 1944.
24. Quoted in Molony, *The Mediterranean and Middle East,* vol. 6, part 1, p. 235.
25. Irving, *Hitler's War, 1942–1945,* p. 634. According to Irving, Kesselring formally suggested to the Vatican that both sides should continue to respect Rome as an "open city," but the Allies ignored the appeal and "appealed to the city's populace to join the battle," and that Maitland Wilson "broadcast the falsehood that the Germans were defending Rome." It is clear from his memoirs that Kesselring's motivation for saving Rome was humane and that despite the military advantages of a prolonged battle, "I refused to budge from my determination to keep the battle out of Rome" (*The Memoirs of Field-Marshal Kesselring,* p. 204).
26. Clark diary, June 2, 1944. Clark was not the only one under great tension. His mother had written him to "Please take Rome soon. I can't stand the wait much longer. I'm all frazzled out" (quoted in Adleman and Walton, *Rome Fell Today,* p. 255).
27. Although Kesselring remained determined to hold Valmontone on June 1 and 2—to the benefit of the Tenth Army—LXXVI Panzer Corps reported that it was utterly "devoid of tangible reserves and predicted the Valmontone sector would collapse on June 2 unless substantial reinforcements were rushed to the front. This was of course impossible; the plight of the Fourteenth Army was such that a hastily alerted police battalion from Rome had to be thrown into the breach at Velletri (a battalion that was

admittedly unsuitable for the purpose, and in the event indeed retreated with the greatest haste). . . . The danger of a deep wedge being driven between LXXVI Panzer Corps and XIV Panzer Corps was very real." What few reserves Kesselring could scrape up at this late date were to be sent to protect the Tenth Army (Report No. 20, "The Italian Campaign, 4 Jan–4 June 1944").

28. Howze, "Armor in the Breakout from the Anzio Beachhead."

29. Ibid. Later, Howze was just settling down for what he hoped was a well-earned nap in a brick farmhouse, when Rogers came in "bringing me, as a personal present, a German colonel he'd picked up. I was too sleepy to object and Rogers departed. Shortly thereafter the Luftwaffe reappeared and really worked over our crossroads, and the German colonel and I were chased around the building as the aircraft changed directions. The German spoke no English and I no German, but we worked very well together in figuring out where to go next."

30. Burhans, *The First Special Service Force*, pp. 238 and 239.

31. Clark diary, June 3, 1944.

32. Quoted in Burhans, p. 240. "68 Northing" was a map reference to all the Tiber bridges north of the Vatican. These were the key objectives in Rome and led to Highways 2 and 3, the key routes to be employed by the Fifth Army in this pursuit of Army Group C.

33. Although aware of Kesselring's "open city" decree, Clark was taking no chances and ordered both II and VI Corps to send flying columns into Rome to prevent the bridges' destruction.

34. Adleman and Walton, *Rome Fell Today*, p. 252. The *Fifth Army History* officially credits the 88th Reconnaissance Troop of the 88th Division with being the first Allied unit to enter Rome the morning of June 4. At 0800 elements of the troop passed a ROMA sign in the suburbs. This claim could certainly be contested by the First Special Service Force. According to its official history, a Force patrol mounted on Shermans of Task Force Howze entered the railway yards of Pietralata, considered a part of Rome, at 0625 hours, June 4. Another account records that yet another patrol of the First Special Service Force passed through the Porta San Giovanni into Rome proper at exactly 0600 hours. In all three instances the small forces that had entered Rome were soon forced back outside the city limits by German fire. In addition to the 88th Division, both the 3d Infantry and 1st Armored divisions also claimed entry sometime between 0800 and 0900 the morning of June 4. Less well known is that a small detachment of a French tank destroyer company of the 3d Algerian Division had not only managed to enter Rome at about 0900, but actually became the first Allied unit to penetrate into the center of the city. Led by a captain, the jeeps drove past the Vatican to the Piazza di Venezia, where Benito Mussolini had trumpeted the glory of Italian Fascism from the balcony of the palazzo. Now it was utterly lifeless. Not an Italian or German was to be seen. Apparently believing the patrol to be German, the Romans remained behind closed shutters. The patrol silently exited Rome, and the captain was ordered to report to his division commander, who sternly informed him he deserved sixty days in prison for entering Rome without permission. "What, after all, would Clark say? . . . The general then walked up and embraced him,

kissing both cheeks. 'You also deserve my embrace,' he said." (Burhans, *The First Special Service Force,* p. 240; and Kurzman, *The Race for Rome,* pp. 477, 479).

35. Kurzman, *The Race for Rome,* part 2, and Burhans, *The First Special Service Force,* chap. 8, passim, contain excellent accounts of the fall of Rome.

36. Kurzman, *The Race for Rome,* pp. 475–76; and Walker, *From Texas to Rome,* pp. 382–83. Roman fever had so infected the participants that some irrational incidents occurred in the haste to lay claim to the Eternal City. When the incursion of the 85th Division near Highway 7 was discovered, the VI Corps chief of staff, Colonel Don Carleton, called his counterpart in II Corps and "began yelling to ours like a pig caught under a fence that if we didn't stop, we'd cross their boundary and their highway, and if we did, he intimated, they were going to shoot it out with us!" (Major General Geoffrey Keyes, quoted in Adleman and Walton, *Rome Fell Today,* p. 255).

37. Truscott, *Command Missions,* p. 378.

38. Harmon, "We Break Out at Anzio."

39. Quoted in Adleman and Walton, *Rome Fell Today,* pp. 253–54. Colonel Andersson commanded the 1108th Engineer Combat Group.

40. Ibid., p. 253. The night of June 4 Colonel Andersson and Frederick had just reached one of the Tiber bridges, which had been seized by a detachment of the First Special Service Force, when a firefight began. The official Force history states that it was Germans, but the official U.S. Army history claims it was a mistaken fight between Forcemen and troops of the 351st Infantry Regiment of the 88th Division, who also had orders to seize the same bridge, mistook the Americans for German troops, and opened fire. Frederick's driver was killed, and Frederick, Andersson, and several others were wounded before the mistake was detected. Frederick was wounded in both the arm and leg and earlier that day had been wounded in the shoulder. Typically, Frederick refused medical treatment, but at the urging of his medical officer finally reported to one of the field hospitals at Anzio. The next morning the MO received a call from Frederick, who told him: "These goddamn German prisoners kept me awake all night with their moaning. I'd advise you to get me the hell out of here fast!" He did, without bothering with the formality of checking out. Years later when Frederick visited a civilian hospital a surgeon told Frederick that he had been the commander of the hospital at Anzio. "You know, you're still AWOL and you owe the Government all the salary you've been drawing since the end of World War II," he said in jest (Fisher, *Cassino to the Alps,* p. 218; William P. Jones Papers, USAMHI; Adleman and Walton, *The Devil's Brigade,* p. 203; and Burhans, *The First Special Service Force,* p. 244).

41. Clark, *Calculated Risk,* p. 332; Kurzman, *The Race for Rome,* pp. 482–83; Fisher, *Cassino to the Alps,* p. 215; and Adleman and Walton, *Rome Fell Today,* p. 254. There is another version of the story, in which Keyes came first to demand that Frederick clear away the obstacle so Clark could have his picture taken entering the city on June 4. The above accounts all verify that Clark and Keyes arrived together.

42. Walker diary, pp. 384 and 387; and Fisher, p. 220.

43. Reconnaissance elements of the British 1st Division, at that time still under

VI Corps, crossed the Tiber south of Rome on June 5, otherwise few British units passed through Rome (Letter, Major General Lowell W. Rooks [(U.S.) Deputy Chief of Staff, AFHQ] to Major General Sir John Kennedy [Director of Military Operations, War Office, London], June 26, 1944, PRO [WO 216/166]).

44. Quoted in Adleman and Walton, *Rome Fell Today,* p. 268. As Tompkins relates, "I was so outraged that some guy would come along and requisition my apartment that I just stomped out of there right down to Clark's office to prove to them that no goddamned brigadier general was going to get my place. And he didn't either. But that was the atmosphere of the immediate post-liberation."

45. Quoted in Desmond Flower and James Reeves, eds., *The Taste of Courage, The War, 1939–1945* (New York, 1969), p. 700. Clark was originally to have entered Rome at the head of a spit-and-polish honor guard provided by the 91st Cavalry Reconnaissance Squadron (assigned to II Corps). The troop could not prepare in time, and when Clark arrived the morning of June 5 he was told there would be a delay of several hours before the preparations were completed. " 'Oh, the hell with that,' he said, 'I don't care whether or not the men have shaves. The important thing is to get into Rome before the Germans do something about it.' Clark picked a jeep at random and off they went" (Adleman and Walton, *Rome Fell Today,* p. 272).

46. Quoted in Sevareid, *Not So Wild a Dream,* p. 414.

47. Ibid. Only Geoffrey Keyes seems to have defended Clark's insincerity. While admitting that it was stage-managed by Clark's public relations officer, Keyes said, "I can understand General Clark. He wanted to make sure that Fifth Army got the glory. I don't think it was intentional that he left the British and French out. But it did kind of hurt them, and, of course, that's what Eric Sevareid objected to so strenuously, in his book—that he left the others out" (Adleman and Walton, *Rome Fell Today,* p. 273).

48. Quoted in Sir David Cole, *Rough Road to Rome* (London, 1983), pp. 229, 231.

Epilogue

1. Graham and Bidwell, *Tug of War,* pp. 395–96. A similar observation was made by U.S. naval historian Samuel Eliot Morison, who wrote: "Invasion made Italy a major battlefield. And, once we were in Italy, there could be no turning back" (*Sicily–Salerno–Anzio,* p. 382).

2. Quoted in Gilbert, *Road to Victory,* p. 769. During the preparations for Overlord, Churchill always seemed to relate a problem, real or perceived, to the experience of Anzio. Whether it was too many vehicles or noncombatants, the inference was always that it had been a lesson learned from Anzio. His chief military deputy, General Sir Hastings Ismay, had better sense than to relate to Churchill how the first crates ashore at Anzio were found to contain harmoniums and hymn books. This anecdote appears in Lord Ismay, *Memoirs* (London, 1960), p. 352, and has never been substantiated. Ismay himself noted that its authenticity was questionable. Nevertheless, had Churchill ever heard this tale, it would undoubtedly have been repeatedly used as an example of bad planning.

3. Long after the war, Churchill revealed he still failed to grasp fully the significance of Anzio. In 1953 he and Montgomery cited Anzio as one of the five capital mistakes made by Americans during World War II: "They had done at Anzio what Stopford did at Suvla Bay: clung to the beaches and failed to establish positions inland as they could well have done" (Colville, *The Fringes of Power,* p. 674).

4. Quoted in Moran, *Winston S. Churchill,* p. 210.

5. Alexander interviews, part 2.

6. Colville, *The Fringes of Power,* p. 470.

7. The pre-Anzio intelligence estimates foretold that some fourteen thousand German troops were based in the Anzio area. By January 23 the Germans could muster another division and as many as three additional regiments. By January 24–25 there might be up to thirty-one thousand opposing VI Corps.

8. Fitzpatrick to Penney, March 8, 1949, Penney Papers.

9. Major General (later Lieutenant-General Sir) Terence S. Airey to Major General W. R. C. Penney, March 31, 1949, Penney Papers.

10. Truscott, *Command Missions,* pp. 311, 549.

11. Harmon and MacKaye, "Our Bitter Days at Anzio."

12. Quoted in Cloake, *Templer: Tiger of Malaya,* p. 130.

13. Penney's notes about Anzio in folder 16/1; and Brigadier Peter Pasley to Penney, February 5, folder 16/18.

14. Clark, *Calculated Risk,* passim. After the war Clark added the following handwritten comments to his diary entry for January 22: "Our hope was that our Anzio threat would be enough to force [a] Ger[man] general withdrawal back of Rome. It would be normal procedure and British intelligence was that [the] Ger[mans] would not maintain their lines or bring in reinforcements.... In [the] actual landing, we went inland as far as feasible. Had we gone any farther we would have been too weak to hold.... We just didn't have [the] build up to go further—[the] German build up was terrific. Air force thought that they could stop [the] enemy move up and 'isolate' [the] bridgehead area. They failed to do it and were astonished when Ed Howard (the Fifth Army G-2) showed that a German division had got there from reserve area between Anzio and Cassino."

15. Marshall interview, part 2, July 25, 1949, USAMHI.

16. Kesselring, quoted in Majdalany, *The Battle of Cassino,* p. 86.

17. Lucas, quoted by Major General Geoffrey Keyes in Adleman and Walton, *Rome Fell Today,* p. 167.

18. Adleman and Walton, *Rome Fell Today,* pp. 167–68.

19. Westphal, *The German Army in the West,* p. 158.

20. Blumenson, *Anzio: The Gamble that Failed,* p. 129.

21. Quoted in Morison, *Sicily-Salerno-Anzio,* p. 383.

22. Ellis, *Cassino: The Hollow Victory,* p. 475.

23. Morison, *Sicily-Salerno-Anzio,* p. 381.

24. Quoted in Bailey, Ms. R-50, p. 27. Although his case for a strategic withdrawal in Italy failed, few could quarrel with his conclusion that, "Our situation is characterized by the fact that the enemy command in Italy is containing the German forces (on the defensive) with an approximate strength ratio of 1:1, while an initial ratio of 1:2 in favor of the enemy may

be expected in the decisive area of northern France." Colonel Roenne was later accused of involvement in the July 20, 1944, plot to assassinate Hitler and was executed.

25. Marshall interview, part 2, July 25, 1949, USAMHI.
26. Trevelyan, *Rome '44*, p. 293.
27. Graham and Bidwell, *Tug of War*, p. 340.
28. Blumenson, *Anzio: The Gamble That Failed*, p. 172.
29. Mathews, "General Clark's Decision to Drive on Rome," in *Command Decision*, p. 284.
30. Truscott, *Command Missions*, p. 550.
31. Field Marshal Earl Alexander of Tunis, *The Alexander Memoirs, 1940–1945* (New York, 1962), p. 127.
32. Alexander interviews, part 3.
33. Ibid.
34. Molony, *The Mediterranean and Middle East*, vol. 6, part 1, p. 288.
35. Quoted in Kurzman, *The Race for Rome*, p. 390. Kurzman's source is Ms. C-025, "71st Infantry Division in Italy," German Report Series.
36. David G. Chandler, *The Military Maxims of Napoleon* (New York, 1988), p. 61.
37. Von Senger, *Neither Fear Nor Hope*, p. 249.
38. Kesselring and Westphal in German Generals' Collection, Liddell Hart Papers.
39. Lewin, *Ultra Goes to War*, pp. 290–91.
40. Hinsley et al., *British Intelligence in the Second World War*, vol. 3, part 1, p. 202.
41. Craven and Cate, *The Army Air Forces in World War II*, vol. 3, *Europe: Argument to V-E Day*, p. 361.
42. Quoted in G. Boulle, *Le Corps Expéditionnaire Français en Italie, 1943–44*, vol. 2 (Paris, 1973), p. 310. Also quoted in Ellis, *Cassino: The Hollow Victory*, p. 449.

Postscript

1. This poem, titled "Reflex," is extracted from Hans Juergensen, *Beachheads and Mountains: Campaigning from Sicily to Anzio* (Tampa, 1984), p. 33. Juergensen was a telephone and radio operator who served with Company A, 84th Chemical Mortar Battalion and wrote this poem on February 1, 1944.
2. War diary, 1st Division, appendix I, narrative of Anzio, PRO (WO 204/8239). In 1944 the average British infantry division was composed of approximately 870 officers and 17,477 Other [Enlisted] Ranks. The figures compiled by the 1st Division included formations attached for varying periods of time during the course of the campaign. The percentages cited are based upon the authorized numbers. As previously noted, the officer casualty rate in many of the infantry battalions exceeded 100 percent.
3. *Fifth Army History*, part 5, chap. 6, appendix B, and Molony, *The Mediterranean and Middle East*, vol. 5, fn., p. 520. None of the official histories and other accounts and monographs provide total statistics solely for Allied forces at Anzio from January 22 to the liberation of Rome on June 4, 1944.

The figures cited above were obtained by extrapolating data from the above sources.

4. Gregory Blaxland, *Alexander's Generals*, (London, 1979), p. 137, and John Ellis, *Cassino: The Hollow Victory*, p. 466. The *Fifth Army History* records capturing 10,539 POWs during Diadem but provides no overall figures solely for Anzio (*Fifth Army History*, part 6, appendix D.)

5. Morison, *Sicily–Salerno–Anzio*, p. 381.

6. Oral history account of Lance Corporal Liebschner, Department of Sound Records, Imperial War Museum. Recorded in 1985, this is a moving account of the experience of a German soldier. Liebschner is a self-described gung-ho young soldier who attempted to join the Waffen SS but was turned down because he was only sixteen. When he saw for himself the "vehicles, tanks, jeeps, guns, lorries in long columns, as long as the road stretched and as far as the eye could see," Liebschner became convinced that Germany could never win the war. The experience of Anzio was so profound that Liebschner became a pacifist after the war.

7. The Nettuno cemetery contains the graves of 647 GIs who were killed elsewhere in the Mediterranean and temporarily buried in Bulgaria, Greece, Corsica, Sardinia, and Malta and later reinterred in Italy in 1946 and 1947 (Edward Steere and Thayer M. Boardman, *Final Disposition of World War II Dead, 1942–51*, QMC Historical Studies, series 2, no. 4, 1957, p. 588; and the *New York Times*, May 29, 1989).

8. Bill Mauldin, *The Brass Ring* (New York, 1971), p. 272.

9. Excellent photographs of the Anzio beachhead in 1944 and today are in *After the Battle*, no. 52, "Anzio."

10. *After the Battle*, no. 52, "Anzio," passim.

11. Ibid.

12. My thanks to former Ranger Jim Brennan, who provided details of the Ranger pilgrimages to Cisterna after the war. Brennan served in the First Ranger Battalion and was captured the morning of January 30, 1944.

13. Dormer Papers, Department of Documents, Imperial War Museum.

14. Notes (undated) of speech by Lieutenant General William P. Yarborough, USA (Ret.).

15. Ibid., and Jesse N. Bradley, "Beachhead Bailout at Anzio," *The Retired Officer*, September 1983.

16. Colville, *The Fringes of Power*, p. 730. Churchill also summoned one of his trusted former military assistants, Lieutenant General Sir Ian Jacob, from his position as Director General of the BBC to become Alexander's principal assistant. In reality, Churchill wanted the cool professionalism of Jacob to guide Alexander through the labyrinth of Whitehall politics. But not even Jacob could keep Alexander from turning into arguably the most ineffective minister of defense in the postwar years of Britain.

17. Nicolson, *Alex*, p. 353.

18. From the Introduction by Edward Seago to *The Paintings of Field Marshal Earl Alexander of Tunis* (London, 1973), p. 19. Seago also notes that Alexander loved Italy and wrote in the foreword to a book of Seago's reproductions of works about Italy: "For all the destruction and suffering that it has inevitably brought in its train, the Italian campaign—more, probably, than any other—none the less abounds with drama and romance. The back-

ground as it unfolded evoked continual memories of Italy's great past; in the foreground in sharp, strident contrast there was the momentous advance of modern armies, bent on restoring the civilisation to which Italy has contributed so much. At every stage of the advance the scene called to mind Italian masters of every age and school; if the ruins of Cassino resembled the cold desolation of Dante's ninth circle of Hell, the countryside very often recalled the canvases of Bellini and the skies those of Canaletto" (quoted by Seago, pp. 17–18).

19. Nicolson, *Alex*, p. 371.

20. Blumenson, *Mark Clark*, passim. Clark wrote two separate memoirs, *Calculated Risk*, and *From the Danube to the Yalu*.

21. Colonel Lucian K. Truscott III, writing in the editor's preface to his father's *The Twilight of the U.S. Cavalry*, p. xii.

22. Edward M. Coffman teaches history at the University of Wisconsin (Madison) and is quoted in the Foreword to Truscott's *The Twilight of the U.S. Cavalry*, p. i.

23. Marshall to McNair, February 20, 1944, Microfilm reel 28, George C. Marshall Papers, Marshall Library. Despite Lucas's protestations in his diary to the contrary, both Clark and Devers independently believed that he was indeed worn out. In an eyes-only cable to Eisenhower on March 1, 1944, Marshall offered Lucas to the SHAEF commander, noting that "according to Devers he 'looked old and completely tired out.' All were agreed that he had done everything that could have been done with the means available" (box 67, folder 4, Marshall Papers). When Lucas's brother wrote to Mark Clark in 1962 to protest his treatment by Wynford Vaughan-Thomas in *Anzio*, Clark replied that he stood by what he had written about Lucas in *Calculated Risk*, which he considered to be both factual and fair. Clark also insisted that in addition to the loss of faith in him by the British, "John was not feeling too well . . . I also knew he was very tired. He had carried a tremendous load." (Charles C. Lucas, Jr., to Clark April 23, 1962, and Clark's reply on April 25, both in box 16, folder 12, Clark Papers, The Citadel Archives).

24. Memorandum, McNair-Marshall, February 21 1944, Microfilm reel 28.

25. Various interviews with Colonel Gordon G. Bartlett, USA (Ret.), 1988–90. According to his son, Colonel John P. Lucas, Jr., USA (Ret.), there were no photographs or news releases about his father during his tenure at Fourth Army. When the diary was revised, Lucas Jr. charges that approval to publish was deliberately withheld until Clark had been promoted to full general. The diary presently utilized by historians is not the original, which apparently no longer exists. Colonel Lucas told the author that the original diary was even more critical than the present version and that he can shed no light on his father's opinion of Clark, which he kept to himself. Lucas later told Bartlett that "I was practically under house arrest" (Lucas Jr., interview of June 19, 1990, and Bartlett, telephone conversation, July 13, 1990).

26. Interview with Col. John P. Lucas, Jr., June 19, 1990.

27. Ibid. Lucas loved to dance and it was while on the dance floor one night in December 1949 that he collapsed and died shortly thereafter at a nearby military hospital.

28. Bartlett interview, October 8, 1988, and Lucas interview with Sidney T. Mathews, May 24, 1948, USAMHI. One of Lucas's problems at Anzio was that he needed an "S.O.B." for his chief of staff instead of the gentlemanly, well-meaning but largely ineffective Colonel "Dutch" Keiser. "It was," observed Colonel Bartlett, "not a good combination. Lucas had a happy staff but they did not produce well under pressure." Bartlett also believed that Lucas's inability to understand the British was a major liability, whereas Truscott had worked closely with them and understood their system of command. Mathews notes that "General Lucas never believed that the time had come for an all-out attack. In the 30 January drive . . . he never thought or felt VI Corps could drive through and take the Alban Hills. That may been cited as the final objective in the order but the most he wanted and expected to do by that operation was to secure the Cisterna-Rome railroad and a firm line based around it and Cisterna. In other words, he wanted to increase the strength of his defensive positions around the port of Anzio. By that time, Lucas says, he knew the German build-up was such that it was silly to expect his small forces to push to the Alban Hills."

29. In 1945 Lucas was also recognized by the Italian government, which decorated him as a "Grand Officer of the Order of Saints Maurice and Lazarus" (U.S. Army Public Information release, 1948, copy in U.S. Army Center of Military History, Washington, D.C.).

30. Greiner, quoted in *From Texas to Rome*, pp. 432–33.

31. Quoted in interview by the Sarasota (Florida) *Herald-Tribune*, February 28, 1971.

32. Letter of February 1, 1944, Strick Papers, Imperial War Museum. Among those devastated by Strick's death was his loyal batman, Rifleman Jack Armstrong, who had been hospitalized and shortly thereafter wrote to his mother that "When I left him, he shook hands with me and said: 'Good luck. Look after yourself.' I told him it was he who needed all the luck. I don't know what I shall do now. . . . On the three occasions when he was wounded before, I was with him each time. We always said to each other, we were each other's luck. . . . I have lost my best friend" (letter of February 20, 1944).

33. Nicolson, *Alex*, p. 344. One of the chief complaints about his trial was that the court seemed not to understand that Kesselring had no authority over the Gestapo and their activities. A member of the tribunal would later admit that he was "a soldier's soldier, through and through" (see Raleigh Trevelyan, *Rome '44*, p. 325).

34. Macksey, *Kesselring: The Making of the Luftwaffe*, p. 257.

35. *Kriegsgräberfürsorge* No. 3, 1976, pp. 80–81. In all, 107,221 German dead from World War II are buried in military cemeteries in Italy. Pomezia is located sixteen miles southeast of Rome and approximately twelve miles northwest of Anzio.

36. *The Fighting Forty-Fifth*, p. 195. Losses during the Italian campaign, mainly at Salerno and Anzio, were 1,808 officers and enlisted men killed in action, 6,060 wounded, 24,110 injured, and 1,927 missing, total: 1,344 officers and 32,561 enlisted men. During all campaigns the division lost 3,547 killed, 14,441 wounded, and 533 missing in action.

37. Quoted in Nicolson, *Alex,* p. 273.
38. Truscott, *Command Missions,* p. 555.
39. Letter to the author, July 6, 1989.
40. Quoted in Merle Miller, *Ike the Soldier* (New York, 1987), p. 561.
41. Ellis, *Cassino: The Hollow Victory,* p. 478.
42. Trevelyan, *The Fortress,* p. 10.
43. Ibid., p. 212.

Sources and Selected Bibliography

UNPUBLISHED SOURCES

Principal institutional collections used are:

Public Record Office, Kew, London

The personal papers of Field Marshal Earl Alexander of Tunis (WO 214); the Churchill papers (PREM 3); papers, Middle East Forces (including 15th Army Group) (WO 201); unit war diaries, Middle East Forces (WO 169); military narratives, Cabinet Office Historical Section (CAB 44); Allied Force Headquarters (AFHQ) papers (WO 204); Official War Histories, Cabinet Office Historical Section (CAB 101); War Office Director of Military Operations & Intelligence papers (WO 106); War Office, Director of Military Training papers (WO 231); Joint Planning Committee papers (CAB 84); British Army Strength Returns (WO 73); Chief of Air Staff papers (AIR 8); Mediterranean Allied Air Forces (AIR 19, 23, and 41); Admiralty papers (ADM 199).

Imperial War Museum, London

Department of Printed Books (printed sources); Department of Documents: the diary and papers of E. P. Danger and Captain J. A. Strick; the papers of Commander J. S. Townson; G. Allnutt; R. H. Turner; Commander G. B. B. Richey; Lieutenant R. Sutton; Lieutenant J. H. Jones, RNVR; and various miscellaneous collections; Department of Photographs; Department of Sound Records, oral histories: Field Marshal Lord Harding of Petherton; Major General T. B. L. Churchill; Colonel F. H. Foster; Hans Paul Joachim Liebschner; various transcripts from the "World at War" television series and from the BBC Sound Archives.

Liddell Hart Centre for Military Archives, King's College, London

The papers and diary of Field Marshal Lord Alanbrooke; the papers of Major General W. R. C. Penney; the papers of Sir Basil Liddell Hart, including the postwar interrogations, correspondence, and notes in the "German Generals' Collection."

Department of Manuscripts, British Library, London

The papers of Admiral of the Fleet Viscount Cunningham of Hyndhope.

Ministry of Defence Library, Whitehall, London

Various postwar War Office monographs.

Library and Special Collections Branch, United States Military Academy, West Point, New York

Various miscellaneous collections.

George C. Marshall Research Library, Virginia Military Institute, Lexington, Virginia

The papers of General of the Army George C. Marshall; the diary and papers of General Lucian K. Truscott, Jr.

Office of Air Force History, Washington, D.C.

Various microfilms of the Foreign Military Studies, German Report Series.

The Citadel Archives, Charleston, South Carolina

The diary and papers of General Mark W. Clark; the papers of Brigadier General Edwin B. Howard; photographs in the Clark collection.

United States Navy Historical Center, Washington, D.C.

The papers of Samuel Eliot Morison; War Diary, Operations Division, German Naval staff, January–June 1944 (microfilm).

United States Army Military History Institute (USAMHI), Carlisle Barracks, Pennsylvania

Archives: various OCMH papers, including: OCMH Collection: World War II, Mediterranean; "Research Notes," World War II, and interviews of Field Marshal Earl Alexander of Tunis, General Mark Clark, General Dwight D. Eisenhower, General Lyman L. Lemnitzer, General George C. Marshall, General Robert J. Wood, Major General John P. Lucas, Major General Fred L. Walker, and Brigadier General Charles E. Saltzman; the Magna E. Bauer collection; the papers of Colonel William P. Jones; the diary and papers of Major General John P. Lucas, including a translation of Kesselring's observations of World War II (Kesselring "diary"); the Ranger collection; the papers of General Hamilton H. Howze (Howze/Hawkins collection); General Robert J. Wood; Lieutenant General John P. O'Daniel; Lieutenant General William P. Yarborough; Major General Ernest N. Harmon; Louis F. Lisko; Oral histories: General Paul D. Adams; General Mark Clark; General Theodore J. Conway; General Michael S. Davison; General Ben Harrell; General William B. Rosson; Lieutenant General Ira C. Eaker; Lieutenant General John A. Heintges; Lieutenant General Harry Lemley, and Brigadier General O. Glenn Goodhand.

Library: OCMH interview of General Lucian K. Truscott, Jr., and notes and extracts from the diary of General Mark Clark; various monographs, including: "The German Operation at Anzio," "Operations of British, Indian and Dominion Forces in Italy," various volumes; U.S. Army Infantry School; Alfred G. Steiger manuscript on German operations in Italy; various manuscripts in the Foreign Military Studies, German Report Series; "A Military Enclyopedia, based on Operations in the Italian Campaigns, 1943–1945" (G-3 Section, 15th Army Group); "American Armor at Anzio" (prepared by the U.S. Army Armor School, Fort Knox, Kentucky); *Fifth Army History;* and British and U.S. Army regimental histories and secondary sources.

Photographic Branch, National Archives, Washington, D.C.

Photographs of Anzio and Cassino, Allied and German commanders.

The Dwight D. Eisenhower Library, Abilene, Kansas

Oral histories: General Arthur S. Nevins and General Jacob L. Devers; the diary of Captain Harry C. Butcher, USNR; various photographs of the Anzio beachhead.

The U.S. Army Center of Military History, Washington, D.C.

OCMH monographs by Britt Bailey and Ralph S. Mavrogordato; various miscellaneous papers.

Manuscript Division, Library of Congress

The papers of General George S. Patton, Jr., and Lieutenant General Ira C. Eaker.

Henry Prescott Chaplin Memorial Library, Norwich University, Northfield, Vermont

The papers of Major General Ernest N. Harmon.

Special Collections Division, Mugar Library, Boston University, Boston, Massachusetts

The papers of Lieutenant General William P. Yarborough.

Houghton Library, Harvard University, Cambridge, Massachusetts

The papers of James Parton.

Research Library, U.S. Army Command & General Staff College, Fort Leavenworth, Kansas

Monographs: Arthur F. Fournier and Teddy D. Bitner.

45th Infantry Division Museum, Oklahoma City, Oklahoma

Various monographs and bibliographies.

Library, U.S. Naval War College, Newport, Rhode Island

Oral histories: Admiral John L. Hall; Admiral H. Kent Hewitt; and Admiral Alan G. Kirk. Monograph: "From Algiers to Anzio," the unpublished diary and recollections of Major General John P. Lucas.

PUBLISHED SOURCES

Alexander, Field Marshal Earl of Tunis. *The Alexander Memoirs, 1940–1945.* New York, 1962.

Adleman, Robert H., and Walton, George. *The Devil's Brigade.* London, 1968.
———. *Rome Fell Today.* London, 1969.

Altieri, James J. *Darby's Rangers.* Durham, N.C., 1945.
———. *The Spearheaders.* New York, 1960.

Aris, G. R., *The Fifth British Division, 1939–1945.* London, 1959.

Baldwin, Hanson. *Battles Lost and Won.* New York, 1966.

Ball, Edmund F. *Staff Officer with the Fifth Army: Sicily, Salerno and Anzio.* New York, 1958.

Barclay, C. N. *The London Scottish in the Second World War, 1939–45.* London, 1952.
———. *The History of the Sherwood Foresters, 1919–57.* London, 1959.

Belchem, David. *All in the Day's March.* London, 1978.

Bennett, Ralph. *Ultra and Mediterranean Strategy.* New York, 1989.

Bidwell, Shelford. "Kesselring," in Correlli Barnett, ed., *Hitler's Generals.* New York/London, 1989.

Blair, Clay. *Ridgway's Paratroopers.* New York, 1985.

Blaxland, Gregory. *Alexander's Generals: The Italian Campaign, 1944–45.* London, 1979.

Blight, G. *The History of the Royal Berkshire Regiment, 1920–1947*. Staples, 1953.

Blumenson, Martin. *Bloody River*. London, 1970.

———. *Anzio: The Gamble That Failed*. New York, 1986.

———. *Salerno to Cassino*. Washington, 1969.

———. *The Patton Papers*, vol. 2. Boston, 1974.

———. *Mark Clark*. New York, 1985.

Blumenson, Martin, and Stokesbury, James L. *Masters of the Art of Command*. Boston, 1975.

Bond, Harold L. *Return to Cassino: A Memoir of the Fight for Rome*. Garden City, 1964.

Bowditch, John III. *The Anzio Beachhead*, vol. 14 in the "American Forces in Action" series. Washington, D.C., 1947.

Bradley, Omar N. *A Soldier's Story*. New York, 1951.

———. *A General's Life*, with Clay Blair. New York, 1983.

Brendon, Piers. *Ike: His Life and Times*. New York, 1986.

Brereton, J. M. *A Guide to the Regiments and Corps of the British Army*. London, 1985.

Brett-Smith, Richard. *Hitler's Generals*. San Rafael, Calif., 1977.

Bryant, Arthur. *The Turn of the Tide*. London, 1957.

———. *Triumph in the West*. London, 1959.

Buckley, Christopher. *Road to Rome*. London, 1945.

Bullen, R. E. *History of the 2/7th Battalion The Queen's Royal Regiment, 1939–1946*. Besley, Exeter, 1958.

Burhans, Robert D. *The First Special Service Force*. Washington, D.C., 1947.

Butcher, Harry C. *Three Years with Eisenhower*. London, 1946.

Carver, Michael. *Harding of Petherton, Field Marshal*. London, 1978.

Cate, J. L., and Craven, W. F., eds. *The Army Air Forces in World War II*, vol. 3, *Europe: ARGUMENT to VE Day, January 1944–May 1945*. Chicago, 1951.

Cave Brown, Anthony. *Bodyguard of Lies*. London, 1976.

———. *Wild Bill Donovan: The Last Hero*. New York, 1982.

Chandler, Alfred D., ed. *The Papers of Dwight David Eisenhower: The War Years*. 5 vols: Baltimore, 1970.

Cheetham, A. M. *Ubique*. Formby, England, 1987.

Churchill, Winston S. *Hinge of Fate*. Boston, 1950.

———. *Closing the Ring*. Boston, 1951.

Clark, Mark. *Calculated Risk*. New York, 1951.

Cloake, John. *Templer: Tiger of Malaya*. London, 1985.

Cole, Sir David. *Rough Road to Rome*. London, 1983.

Colville, John. *The Churchillians*. London, 1981.

———. *The Fringes of Power: Downing Street Diaries, 1939–1955*. London, 1985.

Cunningham, Admiral of the Fleet Viscount. *A Sailor's Odyssey*. London, 1951.

Darby, William O., and Baumer, William H. *We Led the Way: Darby's Rangers*. San Rafael, Calif., 1980.

Dean, C. G. T. *6th Gordons 1939–1945*. Aberdeen, 1946.

———. *The Loyal Regiment, 1919–53*. Preston, Lancashire, 1955.

Ehrman, John. *Grand Strategy*, vol. 5. London, 1956.

546   Sources and Selected Bibliography

Ellis, John. *Cassino: The Hollow Victory.* New York, 1984.

Erskine, D., ed. *The Scots Guards, 1919–55.* London, 1956.

Fifth Army History, vols. 1–9. Privately published, 1946.

The Fighting Forty-Fifth. Nashville, 1978 (reprint).

Fisher, Ernest F., Jr. *Cassino to the Alps.* Washington D.C., 1977.

Fitzgerald, Desmond. *A History of the Irish Guards in the Second World War.* London, 1986 (reprint, 1949 edition).

Foster, R. C. G. *History of the Queen's Royal Regiment,* vol. 8. Aldershot, 1953.

Forty, George. *Fifth Army at War.* London, 1980.

Fraser, David. *Alanbrooke.* London, 1982.

Galloway, Strome. *The General Who Never Was.* Belleville, Ontario, 1981.

Garland, Albert N., and Smyth, Howard McGaw. *Sicily and the Surrender of Italy.* Washington, D.C., 1965.

Gilbert, Martin. *Road to Victory: Winston S. Churchill, 1941–1945.* London, 1986.

Graham, Dominick, and Bidwell, Shelford. *Tug of War: The Battle for Italy, 1943–45.* London/New York, 1986.

Greenfield, Kent Roberts, ed. *Command Decisions.* New York, 1959.

Hamilton, Nigel. *Monty: Master of the Battlefield, 1942–1944.* London/New York, 1983/1984.

Hampshire, Cecil. *The Beachhead Commandos.* London, 1983.

Hapgood, David, and Richardson, David. *Monte Cassino.* New York, 1984.

Harmon, Ernest N. *Combat Commander.* Englewood Cliffs, 1970.

Harpur, Bryan. *The Impossible Victory.* London, 1980.

Harr, Bill. *Combat Boots.* New York, 1952.

Hickey, Des, and Smith, Gus. *Operation Avalanche: The Salerno Landings, 1943.* London, 1983.

Hinsley, F. H., et al. *British Intelligence in the Second World War,* vol. 3, part 1. London, 1984.

History of the First Division. Privately printed in Palestine, 1946.

History of the 157th Regiment (Rifle). Baton Rouge, 1946.

Hobbs, Joseph P. *Dear General: Eisenhower's Wartime Letters to Marshall.* Baltimore, 1971.

Hough, Richard. *The Greatest Crusade: Roosevelt, Churchill and the Naval Wars.* New York, 1986.

Howard, Michael. *The Mediterranean Strategy in World War II.* New York, 1968.

Howe, George F. *The Battle History of the 1st Armored Division, "Old Ironsides."* Washington, D.C., 1954.

Hunt, David. *A Don at War.* London, 1966.

Irving, David. *Hitler's War, 1942–1945.* London, 1983.

Jackson, W. G. F. *The Battle for Rome.* New York, 1969.

James, Robert Rhodes. *Winston Churchill: A Study in Failure, 1900–1939.* London, 1970.

Juergensen, Hans. *Beachheads and Mountains.* Tampa, 1984.

Kemp, J. C. *The History of the Royal Scots Fusiliers, 1919–59.* Glasgow, 1963.

Kemp, P. K. *The Middlesex Regiment, 1919–1952.* Aldershot, 1956.

Kennedy, John. *The Business of War.* London, 1957.

Kesselring, Albert. *The Memoirs of Field-Marshal Kesselrin* (reprint, 1953 edition).

Kimball, Warren F., ed. *Churchill and Roosevelt: The Com* *dence,* vols. 2, 3. Princeton, 1985.

King, Michael. *William Orlando Darby: A Military Biogi* Conn., 1982.

Kurzman, Dan. *The Race for Rome.* New York, 1975.

Lewin, Ronald. *Ultra Goes to War.* London, 1978.

Linklater, Eric. *The Campaign in Italy.* London, 1951.

London Irish Rifles. *The London Irish at War.* Privately published, n.d.

Macksey, Kenneth. *Kesselring: The Making of the Luftwaffe.* New York, 1978.

Macmillan, Harold. *The Blast of War.* London, 1967.

———. *War Diaries: The Mediterranean 1943–1945.* London, 1984.

Majdalany, Fred. *The Battle of Cassino.* London, 1975.

Manchester, William. *The Last Lion: Winston Spencer Churchill; Visions of Glory, 1874–1932.* Boston, 1983.

Masters, John U. A. *The Story of the 2d Battalion the Sherwood Foresters.* Aldershot, 1946.

Matloff, Maurice. *Strategic Planning for Coalition Warfare, 1943–44.* Washington, D.C., 1959.

Mauldin, Bill. *The Brass Ring.* New York, 1971.

Maund, Rear Admiral L. E. H. *Assault from the Sea.* London, 1949.

Miles, Wilfrid. *The Gordon Highlanders, 1919–1945.* London, 1961.

Miller, Merle. *Ike the Soldier.* New York, 1987.

Mitcham, Samuel W., Jr. *Hitler's Legions: The German Army Order of Battle, World War II.* New York, 1985.

Molony, C. J. C. *The Mediterranean and Middle East,* vol. 5. London, 1973.

———. *The Mediterranean and Middle East,* vol. 6, part 1. London, 1986.

Moran, Lord. *Winston S. Churchill: The Struggle for Survival, 1940–1965.* London, 1968 (paperback edition).

Morison, Samuel Eliot. *Sicily–Salerno–Anzio.* Boston, 1954.

Munthe, Malcolm. *War is Sweet.* London, 1954.

Nelson, Guy. *Thunderbird—A History of the 45th Infantry Division.* Oklahoma City, 1970

Neville, J. E. H. *The Oxford and Buckinghamshire Light Infantry Chronicle, 1942–44,* vol. III. Aldershot, 1952

Nichols, David, ed. *Ernie: The Best of Ernie Pyle's World War II Dispatches.* New York, 1986.

Nicolson, Nigel. *The Grenadier Guards in the War of 1939–1945,* vol. 2. Aldershot, 1949.

———. *Alex: The Life of Field Marshal Earl Alexander of Tunis.* London, 1976.

Parton, James. *"Air Force Spoken Here:" General Ira Eaker and the Command of the Air.* Bethesda, 1986.

Pawle, Gerald R. *The War and Colonel Warden.* London, 1963.

Pogue, Forrest C. *George C. Marshall: Organizer of Victory, 1943–1945.* New York, 1973.

Public Record Office. *The Second World War: A Guide to Documents in the Public Record Office.* London, 1972.

Pyle, Ernie. *Brave Men.* New York, 1944.

port by the Supreme Allied Commander Mediterranean to the Combined Chiefs of Staff. London, 1944.

Richards, Denis, and Saunders, Hilary St. George. "The Royal Air Force, 1939–45," vol. 2. *The Fight Avails.* London, 1975.

Richardson, General Sir Charles. *Flashback.* London, 1985.

Ridgway, Matthew B. *Soldier.* New York, 1956.

Roosevelt, Kermit B. *War Report of the OSS,* vol. 2. New York, 1976.

Roskill, S. W. *The War at Sea,* vol. 3, part 1. London, 1960.

———. *Churchill and the Admirals.* London, 1978.

Scrivener, Jane. *Inside Rome with the Germans.* New York, 1945.

Senger und Etterlin, General Fridolin von. *Neither Fear nor Hope.* New York, 1954.

Sevareid, Eric. *Not So Wild a Dream.* New York, 1968.

Shapiro, L. S. B. *They Left the Back Door Open.* Toronto, 1944.

Sheehan, Fred. *Anzio: Epic of Bravery,* Norman, Okla., 1964.

Sheppard, G. A. *The Italian Campaign, 1943–1945.* New York, 1968

Sinclair-Stevenson, Christopher. *The Gordon Highlanders.* London, 1968.

Slessor, Sir John. *The Central Blue.* London, 1956.

Starr, Lieutenant Colonel C. G., ed. *From Salerno to the Alps: A History of Fifth Army 1943–45.* Washington, D.C., 1948.

The Story of the 180th Regiment. San Angelo, Tex., 1947.

Strong, Kenneth. *Intelligence at the Top.* London, 1968.

Sulzberger, C. L. *A Long Row of Candles.* New York, 1969.

Taggart, Donald G., ed. *History of the Third Infantry Division in World War II.* Washington, D.C., 1947.

Tompkins, Peter. *A Spy in Rome.* New York, 1962.

Trevelyan, Raleigh. *The Fortress: A Diary of Anzio and After.* London, 1986 (reprint, 1956 edition).

———. *Rome '44: The Battle for the Eternal City.* London, 1981.

Truscott, Lucian K. *Command Missions.* New York, 1954.

———. *The Twilight of the U.S. Cavalry.* Lawrence, Kans., 1989.

Vaughan-Thomas, Wynford. *Anzio.* New York, 1962 (paperback edition).

Verney, Peter. *Anzio 1944: An Unexpected Fury.* London, 1978.

Walker, Major General Fred L. *From Texas to Rome: A General's Journal.* Dallas, 1969.

Westphal, Siegfried. *The German Army in the West.* London, 1951.

Wilson, Lord. *Eight Years Overseas, 1939–1947.* London, 1948.

Woodruff, William. *Vessel of Sadness.* Carbondale, Ill., 1978 (reprint, 1969 edition).

Acknowledgments

This book could not have been written without the cooperation, comments, recollections, and criticisms of a considerable number of people in several countries. Therefore, it is with special pleasure that I take this opportunity to record publicly my indebtedness to those listed below who have shared their knowledge of the events depicted in *Fatal Decision*. To each I express my deep gratitude for their contribution:

In Canada

Dr. William J. McAndrew of the Directorate of History, National Defence Headquarters, Ottawa, not only provided many important documents from Canadian archives but also read and commented on a portion of the manuscript. For many years Bill has been a valuable sounding board for ideas and a vital source of information, and I am especially grateful for our longtime correspondence, which includes our mutual dismay at the annual demise of the Boston Red Sox. Special thanks to my colleague Dominick Graham, coauthor of the best account yet written of the Italian campaign, *Tug of War: The Battle for Italy, 1943–45,* who read and commented on the introductory chapters of the manuscript and offered his unique and informed perspective on the Italian campaign.

In the United Kingdom

Brigadier Shelford Bidwell, the eminent historian and coauthor of *Tug of War,* once again proved a rich source of information and offered astute advice and encouragement when it was most needed. Lieutenant General Sir Ian Jacob not only provided "Operation Symbol," his personal diary of the Casablanca Conference, but read and offered helpful comments on the introductory chapters, as did General Sir Charles Richardson.

I am indebted to the late Major James C. Williamson, MC, the former adjutant of the 6th Battalion, the Gordon Highlanders, whose tireless efforts on my behalf enabled me to reconstruct the fate of the Gordons at Anzio. Also I express my sincere appreciation to: Lieutenant Colonel Donald A. Young, who carried on the search after Jim Williamson's untimely death; Major Edward N.

Grace, MC, who provided an unpublished account of Anzio and supplied the answers to numerous questions; and to the former members of the 6th Gordons, who contributed recollections of their experiences at Anzio.

Others who contributed were Brian Harpur; General Sir Desmond Fitzpatrick; Lieutenant General Sir James Wilson; Brigadier James A. Oliver; Raleigh Trevelyan; Brigadier D. M. L. Gordon-Watson; and Sir David Hunt.

My thanks to: the keeper and staff of the Public Record Office, Kew, London; the Manuscript Division of the British Library; Miss Patricia Methven, archivist of the Liddell Hart Centre for Military Archives, King's College, London; the librarian and staff of the Ministry of Defence Library, Whitehall; the Commonwealth War Graves Commission; the director and staff of the Imperial War Museum, London: Department of Documents, Department of Printed Books, Department of Photographs, particularly David Parry, and Department of Sound Records. Special thanks to the ever-efficient staffs of the Reading Room and the Department of Sound Records.

In Italy

Silvano Casaldi furnished important background material about Angelita of Anzio and the controversy that has ensued since 1961.

In New Zealand

Dr. Vincent Orange of the History Department, University of Canterbury, Christchurch, New Zealand, kindly furnished extracts from the Stanley Bruce Papers and the Air Marshal Sir Arthur Coningham Papers and supplied data about air operations during Operation Shingle.

In the United States

The staff of the Henry Prescott Chaplin Memorial Library, Norwich University, Northfield, Vermont, particularly, Mrs. Jacqueline S. Painter, university archivist, and my classmate, Colonel Anthony J. Carbone, USA (Ret.), vice president for institutional development, who kindly furnished the photograph of General Harmon; also the staffs of the Operational Archives Branch of the Naval Historical Center, Washington Navy Yard; Manuscript Division, Library of Congress; the helpful and efficient staff of the Library of the U.S. Army Command & General Staff College, Fort Leavenworth, Kansas; the staff of the U.S. Army Center of Military History, Washington, D.C., particularly Miss Hannah Zeidlick, Dr. Edward Drea, and Alexander S. Cochran, Jr.; the Office of Air Force History, especially Dr. Joseph P. Harahan, and the helpful staff of the AF/CHO library; the staff of the Dwight D. Eisenhower Library, Abilene, Kansas; Mr. John N. Jacob, archivist-librarian, George C. Marshall Research Library, Lexington, Virginia, who made my research trip to Lexington both enjoyable and effective; the U.S. Naval Institute, Annapolis, Maryland; and the Library of the Naval War College, Newport, Rhode Island.

Special thanks to Jane Yates, acting director, Archives-Museum, The Citadel, Charleston, South Carolina, whose advice and assistance in locating material in the papers of General Mark Clark was of immense help.

I am indebted to Peter Tompkins, not only for his hospitality, but for permitting me access to his private papers, including copies of his secret messages from Rome to Fifth Army, and for his help in supplying photographs of the Anzio beachhead.

Nigel Hamilton's unique knowledge of World War II resulted in advice and encouragement about many aspects of the book. He also furnished notes and a number of documents dealing with the Italian campaign. As always, I am deeply grateful.

Brigadier General John W. Dobson, USA (Ret.), took considerable time to answer my questions and comment on the chapter dealing with the ill-fated Ranger operation at Cisterna and the late General Theodore J. Conway, USA (Ret.), shared his recollections of the Italian campaign and was especially helpful.

John S. D. Eisenhower kindly furnished a copy of his father's unpublished manuscript. Colonel G. Gordon Bartlett, USA (Ret.), shared his knowledge of Major General Lucas and assisted in many other ways during the research and writing of the book.

I express my heartfelt thanks to the Falmouth, Massachusetts Public Library, especially Toni Robertson and Gail Rose of the Inter-Library Loan Department, who once again, cheerfully and with exceptional efficiency, responded to my endless requests for photocopies, microfilm, and books, most of them long out of print. They were literally my lifeline.

The library and the archives of the U.S. Army Military History Institute, Carlisle Barracks, Pennsylvania, are among the richest sources of both published and archival material relating to Anzio. I am greatly indebted to the former director, Colonel Rod Paschall, archivist-historian Dr. Richard J. Sommers, and assistant archivist David A. Keough, whose encylopedic knowledge of sources both within USAMHI and outside were exceptionally helpful. Librarian John J. Slonaker and his staff patiently answered my many questions and were never at a loss in finding some innovative way of assisting me. To everyone at this superb research facility, my sincerest thanks for making my task infinitely easier. Your efficiency and helpfulness are unexcelled.

The secretaries of various veterans' associations have been extremely helpful in furnishing information and putting me in contact with veterans of Anzio and the Italian campaign. Special thanks to the following: Colonel Walter I. Strong, USA (Ret.) and the Anzio Beachhead Veterans of World War II; William S. Story and the First Special Service Force Association; Ray Daily and the 34th Infantry Division Association; Judge Fred Daugherty and the 45th Infantry Division Musuem; Paul Morin, John W. Trombi, and the 57th Signal Battalion Association; Brigadier General Felix L. Sparks, USA (Ret.) and the 157th Regimental Association; Donald C. Van Roosen and the National Order of Battlefield Commissions; and Raymond Alm and The Ranger Association.

Others whom I thank for their assistance are: Howard D. Anderson; James R. Bird; Clay Blair; Martin Blumenson; Mrs. John K. Boles, Jr.; James Brennan; David Browning; Sid Butterfield; Russell B. Capelle; Colonel John S. Cole, USA (Ret.); Howard W. Connor; John T. Cummings; Lawrence Durigon, editor, the Norwich University *Record;* John R. Fitzgerald; Robert E. Graham; Fitzgerald F. Harder; Arnold W. Hirsch; John A. Hixson; William Hollerbach; General

Hamilton H. Howze, USA (Ret.); George Hunt; John King; I. W. LaLonde; Jerome Lowery; Colonel John P. Lucas, USA (Ret.); Donald E. MacDonald; John R. Martin; Grace C. Newton; Dr. C. L. Oglesbee; Richard O'Rourke; Richard J. Ott; James L. Parton; Kenneth H. Powers; Manuel J. Ramos; Vera Lee Rieck; Colonel Jacob Shapiro, USA (Ret); Richard G. Shaughnessy; Stanley R. Smith; William G. Turner, Jr.; General John W. Vessey, USA (Ret.); Robert M. and Helen Watt; Muriel M. Westover; the Honorable James M. Wilson; Edward G. Winterroth; and Lieutenant General William P. Yarborough, USA (Ret.).

No author could have two more caring or competent editors than Stuart Proffitt of HarperCollins (London) and Buz Wyeth of HarperCollins (New York). Both offered their full assistance, criticism, and advice where and when it was most needed and above all, their patience as the manuscript evolved into this book. Also, my thanks to Susan H. Llewellyn of HarperCollins (New York) for a superb job of copyediting. For many years my literary agent, Julie Fallowfield, has guided me through the good times and the bad and to her I offer my heartfelt appreciation.

Lastly, very special thanks to two dear friends, Harry and Sue Brack, who helped to make my research in London possible. Liane and David Rippingale, my daughter and son-in-law, assisted with research in London, and once again, my indebtedness to my wife, Shirley Ann, whose support and perseverance during the writing of this book were, as always, above and beyond the call of duty.

Index

Note: Ranks and titles are generally the highest mentioned in the text

A Force (British deception unit) 129
Adam, Sir Ronald 47
Adolf Hitler Line (later Senger Line) 330, 349, 352–4
Adrano 152
Airey, Major General Terence 403
Alam Halfa 13
Alamein, El, Battle of, 1942 13, 15
Alatri 376
Alban Hills (Colli Albani, or Colli La Laziali): Lucas fails to seize 6, 133–5, 264, 402–5; plan to capture 72, 74, 111–13, 143, 152, 160, 181; German artillery bombardments from 121, 148, 150–1; in Harding's breakout plan 336–7; Harmon advances on 358, 366; Germans withdraw from 366; in Clark's plan 369–70, 373, 392; German defense of 373–4, 387; defenses breached 390
Albano 381–2, 394
Albano, Lake 137, 178
Alexander, General Sir Harold R. L. G. (later Field Marshal Earl): halted by Kesselring 5; plans Anzio strategy 6, 47–8, 77–8, 105; appointed Middle East Commander 13; mistrust of U.S. fighting performance 16–18, 25, 42, 60; as ground commander for Sicily 19; and Sicily invasion plan 21; conduct of Sicily campaign 24–6, 28, 55; Montgomery criticizes 34, 48–9, 55; doubts on Salerno landings 38; and dismissal of Dawley 42, 63; forecasts rapid advance in Italy 43; pressed to capture Rome 45, 95; and Clark's inexperience 49; personality, background and style 49–58, 60, 65–6; command in Italy 50, 67; relations with Churchill 53–4; relations with Clark 54, 58, 62–3, 112, 184–5, 326, 329, 332, 337–42, 353, 365, 408; anger over reporting of Anzio 57; view of Devers 64; on plans to take Rome 67, 72; fails to win command of Normandy land forces 69; discusses amphibious end runs 70; amphibious landing 71–2; and conduct of Italian campaign 75; and inadequate resources for Anzio 96, 98; optimism over Anzio 105–6; chairs final commanders' conference 106; view of Lucas 106–7, 144, 185; aims at Anzio 111–13; visits

Anzio front 120, 134, 144, 184; and Lucas's over-caution 144; and battles for Cisterna and Campoleone 181; and Clark's proposal for Civitavecchia landing 185; unaware of enemy strength 185–6; presents VC to Sidney 210; sends reinforcements 220; and Anzio stalemate 252, 264–5, 279; attacks and censors defeatist commentators 253; and Cassino 259–60, 263, 329, 406–7; praises German 1st Parachute Division 262; Churchill's dissatisfaction with 264–6, 278; replaces Lucas 266–70, 406; and Tompkins's warning 306; and morale 310–11; Italian offensive plans 329–34, 336; and Leese 337; and Clark's wish to capture Rome 338, 371, 400; reports good progress of Diadem 349; experience 350; and Clark's abandonment of Buffalo and change of direction 366, 371–3, 408–10; and Valmontone Gap 380; and proposed French plan 386; and Walker's breakout success 389; management of Anzio campaign 401–3, 406; promotion and later career 418; as artist 418–19; Lucas's criticism of 421; and Kesselring's sentence 426; on enemy's organizational efficiency 428
Allen, Brigadier General Frank 363
Allied Forces
  AIR
    XII Air Support Command 232
    Desert Air Force 232
    XII Tactical Air Command 363
    Mediterranean Allied Air Force (MAAF) 50, 122, 136, 412
    Mediterranean Allied Strategic Air Force 333
    Mediterranean Allied Tactical Air Force (MATAF) 332, 334
  ARMY
    15th Army Group 5, 36, 47, 56, 75, 96–7, 145, 257
    21st Army Group 69
  NAVAL
    Support Carrier Force 37
    Task Force 81 108, 113–14, 124
    Western Naval Task Force 37
Alnutt, Fusilier Gilbert 325
Altenstadt, Colonel von 343

American Field Service 324

Ambrosio, General Vittorio 31

Anders, Lieutenant General Wladyslaw, 50, 347

Anderson, Lieutenant General Kenneth N. 153

Anderson, 2d Lieutenant Howard D., 1, 4

Anderson, Colonel 395

Anvil, Operation *see* France, Southern

Anziate, Via 146–7, 149, 155, 183, 188, 206, 213, 226, 234, 235, 245; rebuilt 416

Anzio (town): name 2n; port cleared 133

Anzio (Operation Shingle): conditions at 1–4, 6, 140, 190, 206, 299–304, 315–25; landings 4–5, 114–15, 119–23; plans 70–2, 76–7; shortage of landing craft 72–4, 76, 97–8; strength of landing 75–7, 96; aims 76; inadequate Allied resources and supplies 96–8, 100; training and rehearsals for 108; naval force 113, 255; weather 113; naval bombardment 119–20, 149, 151, 214; Allied air support and sorties 121–2, 136, 151, 214, 232–4, 293–4, 412; air losses 123; casualties in landings 123; beachhead 133, 135; German strength 135–6, 146, 174–5, 185; terrain 137–40; road network 140; German artillery bombardments 148, 150–1, 226 & n, 299–300, 454–7; use of tanks 176, 193–7, 214, 223, 228–33, 235; German initiative at 181; first German counterattack 189–216; Allied artillery at 200–1, 205–6, 214, 220, 229–31, 237, 243, 248, 249–50, 293, 303, 453; casualty rate 205, 217–18, 230–3, 250–1, 294, 303, 413; second German counterattack 205–7, 224–41; infiltration tactics 208; night fighting 208; truces for wounded 228, 230; stalemate 251–2, 264–5, 277–8, 298, 326–7; and Cassino 263; ammunition supplies 284–6, 303, 452; propaganda leaflets 301–2; fraternizations 309–10; battle fatigue and morale 310–11; deserters 311; Italian civilians 311–12, 321; entertainments and recreation 312–13; casualty clearing stations and hospitals 323–4; supply by sea 328; Allied forces build up 328–9; breakout plan (Diadem) 333–6; breakout barrage 355; minefields 358; strategy and conduct assessed 400–6, 430; need questioned 406–7; cemeteries 415; postwar development 415–17

Anzio-Albano highway 140

Anzio Annie (German gun; Leopold) 3, 226, 299, 391, 454–7

Anzio Express (German gun; Robert) 3, 226, 299, 391, 454–7

Aprilia ("the Factory"): position 138, 140, 142, 147–9, 156, 183; German counterattack on 186, 188, 190, 205–7; Germans capture 212–14, 217, 219; Allies counterattack 220, 222–4; bombed 234; in Allied breakout 356, 359; captured 384; rebuilt 416

Aquino 352

Arcadia Conference, Washington, 1941 12

Ardea 155, 233, 384

Ardeatine Caves 307, 426, 427

Arnim, General Jürgen von 15–17, 87

Arnold, General H. H. ("Hap") 412

Artemisio, Monte 374, 387–9, 391

Artena 358, 361, 372, 375, 377–80, 384

Asquith, Herbert Henry (1st Earl) 102

Attlee, Clement 426

Auchinleck, General Sir Claude 13, 20

Avalanche, Operation *see* Salerno

Avellino highway 374

Avezzano 71–2, 330

Axis Sally 169, 298

B-17 Flying Fortresses 234, 294, 352

B-24 Liberator bombers 234, 294

Baade, Major General Ernst-Günther 91, 336

Badoglio, Marshal Pietro 31, 33, 38, 88

Barrett, Lieutenant Colonel G. B. 457

Bartlett, Colonel G. Gordon 421

Bastogne (Ardennes) 237

Baynes, Lieutenant Colonel D. C. 284–7

Baytown, Operation *see* Calabria

Beaverbrook, William Maxwell Aitken, 1st Baron 97, 101

Beelitz, Colonel Dietrich 376

Bennett, Ralph 110, 184

Bernhard Line (Winter Line) 47

Biddle, George 59

Bidwell, Shelford *see* Graham, D., and Bidwell, S.

Biscayne, USS 113

Bizerte 15, 17

Blumenson, Martin 250n, 329, 406, 408

"Boot, the" 288, 291, 294–5, 300

Borgo Grappa 363, 367

Borgo Piave 140–1

Borgo Sabotino 322

"Bowling Alley" 140, 148, 241, 245, 249, 416

Bradley, Sergeant Jesse N., 307–8, 418

Bradley, Lieutenant General Omar N. 16–17, 25–7, 50–1, 60–1, 69, 152

Brann, Brigadier General Don 112–13, 367–8, 402

Bridgman, Major R. L. H. 192–4

Britain: grand strategy 12–14, 32–3; manpower limitations 47

Forces and Formations

ARMY

British Expeditionary Force, 1939–40 13

First Army 17

Eighth Army: reverses in North Africa 13; advance in North Africa 15; attitude to British First Army 17; in Sicily 21, 25–6; in Calabria 36, 39; Termoli landings 46; exhaustion 47; Montgomery commands in Italy 50; Leese takes over 65; stalled at Sangro 68; and Harding's Cassino breakthrough plan 334–5; and offensive plan (Diadem) 337–8, 340, 342; and Clark's race for Rome 338, 354, 390; attacks Hitler Line 353; Clark criticizes 385–6; and French plan 386–7; advance 387, 391

CORPS

10th 36–7, 40–1, 46, 79, 81–2, 126, 257

13th 26, 32, 39, 334, 347-9, 352, 354
30th 26
DIVISIONS
1st: casualties 2, 200, 217, 221, 287; in
Anzio landings 95, 113, 119, 122-4; in
rehearsals 108; Moletta River boundary
140; campaign 147; plan captured 156;
prepares for attack 160; forces wedge
179; faces German counteroffensive
184, 188, 190, 198, 210-11, 245;
achievements 217; held in reserve 230;
counters German 10th Parachute
Regiment 232; defensive line 240;
relieved 291; and breakout 336, 356;
later fighting 428
4th 348
5th 79, 81, 291, 296, 311, 316, 356
46th 40-1, 79, 81-2, 84, 141
50th (Northumbrian) 42
51st (Highland) 42
56th: at Salerno 37, 40; river assault
crossings 79, 81; reinforces Lucas 184,
199, 206, 220; faces second German
counteroffensive 229; defensive line
240; casualties 250n, 287, 295; attempts
relief of 157th Regiment 284; relieved
291, 296; and breakout 336; later
activities 428
BRIGADES
2d 146, 156, 190, 206
3d 151, 156, 176, 178, 184, 188, 198, 206,
211
24th Guards 141-2, 146, 148, 206, 211,
214, 287, 325
168th 184, 199, 206, 214
169th 245, 248, 249, 284
Infantry and Other Regiments
Black Watch 179
1st Duke of Wellington's 176-7, 188, 200,
216-17, 224, 288, 290
6th Gordon Highlanders 190, 192-200,
206, 207
5th Grenadier Guards 146-8, 150-1, 190,
199, 206, 208-10, 212, 214, 216-17
2d/4th Hampshires 348
1st Irish Guards 120, 146-50, 155-8;
casualties 149-50, 200, 217, 287, 290;
face German counterattack 188-90,
197-9, 212, 214, 216; and surrender of
Gordons 196; shelter in Pozzolano
Caves 206; in "the Boot" 287-8;
relieved 288
1st King's Shropshire Light Infantry 177,
188, 217
1st London Irish 206-7, 209, 211, 213,
217, 325
1st London Scottish Rifles 199-200, 217
1st Loyal (North Lancashire) 149, 190,
206, 241, 242-3, 245, 248, 250n
2d/7th Middlesex 196, 242
2d North Staffordshire 206, 208, 211-12,
217
2d/7th Queen's Royal Regiment 284-7,
295-6
1st Reconnaissance Regiment 190, 206
10th Royal Berkshire Regiment 206,
213-14, 217
2d Royal Scots Fusiliers 458-62, 464

46th Royal Tank Regiment 134, 146, 157,
177, 193, 199, 242
1st Scots Guards 146-7, 151, 155-8,
189-90, 206, 209, 211-12, 214-17
2d Sherwood Foresters 152, 177-9, 188,
198, 211; casualties 179, 200, 217, 296,
300; at Boot 294-6, 300; conditions
316
Other Units and Formations
Commandos 36-7, 111-12
9th Royal Marine Commandos 296
40th Royal Marine Commandos 296
Royal Artillery 122, 200
80th Medium Regiment, Royal Artillery
(the Scottish Horse) 149-50
ROYAL NAVY 113-14, 232
Brooke, General Sir Alan (*later* Field
Marshal 1st Viscount): assigns Alexander
to Tunisia 16-17; argues at Casablanca for
Sicily invasion 19; Montgomery complains
of Calabria invasion to 34; relations with
Churchill 53, 78, 94-5, 100; view of
Alexander 54-5, 57, 69; desires command
of invasion forces 69; and proposed
amphibious operation 71-2; steps up
Italian campaign 75; supports Anzio plans
78, 94; and Churchill's Rhodes invasion
plan 95; on Anzio stalemate 265-6; and
Lucas's inadequacies 267; on Churchill's
interference 270; on Churchill's fatigue
330; sends Harding to Alexander 334; and
progress of Diadem 349
Brookes, Father (chaplain) 150
Brooklyn, USS 141
Brown, 1st Lieutenant Allen T. 384
Brown, Lieutenant Colonel Lawrence C.
285
Bruce, Stanley 265
Bryant, Sir Arthur 54
Buckley, Christopher 29
Buckley, Francis X. 364
Buffalo, Operation 336-7, 340-41, 353-5,
358, 361, 364, 378; Clark abandons 365-6,
372, 390
Bulge, Battle of the 237, 422n, 423
Buonriposo Ridge 155, 206, 208-11, 214,
232, 242, 246; *see also* Caves
Bush, George 415
Butcher, Captain Harry C. (USNR) 267

Cadogan, Sir Alexander 278, 330
Caesar Line (C-position) 330, 370, 374, 376,
384-5; breached 388-90
Cairn, Lieutenant Colonel Bogardus S. 362
Cairo Conference, 1943 54, 75
Cairo, Monte 330
Calabria: invasion (Operation Baytown) 32,
34-5, 39, 92
Cameron, Sergeant Arky 322
Campbell-Preston, Major, 149-50
Campoleone: position 132, 135, 138; Allies
aim for 141-2, 144, 146, 152; actions at
149, 151, 155-6, 158, 159; Allied attacks
on 160, 176-9; German defenses at 175,
179; in German counterattack 186, 188;
Allies bomb 234; in Allied breakout 356,
383-4; and Clark's changed plan 382
Campoleone station 188-9, 199, 384

556

Index

Canada
  1st Corps 50, 334, 349, 352, 354
  Royal Canadian Air Force 50
Canaris, Admiral Wilhelm 84–5, 126, 183
Cannon, Major General John K. 332
Carano 292
Carleton, Brigadier General (formerly
  Colonel) Don 275, 396
Caro, Monte 151
Carroceto: position 138, 140, 142; actions at
  146–7, 149, 156, 174; strategic
  importance 186; in German counterattack
  188, 199–200, 206, 214, 217; British hold
  213–17; Allies bomb 234; and Angelita
  462–3
Carroceto Creek ("the Ditch") 209–10, 212,
  245
Carthage 70–1, 98
Carver, Field Marshal Michael, Baron 334
Casablanca conference, 1943 18–20, 32
Casaldi, Silvano 2n
Case Richard (German code word) 127,
  129
Casilina, Via 390, 392
Cassino (and Monte Cassino): German
  defenses 5, 44, 127; stalemate at 6, 47,
  181; and Italian strategy 7; position 67;
  and Anzio 98, 263, 329; as target for
  capture 256–7; Abbey 257, 259–60, 352;
  battles for 258–63, 330, 406–7, 430;
  breakout plan 333–4; and Allied artillery
  barrage 347; in Diadem offensive 347–9;
  falls to Poles 352; German dead 427
Castelforte 79
Cava di Pozzolano 206
Caves: battles for 242, 283–6
Ceprano 387
Childers, 2d Lieutenant Ernest 313
Churchill, Lieutenant Colonel J. M. T. F.
  ("Mad Jack") 111
Churchill, Winston S.: interest in Anzio
  operation 6, 72, 75–7, 93–4, 97, 99–103,
  117, 400–1; Mediterranean strategy 8,
  11–12, 18, 32–3; on Alamein 13; policy on
  cross-Channel invasion 14, 18; and
  invasion of Sicily 20; visits Eisenhower in
  North Africa 33; demands capture of
  Rome 45, 67–8, 75–6, 93, 95, 144; on
  Clark 48, 58; favors Alexander 50, 53;
  Brooke restrains 53, 78, 94–5, 100; and
  press reports on Anzio 57; and high
  command reorganization 68–9; illness in
  North Africa 75, 94; and invasion of
  Rhodes 94; on use of British troops in
  Anzio operation 95–6; at Anzio
  conferences 98–9, 101; and admirals 99;
  in World War I 102; as romantic warrior
  102–3; misjudges Anzio battle 144; chafes
  at stalemate 252, 259, 264–5, 277–9;
  defends Alexander's censorship 253; on
  numbers of vehicles at Anzio 256;
  proposes command changes 270; and
  offensive in Italy 329; fatigue 329–30;
  doubts on Operation Anvil 331–2; and
  Valmontone Gap 380; faith in Alexander
  shaken 402; Lucas's bitterness toward
  421; and Kesselring's sentence 426
Ciano, Count Galeazzo, 31

Cisterna: position 132, 135, 138, 140; Allied
  aim for 141–2, 144, 152, 158, 186; attack
  on 159–60, 172–3; U.S. Rangers action at
  160–9; failure at 174; U.S. 3d Division at
  181; in German counteroffensives 186–8,
  225, 230, 291–2; and Allied offensive
  338–40, 355, 358–60; Allies capture
  360–1, 364, 377; postwar development
  417
Cisterna, Fossi di 172
Civitavecchia 119, 129, 185, 187
Clark, Lieutenant General Mark Wayne:
  plans Anzio strategy 6, 32, 78–9, 106;
  opposes Operation Giant II 35; and
  planning for Salerno 37–8, 56; and
  conduct of Salerno landings 40–1, 49, 63,
  133; and capture of Naples 42; and
  Dawley 42; dislikes McCreery 42, 79,
  82–3; on Lucas's command of VI Corps
  45; anti-British attitude 47, 63, 68, 79,
  81–2, 356; Churchill calls "American
  Eagle" 48, 58, 65; Anzio errors 48;
  commands 5th U.S. Army 49–50, 58, 253;
  personality and career 50, 58–63, 65–6;
  relations with Alexander 54, 58, 62–3,
  112, 184–5, 326, 329, 332, 339–40, 353–4,
  408; courage 59, 61, 63; disliked by
  British 60; as commander 61–3; wins DSC
  63, 68; and subordinate commanders 63;
  despises Devers 64; plans for advance on
  Rome 67–8, 79; agrees to amphibious
  operation 70; cancels Shingle 74;
  diversionary river crossing plan 79–84,
  90, 329, 419; refuses to combine British
  and U.S. forces 83; complains of
  inadequate resources for Anzio 96–7; and
  Churchill's intervention 97, 102; absent
  from Marrakech conference 97; doubts on
  Lucas 104, 106; and rehearsals for Anzio
  109; Truscott warns 110; estimate on
  German reaction to Anzio 110; on naval
  diversion 111; use of combat teams
  111–12; instructions to Lucas 112–13;
  advises caution 119, 133–4; lands 123,
  145; disturbed at Rapido failure 142;
  urges offensive on Lucas 143, 145; on
  Alexander's disappointment at slowness
  144; misuses Rangers 170; and Rangers
  disaster at Cisterna 171; criticizes Lucas
  for inaction 171–2; supports Lucas in
  calling off offensive 181; accepts value of
  Ultra 184; visits front 184; proposes
  Civitavecchia landing 185, 187; Lucas
  requests reinforcements from 219;
  relieves Kammerer 244; and Lucas's
  attack 245; and Anzio stalemate 252, 267;
  conflict with British commanders 253–8;
  criticizes Navy 253–5; and Cassino 256–9,
  261, 263, 329, 406–7; and Freyberg
  257–8; and replacement of Lucas 268–70,
  406; and Tompkins's warning 306; and
  Harding's offensive plan (Diadem) 335,
  339–41, 353; obsession with capture of
  Rome 337–8, 341, 366–7, 370–1, 386, 400,
  410, 412; regard for Juin 350; in breakout
  from Anzio 354; and linkup at breakout
  363–4, abandons Buffalo for Turtle and
  changes direction 365, 366–73, 381–3,

390, 408–11; lacks faith in Ultra 381, 411; leaves Valmontone 381; slow advance 385; attacks Caesar Line 385, 389; benefits from Walker's success 389; drive for Valmontone 389–90; and German resistance 392; on conserving Rome 393; and fall of Rome 396–8; responsibility for Anzio operation 401; orders to Lucas 402, 405; misgivings on Anzio campaign 405; promotion, later career and death 419–20

Clarke, General Bruce C. 422n
Clarke, Dudley 129
Clausewitz, Karl von 61
Coffman, Edward M. 420
Cole, Lieutenant David 399
Colli Laziali see Alban Hills
Colville, Sir John 57, 94, 402, 418
Combat Commands see under United States: 1st Armored Division
Combe, Captain Simon 198
Coningham, Air Vice Marshal Sir Arthur 17, 63
Conrath, Lieutenant General Paul 91, 142
Cori 160, 340–1, 353, 358, 361–2, 378
Corsica 12, 127
Crawdad, Operation 337
Crerar, Lieutenant General H. D. G. 50
Crittenberger, Lieutenant General Willis D., 396, 398
Crocetta, Villa 384
Cub aircraft 307
Culvert, the 291
Cummings, 1st Lieutenant John T. 124
Cunningham, Admiral Sir Andrew 19, 21, 37, 41, 57, 69, 99
Cunningham, Admiral Sir John: attends Anzio conferences 97–8; doubts on Anzio plan 98–9, 101; qualities 99; and Lucas's doubts 107, 109; and Clark's proposed Civitavecchia landing 185; relations with Clark 253–6; restricts Anzio supplies 254; criticisms of Anzio stalemate 254–6, 264, 268

D day: term explained 20n
Daly, John Charles 252
Darby, Colonel William Orlando: commands Rangers at Anzio 95, 120, 148, 158; and preparations for Anzio 108; and Rangers attack on Cisterna 160–3, 167–8; and Ranger losses 168–9; forms and trains first Ranger force 170–1, 272, 424; commands 179th Regiment 244; killed 425
Dawley, Major General Ernest J. 36, 42, 63, 105
Dead End Road 235–6, 240–1, 242, 245, 249
deception measures 127, 129, 336, 342
de Guingand, Major General Sir Francis 34
Dempsey, Lieutenant General Sir Miles 26
desertions and absences 2–3, 311
Devers, Lieutenant General Jacob L. 64, 97, 105, 255, 267, 270
Devil's Brigade, The (film) 424
Diadem plan 334–8, 340, 342–3, 347–9, 353
Dill, Field Marshal Sir John 266, 332, 418
Dobson, Major Jack 161, 163–6, 424–5

Donovan, Major General William J. ("Wild Bill") 304
Dormer, Lieutenant Commander G. H. 313–14, 417
Dragoon, Operation see France, Southern
DUKWs 122
Dung Farm (Smelly Farm) 149, 151, 156–8, 190, 199–200
Dunkirk evacuation, 1940 13, 28
Dutko, PFC John W. 359–60

Eagles, Major General William W. 220, 223, 236, 240, 244, 276, 385, 423
Eaker, Lieutenant General Ira C. 122, 136, 186, 253, 260–1, 294
Egypt 13
Ehalt, Sergeant Major Robert 167
Eisenhower, General Dwight D.: and invasion of Italy 11; prepares "Marshall Memorandum" on cross-Channel operation 14; commands Allied forces in North Africa 14, 16; and Anglo–U.S. dispute 17; and planning for Sicily invasion 28; recommends invasion of Italy 31–3; disagrees with Churchill on Mediterranean strategy 33, 94; and Calabria landings 34–5; and Operation Giant II 35; mistrusts planners 37; and Salerno landings 40–1; and dismissal of Dawley 42, 63; Anzio plan 47, 71, 78; view of Alexander 55–6; assessment of Clark 60; leaves to command Overlord 64, 69; pessimism over capture of Rome 69–70; shortage of landing craft 70–1; originates Anzio landings 72, 76; approves Lucas 104–5; summons Harmon 153; concern at Anzio stalemate 267; supports landings in Southern France 331; letter from Churchill on Anzio 400; declines Lucas's services 421; and Harmon 422
Ellis, John 261, 347, 406, 428; Cassino: The Hollow Victory 428n, 429
Embankment, the 147–9, 155, 176, 212–13, 216, 224; bombed 234
Evelegh, Major General Vivian 267, 276

"Factory, the" see Aprilia
Ferentino 387
Ferriere, La 140
Ficoccia, Fosso della 213
Fielschmidt, Captain Hugo 311
Fifth Army History 250
Fischfang 278, 287, 291
Fisher, Ernest F., Jr. 368
Fitzpatrick, Colonel (later General Sir) Desmond 403
Fiuggi 376
"Flyover, the" (overpass) 146–7, 155, 234, 235, 240–41, 248, 249, 416
Foggia 68, 70, 75
Fondi 374
Fortress, the 316
Fowler, Bob 51n
France: 1940 defeat 13; and 1942 North African invasion 15
France, Southern: invasion (Operation Anvil, later Dragoon) 12, 32n, 76, 253–4, 331–2, 335

France: armed forces
Corps Expéditionnaire Français 50, 334,
350, 353–4, 386, 389, 411; *see also* Juin,
General Alphonse
Fredendall, Major General Lloyd R. 16,
153, 269
Frederick, Brigadier General Robert E.:
commands 1st Special Service Force 143,
184, 276, 318–23, 336, 379, 389; in drive
for Rome 393–4, 396; wounded 395; later
career and death 424
Freyberg, Lieutenant General Sir Bernard,
VC 50, 257–9, 261, 350
Fries, Major General Walter 91, 297
Frosinone 70, 72, 74, 78, 374–6, 386–7

Gaeta 97, 407
Gari River 348
Gariglione River 47, 67, 79, 81–4, 126, 129,
132, 257, 350, 420
Garioch, Lieutenant Harry 195
Gavin, Lieutenant General James M. 104
Gebhart, Private 59
Genazzano 376
Germany: and Italian collapse 31; forced on
defensive 91–2; expected reaction to
Anzio 110–11; surprised by Anzio landing
124, 126, 129; Anzio casualties 200, 221,
232–3, 237, 239, 246, 250, 293–4, 296,
414; morale declines 249, 251; Italian
defensive lines 330
LUFTWAFFE (German air force):
crippled before Sicily landings 24;
attacks Salerno landing forces 39;
operations at Anzio 121, 135, 148,
232–3, 300; radio-controlled
glider-bombs, 300; sinks HMS *Spartan*
314; operations against Diadem 352
Army Group Afrika 17–18, 91
Army Group B 31
Army Group C 89, 129, 133, 297, 374,
391, 402
Army Group von Zangen 145
Panzerarmee Afrika 13, 15
Fifth Panzer Army 15
Sixth Army 91
Tenth Army: at Cassino 5; at Salerno 35,
39, 41–2, 44; and Italian capitulation
38; defenses 46; Vietinghoff commands
89, 174; reserves committed 126,
132–3; composition 187–8; and
Harding's offensive plan 335–6, 340,
342; and Clark's plans 337, 369–70,
372–3, 390; defensive disposition 374–5;
threatened 376–7, 408–9, 411; air
attacks on 376; transfers troops to
LXXVI Panzer Corps 378; escapes 390;
casualties 414; retreat 428
Fourteenth Army: opposes Anzio landings
5, 130, 145; Mackensen commands 5,
89, 174; HQ 135; strength and
composition 174, 187–8, 326–7;
counteroffensives 183–4, 186–7, 206,
246, 263; takes prisoners 218;
reinforced 224; thwarted 237; Hitler's
orders to 292; divisions withdrawn to
reserve 326; center collapses 364;
defeat of 370; reserves 374; defensive

disposition 375, 377; deterioration 380;
line breached 388; retreats, 391, 411,
428; casualties 414
Group Pfeiffer 183
Group Gräser 183, 186–9, 198, 200, 206,
213
CORPS
I Parachute: disposition 130, 132; in
counteroffensives 183, 205–6, 224–5,
239, 246; HQ bombed 306; at Caesar
Line 385; penetrated 388; opposes VI
Corps 392
XIV Panzer: in Sicily 25–6; at Salerno 42;
defends route to Rome 44, 46; and
Allied diversionary assaults 79; Senger
commands 80, 89–90; deceived by
Allied offensive plan 342; faces Diadem
offensive 349–50; threatened 376, and
French plan 386; proposed stand at
Valmontone 390, 410; withdrawal
requested 391
LI Mountain 348, 354, 386
LXXVI: at Salerno 42; in defense of
Anzio 174; in counteroffensives 206,
208, 224, 292; losses 359; disintegration
377; reinforced from Tenth Army 378;
penetrated 388
Airborne Divisions
1st Parachute 91, 174–5, 260, 262–3
4th Parachute: disposition 92, 130, 132; at
Cisterna 159; in counterattacks 215,
229; qualities 263; fights Sherwood
Foresters 295; casualties 296; holds up
Clark 385; in defense of Rome 394
Panzer Divisions
Hermann Göring Parachute Panzer: in
Sicily 22, 24, 109, 142; commanders 91;
recaptures Canal bridges 124;
reinforcement units 130; role 132;
actions 141–2; defends Cisterna 159–61,
175; captures U.S. Rangers 168;
casualties 168; in counterattack 187;
Parachute Demonstration Battalion
230; and 1st Special Service Force
319–20; retained at Anzio 327; sent to
Livorno 336; returns to Anzio 359;
delays Allied advance 372, 375; at
Artena 378–9; counterattacks at Monte
Artemisio 388; in defense of Rome 394,
396, 410
2d Panzer 423
3d Panzer Grenadier: disposition 130,
132; in action 147, 158, 177, 181; in
second counteroffensive 225, 230, 232,
240; casualties 250; holds up Clark 385;
Battle Group Gericke 130
10th Panzer 153, 159
15th Panzer Grenadier 22, 24, 80, 83,
91
16th Panzer 39–40, 46, 87
26th Panzer 40, 174–5, 183, 225, 232,
239–40, 246, 336, 352
29th Panzer Grenadier: Fries commands
91; engineer battalion 120; committed
from reserve 126–7, 129; in
counteroffensives 211, 215, 225, 232,
239–40; demoralized 249; moved 336;
brought back from reserve 352; on

Tenth Army front 374; in Velletri sector 378
90th Panzer Grenadier, 126–7, 130, 257, 336, 390; Battle Group von Behre 130
Infantry Divisions
65th 145, 158, 179, 206, 208–9, 215, 229, 250, 385
71st 130, 132
114th Jäger 224, 240, 246
362d 224, 359, 361, 373
715th 183, 225, 233, 237, 240, 246, 359, 378
Regiments
3d Parachute 257, 262
4th Parachute 175
10th Parachute 226, 232
Panzer Grenadier 177
1st Panzer Grenadier 248
Infantry Lehr 225, 232, 235, 241, 242
725th Grenadier 233
7th Luftwaffe Jägers 172
Giant II, Operation 35–6
Giap, General Vo Nguyen 422n
Gibson, T/5 Eric G. 174
Giglio, Lieutenant Maurizio 307
Gilliam, Staff Sergeant Sidney 2
Giulianello. 362, 377
Gordon-Watson, Major D. M. L. 189–90
Gothic Line 398, 407
Grace, Lieutenant Edward 190, 192–4
Graffagnino, Captain (Dr.) Peter 285, 311
Graham, Dominick, and Bidwell, Shelford 61, 82, 86–7, 259, 334, 341, 352, 354, 386, 400, 406, 408
Grainger, Private H. W. 348
Gräser, Lieutenant General Fritz Hubert 223
Grasshopper, Operation 337
Gregson-Ellis, Major General P. G. S. 356
Greener, Lieutenant General Heinz 421–2
Gruenther, Major General Alfred 109, 368, 371–2, 389, 392–3, 397, 409
Guderian, General Heinz 89
Guettar, El (Tunisia) 16, 170
Gully, the 209–10, 212
Gustav Line: protected 5, 45, 80; importance 7, 44; fortification 46; untested 47; Allied aims to breach 68, 70, 79, 81, 83–4, 105, 134, 329, 407; Allied operations stalled at 74; and Kesselring's defensive policy 88, 257; Hitler orders defense of 131; attacked 258, 334–5; Special Service Force breaches 319; collapses 352
"Gusville" 320–2
Guzzoni, General Alfredo 22, 24, 87, 90

Force H 249
Hankey, Sir Maurice 102
Harding, Lieutenant General Sir John (later Field Marshal Baron): on Alexander 56–7; briefed on Shingle 97; at Marrakesh conference 97–8; recommends replacement of Lucas 107, 266; rejects Clark's Civitavecchia landing proposal 185; on Lucas's replacement 268; on Clark's aim to reach Rome 326; breakout plan (Diadem) 333–8, 340–1, 350, 365;

deception plan 336; meets Clark 353; and drive for Rome 393; later career 419; commutes Kesselring's sentence 426
Harmon, Major General Ernest Nason: in Tunisia 16, 152–3; and Rapido crossing 80; and German artillery fire 151; arrives at Anzio 152, 154; character and qualities 152–4; commands 1st Armoured Division 152–3, 176; booed 154; leadership 154–5; on casualties 159, 178; attack on Alban Hills 160, 174; attack on Campoleone 175–6, 178; counterattacks to relieve 45th Division 235, 270; defensive lines 240; urges Lucas to attack 245, 249; orders artillery on own troops 249; on will to win 251; and replacement of Lucas 269; relations with Truscott 276; on unity at Anzio 299; command truck 302–3; and local civilians 312; on rest and recuperation 313; on atmosphere at Anzio 326; deception 355; involves troops in plan 355–6; attacks 358, 362; and Clark's abandonment of Buffalo for Turtle 365, 377, 380, 382; on road to Rome 366; protests at Clark's change of plan 369; Clark rebukes 385; in Rome 395–6; assessment of Anzio action 404–5; later career 422–3; in Battle of Bulge 422–3; praises British troops 429
Harrell, Lieutenant Colonel Ben 272
Hauser, Major General Wolf 225, 246
Hawkesworth, Major General J. L. 82
Hayes, Corporal Christopher C. 458–64
Heidrich, Lieutenant General Richard 91, 174–5, 261–2, 348
Heilman, Lieutenant Gus 320
Heilmann, Lieutenant Colonel Ludwig 257
Herr, General der Panzertruppen Traugott 174, 233, 427
Hewitt, Vice Admiral H. Kent 24, 37–8, 63
Hewitt, Captain P. A. 296
Hightower, Lieutenant Colonel Louis V. 394–5
Highway 6 79, 135, 160, 336, 358, 369, 372, 375, 377–80, 387, 390, 392
Highway 7 (Appian Way) 135, 140
Hill, Colonel William H. 97, 100, 176
Hitler, Adolf: orders on Anzio 5–6; forces kept in Italy 12; on Mediterranean theater 13; and German forces in Africa 15, 17–18; and defense of Sicily 22; on defection of Italy 31; and defense of southern Italy 43–4, 407; and capture of Rome 45, 391–2; on Kesselring 88; and Senger 90; orders to troops in Italy 131, 186, 226; on battle for Rome 182–3; on wiping out Anzio forces 203; operational intervention 225, 292, 298, 326–8, 376; and Allied artillery 293; Westphal reports impasse to 296–7
Hitler Line see Adolf Hitler Line
Holden, William 424
Hollis, Major General Leslie 101
Holt, Corporal George 234
Holwell, Lance Corporal G. 157–8
Hough, Richard 99

Howze, Colonel Hamilton H.: Task Force
362-3, 365, 375, 377-8; in drive for Rome
392-4, 396
Hube, General Hans Valentin 22, 26-7, 44,
89-90
Hunt, Sir David 43, 373
Huntington, Lieutenant Colonel A. C. 212,
306
Husky, Operation, 19-20, 24, 29-30; see
also Sicily
Hutcheon, Major David 195, 197

Imiri, Monte 378
Indian Divisions
4th 260-62
8th 348
10th 328
intelligence services 411; see also
Tompkins, Peter; Ultra
Irving, David 392
Isola Bella (Femmina Morta) 160, 162, 164,
167, 172-4, 225
Italy: strategy of campaign in 11, 75; North
African forces defeated 13; and Sicily
campaign 24; and fall of Mussolini 30-1;
Germans plan defence of north 31, 43;
Allied invasion plans 32-3; capitulation
33, 38; terrain 45-6; military stagnation in
75-6; Kesselring's defense policy 88-9,
407; German forces in 88-92; German
defense lines 330; Allied tactical offensive
in 332-3
Sixth Army 22

Jackson, Major (later General) W. G. F. 387
Jacob, Brigadier Ian 14
James, Brigadier J. G. 178-9, 199
James, Robert Rhodes 103
Japan 13
Jennings, Lieutenant jg Stephenson 314-15
Jodl, General Alfred 88, 225, 296-7, 327
Johnson, PFC William T. 235-6
Jones, Major A. T. 196-8
Jürgensen, PFC Hans 413
Juin, General Alphonse, 50, 334-5; on
advance 345; in Diadem offensive 350,
352-3; on entry into Rome 383, 398, 412;
Corps pinched out 386; attack plan 386-7

Kasserine Pass (Tunisia) 16-17, 152, 154
Keiser, Brigadier General Lawrence B.
("Dutch") 275
Keitel, Field Marshal Wilhelm 88, 296-7
Kelley, Private Charles R. 360
Kesselring, Generalfeldmarschall Albert:
orders to Mackensen 5; and defense of
Sicily 22, 24; criticizes Allied Sicily
campaign 28; reinforced in north 31; and
Italian capitulation 38, 88; orders
withdrawal from Salerno 42; plan of
defense of southern Italy 43-4, 80, 87-9,
92, 407; helped by mountainous terrain
45; and Termoli landings 46; attempts to
outflank at Anzio 47, 74; response to
Anzio assaults 76, 79, 81-2, 127, 129-32,
134-5, 144-5, 182, 402; commits reserves
on Garigliano 82, 84; qualities and
background 86-8, 426; flying 87;

animosity for Rommel 87, 89; relations
with Hitler 88-9; differences with OKW
88-9; and Allied aims at Anzio 111;
preparations for Anzio landings 114;
responds to Civitavecchia diversion 119;
surprised by Anzio landings 124, 126-7,
129; commits reserves against landings
126, 132-3, 374; troop dispositions and
reinforcements 129-32, 174, 181, 326;
confidence 132, 134-6; given copy of
Allied plan 132; first counteroffensive
136, 143, 182-4, 200; attitude to Lucas
143; Ultra intercepts of 145, 184; defense
of Cisterna and Campoleone 159, 175;
differences with Mackensen 187-8, 359,
373-4; and time constraints 224; and
second counteroffensive 225; criticizes
Infantry Lehr Regiment 232; takes troops
from Cassino 257; and battles for Cassino
258, 327; on impasse in Italy 291; plans
attack on Cisterna 291-2; interference
from Hitler 292, 298; and Allied artillery
293; sends report to Hitler 296; supply
problems 333; Harding plans destruction
of 335, 342; and Harding's deception plan
336; surprised by Allied offensive 343;
withdraws to Hitler Line 349; respect for
Juin 350; and breach of Gustav Line 352;
and British achievements 356; defends
against Clark 373-4; and Berlin
interference 377; and Valmontone sector
378, 380-1, 390; uninformed of von
Mackensen's line at Monte Artemisio 388;
and battle for Rome 391, 393; troop
shortage 392; retreats to Gothic Line 398;
Allied underestimation of 401-3; on
Allied weakness at Anzio 405; on effect of
Anzio 406; criticized 407; on success of
German withdrawal 411; postwar
sentence and imprisonment 426; death
426
Keyes, Major General Geoffrey: commands
II Corps 79, 335; and river crossing plan
81, 84; at Cassino 257; offensive 390; in
race for Rome 393, 395-6; in Rome
398
Kilby, Captain C. 295
King, Admiral Ernest J. 19
King, William Lyon Mackenzie 252
Knowlton, 1st Lieutenant Donald T. 313
Korean War 420
Krasvac, Lieutenant George 322
Kursk 12, 91

Labico 374
landing craft (LSTs, LSIs): shortage 70-2,
74-6, 96; described 72n; made available
for Anzio 77-8, 97-8, 100; in landings
122; retained 136; used for supply 328;
torpedoed (LST 348) 314-15
Lanuvio 381, 383-4, 394
Lariano 389
Lateral Road 240
Laziali, Colli see Alban Hills
Leese, Lieutenant General Sir Oliver:
succeeds Montgomery as Eighth Army
commander 65; in Cassino breakthrough
334-5, 349; quarrel with Clark 337-8;

attack on Hitler Line 354; and advance on Rome 390; and Cassino battles 407; in S. E. Asia 420
Leghorn see Livorno
Lemelsen, General der Panzertruppen Joachim 375
Lemnitzer, Brigadier General Lyman L. 62, 64, 134, 353
Lepini Mountains 361, 378
Lewin, Ronald 381, 411
Liddell Hart, Sir Basil 7
Liebenstein, Captain Gustav von, Baron 452
Liebschner, Lance Corporal Hans Paul Joachim 414
Liri Valley 5, 44, 47, 67, 70, 72, 80, 126, 256, 260, 335, 337, 386, 407; and Diadem offensive 342, 348–50, 352
Littoria 141
Livorno (Leghorn) 336, 342
Lobster Claw (or Boot) 242, 291; see also "Boot, the"
Lowrey, First Sergeant Jerome 2
Lowry, Admiral Frank J. 108–9, 113, 151
Loyal, HMS 149
Luca, Angelina de 459–61
Lucas, Major General John Porter: commands Anzio force 4, 95, 104; assessed 6–7, 400–5, 407; replaces Dawley as VI Corps commander 45; on hardships of Italian fighting 45–6; view of Clark 59, 185; supplies 96; and Anzio aims 97, 112–13; absent from Marrakech conference 97–8; misgivings on Anzio 99–100, 104–7, 109–10, 114, 117; background 104; and superiors' attitude to Anzio 105–6; training and preparations for Anzio 108; Ultra information withheld from 109–10, 145; Clark grants discretion to 112–13, 119; in Operation Husky 114; at Anzio landings 114, 119, 121; self-confidence 114; assessment of opposition 114–15; prepares for enemy counterattack 124; decides against Alban Hills advance 133, 402–5; and Clark's caution 133–4, 144; Alexander advises on visit 134; growing pessimism 134, 185; isolation 136; delays 141–3, 145, 160, 174; mixed orders from superiors 143–4; overestimates enemy strength 145; offensive to expand beachhead 152, 159–60, 175; welcomes Harmon 155; and Rangers disaster at Cisterna 171; Clark blames for inaction 171–2; calls off offensive 181; loses initiative 182; reinforcements 184, 218; visits front 184; and Alexander's unawareness of dangers, 185–6; withdraws and withholds 1st Armored Division 188, 199; disagreements with Penney 200–1, 217–19; defiance 205; artillery support 214, 232; anti-British attitude 219; reluctance to visit front 219–20, 269; resolution to win 222; strength 224, 232; maintains reserves 231; designates line of no retreat 235; decides to attack 245, 249; and closing of Anzio port 248; and Alexander's attack on defeatism 253;

requests naval gunfire 255; blamed and replaced 264–71; Truscott on 275; Churchill criticizes 278; and Tompkins's warning 306; responsibility and command 400–5, 407; later career, honors and death 420–1
Luy, Staff Sergeant Bernhard 221

McCreery, Lieutenant General Richard: commands 10th Corps in Salerno landings 36; contempt for Clark 42, 79, 82–3; battle experience 49; postpones assault on Sant'Ambrogio 81; success in crossing Garigliano 81–2, 84, 90, 257, 350, 420; Kesselring counters 132; at Cassino 259; suggested for Anzio 266; made commander of Eighth Army 420
McGeogh, Tommy 309
Mackensen, Colonel General Eberhard von: commands German 14th Army 5, 89, 146, 174; surprised by landing 126; HQ 130, 135; counterattacks 136, 159, 181–3, 186, 200–1, 205, 219; differences with Kesselring 187–8, 359, 373–4; regroups 217, 221; and time constraints 224; second counteroffensive 224, 233, 239–40; presents plan to Hitler 225; and loss of railway guns 226n; use of armor limited 231; criticizes Infantry Lehr Regiment 232; and Allied artillery 293; controls reserve division 327; supplies reduced 333; on decisive battle 347; defense of Alban Hills 370, 373–4; resigns 375; line breached 388; and Clark's drive for Valmontone 390; trial, later career and death 427
Macksey, Kenneth 426
Macmillan, Harold 51, 56–7, 372
McNair, Lieutenant General Lesley J. 421
McPheeters, Lieutenant Colonel John W. 303
Majdalany, Fred 263
Manchester, William 102
Mansell, Captain Nicholas 220, 242
Mansfield, Rear Admiral J. M. 255–6
Manstein, General Erich von 89
Manteuffel, General der Panzertruppen Hasso von 422n
Marrakech 98, 101, 106, 111
Marshall, General George C.: opposes Mediterranean strategy 12, 19, 43, 77; argues for cross-Channel invasion 14, 94; and Eisenhower's relations with British in North Africa 17; criticizes Hitler's Italy defence strategy 43; receives Eisenhower's view of Clark 60; relations with Clark 61; appoints Devers 64; desires command of invasion forces 69; and LST requirements for Anzio 77; approves Lucas 104–5; forms U.S. Rangers 169; supports landings in Southern France 331–2; and capture of Rome 338; defends Lucas's conduct of campaign 405; and German defence of Italy 408; and Lucas's later career 420–1; and Harmon's later career 422n
Martin, First Lieutenant John R. 292
Mateur, Battle of (Tunisia) 152

Mathews, Sidney T. 338, 368–9, 381, 408
Mauldin, Bill 276, 415
Mediterranean: Allied strategy in 11–13,
    18–19, 32–3, 75, 77, 94
Mencken, H. L. 345
Menicante, Clemente 306
Messina (Sicily) 25–7, 91
Messina, Strait of 27–8, 34
Middleton, Major General Troy H. 36
Miller, Major Alvah M. 162
Mills, Private James H. 361
mines and minesweeping (sea) 313
Minturno 79
Moletta River 124, 140, 149, 287, 356, 359
Montagu-Douglas-Scott, Lieutenant Colonel
    C. A. 157–8, 294
Montecorvino airfield 40
Montgomery, General Sir Bernard Law
    (later Field Marshal 1st Viscount): North
    African campaign 13, 15; command in
    Sicily 19; criticizes Sicily plan 20–1;
    conduct of Sicily campaign 24–8, 55, 91;
    and invasion of Italy 32, 34–5; criticizes
    Alexander 34, 48–9, 55; on imperfect
    planning 37, 96; blamed for inaction
    48–9, 56; commands Eighth Army in Italy
    50; personality 51; relations with
    Churchill 53; working relations with
    Alexander 63; leaves Italy to command
    Overlord land forces 65, 69; takes Foggia
    airfield 68; and Gustav Line 68; bogged
    down 71
Moore, Lieutenant Colonel Harold G.
    422n
Moran, Charles McMoran Wilson, 1st Baron
    53–4, 103, 401
Morison, Samuel Eliot 407
Mountbatten, Admiral Lord Louis (later 1st
    Earl) 68
Mulreaney, Private Eugene 1
Mulreaney, Private Robert P. 1
Murray, Brigadier A. S. P. 156, 199, 212,
    223
Mussolini, Benito: and Mediterranean
    theater 13; British policy to remove 18;
    and defence of Sicily 22; downfall 30–1;
    rescued by Skorzeny 31; drains Pontine
    marshes 137–8; and fall of Rome 392
Mussolini Canal (now Canale di Moscarello)
    123–4, 137, 140, 160, 226, 231, 319;
    renamed 417

Naples 42, 100, 113, 313, 328
Napoleon I (Bonaparte), Emperor of France
    29, 61, 366
Nemi, Lake 137
Nero, Roman Emperor 2, 137
Nettuno: name 2 & n; landing at 4; position
    138; shelled 205; U.S. cemetery at 415;
    postwar rebuilding 416–17
Newman, Lieutenant 166
Newton, Nurse Grace 3
New Zealand Corps 50, 257–9
    2d New Zealand Division 262
    4th New Zealand Armored Brigade 262
Nickforce 153
Normandy invasion, 1944 (Operation
    Overlord) 12, 29, 32; date and place

agreed 44; given priority for resources 70;
    planning 330; support from Italian
    campaign 331–2, 334–5; Churchill's
    anxieties over 400–1; landings 412
North Africa 13–15, 18, 22; see also Tunisia
Norwich University (USA) 423

OKW (Oberkommando der Wehrmacht) 38,
    88–9, 376
O'Brien, John J. 314
O'Connor, Lieutenant General Sir Richard
    13
O'Daniel, Brigadier General John W. ("Iron
    Mike") 162, 275, 293, 358, 369, 377–9;
    later career 423, 425
O'Neill, Colonel E. J. 97, 100
O'Reilly, T/S James P. 166–7
OSS (Office of Strategic Services) 304–6
Overlord, Operation see Normandy invasion

Pacific theater 19, 70
Padiglione 138, 140, 179, 382
Padiglione Woods 140, 382
Paisley, Brigadier Peter, 220
Palermo (Sicily) 26
Pantano Ditch (Fosso di Pantano; renamed
    Ditch of Holy Souls) 161, 164, 416
Pantelleria 123
Pantoni (track junction) 295
Parton, James 260
Patton, Lieutenant General George S., Jr:
    appointed to command II Corps 16, 153;
    dispute with Coningham 17; command in
    Sicily 19; in Sicily plan 21; and conduct of
    Sicily campaign 24–7, 55–6; relations with
    Alexander 50, 54, 56; as commander 61,
    155; disgrace and exile 69; friendship
    with Lucas at Anzio 106; doubts on Anzio
    106; and Harmon 152–3; decorates Darby 170;
    proposed to take over at Anzio 264,
    267–8
Paulus, Field Marshal Friedrich von 91
Pearl Harbor 12
Peddie, Lieutenant Colonel James 190,
    192–7
Penney, Major General W. R. C. (later Sir
    Ronald): dismisses advance on Rome 7;
    Clark and Alexander differ on 62–3;
    commands 1st Division in Anzio landings
    95, 113; dines with Patton 106; on
    preparation for Anzio landings 107–8;
    conduct of campaign 142, 146, 151, 174,
    176; disbelieves presence of German
    paratroopers 156; approves Harmon's
    plan 176; and German counteroffensive
    184, 188, 200–1, 206; requests
    reinforcements 199, 218–20;
    disagreements with Lucas 200, 217–20;
    and artillery support 214; warns of
    untenable position 218; urges
    counterattack 218–20; wounded 236, 423;
    and Lucas's replacement 268; and
    Wedderburn's death 294; on quality of
    replacement troops 311; assessment of
    Anzio action 404; later career and death
    423–4
Pescara 330
Pestell, Sergeant Major 310

Peter Beach (Anzio) 122–3
Pettigrew, Captain (*later* Major) W. E. 459, 461–2, 464
Pico 353
Pisa-Rimini Line 43
Pointblank offensive 70
Point 593 (Cassino) 258, 261
Polish 2d Corps 50, 334, 347–8
Pomezia: German cemetery 427
Pontecorvo 350, 352–3
Ponte Rotto 230, 359
Pontina, Via 416
Pontine Marshes 2, 137–8
Portal, Marshal of the RAF Sir Charles 53
Portent (minesweeper) 123
Pound, Admiral Sir Dudley 69
Power, Captain Manley 99–101
Practica di Mare 306, 337
Preston's Farm 149–50
Pyle, Ernie 3–4, 301

Quebec Conference, 1943 (Quadrant) 11, 32, 44, 94

Ramos, PFC Manny 413, 429
Ramsay, Admiral Sir Bertram 24
Ranger Houdini Club 169
Ranger, Via 416
Rapido River 67, 79–84, 106, 126, 142, 256–7, 329, 348, 419
Red Army (USSR) 12, 14, 18
Red Beach (Anzio) 123
Rhodes 94
Richardson, Brigadier Charles (*later* General Sir) 277, 403
Richthofen, Field Marshal Wolfgang von 183
Ridgway, Major General Matthew B. 35
Robertson, Major General Sir Brian 386
Robertson, First Lieutenant Joe 229
Rodt, Major General Eberhard 91
Roenne, Colonel Alexis Freiherr von 407
Rogers, Lieutenant Colonel Glenn 393
Rome: Allies aim to capture 6–7, 43, 45–6, 49, 67, 69–72, 95; bombed 30; proposed airborne capture of 35–6; Clark's plans for and obsession with 68, 337–8, 341, 370–1, 386, 390, 410, 412; battle for 92; roads to 140; Tompkins and OSS in 304–6, 425; Allied advance on 390–6; declared "open city" 391; fall and liberation 394, 396–9
Rommel, Field Marshal Erwin 13, 15–16, 31, 87, 89, 350, 407
Roosevelt, Franklin Delano: and Churchill's Mediterranean strategy 12, 14, 18, 95; and invasion of Sicily 20; and reorganization of high command 68; and Churchill's plans for Anzio 77–8, 101; decorates Johnson 236; on Anzio stalemate 252; and delays in Italy 330; supports Operation Anvil 331
Roskill, Stephen 94, 99, 101
Rossi, Angelita (Angelita of Anzio) 458–64
Roundup, Operation 14, 19
Royal Canadian Air Force *see under* Canada
Rundstedt, Field Marshal Gerd von 423n

Russia (USSR) 12, 14
Ryder, Major General Charles W. 258, 361, 384–5

Salerno: landings (Operation Anvil) 32, 34–7, 39–41, 49, 92; planning for 37–8; German withdrawal 42, 44; British mutiny at 42; Alexander's generalship at 56; Clark at 63; Rangers at 170–1; German defense 403
San Gennaro ridgeline 384
Sangro River 68
San Pietro 84, 389
Sant'Ambrogio 79, 81
Sant'Angelo 80, 82
Sardinia 12, 22, 127
Schaefer, First Lieutenant Bernard J., 211
Schlemm, General Alfred 131, 183, 233, 392, 427
Schlemmer, Brigadier General 131
Schmalz, Lieutenant General Wilhelm 91, 375, 378, 427
Scott, Colonel, 212, 216
Seago, William 419
Sele River 36–7, 49
Senger und Etterlin, Lieutenant General Fridolin von: commands XIV Panzer Corps 80, 89; defends against river crossings 80–1; qualities 89–90; on bombing of Cassino Abbey 251, 260; and battles for Cassino 256–7, 259; deceived by Allied offensive plan 342; absence on leave 343; and German defensive position 376; in ordered retreat 387; Vietinghoff requests withdrawal 391; on weakness of Valmontone 410; later career and death 427
Senger Line *see* Adolf Hitler Line
Sevareid, Eric 59, 361, 364, 370, 388–9, 398
Sheehan, Fred 317–18
Sherrick, 1st Lieutenant James M. 244
Shingle, Operation (Anzio campaign): landings 4–5; planning 72, 74–8, 96, 101–3; Churchill supports 93–4, 101–3, 400; logistical restrictions 401; air support 412; *see also* Anzio
Sicily: campaign in (Operation Husky) 11, 24–9, 92; invasion of 18–19; plan 20–2; Axis forces and defense in 22, 24, 403; landings 24; Germans evacuate 27–9; Ultra intelligence on 109; Rangers in 170
Sidi Bou Zid 11, 154
Sidney, Major W. Philip, VC (*later* Viscount De l'Isle), 209–10, 424
Silvestri, Ennio 458n, 459, 461–2
Singapore 13
Singleton, Ronald 460
Skorzeny, Lieutenant Colonel Otto 31
Slim, Field Marshal Sir William 420
Smith, Major General Walter Bedell 35–6, 97
Smuts, Field Marshal Jan Christian 278
Snakeshead Ridge (Cassino) 258
South African 6th Armoured Division 397
Souza, Captain Ben 364
SOE (Special Operations Executive) 305
Spaccasassi Creek (Fosso di Spaccasassi) 148, 241

Sparks, Captain (*later* Brigadier General) Felix L. 228, 234, 246, 264, 278, 285, 315; later career 424

Spartan, HMS 314

Special Service Force, First (U.S.–Canadian): activities 143, 276, 318–23, 424; casualties 323; and breakout plan 336; attacks 358–62; advance 367, 371, 378, 389; in Valmontone Gap 378–9; at Artena 379; in drive on Rome 393–4, 396; in Rome 397

Stalin, Josef V. 12, 18

Stalingrad 12, 18, 91

Stallings, Sergeant Jack W. 321

Stange, Colonel Klaus 333

Stanley, Colonel Thomas H. 133

Stars and Stripes (newspaper) 321

Stempkofski (Polish deserter), 175

Stokesbury, James L. 429

Strangle, Operation 332–3

Strick, Captain John 425–6

Strong, Brigadier Kenneth 70, 98, 100, 111

Subaico 375

Sulzberger, C. L. 52, 59

Sunday Independent (newspaper) 463n, 464

superstitions and intuition 307

survival "miracles" 308–9

Sutherland, Lieutenant Colonel Arthur 62

Taylor, Brigadier General Maxwell 36

Tedder, Air Chief Marshal Sir Arthur: and Anglo–U.S. relations 17; and Sicily plan 21; and Salerno landings 34, 37, 41; relations with Churchill 53; Clark's view of 63; as Eisenhower's deputy for Overlord 69; meets Churchill 76

Templer, Major General Sir Gerald W. R. (*later* Field Marshal): Alexander visits 52–3; reinforces Lucas 184, 220; takes over 1st Division from Penney 236; character 239; commands defensive line 239–40; in attack 248, 249; criticizes Lucas 271; relations with Truscott 276; and relief of 157th Regiment 284; and Queen's Regiment action 287; assessment of Anzio 404–5; later career 424

Termoli: landings at 46, 68

Terracina 364, 374, 407

"Thumb, the" 179, 181, 186–7, 189, 197–8, 200–1

Tiger tanks 194–7

Tobruk (Libya) 15

Tompkins, Peter 304–7, 397, 425, 455

Torch, Operation, 1942 14–15, 29

Traietti, Luciano 461

Trevelyan, Raleigh 221, 316, 408, 430; *Rome '44* 463

Troina (Sicily) 27

Troubridge, Rear Admiral Thomas H. 113, 120

Truscott, Major General Lucias K.: and diversionary assault 79; commands US 3d Division in Anzio landings 95, 272; and rehearsal for Anzio 108–9; scepticism over Anzio 110; on smooth landings 120; lands 123; tanks 134; regroups for attack 141–2, 146; wounded 141; attacks Cisterna 160–1, 172–3, 175, 186; and loss of Ranger force 168, 171; forms U.S.

Rangers 169, 272; criticizes Eagles at Factory 223; and second German counterattack 229–30; urges Lucas to attack 245; replaces Lucas as VI Corps commander 268–71, 273–9; qualities, behavior and background 271–7; relations with British 276–7; and relief of 157th Regiment 284; use of artillery 293; witnesses Allied air bombardment 294; plundered by Special Service Force 321; offensive plans 327, 337, 339–41, 354; troop strength 329, 336; and Clark's opposition to British plan 340–1, 353; in breakout offensive 355–6, 358, 378; Harmon's disagreement with 358; and Clark's abandonment of Buffalo for Turtle 366–70, 382, 384, 408; reinforces O'Daniel 379; on reaching Rome 383; commits reserves 384; Clark rebukes 385; and Walker's breakthrough 388–9; and drive for Rome 392, 395; in Rome 398; assessment of Anzio strategy 404–5; at 1945 U.S. cemetery memorial 415–16; promotion and later career 420, 427; praises Darby 425; praises British troops 429; *Command Missions* 420

Truscott Boulevard (road) 317

Tucker, Colonel Reuben H. 95, 141, 160, 206, 276

Tunisia 15–20, 22

Turkey 94–5

Turtle, Operation 336, 358, 366, 368–9, 372, 374, 381–3

Twining, Major General Nathan F. 122, 260, 333

Ultra: and advance on Rome 43; and Kesselring's position 89, 144, 184; Lucas deprived of intelligence from 109, 145; secrecy over 109–10; value assessed 145; aids Truscott's artillery 293; and Radio Vittoria 306; and Allied breakout plan 333; on deterioration of German Fourteenth Army 380–1; Clark discounts 381, 411

United States of America: enters war 12; and Mediterranean strategy 14–15, 32–3

AIR

Fifteenth Air Force 122, 260

721st Squadron, 450th Heavy Bombardment Group 115

ARMY

Fifth Army: organized for Italian campaign 32; in Salerno landings 34–6, 40, 42; and planning for Salerno 37; advance opposed 44, 46–7; and Anzio plan 48, 77–9, 98; aim to take Rome 49; Clark commands 50, 58, 67–8; and proposed amphibious operation 70–2, 74; stalled by failure of Rapido-Garigliano crossings 83, 96; Kesselring obstructs 89; operational order for Anzio 112; attacks towards Cassino line 114, 152; forward command post 143; and Ultra intelligence 145; British interference in 253; in Cassino breakthrough 334; and Harding offensive plan 337–8, 340–3;

and race for Rome 338, 390; success in
breakthrough 364; turns from
Valmontone 381, 410; slow advance
398; casualties 414
Seventh Army 21, 24, 26–7
CORPS
II: in Tunisia 16–17, 153; in Sicily 25–6;
stalled in southern Italy 79; attacks
Gustav Line 258; at Cassino 258–9, 335;
in Diadem offensive 350, 354; in
link-up at Anzio breakout 363–4; and
French Corps 386; and destruction of
Fourteenth Army 389; drive for Rome
390, 392; in capture of Rome 394–5
IV 396
VI: in Anzio landings 4–5, 95, 111, 122–3;
at Salerno 36–7, 40–1; Lucas commands
45, 96; offensive 46; in Operation
Shingle 72, 74, 79; and Rapido crossing
failure 84; supplies 97–8, 100, 133, 327;
amphibious training 107; expected
German opposition 111; post-beachhead
plans 111; aims and objectives at Anzio
112, 133; bridgehead 124; and German
strength 145, 224; inadequate
battlefield intelligence 156; left flank
overextended 181; forced onto
defensive 182; faces German
counterattack 188, 205–7; supporting
gunfire 232, 293; casualties 251;
stalemate 266; Lucas relieved of
command 264–71; Truscott takes over
270–1, 275; and Kesselring's third
attack 291; and Harding's breakout
plan 335–8, 340–1, 353; advance 362–3,
367; and Clark's change of plan and
direction 369–70, 372, 375, 377, 384,
408–10; at Caesar Line 385; and
destruction of Fourteenth Army 389;
drive for Rome 390, 394–6; meets
resistance 392; unsupported in allotted
task 403; in invasion of Southern
France 427
Airborne Divisions
82d 21, 35–6, 41, 56, 49, 109
101st 237
Armored Divisions
1st: at Rapido crossing 80; presence at
Anzio 142–3, 152–5, 174, 181, 403;
attack on Campoleone 175–6, 178–9;
and German counteroffensive 188, 199,
201, 214; held in reserve 230; in attack
245; casualties 250n, 359; in breakout
254–6, 358–63; attack on Valmontone
367; at Albano 381; at Velletri 382;
advance 384; at Caesar Line 385; and
drive for Rome 392, 394–6; later
activities 428
Combat Commands: A 142, 155, 160,
384; B 328, 359
2d 153, 222, 223n
Infantry Divisions
1st: in Sicily 21, 24–5, 80, 142; attack plan
160; artillery 249; deserters 311; tanks
occupy farmhouses 312; and breakout
plan 336; casualties 413
3d: enters Messina 27; and diversionary
assault 79; in Anzio landings 95, 113;

123–4; Truscott commands 95, 272–3;
turnover and inexperience 100; in
Anzio rehearsal 108; scepticism over
Anzio 110; meets resistance 124;
terrain 140; early advance 141;
proposed offensive by 143, 146;
artillery 160, 293; in attack on Cisterna
160, 162, 172–3, 175, 181; awards for
bravery 173, 360–1, 428; maintains
front 230; training and experience
272–3; German attack on 291–2; repels
attacks 294; and breakout plan 336,
355–6, 358–62; advance 367; on
Valmontone Gap 378; controls Artena
379, 389; enters Valmontone 390; in
drive for Rome 393; later fighting 428;
casualties 428
9th 153
34th: at Cassino 257–8, 261; sent to Anzio
328, 336; in breakout 361; advance 367,
381, 383–5, 394; replaced 388
36th (Texas National Guard): at Salerno
36–7, 40; in diversionary river assault
79–84, 348, 419; casualties 83; sent to
Anzio 328, 336, 317; advance 367; on
Monte Artemisio 374, 387; at Velletri
382–3, 421–2; effects breakthrough
387–90, 394; and capture of Rome 396;
veterans' association brings charge
against Clark 419, 421
45th ("Thunderbirds") 1; in Sicily 25–6; at
Salerno 36; reinforces Lucas 184, 218;
counterattacks 218, 220; attack on
Factory 224; in second German
counteroffensive 229, 233, 235, 237,
239ND40, 243; artillery fire 250;
casualties 250–1, 428; and Caves 285;
and breakout plan 336, 356; advance
367, 394; and Clark's attack 381, 383;
and German I Parachute Corps 392;
later actions 428
85th 389, 393
88th 350, 389, 392–3
Armored Regiments
1st 178, 214
13th 362
Infantry Regiments
6th Armored Infantry 245; 1st Battalion
378
7th 160, 230, 358, 379; 1st Battalion
172–3
15th 160, 172–3, 358, 379; 2d Battalion
173
30th 124, 230, 245, 358–9, 379; 1st
Battalion 173; 2d Battalion 293; 3d
Battalion 359
141st 388
157th: 2d Battalion, E Company 228–9,
233–4, 246, 251, 283–5, 295; 3d
Battalion 236–7; D Company 285; I
Company 241, 243–4
179th: as reserve 141–2; at Cisterna 142
146; casualties 229, 246, 250; faces
German counteroffensive 233, 236;
destroyed 233, 236; command change
244–5; courts martial 310; Combat
Team 160; 1st Battalion 222–4, 240,
243; 2d & 3d Battalions 236

United States of America *(cont'd)*
 180th 235, 237, 243, 245–6; 1st Battalion
  241; 2d Battalion 243
 362d 358
 504th Parachute Infantry 95, 113, 160,
  169, 206, 209, 211, 230; 2d Battalion
  141; 3d Battalion 172, 188
 715th 358
 Other Regiments
 36th Engineer Combat 124, 133, 287,
  317, 322, 363, 388
 48th Engineer 363
 540th Engineer 114; Combat Group 457
 91st Reconnaissance 363
 Other Units and Formations
 10th Engineer Battalion 363
 191st Tank Battalion 222–3, 233
 509th Parachute Infantry Battalion 120,
  148, 292
 751st Tank Battalion 134
 894th Tank Destroyer Battalion 158, 211
 Rangers: at Salerno 36–7, 170–1; at Anzio
  95, 120, 148, 158; casualties 159, 164,
  166–7; in attack on Cisterna 160–9,
  175; escapes by 169; first formed
  169–71; disbanded 171; reunion 417;
  1st Battalion 148, 160–5, 167–8, 170; 3d
  Battalion 148, 160–2, 164–7; 4th
  Battalion 148, 160–2, 164, 167, 169,
  172–3
 56th Evacuation Hospital 308
 93d Evacuation Hospital 3
 95th Evacuation Hospital 1, 207
 160th Field Artillery Battalion 244
 3d Reconnaissance Troop 172
 NAVY
 15th Cruiser Squadron 255

Vallelata Farm 149
Vallelata Ridge 149, 158, 188, 190
Valmontone 160, 336–40, 353, 358, 362–3,
 365, 367, 371–3, 378, 381–2, 389–90, 403,
 408–11; captured 390–1
Valmontone Gap 366–7, 374–5, 377, 379–80
Vaughan-Thomas, Wynford 4, 199, 201,
 209, 277
Velletri 160, 369, 384, 387–8
Velletri Gap 358, 361–2, 372, 374–5, 377–8,
 380–2, 410
Verney, Peter 240, 242
Vian, Rear Admiral Sir Philip 37, 99
Victor Emmanuel III, King of Italy 2n, 30–1
Vietinghoff, General der Panzertruppen
 Heinrich von: command at Cassino 5; at
 Salerno 35, 39, 41; withdraws from
 Salerno 42; defensive line 46, 80; and
 Kesselring's flying 87; commands Tenth
 Army 89, 174; qualities 89; surprised by
 landings 126; and reserves 127; releases
 Corps HQ and troops 130; praises 1st
 Parachute Division at Cassino 262;

shortage of intelligence on battlefield
 327–8; supplies reduced 333; and
 Harding's offensive plan 335, 343;
 decorated by Hitler 343; repels Polish
 attack 348; withdraws to Hitler Line 349;
 and Valmontone Gap 375; defensive
 position 376–7; and French plan 386;
 requests withdrawal of XIV Panzer Corps
 391; criticizes Clark's change of plan 410;
 later career 427
Vittoria, Radio (OSS clandestine) 305–7, 455
Volturno River 35, 46–7, 273

Walker, Major General Fred L.: commands
 36th Division at Salerno 36; relations with
 Clark 63, 421; and diversionary river
 assault 79–80, 83–4, 106; and Harding's
 breakout plan 336; Clark visits 371;
 effects breakthrough 387–9; and race for
 Rome 394–6; later career 421–2
Ward, Charles M. 315
Ward, Major General Orlando 154
Webb-Carter, Lieutenant Colonel B. W. 290
Wedderburn, Lieutenant Colonel David
 157, 215–17; death 294
Wedemeyer, Brigadier General Albert C.
 60
Weekend (magazine) 459–60, 462–4
Wentzell, Major General Fritz 328, 376
Westphal, General Siegfried 126, 131, 187,
 297, 343, 406
Wigan Street 241, 243
Williams, Captain Donald 308
Williamson, Captain James C. 194, 197
Wilson, Lieutenant 294, 369
Wilson, Corporal George 195
Wilson, General Sir Henry Maitland
 ("Jumbo"): replaces Eisenhower as
 Mediterranean commander 64–5, 69;
 Churchill meets 76, 252; and British
 forces at Anzio 95; at Marrakech
 conference 97; on "Salerno complex" 133;
 attends meeting with Clark 253–4; and
 naval support 256; and Cassino 259; and
 Anzio stalemate 267; Churchill proposes
 to command 15th Army Group 270; and
 Operation Anvil 331; on objective of
 Italian offensive 332; and Clark's change
 of plan 372
Wilson, James 276
Winter Line *see* Bernhard Line
Wunn, Lieutenant Heinrich 209–10, 221
Wylie, Sergeant Jimmy 290

X-Ray Beach 417

"Y" Service (intelligence) 411
Yarborough, Lieutenant Colonel *(later*
 Lieutenant General) William P. 120, 148,
 292–3, 309, 417–18
Young, Major H. L. S. 302